Rule-Based Expert Systems

The Addison-Wesley Series in Artificial Intelligence

Buchanan and Shortliffe (eds.): *Rule-Based Expert Systems: The MYCIN Experiments of the Stanford Heuristic Programming Project.* (1984)

Clancey and Shortliffe (eds.): *Readings in Medical Artificial Intelligence: The First Decade.* (1984)

Pearl: *Heuristics: Intelligent Search Strategies for Computer Problem Solving.* (1984)

Sager: *Natural Language Information Processing: A Computer Grammar of English and Its Applications.* (1981)

Wilensky: *Planning and Understanding: A Computational Approach to Human Reasoning.* (1983)

Winograd: *Language as a Cognitive Process Vol. I: Syntax.* (1983)

Winston: *Artificial Intelligence,* Second Edition. (1984)

Winston and Horn: *LISP.* (1981)

Rule-Based Expert Systems

The MYCIN Experiments of the Stanford Heuristic Programming Project

Edited by

Bruce G. Buchanan
Department of Computer Science
Stanford University

Edward H. Shortliffe
Department of Medicine
Stanford University School of Medicine

Addison-Wesley Publishing Company
Reading, Massachusetts • Menlo Park, California
London • Amsterdam • Don Mills, Ontario • Sydney

This book is in The Addison-Wesley Series in Artificial Intelligence.

Library of Congress Cataloging in Publication Data

Main entry under title:

Rule-based expert systems.

Bibliography: p.
Includes index.
1. Expert systems (Computer science) 2. MYCIN (Computer system) I. Buchanan, Bruce G. II. Shortliffe, Edward Hance.
QA76.9.E96R84 1984 001.53'5 83-15822
ISBN 0-201-10172-6

ABCDEFGHIJ-MA-8987654

For Sally and Linda

Contents

Contributors

J. Barclay Adams, M.D., Ph.D.
Associate Physician
Department of Medicine
Brigham and Women's Hospital
Harvard Medical School
Boston, Massachusetts 02115

Janice S. Aikins, Ph.D.
Research Computer Scientist
IBM Palo Alto Scientific Center
1530 Page Mill Road
Palo Alto, California 94304

James S. Bennett, M.S.
Senior Knowledge Engineer
Teknowledge, Inc.
525 University Avenue
Palo Alto, California 94301

Sharon Wraith Bennett, R.Ph.
Clinical Pharmacist
University Hospital, RC32
University of Washington
Seattle, Washington 98109

Miriam B. Bischoff, M.S.
Research Affiliate
Medical Computer Science, TC-135
Stanford University Medical Center
Stanford, California 94305

Robert L. Blum, M.D., Ph.D.
Research Associate
Department of Computer Science
Stanford University
Stanford, California 94305

Alain Bonnet, Ph.D.
Professor
Ecole Nationale Superieure des Telecommunications
46, rue Barrault
75013 Paris
France

Bruce G. Buchanan, Ph.D.
Professor of Computer Science (Research)
Department of Computer Science
Stanford University
Stanford, California 94305

A. Bruce Campbell, M.D., Ph.D.
Practice of Hematology/Oncology
9834 Genesee Avenue, Suite 311
La Jolla, California 92037

William J. Clancey, Ph.D.
Research Associate
Department of Computer Science
Stanford University
Stanford, California 94305

Jan E. Clayton, M.S.
Knowledge Engineer
Teknowledge, Inc.
525 University Avenue
Palo Alto, California 94301

Stanley N. Cohen, M.D.
Professor of Genetics and Medicine
Stanford University Medical Center
Stanford, California 94305

Randall Davis, Ph.D.
Assistant Professor of Computer Science
Artificial Intelligence Laboratory
Massachusetts Institute of Technology
Cambridge, Massachusetts 02139

Robert S. Engelmore, Ph.D.
Director, Knowledge Systems Development
Teknowledge, Inc.
525 University Avenue
Palo Alto, California 94301

Lawrence M. Fagan, M.D., Ph.D.
Senior Research Associate
Department of Medicine
Stanford University Medical Center
Stanford, California 94305

Edward A. Feigenbaum, Ph.D.
Professor of Computer Science
Department of Computer Science
Stanford University
Stanford, California 94305

Jean Gordon, Ph.D.
Research Assistant
Medical Computer Science, TC-135
Stanford University Medical Center
Stanford, California 94305

John F. Hannigan, Ph.D.
Statistician
Northern California Cancer Program
1801 Page Mill Road
Palo Alto, California 94304

Charlotte D. Jacobs, M.D.
Assistant Professor of Medicine (Oncology)
Stanford University Medical Center
Stanford, California 94305

Jonathan J. King, Ph.D.
Knowledge Engineer
Teknowledge, Inc.
525 University Avenue
Palo Alto, California 94301

John C. Kunz
Manager, Custom Systems
IntelliGenetics
124 University Avenue
Palo Alto, California 94301

John J. Osborn, M.D.
President
Jandel Corporation
3030 Bridgeway
Sausalito, California 94965

A. Carlisle Scott, M.S.
Senior Knowledge Engineer
Teknowledge, Inc.
525 University Avenue
Palo Alto, California 94301

Edward H. Shortliffe, M.D., Ph.D.
Assistant Professor of Medicine and Computer Science
Medical Computer Science, TC-135
Stanford University Medical Center
Stanford, California 94305

David E. Smith
Research Assistant
Department of Computer Science
Stanford University
Stanford, California 94305

Motoi Suwa, Ph.D.
Chief, Man-Machine Systems Section, Computer Systems Division
Electrotechnical Laboratory
1-1-4 Umezono, Sakura-mura
Niihari-gun, Ibaraki 305
Japan

Randy L. Teach
Deputy Assistant Secretary for Evaluation and Technical Analysis
Department of Health and Human Services
Washington, D.C. 20201

William van Melle, Ph.D.
Computer Scientist
Xerox Palo Alto Research Center
3333 Coyote Hill Road
Palo Alto, California 94304

Jerold W. Wallis, M.D.
Resident in Medicine
University of Michigan Hospital
Ann Arbor, Michigan 48105

Victor L. Yu, M.D.
Associate Professor of Medicine
Division of Infectious Disease
968 Scaife Hall
University of Pittsburgh School of Medicine
Pittsburgh, Pennsylvania 15261

Foreword

The last seven years have seen the field of artificial intelligence (AI) transformed. This transformation is not simple, nor has it yet run its course. The transformation has been generated by the emergence of *expert systems*. Whatever exactly these are or turn out to be, they first arose during the 1970s, with a triple claim: to be AI systems that used large bodies of heuristic knowledge, to be AI systems that could be applied, and to be the wave of the future. The exact status of these claims (or even whether my statement of them is anywhere close to the mark) is not important. The thrust of these systems was strong enough and the surface evidence impressive enough to initiate the transformation. This transformation has at least two components. One comes from the resulting societal interest in AI, expressed in the widespread entrepreneurial efforts to capitalize on AI research and in the Japanese Fifth-Generation plans with their subsequent worldwide ripples. The other component comes from the need to redraw the intellectual map of AI to assimilate this new class of systems—to declare it a coherent subarea, or to fragment it into intellectual subparts that fit the existing map, or whatever.

A side note is important. Even if the evidence from politics is not persuasive, science has surely taught us that more than one revolution can go on simultaneously. Taken as a whole, science is currently running at least a score of revolutions—not a small number. AI is being transformed by more than expert systems. In particular, robotics, under the press of industrial productivity, is producing a revolution in AI in its own right. Although progressing somewhat more slowly than expert systems at the moment, robotics in the end will produce an effect at least as large, not just on the applied side, but on the intellectual structure of the field as well. Even more, both AI and robotics are to some degree parts of an overarching revolution in microelectronics. In any event, to focus on one revolution, namely expert systems, as I will do here for good reason, is not to deny the importance of the others.

The book at whose threshold this foreword stands has (also) a triple claim on the attention of someone interested in expert systems and AI. First, it provides a detailed look at a particular expert system, MYCIN. Second, it is of historical interest, for this is not just any old expert system, but the granddaddy of them all—the one that launched the field. Third, it is an attempt to advance the science of AI, not just to report on a system or project. Each of these deserves a moment's comment, for those readers who will tarry at a foreword before getting on with the real story.

MYCIN as Example It is sometimes noted that the term *expert system* is a pun. It designates a system that is expert in some existing human art, and thus that operates at human scale—not on some trifling, though perhaps illustrative task, not on some *toy* task, to use the somewhat pejorative term popular in the field. But it also designates a system that plays the role of a consultant, i.e., an expert who gives advice to someone who has a task. Such a dual picture cannot last long. The population of so-called expert systems is rapidly becoming mongrelized to include any system that is applied, has some vague connection with AI systems and has pretentions of success. Such is the fate of terms that attain (if only briefly) a positive halo, when advantage lies in shoehorning a system under its protective and productive cover.

MYCIN provides a pure case of the original pun. It is expert in an existing art of human scale (diagnosing bacterial infections and prescribing treatment for them) and it operates as a consultant (a physician describes a patient to MYCIN and the latter then returns advice to the physician). The considerations that came to the fore because of the consultant mode—in particular, explanation to the user—play a strong role throughout all of the work. Indeed, MYCIN makes explicit most of the issues with which any group who would engineer an expert system must deal. It also lays out some of the solutions, making clear their adequacies and inadequacies. Because the MYCIN story is essentially complete by now and the book tells it all, the record of initial work and response gives a perspective on the development of a system over time. This adds substantially to the time-sliced picture that constitutes the typical system description. It is a good case to study, even though, if we learn our lessons from it and the other early expert systems, we will not have to recapitulate exactly this history again.

One striking feature of the MYCIN story, as told in this book, is its eclecticism. Those outside a system's project tend to build brief, trenchant descriptions of a system. MYCIN is an example of approach X leading to a system of type Y. Designers themselves often characterize their own systems in such abbreviated terms, seeking to make particular properties stand out. And, of course, critics do also, although the properties they choose to highlight are not usually the same ones. Indeed, I myself use such simplified views in this very foreword. But if this book makes anything clear, it is that the MYCIN gang (as they called themselves) continually explored, often with experimental variants, the full range of ideas in the AI armamentarium. We would undoubtedly see that this is true of many projects if we were to follow their histories carefully. However, it seems to have been particularly true of the effort described here.

MYCIN as History MYCIN comes out of the Stanford Heuristic Programming Project (HPP), the laboratory that without doubt has had the most impact in setting the expert-system transformation in motion and determining its initial character. I said that MYCIN is the granddaddy of expert systems. I do not think it is so viewed in HPP. They prefer to talk about DENDRAL, the system for identifying chemical structures from mass spectrograms (Lindsay, Buchanan, Feigenbaum, and Lederberg,

1980), as the original expert system (Feigenbaum, 1977). True, DENDRAL was the original system built by the group that became HPP, and its origins go back into the mid-1960s. Also true is that many basic design decisions that contributed to MYCIN came from lessons learned in DENDRAL. For instance, the basic production-system representation had been tried out in DENDRAL for modeling the mass spectrometer, and it proved highly serviceable, as seen in all the work on Meta-DENDRAL, which learned production rules. And certainly true, as well, is that the explicit focus on the role of expertise in AI systems predates MYCIN by a long stretch. I trace the focus back to Joel Moses's dissertation at M.I.T. in symbolic integration (Moses, 1967), which led to the MACSYMA project on symbolic mathematics (Mathlab Group, 1977), a system often included in the roster of early expert systems.

Even so, there are grounds for taking DENDRAL and MACSYMA as precursors. DENDRAL has strong links to classical problem-solving programs, with a heuristically shaped combinatorial search in a space of all isomers at its heart and a representation (the chemical valence model) that provided the clean space within which to search. DENDRAL started out as an investigation into scientific induction (on real tasks, to be sure) and only ended up becoming an expert system when that view gradually emerged. MYCIN, on the other hand, was a pure rule-based system that worked in an area unsupported by a clean, scientifically powerful representation. Its search was limited enough (being nongenerative in an important sense) to be relegated to the background; thus MYCIN could be viewed purely as a body of knowledge. MYCIN embodied all the features that have (it must be admitted) become the clichés of what expert systems are. MACSYMA also wears the mantle of original expert system somewhat awkwardly. It has never been an AI system in any central way. It has been regarded by those who created it, and now nurture it, as not belonging to the world of AI at all, but rather to the world of symbolic mathematics. Only its roots lie in AI—though they certainly include the attitude that computer systems should embody as much expertise as possible (which may or may not imply a large amount of knowledge).

My position here is as an outsider, for I did not witness the day-to-day development of MYCIN in the research environment within which (in the early 1970s) DENDRAL was the reigning success and paradigm. But I still like my view that MYCIN is the original expert system that made it evident to all the rest of the world that a new niche had opened up. Indeed, an outsider's view may have a validity of its own. It is, at least, certain that in the efflorescence of medical diagnostic expert systems in the 1970s (CASNET, INTERNIST, and the Digitalis Therapy Advisor; see Szolovits, 1982), MYCIN epitomized the new path that had been created. Thus, gathering together the full record of this system and the internal history of its development serves to record an important event in the history of AI.

MYCIN as Science The first words of this foreword put forth the image of a development within AI of uncertain character, one that needed to be assimilated. Whatever effects are being generated on the social organization of the field by the development of an applied wing of AI, the more important requirement for assimilation, as far as I am concerned, comes from the scientific side. Certainly, there is nothing very natural about expert systems as a category, although the term is useful for the cluster of systems that is causing the transformation.

AI is both an empirical discipline and an engineering discipline. This has many consequences for its course as a science. It progresses by building systems and demonstrating their performance. From a scientific point of view, these systems are the data points out of which a cumulative body of knowledge is to develop. However, an AI system is a complex join of many mechanisms, some new, most familiar. Of necessity, on the edge of the art, systems are messy and inelegant joins—that's the nature of frontiers. It is difficult to extract from these data points the scientific increments that should be added to the cumulation. Thus, AI is case-study science with a vengeance. But if that were not enough of a problem, the payoff structure of AI permits the extraction to be put off, even to be avoided permanently. If a system performs well and breaks new ground—which can often be verified by global output measures and direct qualitative assessment—then it has justified its construction. Global conclusions, packaged as the discursive views of its designers, are often the only increments to be added to the cumulated scientific base.

Of course, such a judgment is too harsh by half. The system itself constitutes a body of engineering know-how. Through direct study and emulation, the next generation of similar systems benefits. However, the entire history of science shows no alternative to the formation of explicit theories, with their rounds of testing and modification, as the path to genuine understanding and control of any domain, whether natural or technological. In the present state of AI, it is all too easy to move on to the next system without devoting sufficient energies to trying to understand what has already been wrought and to doing so in a way that adds to the explicit body of science. An explosive development, such as that of expert systems, is just the place where engineering progress can be expected to occur pell-mell, with little attention to obtaining other than global scientific lessons.

This situation is not to be condemned out of hand, but accepted as a basic condition of our field. For the difficulties mentioned above stem from the sources that generate our progress. Informal and experiential techniques work well because programmed systems are so open to direct inspection and assessment, and because the loop to incremental change and improvement is so short, with interactive creation and modification. AI, like any other scientific field, must find its own particular way to science, building on its own structure and strengths. But the field is young, and that way is not yet clear. We must continue to struggle to find out how to extract scientific knowledge from our data points. The situation is hardly unappreciated, and many people in the field are trying their hands at varying approaches, from formal theory to more controlled system experimentation. There has been exhortation as well. Indeed, I seem to have done my share of exhortation, especially with respect to expert systems. The editors of the present volume, in inviting me to provide a foreword to it, explicitly noted that the book was (in small part) an attempt to meet the calls I had made for more science from our expert-systems experiments. And recently, Harry Pople asserted that his attempt at articulating the task domain of medical diagnosis for INTERNIST was (again, in small part) a response to exhortation (he called it criticism) of mine (Pople, 1982). I am not totally comfortable with the role of exhorter—I prefer to be in the trenches. However, if comments of mine have helped move anyone to devote energy to extracting the science from our growing experience with expert systems, I can only rejoice.

The third claim of this book, then, is to extract and document the scientific lessons from the experience with MYCIN. This extraction and documentation occurs at two levels. First, there has been a very substantial exploration in the last decade of many of the questions that were raised by MYCIN. Indeed, there are some 26 contributors to this book, even though the number of people devoted to MYCIN proper at any one time was never very large. Rather, the large number of contributors reflects the large number of follow-on and alternative-path studies that have been undertaken. This book documents this work. It does so by collecting the papers and reports of the original researchers that did the work, but the present editors have made substantial revisions to smooth the whole into a coherent story. This story lays to rest the simplified view that MYCIN was a single system that was designed, built, demonstrated and refined; or even that it was only a two-stage affair—MYCIN, the original task-specific system, followed by a single stage of generalization into EMYCIN, a kernel system that could be used in other tasks. The network of studies was much more ramified, and the approaches considered were more diverse.

The step to EMYCIN does have general significance. It represents a major way we have found of distilling our knowledge and making it available to the future. It is used rather widely; for example, the system called EXPERT (Kulikowski and Weiss, 1982) bears the same relation to the CASNET system as EMYCIN does to MYCIN. It is of a piece with the strategy of building special-purpose problem-oriented programming languages to capture a body of experience about how to solve a class of problems, a strategy common throughout computer science. The interesting aspect of this step, from the perspective of this foreword, is its attempt to capitalize on the strong procedural aspects of the field. The scientific abstraction is embodied in the streamlined and clean structure of the kernel system (or programming language). The scientific advance is communicated by direct study of the new artifact and, importantly, by its use. Such kernel systems still leave much to be desired as a vehicle for science. For example, evaluation still consists in global discussion of features and direct experience, and assessment of its use. (Witness the difficulty that computer science has in assessing programming languages, an entirely analogous situation.) Still, the strategy represented by EMYCIN is an important and novel response by AI to producing science.

The second level at which this book addresses the question of science is in surveying the entire enterprise and attempting to draw the major lessons (see especially the last chapter). Here the editors have faced a hard task. Of necessity, they have had to deal with all the complexity of a case study (more properly, of a collection of them). Thus, they have had to settle for reflecting on the enterprise and its various products and experiences, and to encapsulate these in what I referred to above as qualitative discussion. But they have a long perspective available to them, and there is a lot of substance in the individual studies. Thus, the lessons that they draw are indeed a contribution to our understanding of expert systems.

In sum, for all these reasons I've enumerated, I commend to you a volume that is an important addition to the literature on AI expert systems. It is noteworthy that the Stanford Heuristic Programming Project previously produced an analogous book describing the DENDRAL effort and summarizing their experience with it (Lindsay, Buchanan, Feigenbaum and Lederberg, 1980). Thus, HPP has done its bit twice. It is well ahead of many of the rest of us in providing valuable increments to the accumulation of knowledge about expert systems.

Pittsburgh, Pennsylvania Allen Newell
March 1984

REFERENCES

Feigenbaum, E. A. The art of artificial intelligence: Themes and case studies in knowledge engineering. In *Proceedings of the Fifth International Joint Conference on Artificial Intelligence.* Pittsburgh, PA: Computer Science Department, Carnegie-Mellon University, 1977.

Kulikowski, C. A., and Weiss, S. M. Representation of expert knowledge for consultation: The CASNET and EXPERT projects. In P. Szolovits (ed.), *Artificial Intelligence in Medicine.* Boulder, CO: Westview Press, 1982.

Lindsay, R. K., Buchanan, B. G., Feigenbaum, E. A., and Lederberg, J. *Applications of Artificial Intelligence to Chemistry: The DENDRAL Project.* New York: McGraw-Hill, 1980.

Mathlab Group. *MACSYMA Reference Manual* (Tech. Rep.). Computer Science Laboratory, M.I.T., 1977.

Moses, J. *Symbolic Integration.* Doctoral dissertation, M.I.T., 1967.

Pople, H. E., Jr. Heuristic methods for imposing structure on ill-structured problems: The structuring of medical diagnosis. In P. Szolovits, (ed.), *Artificial Intelligence in Medicine.* Boulder, CO: Westview Press, 1982.

Szolovits, P. *Artificial Intelligence in Medicine,* Boulder, CO: Westview Press, 1982.

Preface

Artificial intelligence, or AI, is largely an experimental science—at least as much progress has been made by building and analyzing programs as by examining theoretical questions. MYCIN is one of several well-known programs that embody some intelligence and provide data on the extent to which intelligent behavior can be programmed. As with other AI programs, its development was slow and not always in a forward direction. But we feel we learned some useful lessons in the course of nearly a decade of work on MYCIN and related programs.

In this book we share the results of many experiments performed in that time, and we try to paint a coherent picture of the work. The book is intended to be a critical analysis of several pieces of related research, performed by a large number of scientists. We believe that the whole field of AI will benefit from such attempts to take a detailed retrospective look at experiments, for in this way the scientific foundations of the field will gradually be defined. It is for all these reasons that we have prepared this analysis of the MYCIN experiments.

The MYCIN project is one of the clearest representatives of the experimental side of AI. It was begun in the spring of 1972 with a set of discussions among medical school and computer science researchers interested in applying more intelligence to computer programs that interpret medical data. Shortliffe's Ph.D. dissertation in 1974 discussed the problem and the MYCIN program that implemented a solution. In itself, the 1974 version of MYCIN represents an experiment. We were testing the hypothesis, advanced in previous work at Stanford, that a rule-based formalism was sufficient for the high performance, flexibility, and understandability that we demanded in an expert consultation system. The positive answer to this question is one of the best-known lessons in the history of AI.

In addition to, or rather because of, the original MYCIN program and the medical knowledge base that was accumulated for that work, many derivative projects explored variations on the original design. EMYCIN[1] is among the best known of these, but there are several others. In this book we discuss many of the experiments that evolved in the period from 1972

[1]We use the name EMYCIN for the system that evolved from MYCIN as a framework for building and running new expert systems. The name stands for "essential MYCIN," that is, MYCIN's framework without its medical knowledge base. We have been reminded that E-MYCIN is the name of a drug that Upjohn Corp. has trademarked. The two names should not be confused: EMYCIN should not be ingested, nor should E-MYCIN be loaded into a computer.

to 1982 based on the 1972–1974 design effort. We have chosen those pieces of work that, at least in retrospect, can be seen as posing clear questions and producing clear results, most of which were documented in the AI or medical literature and in technical reports.

We are taking a retrospective view, so as to restate questions and reinterpret results in a more meaningful way than that in which they were originally documented. Among other things, we now present these pieces of work as a collected whole, whereas they were not originally written as such. Each paper is heavily edited—new sections have been added to put the work in context, old sections have been deleted to avoid redundancies and "red herrings," and the entire text has been reworked to fit each paper into the unified picture. Each part begins with an overview chapter posing the central question of the section, discussing the implications of the question in its historical context, and providing a current framework for interpreting the results. Some entirely new papers were prepared specifically for this book. In addition, we are including several papers and technical reports that have previously been difficult to find and will therefore be generally available for the first time.

The last chapter is entirely new and could not have been written until the experiments were performed. It presents a set of conclusions that we have drawn from the experimental results. In a sense, the rest of the book discusses the data that support these conclusions. We believe this book is unique in its attempt to synthesize 10 years of work in order to demonstrate scientific foundations and the way in which AI research evolves as key issues emerge.

Acknowledgments

We gratefully acknowledge the help and friendship of Edward Feigenbaum and Joshua Lederberg. Over many years not only did they motivate and encourage our work in applying artificial intelligence to medicine, but they also created the intellectual and computing environment at Stanford that made this work possible.

Many individuals have contributed to the varied aspects of MYCIN and to the ideas in this book. In the past we have affectionately referred to each other as "the MYCIN gang." All of the authors of chapters built parts of MYCIN, performed experiments, contributed to overall design, and/or wrote the original articles on which the chapters are based. The persons who have been part of the MYCIN gang with us over the years are Janice S. Aikins, Stanton G. Axline, Timothy F. Beckett, James S. Bennett, Sharon Wraith Bennett, Robert L. Blum, Miriam B. Bischoff, Alain Bonnet, A. Bruce Campbell, Robert Carlson, Ricardo Chavez-Pardo, William J. Clancey, Jan E. Clayton, Stanley N. Cohen, Gregory F. Cooper,

Randall Davis, Robert S. Engelmore, Lawrence M. Fagan, Robert Fallat, Edward A. Feigenbaum, John Foy, Jean Gordon, Cordell Green, John F. Hannigan, Diane Warner Hasling, Robert Illa, Charlotte D. Jacobs, Jonathan J. King, John C. Kunz, Reed Letsinger, Robert London, Dana Ludwig, Thomas C. Merigan, John J. Osborn, Frank Rhame, Louis Sanner, A. Carlisle Scott, David E. Smith, Motoi Suwa, Randy L. Teach, William J. van Melle, Jerold Wallis, and Victor L. Yu.

We wish to thank, also, the numerous other persons in the AI, particularly the AIM (AI in Medicine), community with whom conversations over the years have been valuable sources of ideas. In particular, Randy Davis, John McDermott, Carli Scott, Bill van Melle, Bill Clancey, and Jim Bennett gave us help in clearly formulating Chapter 36.

We were fortunate in having Joan Differding and Dikran Karaguezian organize and edit much of the material here. Their help was invaluable. Jane Hoover carefully copyedited the manuscript and substantially contributed to its readability. We also wish to thank Darlene Vian, Juanita Mullen, Susan Novak, Cindy Lawton, and Barbara Elspas for assistance in preparing the manuscript.

Almost all of the computing work reported here (and the manuscript preparation) was done on the SUMEX-AIM computer at Stanford. Mr. Thomas Rindfleisch, former director of SUMEX, made it possible for us to attend to the research without undue worry about system reliability by making SUMEX a stable, high-quality computing environment. We also wish to acknowledge the importance of SUMEX funding from the National Institutes of Health, Division of Research Resources (RR-00785) and to thank, particularly, Dr. William Baker for his leadership in sustaining the quality of the resource.

Finally, the individual projects described here were funded by a variety of agencies over the years. We gratefully acknowledge the assistance of the Bureau of Health Services Research and Evaluation (HS-01544), the National Institutes of Health, General Medical Sciences (GM 01922 and GM 29662), the National Science Foundation (MCS-7903753), the Defense Advanced Research Projects Agency (MDA-903-77-C-0322), the Office of Naval Research (N0014-79-C-0302, NR-049-479), the National Library of Medicine (LM-03395, LM-00048), and the Henry J. Kaiser Family Foundation.

Stanford University
March 1984

B.G.B.
E.H.S.

In the early stages of the development of any science different men confronting the same range of phenomena, but not usually all the same particular phenomena, describe and interpret them in different ways. What is surprising, and perhaps also unique in its degree to the fields we call science, is that such initial divergences should ever largely disappear.

T. S. Kuhn, *The Structure of Scientific Revolutions (International Encyclopedia of Unified Science,* vol. II, no. 2). Chicago: University of Chicago Press, 1962.

The philosopher's treatment of a question is like the treatment of an illness.

L. Wittgenstein, *Philosophical Investigations,* para. 255 (trans. G. E. M. Anscombe). New York: Macmillan, 1953.

Every one then who hears these words of mine and does them will be like a wise man who built his house upon the rock; and the rain fell, and the floods came, and the winds blew and beat upon that house, but it did not fall, because it had been founded on the rock. And every one who hears these words of mine and does not do them will be like a foolish man who built his house upon the sand; and the rain fell, and the floods came, and the winds blew and beat against that house, and it fell; and great was the fall of it.

Matthew 7:24–27
(Revised Standard Version)

PART ONE

Background

1

The Context of the MYCIN Experiments

Artificial Intelligence (AI) is that branch of computer science dealing with symbolic, nonalgorithmic methods of problem solving. Several aspects of this statement are important for understanding MYCIN and the issues discussed in this book. First, most uses of computers over the last 40 years have been in numerical or data-processing applications, but most of a person's knowledge of a subject like medicine is not mathematical or quantitative. It is symbolic knowledge, and it is used in a variety of ways in problem solving. Also, the problem-solving methods themselves are usually not mathematical or data-processing procedures but qualitative reasoning techniques that relate items through judgmental rules, or heuristics, as well as through theoretical laws and definitions. An algorithm is a procedure that is guaranteed either to find the correct solution to a problem in a finite time or to tell you there is no solution. For example, an algorithm for opening a safe with three dials is to set the dials on every combination of numbers and try the lock after each one. Heuristic methods, on the other hand, are not guaranteed to work, but will often find solutions in much shorter times than will exhaustive trial and error or other algorithms. For the example of the safe, one heuristic is to listen for tumblers to drop into place. Few problems in medicine have algorithmic solutions that are both practical and valid. Physicians are forced to reason about an illness using judgmental rules and empirical associations along with definitive truths of physiology.

MYCIN is an expert system (Duda and Shortliffe, 1983). By that we mean that it is an AI program designed (a) to provide expert-level solutions to complex problems, (b) to be understandable, and (c) to be flexible enough to accommodate new knowledge easily. Because we have designed MYCIN to provide advice through a consultative dialogue, we sometimes refer to it as a consultation system.

There are two main parts to an expert system like MYCIN: a knowledge base and an inference mechanism, or engine (Figure 1-1). In addition, there are often subprograms designed to facilitate interaction with users,

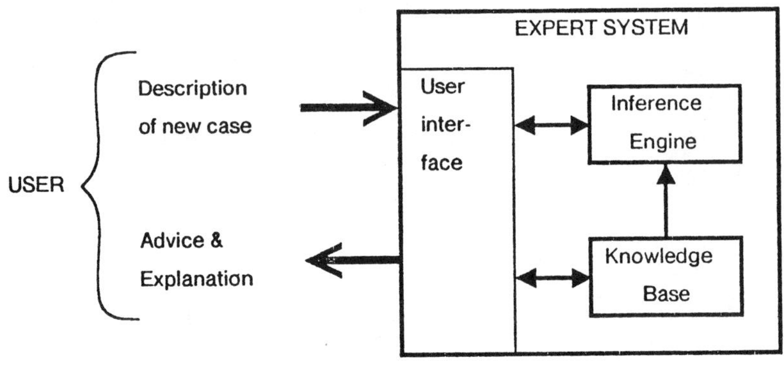

FIGURE 1-1 Major parts of an expert system. Arrows indicate information flow.

to help build a knowledge base, to explain a line of reasoning, and so forth.

The knowledge base is the program's store of facts and associations it "knows" about a subject area such as medicine. A critical design decision is how such knowledge is to be represented within the program. There are many choices, in general. For MYCIN, we chose to represent knowledge mostly as conditional statements, or rules, of the following form:

IF: There is evidence that A and B are true,

THEN: Conclude there is evidence that C is true.

This form is often abbreviated to one of the following:

If A and B, then C

$A \& B \rightarrow C$

We refer to the antecedent of a rule as the premise or left-hand side (LHS) and to the consequent as the action or right-hand side (RHS).

The inference mechanism can take many forms. We often speak of the control structure or control of inference to reflect the fact that there are different controlling strategies for the system. For example, a set of rules may be chained together, as in this example:

If A, then B	(Rule 1)
If B, then C	(Rule 2)
A	(Data)
$\therefore$C	(Conclusion)

This is sometimes called forward chaining, or data-directed inference, because the data that are known (in this case A) drive the inferences from left to right in rules, with rules chaining together to deduce a conclusion (C).

MYCIN primarily uses backward chaining, or a goal-directed control strategy. The deductive validity of the argument is established in the same way, but the system's behavior is quite different. In goal-directed reasoning a system starts with a statement of the goal to achieve and works "backward" through inference rules, i.e., from right to left, to find the data that establish that goal, for example:

Find out about C	(Goal)
If B, then C	(Rule 1)
If A, then B	(Rule 2)
∴If A, then C	(Implicit rule)
Question: Is A true?	(Data)

Since there are many rule chains and many pieces of data about which the system needs to inquire, we sometimes say that MYCIN is an evidence-gathering program.

The whole expert system is used to perform a task, in MYCIN's case to provide diagnostic and therapeutic advice about a patient with an infection as described in Section 1.2. We sometimes refer to the whole system, shown in Figure 1-1, as the *performance system* to contrast it with other subsystems not so directly related to giving advice. MYCIN contains an explanation subsystem, for example, which explains the reasoning of the performance system (see Part Six).

Several of the chapters in this book deal with the problems of constructing a performance system in the first place. We have experimented with different kinds of software tools that aid in the construction of a new system, mostly by helping with the formulation and understanding of a new knowledge base. We refer to the process of mapping an expert's knowledge into a program's knowledge base as *knowledge engineering*.[1] The intended users of these kinds of tools are either (a) the so-called knowledge engineers who help an expert formulate and represent domain-specific knowledge for the performance system or (b) the experts themselves. Al-

[1]The term *knowledge engineering* was, to the best of our knowledge, coined by Edward Feigenbaum after Donald Michie's phrase *epistemological engineering*. Like the phrases *expert system* and *knowledge-based system*, however, it did not come into general use until about 1975. For more discussion of expert systems, see Buchanan and Duda (1983).

though either group might also run the performance system to test it, neither overlaps with the intended routine users of the performance system. Our model is that engineers help experts build a system that others later use to get advice. Elaborating on the previous diagrams, we show this model in Figure 1-2.

Choice of Programming Language

LISP has been the programming language of choice for AI programs for nearly two decades (McCarthy et al., 1962). It is a symbol manipulation language of extreme flexibility based on a small number of simple constructs.[2] We are often asked why we chose LISP for work on MYCIN, so a brief answer is included here. Above all, we needed a language and programming environment that would allow rapid modification and testing and in which it was easy and natural to separate medical rules in the knowledge base from the inference procedures that *use* the rules. LISP is an interpretive language and thus does not require that programs be recompiled after they have been modified in order to test them. Moreover, LISP removes the distinction between programs and data and thus allows us to *use* rules as parts of the program and to *examine* and *edit* them as data structures. The editing and debugging facilities of Interlisp also aided our research greatly.

Successful AI programs have been written in many languages. Until recently LISP was considered to be too slow and too large for important applications. Thus there were reasons to consider other languages. But for a research effort, such as this one, we were much more concerned with saving days during program development than with saving seconds at run time. We needed the flexibility that LISP offered. When Interlisp became available, we began using it because it promised still more convenience than other versions. Now that additional tools, such as EMYCIN, have been built on top of Interlisp, more savings can be realized by building new systems using those tools (when appropriate) than by building from the base-level LISP system. At the time we began work on MYCIN, however, we had no choice.

1.1 Historical Perspective on MYCIN

As best as we can tell, production rules were brought into artificial intelligence (AI) by Allen Newell, who had seen their power and simplicity demonstrated in Robert Floyd's work on formal languages and compilers

[2]See Winston and Horn (1981), Charniak et al. (1980), and Allen (1978) for more information about the language itself.

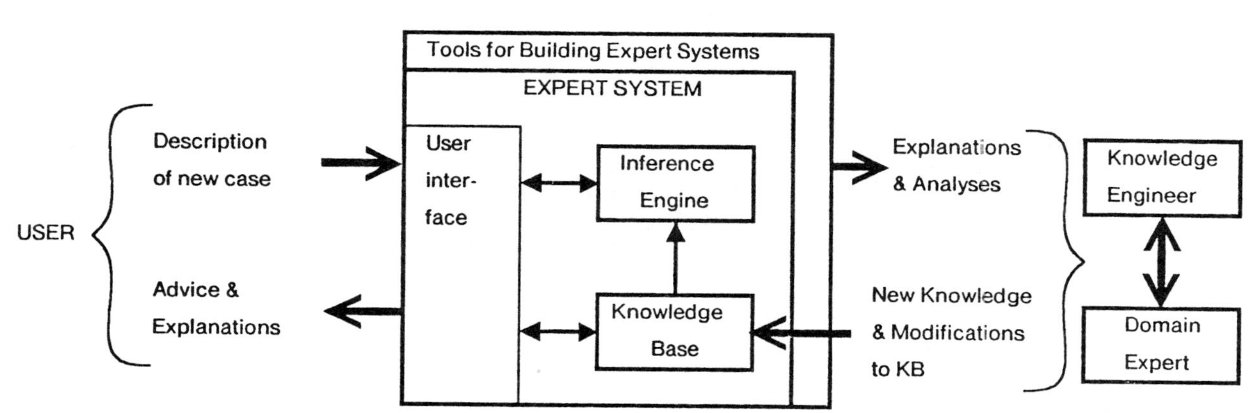

FIGURE 1-2 Interaction of a knowledge engineer and domain expert with software tools that aid in building an expert system. Arrows indicate information flow.

(Floyd, 1961) at Carnegie-Mellon University. Newell saw in production systems an elegant formalism for psychological modeling, a theme still pursued at Carnegie-Mellon University and elsewhere. Through conversations between Newell and himself at Stanford in the 1960s (see Newell, 1966), Edward Feigenbaum began advocating the use of production rules to encode domain-specific knowledge in DENDRAL. Don Waterman picked up on the suggestion, but decided to work with rules and heuristics of the game of poker (Waterman, 1970) rather than of mass spectrometry. His success, and Feigenbaum's continued advocacy, led to recoding much of DENDRAL's knowledge into rules (Lindsay et al., 1980).

The DENDRAL program was the first AI program to emphasize the power of specialized knowledge over generalized problem-solving methods (see Feigenbaum et al., 1971). It was started in the mid-1960s by Joshua Lederberg and Feigenbaum as an investigation of the use of AI techniques for hypothesis formation. It constructed explanations of empirical data in organic chemistry, specifically, explanations of analytic data about the molecular structure of an unknown organic chemical compound.[3] By the mid-1970s there were several large programs, collectively called DENDRAL, which interacted to help organic chemists elucidate molecular structures. The programs are knowledge-intensive; that is, they require very specialized knowledge of chemistry in order to produce plausible explanations of the data. Thus a major concern in research on DENDRAL was how to represent specialized knowledge of a domain like chemistry so that a computer program could use it for complex problem solving.

MYCIN was an outgrowth of DENDRAL in the sense that many of the lessons learned in the construction of DENDRAL were used in the design and implementation of MYCIN. Foremost among these was the newfound power of production rules, as discussed in Chapter 2. The senior members of the DENDRAL team, Lederberg and Feigenbaum, had convinced themselves and Bruce Buchanan that the AI ideas that made DENDRAL work could be applied to a problem of medical import. At about that time, Edward Shortliffe had just discovered AI as a medical student enrolled in a Computer Science Department course entitled "Models of Thought Processes," taught at the time by Jerome Feldman. Also, Stanley Cohen, then Chief of Clinical Pharmacology at the Stanford University Medical School, had been working on a medical computing project, the MEDIPHOR drug interaction warning system (Cohen et al., 1974). He had sought Buchanan's involvement and had also just accepted Shortliffe as a research assistant on the project. In addition, the late George Forsythe, then Chairman of the Computer Science Department, was strongly supportive of this kind of interdisciplinary research project and encouraged

[3]Even more specifically, the data about the unknown compound were data from a mass spectrometer, an instrument that bombards a small sample of a compound with high-energy electrons and produces data on the resulting fragments.

Shortliffe in his efforts to obtain formal training in the field. Thus the scene was set for a collaborative effort involving Cohen, Buchanan, and Shortliffe—an effort that ultimately grew into Shortliffe's dissertation.

After six months of collaborative effort on MEDIPHOR, our discussions began to focus on a computer program that would monitor physicians' prescriptions for antibiotics and generate warnings on inappropriate prescriptions in the same way that MEDIPHOR produced warnings regarding potential drug-drug interactions. Such a program would have needed to access data bases on three Stanford computers: the pharmacy, clinical laboratory, and bacteriology systems. It would also have required considerable knowledge about the general and specific conditions that make one antibiotic, or combination of antibiotics, a better choice than another. Cohen interested Thomas Merigan, Chief of the Infectious Disease Division at Stanford, in lending both his expertise and that of Stanton Axline, a physician in his division. In discussing this new kind of monitoring system, however, we quickly realized that it would require much more medical knowledge than had been the case for MEDIPHOR. Before a system could monitor for inappropriate therapeutic decisions, it would need to be an "expert" in the field of antimicrobial selection. Thus, with minor modifications for direct data entry from a terminal rather than from patient data bases, a monitoring system could be modified to provide consultations to physicians. Another appeal of focusing on an interactive system was that it provided us with a short-term means to avoid the difficulty of linking three computers together to provide data to a monitoring system. Thus our concept of a computer-based consultant was born, and we began to model MYCIN after infectious disease consultants. This model also conformed with Cohen's strong belief that a computer-based aid for medical decision making should suggest therapy as well as diagnosis.

Shortliffe synthesized medical knowledge from Cohen and Axline and AI ideas from Buchanan and Cordell Green. Green suggested using Interlisp (then known as BBN-LISP), which was running at SRI International (then Stanford Research Institute) but was not yet available at the university. Conversations with him also led to the idea of using Carbonell's program, SCHOLAR (Carbonell, 1970a), as a model for MYCIN. SCHOLAR represented facts about the geography of South America in a large semantic network and answered questions by making inferences over the net. However, this model was not well enough developed for us to see how a long dialogue with a physician could be focused on one line of reasoning at a time. We also found it difficult to construct semantic networks for the ill-structured knowledge of infectious disease. We turned instead to a rule-based approach that Cohen and Axline found easier to understand, particularly because chained rules led to lines of reasoning that they could understand and critique.

One important reason for the success of our early efforts was Shortliffe's ability to provide quickly a working prototype program that would show Cohen and Axline the consequences of the rules they had stated at each meeting. The modularity of the rules was an important benefit in providing rapid feedback on changes. Focusing early on a working program not only kept the experts interested but also allowed us to design the emerging program in response to real problems instead of trying to imagine the shape of the problems entirely in advance of their manifestations in context.

Green recommended hiring Carli Scott as our first full-time employee, and the MYCIN research began to take shape as a coordinated project. Axline subsequently enlisted help from infectious disease fellows to complement the expertise of Cohen's clinical pharmacology fellow. Graduate students from the Computer Science Department were also attracted to the work, partly because of its social relevance and partly because it was new and exciting. Randall Davis, for example, had been working on vision understanding at the Stanford AI Lab and had been accepted for medical school when he heard about MYCIN and decided to invest his research talents with us.

In our first grant application (October, 1973), we described the goals of the project.

> For the past year and a half the Divisions of Clinical Pharmacology and Infectious Disease plus members of the Department of Computer Science have collaborated on initial development of a computer-based system (termed MYCIN) that will be capable of using both clinical data and judgmental decisions regarding infectious disease therapy. The proposed research involves development and acceptable implementation of the following:
>
> A. CONSULTATION PROGRAM. The central component of the MYCIN system is an interactive computer program to provide physicians with consultative advice regarding an appropriate choice of antimicrobial therapy as determined from data available from the microbiology and clinical chemistry laboratories and from direct clinical observations entered by the physician in response to computer-generated questions;
>
> B. INTERACTIVE EXPLANATION CAPABILITIES. Another important component of the system permits the consultation program to explain its knowledge of infectious disease therapy and to justify specific therapeutic recommendations;
>
> C. COMPUTER ACQUISITION OF JUDGMENTAL KNOWLEDGE. The third aspect of this work seeks to permit experts in the field of infectious disease therapy to teach the MYCIN system the therapeutic decision rules that they find useful in their clinical practice.

The submission of our initial grant application encouraged us to choose a name for the project on which we had already been working for two years. After failing to find a suitable acronym, we selected the name MYCIN at Axline's suggestion. This name is simply the common suffix associated with many antimicrobial agents.

Although we were aiming at a program that would help physicians, we also realized that there were many computer science problems with

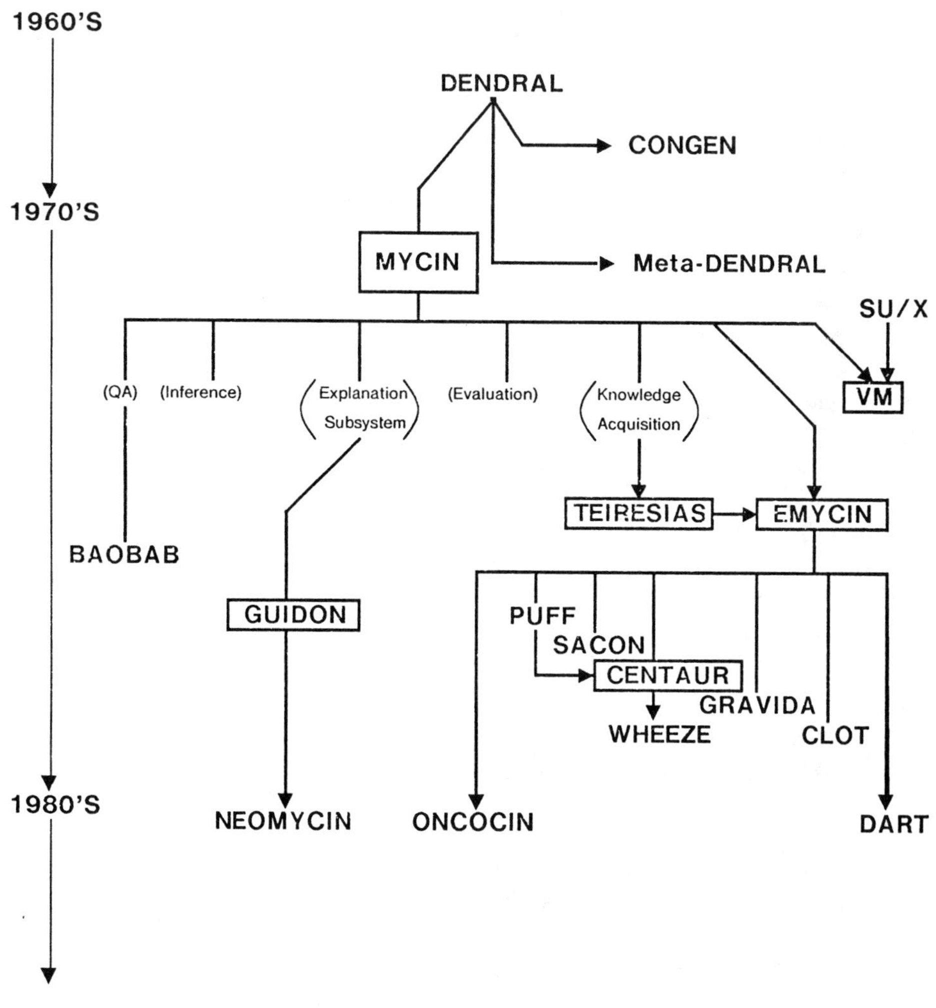

FIGURE 1-3 HPP programs relating to MYCIN. (Program names in boxes were Ph.D. dissertation research programs.)

which we had to grapple. No other AI program, including DENDRAL, had been built using so much domain-specific knowledge so clearly separated from the inference procedures.

A schematic review of the history of the work on MYCIN and related projects is shown in Figure 1-3. MYCIN was one of several projects in the Stanford Heuristic Programming Project (HPP); others were DENDRAL, CONGEN, Meta-DENDRAL, and SU/X.[4] There was much interaction

[4]Later renamed HASP/SIAP (Nii and Feigenbaum, 1978; Nii et al., 1982).

among the individuals working in HPP that is not shown in this simplified diagram, of course. Within the MYCIN project individuals were working on several nearly separable subprojects, some of which are shown: Question Answering (QA), Inference (including certainty factors, or CF's, and the therapy recommendation code), Explanation, Evaluation, and Knowledge Acquisition. These subprojects formed the basis of several of the experiments reported in this volume. All were well-focused projects since we were undertaking them partly to improve the knowledge base and the performance of MYCIN. Figure 1-3 shows roughly the chronology of work; however, in the organization of this book chronology is not emphasized.

Ancient History

Jaynes (1976) refers to a collection of 20,000–30,000 Babylonian tablets, about 20% of which contain sets of production rules ("omens") for governing everyday affairs.[5] These were already written and catalogued by about 650 B.C. He describes the form of each entry as "an if-clause or protasis followed by a then-clause or apodosis." For example,

> "If a horse enters a man's house and bites either an ass or a man,
> the owner of the house will die and his household will be scattered."
>
> "If a man unwittingly treads on a lizard and kills it,
> he will prevail over his adversary."

Included in these are medical rules, correlating symptoms with prognoses. According to one of Jaynes' sources (Wilson, 1956; 1962), these tablets of scientific teachings were catalogued by subject matter around 700 B.C. Among the left-hand sides quoted from the medical tablets are the following (Wilson, 1956):

> "If, after a day's illness, he begins to suffer from headache . . ."
>
> "If, at the onset of his illness, he had prickly heat . . ."
>
> "If he is hot (in one place) and cold (in another) . . ."
>
> "If the affected area is clammy with sweat . . ."

Each clause is catalogued as appearing in 60–150 entries on the tablets. One right-hand side for the medical rules cited by Wilson is the following:

> ". . . he will die suddenly."

[5]We are indebted to James Bennett for pointing out this reference.

Thus we see that large collections of simple rules were used for medical diagnosis long before MYCIN and that some thought had been given to the organization of the knowledge base.[6]

1.2 MYCIN's Task Domain—Antimicrobial Selection

Because a basic understanding of MYCIN's task domain is important for understanding much of what follows, we include here a brief description of infectious disease diagnosis and therapy.[7]

1.2.1 The Nature of the Decision Problem

An antimicrobial agent is any drug designed to kill bacteria or to arrest their growth. Thus the selection of antimicrobial therapy refers to the problem of choosing an agent (or combination of agents) for use in treating a patient with a bacterial infection. The terms *antimicrobial* and *antibiotic* are often used interchangeably, even though the latter actually refers to any one of a number of drugs that are isolated as naturally occurring products of bacteria or fungi. Thus the well-known penicillin mold is the source of an antibiotic, penicillin, that is used as an antimicrobial. Some antibiotics are too toxic for use in treating infectious diseases but are still used in research laboratories (e.g., dactinomycin) or in cancer chemotherapy (e.g., daunomycin). Furthermore, some antimicrobials (such as the sulfonamides) are synthetic drugs and are therefore not antibiotics. There are also semisynthetic antibiotics (e.g., methicillin) that are produced in chemical laboratories by manipulating a naturally occurring antibiotic molecule. In writing about MYCIN we have tended not to rely on this formal distinction between antimicrobial and antibiotic and have used the terms as though they were synonymous.

Antimicrobial selection would be a trivial problem if there were a single nontoxic agent effective against all bacteria capable of causing human disease. However, drugs that are highly useful against certain organisms are often not the most effective against others. The identity (genus) of the organism causing an infection is therefore an important clue for deciding

[6]The fact that the rules on the tablets were themselves indexed by premise clauses would suggest that they were used in data-directed fashion. Yet the global organization of rules on tablets was by subject matter, so that medical rules were together, house-building rules together, and so on. This "big switch" organization of the knowledge base is an early instance of using rule groups to focus the attention of the problem solver, a pressing problem, especially in large, data-directed systems such as the Babylonian omens.

[7]This section is based on a similar discussion by Shortliffe (1974).

what drugs are apt to be beneficial for the patient. Initially, MYCIN did not consider infections caused by viruses or pathogenic fungi, but since these other kinds of organisms are particularly significant as causes of meningitis, they were later added when we began to work with that domain.

Selection of therapy is a four-part decision process. First, the physician must decide whether or not the patient has a significant infection requiring treatment. If there is significant disease, the organism must be identified or the range of possible identities must be inferred. The third step is to select a set of drugs that may be appropriate. Finally, the most appropriate drug or combination of drugs must be selected from the list of possibilities. Each step in this decision process is described below.

Is the Infection Significant?

The human body is normally populated by a wide variety of bacteria. Organisms can invariably be cultured from samples taken from a patient's skin, throat, or stool. These normal flora are not associated with disease in most patients and are, in fact, often important to the body's homeostatic balance. The isolation of bacteria from a patient is therefore not presumptive evidence of significant infectious disease.

Another complication is the possibility that samples obtained from normally sterile sites (such as the blood, cerebrospinal fluid, or urinary tract) will be contaminated with external organisms either during the collection process itself or in the microbiology laboratory where the cultures are grown. It is therefore often wise to obtain several samples and to see how many contain organisms that may be associated with significant disease.

Because the patient does have a normal bacterial flora and contamination of cultures may occur, determination of the significance of an infection is usually based on clinical criteria. Does the patient have a fever? Is he or she coughing up sputum filled with bacteria? Does the patient have skin or blood findings suggestive of serious infection? Is his or her chest x-ray normal? Does the patient have pain or inflammation? These and similar questions allow the physician to judge the seriousness of the patient's condition and often demonstrate why the possibility of infection was considered in the first place.

What Is the Organism's Identity?

There are several laboratory tests that allow an organism to be identified. The physician first obtains a sample from the site of suspected infection (e.g., a blood sample, an aspirate from an abscess, a throat swabbing, or a urine specimen) and sends it to the microbiology laboratory for culture.

There the technicians first attempt to grow organisms from the sample on an appropriate nutritional medium. Early evidence of growth may allow them to report the morphological and staining characteristics of the organism. However, complete testing of the organism to determine a definite identity usually requires 24–48 hours or more.

The problem with this identification process is that the patient may be so ill at the time when the culture is first obtained that the physician cannot wait two days before beginning antimicrobial therapy. Early data regarding the organism's staining characteristics, morphology, growth conformation, and ability to grow with or without oxygen may therefore become crucially important for narrowing down the range of possible identities. Furthermore, historical information about the patient and details regarding his or her clinical status may provide additional useful clues as to the organism's identity.

What Are the Potentially Useful Drugs?

Even once the identity of an organism is known with certainty, its range of antimicrobial sensitivities may be unknown. For example, although a *Pseudomonas* is usually sensitive to gentamicin, an increasing number of gentamicin-resistant *Pseudomonae* are being isolated. For this reason the microbiology technicians will often run *in vitro* sensitivity tests on an organism they are growing, exposing the bacterium to several commonly used antimicrobial agents. This sensitivity information is reported to the physician so that he or she will know those drugs that are likely to be effective *in vivo* (i.e., in the patient).

Sensitivity data do not become available until one or two days after the culture is obtained, however. The physician must therefore often select a drug on the basis of the list of possible identities plus the antimicrobial agents that are statistically likely to be effective against each of the identities. These statistical data are available from many hospital laboratories (e.g., 82% of *E. coli* isolated at Stanford Hospital are sensitive *in vitro* to gentamicin), although, in practice, physicians seldom use the probabilistic information except in a rather intuitive sense (e.g., "Most of the *E. coli* infections I have treated recently have responded to gentamicin.").

Which Drug Is Best for This Patient?

Once a list of drugs that may be useful has been considered, the best regimen is selected on the basis of a variety of factors. These include the likelihood that the drug will be effective against the organism, as well as a number of clinical considerations. For example, it is important to know whether or not the patient has any drug allergies and whether or not the drug is contraindicated because of age, sex, or kidney status. If the patient has meningitis or brain involvement, whether or not the drug crosses the blood-brain barrier is an important question. Since some drugs can be given only orally, intravenously (IV), or intramuscularly (IM), the desired route of administration may become an important consideration. The severity of the patient's disease may also be important, particularly for those drugs whose use is restricted on ecological grounds or which are particularly likely to cause toxic complications. Furthermore, as the patient's clinical status varies over time and more definitive information becomes available from the microbiology laboratory, it may be wise to change the drug of choice or to modify the recommended dosage.

1.2.2 Evidence That Assistance Is Needed

The "antimicrobial revolution" began with the introduction of the sulfonamides in the 1930s and penicillin in 1943. The beneficial effects that these and subsequent drugs have had on humanity cannot be overstated. However, as early as the 1950s it became clear that antibiotics were being misused. A study of office practice involving 87 general practitioners (Peterson et al., 1956) revealed that antibiotics were given indiscriminately to all patients with upper respiratory infections by 67% of the physicians, while only 33% ever tried to separate viral from bacterial etiologies. Despite attempts to educate physicians regarding this kind of inappropriate therapy, similar data have continued to be reported (Kunin, 1973).

At the time we began work on MYCIN, antibiotic misuse was receiving wide attention (Scheckler and Bennett, 1970; Roberts and Visconti, 1972; Kunin, 1973; Simmons and Stolley, 1974; Carden, 1974). The studies showed that very few physicians go through the methodical decision process that was described above. In the outpatient environment antibiotics are often prescribed without the physician's having identified or even cultured the offending organism (Kunin, 1973). In 1972 the FDA certified enough (2,400,000 kg) of the commonly used antibiotics to treat two illnesses of average duration in every man, woman, and child in the country. Yet it has been estimated that the average person has an illness requiring antibiotic treatment no more often than once every five to ten years (Kunin, 1973). Part of the reason for such overprescribing is the patient's demand for some kind of prescription with every office visit (Muller, 1972). It is difficult for many physicians to resist such demands; thus improved public education is one step toward lessening the problem.

However, antibiotic use is widespread among hospitalized patients as well. Studies have shown that, on any given day, one-third of the patients in a general hospital are receiving at least one systemic antimicrobial agent (Roberts and Visconti, 1972; Scheckler and Bennett, 1970; Resztak and Williams, 1972). The monetary cost to both patients and hospitals is enormous (Reimann and D'ambola, 1966; Kunin, 1973). Simmons and Stolley (1974) have summarized the issues as follows:

1. Has the wide use of antibiotics led to the emergence of new resistant bacterial strains?
2. Has the ecology of "natural" or "hospital" bacterial flora been shifted because of antibiotic use?
3. Have nosocomial (i.e., hospital-acquired) infections changed in incidence or severity due to antibiotic use?
4. What are the trends of antibiotic use?
5. Are antibiotics properly used in practice?
   - Is there evidence that prophylactic use of antibiotics is harmful, and how common is it?
   - Are antibiotics often prescribed without prior bacterial culture?
   - When cultures are taken, is the appropriate antibiotic usually prescribed and correctly used?
6. Is the increasingly more frequent use of antibiotics presenting the medical community and the public with a new set of hazards that should be approached by some new administrative or educational measures?

Having stated the issues, these authors proceed to cite evidence that indicates that each of these questions has frightening answers—that the effects of antibiotic misuse are so far-reaching that the consequences may often be worse than the disease (real or imagined) being treated!

Our principal concern has been with the fifth question: are physicians rational in their prescribing habits and, if not, why not? Roberts and Visconti examined these issues in 1,035 patients consecutively admitted to a 500-bed community hospital (Roberts and Visconti, 1972). Of 340 patients receiving systemic antimicrobials, only 35% were treated for infection. The rest received either prophylactic therapy (55%) or treatment for symptoms without verified infection (10%). A panel of expert physicians and pharmacists evaluated these therapeutic decisions, and only 13% were judged to be rational, while 66% were assessed as clearly irrational. The remainder were said to be questionable.

Of particular interest were the reasons why therapy was judged to be irrational in those patients for whom some kind of antimicrobial therapy was warranted. This group consisted of 112 patients, or 50.2% of the 223 patients who were treated irrationally. It is instructive to list the reasons that were cited, along with the percentages indicating how many of the 112 patients were involved:

Antimicrobial contraindicated in patient	7.1%
Patient allergic	2.7
Inappropriate sequence of antimicrobials	26.8
Inappropriate combination of antimicrobials	24.1
Inappropriate antimicrobial used to treat condition	62.5
Inappropriate dose	18.7

Inappropriate duration of therapy	9.8
Inappropriate route	3.6
Culture and sensitivity needed	17.0
Culture and sensitivity indicate wrong antibiotic being used	16.1

The percentages add up to more than 100% because a given therapy may have been judged inappropriate for more than one reason. Thus 62.5% of the 112 patients who required antimicrobial therapy but were treated irrationally were given a drug that was inappropriate for their clinical condition. This observation reflects the need for improved therapy selection for patients requiring therapy—precisely the decision task that MYCIN was designed to assist.

Once a need for improved continuing medical education in antimicrobial selection was recognized, there were several valid ways to respond. One was to offer appropriate post-graduate courses for physicians. Another was to introduce surveillance systems for the monitoring and approval of antibiotic prescriptions within hospitals (Edwards, 1968; Kunin, 1973). In addition, physicians were encouraged to seek consultations with infectious disease experts when they were uncertain how best to proceed with the treatment of a bacterial infection. Finally, we concluded that an automated consultation system that could substitute for infectious disease experts when they are unavailable or inaccessible could provide a valuable partial solution to the therapy selection problem. MYCIN was conceived and developed in an attempt to fill that need.

1.3 Organization of the Book

This volume is organized into twelve parts of two to four chapters, each highlighting a fundamental theme in the development and evolution of MYCIN. This introductory part closes with a classic review paper that outlines the production rule methodology.

The design and implementation of MYCIN are discussed in Part Two. Shortliffe's thesis was the beginning, but the original system he developed was modified as required.

In Part Three we focus on the problems of building a knowledge base and on knowledge acquisition in general. TEIRESIAS, the program resulting from Randy Davis' dissertation research, is described.

In Part Four we address the problems of reasoning under uncertainty. The certainty factor model, one answer to the question of how to propagate uncertainty in an inference mechanism, forms the basis of this part.

Part Five discusses the generality of the MYCIN formalism. The EMYCIN system, written largely by William van Melle as part of his dissertation work, is a strongly positive answer to the question of whether MYCIN could be generalized.

Work on explanation is reviewed in Part Six. Explanation was a major design requirement from the start, and many persons contributed to MYCIN's explanation capabilities.

In Part Seven we discuss some of the experimentation we were doing with alternative representations. Jan Aikins' thesis work on CENTAUR examined the advantages of combining frames and production rules. Larry Fagan's work on VM examined the augmentations to a production rule system that are needed to reason effectively with data monitored over time.

As an outgrowth of the explanation work, we came to believe that MYCIN had some pedagogical value to students trying to learn about infectious disease diagnosis and therapy. William Clancey took this idea one step further in his research on the GUIDON system, described in Part Eight. GUIDON is an intelligent tutor that we initially believed could tutor students about the contents of any knowledge base for an EMYCIN system. There is now strong evidence that this hypothesis was false because more knowledge is needed for tutoring than for advising.

In Part Nine we discuss the concept of meta-level knowledge, some of which we found to be necessary for intelligent tutoring. We first examined rules of strategy and control, called meta-rules, in the context of the TEIRESIAS program. One working hypothesis was that meta-rules could be encoded as production rules similar to those at the object level (medical rules) and that the same inference and explanation routines could work with them as well.

From the start of the project, we had been concerned about performance evaluation, as described in Part Ten. We undertook three different evaluation experiments, each simpler and more realistic but somewhat more limited than the last.

Another primary design consideration was human engineering, the subject of Part Eleven. We knew that a useful system had to be well enough engineered to make people want to use it; high performance alone was not sufficient. The chapters in this part discuss experiments with both natural language interfaces and customized hardware and system architectures.

Finally, in Part Twelve, we attempt to summarize the lessons about rule-based expert systems that we have learned in nearly a decade of research on the programs named in Figure 1-3. We believe that AI is largely an experimental science in which ideas are tested in working programs. Although there are many experiments we neglected to perform, we believe the descriptions of several that we did undertake will allow others to build on our experience and to compare their results with ours.

2

The Origin of Rule-Based Systems in AI

Randall Davis and Jonathan J. King

Since production systems (PS's) were first proposed by Post (1943) as a general computational mechanism, the methodology has seen a great deal of development and has been applied to a diverse collection of problems. Despite the wide scope of goals and perspectives demonstrated by the various systems, there appear to be many recurrent themes. We present an analysis and overview of those themes, as well as a conceptual framework by which many of the seemingly disparate efforts can be viewed, both in relation to each other and to other methodologies. Accordingly, we use the term *production system* in a broad sense and show how most systems that have used the term can be fit into the framework. The comparison to other methodologies is intended to provide a view of PS characteristics in a broader context, with primary reference to procedurally based techniques, but also with reference to more recent developments in programming and the organization of data and knowledge bases.

This chapter begins by offering a review of the essential structure and function of a PS, presenting a picture of a "pure" PS to provide a basis for subsequent elaborations. Current views of PS's fall into two distinct classes, and we shall demonstrate that this dichotomy may explain much of the existing variation in goals and methods. This is followed by some speculations on the nature of appropriate and inappropriate problem domains for PS's—i.e., what is it about a problem that makes the PS methodology appropriate, and how do these factors arise out of the system's basic structure and function? Next, we review characteristics common to all systems, explaining how they contribute to the basic character and noting their

This chapter is based on an article taken with permission from *Machine Intelligence 8: Machine Representations of Knowledge*, edited by E. W. Elcock and D. Michie, published in 1977 by Ellis Horwood Ltd., Chichester, England.

interrelationships. Finally, we present a taxonomy for PS's, selecting four dimensions of characterization and indicating the range of possibilities suggested by recent efforts.

Two points of methodology should be noted. First, we make frequent reference to what is "typically" found, and what is "in the spirit of things." Since there is really no one formal design for PS's and recent implementations have explored variations on virtually every aspect, their use becomes more an issue of a programming *style* than of anything else. It is difficult to exclude designs or methods on formal grounds, and we refer instead to an informal but well-established style of approach. A second, related point is important to keep in mind as we compare the capabilities of PS's with those of other approaches. Since it is possible to imagine coding any given Turing machine in either procedural or PS terms [see Anderson, (1976) for a formal proof of the latter], in the formal sense their computational power is equivalent. This suggests that, given sufficient effort, they are ultimately capable of solving the same problems. The issues we wish to examine are not, however, questions of absolute computational power but of the impact of a particular methodology on program structure, as well as of the relative ease or difficulty with which certain capabilities can be achieved.

2.1 "Pure" Production Systems

A production system may be viewed as consisting of three basic components: a set of rules, a data base, and an interpreter for the rules. In the simplest design a rule is an ordered pair of symbol strings, with a left-hand side and a right-hand side (LHS and RHS). The rule set has a predetermined, total ordering, and the data base is simply a collection of symbols. The interpreter in this simple design operates by scanning the LHS of each rule until one is found that can be successfully matched against the data base. At that point the symbols matched in the data base are replaced with those found in the RHS of the rule and scanning either continues with the next rule or begins again with the first. A rule can also be viewed as a simple conditional statement, and the invocation of rules as a sequence of actions chained by *modus ponens*.

2.1.1 Rules

More generally, one side of a rule is *evaluated* with reference to the data base, and if this succeeds (i.e., evaluates to TRUE in some sense), the action specified by the other side is performed. Note that *evaluate* is typically taken to mean a passive operation of "perception," or "an operation involving only matching and detection" (Newell and Simon, 1972), while the action is generally one or more conceptually primitive operations (although more complex constructs are also being examined; see Section 2.4.9). As noted, the simplest evaluation is a matching of literals, and the simplest action, a replacement.

Note that we do not specify which side is to be matched, since either is possible. For example, given a grammar written in production rule form,[1]

$$\begin{aligned}
S &\rightarrow A\,B\,A\\
A &\rightarrow A\,1\\
A &\rightarrow 1\\
B &\rightarrow B\,0\\
B &\rightarrow 0
\end{aligned}$$

matching the LHS on a data base that consists of the start symbol S gives a generator for strings in the language. Matching on the RHS of the same set of rules gives a recognizer for the language. We can also vary the methodology slightly to obtain a top-down recognizer by interpreting elements of the LHS as goals to be obtained by the successful matching of elements from the RHS. In this case the rules "unwind." Thus we can use the same set of rules in several ways. Note, however, that in doing so we obtain quite different systems, with characteristically different control structures and behavior.

The organization and accessing of the rule set is also an important issue. The simplest scheme is the fixed, total ordering already mentioned, but elaborations quickly grow more complex. The term *conflict resolution* has been used to describe the process of selecting a rule. These issues of rule evaluation and organization are explored in more detail below.

2.1.2 Data Base

In the simplest production system the data base is simply a collection of symbols intended to reflect the state of the world, but the interpretation of those symbols depends in large part on the nature of the application. For those systems intended to explore symbol-processing aspects of human cognition, the data base is interpreted as modeling the contents of some memory mechanism (typically short-term memory, STM), with each symbol representing some "chunk" of knowledge; hence its total length (typically around seven elements) and organization (linear, hierarchical, etc.) are im-

[1]One class of production systems we will not address at any length is that of grammars for formal languages. While the intellectual roots are similar (Floyd, 1961; Evans, 1964), their use has evolved a distinctly different flavor. In particular, their nondeterminism is an important factor that provides a different perspective on control and renders the question of rule selection a moot point.

portant theoretical issues. Typical contents of STM for psychological models are those of PSG (Newell, 1973), where STM might contain purely content-free symbols such as:

```
QQ
(EE FF)
TT
```

or of VIS (Moran, 1973a), where STM contains symbols representing directions on a visualized map:

```
(NEW C-1 CORNER WEST L-1 NORTH L-2)
(L-2 LINE EAST P-2 P-1)
(HEAR NORTH EAST % END)
```

For systems intended to be knowledge-based experts, the data base contains facts and assertions about the world, is typically of arbitrary size, and has no *a priori* constraints on the complexity of organization. For example, the MYCIN system uses a collection of quadruples, consisting of an associative triple and a *certainty factor* (CF), which indicates (on a scale from -1 to 1) how strongly the fact has been confirmed (CF $>$ 0) or disconfirmed (CF $<$ 0):

```
(IDENTITY ORGANISM-1 E.COLI .8)
(SITE CULTURE-2 BLOOD 1.0)
(SENSITIVE ORGANISM-1 PENICILLIN -1.0)
```

As another example, in the DENDRAL system (Feigenbaum et al., 1971; Lindsay et al., 1980) the data base contains complex graph structures that represent molecules and molecular fragments.

A third style of organization for the data base is the "token stream" approach used, for example, in LISP70 (Tesler et al., 1973). Here the data base is a linear stream of tokens, accessible only in sequence. Each production in turn is matched against the beginning of the stream (i.e., if the first character of a production and the first character of the stream differ, the whole match fails), and if the rule is invoked, it may act to add, delete, or modify characters in the matched segment. The anchoring of the match at the first token offers the possibility of great efficiency in rule selection since the productions can be "compiled" into a decision tree that keys off sequential tokens from the stream. A very simple example is shown in Figure 2-1.

Whatever the organization of the data base, one important characteristic that should be noted is that it is the sole storage medium for all state variables of the system. In particular, unlike procedurally oriented languages, PS's do not provide for separate storage of control state information—there is no separate program counter, pushdown stack, etc.—and all information to be recorded must go into the single data base. We refer to this as *unity of data and control store* and examine some of its implications below. This store is, moreover, universally accessible to every rule in the

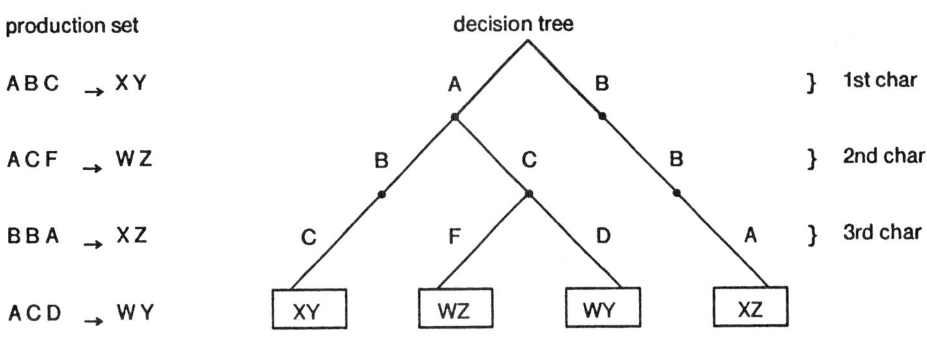

FIGURE 2-1 Production rule and decision tree representations of a simple system that replaces sequences of three symbols in the data base with sequences of two others.

system, so that anything put there is potentially detectable by any rule. We shall see that both of these points have significant consequences for the use of the data base as a communication channel.

2.1.3 Interpreter

The interpreter is the source of much of the variation found among different systems, but it may be seen in the simplest terms as a *select-execute* loop in which one rule applicable to the current state of the data base is chosen and then executed. Its action results in a modified data base, and the select phase begins again. Given that the selection is often a process of choosing the first rule that matches the current data base, it is clear why this cycle is often referred to as a *recognize-act*, or *situation-action*, loop. The range of variations on this theme is explored in Section 2.5.3 on control cycle architecture.

This alternation between selection and execution is an essential element of PS architecture, which is responsible for one of its most fundamental characteristics. By choosing each new rule for execution on the basis of the total contents of the data base, we are effectively performing a complete reevaluation of the control state of the system at every cycle. This is distinctly different from procedurally oriented approaches in which control flow is typically the decision of the process currently executing and is commonly dependent on only a small fraction of the total number of state variables. PS's are thus sensitive to any change in the entire environment, and potentially responsive to such changes within the scope of a single execution cycle. The price of such responsiveness is, of course, the computation time required for the reevaluation.

An example of one execution of the recognize-act loop for a greatly simplified version of Newell's PSG system will illustrate some of the foregoing notions. The production system, called PS.ONE, is assumed for this example to contain two productions, PD_1 and PD_2. We indicate this as follows:

PS.ONE: (PD_1 PD_2)

PD_1: (DD AND (EE) → BB)
PD_2: (XX → CC DD)

PD_1 says that if the symbol DD and some expression beginning with EE, i.e., (EE . . .), is found in STM, then insert the symbol BB at the front of STM. PD_2 says that if the symbol XX is found in STM, then first insert the symbol CC, then the symbol DD, at the front of STM.

The initial contents of STM are

STM: (QQ (EE FF) RR XX SS)

This STM is assumed to have a fixed maximum capacity of five elements. As new elements are inserted at the front (left) of STM, therefore, other elements will be lost (forgotten) off the right end. In addition, elements accessed when matching the condition of a rule are *refreshed* (pulled to the front of STM) rather than replaced.

The production system scans the productions in order: PD_1, then PD_2. Only PD_2 matches, so it is evoked. The contents of STM after this step are

STM: (DD CC XX QQ (EE FF))

PD_1 will match during the next cycle to yield

STM: (BB DD (EE FF) CC XX)

completing two cycles of the system.

2.2 Two Views of Production Systems

Prior work has suggested that there are two major views of PS's, characterized on one hand by psychological modeling efforts (PSG, PAS II, VIS, etc.) and on the other by performance-oriented, knowledge-based expert systems (e.g., MYCIN, DENDRAL). These distinct efforts have arrived at similar methodologies while pursuing differing goals.

The psychological modeling efforts are aimed at creating a program that embodies a theory of human performance of simple tasks. From the performance record of experimental human subjects, the modeler formulates the minimally competent set of production rules that is able to reproduce the behavior. Note that "behavior" here is meant to include *all* aspects of human performance (mistakes, the effects of forgetting, etc.), including all shortcomings or successes that may arise out of (and hence may be clues to) the "architecture" of human cognitive systems.[2]

An example of this approach is the PSG system, from which we constructed the example above. This system has been used to test a number of theories to explain the results of the Sternberg memory-scanning tasks (Newell, 1973), with each set of productions representing a different theory of how the human subject retains and recalls the information given to him or her during the psychological task. Here the subject first memorizes a small subset of a class of familiar symbols (e.g., digits) and then attempts to respond to a symbol flashed on a screen by indicating whether or not it was in the initial set. His or her response times are noted.

The task was first simulated with a simple production system that performed correctly but did not account for timing variations (which were due to list length and other factors). Refinements were then developed to incorporate new hypotheses about how the symbols were brought into memory, and eventually a good simulation was built around a small number of productions. Newell has reported (Newell, 1973) that use of a PS methodology led in this case to the novel hypothesis that certain timing effects are caused by a decoding process rather than by a search process. The experiment also clearly illustrated the possible tradeoffs in speed and accuracy between differing processing strategies. Thus the PS model was an effective vehicle for the expression and evaluation of theories of behavior.

The performance-oriented expert systems, on the other hand, start with productions as a representation of knowledge about a task or domain and attempt to build a program that displays competent behavior in that domain. These efforts are not concerned with similarities between the resulting systems and human performance (except insofar as the latter may provide a possible hint about ways to structure the domain or to approach the problem or may act as a yardstick for success, since few AI programs approach human levels of competence). They are intended simply to perform the task without errors of any sort, humanlike or otherwise. This approach is characterized by the DENDRAL system, in which much of the development has involved embedding a chemist's knowledge about mass spectrometry into rules usable by the program, without attempting to model the chemist's thinking. The program's knowledge is extended by adding rules that apply to new classes of chemical compounds. Similarly, much of the work on the MYCIN system has involved crystallizing informal knowledge of clinical medicine in a set of production rules.

Despite the difference in emphasis, researchers in both fields have

---

[2]For example, the critical evaluation of EPAM must ultimately depend not on the interest it may have as a learning machine, but on its ability to explain and predict phenomena of verbal learning (Feigenbaum, 1963). These phenomena include stimulus and response generalization, oscillation, retroactive inhibition, and forgetting—all of which are "mistakes" for a system intended for high performance but are important in a system meant to model human learning behavior.

been drawn to PS's as a methodology. For the psychological modelers, production rules offer a clear, formal, and powerful way of expressing basic symbol-processing acts that form the primitives of information-processing psychology (cf. Newell and Simon, 1972). For the designer of knowledge-based systems, production rules offer a representation of knowledge that can be accessed and modified with relative ease, making it quite useful for systems designed for incremental approaches to competence. For example, much of the MYCIN system's capability for explaining its actions is based on the representation of knowledge as individual production rules. This makes the knowledge far more accessible to the program itself than it might be if it were embodied in the form of ALGOL-like procedures. As in DENDRAL, the modification and upgrading of the system occur via incremental modification of, or addition to, the rule set.

Note that we are suggesting that it is possible to view a great deal of the work on PS's in terms of a unifying formalism. The intent is to offer a conceptual structure that can help organize what may appear to be a disparate collection of efforts. The presence of such a formalism should not, however, obscure the significant differences that arise from the various perspectives. For example, the decision to use RHS-driven rules in a goal-directed fashion implies a control structure that is simple and direct but relatively inflexible. This offers a very different programming tool than the LHS-driven systems do. The latter are capable of much more complex control structures, giving them capabilities much closer to those of a complete programming language. Recent efforts have begun to explore the issues of more complex, higher-level control within the PS methodology (see Section 2.4.9).

Production systems are seen by some as more than a convenient paradigm for approaching psychological modeling—rather as a methodology whose power arises out of its close similarity to fundamental mechanisms of human cognition. Newell and Simon (1972, pp. 803–804, 806) have argued that human problem-solving behavior can be modeled easily and successfully by a production system because it in fact is being generated by one:

> We confess to a strong premonition that the actual organization of human programs[4] closely resembles the production system organization. . . . We cannot yet prove the correctness of this judgment, and we suspect that the ultimate verification may depend on this organization's proving relatively satisfactory in many different small ways, no one of them decisive.
>
> In summary, we do not think a conclusive case can be made yet for production systems as *the* appropriate form of [human] program organization. Many of the arguments . . . raise difficulties. Nevertheless, our judgment stands that we should choose production systems as the preferred language for expressing programs and program organization.

Observations such as this have led to speculation that the interest in production systems on the part of those building high-performance knowledge-based systems is more than a coincidence. Some suggest that this is occurring because current research is (re)discovering what has been learned by naturally intelligent systems through evolution—that structuring knowledge in a production system format is an effective approach to the organization, retrieval, and use of very large amounts of knowledge.

The success of some rule-based AI systems does lend weight to this argument, and the PS methodology is clearly powerful. But whether or not this is a result of its equivalence to human cognitive processes and whether or not this implies that artificially intelligent systems ought to be similarly structured are still open questions, in our opinion.

2.3 Appropriate and Inappropriate Domains

Program designers have found that PS's easily model problems in some domains but are awkward for others. Let us briefly investigate why this may be so, and relate it to the basic structure and function of a PS.

We can imagine two very different classes of problems—the first is best viewed and understood as consisting of many independent states, while the second seems best understood via a concise, unified theory, perhaps embodied in a single law. Examples of the former include some views of perceptual psychology or clinical medicine, in which there are many states relative to the number of actions (this may be due either to our lack of a cohesive theory or to the basic complexity of the system being modeled). Examples of the latter include well-established areas of physics and mathematics, in which a few basic tenets serve to embody much of the required knowledge, and in which the discovery of unifying principles has emphasized the similarities in seemingly different states. This first distinction appears to be one important factor in distinguishing appropriate from inappropriate domains.

A second distinction concerns the complexity of control flow. At two extremes, we can imagine two processes, one of which is a set of independent actions and the other of which is a complex collection of multiple, parallel processes involving several dependent subprocesses.

A third distinction concerns the extent to which the knowledge to be embedded in a system can be separated from the manner in which it is to be used [also known as the controversy between declarative and procedural representations; see Winograd (1975) for an extensive discussion]. As one example, we can imagine simply stating facts, perhaps in a language like predicate calculus, without assuming how those facts will be employed. Alternatively, we could write procedural descriptions of how to accomplish a stated goal. Here the use of the knowledge is for the most part predetermined during the process of embodying it in this representation.

In all three of these distinctions, a PS is well-suited to the first description and ill-suited to the latter. The existence of multiple, nontrivially different, independent states is an indication of the feasibility of writing multiple, nontrivial, modular rules. A process composed of a set of independent actions requires only limited communication between the actions, and, as we shall see, this is an important characteristic of PS's. The ability to state what knowledge ought to be in the system without also describing its use greatly improves the ease with which a PS can be written (see Section 2.4.9).

For the second class of problems (unified theory, complex control flow, predetermined use for the knowledge), the economy of the relevant basic theory makes for either trivial rules or multiple, almost redundant, rules. In addition, a complex looping and branching process requires explicit communication between actions, in which one action explicitly invokes the next, while interacting subgoals require a similarly advanced communication process to avoid conflict. Such communication is not easily supplied in a PS-based system. The same difficulty also makes it hard to specify in advance exactly how a given fact should be used.

It seems also to be the nature of production systems to focus upon the variations within a domain rather than upon the common threads that link different facts or operations. Thus, for example, the process of addition is naturally expressed via productions as n^2 rewrite operations involving two symbols (the digits being added). The fact that addition is commutative, or rather that there is a property of "commutativity" shared by all operations that we consider to be addition, is a rather awkward one to express in production system terms. This same characteristic may, conversely, be viewed as a capability for focusing on and handling significant amounts of detail. Thus, where the emphasis of a task is on recognition of large numbers of distinct states, PS's provide a significant advantage. In a procedurally oriented approach, it is both difficult to organize and troublesome to update the repeated checking of large numbers of state variables and the corresponding transfers of control. The task is far easier in PS terms, where each rule can be viewed as a "demon" awaiting the occurrence of a specific state.[3]

The potential sensitivity and responsiveness of PS's, which arise from their continual reevaluation of the control state, has also been referred to as the *openness* of rule-based systems. It is characterized by the principle that "any rule can fire at any time," which emphasizes the fact that at any point in the computation any rule could be the next to be selected, depending only on the state of the data base at the end of the current cycle. Compare this to the normal situation in a procedurally oriented language,

[3]In the case of one PS (DENDRAL) the initial, procedural approach proved sufficiently inflexible that the entire system was rewritten in production rule terms (Lindsay et al., 1980).

where such a principle is manifestly untrue: it is simply not typically the case that, depending on the contents of that data base, any procedure in the entire program could potentially be the next to be invoked.

We do not mean to imply that both approaches *couldn't* perform in both domains, but that there are tasks for which one of them would prove awkward and the resulting system unenlightening. Such tasks are far more elegantly accomplished in only one of the two methodologies. The main point is that we can, to some extent, formalize our intuitive notion of which approach seems more appropriate by considering two essential characteristics of any PS: its set of multiple, independent rules and its limited, indirect channel of interaction via the data base.

2.4 Production System Characteristics

Despite the range of variation in methodologies, there appear to be many characteristics common to almost all PS's. It is the presence of these and their interactions that contribute to the "nature" of a PS, its capabilities, deficiencies, and characteristic behavior.

The network of Figure 2-2 is a summary of features and relationships. Each box represents some feature, capability, or parameter of interest, with arrows labeled with +'s and −'s suggesting the interactions between them. This rough scale of facilitation and inhibition is naturally very crude, but does indicate the interactions as we see them. Figure 2-2 contains at least three conceptually distinct sorts of factors: (a) those fundamental characteristics of the basic PS scheme (e.g., indirect, limited channel, constrained format); (b) secondary effects (e.g., automated modifiability of behavior); and (c) performance parameters of implementation (e.g., visibility of behavior flow, extensibility), which are helpful in characterizing PS strengths and weaknesses.

2.4.1 Indirect, Limited Channel of Interaction

Perhaps the most fundamental and significant characteristic of PS's is their restriction on the interactions between rules. In the simplest model, a pure PS, we have a completely ordered set of rules, with no interaction channel other than the data base. The total effect of any rule is determined by its modifications to the data base, and hence subsequent rules must "read" there any traces the system may leave behind. Winograd (1975, p. 194) characterizes this feature in discussing global modularity in programming:

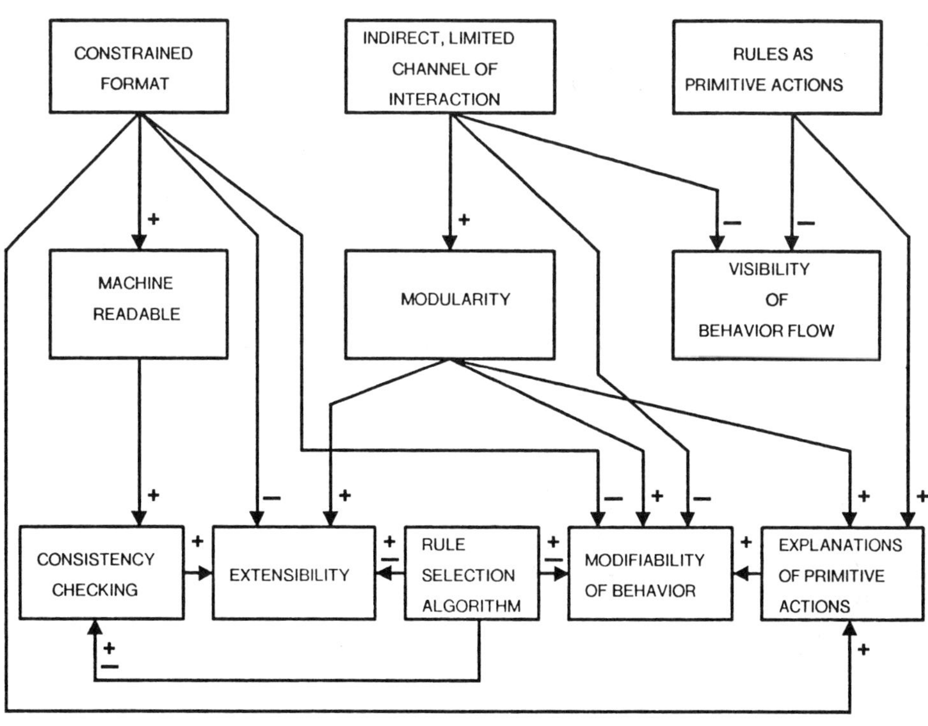

FIGURE 2-2 Basic features and relationships of a production system. Links labeled with a + indicate a facilitating relationship, while those labeled with a − indicate an inhibiting relationship.

> We can view production systems as a programming language in which all interaction is forced through a very narrow channel. . . . The temporal interaction [of individual productions] is completely determined by the data in this STM, and a uniform ordering regime for deciding which productions will be activated in cases where more than one might apply. . . . Of course it is possible to use the STM to pass arbitrarily complex messages which embody any degree of interaction we want. But the spirit of the venture is very much opposed to this, and the formalism is interesting to the degree that complex processes can be described without resort to such kludgery, maintaining the clear modularity between the pieces of knowledge and the global process which uses them.

While this characterization is clearly true for a pure PS, with its limitations on the size of STM, we can generalize on it slightly to deal with a broader class of systems. First, in the more general case, the channel is not so much narrow as *indirect* and *unique*. Second, the kludgery[4] arises not from arbitrarily complex messages but from *specially crafted* messages, which force highly specific, carefully chosen interactions.

With reference to the first point, one of the most fundamental characteristics of the pure PS organization is that rules must interact indirectly through a single channel. Indirection implies that all interaction must occur by the effect of modifications written in the data base; uniqueness of the channel implies that these modifications are accessible to every one of the rules. Thus, to produce a system with a specified behavior, one must not think in the usual terms of having one section of code call another explicitly, but rather use an indirect approach in which each piece of code (i.e., each rule) leaves behind the proper traces to trigger the next relevant piece. The uniform access to the channel, along with the openness of PS's, implies that those traces must be constructed in the light of a potential response from any rule in the system.

With reference to Winograd's second point, in many systems the action of a single rule may, quite legitimately, result in the addition of very complex structures to the data base (e.g., DENDRAL; see Section 2.5). Yet another rule in the same system may deposit just one carefully selected symbol, chosen solely because it will serve as an unmistakable symbol for precisely one other (carefully preselected) rule. Choosing the symbol carefully provides a way of sending what becomes a private message through a public channel; the continual reevaluation of the control state assures that the message can take immediate effect. The result is that one rule has effectively called another, procedure style, and this is the variety of kludgery that is contrary to the style of knowledge organization typically associated with a PS. It is the premeditated nature of such message passing (typically in an attempt to "produce a system with specified behavior") that is the primary violation of the "spirit" of PS methodology.

The primary effect of this indirect, limited interaction is the development of a system that is strongly modular, since no rule is ever called directly. The indirect, limited interaction is also, however, the most significant factor that makes the behavior of a PS more difficult to analyze. This results because, even for very simple tasks, overall behavior of a PS may not be at all evident from a simple review of its rules.

To illustrate many of these issues, consider the algorithm for addition of positive, single-digit integers used by Waterman (1974) with his PAS II production system interpreter. First, the procedural version of the algorithm, in which transfer of control is direct and simple.

```
          add(m,n)  ::=
A]                  count←0; nn←n;
B]             L1:  if count = m then return(nn);
```

[4]Kludge is a term drawn from the vernacular of computer programmers. It refers to a "patch" or "trick" in a program or system that deals with a potential problem, usually in an inelegant or nongeneralized way. Thus kludgery refers to the use of kludges.

```
C]          count←successor(count);
D]          nn←successor(nn);
E]          go(L1);
```

Compare this with the set of productions for the same task in Figure 2-3. The S in Rules 2, 3, and 5 indicates the successor function. After initialization (Rules 1 and 2), the system loops around Rules 4 and 5 producing the successor rules it needs (Rule 5) and then incrementing NN by 1 for M iterations. In this loop, intermediate calculations (the results of successor function computations) are saved via (PROD) in Rule 5, and the final answer is saved by (PROD) in Rule 3. Thus, as shown in Figure 2-4, after computing 4 + 2 the rule set will contain seven additional rules; it is recording its intermediate and final results by writing new productions and in the future will have these answers available in a single step. Note that the set of productions therefore *is* memory (and in fact long-term memory, or LTM, since productions are never lost from the set). The two are not precisely analogous, since the procedural version does simple addition, while the production set both adds and "learns." As noted by Waterman (1974), the production rule version does not assume the existence of a successor function. Instead Rule 5 writes new productions that give the successor for specific integers. Rule 3 builds what amounts to an addition table, writing a new production for each example that the system is given. Placing these new rules at the front of the rule set (i.e., before Rule 1) means that the addition table and successor function table will always be consulted before a computation is attempted, and the answer obtained in one step if possible. Without these extra steps, and with a successor function, the production rule set could be smaller and hence slightly less complex.

Waterman also points out some direct correspondences between the production rules in Figure 2-3 and the statements in the procedure above. For example, Rules 1 and 2 accomplish the initialization of line A, Rule 3 corresponds to line B, and Rule 4 to lines C and D. There is no production equivalent to the "goto" of line E because the production system execution cycle takes care of that implicitly. On the other hand, note that in the procedure there is no question whatsoever that the initialization step nn ← n is the second statement of "add" and that it is to be executed just once, at the beginning of the procedure. In the productions, the same action is predicated on an unintuitive condition of the STM (essentially it says that if the value of N is known, but NN has never been referenced or incremented, then initialize NN to the value that N has at that time). This degree of explicitness is necessary because the production system has no notion that the initialization step has already been performed in the given ordering of statements, so the system must check the conditions each time it goes through a new cycle.

Thus procedural languages are oriented toward the explicit handling of control flow and stress the importance of its influence on the fundamental organization of the program (as, for example, in recent develop-

Production Rules:

Condition (LHS)		*Action (RHS)*
1] (READY) (ORDER X_1)	→	(REP (READY) (COUNT X_1)) (ATTEND)
2] (N X_1) -(NN) -(S NN)	→	(DEP (NN X_1))
3] (COUNT X_1) (M X_1) (NN X_2) (N X_3)	→	(SAY X_2 IS THE ANSWER) (COND (M X_1) (N X_3)) (ACTION (STOP)) (ACTION (SAY X_2 IS THE ANSWER)) (PROD) (STOP)
4] (COUNT) (NN)	→	(REP (COUNT) (S COUNT)) (REP (NN) (S NN))
5] (ORDER X_1 X_2)	→	(REP (X_1 X_2) (X_2)) (COND (S X_3 X_1)) (ACTION (REP (S X_3 X_1) (X_3 X_2))) (PROD)

Initial STM:

(READY) (ORDER 0 1 2 3 4 5 6 7 8 9)

Notation:

- The X_1's in the condition are variables in the pattern match; all other symbols are literals. An X_1 appearing *only* in the action is also taken as a literal. Thus if Rule 5 is matched with $X_1=4$ and $X_2=5$, as its second action it would deposit (COND (S X_3 4)) in STM. These variables are local to each rule; that is, their previous bindings are disregarded.
- All elements of the LHS must be matched for a match to succeed.
- A hyphen indicates the ANDNOT operation.
- An expression enclosed in parentheses and starting with a literal [e.g., (COUNT) in Rule 4] will match any expression in STM that starts with the same literal [e.g., (COUNT 2)]. The expression (ORDER X_1 X_2) will match (ORDER 0 1 2 3 . . . 9) and bind $X_1=0$ and $X_2=1$.
- REP stands for REPlace, so that, for example, the RHS of Rule 1 will replace the expression (READY) in the data base with the expression (COUNT X_1) [where the variable X_1 stands for the element matched by the X_1 in (ORDER X_1)].
- DEP stands for DEPosit symbols at front of STM.
- ATTEND means wait for input from computer terminal. For this example, typing (M 4)(N 2) will have the system add 4 and 2.
- SAY means output to terminal.

FIGURE 2-3 A production system for the addition of two single-digit integers [after Waterman (1974), simplified slightly].

- (COND . . .) is shorthand for (DEP (COND . . .)).
- (ACTION . . .) is shorthand for (DEP (ACTION . . .)).
- PROD means gather all items in the STM of the form (COND . . .) and put them together into an LHS, gather all items of the form (ACTION . . .) and put them together into an RHS, and remove all these expressions from the STM. Form a production from the resulting LHS and RHS, and add it to the front of the set of productions (i.e., before Rule 1).

FIGURE 2-3 continued

ments in structured programming). PS's, on the other hand, emphasize the statement of independent chunks of knowledge from a domain and make control flow a secondary issue. Given the limited form of communication available in PS's, it is more difficult to express concepts that require structures larger than a single rule. Thus, where the emphasis is on global behavior of a system rather than on the expression of small chunks of knowledge, PS's are, in general, less transparent than equivalent procedural routines.

2.4.2 Constrained Format

While there are wide variations in the format permitted by various PS's, in any given system the syntax is traditionally quite restrictive and generally follows the conventions accepted for PS's.[5] Most commonly this means, first, that the side of the rule to be matched should be a simple predicate built out of a Boolean combination of computationally primitive operations; these involve (as noted above) only matching and detection. Second, it means the side of the rule to be executed should perform conceptually simple operations on the data base. In many of the systems oriented toward psychological modeling, the side to be matched consists of a set of literals or simple patterns, with the understanding that the set is to be taken as a conjunction, so that the predicate is an implicit one regarding the success or failure of matching all of the elements. Similarly, the side to be executed performs a simple symbol replacement or rearrangement.

Whatever the format, though, the conventions noted lead to clear restrictions for a pure production system. First, as a predicate, the matching side of a rule should return only some indication of the success or failure of the match.[6] Second, as a simple expression, the matching operation is

[5]Note, however, that the tradition arises out of a commonly followed convention rather than any essential characteristic of a PS.

[6]While binding individual variables or segments in the process of pattern matching is quite often used, it would be considered inappropriate to have the matching process produce a complex data structure intended for processing by another part of the system.

RULE	STATUS	STM AFTER RULE SUCCEEDS	NEW RULES/COMMENTS
CYCLE #1			
		(READY)(ORDER 0 1 2 3 4 5 6 7 8 9)	initial state
Rule 1	Succeeds	(COUNT 0)(ORDER 0 1 2 3 4 5 6 7 8 9) (N 2)(M 4)(COUNT 0) (ORDER 0 1 2 3 4 5 6 7 8 9)	awaits input (M 4)(N 2) after input
Rule 2	Succeeds	(NN 2)(N 2)(M 4)(COUNT 0) (ORDER 0 1 2 3 4 5 6 7 8 9)	X_1 bound to 2
Rule 3	Fails		
Rule 4	Succeeds	(S NN 2)(N 2)(M 4)(S COUNT 0) (ORDER 0 1 2 3 4 5 6 7 8 9)	
Rule 5	Succeeds	(S NN 2)(N 2)(M 4)(S COUNT 0) (ORDER 1 2 3 4 5 6 7 8 9)	X_1 bound to 0 New Rule 6: (S X_3 0) $\rightarrow$ (REP(S X_3 0)(X_3 1)
CYCLE #2			
Rule 6	Succeeds	(S NN 2)(N 2)(M 4)(COUNT 1) (ORDER 1 2 3 4 5 6 7 8 9)	X_3 bound to the literal COUNT
Rule 1	Fails		
Rule 2	Fails		
Rule 3	Fails		
Rule 4	Fails		
Rule 5	Succeeds	(S NN 2)(N 2)(M 4)(COUNT 1) (ORDER 2 3 4 5 6 7 8 9)	New Rule 7: (S X_3 1) $\rightarrow$ (REP(S X_3 1)(X_3 2))
CYCLE #3			
Rule 7	Fails		
Rule 6	Fails		
Rule 1	Fails		
Rule 2	Fails		
Rule 3	Fails		
Rule 4	Fails		
Rule 5	Succeeds	(S NN 2)(N 2)(M 4)(COUNT 1) (ORDER 3 4 5 6 7 8 9)	New Rule 8: (S X_3 2) $\rightarrow$ (REP(S X_3 2)(X_3 3))
CYCLE #4			
Rule 8	Succeeds	(NN 3)(N 2)(M 4)(COUNT 1) (ORDER 3 4 5 6 7 8 9)	X_3 bound to NN
Rule 7	Fails		
Rule 6	Fails		
Rule 1	Fails		
Rule 2	Fails		
Rule 3	Fails		
Rule 4	Succeeds	(S NN 3)(N 2)(M 4)(S COUNT 1) (ORDER 3 4 5 6 7 8 9)	
Rule 5	Succeeds	(S NN 3)(N 2)(M 4)(S COUNT 1) (ORDER 4 5 6 7 8 9)	New Rule 9: (S X_3 3) $\rightarrow$ (REP(S X_3 3)(X_3 4))
CYCLE #5			
Rule 9	Succeeds	(NN 4)(N 2)(M 4)(S COUNT 1) (ORDER 4 5 6 7 8 9)	
	. . etc. . .	<continued cycling>	Rules 10 and 11 generated
Rule 3	Succeeds	(NN 6)(N 2)(M 4)(COUNT 4) (ORDER 6 7 8 9)	Bind X_1 to 4, X_2 to 6, X_3 to 2; Prints '6 IS THE ANSWER'; Rule 12 produced; Terminates.

FIGURE 2-4 Trace of production system shown in Figure 2-3. Adding 4 and 2.

precluded from using more complex control structures like iteration or recursion within the expression itself (although such operations can be constructed from multiple rules). Finally, as a matching and detection operation, it must only "observe" the state of the data base and not change it in the operation of testing it.

We can characterize a continuum of possibilities for the side of the rule to be executed. There might be a single primitive action, a simple collection of independent actions, a carefully ordered sequence of actions, or even more complex control structures. We suggest that there are two related forms of simplicity that are important here. First, each action to be performed should be one that is a conceptual primitive for the domain. In the DENDRAL system, for example, it is appropriate to use chemical bond breaking as the primitive, rather than to describe the process at some lower level. Second, the complexity of control flow for the execution of these primitives should be limited—in a pure production system, for example, we might be wary of a complex set of actions that is, in effect, a small program of its own. Again, it should be noted that the system designer may of course follow or disregard these restrictions.

These constraints on form make the dissection and "understanding" of productions by other parts of the program a more straightforward task, strongly enhancing the possibility of having the program itself read and/or modify (rewrite) its own productions. For example, the MYCIN system makes strong use of the concept of allowing one part of the system to read the rules being executed by another part. The system does a partial evaluation of rule premises. Since a premise is a Boolean combination of predicate functions such as

```
($AND (SAME CNTXT SITE)                (the site of the culture is blood and
      (SAME CNTXT GRAM GRAMPOS)         the gramstain is grampositive and
      (DEF IS CNTXT AIR AEROBIC))       the aerobicity is definitely aerobic)
```

and since clauses that are unknown cause subproblems that may involve long computations to be set up, it makes sense to check to see if, based on what is currently known, the entire premise is sure to fail (e.g., if any clause of a conjunction is known to be false). We cannot simply EVAL each clause, since this will trigger a search if the value is still unknown. But if the clause can be "unpacked" into its proper constituents, it is possible to determine whether or not the value is known as yet, and if so, what it is. This is done via a *template* associated with each predicate function. For example, the template for SAME is

```
(SAME CNTXT PARM VALUE)
```

and it gives the generic type and order of arguments for the function (much like a simplified procedure declaration). By using this as a guide to unpack and extract the needed items, we can safely do a partial evaluation of the rule premise. A similar technique is used to separate the known and unknown clauses of a rule for the user's benefit when the system is explaining itself (see Chapter 18 for several examples).

Note that part of the system is reading the code being executed by the other part. Furthermore, note that this reading is guided by information carried in the rule components themselves. This latter characteristic assures that the capability is unaffected by the addition of new rules or predicate functions to the system.

This kind of technique limits expressibility, however, since the limited syntax may not be sufficiently powerful to make expressing each piece of knowledge an easy task. This in turn both restricts extensibility (adding something is difficult if it is hard to express it) and makes modification of the system's behavior more difficult (e.g., it might not be particularly attractive to implement a desired iteration if doing so requires several rules rather than a line or two of code).

2.4.3 Rules as Primitive Actions

In a pure PS, the smallest unit of behavior is a rule invocation. At its simplest, this involves the matching of literals on the LHS, followed by replacement of those symbols in the data base with the ones found on the RHS. While the variations can be more complex, it is in some sense a violation of the spirit of things to have a sequence of actions in the RHS.

Moran (1973b), for example, acknowledges a deviation from the spirit of production systems in VIS when he groups rules in "procedures" within which the rules are totally ordered for the purpose of conflict resolution. He sees several advantages in this departure. It is "natural" for the user (a builder of psychological models) to write rules as a group working toward a single goal. This grouping restricts the context of the rules. It also helps minimize the problem of implicit context: when rules are ordered, a rule that occurs later in the list may really be applicable only if some of the conditions checked by earlier rules are untrue. This dependency, referred to as implicit context, is often not made explicit in the rule, but may be critical to system performance. The price paid for these advantages is twofold: first, extra rules, less directly attributable to psychological processes, are needed to switch among procedures; second, it violates the basic production system tenet that any rule should (in principle) be able to fire at any time—here only those in the currently active procedure can fire.

To the extent that the pure production system restrictions are met, we can consider rules as the quanta of intelligent behavior in the system. Otherwise, as in the VIS system, we must look at larger aggregations of rules to trace behavior. In doing so, we lose some of the ability to quantify and measure behavior, as is done, for example, with the PSG system simulation of the Sternberg task, where response times are attributed to individual production rules and then compared against actual psychological data.

A different sort of deviation is found in the DENDRAL system, and in a few MYCIN rules. In both, the RHS is effectively a small program, carrying out complex sequences of actions. In this case, the quanta of behavior are the individual actions of these programs, and understanding the system thus requires familiarity with them. By embodying these bits of behavior in a stylized format, we make it possible for the system to "read" them to its users (achieved in MYCIN as described above) and hence provide some explanation of its behavior, at least at this level. This prohibition against complex behaviors within a rule, however, may force us to implement what are (conceptually) simple control structures by using the combined effects of several rules. This of course may make overall behavior of the system much more opaque (see Section 2.4.5).

2.4.4 Modularity

We can regard the *modularity* of a program as the degree of separation of its functional units into isolatable pieces. A program is *highly modular* if any functional unit can be changed (added, deleted, or replaced) with no unanticipated change to other functional units. Thus program modularity is inversely related to the strength of coupling between its functional units.

The modularity of programs written as pure production systems arises from the important fact that the next rule to be invoked is determined solely by the contents of the data base, and no rule is ever called directly. Thus the addition (or deletion) of a rule does not require the modification of any other rule to provide for or delete a call to it. We might demonstrate this by repeatedly removing rules from a PS: many systems will continue to display some sort of "reasonable" behavior.[7] By contrast, adding a procedure to an ALGOL-like program requires modification of other parts of the code to insure that the procedure is invoked, while removing an arbitrary procedure from such a program will generally cripple it.

Note that the issue here is more than simply the "undefined function" error message, which would result from a missing procedure. The problem would persist even if the compiler or interpreter were altered to treat undefined functions as no-ops. The issue is a much more fundamental one concerning organization of knowledge: programs written in procedure-oriented languages stress the kind of explicit passing of control from one section of code to another that is characterized by the calling of procedures.

[7]The number of rules that could be removed without performance degradation (short of redundancies) is an interesting characteristic that would appear to be correlated with which of the two common approaches to PS's is taken. The psychological modeling systems would apparently degenerate fastest, since they are designed to be minimally competent sets of rules. Knowledge-based expert systems, on the other hand, tend to embody numerous independent subproblems in rules and often contain overlapping or even purposefully redundant representations of knowledge. Hence, while losing their competence on selected problems, it appears they would often function reasonably well, even with several rules removed.

This is typically done at a selected time and in a particular context, both carefully chosen by the programmer. If a no-op is substituted for a missing procedure, the context upon returning will not be what the programmer expected, and subsequent procedure calls will be executed in increasingly incorrect environments. Similarly, procedures that have been added must be called from *somewhere* in the program, and the location of the call must be chosen carefully if the effect is to be meaningful.

Production systems, on the other hand, especially in their pure form, emphasize the decoupling of control flow from the writing of rules. Each rule is designed to be, ideally, an independent chunk of knowledge with its own statement of relevance (either the conditions of the LHS, as in a data-driven system, or the action of the RHS, as in a goal-directed system). Thus, while the ALGOL programmer carefully chooses the order of procedure calls to create a selected sequence of environments, in a production system it is the environment that chooses the next rule for execution. And since a rule can only be chosen if its criteria of relevance have been met, the choice will continue to be a plausible one, and system behavior will remain "reasonable," even as rules are successively deleted.

This inherent modularity of pure production systems eases the task of programming in them. Given some primitive action that the system fails to perform, it becomes a matter of writing a rule whose LHS matches the relevant indicators in the data base, and whose RHS performs the action. Whereas the task is then complete for a pure PS, systems that vary from this design have the additional task of assuring proper invocation of the rule (not unlike assuring the proper call of a new procedure). The difficulty of this varies from trivial in the case of systems with goal-oriented behavior (like MYCIN) to substantial in systems that use more complex LHS scans and conflict resolution strategies.

For systems using the goal-oriented approach, rule order is usually unimportant. Insertion of a new rule is thus simple and can often be totally automated. This is, of course, a distinct advantage where the rule set is large and the problems of system complexity are significant. For others (like PSG and PAS II) rule order can be critical to performance and hence requires careful attention. This can, however, be viewed as an advantage, and indeed, Newell (1973) tests different theories of behavior by the simple expedient of changing the order of rules. The family of Sternberg task simulators includes a number of production systems that differ only by the interchange of two rules, yet display very different behavior. Waterman's system (Waterman, 1974) accomplishes "adaptation" by the simple heuristic of placing a new rule immediately before a rule that causes an error.[8]

---

[8]One specific example of the importance of rule order can be seen in our earlier example of addition (Figure 2-3). Here Rule 5 assumes that an ordering of the digits exists in STM in the form (ORDER 0 1 2 . . .) and from this can be created the successor function for each digit. If Rule 5 were placed before Rule 1, the system wouldn't add at all. In addition, acquiring the notion of successor in subsequent runs depends entirely on the placement of the new successor productions *before* Rule 3, or the effect of this new knowledge would be masked.

2.4.5 Visibility of Behavior Flow

Visibility of behavior flow is the ease with which the overall behavior of a PS can be understood, either by observing the system or by reviewing its rule base. Even for conceptually simple tasks, the stepwise behavior of a PS is often rather opaque. The poor visibility of PS behavior compared to that of the procedural formalism is illustrated by the Waterman integer addition example outlined in Section 2.4.1. The procedural version of the iterative loop there is reasonably clear (lines B, C, and E), and an ALGOL-type

```
FOR I := 1 UNTIL N DO . . .
```

would be completely obvious. Yet the PS formalism for the same thing requires nonintuitive productions (like 1 and 2) and symbols like NN whose only purpose is to "mask" the condition portion of a rule so it will not be invoked later [such symbols are termed *control elements* (Anderson, 1976)].

The requirement for control elements, and much of the opacity of PS behavior, is a direct result of two factors noted above: the unity of control and data store, and the reevaluation of the data base at every cycle. Any attempt to "read" a PS requires keeping in mind the entire contents of the data base and scanning the entire rule set at every cycle. Control is much more explicit and localized in procedural languages, so that reading ALGOL code is a far easier task.[9]

The perspective on knowledge representation implied by PS's also contributes to this opacity. As suggested above, PS's are appropriate when it is possible to specify the content of required knowledge without also specifying the way in which it is to be used. Thus, reading a PS does not generally make clear how it works so much as what it may know, and the behavior is consequently obscured. The situation is often reversed in procedural languages: program behavior may be reasonably clear, but the domain knowledge used is often opaquely embedded in the procedures. The two methodologies thus emphasize different aspects of knowledge and program organization.

2.4.6 Machine Readability

Several interesting capabilities arise from making it possible for the system to examine its own rules. As one example, it becomes possible to implement automatic consistency checking. This can proceed at several levels. In the simplest approach we can search for straightforward syntactic problems such as contradiction (e.g., two rules of the form A & B → C and A & B → -C) or subsumption (e.g., two rules of the form D & E & F → G and D

[9]One of the motivations for the interest in structured programming is the attempt to emphasize still further the degree of explicitness and localization of control.

& F → G). A more sophisticated approach, which would require extensive domain-specific knowledge, might be able to detect "semantic" problems, such as, for example, a rule of the form A & B → C when it is known from the meanings of A and B that A → B. Many other (domain-specific) tests may also be possible. The point is that by automating the process, extensive (perhaps exhaustive) checks of newly added productions are possible (and could perhaps be run in background mode when the system is otherwise idle).

A second sort of capability (described in the example in Section 2.4.2) is exemplified by the MYCIN system's approach to examining its rules. This is used in several ways (Davis, 1976) and produces both a more efficient control structure and precise explanations of system behavior.

2.4.7 Explanation of Primitive Actions

Production system rules are intended to be modular chunks of knowledge and to represent primitive actions. Thus explaining primitive acts should be as simple as stating the corresponding rule—all necessary contextual information should be included in the rule itself. Achieving such clear explanations, however, strongly depends on the extent to which the assumptions of modularity and explicit context are met. In the case where stating a rule does provide a clear explanation, the task of modification of program behavior becomes easier.

As an example, the MYCIN system often successfully uses rules to explain its behavior. This form of explanation fails, however, when considerations of system performance or human engineering lead to rules whose context is obscure. One class of rule, for example, says, in effect, "If A seems to be true, and B seems to be true, then that's (more) evidence in favor of A."[10] It is phrased this way rather than simply "If B seems true, that's evidence in favor of A," because B is a very rare condition, and it appears counterintuitive to ask about it unless A is suspected to begin with. The first clause of the rule is thus acting as a strategic filter, to insure that the rule is not even tried unless it has a reasonable chance of succeeding. System performance has been improved (especially as regards human engineering considerations), at the cost of a somewhat more opaque rule.

2.4.8 Modifiability, Consistency, and Rule Selection Mechanism

As noted above, the tightly constrained format of rules makes it possible for the system to examine its own rule base, with the possibility of modifying it in response to requests from the user or to ensure consistency with

[10]These are known as *self-referencing rules*; see Chapter 5.

respect to newly added rules. While all these are conceivable in a system using a standard procedural approach, the heavily stylized format of rules, and the typically simple control structure of the interpreters, makes them all realizable prospects in a PS.

Finally, the relative complexity of the rule selection mechanism will have varying effects on the ability to automate consistency checks, or behavior modification and extension. An RHS scan with backward chaining (i.e., a goal-directed system; see Section 2.5.3) seems to be the easiest to follow since it mimics part of human reasoning behavior, while an LHS scan with a complex conflict resolution strategy makes the system generally more difficult to understand. As a result, predicting and controlling the effects of changes in, or additions to, the rule base are directly influenced in either direction by the choice of rule selection mechanism.

2.4.9 Programmability

The answer to "How easy is it to program in this formalism?" is "It's reasonably difficult." The experience has been summarized (Moran, 1973a):

> Any structure which is added to the system diminishes the explicitness of rule conditions. . . . Thus rules acquire implicit conditions. This makes them (superficially) more concise, but at the price of clarity and precision. . . . Another questionable device in most present production systems (including mine) is the use of tags, markers, and other cute conventions for communicating between rules. Again, this makes for conciseness, but it obscures the meaning of what is intended. The consequence of this in my program is that it is very delicate: one little slip with a tag and it goes off the track. Also, it is very difficult to alter the program; it takes a lot of time to readjust the signals.

One source of the difficulties in programming production systems is the necessity of programming "by side effect." Another is the difficulty of using the PS methodology on a problem that cannot be broken down into the solution of independent subproblems or into the synthesis of a behavior that is neatly decomposable.

Several techniques have been investigated to deal with this difficulty. One of them is the use of tags and markers (control elements), referred to above. We have come to believe that the manner in which they are used, particularly in psychological modeling systems, can be an indication of how successfully the problem has been put into PS terms. To demonstrate this, consider two very different (and somewhat idealized) approaches to writing a PS. In the first, the programmer writes each rule independently of all the others, simply attempting to capture in each some chunk of required knowledge. The creation of each rule is thus a separate task. Only when all of them have been written are they assembled, the data base initialized, and the behavior produced by the entire set of rules noted. As a second approach, the programmer starts out with a specific behavior that he or she wants to recreate. The entire rule set is written as a group with this in mind, and, where necessary, one rule might deposit a symbol like A00124 in STM solely to trigger a second specific rule on the next cycle.

In the first case the control elements would correspond to recognizable states of the system. As such, they function as indicators of those states and serve to trigger what is generally a large class of potentially applicable rules.[11] In the second case there is no such correspondence, and often only a single rule recognizes a given control element. The idea here is to insure the execution of a specific sequence of rules, often because a desired effect could not be accomplished in a single rule invocation. Such idiosyncratic use of control elements is formally equivalent to allowing one rule to call a second, specific rule and hence is very much out of character for a PS. To the extent that such use takes place, it appears to us to be suggestive of a failure of the methodology—perhaps because a PS was ill-suited to the task to begin with or because the particular decomposition used for the task was not well chosen.[12] Since one fundamental assumption of the PS methodology as a psychological modeling tool is that states of the system correspond to what are at least plausible (if not immediately recognizable) individual "states of mind," the relative abundance of the two uses of control elements mentioned above can conceivably be taken as an indication of how successfully the methodology has been applied.

A second approach to dealing with the difficulty of programming in PS's is the use of increasingly complex forms within a single rule. Where a pure PS might have a single action in its RHS, several psychological modeling systems (PAS II, VIS) have explored the use of more complex sequences of actions, including the use of conditional exits from the sequence.

Finally, one effort (Rychener, 1975) has investigated the use of PS's that are unconstrained by prior restrictions on rule format, use of tags, etc. The aim here is to employ the methodology as a formalism for explicating knowledge sources, understanding control structures, and examining the effectiveness of PS's for attacking the large problems typical of artificial intelligence. The productions in this system often turn out to have a relatively simple format, but complex control structures are built via carefully orchestrated interaction of rules. This is done with several techniques, including explicit reliance on both control elements and certain characteristics of the data base architecture. For example, iterative loops

---

[11]This basic technique of "broadcasting" information and allowing individual segments of the system to determine their relevance has been extended and generalized in systems like HEARSAYII (Lesser et al., 1974) and BEINGS (Lenat, 1975).

[12]The possibility remains, of course, that a "natural" interpretation of a control element will be forthcoming as the model develops, and additional rules that refer to it will be added. In that case the ease of adding the new rules arises out of the fact that the technique of allowing one rule to call another was not used.

are manufactured via explicit use of control elements, and data are (redundantly) reasserted in order to make use of the "recency" ordering on rules (the rule that mentions the most recently asserted data item is chosen first; see Section 2.5.3). These techniques have supported the reincarnation as PS's of a number of sizable AI programs [e.g., STUDENT (Bobrow, 1968)], but, Bobrow notes, "control tends to be rather inflexible, failing to take advantage of the openness that seems to be inherent in PS's."

This reflects something of a new perspective on the use of PS's. Previous efforts have used them as tools for analyzing both the core of knowledge essential to a given task and the manner in which such knowledge is used. Such efforts relied in part on the austerity of the available control structure to keep all of the knowledge explicit. The expectation is that each production will embody a single chunk of knowledge. Even in the work of Newell (1973), which used PS's as a medium for expressing different theories in the Sternberg task, an important emphasis is placed on productions as a model of the detailed control structure of humans. In fact, every aspect of the system is assumed to have a psychological correlate.

The work reported by Rychener (1975), however, after explicitly detailing the chunks of knowledge required in the word problem domain of STUDENT, notes a many-to-many mapping between its knowledge chunks and productions. That work also focuses on complex control regimes that can be built using PS's. While still concerned with knowledge extraction and explication, it views PS's more as an abstract programming language and uses them as a vehicle for exploring control structures. While this approach does offer an interesting perspective on such issues, it should also be noted that as productions and their interactions grow more complex, many of the advantages associated with traditional PS architecture may be lost (for example, the loss of openness noted above). The benefits to be gained are roughly analogous to those of using a higher-level programming language: while the finer grain of the process being examined may become less obvious, the power of the language permits large-scale tasks to be undertaken and makes it easier to examine phenomena like the interaction of entire categories of knowledge.

The use of PS's has thus grown to encompass several different forms, many of which are far more complex than the pure PS model described initially.

2.5 Taxonomy of Production Systems

In this section we suggest four dimensions along which to characterize PS's: form, content, control cycle architecture, and system extensibility. For each dimension we examine related issues and indicate the range as evidenced by systems currently (or recently) in operation.

2.5.1 Form—How Primitive or Complex Should the Syntax of Each Side Be?

There is a wide variation in the syntax used by PS's and corresponding differences in both the matching and detection process and the subsequent action caused by rule invocation. For matching, in the simplest case only literals are allowed, and it is a conceptually trivial process (although the rule and data base may be so large that efficiency becomes a consideration). Successively more complex approaches allow free variables [Waterman's poker player (Waterman, 1970)], syntactic classes (as in some parsing systems), and increasingly sophisticated capabilities of variable and segment binding and of pattern specification (PAS II, VIS, LISP70).[13]

The content of the data base also influences the question of form. One interesting example is Anderson's ACT system (Anderson, 1976), whose rules have node networks in their LHS's. The appearance of an additional piece of network as input results in a "spread of activation" occurring in parallel through the LHS of each production. The rule that is chosen is the one whose LHS most closely matches the input and that has the largest subpiece of network already in its working memory.

As another example, the DENDRAL system uses a literal pattern match, but its patterns are graphs representing chemical classes. Each class is defined by a basic chemical structure, referred to as a *skeleton*. As in the data base, atoms composing the skeleton are given unique numbers, and chemical bonds are described by the numbers of the atoms they join (e.g., "5 6"). The LHS of a rule is the name of one of these skeletons, and a side effect of a successful match is the recording of the structural correspondence between atoms in the skeleton and those in the molecule. The action parts of these rules describe a sequence of actions to perform: *break* one or more bonds, saving a molecular fragment, and *transfer* one or more hydrogen atoms from one fragment to another. An example of a simple rule is

```
ESTROGEN  →  (BREAK (14 15) (13 17))
             (HTRANS +1 +2)
```

The LHS here is the name of the graph structure that describes the estrogen class of molecules, while the RHS indicates the likely locations for bond breakages and hydrogen transfers when such molecules are subjected to mass spectral bombardment. Note that while both sides of the rule are relatively complex, they are written in terms that are conceptual primitives in the domain.

A related issue is illustrated by the rules used by MYCIN, where the LHS consists of a Boolean combination of standardized predicate functions. Here the testing of a rule for relevance consists of having the stan-

---

[13]For an especially thorough discussion of pattern-matching methods in production systems as used in VIS, see Moran (1973a, pp. 42–45).

dard LISP evaluator assess the LHS, and all matching and detection are controlled by the functions themselves. While using functions in LHS's provides power that is missing from using a simple pattern match, that creates the temptation to write one function to do what should be expressed by several rules. For example, one small task in MYCIN is to deduce that certain organisms are present, even though they have not been recovered from any culture. This is a conceptually complex, multistep operation, which is currently (1975) handled by invocation of a single function. If one succumbs often to the temptation to write one function rather than several rules, the result can be a system that may perform the initial task but that loses a great many of the other advantages of the PS approach. The problem is that the knowledge embodied in these functions is unavailable to anything else in the system. Whereas rules can be accessed and their knowledge examined (because of their constrained format), chunks of ALGOL-like code are not nearly as informative. The availability of a standardized, well-structured set of operational primitives can help to avoid the temptation to create new functions unnecessarily.

2.5.2 Content—Which Conceptual Levels of Knowledge Belong in Rules?

The question here is how large a reasoning step should be embodied in a single rule, and there seem to be two distinct approaches. Systems designed for psychological modeling (PAS II, PSG, etc.) try to measure and compare tasks and determine required knowledge and skills. As a result, they try to dissect cognition into its most primitive terms. While there is, of course, a range of possibilities, from the simple literal replacement found in PSG to the more sophisticated abilities of PAS II to construct new productions, rules in these systems tend to embody only the most basic conceptual steps. Grouped at the other end of this spectrum are the task-oriented systems, such as DENDRAL and MYCIN, which are designed to be competent at selected real-world problems. Here the conceptual primitives are at a much higher level, encompassing in a single rule a piece of reasoning that may be based both on experience and on a highly complex model of the domain. For example, the statement "a gram-negative rod in the blood is likely to be an *E. coli*" is based in part on knowledge of physiological systems and in part on clinical experience. Often the reasoning step is sufficiently large that the rule becomes a significant statement of a fact or principle in the domain, and, especially where reasoning is not yet highly formalized, a comprehensive collection of such rules may represent a substantial portion of the knowledge in the field.

An interesting, related point of methodology is the question of what kinds of knowledge ought to go into rules. Rules expressing knowledge about the domain are the necessary initial step, but interest has been generated lately in the question of embodying strategies in rules. We have been actively pursuing this in the implementation of *meta-rules* in the MYCIN system (Davis et al., 1977). These are "rules about rules," and they contain strategies and heuristics. Thus, while the ordinary rules contain standard object-level knowledge about the medical domain, meta-rules contain information about rules and embody strategies for selecting potentially useful paths of reasoning. For example, a meta-rule might suggest:

> If the patient has had a bowel tumor, then in concluding about organism identity, rules that mention the gastrointestinal tract are more likely to be useful.

There is clearly no reason to stop at one level, however—third-order rules could be used to select from or order the meta-rules, by using information about how to select a strategy (and hence represent a search through "strategy space"); fourth-order rules would suggest how to select criteria for choosing a strategy; etc.

This approach appears to be promising for several reasons. First, the expression of any new level of knowledge in the system can mean an increase in competence. This sort of strategy information, moreover, may translate rather directly into increased speed (since fewer rules need be tried) or no degradation in speed even with large increases in the number of rules. Second, since meta-rules refer to rule content rather than rule names, they automatically take care of new object-level rules that may be added to the system. Third, the possibility of expressing this information in a format that is essentially the same as the standard one means a uniform expression of many levels of knowledge. This uniformity in turn means that the advantages that arise out of the embodiment of any knowledge in a production rule (accessibility and the possibility of automated explanation, modification, and acquisition of rules) should be available for the higher-order rules as well.

2.5.3 Control Cycle Architecture

The basic control cycle can be broken down into two phases called *recognition* and *action*. The recognition phase involves selecting a single rule for execution and can be further subdivided into *selection* and *conflict resolution*.[14] In the selection process, one or more potentially applicable rules are chosen from the set and passed to the conflict resolution algorithm, which chooses one of them. There are several approaches to selection, which can be categorized by their rule scan method. Most systems (e.g., PSG, PAS II) use some variation of an LHS scan, in which each LHS is evaluated in turn. Many stop scanning at the first successful evaluation (e.g., PSG), and

[14]The range of conflict resolution algorithms in this section was suggested in a talk by Don Waterman.

hence conflict resolution becomes a trivial step (although the question then remains of where to start the scan on the next cycle: to start over at the first rule or to continue from the current rule).

Some systems, however, collect all rules whose LHS's evaluate successfully. Conflict resolution then requires some criterion for choosing a single rule from this set (called the conflict set). Several have been suggested, including:

(i) Rule order—there is a complete ordering of all rules in the system, and the rule in the conflict set with the highest priority is chosen.
(ii) Data order—elements of the data base are ordered, and that rule is chosen which matches element(s) in the data base with highest priority.
(iii) Generality order—the most specific rule is chosen.
(iv) Rule precedence—a precedence network (perhaps containing cycles) determines the hierarchy.
(v) Recency order—either the most recently executed rule or the rule containing the most recently updated element of the data base is chosen.

For example, the LISP70 interpreter uses (iii), while DENDRAL uses (iv).

A different approach to the selection process is used in the MYCIN system. The approach is goal-oriented and uses an RHS scan. The process is quite similar to the unwinding of consequent theorems in PLANNER (Hewitt, 1972): given a required subgoal, the system retrieves the (unordered) set of rules whose actions conclude something about that subgoal. The evaluation of the first LHS is begun, and if any clause in it refers to a fact not yet in the data base, a generalized version of this fact becomes the new subgoal, and the process recurs. However, because MYCIN is designed to work with judgmental knowledge in a domain where collecting all relevant data and considering all possibilities are very important, in general, it executes *all* rules from the conflict set rather than stopping after the first success.

The meta-rules mentioned above may also be seen as a way of selecting a subset of the conflict set for execution. There are several advantages to this. First, the conflict resolution algorithm is stated explicitly in the meta-rules (rather than implicitly in the system's interpreter) and in the same representation as the rest of the rule-based knowledge. Second, since there can be a set of meta-rules for each subgoal type, MYCIN can specify distinct, and hence potentially more customized, conflict resolution strategies for each individual subgoal. Since the backward chaining of rules may also be viewed as a depth-first search of an AND/OR goal tree,[15] we may view

[15]An AND/OR goal tree is a reasoning network in which AND's (conjunctions of LHS conditionals) and OR's (disjunctions of multiple rules that all allow the same goal/conclusion to be reached) alternate. This structure is described in detail during the discussion of MYCIN's control structure in Chapter 5.

the search tree as storing at every branch point a collection of specific heuristics about which path to take. In addition, rules in the system are inexact, judgmental statements with a model of "approximate implication" in which the user may specify a measure of how firmly he or she believes that a given LHS implies its RHS (Shortliffe and Buchanan, 1975). This admits the possibility of writing numerous, perhaps conflicting heuristics, whose *combined* judgment forms the conflict resolution algorithm.

Control cycle architecture affects the rest of the production system in several ways. Overall efficiency, for example, can be strongly influenced. The RHS scan in a goal-oriented system insures that only relevant rules are considered in the conflict set. Since this is often a small subset of the total, and one that can be computed once and stored for reference, there is no search necessary at execution time; thus the approach can be quite efficient. In addition, since this approach seems natural to humans, the system's behavior becomes easier to follow.

Among the conflict resolution algorithms mentioned, rule order and recency order require a minimal amount of checking to determine the rule with highest priority. Generality order can be efficiently implemented, and the LISP70 compiler uses it effectively. Data order and rule precedence require a significant amount of bookkeeping and processing, and hence may be slower (PSH, a development along the lines of PSG, attacks precisely this problem).

The relative difficulty of adding a new rule to the system is also determined to a significant degree by the choice of control cycle architecture. Like PLANNER with its consequent theorems, the goal-oriented approach makes it possible to simply "throw the rule in the pot" and still be assured that it will be retrieved properly. The generality-ordering technique also permits a simple, automatic method for placing the new rule, as do the data-ordering and recency strategies. In the latter two cases, however, the primary factor in ordering is external to the rule, and hence, while rules may be added to the rule set easily, it is somewhat harder to predict and control their subsequent selection. For both rule order and rule precedence networks, rule addition may be a substantially more difficult problem that depends primarily on the complexity of the criteria used to determine the hierarchy.

2.5.4 System Extensibility

Learning, viewed as augmentation of the system's rule base, is of concern both to the information-processing psychologists, who view it as an essential aspect of human cognition, and to designers of knowledge-based systems, who acknowledge that building truly expert systems requires an incremental approach to competence. As yet we have no range or even points of comparison to offer because of the scarcity of examples. Instead, we suggest some standards by which the ease of augmentation may be judged.[16]

Perhaps the most basic question is "How automatic is it?" The ability to learn is clearly an area of competence by itself, and thus we are really asking how much of that competence has been captured in the system, and how much the user has to supply. Some aspects of this competence include:

- If the current system displays evidence of a bug caused by a missing or incorrect rule, how much of the diagnosing of the bug is handled by the system, and how much tracing must be done by the user?
- Once the bug is uncovered, who fixes it? Must the user modify the code by hand? . . . tell the system in some command language what to do? . . . indicate the generic type of the error? Can the user simply point out the offending rule, or can the system locate and fix the bug itself?
- Can the system indicate whether the new rule will in fact fix the bug or if it will have side effects or undesired interactions?
- How much must the user know about rule format conventions when expressing a new (or modified) rule? Must he or she know how to code it explicitly? . . . know precisely the vocabulary to use? . . . know generally how to phrase it? Or can the user indicate in some general way the desired rule and allow the system to make the transformation? Who has to know the semantics of the domain? For example, can the system detect impossible conjunctions (A & B, where A → not-B), or trivial disjunctions (A $\vee$ B, where A → not-B)? Who knows enough about the system's idiosyncrasies to suggest optimally fast or powerful ways of expressing rules?
- How difficult is it to enter strategies?
- How difficult is it to enter control structure information? Where is the control structure information stored: in aggregations of rules or in higher-order rules? The former makes augmentation or modification a difficult problem; the latter makes it somewhat easier, since the information is explicit and concentrated in one place.
- Can you assure continued consistency of the rule base? Who has to do the checking?

These are questions that will be important and useful to confront in designing any system intended to do knowledge acquisition, especially any built around production rules as underlying knowledge representation.

---

[16]It should be noted that this discussion is oriented primarily toward an interactive, mixed-initiative view of learning, in which the human expert teaches the system and answers questions it may generate. It has also been influenced by our experience in attacking this problem for the MYCIN system (Davis, 1976). Many other models of the process (e.g., teaching by selected examples) are of course possible.

2.6 Conclusions

In artificial intelligence research, production systems were first used to embody primitive chunks of information-processing behavior in simulation programs. Their adaptation to other uses, along with increased experience with them, has focused attention on their possible utility as a general programming mechanism. Production systems permit the representation of knowledge in a highly uniform and modular way. This may pay off handsomely in two areas of investigation: development of programs that can manipulate their own representations and development of a theory of loosely coupled systems, both computational and psychological. Production systems are potentially useful as a flexible modeling tool for many types of systems; current research efforts are sufficiently diverse to discover the extent to which this potential may be realized.

Information-processing psychologists continue to be interested in production systems. PS's can be used to study a wide range of tasks (Newell and Simon, 1972). They constitute a general programming system with the full power of a Turing machine, but use a homogeneous encoding of knowledge. To the extent that the methodology is that of a pure production system, the knowledge embedded is completely explicit and thus aids experimental verification or falsifiability of theories that use PS's as a medium of expression. Productions may correspond to verifiable bits of psychological behavior (Moran, 1973a), reflecting the role of postulated human information-processing structures such as short-term memory. PS's are flexible enough to permit a wide range of variation based on reaction times, adaptation, or other commonly tested psychological variables. Finally, they provide a method for studying learning and adaptive behavior (Waterman, 1974).

For those wishing to build knowledge-based expert systems, the homogeneous encoding of knowledge offers the possibility of automating parts of the task of dealing with the growing complexity of such systems. Knowledge in production rules is both accessible and relatively easy to modify. It can be executed by one part of the system as procedural code and examined by another part as if it were a declarative expression. Despite the difficulties of programming PS's, and their occasionally restrictive syntax, the fundamental methodology suggests a convenient and appropriate framework for the task of structuring and specifying large amounts of knowledge. (See Hayes-Roth et al., 1983, for recent uses of production systems.) It may thus prove to be of great utility in dealing with the problems of complexity encountered in the construction of large knowledge bases.

PART TWO

Using Rules

3

The Evolution of MYCIN's Rule Form

There is little doubt that the decision to use rules to encode infectious disease knowledge in the nascent MYCIN system was largely influenced by our experience using similar techniques in DENDRAL. However, as mentioned in Chapter 1, we did experiment with a semantic network representation before turning to the production rule model. The impressive published examples of Carbonell's SCHOLAR system (Carbonell, 1970a; 1970b), with its ability to carry on a mixed-initiative dialogue regarding the geography of South America, seemed to us a useful model of the kind of rich interactive environment that would be needed for a system to advise physicians.

Our disenchantment with a pure semantic network representation of the domain knowledge arose for several reasons as we began to work with Cohen and Axline, our collaborating experts. First, the knowledge of infectious disease therapy selection was ill-structured and, we found, difficult to represent using labeled arcs between nodes. Unlike South American geography, our domain did not have a clear-cut hierarchical organization, and we found it challenging to transfer a page or two from a medical textbook into a network of sufficient richness for our purposes. Of particular importance was our need for a strong inferential mechanism that would allow our system to reason about complex relationships among diverse concepts; there was no precedent for inferences on a semantic net that went beyond the direct, labeled relationships between nodes.[1]

Perhaps the greatest problem with a network representation, and the greatest appeal of production rules, was our gradually recognized need to deal with small chunks of domain knowledge in interacting with our expert collaborators. Because they were not used to dissecting their clinical reasoning processes, it was totally useless to ask them to "tell us all that you know." However, by discussing specific difficult patients, and by encour-

[1]The PROSPECTOR system (Duda et al., 1978a; 1978b), which was developed shortly after MYCIN, uses a network of inferential relations—a so-called *inference net*—to combine a semantic network with inference rules.

aging our collaborators to justify their questions or decisions, those of us who were not expert in the field began to tease out "nuggets" of domain knowledge—individual inferential facts that the experts identified as pertinent for problem solving in the domain. By encoding these facts as individual production rules, rather than attempting to decompose them into nodes and links in a semantic network, we found that the experts were able to examine and critique the rules without difficulty. This transparency of the knowledge base, coupled with the inherent modularity of knowledge expressed as rules, allowed us to build a prototype system quickly and allowed the experts to identify sources of performance problems with relative ease. They particularly appreciated having the ability to observe the effects of chained reasoning based on individual rules that they themselves had provided to us. In current AI terminology, the organization of knowledge was not object-centered but was centered around inferential *processes*.

Our early prototype rapidly diverged from DENDRAL because we were driven by different performance goals and different characteristics of the knowledge in the domain. Of particular importance was the need to deal with inexact inference; unlike the categorical conclusions in DENDRAL's rules, the actions in MYCIN's productions were typically conclusions about the state of the world that were not known with certainty. We soon recognized the need to accumulate evidence regarding alternative hypotheses as multiple rules lent credence to the conclusions. The need for a system to measure the weight of evidence of competing hypotheses was not surprising; it had also characterized conventional statistical approaches to computer-based medical decision making. Our certainty factor model, to which we refer frequently throughout this book (and which is the subject of Part Four), was developed in response to our desire to deal with uncertainty while attempting to keep knowledge modular and in rules.

The absence of complete certainty in most of our rules meant that we needed a control structure that would consider *all* rules regarding a given hypothesis and not stop after the first one had succeeded. This need for exhaustive search was distinctly different from control in DENDRAL, where the hierarchical ordering of rules was particularly important for correct prediction and interpretation (see Chapter 2). Because rule ordering was not important in MYCIN, the modularity of rules was heightened; the experts did not need to worry about ordering the rules they gave us or about other details of control.[2]

Another important distinction between the reasoning paradigms of DENDRAL and MYCIN was recognized early. DENDRAL generated hypotheses regarding plausible chemical structures and used its rule set to

---

[2]The arbitrary order of MYCIN's rules did lead to some suboptimal performance characteristics, however. In particular, the ordering of questions to the user often seemed unfocused. It was for this reason that the MAINPROPS (later known as INITIALDATA) feature was devised (see Chapter 5), and the concept of meta-rules was developed to allow rule selection and ordering based on strategic knowledge of the domain (see Chapter 28). The development of *prototypes* in CENTAUR (Chapter 23) was similarly motivated.

test these hypotheses and to select the best ones. Thus DENDRAL's control scheme involved forward invocation of rules for the last phase of the plan-generate-and-test paradigm. On the other hand, it was unrealistic for MYCIN to start by generating hypotheses regarding likely organisms or combinations of pathogens; there were no reasonable heuristics for pruning the search space, and there was no single piece of orienting information similar to the mass spectrum, which provided the planning information to constrain DENDRAL's hypothesis generator. Thus MYCIN was dependent on a reasoning model based on evidence gathering, and its rules were used to guide the process of input data collection. Because we wanted to avoid problems of natural language understanding, and also did not want to teach our physician users a specialized input language, we felt it was unreasonable to ask the physician to enter some subset of the relevant patient descriptors and then to have the rules fire in a data-driven fashion. Instead, we chose a goal-directed control structure that allowed MYCIN to ask the relevant questions and therefore permitted the physician to respond, in general, with simple one-word answers. Thus domain characteristics led to forward-directed use of the generate-and-test paradigm in DENDRAL and to goal-directed use of the evidence-gathering paradigm in MYCIN.

We were not entirely successful in putting all of the requisite medical knowledge into rules. Chapter 5 describes the problems encountered in trying to represent MYCIN's therapy selection algorithm as rules. Because therapy selection was initially implemented as LISP code rather than in rules, MYCIN's explanation system was at that time unable to justify specific therapy decisions in the same way it justified its diagnostic decisions. This situation reflects the inherent tension between procedural and production-based representation of this kind of algorithmic knowledge. The need for further work on the problem was clear. A few years later Clancey assumed the challenge of rewriting the therapy selection part of MYCIN so that appropriate explanations could be generated for the user. We were unable to encode the entire algorithm in rules, however, and instead settled on a solution reminiscent of the generate-and-test approach used in DENDRAL: rules were used to evaluate therapeutic hypotheses after they had been proposed (generated) by an algorithm that was designed to support explanations of its operation. This clever solution, described in Chapter 6, seemed to provide an optimal mix of procedural and rule-based knowledge.

3.1 Design Considerations

Many of the decisions that led to MYCIN's initial design resulted from a pragmatic response to perceived demands of physicians as computer users. Our perceptions were largely based on our own intuitions and observations about problems that had limited the success of previous computer-based medical decision-making systems. More recently we have undertaken formal studies of physician attitudes (Chapter 34), and the data that resulted, coupled with our prior experience building MYCIN, have had a major impact on our more recent work with ONCOCIN (Chapter 35). These issues are addressed in detail in Part Eleven.

However, since many of the features and technical decisions that are reflected in the other chapters in Part Two are based on our early analysis of design considerations for MYCIN (Shortliffe, 1976), we summarize those briefly here. We have already alluded to several ways in which MYCIN departed from the pure production systems described in Chapter 2. These are further discussed throughout the book (see especially Chapter 36), but it is important to recognize that the system's development was evolutionary. Most such departures resulted from characteristics of the medical domain, from our perceptions of physicians as potential computer users, or from unanticipated problems that arose as MYCIN grew in size and complexity.

We recognized at the outset that educational programs designed for instruction of medical students had tended to meet with more long-term success than had clinical consultation programs. A possible explanation, we felt, was that instructional programs dealt only with hypothetical patients in an effort to teach diagnostic or therapeutic concepts, whereas consultation systems were intended to assist physicians with the management of real patients in the clinical setting. A program aiding decisions that can directly affect patient well-being must fulfill certain responsibilities to physicians if they are to accept the computer and make use of its knowledge. For example, we observed that physicians had tended to reject computer programs designed as decision-making aids unless they were accessible, easy to use, forgiving of simple typing errors,. reliable, and fast enough to save time. Physicians also seemed to prefer that a program function as a *tool*, not as an "all-knowing" machine that analyzes data and then states its conclusions as dogma without justifying them. We had also observed that physicians are most apt to need advice from consultation programs when an unusual diagnostic or therapeutic problem has arisen, which is often the circumstance when a patient is acutely ill. Time is an important consideration in such cases, and a physician will probably be unwilling to experiment with an "unpolished" prototype. In fact, time will *always* be an important consideration given the typical daily schedule of a practicing physician.

With considerations such as these in mind from the start, we defined the following list of prerequisites for the acceptance of a clinical consultation program (Shortliffe et al., 1974):[3]

[3]This analysis was later updated, expanded, and analyzed after we gained more experience with MYCIN (Shortliffe, 1980).

1. The program should be *useful*; i.e., it should respond to a well-documented clinical need and, ideally, should tackle a problem with which physicians have explicitly requested assistance.
2. The program should be *usable*; i.e., it should be fast, accessible, easy to learn, and simple for a novice computer user.
3. The program should be *educational when appropriate*; i.e., it should allow physicians to access its knowledge base and must be capable of conveying pertinent information in a form that they can understand and from which they can learn.
4. The program should be able to *explain its advice*; i.e., it should provide the user with enough information about its reasoning so that he or she can decide whether to follow the recommendation.
5. The program should be able to *respond to simple questions*; i.e., it should be possible for the physician to request justifications of specific inferences by posing questions, ideally using natural language.
6. The program should be able to *learn new knowledge*; i.e., it should be possible to tell it new facts and have them easily and automatically incorporated for future use, or it should be able to learn from experience as it is used on large numbers of cases.
7. The program's knowledge should be *easily modified*; i.e, adding new knowledge or correcting errors in new knowledge should be straightforward, ideally accomplished without having to make explicit changes to the program (code) itself.

This list of design considerations played a major role in guiding our early work on MYCIN, and, as we suggested earlier in this chapter, they largely account for our decision to implement MYCIN as a rule-based system. In Chapters 4 through 6, and in subsequent discussions of knowledge acquisition (Part Three) and explanation (Part Six), it will become clear how the production system formalism provided a powerful foundation for an evolving system intended to satisfy the design goals we have outlined here.

3.2 MYCIN as an Evolutionary System

One of the lessons of the MYCIN research has been the way in which the pure theory of production systems, as described in Chapter 2, has required adaptation in response to issues that arose during system development. Many of these deviations from a pure production system approach with backward chaining will become clear in the ensuing chapters. For reference we summarize here some of those deviations, citing the reasons for changes that were introduced, even though this anticipates more complete discussions in later chapters.

1. *The context tree*: We realized the need to allow our rules to make conclusions about multiple objects and to keep track of the hierarchical relationships among them. The context tree (described in Chapter 5) was created to provide a mechanism for representing hierarchical relationships and for quantifying over multiple objects. For instance, ORGANISM-1 and ORGANISM-2 are contexts of the same type that are related to cultures in which they are observed to be growing and that need to be compared, collected, and reasoned with together at times.

2. *Instantiation of contexts*: When a new object required attention, we needed a mechanism for creating it, naming it, and recording its associations with other contexts in the system. Prototypical contexts, similar in concept to the "frames" of more recent AI work (Minsky, 1975), provided a mechanism for creating new objects when they were needed. These are called *context-types* to distinguish them from individual contexts. For instance, ORGANISM is a context-type.

3. *Development of MAINPROPS*: Physicians using the evolving system began to complain that MYCIN did not ask questions in the order they were used to. For example, they indicated it was standard practice to discuss the site, timing, and method of collection for a culture as soon as it was first mentioned. Thus we created a set of parameters called the MAINPROPS for each prototypical context.[4] The values of these parameters were automatically asked for when a context was first created, thereby providing the kind of focused questioning with which physicians felt most comfortable. The benefit was in creating a more natural sequence of questions. The risk was in asking a few more questions than might be logically necessary for some cases. This was a departure from the pure production system aproach of asking questions only when the information was needed for evaluating the premise of a rule.

4. *Addition of antecedent rules*: The development of MAINPROPS meant that we knew there were a small number of questions that would be asked every time a context was created. In a pure backward-chaining system, rules that had premise conditions that depended *only* on the values of parameters on MAINPROPS lists would be invoked when needed so there was no *a priori* reason to do anything special with such rules. However, two situations arose that made us flag such rules as antecedent rules to be invoked in a data-driven fashion rather than await goal-oriented invocation. First, there were cases in which an answer to one MAINPROPS

[4]This name was later changed to INITIALDATA in EMYCIN systems.

question could uniquely determine (via a definitional antecedent rule) the value of another subsequent MAINPROPS property for the same context (e.g., if an organism's identity was known, its gram stain and morphology were of course immediately determined). By implementing such rules as antecedent rules and by checking to see if the value of a MAINPROPS parameter was known before asking the user, we avoided inappropriate or unnecessary questions.

The second use of antecedent rules arose when the preview mechanism was implemented (see paragraph 12 below). Because an antecedent rule could determine that a premise condition of another rule was false, such rules could be rejected immediately during the preview phase. If antecedent rules had been saved for backward-chained invocation, however, the preview mechanism would have failed to reject the rule in question. Thus the MONITOR would have inappropriately pursued the first two or three conditions in the premise of the rule, perhaps at considerable computational expense, only to discover that the subsequent clause was clearly false due to an answer of an earlier MAINPROPS question. Thus antecedent rules offered a considerable enhancement to efficiency in such cases.

5. *Self-referencing rules*: As will be discussed in Chapter 5, it became necessary to write rules in which the same parameter appeared in both the premise and the action parts. Self-referencing rules of the form A & B & C → A are a departure from the pure production system approach, and they required changes to the goal-oriented rule invocation mechanism. They were introduced for three purposes: default reasoning, screening, and using information about risks and utilities.

a. *Default reasoning*: MYCIN makes no inferences except those that are explicitly stated in rules, as executed under the certainty factor (CF) model (see Chapter 11) and backward-chaining control. There are no implicit ELSE clauses in the rules that assign default values to parameters.[5] When rules fail to establish a value for a parameter, its value is considered to be UNKNOWN—no other defaults are used. One use of the self-referencing rules is to assign a default value to a parameter explicitly:

> IF a value for X is not known (after trying to establish one),
> THEN conclude that the value of X is Z.

Thus, reasoning with defaults is done in the rules and can be explained in the same way as any other conclusions. The control structure had to be changed, however, to delay executing these rules until all other relevant rules had been tried.

b. *Screening*: For purposes of human engineering, we needed a screen-

[5]Explicit else clauses were defined in the syntax (see Chapter 5) but were eliminated, mostly for the sake of simplicity.

ing mechanism to avoid asking about unusual parameters (B and C, above) unless there is already some *other* evidence for the hypothesis (A) under consideration. For example, we did not want MYCIN to use the simple rule

Pseudomonas-type skin lesions → *Pseudomonas*

unless there already was evidence for *Pseudomonas*—otherwise, the program would appear to be asking for minute pieces of data inappropriately.

c. *Utilities*: Self-referencing rules gave us a way to consider the risks of failing to consider a hypothesis. Once there is evidence for *Pseudomonas*, say, being a possible cause of an infection, then a self-referencing rule can boost the importance of considering it in therapy, based on the high risk of failing to treat for it.

6. *Mapping rules*: We soon recognized the need for rules that could be applied iteratively to a set of contexts (e.g., a rule comparing a current organism to each bacterium in the set of all previous organisms in the context tree). Special predicate functions (e.g., THERE-IS, FOR-EACH, ONE-OF) were therefore written so that a condition in a rule premise could map iteratively over a set of contexts. This was a partial solution to the general representation problem of expressing universal and existential quantification. Only by considering all contexts of a type could we determine if all or some of them had specified properties. The context tree allowed easy comparisons within any parent context (e.g., all the organisms growing in CULTURE-2) but did not allow easy comparison across contexts (e.g., all organisms growing in all cultures).

7. *Tabular representation of knowledge*: When large numbers of rules had been written, each having essentially the same form, we recognized the efficiency of collapsing them into a single rule that read the values for its premise conditions and action from a specialized table. (A related concept was implemented in changes that allowed physicians to enter information in a more natural way. If they were looking at a patient's record for answers to questions, it was more convenient to enter many items at once into a table of related parameters. There was, however, the attendant risk of asking for information that would not actually be used in some cases.) Chapter 5 describes the implementation of this feature.

8. *Augmentation of rules*: As multiple experts joined to collaborate on development of the knowledge base, we recognized the need to keep track of who wrote individual rules. Thus extra properties were added to rules that allowed us to keep track of authorship, to record literature references that defended the inference stored in the rule, and to allow recording of free-form text justification of certain complicated rules for which the normal rule translation was somewhat cryptic. These extra *slots* associated with

rules gave the latter more the character of frames than of pure productions.

9. *The therapy algorithm*: As described in Chapter 5, the final step in MYCIN's decision process was largely algorithmic and proved difficult to encode in rules. Chapter 6 describes our eventual solution, in which we integrated algorithmic and rule-based approaches in a novel manner.

10. *Management of uncertainty*: Previous PS's had not encoded the uncertainty in rules. Thus MYCIN's certainty factor model (see Part Four) was an augmentation mandated by the nature of decision making in this complex medical domain.

11. *Addition of meta-rules*: As mentioned in Chapter 2 and described in Chapter 28, we began to realize that strategies for optimal rule invocation could themselves be encoded in rules. MYCIN's PS approach was modified to manage high-level meta-rules that could be invoked via the usual rule monitor and that would assist in determining optimal problem-solving strategies.

12. *Addition of a preview mechanism*: It became clear that it was inefficient for the rule interpreter to assess the first few conditions in a rule premise if it was already known that a subsequent condition was false. Thus a preview mechanism was added to the interpreter so that it first examined the whole premise to see if there were parameters whose values had previously been determined. The addition of the preview mechanism made it important to add antecedent rules, as mentioned above (paragraph 4).

13. *The concept of a unity path*: Because many MYCIN rules reached conclusions with less than certainty, it was generally necessary to invoke *all* rules that could bear on the value of a parameter under consideration. This is part of MYCIN's cautious evidence-gathering strategy in which *all* relevant evidence available at the time of a consultation is used. However, if a rule successfully reaches a conclusion with certainty (i.e., it has CF = 1), then it is not necessary to try alternate rules. Thus the rule monitor was altered to try first those rules that could reach a conclusion with certainty, either through a single rule with CF = 1 or through a chain of rules, each with CF = 1 (a so-called unity path). When certain rules succeeded, the alternate rules were ignored, and this prevented inefficiencies in the development of the reasoning network and in the generation of questions to the user.

14. *Prevention of circular reasoning*: The issue of circular reasoning does not normally arise in pure production systems but was a serious potential problem for MYCIN. (Self-referencing rules, discussed in paragraph 5 above, are a special case of the general circular reasoning problem

involving any number of rules.) Special changes to the rule monitor were required to prevent this undesirable occurrence (see Chapter 5).

15. *The tracing mechanism*: As is described in Chapter 5, we made the decision to determine *all* possible values of a parameter instead of determining only the value specified in the premise condition of interest. This potential inefficiency was tolerated for reasons of user acceptance. We found that physicians preferred a focused and exhaustive consideration of one topic at a time, rather than having the system return subsequently to the subject when another possible value of the same parameter was under consideration.

16. *The ASKFIRST concept*: Pure production systems have not generally distinguished between attributes that the user may already know with certainty (such as values of laboratory tests) and those that inherently require inference. In MYCIN this became an important distinction, which required that each parameter be labeled as an ASKFIRST attribute (originally named LABDATA as discussed in Chapter 5) or as a parameter that should first be determined by using rules rather than by asking the user.

17. *Procedural conditions associated with parameters*: We also discovered unusual circumstances in which a special test was necessary before MYCIN could decide whether it was appropriate to ask the user for the value of a parameter. This was solved through a kind of procedural attachment, i.e., an executable piece of conditional code associated with a parameter, which would allow the rule monitor to decide whether a question to the user was appropriate. Each parameter thus began to be represented as a frame with several slots, including some whose values were procedures.

18. *Rephrasing prompts*: As users became more familiar with MYCIN, we found that they preferred short, less detailed prompts when the program requested information. Thus a "terse" mode was implemented and could be selected by an experienced user. Similarly, a reprompt mechanism was developed so that a novice user, puzzled by a question, could be given a more detailed explanation of what MYCIN needed to know. These features were added to an already existing HELP facility, which showed examples of acceptable answers to questions.

19. *Multiple instances of contexts*: Some of the questions asked by MYCIN are necessary for deciding whether or not to create contexts (rather than for determining the value of a parameter). Furthermore, optimal human engineering requires that this kind of question be phrased differently for the first instance of a context-type than for subsequent instances. These alternate prompts are discussed in Chapter 5.

20. *HERSTORY List*: Another addition to the rule monitor in MYCIN was a mechanism for keeping track of all rules invoked, failing, succeeding, etc., and the reasons for these various outcomes. The so-called HERSTORY List, or history tree, then provided the basis for MYCIN's explanations in response to users' queries.

21. *Creation of a Patient Data Table*: Finally, we recognized the need to develop mechanisms for (a) reevaluating cases when more information became available and (b) assessing the impact of modifications to the knowledge base on a library of cases previously handled well. These goals were achieved by the development of a Patient Data Table, i.e., a mechanism for storing and accessing the initializing conditions necessary for full consideration of cases. See Chapter 5 for further discussions of this feature.

3.3 A Word About the Logic of MYCIN

The logic of MYCIN's reasoning is propositional logic, where the elementary propositions are fact triples and the primary rule of inference is *modus ponens* (A and A $\supset$ B implies B). It is extended (and somewhat complicated) in the following respects:

- Certainty factors (CF's) are attached (or propagated) to all propositions.
- CF's are associated with all implications.
- Predicates are associated with fact triples to change the way facts stated in rules are matched against facts in the dynamically constructed case record. A variety of predicates have been defined (see Section 5.1.5); some refer to values of attributes (e.g., NOT-SAME, ONE-OF) and some reference values of CF's (e.g., KNOWN, DEFINITE).
- Limited quantification is allowed over conjunctions of propositions (e.g., THERE-IS, FOR-EACH).
- Meta-level reasoning is allowed in order to increase efficiency (e.g., using meta-rules or looking for a unity path).

MYCIN's logic is incomplete in the sense that we know there are propositions that can be expressed in the language but are not provable as theorems. MYCIN's logic is not inconsistent in itself (we believe), but it is *not* immune to inconsistencies introduced into its knowledge base.

3.4 Overview of Part Two

The remainder of this part consists of three papers that summarize MYCIN and its use of production rules. In order to orient the reader to MYCIN's overall motivation and design, we first include as Chapter 4 an introductory paper that provides an overview of the system as of 1978 (approximately the time when development of the medical knowledge base stopped). Chapter 5 is the original detailed description of MYCIN from 1975. It provides technical information on the system's representation and control mechanisms. Chapter 6 is a brief paper from 1977 that discusses the way in which production rules were adapted to deal with the algorithmic knowledge regarding therapy selection.

4

The Structure of the MYCIN System

William van Melle

A number of constraints influenced the design of the MYCIN system. In order to be useful, the system had to be easy to use and had to provide consistently reliable advice. It needed to be able to accommodate the large body of task-specific knowledge required for high performance, a knowledge base that is subject to change over time. The system also had to be able to use inexact or incomplete information. This applies not only to the absence of definitive laboratory data, but also to the medical domain itself (which is characterized by much judgmental knowledge). Finally, to be a useful interactive system, MYCIN needed to be capable of supplying explanations for its decisions and responding to physicians' questions, rather than simply printing orders.

The MYCIN system comprises three major subprograms, as depicted in Figure 4-1. The *Consultation Program* is the core of the system; it interacts with the physician to obtain information about the patient, generating diagnoses and therapy recommendations. The *Explanation Program* provides explanations and justifications for the program's actions. The *Knowledge-Acquisition Program* is used by experts to update the system's knowledge base.

This chapter is based on an article originally appearing under the title "MYCIN: A knowledge-based consultation program for infectious disease diagnosis" in *International Journal of Man-Machine Studies* 10: 313–322 (1978).

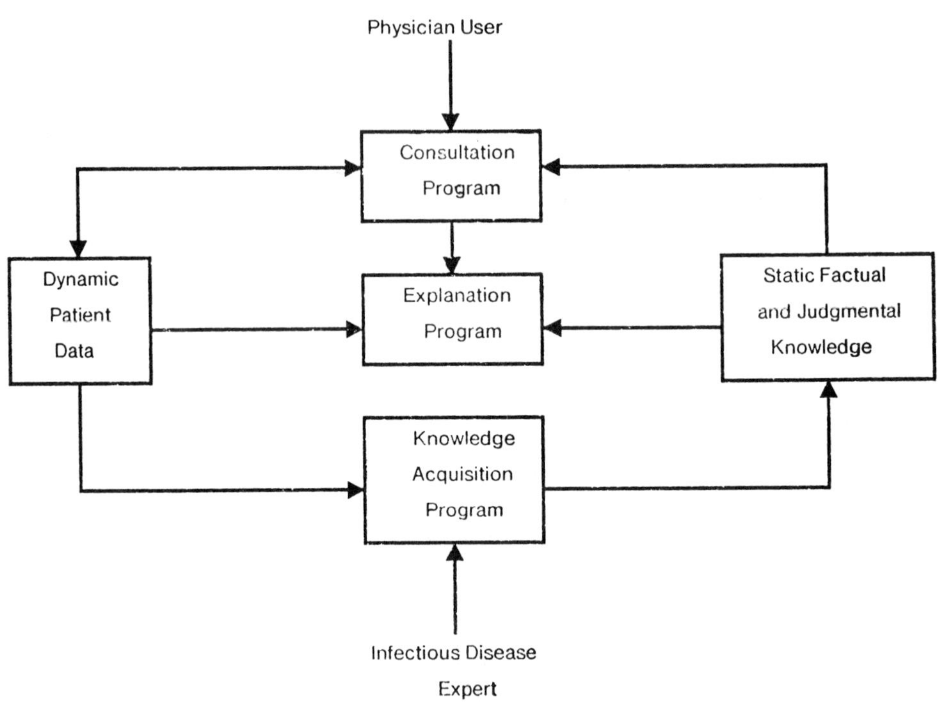

FIGURE 4-1 Organization of the MYCIN system. Arrows denote information flow between modules, knowledge base, and users.

4.1 The Consultation Program

Excerpts from a sample consultation are shown in Figure 4-2. (A complete annotated typescript is shown in the Appendix.) The doctor's responses are in upper-case letters following the double-asterisk prompt. Considerable effort has gone into the human engineering aspects of the system, to make the interaction as smooth as possible. If the user finds a question unclear, he or she can request a rephrasing with a list of sample responses. A large dictionary of synonyms allows the user great latitude in choice of responses, and simple typing or spelling errors are automatically corrected.

4.1.1 Knowledge Organization

Information about the patient and conclusions drawn during the consultation are represented as associative (object-attribute-value) triples. The

1) Patient's name: (first-last)
**** FRED BRAUN**
2) Sex:
**** M**
3) Age:
**** 55**

(Questions 1-3 request background patient data.)

4) Are there any cultures for Fred Braun which may be related to the present illness, and from which organisms have been grown successfully in the microbiology laboratory?
**** Y**

--------CULTURE-1--------
5) From what site was the specimen for CULTURE-1 taken?
**** BLOD**
=BLOOD

(System corrects typing error.)

6) Please give the date and time when CULTURE-1 was obtained. (mo/da/yr time)
**** JUN 20, 1977**
The first organism isolated from the blood culture of 20-JUN-77 (CULTURE-1) will be referred to as:

--------ORGANISM-1--------
7) Enter the laboratory-reported identity of ORGANISM-1:
****UNKNOWN**

(Typically identity is not yet known.)

8) The stain (gram or Ziehl-Neelsen acid-fast) of ORGANISM-1:
**** NEG**

(Preliminary lab results give some clues.)

9) Is ORGANISM-1 rod or coccus (etc.):
**** ROD**
10) What is the form of the individual organisms (e.g. lancet-shaped for cocci, fusiform for rods, etc.)?
**** FUSIFORM**

(. . . more questions follow in order to gather sufficient information to infer the identity and significance of the infecting organisms . . .)

23) What is the suspected portal of entry of the gramneg rod from the blood culture of 20-JUN-77 (ORGANISM-1) into this sterile site?
**** GI (6)**

(User indicates the uncertainty of his response.)

24) Is Fred Braun a burn patient?
**** N**
25) Is Fred Braun a compromised host (e.g. alcoholic, sickle-cell-disease, immunosuppressed)?
**** N**
26) Is Fred Braun febrile?
**** Y**

(. . . after about 50–60 questions, MYCIN prints the diagnostic hypotheses on which therapy will be based . . .)

My therapy recommendations will be designed to treat for organisms that are either very likely or, although less likely, would have a significant effect on therapy selection if they were present. It is important to cover for the following probable infection(s) and associated organism(s):

INFECTION-1 is BACTEREMIA

<ITEM-1> E.COLI [ORGANISM-1]
<ITEM-2> KLEBSIELLA [ORGANISM-1]
<ITEM-3> ENTEROBACTER [ORGANISM-1]
<ITEM-4> KLEBSIELLA-PNEUMONIAE [ORGANISM-1]

FIGURE 4-2 Excerpts from a MYCIN consultation. (Comments in italics are not part of the actual interaction.)

(. . . questions follow to evaluate possible therapy choices, and finally MYCIN prints its therapy recommendations . . .)

```
[REC-1] My preferred therapy recommendation is as follows:
  In order to cover for items <1 2 3 4>:
    Give: GENTAMICIN                         (One drug covers 4 possible identities.)
    Dose: 119 mg (6.0 ml) q8h IV for 10 days [calculated on basis of
          1.7 mg/kg]
    Comments: Modify dose in renal failure.
```

FIGURE 4-2 continued

objects, known as *contexts* in MYCIN, are such things as individual cultures taken from the patient, organisms that grew out of them, and drugs the patient is currently receiving. Various attributes, termed *clinical parameters*, characterize these objects. Questions asked during the consultation attempt to fill in the values for relevant attributes of these objects. To represent the uncertainty of data or competing hypotheses, attached to each triple is a *certainty factor* (CF), a number between -1 and 1 indicating the strength of the belief in (or a measure of the importance of) that fact. A CF of 1 represents total certainty of the truth of the fact, while a CF of -1 represents certainty regarding the negation of the fact. While certainty factors are *not* conditional probabilities, they are informally based on probability theory (see Part Four). Some triples (with CF's) from a typical consultation might be as follows:

```
(IDENTITY ORGANISM-1 PSEUDOMONAS 0.8)
(IDENTITY ORGANISM-1 E. COLI 0.15)
(SITE CULTURE-2 THROAT 1.0)
(BURNED PATIENT-298 YES -1.0)
```

Here ORGANISM-1 is probably *Pseudomonas*, but there is some evidence to believe it is *E. coli*; the site of CULTURE-2 is (without doubt) the throat; and PATIENT-298 is known *not* to be a burn patient.

4.1.2 Production Rules

MYCIN reasons about its domain using judgmental knowledge encoded as production rules. Each rule has a *premise*, which is a conjunction of predicates regarding triples in the knowledge base. If the premise is true, the conclusion in the *action* part of the rule is drawn. If the premise is known with less than certainty, the strength of the conclusion is modified accordingly.

A typical rule is shown in Figure 4-3. The predicates (such as SAME) are simple LISP functions operating on associative triples, which match the declared facts in the premise clause of the rule against the dynamic data known so far about the patient. $AND, the multi-valued analogue of

```
RULE035

PREMISE:  ($AND (SAME CNTXT GRAM GRAMNEG)
                (SAME CNTXT MORPH ROD)
                (SAME CNTXT AIR ANAEROBIC))
ACTION:   (CONCLUDE CNTXT IDENTITY BACTEROIDES TALLY .6)

IF:  1) The gram stain of the organism is gramneg, and
     2) The morphology of the organism is rod, and
     3) The aerobicity of the organism is anaerobic
THEN:  There is suggestive evidence (.6) that the identity
       of the organism is bacteroides
```

FIGURE 4-3 A MYCIN rule, in both its internal (LISP) form and English translation. The term CNTXT appearing in every clause is a variable in MYCIN that is bound to the current context, in this case a specific organism (ORGANISM-2), to which the rule may be applied.

the Boolean AND function, performs a minimization operation on CF's. The body of the rule is actually an executable piece of LISP code, and "evaluating" a rule entails little more than the LISP function EVAL. However, the highly stylized nature of the rules permits the system to examine and manipulate them, enabling many of the system's capabilities discussed below. One of these is the ability to produce an English translation of the LISP rule, as shown in the example. This is possible because each of the predicate functions has associated with it a translation pattern indicating the logical roles of the function's arguments.

It is intended that each rule be a single, modular chunk of medical knowledge. The number of rules in the MYCIN system grew to about 500.

4.1.3 Application of Rules—The Rule Interpreter

The control structure is a goal-directed backward chaining of rules. At any given time, MYCIN is working to establish the value of some clinical parameter. To this end, the system retrieves the (precomputed) list of rules whose conclusions bear on this goal. The rule in Figure 4-3, for example, would be retrieved in the attempt to establish the identity of an organism. If, in the course of evaluating the premise of one of these rules, some other piece of information that is not yet known is needed, MYCIN sets up a subgoal to find out that information; this in turn causes other rules to be tried. Questions are asked during the consultation when rules fail to deduce the necessary information. If the user cannot supply the requested information, the rule is simply ignored. This control structure results in a highly focused search through the rule base.

4.1.4 Advantages of the Rule Methodology

The modularity of rules simplifies the task of updating the knowledge base. Individual rules can be added, deleted, or modified without drastically affecting the overall performance of the system. And because each rule is a coherent chunk of knowledge, it is a convenient unit for explanation purposes. For example, to explain why the system is asking a question during the consultation, a first approximation is simply to display the rule currently under consideration.

The stylized nature of the rules is useful for many operations. While the syntax of the rules permits the use of any LISP function, there is a small set of standard predicates that make up the vast majority of the rules. The system contains information about the use of these predicates in the form of function *templates*. For example, the predicate SAME is described as follows:

function template: (SAME CNTXT PARM VALUE)

sample function call: (SAME CNTXT SITE BLOOD)

The system can use these templates to "read" its own rules. For example, the template shown here contains the standard tokens CNTXT, PARM, and VALUE (for context, parameter, and corresponding value), indicating the components of the associative triple that SAME tests. If the clause above appears in the premise of a given rule, the system can determine that the rule needs to know the site of the culture, and that the rule can only succeed if that site is, in fact, blood. When asked to display rules that are relevant to blood cultures, MYCIN will be able to choose that rule.

An important function of the templates is to permit MYCIN to pre-compute automatically (at system generation time) the set of rules that conclude about a particular parameter; it is this set that the rule monitor retrieves when the system needs to deduce the value of that parameter.

The system can also read rules to eliminate obviously inappropriate ones. It is often the case that, of a large set of rules under consideration, several are provably false by information already known. That is, the information needed to evaluate one of the clauses in the premise has already been determined, and that clause is false, thereby making the entire premise false. By reading the rules before actually invoking them, many can be immediately discarded, thereby avoiding the deductive work necessary in evaluating the premise clauses that precede the false one (this is called the *preview mechanism*). In some cases this means the system avoids the useless search of one or more subgoal trees, when the information thereby deduced would simply be overridden by the demonstrably false premise.

Another more dramatic case occurs when it is possible, on the basis of information currently available, to deduce with certainty the value of some parameter that is needed by a rule. This is the case when there exists a chain of one or more rules whose premises are known (or provable, as above) with certainty and that ultimately conclude the desired value with certainty. Since each rule in this chain must have a certainty factor of 1.0, we term such a chain a *unity path*; and since a value known with certainty excludes all other potential values, no other rules need be tried. MYCIN always seeks a unity path before trying a set of rules or asking a question; typically, this means "commonsense" deductions are made directly, without asking the user "silly" questions or blindly invoking all the rules pertaining to the goal. Since there are usually few rules on any potential unity path, the search tends to be small.

The ability to read rules opens the way to the writing of rules that manipulate other rules. We term such rules *meta-rules* (see Part Nine); they are used to make deductions not about the medical entities of the domain but about strategies to be used by the system. Whenever the rule interpreter is about to invoke a list of rules to establish some goal, it first applies any meta-rules associated with that goal. These meta-rules can reorder or prune the rule list to make the search more suitable for the given case.

4.2 Explanation Capability

A major subprogram of MYCIN is a general *Question-Answering* (QA) *Module*, which answers simple English-language questions concerning the system's decisions in a particular consultation or about the system's general knowledge. A limited set of commonly desired explanations is also provided in a command style during the consultation by the *Reasoning Status Checker*. This special module explains the system's current line of reasoning and motivation for the questions asked. (A more detailed study of explanation in MYCIN is included in Part Six of this book.) The QA Module is entered automatically at the end of each consultation and is also available to the user during the consultation if the need arises. The user is encouraged to ask questions about any aspect of MYCIN's performance.

Because of the relatively unambiguous vocabulary used in the medical domain, and because of our desire to minimize the delay in answering questions, we have forgone any complicated parsing techniques in the QA Module. Rather, we use a simple pattern-matching approach, relying on the strong implications of certain keywords in the user's questions. The words in the translation of a clinical parameter, and values of that parameter, are tagged in the system dictionary as implying that parameter. By suitably weighing the implications of each word in the sentence, the system determines one or more parameter/value pairs being asked about. Pattern matching is used to determine the general type of the question, which indicates what is being asked about those parameter/value pairs. Typical

**** IS ORGANISM-1 A STREPTOCOCCUS?**
No. The identity of ORGANISM-1 is e.coli (.74) bacteroides (.7)
klebsiella-pneumoniae (.4) pseudomonas-aeruginosa (.22) enterobacter
(.21) proteus-non-mirabilis (.19) serratia (.03) salmonella (.02)

****WHY DID YOU RULE OUT STREPTOCOCCUS AS A POSSIBILITY FOR ORGANISM-1?**
RULE033 could have been used to determine that the identity of
ORGANISM-1 is streptococcus. However, clause 2 of RULE033 ["the
morphology of the organism is coccus"] was already known to be false
for ORGANISM-1, so the rule was never tried.

**** HOW DO YOU KNOW THAT CULTURE-1 WAS FROM A STERILE SOURCE?**
I used RULE189 to conclude that this blood culture was taken from a
sterile source. This gave a cumulative CF of (1.0). The last
question asked before the conclusion was made was 7.

**** WHAT DOES GU MANIPULATION TELL YOU ABOUT THE IDENTITY OF AN ORGANISM?**
The rules listed below use:
whether the patient has had a genito-urinary manipulative procedure
to conclude about:
the identity of the organism

156, 163, 190
Which do you wish to see?
**** 156**

RULE156
IF: 1) The site of the culture is blood, and
2) The gram stain of the organism is gramneg, and
3) The morphology of the organism is rod, and
4) The portal of entry of the organism is urine, and
5) The patient has not had a genito-urinary manipulative procedure, and
6) Cystitis is not a problem for which the patient has been treated
THEN: There is suggestive evidence (.6) that the identity of the organism is e.coli

**** IS BLOOD A STERILE SITE?**
Yes. Blood is one of those sites that is normally sterile.

**** WHAT ARE THE NONSTERILE SITES?**
Those sites that are normally nonsterile are: CERVIX, CUTANEOUS-ULCER, LOCHIA, NOSE, SKIN, STOOL, THROAT, URETHRA, VAGINA.

**** IS BACTEROIDES AEROBIC?**
No, the aerobicity of bacteroides is anaerobic.

FIGURE 4-4 Interaction with the QA Module. The user's questions follow the double-asterisk prompt.

questions (see Figure 4-4) seek the value of a certain parameter, how this value was concluded, and how this parameter was used. Questions about the value of a given parameter of an object are answered by simply displaying the current hypothesis regarding it. To explain how the value of a parameter was concluded, MYCIN retrieves the list of rules that were successfully applied and prints them, along with the conclusions drawn. Alternatively, if the user supplied the value by answering a previous question, this is noted. More general questions about how information is used or concluded are answered by retrieving the relevant rules from the rule base.

```
    34) Was penicillinase added to this blood culture (CULTURE-1)?
    ** WHY

[i.e. WHY is it important to determine whether penicillinase was added to
CULTURE-1?]

[3.0] This will aid in determining whether ORGANISM-1 is a contaminant.
  It has already been established that
    [3.1] the site of CULTURE-1 is blood, and
    [3.2] the gram stain of ORGANISM-1 is grampos
  Therefore, if
    [3.3] penicillinase was added to this blood culture
  then
    there is weakly suggestive evidence (.4) that ORGANISM-1 is a
contaminant [RULE039]

    ** WHY

[i.e. WHY is it important to determine whether ORGANISM-1 is a
contaminant?]

[4.0] . . . In order to determine whether there is significant disease
  associated with this occurrence of ORGANISM-1.
  It has already been established that
    [4.1] this blood culture was taken from a sterile source
  Therefore, if
    [4.2] ORGANISM-1 is not a contaminant
  then
    there is strongly suggestive evidence (.9) that there is
    significant disease associated with this occurrence of ORGANISM-1
  [RULE032]

    ** WHY

[i.e. WHY is it important to determine whether there is significant
  disease associated with this occurrence of ORGANISM-1]

[5.0] . . . In order to determine the organisms which require therapy.
  It has already been established that
    [5.1] the infection is known, and
    [5.2] the identity of ORGANISM-1 is known
  Therefore, if
    [5.3] there is significant disease associated with this occurrence
    of ORGANISM-1
  then
    it is definite (1.0) that ORGANISM-1 is one of the organisms which
    require therapy
  [RULE090]

    ** HOW 5.2

[i.e. HOW was it established that the identity of ORGANISM-1 is known?]

Question 9 was asked, but you weren't sure; so the following was used:

  [5.5] RULE084 was used to conclude that the identity of ORGANISM-1 is
  streptococcus-group-a (.29).
```

FIGURE 4-5 Use of the Reasoning Status Checker during the consultation to explain MYCIN's line of reasoning.

As shown in Figure 4-5, the Reasoning Status Checker is invoked by the HOW and WHY commands. At any time during the consultation, when the user is asked a question, he or she can delay answering it and instead ask why the question was asked. Since questions are asked in order to establish the truth of the premise of some rule, a simple answer to WHY is "because I'm trying to apply the following rule." Successive WHY questions unwind the chain of subgoals, citing the rules that led to the current rule being tried.

Besides examining the current line of reasoning, the user can also ask about previous decisions, or about how future decisions might be made, by giving the HOW command. Explaining how the truth of a certain clause was established is accomplished as described above for the general QA Module. To explain how a presently unknown clause might be established, MYCIN retrieves the set of rules that the rule interpreter would select to establish that clause and selects the relevant rules from among them by "reading" the premises for applicability and the conclusions for relevance to the goal.

4.3 Knowledge Acquisition

The knowledge base is expanded and improved by acquiring new rules, or modifications to old rules, from experts. Ordinarily, this process involves having the medical expert supply a piece of medical knowledge in English, which a system programmer converts into the intended LISP rule. This mode of operation is suitable when the expert and the skilled programmer can work together. Ideally, however, the expert should be able to convey his or her knowledge directly to the system.

Work has been undertaken (see Part Three) to allow experts to update the rule base directly. A rule-acquisition routine parses an English-language rule by methods similar to those used in parsing questions in the QA Module. Each clause is broken down into one or more object-attribute-value triples, which are fitted into the slots of the appropriate predicate function template. This process is further guided by *rule models* (see Chapter 28), which supply expectations about the structure of rules and the interrelationships of the clinical parameters.

One mode of acquisition that has received special attention is acquiring new rules in the context of an error. In this case, the user is trying to correct a localized deficiency in the rule base; if a new rule is to correct the program's faulty behavior, it must at the very least apply to the consultation at hand. In particular, each of the premises must evaluate to TRUE for the given case. These expectations greatly simplify the task of the acquisition program, and also aid the expert in formulating new rules.

One difficult aspect of rule acquisition is the actual formulation of medical knowledge into decision rules. Our desire to keep the rule format simple is occasionally at odds with the need to encode the many aspects of medical decision making. The backward chaining of rules by the deductive system is also often a stumbling block for experts who are new to the system. However, they soon learn to structure their knowledge appropriately. In fact, some experts have felt that encoding their knowledge into rules has helped them formalize their own view of the domain, leading to greater consistency in their decisions.

5

Details of the Consultation System

Edward H. Shortliffe

In this chapter MYCIN's implementation is presented in considerable detail. Our goals are to explain the data and control structures used by the program and to describe some of the complex and often unexpected problems that arose during system implementation. In Chapter 1 the motivations behind many of MYCIN's capabilities were mentioned. The reader is encouraged to bear those design criteria in mind throughout this chapter.

This chapter specifically describes the *Consultation System*. This subprogram uses both system knowledge from the corpus of rules and patient data entered by the physician to generate advice for the user. Furthermore, the program maintains a dynamic data base, which provides an ongoing record of the current consultation. As a result, this chapter must discuss both the nature of the various data structures and how they are used or maintained by the Consultation System.

Section 5.1 describes the corpus of rules and the associated data structures. It provides a formal description of the rules used by MYCIN. Our quantitative truth model is briefly introduced, and the mechanism for rule evaluation is explained. This section also describes the clinical parameters with which MYCIN is familiar and which form the basis for the conditional expressions in the premise of a rule.

In Section 5.2 MYCIN's goal-oriented control structure is described. Mechanisms for rule invocation and question selection are explained at that time. The section also discusses the creation of the dynamic data base,

---

This chapter is condensed from Chapter 3 of *Computer-Based Medical Consultations: MYCIN*. New York: Elsevier/North-Holland, 1976.

which is the foundation for both the system's advice and its explanation capabilities (to be described in Part Six).

Section 5.3 is devoted to an explanation of the program's context tree, i.e., the network of interrelated organisms, drugs, and cultures that characterize the patient and his or her current clinical condition. The need for such a data structure is clarified, and the method for propagation (growth) of the tree is described.

The final tasks in MYCIN's clinical problem area are the identification of potentially useful drugs and the selection of the best drug or drugs from that list. MYCIN's early mechanism for making these decisions is discussed in Section 5.4 of this chapter. Later refinements are the subject of Chapter 6.

Section 5.5 discusses MYCIN's mechanisms for storing patient data and for permitting a user to change the answer to a question. As will be described, these two capabilities are closely interrelated.

In Section 5.6 we briefly mention extensions to the system that were contemplated when this material was written in 1975. Several of these capabilities were eventually implemented.

5.1 System Knowledge

5.1.1 Decision Rules

Automated problem-solving systems use criteria for drawing conclusions that often support a direct analogy to the rule-based knowledge representation used by MYCIN. Consider, for example, the conditional probabilities that underlie Bayesian diagnosis programs. Each probability provides information that may be stated in an explicit rule format:

$P(h|e) = X$ means
IF: e is known to be true
THEN: conclude that h is true with probability X

It is important to note, therefore, that the concept of rule-based knowledge is not unique, even for medical decision-making programs.

Representation of the Rules

The 200 rules in the original MYCIN system consisted of a *premise*, an *action*, and sometimes an *else* clause. Else clauses were later deleted from the system because they were seldom used, and a general representation of inference statements could be achieved without them. Every rule has a name of the form RULE### where ### represents a three-digit number.

The details of rules and how they are used are discussed throughout the remainder of this chapter. We therefore offer a formal definition of rules, which will serve in part as a guide for what is to follow. The rules are stored as LISP data structures in accordance with the following Backus-Nauer Form (BNF) description:

<rule> ::= <premise> <action> | <premise> <action> <else>

<premise> ::= ($AND <condition> . . . <condition>)

<condition> ::= (<func1> <context> <parameter>) |
(<func2> <context> <parameter> <value>) |
(<special-func> <arguments>) |
($OR <condition> . . . <condition>)

<action> ::= <concpart>

<else> ::= <concpart>

<concpart> ::= <conclusion> | <actfunc> |
(DO-ALL <conclusion> . . . <conclusion>) |
(DO-ALL <actfunc> . . . <actfunc>)

<context> ::= *see* Section 5.1.2

<parameter> ::= *see* Section 5.1.3

<value> ::= *see* Section 5.1.4

<func1> ::= *see* Section 5.1.5

<func2> ::= *see* Section 5.1.5

<special-func> ::= *see* Section 5.1.6

<arguments> ::= *see* Section 5.1.6

<conclusion> ::= *see* Section 5.2.3

<actfunc> ::= *see* Section 5.4

Thus the premise of a rule consists of a conjunction of conditions, each of which must hold for the indicated action to be taken. Negations of conditions are handled by individual predicates (<func1> and <func2>) and therefore do not require a $NOT function to complement the Boolean functions $AND and $OR. If the premise of a rule is known to be false, the conclusion or action indicated by the else clause is taken. If the truth of the premise cannot be ascertained or the premise is false but no else condition exists, the rule is simply ignored.

The premise of a rule is always a conjunction of one or more conditions. Disjunctions of conditions may be represented as multiple rules with identical action clauses. A condition, however, may itself be a disjunction of conditions. These conventions are somewhat arbitrary but do provide sufficient flexibility so that any Boolean expression may be represented by one or more rules. As is discussed in Section 5.2, multiple rules are effectively ORed together by MYCIN's control structure.

For example, two-leveled Boolean nestings of conditions are acceptable as follows:

Legal:

[1] A & B & C → D

[2] A & (B or C) → D

[3] (A or B or C) & (D or E) → F

Illegal:

[4] A or B or C → D

[5] A & (B or (C & D)) → E

Rule [4] is correctly represented by the following three rules:

[6] A → D

[7] B → D

[8] C → D

whereas [5] must be written as:

[9] A & C & D → E

[10] A & B → E

Unlike rules that involve strict implication, MYCIN's rules allow the strength of an inference to be modified by a certainty factor (CF). A CF is a number from −1 to +1, the nature of which is described in Section 5.1.4 and in Chapter 11.

The following three examples are rules from MYCIN that have been translated into English from their internal LISP representation (Section 5.1.7). They represent the range of rule types available to the system. The details of their internal representation will be explained as we proceed.

RULE037

IF: 1) The identity of the organism is not known with certainty, and
2) The stain of the organism is gramneg, and
3) The morphology of the organism is rod, and
4) The aerobicity of the organism is aerobic

THEN: There is strongly suggestive evidence (.8) that the class of the organism is enterobacteriaceae

RULE145

IF: 1) The therapy under consideration is one of: cephalothin clindamycin erythromycin lincomycin vancomycin, and
2) Meningitis is an infectious disease diagnosis for the patient

THEN: It is definite (1) the therapy under consideration is not a potential therapy for use against the organism

RULE060

IF: The identity of the organism is bacteroides

THEN: I recommend therapy chosen from among the following drugs:

1 - clindamycin	(.99)
2 - chloramphenicol	(.99)
3 - erythromycin	(.57)
4 - tetracycline	(.28)
5 - carbenicillin	(.27)

Before we can explain how rules such as these are invoked and evaluated, it is necessary to describe further MYCIN's internal organization. We shall therefore temporarily digress in order to lay some groundwork for the description of the evaluation functions in Section 5.1.5.

5.1.2 Categorization of Rules by Context

The Context Tree

Although it is common to describe diagnosis as inference based on attributes of the patient, MYCIN's decisions must necessarily involve not only the patient but also the cultures that have been grown, organisms that have been isolated, and drugs that have been administered. Each of these is termed a *context* of the program's reasoning (see <context> in the BNF description of rules).[1]

MYCIN currently (1975) knows about ten different context-types:

[1]The use of the word *context* should not be confused with its meaning in high-level languages that permit temporary saving of all information regarding a program's current status—a common mechanism for backtracking and parallel-processing implementations.

CURCULS	A current culture from which organisms were isolated
CURDRUGS	An antimicrobial agent currently being administered to a patient
CURORGS	An organism isolated from a current culture
OPDRGS	An antimicrobial agent administered to the patient during a recent operative procedure
OPERS	An operative procedure the patient has undergone
PERSON	The patient
POSSTHER	A therapy being considered for recommendation
PRIORCULS	A culture obtained in the past
PRIORDRGS	An antimicrobial agent administered to the patient in the past
PRIORORGS	An organism isolated from a prior culture

Except for PERSON, each of these context-types may be instantiated more than once during any given run of the consultation program. Some may not be created at all if they do not apply to the given patient. However, each time a context-type is instantiated, it is given a unique name. For example, CULTURE-1 is the first CURCUL and ORGANISM-1 is the first CURORG. Subsequent CURCULS or PRIORCULS are called CULTURE-2, CULTURE-3, etc.

The context-types instantiated during a run of the consultation program are arranged hierarchically in a data structure termed the *context tree*. One such tree is shown in Figure 5-1. The context-type for each instantiated context is shown in parentheses near its name. Thus, to clarify terminology, we note that a node in the context tree is called a *context* and is created as an instantiation of a context-type. This sample context tree corresponds to a patient from whom two current cultures and one prior culture were obtained. One organism was isolated from each of the current cultures, but the patient is being treated (with two drugs) for only one of the current organisms. Furthermore, two organisms were grown from the prior culture, but therapy was instituted to combat only one of these. Finally, the patient has had a recent operative procedure during which he or she was treated with an antimicrobial agent.

The context tree is useful not only because it gives structure to the clinical problem (Figure 5-1 already tells us a good deal about PATIENT-1), but also because we often need to be able to relate one context to another. For example, in considering the significance of ORGANISM-2, MYCIN may well want to be able to reference the site of the culture from which ORGANISM-2 was obtained. Since the patient has had three different cultures, we need an explicit mechanism for recognizing that ORGANISM-2 came from CULTURE-2, not from CULTURE-1 or CULTURE-3. The technique for dynamic propagation (i.e., growth) of the context tree during a consultation is described in Section 5.3.

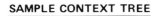

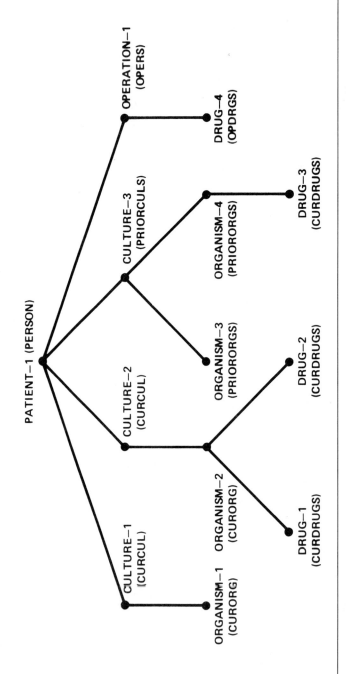

FIGURE 5-1 Context tree for a sample patient with two recent positive cultures, an older one, and a recent significant operative procedure. Nodes in the tree are termed *contexts*.

Interrelationship of Rules and the Tree

The 200 rules currently used by MYCIN[2] are not explicitly linked in a decision tree or reasoning network. This feature is in keeping with our desire to keep system knowledge modular and manipulable. However, rules are subject to categorization in accordance with the context-types for which they are most appropriately invoked. For example, some rules deal with organisms, some with cultures, and still others deal solely with the patient. MYCIN's current rule categories are as follows (context-types to which they may be applied are enclosed in parentheses):

CULRULES	Rules that may be applied to any culture (CURCULS or PRIORCULS)
CURCULRULES	Rules that may be applied only to current cultures (CURCULS)
CURORGRULES	Rules that may be applied only to current organisms (CURORGS)
DRGRULES	Rules that may be applied to any antimicrobial agent that has been administered to combat a specific organism (CURDRUGS or PRIORDRGS)
OPRULES	Rules that may be applied to operative procedures (OPERS)
ORDERRULES	Rules that are used to order the list of possible therapeutic recommendations (POSSTHER)
ORGRULES	Rules that may be applied to any organism (CURORGS or PRIORORGS)
PATRULES	Rules that may be applied to the patient (PERSON)
PDRGRULES	Rules that may be applied only to drugs given to combat prior organisms (PRIORDRGS)
PRCULRULES	Rules that may be applied only to prior cultures (PRIORCULS)
PRORGRULES	Rules that may be applied only to organism isolated from prior cultures (PRIORORGS)
THERULES	Rules that store information regarding drugs of choice (Section 5.4.1)

Every rule in the MYCIN system belongs to one, and only one, of these categories. Furthermore, selecting the proper category for a newly acquired rule does not present a problem. In fact, category selection can be automated to a large extent.

Consider a rule such as this:

[2] *Ed. note:* This number increased to almost 500 by 1978.

RULE124

IF: 1) The site of the culture is throat, and
2) The identity of the organism is streptococcus
THEN: There is strongly suggestive evidence (.8) that the subtype of the organism is not group-D

This is one of MYCIN's ORGRULES and may thus be applied to either a CURORGS context or a PRIORORGS context. Referring back to Figure 5-1, suppose RULE124 were applied to ORGANISM-2. The first condition in the premise refers to the site of the culture from which ORGANISM-2 was isolated (i.e., CULTURE-2) and not to the organism itself (i.e., organisms do not have sites, but cultures do). The context tree is therefore important for determining the proper context when a rule refers to an attribute of a node in the tree other than the context to which the rule is being explicitly applied. Note that this means that a single rule may refer to nodes at several levels in the context tree. The rule is categorized simply on the basis of the lowest context-type (in the tree) that it may reference. Thus RULE124 is an ORGRULE rather than a CULRULE.

5.1.3 Clinical Parameters

This subsection describes the data types indicated by <parameter> and <value> in the BNF description of rules. Although we have previously asserted that all MYCIN's knowledge is stored in its corpus of rules, the clinical parameters and their associated properties comprise an important class of second-level knowledge. We shall first explain the kind of parameters used by the system and then describe their representation.

A clinical parameter is a characteristic of one of the contexts in the context tree, i.e., the name of the patient, the site of a culture, the morphology of an organism, the dose of a drug, etc. A patient's status would be completely specified by a context tree in which values were known for all the clinical parameters characterizing each node in the tree (assuming the parameters known to MYCIN encompass all those that are clinically relevant—a dubious assumption at present). In general, this is more information than is needed, however, so one of MYCIN's tasks is to identify those clinical parameters that need to be considered for the patient about whom advice is being sought.

The concept of an attribute-object-value triple is common within the AI field. This associative relationship is a basic data type for the SAIL language (Feldman et al., 1972) and is the foundation for the property-list formalism in LISP (McCarthy et al., 1962). Relational predicates in predicate calculus also represent associative triples. The point is that many facts may be expressed as triples that state that some object has an attribute with some specified value. Stated in the order <attribute object value>, examples include:

(COLOR BALL RED)
(OWNS FIREMAN RED-SUSPENDERS)

```
(AGE BOB 22)
(FATHER CHILD 'DADDY')
(GRAMSTAIN ORGANISM GRAM-POSITIVE)
(DOSE DRUG 1.5-GRAMS)
(MAN BOB TRUE)
(WOMAN BOB FALSE)
```

Note that the last two examples are different from the others in that they represent a rather different kind of relationship. In fact, several authors would classify the first six as "relations" and the last two as "predicates," using the simpler notation:

```
MAN (BOB)
-WOMAN (BOB)
```

Regardless of whether it is written as MAN(BOB) or (MAN BOB TRUE), this binary predicate statement has rather different characteristics from the relations that form natural triples. This distinction will become clearer later (see yes-no parameters below).

MYCIN stores inferences and data using the attribute-object-value concept. The object is always some context in the context tree, and the attribute is a clinical parameter appropriate for that context. Information stored using this mechanism may be retrieved and updated in accordance with a variety of conventions described throughout this chapter.

The Three Kinds of Clinical Parameters

There are three fundamentally different kinds of clinical parameters. The simplest variety is *single-valued parameters*. These are attributes such as the name of the patient and the identity of the organism. In general, they have a large number of possible values that are mutually exclusive. As a result, only one can be the true value, although several may seem likely at any point during the consultation.

Multi-valued parameters also generally have a large number of possible values. The difference is that the possible values need not be mutually exclusive. Thus such attributes as a patient's drug allergies and a locus of an infection may have multiple values, each of which is known to be correct.

The third kind of clinical parameter corresponds to the binary predicate discussed above. These are attributes that are either true or false for the given context. For example, the significance of an organism is either true or false (yes or no), as is the parameter indicating whether the dose of a drug is adequate. Attributes of this variety are called *yes-no parameters*. They are, in effect, a special kind of single-valued parameter for which there are only two possible values.

Classification and Representation of the Parameters

The clinical parameters known to MYCIN are categorized in accordance with the context to which they apply. These categories include:

PROP-CUL	Those clinical parameters which are attributes of cultures (e.g., site of the culture, method of collection)
PROP-DRG	Those clinical parameters which are attributes of administered drugs (e.g., name of the drug, duration of administration)
PROP-OP	Those clinical parameters which are attributes of operative procedures (e.g., the cavity, if any, opened during the procedure)
PROP-ORG	Those clinical parameters which are attributes of organisms (e.g., identity, gram stain, morphology)
PROP-PT	Those clinical parameters which are attributes of the patient (e.g., name, sex, age, allergies, diagnoses)
PROP-THER	Those clinical parameters which are attributes of therapies being considered for recommendation (e.g., recommended dosage, prescribing name)

These categories encompass all clinical parameters used by the system. Note that any of the nodes (contexts) in the context tree for the patient may be fully characterized by the values of the set of clinical parameters in one of these categories.

Each of the 65 clinical parameters currently (1975) known to MYCIN has an associated set of properties that is used during consideration of the parameter for a given context. Figure 5-2 presents examples of the three types of clinical parameters, which together demonstrate several of these properties:

EXPECT	This property indicates the range of expected values that the parameter may have. IF equal to (YN), then the parameter is a yes-no parameter. IF equal to (NUMB), then the expected value of the parameter is a number. IF equal to (ONE-OF <list>), then the value of the parameter must be a member of <list>. IF equal to (ANY), then there is no restriction on the range of values that the parameter may have.
PROMPT	This property is a sentence used by MYCIN when it requests the value of the clinical parameter from the user; if there is an asterisk in the phrase (see Figure 5-2), it is replaced by the name of the context about which the question is being asked; this property is used only for yes-no or single-valued parameters.
PROMPT1	This property is similar to PROMPT but is used if the clinical parameter is a multi-valued parameter; in these cases MYCIN only asks the question about

Yes-No Parameter

FEBRILE: <FEBRILE is an attribute of a patient and is therefore a member of the list PROP-PT>

EXPECT: (YN)
LOOKAHEAD: (RULE149 RULE109 RULE045)
PROMPT: (Is * febrile?)
TRANS: (* IS FEBRILE)

Single-Valued Parameter

IDENT: <IDENT is an attribute of an organism and is therefore a member of the list PROP-ORG>

CONTAINED-IN: (RULE030)
EXPECT: (ONEOF (ORGANISMS))
LABDATA: T
LOOKAHEAD: (RULE004 RULE054 . . . RULE168)
PROMPT: (Enter the identity (genus) of *:)
TRANS: (THE IDENTITY OF *)
UPDATED-BY: (RULE021 RULE003 . . . RULE166)

Multi-Valued Parameter

INFECT: <INFECT is an attribute of a patient and is therefore a member of the list PROP-PT>

EXPECT: (ONEOF (PERITONITIS BRAIN-ABCESS MENINGITIS BACTEREMIA UPPER-URINARY-TRACT-INFECTION . . . ENDOCARDITIS))
LOOKAHEAD: (RULE115 RULE149 . . . RULE045)
PROMPT1: (Is there evidence that the patient has a (VALU)?)
TRANS: (AN INFECTIOUS DISEASE DIAGNOSIS FOR *)
UPDATED-BY: (RULE157 RULE022 . . . RULE105)

FIGURE 5-2 Examples of the three types of clinical parameters. As shown, each clinical parameter is characterized by a set of properties described in the text.

	a single one of the possible parameter values; the value of interest is substituted for (VALU) in the question.
LABDATA	This property is a flag, which is either T or NIL; if T it indicates that the clinical parameter is a piece of primitive data, the value of which may be known with certainty to the user (see Section 5.2.2).
LOOKAHEAD	This property is a list of all rules in the system that reference the clinical parameter in the premise.

UPDATED-BY	This property is a list of all rules in the system in which the action or else clause permits a conclusion to be made regarding the value of the clinical parameter.
CONTAINED-IN	This property is a list of all rules in the system in which the action or else clause references the clinical parameter but does not cause its value to be updated.
TRANS	This property is used to translate an occurrence of this parameter into its English representation; the context of the parameter is substituted for the asterisk during translation.
DEFAULT	This property is used only with clinical parameters for which EXPECT = (NUMB); it gives the expected units for numerical answers (days, years, grams, etc.).
CONDITION	This property, when utilized, is an executable LISP expression that is evaluated before MYCIN requests the value of the parameter; if the CONDITION is true, the question is not asked (e.g., "Don't ask for an organism's subtype if its genus is not known by the user").

The uses of these properties will be discussed throughout the remainder of this chapter. However, a few additional points are relevant here. First, it should be noted that the order of rules for the properties LOOKAHEAD, UPDATED-IN, and CONTAINED-IN is arbitrary and does not affect the program's advice. Second, EXPECT and TRANS are the only properties that *must* exist for every clinical parameter. Thus, for example, if there is no PROMPT or PROMPT1 stored for a parameter, the system assumes that it simply cannot ask the user for the value of the parameter. Finally, note in Figure 5-2 the difference in the TRANS property for yes-no and non–yes-no parameters. In general, a parameter and its value may be translated as follows:

THE <attribute> OF <object> IS <value>

However, for a yes-no parameter such as FEBRILE, it is clearly necessary to translate the parameter in a fashion other than this:

THE FEBRILE OF PATIENT-1 IS YES

Our solution has been to suppress the YES altogether and simply to say:

PATIENT-1 IS FEBRILE

5.1.4 Certainty Factors

Chapter 11 presents a detailed description of certainty factors and their theoretical foundation. This section therefore provides only a brief overview of the subject. A familiarity with the characteristics of certainty factors (CF's) is necessary for the discussion of MYCIN during the remainder of this chapter.

The value of every clinical parameter is stored by MYCIN along with an associated certainty factor that reflects the system's "belief" that the value is correct. This formalism is necessary because, unlike domains in which objects either have or do not have some attribute, in medical diagnosis and treatment there is often uncertainty regarding attributes such as the significance of the disease, the efficacy of a treatment, or the diagnosis itself. CF's are an alternative to conditional probability that has several advantages in MYCIN's domain.

A certainty factor is a number between -1 and $+1$ that reflects the degree of belief in a hypothesis. Positive CF's indicate there is evidence that the hypothesis is valid. The larger the CF, the greater is the belief in the hypothesis. When CF = 1, the hypothesis is known to be correct. On the other hand, negative CF's indicate that the weight of evidence suggests that the hypothesis is false. The smaller the CF, the greater is the belief that the hypothesis is invalid. CF = -1 means that the hypothesis has been effectively disproven. When CF = 0, there is either no evidence regarding the hypothesis or the supporting evidence is equally balanced by evidence suggesting that the hypothesis is not true.

MYCIN's hypotheses are statements regarding values of clinical parameters for the various nodes in the context tree. For example, sample hypotheses are

h_1 = The identity of ORGANISM-1 is streptococcus
h_2 = PATIENT-1 is febrile
h_3 = The name of PATIENT-1 is John Jones

We use the notation CF[h,E]=X to represent the certainty factor for the hypothesis h based on evidence E. Thus, if CF[h_1,E] = .8, CF[h_2,E] = $-.3$, and CF[h_3,E] = $+1$, the three sample hypotheses above may be qualified as follows:

CF[h_1,E] = .8 : There is strongly suggestive evidence (.8) that the identity of ORGANISM-1 is streptococcus

CF[h_2,E] = $-.3$: There is weakly suggestive evidence (.3) that PATIENT-1 is not febrile

CF[h_3,E] = $+1$: It is definite (1) that the name of PATIENT-1 is John Jones

Certainty factors are used in two ways. First, as noted, the value of every clinical parameter is stored with its associated certainty factor. In this case the evidence E stands for all information currently available to MY-

CIN. Thus, if the program needs the identity of ORGANISM-1, it may look in its dynamic data base and find:

IDENT of ORGANISM-1 = ((STREPTOCOCCUS .8))

The second use of CF's is in the statement of decision rules themselves. In this case the evidence E corresponds to the conditions in the premise of the rule. Thus

$$A \ \& \ B \ \& \ C \xrightarrow{X} D$$

is a representation of the statement CF[D,(A & B & C)] = X. For example, consider the following rule:

IF: 1) The stain of the organism is grampos, and
2) The morphology of the organism is coccus, and
3) The growth conformation of the organism is chains
THEN: There is suggestive evidence (.7) that the identity of the organism is streptococcus

This rule may also be represented as CF[h_1,e] = .7, where h_1 is the hypothesis that the organism (context of the rule) is a *Streptococcus* and e is the evidence that it is a gram-positive coccus growing in chains.

Since diagnosis is, in effect, the problem of selecting a disease from a list of competing hypotheses, it should be clear that MYCIN may simultaneously be considering several hypotheses regarding the value of a clinical parameter. These hypotheses are stored together, along with their CF's, for each node in the context tree. We use the notation Val[C,P] to signify the set of all hypotheses regarding the value of the clinical parameter P for the context C. Thus, if MYCIN has reason to believe that ORGANISM-1 may be either a *Streptococcus* or a *Staphylococcus,* but *Pneumococcus* has been ruled out, its dynamic data base might well show:

Val[ORGANISM-1,IDENT] = ((STREPTOCOCCUS .6)(STAPHYLOCOCCUS .4)
(DIPLOCOCCUS-PNEUMONIAE -1))

It can be shown that the sum of the CF's for supported hypotheses regarding a single-valued parameter (i.e., those parameters for which the hypotheses are mutually exclusive) cannot exceed 1 (Shortliffe and Buchanan, 1975). Multi-valued parameters, on the other hand, may have several hypotheses that are all known to be true, for example:

Val[PATIENT-1,ALLERGY] = ((PENICILLIN 1)(AMPICILLIN 1)
(CARBENICILLIN 1)(METHICILLIN 1))

As soon as a hypothesis regarding a single-valued parameter is proved to be true, all competing hypotheses are effectively disproved:

Val[ORGANISM-1,IDENT] = ((STREPTOCOCCUS 1)(STAPHYLOCOCCUS -1)
(DIPLOCOCCUS-PNEUMONIAE -1))

In Chapter 11 we demonstrate that $CF[h,E] = -CF[\neg h,E]$. This observation has important implications for the way MYCIN handles the binary-valued attributes we call yes-no parameters. Since "yes" is "¬no," it is not necessary to consider "yes" and "no" as competing hypotheses for the value of a yes-no parameter (as we do for single-valued parameters). Instead, we can always express "no" as "yes" with a reversal in the sign of the CF. This means that Val[C,P] is always equal to the single value "yes," along with its associated CF, when P is a yes-no parameter.

We discuss below MYCIN's mechanism for adding to the list of hypotheses in Val[C,P] as new rules are invoked and executed. However, the following points should be emphasized here:

1. The strength of the conclusion associated with the execution of a rule reflects not only the CF assigned to the rule, but also the program's degree of belief regarding the validity of the premise.
2. The support of several rules favoring a single hypothesis may be assimilated incrementally on the list Val[C,P] by using the special combining functions described in Chapter 11.

5.1.5 Functions for the Evaluation of Premise Conditions

This section describes the evaluation of the individual conditions (see <condition>, Section 5.1.1) in the premise of rules. Conditions in general evaluate to true or false (T or NIL). Thus they may at first glance be considered simple predicates on the values of clinical parameters. However, since there may be several competing hypotheses on the list Val[C,P], each associated with its own degree of belief as reflected by the CF, conditional statements regarding the value of parameters can be quite complex. All predicates are implemented as LISP functions. The functions that undertake the required analysis are of three varieties, specified by the designations <func1>, <func2>, and <special-func> in the BNF rule description. This section explains the <func1> and <func2> predicates. The <special-func> category is deferred until later, however, so that we may first introduce our specialized knowledge structures.

There are four predicates in the category <func1>. These functions do not form conditionals on specific values of a clinical parameter but are concerned with the more general status of knowledge regarding the attributes in question. For example, KNOWN[ORGANISM-1,IDENT] is an invocation of the <func1> predicate KNOWN; it would return true if the identity of ORGANISM-1 were known, regardless of the value of the clinical parameter IDENT. KNOWN and the other <func1> predicates may be formally defined as follows:

Predicates of the Category <func1>

Let V = Val[C,P] be the set of all hypotheses regarding the value of the clinical parameter P for the context C.

Let Mv = Max[V] be the most strongly supported hypothesis in V (i.e., the hypothesis with the largest CF).

Let CFmv = CF[Mv,E] where E is the total available evidence.

Then, if P is either a single-valued or multi-valued parameter, the four predicates (functions) may be specified as follows:

Function	*If*	*Then*	*Else*
KNOWN[C,P]	CFmv > .2	T	NIL
NOTKNOWN[C,P]	CFmv ≤ .2	T	NIL
DEFINITE[C,P]	CFmv = 1	T	NIL
NOTDEFINITE[C,P]	CFmv < 1	T	NIL

In words, these definitions reflect MYCIN's convention that the value of a parameter is known if the CF of the most highly supported hypothesis exceeds .2. The .2 threshold was selected empirically. The implication is that a positive CF less than .2 reflects so little evidence supporting the hypothesis that there is virtually no reasonable hypothesis currently known. The interrelationships among these functions are diagrammed on a CF number line in Figure 5-3. Regions specified are the range of values for CFmv over which the function returns T.

As was pointed out in the preceding section, however, yes-no parameters are special cases because we know CF[YES,E] = −CF[NO,E]. Since the values of yes-no parameters are always stored in terms of YES, MYCIN must recognize that a YES with CF = −.9 is equivalent to a NO with CF = .9. The definitions of the four <func1> predicates above do not reflect this distinction. Therefore, when P is a yes-no parameter, the four functions are specified as follows:

Function	*If*	*Then*	*Else*
KNOWN[C,P]	|CFmv| > .2	T	NIL
NOTKNOWN[C,P]	|CFmv| ≤ .2	T	NIL
DEFINITE[C,P]	|CFmv| = 1	T	NIL
NOTDEFINITE[C,P]	|CFmv| < 1	T	NIL

Figure 5-4 shows the relationship among these functions for yes-no parameters.

There are nine predicates in the category <func2>. Unlike the <func1> predicates, these functions control conditional statements regarding specific values of the clinical parameter in question. For example, SAME[ORGANISM-1,IDENT,E.COLI] is an invocation of the <func2>

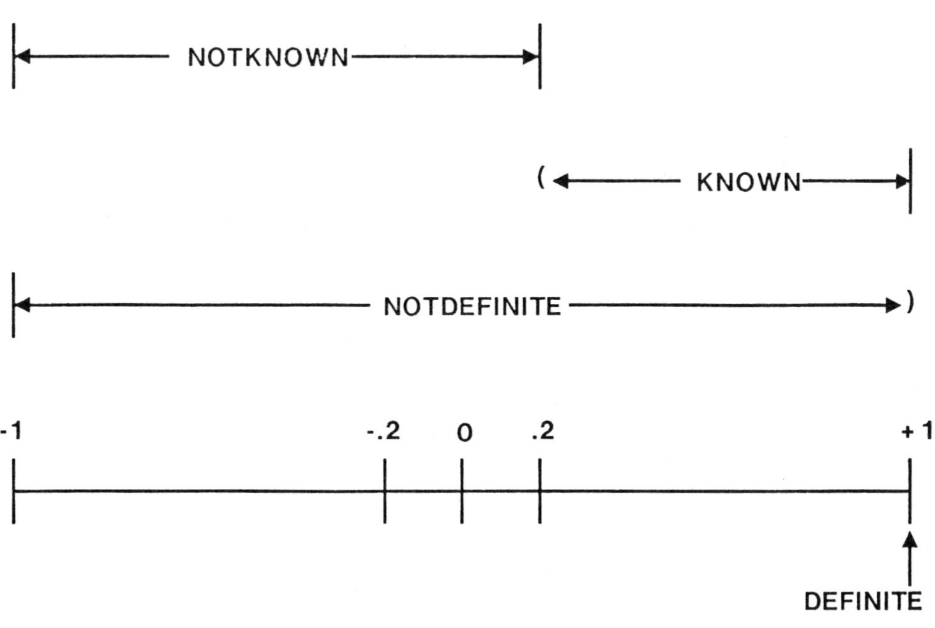

FIGURE 5-3 Diagram indicating the range of CF values over which the <func1> predicates hold true when applied to multi-valued or single-valued (i.e., non–yes-no) clinical parameters. Vertical lines and parentheses distinguish closed and non-closed certainty factor ranges, respectively.

predicate SAME; it would return a non-NIL value if the identity of ORGANISM-1 were known to be *E. coli*. SAME and the other <func2> predicates may be formally defined as follows:

Predicates of the Category <func2>

Let V = Val[C,P] be the set of all hypotheses regarding the value of the clinical parameter P for the context C.

Let I = Intersection[V,LST] be the set of all hypotheses in V that also occur in the set LST; LST contains the possible values of P for comparison by the predicate function; it usually contains only a single element; if no element in LST is also in V, I is simply the empty set.

Let M_i = Max[I] be the most strongly confirmed hypothesis in I; thus M_i is NIL if I is the empty set.

Let CFmi = CF[M_i,E] where CFmi = 0 if M_i is NIL.

Then the <func2> predicates are specified as follows:

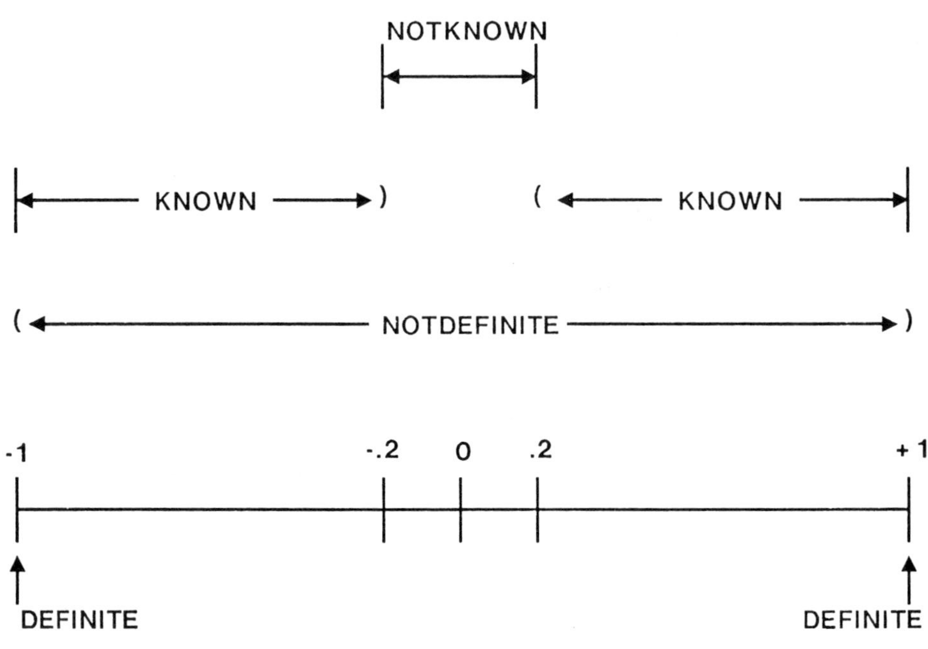

FIGURE 5-4 Diagram indicating the range of CF values over which the <func1> predicates hold true when applied to yes-no clinical parameters.

Function	*If*	*Then*	*Else*
SAME[C,P,LST]	CFmi > .2	CFmi	NIL
THOUGHTNOT[C,P,LST]	CFmi < −.2	−CFmi	NIL
NOTSAME[C,P,LST]	CFmi ≤ .2	T	NIL
MIGHTBE[C,P,LST]	CFmi ≥ −.2	T	NIL
VNOTKNOWN[C,P,LST]	|CFmi| ≤ .2	T	NIL
DEFIS[C,P,LST]	CFmi = +1	T	NIL
DEFNOT[C,P,LST]	CFmi = −1	T	NIL
NOTDEFIS[C,P,LST]	.2 < CFmi < 1	T	NIL
NOTDEFNOT[C,P,LST]	−1 < CFmi < −.2	T	NIL

The names of the functions have been selected to reflect their semantics. Figure 5-5 shows a graphic representation of each function and also explicitly states the interrelationships among them.

Note that SAME and THOUGHTNOT are different from all the other functions in that they return a number (CF) rather than T if the defining condition holds. This feature permits MYCIN to record the degree to which premise conditions are satisfied. In order to explain this

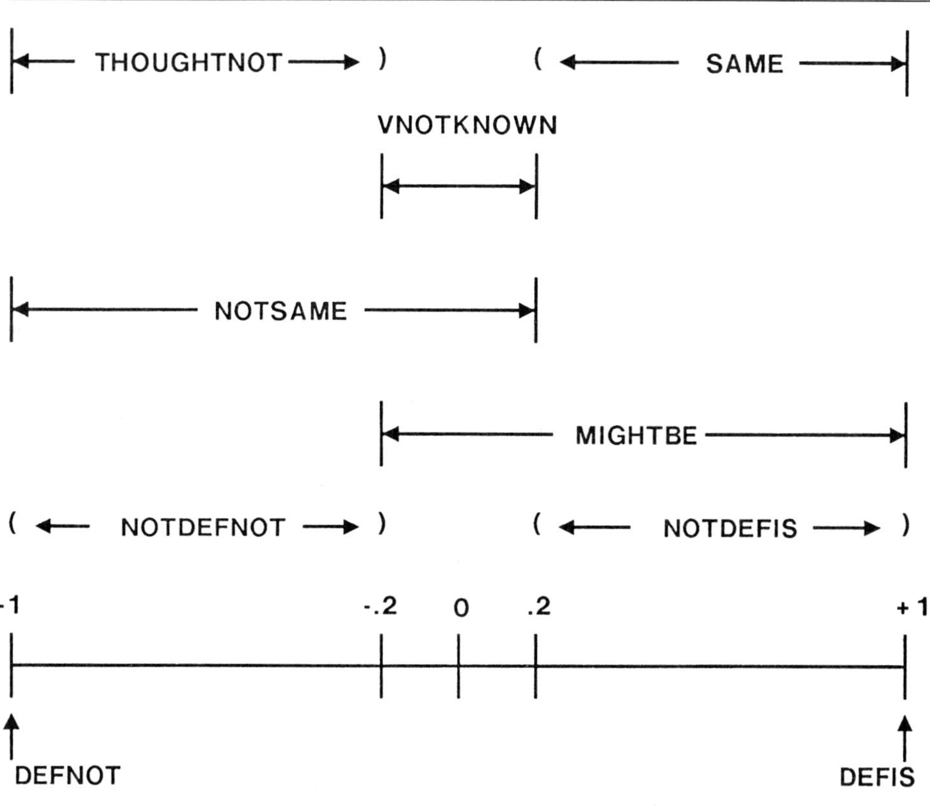

FIGURE 5-5 Diagram indicating the range of CF values over which the <func2> predicates hold true. The logical relationships of these predicates are summarized below the diagram.

point, we must discuss the $AND function that oversees the evaluation of the premise of a rule. The reader will recall the BNF description:

<premise> ::= ($AND <condition> . . . <condition>)

$AND is similar to the standard LISP AND function in that it evaluates its conditional arguments one at a time, returning false (NIL) as soon as a condition is found to be false, and otherwise returning true (T). The difference is that $AND expects some of its conditions to return numerical values rather than simply T or NIL. If an argument condition returns NIL (or a number equal to .2 or less), it is considered false and $AND stops considering subsequent arguments. On the other hand, nonnumeric values of conditions are interpreted as indicating truth with CF = 1. Thus each true condition either returns a number or a non-NIL value that is interpreted as 1. $AND then maintains a record of the lowest value returned by any of its arguments. This number, termed TALLY, is a certainty tally, which indicates MYCIN's degree of belief in the premise (see Combining Function 2 in Chapter 11). Thus $.2 < \text{TALLY} \leq 1$, where TALLY = 1 indicates that MYCIN believes the premise to be true with certainty.

Most of the predicates that evaluate conditions in the premise of a rule return either T or NIL as we have shown. Consider, however, the semantics of the most commonly used function, SAME, and its analogous function, THOUGHTNOT. Suppose MYCIN knows:

```
Val[ORGANISM-1,IDENT] = ((STREPTOCOCCUS .7)(STAPHYLOCOCCUS .3))
```

Then it seems clear that

```
SAME[ORGANISM-1,IDENT,STREPTOCOCCUS]
```

is in some sense "more true" than

```
SAME[ORGANISM-1,IDENT,STAPHYLOCOCCUS]
```

even though both hypotheses exceed the threshold CF = .2. If SAME merely returned T, this distinction would be lost. Thus, for this example:

```
          SAME[ORGANISM-1,IDENT,STREPTOCOCCUS] = .7
          SAME[ORGANISM-1,IDENT,STAPHYLOCOCCUS] = .3
whereas   KNOWN[ORGANISM-1,IDENT] = T
and       NOTDEFIS[ORGANISM-1,IDENT,STREPTOCOCCUS] = T
```

A similar argument explains why THOUGHTNOT returns a CF rather than T. It is unclear whether any of the other <func2> predicates should return a CF rather than T; our present conviction is that the semantics of those functions do not require relative weightings in the way that SAME and THOUGHTNOT do.

Consider a brief example, then, of the way in which the premise of a rule is evaluated by $AND. The following ORGRULE:

```
IF:   1) The stain of the organism is gramneg, and
      2) The morphology of the organism is rod, and
      3) The aerobicity of the organism is aerobic
THEN:    There is strongly suggestive evidence (.8) that
         the class of the organism is enterobacteriaceae
```

is internally coded in LISP as:

```
PREMISE: ($AND (SAME CNTXT GRAM GRAMNEG)
               (SAME CNTXT MORPH ROD)
               (SAME CNTXT AIR AEROBIC))
ACTION:  (CONCLUDE CNTXT CLASS ENTEROBACTERIACEAE TALLY .8)
```

Suppose this rule has been invoked for consideration of ORGANISM-1; i.e., the context of the rule (CNTXT) is the node in the context tree termed ORGANISM-1. Now suppose that MYCIN has the following information in its data base (we will discuss later how it gets there):

```
Val[ORGANISM-1,GRAM] = ((GRAMNEG 1.0))
Val[ORGANISM-1,MORPH] = ((ROD .8)(COCCUS .2))
Val[ORGANISM-1,AIR] = ((AEROBIC .6)(FACUL .4))
```

$AND begins by evaluating SAME[ORGANISM-1,GRAM,GRAMNEG]. The function returns CF = 1.0, so TALLY is set to 1.0 (see definition of TALLY in the description of $AND above). Next $AND evaluates the second premise condition, SAME[ORGANISM-1,MORPH,ROD], which returns .8. Since the first two conditions both were found to hold, $AND evaluates SAME[ORGANISM-1,AIR,AEROBIC], which returns .6. Thus TALLY is set to .6, and $AND returns T. Since the premise is true, MYCIN may now draw the conclusion indicated in the action portion of the rule. Note, however, that CONCLUDE has as arguments both .8 (i.e., the CF for the rule as provided by the expert) and TALLY (i.e., the certainty tally for the premise). CONCLUDE and the other functions that control inferences are described later.

5.1.6 Static Knowledge Structures

Although all MYCIN's inferential knowledge is stored in rules, there are various kinds of static definitional information, which are stored differently even though they are accessible from rules.

Tabular and List-Based Knowledge

There are three categories of knowledge structures that could be discussed in this section. However, one of them, MYCIN's dictionary, is used principally for natural language understanding and will therefore not be described. The other two data structures are simple lists and knowledge tables.

Simple lists: Simple lists provide a mechanism for simplifying references to variables and optimizing knowledge storage by avoiding unnecessary duplication. Two examples should be sufficient to explain this point.

As was shown earlier, the EXPECT property for the clinical parameter IDENT is

```
(ONEOF (ORGANISMS))
```

ORGANISMS is the name of a linear list containing the names of all bacteria known to MYCIN. There is also a clinical parameter named COVERFOR for which the EXPECT property is

```
(ONEOF ENTEROBACTERIACEAE (ORGANISMS) G+COCCI C-COCCI)
```

Thus, by storing the organisms separately on a list named ORGANISMS, we avoid having to duplicate the list of names in the EXPECT property of both IDENT and COVERFOR. Furthermore, using the variable name rather than internal pointers to the list structure facilitates references to the list of organisms whenever it is needed.

A second example involves the several rules in the system that make conclusions based on whether an organism was isolated from a site that is normally sterile or nonsterile. STERILESITES is the name of a simple list containing the names of all normally sterile sites known to the system. There is a similar list named NONSTERILESITES. Thus many rules can have the condition (SAME CNTXT SITE STERILESITES), and the sites need not be listed explicitly in each rule.

Knowledge tables: In conjunction with the special functions discussed in the next subsection, MYCIN's knowledge tables permit a single rule to accomplish a task that would otherwise require several rules. A knowledge table contains a comprehensive record of certain clinical parameters plus the values they take on under various circumstances. For example, one of MYCIN's knowledge tables itemizes the gram stain, morphology, and aerobicity for every bacterial genus known to the system. Consider, then, the task of inferring an organism's gram stain, morphology, and aerobicity if its identity is known with certainty. Without the knowledge table, MYCIN would require several rules of the following form:

```
IF:    The identity of the organism is definitely W
THEN:  1) It is definite (1) that the gramstain of the
          organism is X, and
       2) It is definite (1) that the morphology of the
          organism is Y, and
       3) It is definite (1) that the aerobicity of the
          organism is Z
```

Instead, MYCIN contains a single rule of the following form:

RULE030

```
IF:    The identity of the organism is known with certainty
THEN:  It is definite (1) that these parameters - GRAM
       MORPH AIR - should be transferred from the identity
       of the organism to this organism
```

Thus if ORGANISM-1 is known to be a *Streptococcus,* MYCIN can use RULE030 to access the knowledge table to look up the organism's gram stain, morphology, and aerobicity.

Specialized Functions

The efficient use of knowledge tables requires the existence of four specialized functions (the category <special-func> from Section 5.1.1). As explained below, each function attempts to add members to a list named GRIDVAL and returns T if at least one element has been found to be placed in GRIDVAL.

Functions of the Category <special-func>

Let V = Val[C,P] be the set of all hypotheses regarding the value of the clinical parameter P for the context C.

Let CLST be a list of objects that may be characterized by clinical parameters.

Let PLST be a list of clinical parameters.

Then:

Function	*Value of GRIDVAL*
SAME2[C,CLST,PLST]	{X | X ∊ CLST & (for all P in PLST) SAME [C,P,Val[X,P]]}
NOTSAME2[C,CLST,PLST]	{X | X ∊ CLST & (for at least one P in PLST) NOTSAME[C,P,Val[X,P]]}
SAME3[C,P,CLST,P*]	{X | X ∊ CLST & SAME[C,P,Val[X,P*]]}
NOTSAME3[C,P,CLST,P*]	{X | X ∊ CLST & NOTSAME [C,P,Val[X,P*]]}
GRID[<object>,<attribute>]	{X | X is a value of the <attribute> of <object>}

GRID is merely a function for looking up information in the specialized knowledge table.

The use of these functions is best explained by example. Consider the following verbalization of a rule given us by one of our collaborating experts:

> If you know the portal of entry of the current organism and also know the pathogenic bacteria normally associated with that site, you have evidence that the current organism is one of those pathogens so long as there is no disagreement on the basis of gram stain, morphology, or aerobicity.

This horrendous sounding rule is coded quite easily using SAME2[C,CLST,PLST], where C is the current organism, CLST is the list of pathogenic bacteria normally associated with the portal of entry of C, and PLST is the set of properties (GRAM MORPH AIR). GRID is used to set up CLST. The LISP version of the rule is

```
PREMISE: ($AND (GRID (VAL CNTXT PORTAL) PATH-FLORA)
                   (SAME2 CNTXT GRIDVAL (QUOTE (GRAM MORPH AIR))))
ACTION:  (CONCLIST CNTXT IDENT GRIDVAL .8)
```

Note that GRID sets up the initial value of GRIDVAL for use by SAME2, which then redefines GRIDVAL for use in the action clause. This rule is translated (to somewhat stilted English) as follows:

```
IF:   1) The list of likely pathogens associated with the
         portal of entry of the organism is known, and
      2) This current organism and the members you are
         considering agree with respect to the following
         properties: GRAM MORPH AIR
THEN:    There is strongly suggestive evidence (.8) that
         each of them is the identity of this current
         organism
```

SAME2 and NOTSAME2 can also be used for comparing the values of the same clinical parameters for two or more different contexts in the context tree, for example:

```
SAME2[ORGANISM-1 (ORGANISM-2 ORGANISM-3) (GRAM MORPH)]
```

On the other hand, SAME3 and NOTSAME3 are useful for comparing different parameters of two or more contexts. Suppose you need a predicate that returns T if the site of a prior organism (ORGANISM-2) is the same as the portal of entry of the current organism (ORGANISM-1). This is accomplished by the following:

```
SAME3[ORGANISM-1 PORTAL (ORGANISM-2) SITE]
```

5.1.7 Translation of Rules into English

Rules are translated into a subset of English using a set of recursive functions that piece together bits of text. We shall demonstrate the process using the premise condition (GRID (VAL CNTXT PORTAL) PATH-FLORA), which is taken from the rule in the preceding section.

The reader will recall that every clinical parameter has a property named TRANS that is used for translation (Section 5.1.3). In addition, every function, simple list, or knowledge table that is used by MYCIN's rules also has a TRANS property. For our example the following TRANS properties are relevant:

```
GRID:        (THE (2) ASSOCIATED WITH (1) IS KNOWN)
VAL:         (((2 1)))
PORTAL:      (THE PORTAL OF ENTRY OF *)
PATH-FLORA:  (LIST OF LIKELY PATHOGENS)
```

The numbers in the translations of functions indicate where the translation of the corresponding argument should be inserted. Thus the translation of GRID's second argument is inserted for the (2) in GRID's TRANS property. The extra parentheses in the TRANS for VAL indicate that the translation of VAL's first argument should be substituted for the asterisk in the translation of VAL's second argument. Since PORTAL is a PROP-ORG, CNTXT translates as "the organism," and the translation of (VAL CNTXT PORTAL) becomes

The portal of entry of the organism

Substituting VAL's translation for the (1) in GRID's TRANS and PATH-FLORA's translation for the (2) yields the final translation of the conditional clause:

The list of likely pathogens associated with the portal of entry of the organism is known

Similarly, (GRID (VAL CNTXT CLASS) CLASSMEMBERS)

translates as: The list of members associated with the class of the organism is known

All other portions of rules use essentially this same procedure for translation. An additional complexity arises, however, if it is necessary to negate the verbs in action or else clauses when the associated CF is negative. The translator program must therefore recognize verbs and know how to negate them when evidence in a premise supports the negation of the hypothesis that is referenced in the action of the rule.

5.2 Use of the Rules to Give Advice

The discussion in Section 5.1 was limited to the various data structures used to represent MYCIN's knowledge. The present section proceeds to an explanation of how MYCIN uses that knowledge in order to give advice.

5.2.1 MYCIN's Control Structure

MYCIN's rules are directly analogous to the consequent theorems introduced by Hewitt in his PLANNER system (Hewitt, 1972). They permit a reasoning chain to grow dynamically on the basis of the user's answers to questions regarding the patient. This subsection describes that reasoning network, explaining how it grows and how MYCIN manages to ask questions only when there is a reason for doing so.

Consequent Rules and Recursion

MYCIN's task involves a four-stage decision problem:

1. Decide which organisms, if any, are causing significant disease.
2. Determine the likely identity of the significant organisms.
3. Decide which drugs are potentially useful.
4. Select the best drug or drugs.

Steps 1 and 2 are closely interrelated since determination of an organism's significance may well depend on its presumed identity. Furthermore, MYCIN must consider the possibility that the patient has an infection with an organism not specifically mentioned by the user (e.g., an occult abscess suggested by historical information or subtle physical findings). Finally, if MYCIN decides that there is no significant infection requiring antimicrobial therapy, it should skip Steps 3 and 4, advising the user that no treatment is thought to be necessary. MYCIN's task area therefore can be defined by the following rule:

RULE092

IF: 1) There is an organism which requires therapy, and
    2) Consideration has been given to the possible existence of additional organisms requiring therapy, even though they have not actually been recovered from any current cultures
THEN: Do the following:
    1) Compile the list of possible therapies which, based upon sensitivity data, may be effective against the organisms requiring treatment, and
    2) Determine the best therapy recommendations from the compiled list
OTHERWISE: Indicate that the patient does not require therapy

This rule is one of MYCIN's PATRULES (i.e., its context is the patient) and is known as the *goal rule* for the system. A consultation session with MYCIN results from a simple two-step procedure:

1. Create the patient context as the top node in the context tree (see Section 5.3 for an explanation of how nodes are added to the tree).
2. Attempt to apply the goal rule to the newly created patient context.

After the second step, the consultation is over. Thus we must explain how the simple attempt to apply the goal rule to the patient causes a lengthy consultation with an individualized reasoning chain.

When MYCIN first tries to evaluate the premise of the goal rule, the first condition requires that it know whether there is an organism that requires therapy. MYCIN then reasons backwards in a manner that may be informally paraphrased as follows:

How do I decide whether there is an organism requiring therapy? Well, RULE090 tells me that organisms associated with significant disease require therapy. But I don't even have any organisms in the context tree yet, so I'd better ask first if there are any organisms, and if there are I'll try to apply RULE090 to each of them. However, the premise of RULE090 requires that I know whether the organism is significant. I have a bunch of rules for making this decision (RULE038 RULE042 RULE044 RULE108 RULE122). For example, RULE038 tells me that if the organism came from a sterile site it is probably significant. Unfortunately, I don't have any rules for inferring the site of a culture, however, so I guess I'll have to ask the user for this information when I need it . . .

This goal-oriented approach to rule invocation and question selection is automated via two interrelated procedures, a MONITOR that analyzes rules and a FINDOUT mechanism that searches for data needed by the MONITOR.

The MONITOR analyzes the premise of a rule, condition by condition, as shown in Figure 5-6.[3] When the value of the clinical parameter referenced in a condition is not yet known to MYCIN, the FINDOUT mechanism is invoked in an attempt to obtain the missing information. FINDOUT then either derives the necessary information (from other rules) or asks the user for the data.

FINDOUT has a dual strategy depending on the kind of information required by the MONITOR. This distinction is demonstrated in Figure 5-7. In general, a piece of data is immediately requested from the user (an ASK1 question) if it is considered in some sense "primitive," as are, for example, most laboratory data. Thus, if the physician knows the identity of an organism (e.g., from a lab report), we would prefer that the system request that information directly rather than try to deduce it via decision rules. However, if the user does not know the identity of the organism, MYCIN uses its knowledge base in an effort to deduce the range of likely organisms. Nonlaboratory data are those kinds of information that require inference even by the clinician, e.g., whether or not an organism is a contaminant or whether or not a previously administered drug was effective. FINDOUT always attempts to deduce such information first, asking the physician only when MYCIN's knowledge base of rules is inadequate for making the inference from the information at hand (an ASK2 question).

We have previously described the representation of clinical parameters and their associated properties. The need for two of these properties, LABDATA and UPDATED-BY, should now be clear. The LABDATA flag for a parameter allows FINDOUT to decide which branch to take through

[3]As discussed in Section 5.1.5, the MONITOR uses the $AND function to oversee the premise evaluation.

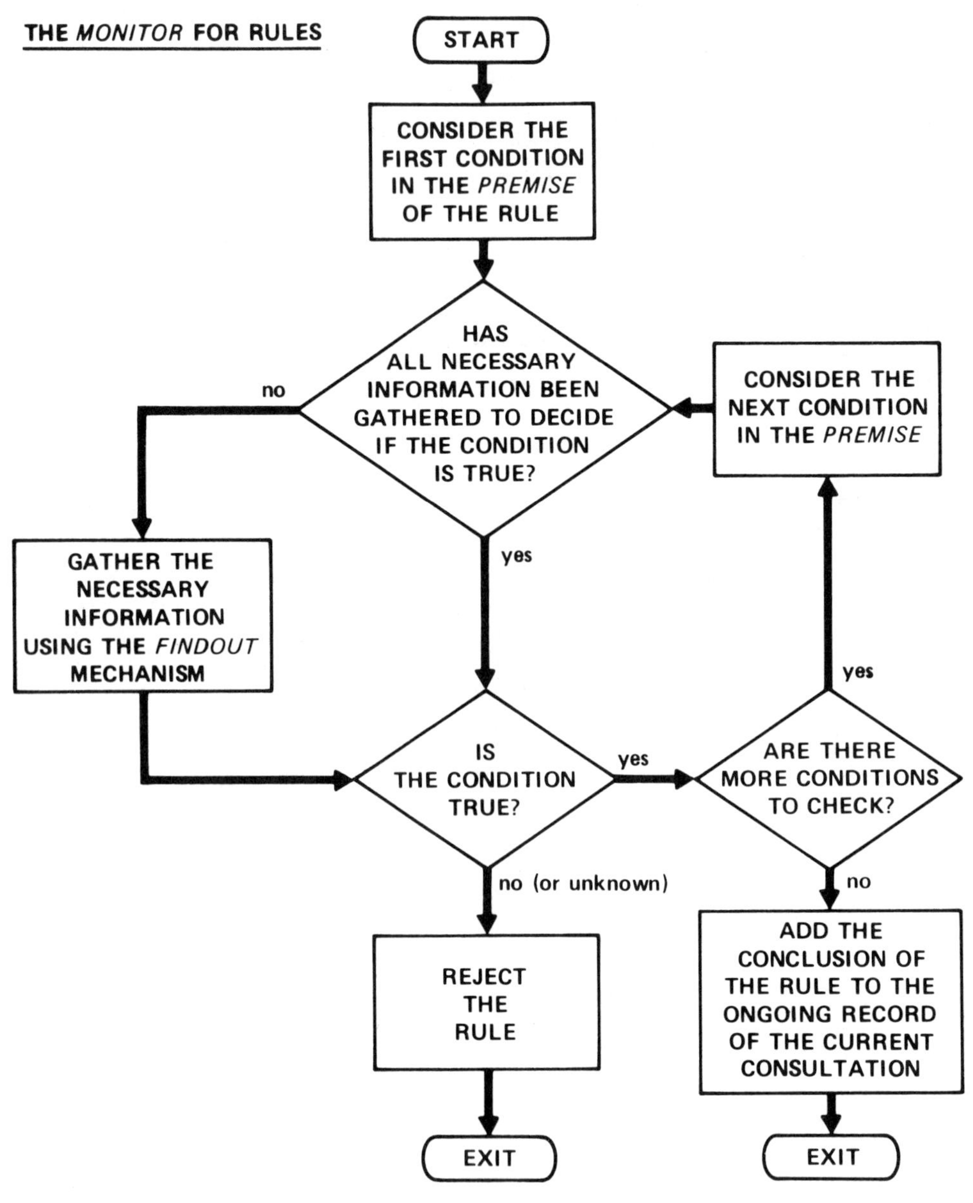

FIGURE 5-6 Flow chart describing how the MONITOR analyzes a rule and decides whether or not it applies in the clinical situation under consideration. Each condition in the premise of the rule references some clinical parameter, and all such conditions must be true for the rule to be accepted (Shortliffe et al., 1975).

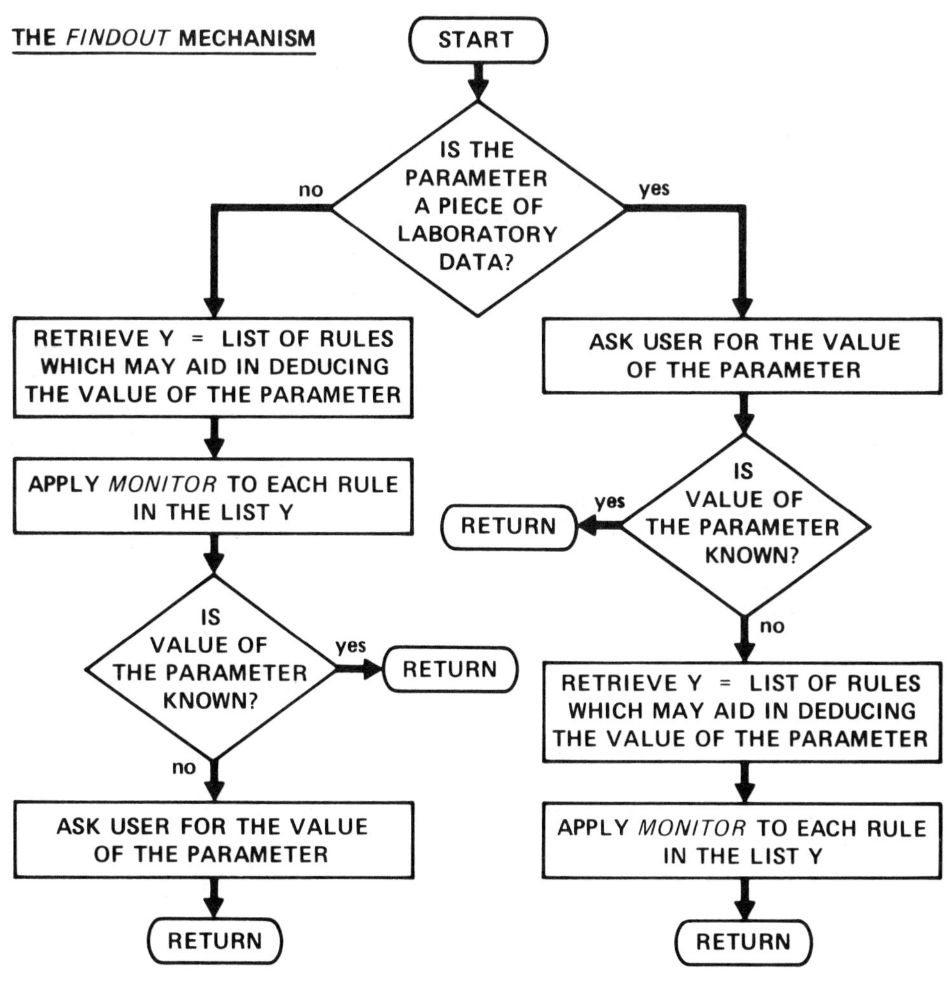

FIGURE 5-7 Flow chart describing the strategy for determining which questions to ask the physician. The derivation of values of parameters may require recursive calls to the MONITOR, thus dynamically creating a reasoning chain specific to the patient under consideration (Shortliffe et al., 1975).

its decision process (Figure 5-7). Thus IDENT is marked as being LABDATA in Figure 5-2.

Recall that the UPDATED-BY property is a list of all rules in the system that permit an inference to be made regarding the value of the indicated parameter. Thus UPDATED-BY is precisely the list called Y in Figure 5-7. Every time a new rule is added to MYCIN's knowledge base, the name of the rule is added to the UPDATED-BY property of the clinical parameter referenced in its action or else clause. Thus the new rule immediately becomes available to FINDOUT at times when it may be useful. It is not necessary to specify explicitly its interrelationships with other rules in the system.

Note that FINDOUT is accessed from the MONITOR, but the MONITOR may also be accessed from FINDOUT. This recursion allows self-propagation of a reasoning network appropriate for the patient under consideration and selects only the necessary questions and rules. The first rule passed to the MONITOR is always the goal rule. Since the first condition in the premise of this rule references a clinical parameter named TREATFOR, and since the value of TREATFOR is of course unknown before any data have been gathered, the MONITOR asks FINDOUT to trace the value of TREATFOR. This clinical parameter is not LABDATA, so FINDOUT takes the left-hand pathway in Figure 5-7 and sets Y to the UPDATED-BY property of TREATFOR, the two-element list (RULE090 RULE149). The MONITOR is then called again with RULE090 as the rule for consideration, and FINDOUT is used to trace the values of clinical parameters referenced in the premise of RULE090. Note that this process parallels the informal paraphrase of MYCIN's reasoning given above.

It is important to recognize that FINDOUT does not check to see whether the premise condition is true. Instead, the FINDOUT mechanism traces the clinical parameter *exhaustively* and returns its value to the MONITOR, where the conditional expression may then be evaluated.[4] Hence FINDOUT is called one time at most for a clinical parameter (in a given context—see Section 5.3). When FINDOUT returns a value to the MONITOR, it marks the clinical parameter as having been traced. Thus when the MONITOR reaches the question "HAS ALL NECESSARY INFORMATION BEEN GATHERED TO DECIDE IF THE CONDITION IS TRUE?" (Figure 5-6), the parameter is immediately passed to FINDOUT unless it has been previously marked as traced.

Figure 5-8 is a portion of MYCIN's initial reasoning chain. In Figure 5-8 the clinical parameters being traced are underlined. Thus REGIMEN is the top goal of the system (i.e., it is the clinical parameter in the action clause of the goal rule). Below each parameter are the rules (from the UPDATED-BY property) that may be used for inferring the parameter's value. Clinical parameters referenced in the premise of each of these rules are then listed at the next level in the reasoning network. Rules with multiple premise conditions have their links numbered in accordance with the order in which the parameters are traced (by FINDOUT). ASK1 indicates that a parameter is LABDATA, so its value is automatically asked of the user when it is needed. ASK2 refers to parameters that are not LABDATA but for which no inference rules currently exist, e.g., if the dose of a drug is adequate. One of the goals in the future development of MYCIN's knowl-

[4]The process is slightly different for multi-valued parameters; see Section 5.2.1.

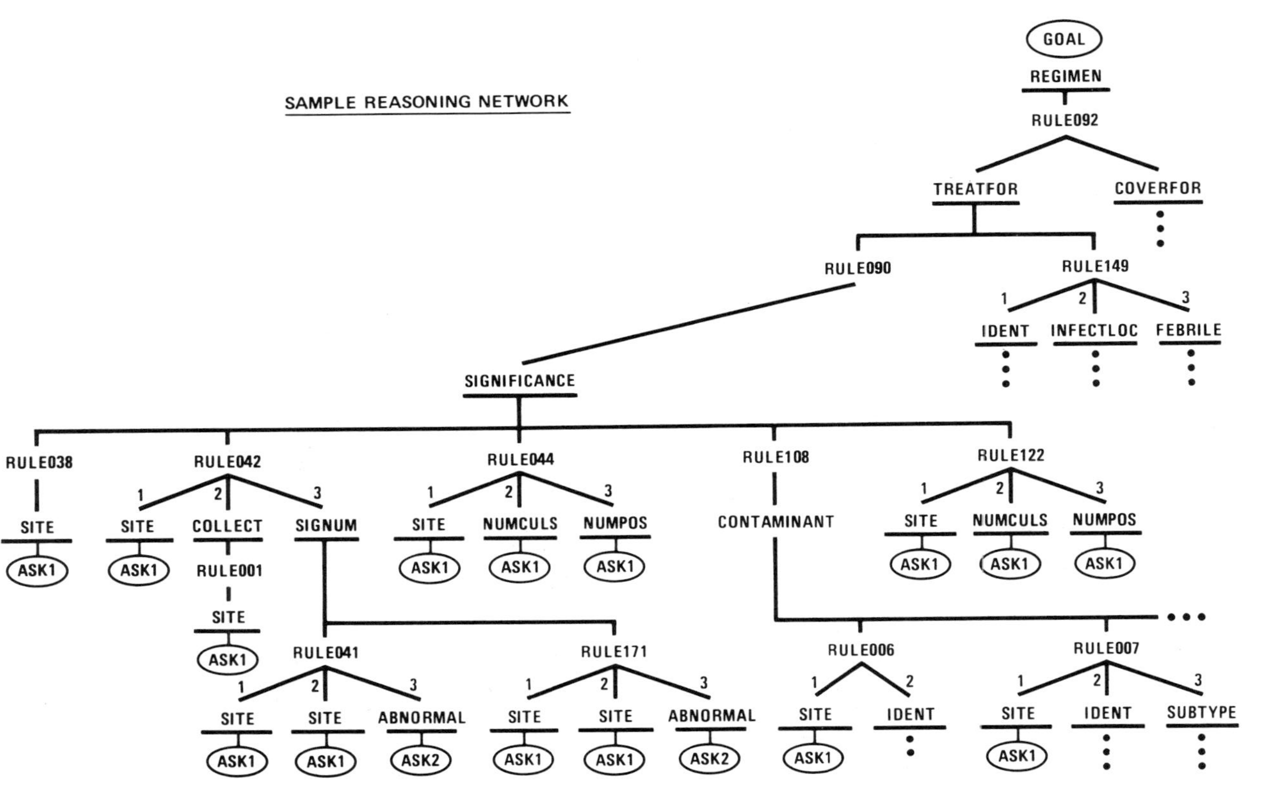

FIGURE 5-8 An example of the kind of reasoning network generated by the MONITOR and FINDOUT mechanisms. Names of clinical parameters are underlined. When a rule has multiple conditions in its premise, numbers have been included to specify the positions of the associated clinical parameters within the premise conditions.

edge base is to acquire enough rules allowing the values of non-LABDATA parameters to be inferred so that ASK2 questions need no longer occur.

Note that the reasoning network in Figure 5-8 is drawn to reflect maximum size. In reality many portions of such a network need not be considered. For example, RULE042 (one of the UPDATED-BY rules under SIGNIFICANCE) is rejected if the SITE condition is found to be false by the MONITOR. When that happens, neither COLLECT nor SIGNUM needs to be traced by FINDOUT, and those portions of the reasoning network are not created. Thus the order of conditions within a premise is highly important. In general, conditions referencing the most common parameters (i.e., those that appear in the premises of the most rules) are put first in the premises of new rules to act as an effective screening mechanism.

A final comment is necessary regarding the box labeled "REJECT THE RULE" in Figure 5-6. This step in the MONITOR actually must check to see if the rule has an else clause. If so, and if the premise is known to be false, the conclusion indicated by the else clause is drawn. If there is no else clause, or if the truth status of the premise is uncertain (e.g., the user has entered UNKNOWN when asked the value of one of the relevant parameters), the rule is simply ignored without any conclusion having been reached.

Asking Questions of the User

The conventions for communication between a program and a physician are a primary factor determining the system's acceptability. We have therefore designed a number of features intended to simplify the interactive process that occurs when FINDOUT reaches one of the boxes entitled "ASK USER FOR THE VALUE OF THE PARAMETER" (Figure 5-7).

When MYCIN requests the value of a single-valued or yes-no parameter, it uses the PROMPT property of the parameter. The user's response is then compared with the EXPECT property of the parameter. If the answer is one of the expected responses, the program simply continues through the reasoning network. Otherwise, MYCIN checks the system dictionary to see if the user's response is a synonym for one of the recognized answers. If this attempt also fails, MYCIN uses Interlisp spelling-correction routines (Teitelman, 1974) to see if a simple spelling or typographical error will account for the unrecognized response. If so, the program makes the correction, prints its assumption, and proceeds as though the user had made no error. If none of these mechanisms succeeds, MYCIN tells the user that the response is not recognized, displays a list of sample responses, and asks the question again.

Multi-valued parameters are handled somewhat differently. FINDOUT recursively traces such parameters in the normal fashion, but when forced to ask a question of the user, it customizes its question to the condition being evaluated in the MONITOR. Suppose, for example, the MONITOR were evaluating the condition (SAME CNTXT INFECT MENINGITIS), i.e., "Meningitis is an infectious disease diagnosis for the patient." If FINDOUT were to ask the question using the regular PROMPT strategy, it would request:

What is the infectious disease diagnosis for PATIENT-1?

The problem is that the patient may have several diagnoses, each of which can be expressed in a variety of ways. If the physician were to respond:

A meningeal inflammation that is probably of infectious origin

MYCIN would be forced to try to recognize that this answer implies meningitis. Our solution has been to customize questions for multi-valued parameters to reflect the value being checked in the current premise condition. The PROMPT1 property is used, and questions always expect a yes or no response:

Is there evidence that the patient has a meningitis?

The advantages of this approach are the resulting ability to avoid natural language processing during the consultation itself and the posing of questions that are specific to the patient under consideration.

In addition to the automatic spelling-correction capability described above, there are a number of options that may be utilized whenever MYCIN asks the user a question:

UNKNOWN	Used to indicate that the physician does not know the answer to the question, usually because the data are unavailable (may be abbreviated U or UNK)
?	Used to request a list of sample recognized responses
??	Used to request a list of *all* recognized responses
RULE	Used to request that MYCIN display the translation of the current decision rule. FINDOUT simply translates the rule being considered by the MONITOR. This feature provides a simple capability for explaining why the program is asking the question. However, it cannot explain motivation beyond the current decision rule.
QA	Used to digress temporarily in order to use the Explanation System. The features of this system are explained in Chapter 18.
WHY	Used to request a detailed explanation of the question being asked. This feature is much more conversational than the RULE option above and permits investigation of the current state of the entire reasoning chain.

CHANGE ###	Used to change the answer to a previous question. Whenever MYCIN asks a question, it prints a number in front of the prompt. Thus CHANGE 4 means "Go back and let me reanswer question 4." The complexities involved in this process are discussed below.
STOP	Halts the program without completing the consultation
HELP	Prints this list

5.2.2 Creation of the Dynamic Data Base

The Consultation System maintains an ongoing record of the consultation. These dynamic data include information entered by the user, inferences drawn using decision rules, and record-keeping data structures that facilitate question answering by the Explanation System (Chapter 18).

Data Acquired from the User

Except for questions related to propagation of the context tree, all queries from MYCIN to the physician request the value of a specific clinical parameter for a specific node in the context tree. The FINDOUT mechanism screens the user's response, stores it in MYCIN's dynamic data base, and returns the value to the MONITOR for evaluation of the conditional statement that generated the question in the first place. The physician's response is stored, of course, so that future rules containing conditions referencing the same clinical parameter will not cause the question to be asked a second time.

As has been noted, however, the values of clinical parameters are always stored along with their associated certainty factors. A physician's response must therefore have a CF associated with it. MYCIN's convention is to assume CF = 1 for the response unless the physician explicitly states otherwise. Thus the following exchange:

```
7) Staining characteristics of ORGANISM-1 (gram):
**GRAMNEG
```

results in: Val[ORGANISM-1,GRAM] = ((GRAMNEG 1.0))

If, on the other hand, the user is fairly sure of the answer to a question but wants to indicate uncertainty, he or she may enter a certainty factor in parentheses after the response. MYCIN expects the number to be an integer between −10 and +10; the program divides the number by 10 to obtain a CF. Using integers simplifies the user's response and also discourages comparisons between the number and a probability measure. Thus the following exchange:

```
8) Enter the identity (genus) of ORGANISM-1:
** ENTEROCOCCUS (8)
```

results in: Val[ORGANISM-1,IDENT] = ((STREPTOCOCCUS-GROUP-D .8))

This example also shows how the dictionary is used to put synonyms into standardized form for the patient's data base (i.e., *Enterococcus* is another name for a group-D *Streptococcus*).

A variant of this last example is the user's option to enter multiple responses to a question, as long as each is modified by a CF. For example:

```
13) Did ORGANISM-2 grow in clumps, chains, or pairs?
** CLUMPS (6) CHAINS (3) PAIRS (-8)
```

results in: Val[ORGANISM-2,CONFORM] = ((CLUMPS .6)(CHAINS .3)(PAIRS -.8))

The CF's associated with the parameter values are then used for evaluation of premise conditions as described earlier. Note that the user's freedom to modify answers increases the flexibility of MYCIN's reasoning. Without the CF option, the user might well have responded UNKNOWN to question 13 above. The demonstrated answer, although uncertain, gives MYCIN much more information than would have been provided by a response of UNKNOWN.

Data Inferred by the System

This subsection explains the <conclusion> item from the BNF rule description, i.e., the functions that are used in action or else clauses when a premise has shown that an indicated conclusion may be drawn. There are only three such functions, two of which (CONCLIST and TRANSLIST) reference knowledge tables (Section 5.1.6) but are otherwise dependent on the third, a function called CONCLUDE. CONCLUDE takes five arguments:

CNTXT	The node in the context tree about which the conclusion is being made
PARAM	The clinical parameter whose value is being added to the dynamic data base
VALUE	The inferred value of the clinical parameter
TALLY	The certainty tally for the premise of the rule (see Section 5.1.5)

CF	The certainty factor for the rule as judged by the expert from whom the rule was obtained

The translation of CONCLUDE depends on the size of CF:

$\lvert CF \rvert \geq .8$	"There is strongly suggestive evidence that . . . "
$.4 \leq \lvert CF \rvert < .8$	"There is suggestive evidence that . . . "
$\lvert CF \rvert < .4$	"There is weakly suggestive evidence that . . . "
Computed CF	"There is evidence that . . . "

Thus the following conclusion:

```
(CONCLUDE CNTXT IDENT STREPTOCOCCUS TALLY .7)
```

translates as:

There is suggestive evidence (.7) that the identity of the organism is streptococcus

If, for example, the rule with this action clause were successfully applied to ORGANISM-1, an organism for which no previous inferences had been made regarding identity, the result would be:

```
Val[ORGANISM-1,IDENT] = ((STREPTOCOCCUS X))
```

where X is the product of .7 and TALLY (see Combining Function 4, Chapter 11). Thus the strength of the conclusion reflects both the CF for the rule *and* the extent to which the premise of the rule is believed to be true for ORGANISM-1.

Suppose a second rule were now found that contains a premise true for ORGANISM-1 and that adds additional evidence to the assertion that the organism is a *Streptococcus*. This new evidence somehow has to be combined with the CF (=X) that is already stored for the hypothesis that ORGANISM-1 is a *Streptococcus*. If Y is the CF calculated for the second rule (i.e., the product of the TALLY for that rule and the CF assigned to the rule by the expert), the CF for the hypothesis is updated to Z so that:

```
Val[ORGANISM-1,IDENT] = ((STREPTOCOCCUS Z))
```

where Combining Function 1 gives $Z = X + Y(1 - X)$. This function is justified and discussed in detail in Chapter 11.

Similarly, additional rules leading to alternate hypotheses regarding the identity of ORGANISM-1 may be successfully invoked. The new hypotheses, along with their associated CF's, are simply appended to the list of hypotheses in Val[ORGANISM-1,IDENT]. Note, of course, that the CF's of some hypotheses may be negative, indicating that there is evidence suggesting that the hypothesis is not true. When there is both positive and negative evidence for a hypothesis, Combining Function 1 must be used in a modified form.

A final point to note is that values of parameters are stored identically regardless of whether the information has been inferred or acquired from the user. The source of a piece of information is maintained in a separate record. It is therefore easy to incorporate new rules that infer values of parameters for which ASK2 questions to the user were once necessary.

Creating an Ongoing Consultation Record

In addition to information provided or inferred regarding nodes in the context tree, MYCIN's dynamic data base contains a record of the consultation session. This record provides the basis for answering questions about the consultation (Chapter 18).

Two general types of records are kept. One type is information about how values of clinical parameters were obtained. If the value was inferred using rules, a record of those inferences is stored with the rules themselves. Thus whenever an action or else clause is executed, MYCIN keeps a record of the details. The second type of record provides a mechanism for explaining why questions were asked. MYCIN maintains a list of questions, their identifying numbers, the clinical parameter and context involved, plus the rule that led to generation of the question. This information is useful when the user retrospectively requests an explanation for a previous question (Chapter 18).

5.2.3 Self-Referencing Rules

As new rules were acquired from the collaborating experts, it became apparent that MYCIN would need a small number of rules that departed from the strict modularity to which we had otherwise been able to adhere. For example, one expert indicated that he would tend to ask about the typical *Pseudomonas*-type skin lesions only if he already had reason to believe that the organism was a *Pseudomonas*. If the lesions were then said to be evident, however, his belief that the organism was a *Pseudomonas* would be increased even more. A rule reflecting this fact must somehow imply an orderedness of rule invocation; i.e., "Don't try this rule until you have already traced the identity of the organism by using other rules in the system." Our solution has been to reference the clinical parameter early in the premise of the rule as well as in the action, for example:

RULE040

IF: 1) The site of the culture is blood, and
2) The identity of the organism may be pseudomonas, and
3) The patient has ecthyma gangrenosum skin lesions
THEN: There is strongly suggestive evidence (.8) that the identity of the organism is pseudomonas

Note that RULE040 is thus a member of both the LOOKAHEAD property and the UPDATED-BY property for the clinical parameter IDENT. Rules having the same parameter in both premise and action are termed *self-referencing rules.* The ordered invocation of such rules is accomplished by a generalized procedure described below.

As discussed in Section 5.2.1, a rule such as RULE040 is originally invoked because MYCIN is trying to infer the identity of an organism; i.e., FINDOUT is asked to trace the parameter IDENT and recursively sends the UPDATED-BY list for that parameter to the MONITOR. When the MONITOR reaches RULE040, however, the second premise condition references the same clinical parameter currently being traced by FINDOUT. If the MONITOR merely passed IDENT to FINDOUT again (as called for by the simplified flow chart in Figure 5-6), FINDOUT would begin tracing IDENT for a second time, RULE040 would be passed to the MONITOR yet again, and an infinite loop would occur.

The solution to this problem is to let FINDOUT screen the list called Y in Figure 5-7, i.e., the UPDATED-BY property for the parameter it is about to trace. Y is partitioned by FINDOUT into regular rules and self-referencing rules (where the latter category is defined as those rules that also occur on the LOOKAHEAD list for the clinical parameter). FINDOUT passes the first group of rules to the MONITOR in the normal fashion. After all these rules have been tried, FINDOUT marks the parameter as having been traced and then passes the self-referencing rules to the MONITOR. In this way, when the MONITOR considers the second condition in the premise of RULE040, the condition is evaluated without a call to FINDOUT because the parameter has already been marked as traced. Thus the truth of the premise of a self-referencing rule is determined on the basis of the set of non–self-referencing rules, which were evaluated first. If one of the regular rules permitted MYCIN to conclude that an organism might be a *Pseudomonas*, RULE040 might well succeed when passed to the MONITOR. This mechanism for handling self-referencing rules satisfies the intention of an expert when he or she gives us decision criteria in self-referencing form.

It should be noted that this approach minimizes the potential for self-referencing rules to destroy certainty factor commutativity. By holding these rules until last, we insure that the certainty tally for any of their premises (see Section 5.1.5) is the same regardless of the order in which the non–self-referencing rules were executed. If there is more than one self-referencing rule successfully executed for a given context and parameter, however, the order of their invocation may affect the final CF. The approach we have implemented thus seeks merely to minimize the potential undesirable effects of self-referencing rules.

5.2.4 Preventing Reasoning Loops

Self-referencing rules are actually a special case of a more general problem. Reasoning loops involving multiple rules cannot be handled by the mechanism described above. The difference is that self-referencing rules are intentional parts of MYCIN's knowledge base whereas reasoning loops are artifacts that must somehow be avoided.

For the following discussion we introduce the following notation:

[q] X ::> Y

means that decision rule [q] uses clinical parameter X to reach a conclusion regarding the value of clinical parameter Y. Thus a self-referencing rule may be represented by:

[a] E ::> E

where E is the clinical parameter that is referenced in both the premise and the action of the rule. Consider now the following set of rules:

[1] A ::> B

[2] B ::> C

[3] C ::> D

[4] D ::> A

Rule [1], for example, says that under certain unspecified conditions, the value of A can be used to infer the value of B. Now suppose that the MONITOR asks FINDOUT to trace the clinical parameter D. Then MYCIN's recursive mechanism would create the following reasoning chain:

```
    [4]   [1]   [2]   [3]
...D ::> A ::> B ::> C ::> D
```

The difference between this looped reasoning chain and a self-referencing rule is that Rule [4] was provided as a mechanism for deducing the value of A, not for reinforcing the system's belief in the value of D. In cases where the value of A is of primary interest, the use of Rule [4] would be appropriate.

MYCIN solves this problem by keeping track of all parameters currently being traced by the FINDOUT mechanism. The MONITOR then simply ignores a rule if one of the parameters checked in its premise is already being traced. The result, with the value of D as the goal, is a three-membered reasoning chain in the case above:

```
  [1]   [2]   [3]
A ::> B ::> C ::> D
```

Rule [4] is rejected because parameter D is already being traced elsewhere in the current reasoning chain. If the value of A were the main goal, however, the chain would be

```
        [2]     [3]     [4]
    B ::> C ::> D ::> A
```

Note that this simple mechanism allows us to have potential reasoning loops in the knowledge base but to select only the relevant nonlooping portions for consideration of a given patient.

A similar problem can occur when a rule permits two conclusions to be made, each about a different clinical parameter. MYCIN prevents loops in such circumstances by refusing to permit the same rule to occur twice in the current reasoning chain.

5.3 Propagation of the Context Tree

The mechanism by which the context tree is customized for a given patient has not yet been discussed. As described in Section 5.2.2, the consultation system begins simply by creating the patient context and then attempting to execute the goal rule. All additional nodes in the context tree are thus added automatically during the unwinding of MYCIN's reasoning regarding the premise of the goal rule. This section first explains the data structures used for creating new nodes. Mechanisms for deciding when new nodes should be added are then discussed.

5.3.1 Data Structures Used for Sprouting Branches

Section 5.1.2 was devoted to an explanation of the context tree. At that time we described the different kinds of contexts and explained that each node in the tree is an instantiation of the appropriate context-type. Each context-type is characterized by the following properties:

PROMPT1	A sentence used to ask the user whether the first node of this type should be added to the context tree; expects a yes-no answer
PROMPT2	A sentence used to ask the user whether subsequent nodes of this type should be added to the context tree
PROMPT3	Replaces PROMPT1 when it is used. This is a message to be printed out if MYCIN assumes that there is at least one node of this type in the tree.
PROPTYPE	Indicates the category of clinical parameters (see Section 5.1.3) that may be used to characterize a context of this type

SUBJECT	Indicates the categories of rules that may be applied to a context of this type
SYN	Indicates a conversational synonym for referring to a context of this type. MYCIN uses SYN when filling in the asterisk of PROMPT properties for clinical parameters.
TRANS	Used for English translations of rules referencing this type of context
TYPE	Indicates what kind of internal name to give a context of this type
MAINPROPS	Lists the clinical parameters, if any, that are to be automatically traced (by FINDOUT) whenever a context of this type is created
ASSOCWITH	Gives the context-type of nodes in the tree immediately above contexts of this type

Two sample context-types are shown in Figure 5-9. The following observations may help clarify the information given in that figure:

1. PRIORCULS: Whenever a prior culture is created, it is given the name CULTURE-# (see TYPE), where # is the next unassigned culture number. The values of SITE and WHENCUL are immediately traced using the FINDOUT mechanism (see MAINPROPS). The culture node is put in the context tree below a node of type PERSON (see ASSOCWITH), and the new context may be characterized by clinical parameters of the type PROP-CUL (see PROPTYPE). The prior culture may be the context for either PRCULRULES or CULRULES (see SUBJECT) and is translated, in questions to the user, as "this (site) culture" (see SYN) where (site) is replaced by the site of the culture if it is known.
2. CURORG: Since there is a PROMPT3 rather than a PROMPT1, MYCIN prints out the PROMPT3 message and assumes (without asking) that there is at least one CURORG for each CURCUL (see ASSOCWITH); the other CURORG properties correspond to those described above for PRIORCULS.

Whenever MYCIN creates a new context using these models, it prints out the name of the new node in the tree, e.g.:

------ORGANISM-1------

Thus the user is familiar with MYCIN's internal names for the cultures, organisms, and drugs under discussion. The node names may then be used in MYCIN's questions at times when there may be ambiguity regarding which node is the current context, e.g.:

Is the patient's illness with the staphylococcus (ORGANISM-2) a hospital-acquired infection?

PRIORCULS

ASSOCWITH: PERSON
MAINPROPS: (SITE WHENCUL)
PROMPT1: (Were any organisms that were significant (but no longer require therapeutic attention) isolated within the last approximately 30 days?)
PROMPT2: (Any other significant earlier cultures from which pathogens were isolated?)
PROPTYPE: PROP-CUL
SUBJECT: (PRCULRULES CULRULES)
SYN: (SITE (this * culture))
TRANS: (PRIOR CULTURES OF *)
TYPE: CULTURE-

CURORG

ASSOCWITH: CURCUL
MAINPROPS: (IDENT GRAM MORPH SENSITIVS)
PROMPT2: (Any other organisms isolated from * for which you would like a therapeutic recommendation?)
PROMPT3: (I will refer to the first offending organism from * as:)
PROPTYPE: PROP-ORG
SUBJECT: (ORGRULES CURORGRULES)
SYN: (IDENT (the *))
TRANS: (CURRENT ORGANISMS OF *)
TYPE: ORGANISM-

FIGURE 5-9 Context trees such as that shown in Figure 5-1 are generated from prototype context-types such as those shown here. The defining properties are described in the text.

It should also be noted that when PROMPT1 or PROMPT2 is used to ask a question, the physician need not be aware that the situation is different from that occurring when FINDOUT asks questions. All the user options described in Section 5.2.1 operate in the normal fashion.

Finally, the MAINPROPS property (later called INITIALDATA) requires brief explanation. The claim was previously made that clinical parameters are traced and their values requested by FINDOUT only when they are needed for evaluation of a rule that has been invoked. Yet we must now acknowledge that certain LABDATA parameters are automatically traced whenever a node for the context tree is created. The reason for this departure is an attempt to keep the program acceptable to physicians. Since the order of rules on UPDATED-BY lists is arbitrary, the order in which questions are asked is somewhat arbitrary as well. We have found that physicians are annoyed if the "basic" questions are not asked first, as soon as the context is created. The MAINPROPS convention forces certain standard questions early in the characterization of a node in the context tree. Parameters not on the MAINPROPS list are then traced in an arbitrary order that depends on the order in which rules are invoked. Since the parameters on MAINPROPS lists are important pieces of information that would uniformly be traced by FINDOUT anyway, the convention we have implemented forces a standardized ordering of the "basic" questions without generating useless information.

5.3.2 Explicit Mechanisms for Branching

There are two situations under which MYCIN attempts to add new nodes to the context tree. The simpler case occurs when rules explicitly reference contexts that have not yet been created. Suppose, for example, MYCIN is trying to determine the identity of a current organism and therefore invokes the following CURORGRULE:

```
IF:   1) The identity of the organism is not known
         with certainty, and
      2) This current organism and prior organisms of
         the patient agree with respect to the following
         properties: GRAM MORPH
THEN:  There is weakly suggestive evidence that each of
       them is a prior organism with the same identity
       as this current organism
```

The second condition in the premise of this rule references other nodes in the tree, namely nodes of the type PRIORORGS. If no such nodes exist, the MONITOR asks FINDOUT to trace PRIORORGS in the normal fashion. The difference is that PRIORORGS is not a clinical parameter but a context-type. FINDOUT therefore uses PROMPT1 of PRIORORGS to ask the user if there is at least one organism. If so, an instantiation of PRIORORGS is added to the context tree, and its MAINPROPS are traced. PROMPT2 is then used to see if there are any additional prior organisms, and the procedure continues until the user indicates there are no more PRIORORGS that merit discussion. Finally, FINDOUT returns the list of prior organisms to the MONITOR so that the second condition in the rule above can be evaluated.

5.3.3 Implicit Mechanisms for Branching

There are two kinds of implicit branching mechanisms. One of these is closely associated with the example of the preceding section. As shown in Figure 5-1, a prior organism is associated with a prior culture. But the explicit reference to prior organisms in the rule above made no mention of prior cultures. Thus if FINDOUT tries to create a PRIORORGS in response to an explicit reference but finds there are no PRIORCULS, the program knows there is an implied need to ask the user about prior cultures before asking about prior organisms. Since PRIORCULS are associated with the patient, and since the patient node already exists in the context tree, only one level of implicit branching is required in the evaluation of the rule.

The other kind of implicit branching occurs when the MONITOR attempts to evaluate a rule for which no appropriate context exists. For example, the first rule invoked in an effort to execute the goal rule is a CURORGRULE (see RULE090, Figure 5-8). Since no current organism has been created at the time the MONITOR is passed this CURORGRULE, MYCIN automatically attempts to create the appropriate nodes and then to apply the invoked rule to each.

5.4 Selection of Therapy

The preceding discussion concentrated on the premise of MYCIN's principal goal rule (RULE092). This section explains what happens when the premise is found to be true and the two-step action clause is executed. Unlike other rules in the system, the goal rule does not lead to a conclusion (Section 5.2.2) but instead instigates actions. The functions in the action of the goal rule thus correspond to the <actfunc> class that was introduced in the BNF description. The first of these functions causes a list of potential therapies to be created. The second allows the best drug or drugs to be selected from the list of possibilities.

5.4.1 Creation of the Potential Therapy List

There is a class of decision rules, the THERULES, that are never invoked by MYCIN's regular control structure because they do not occur on the UPDATED-BY list of any clinical parameter. These rules contain sensitivity information for the various organisms known to the system, for example:

```
IF:   The identity of the organism is pseudomonas
THEN: I recommend therapy chosen from among the following drugs:
                1 - colistin          (.98)
                2 - polymyxin         (.96)
                3 - gentamicin        (.96)
                4 - carbenicillin     (.65)
                5 - sulfisoxazole     (.64)
```

The numbers associated with each drug are the probabilities that a *Pseudomonas* isolated at Stanford Hospital will be sensitive (*in vitro*) to the indicated drug. The sensitivity data were acquired from Stanford's microbiology laboratory (and could easily be adjusted to reflect changing resistance patterns at Stanford or the data for some other hospital desiring a version of MYCIN with local sensitivity information). Rules such as the one shown here provide the basis for creating a list of potential therapies. There is one such rule for every kind of organism known to the system.

MYCIN selects drugs only on the basis of the identity of offending organisms. Thus the program's first task is to decide, for each current organism deemed to be significant, which hypotheses regarding the organism's identity (IDENT) are sufficiently likely that they must be considered in choosing therapy. MYCIN uses the CF's of the various hypotheses in order to select the most likely identities. Each identity is then given an *item number* (see below) and the process is repeated for each significant current organism. The *Set of Indications* for therapy is then printed out, e.g.:

```
My therapy recommendation will be based on the following possible
identities of the organism(s) that seem to be significant:

  <Item 1>  The identity of ORGANISM-1 may be
            STREPTOCOCCUS-GROUP-D
  <Item 2>  The identity of ORGANISM-1 may be
            STREPTOCOCCUS-ALPHA
  <Item 3>  The identity of ORGANISM-2 is PSEUDOMONAS
```

Each item in this list of therapy indications corresponds to one of the THERULES. Thus MYCIN retrieves the list of potential therapies for each indication from the associated THERULE. The default (*in vitro*) statistical data are also retrieved. MYCIN then replaces the default sensitivity data with real data about those of the patient's organisms, if any, for which actual sensitivity information is available from the laboratory. Furthermore, if MYCIN has inferred sensitivity information from the *in vivo* performance of a drug that has already been administered to the patient, this information also replaces the default sensitivity data. Thus the compiled list of potential therapies is actually several lists, one for each item in the Set of Indications. Each list contains the names of drugs and, in addition, the associated numbers representing MYCIN's judgment regarding the organism's sensitivity to each of the drugs.

5.4.2 Selecting the Preferred Drug from the List

When MYCIN recommends therapy, it tries to suggest a drug for each of the items in the Set of Indications. Thus the problem reduces to selecting the best drug from the therapy list associated with each item. Clearly, the probability that an organism will be sensitive to a drug is an important factor in this selection process. However, there are several other considerations. MYCIN's strategy is to select the best drug on the basis of sensitivity information but then to consider contraindications for that drug. Only if a drug survives this second screening step is it actually recommended. Furthermore, MYCIN also looks for ways to minimize the number of drugs recommended and thus seeks therapies that cover for more than one of the items in the Set of Indications. The selection/screening process is described in the following two subsections.

Choosing the Apparent First-Choice Drug

The procedure used for selecting the apparent first-choice drug is a complex algorithm that is somewhat arbitrary and is thus currently (1974) under revision. This section describes the procedure in somewhat general terms since the actual LISP functions and data structures are not particularly enlightening.

There are three initial considerations used in selecting the best therapy for a given item:

1. the probability that the organism is sensitive to the drug;
2. whether the drug is already being administered;
3. the relative efficacy of drugs that are otherwise equally supported by the first two criteria.

As is the case with human consultants, MYCIN does not insist on a change in therapy if the physician has already begun a drug that may work, even if that drug would not otherwise be MYCIN's first choice. Drugs with sensitivity numbers within .05 of one another are considered to be almost identical on the basis of the first criterion. Thus the rule in the previous section, for example, indicates no clear preference among colistin, polymyxin, and gentamicin[5] for *Pseudomonas* infections (if default sensitivity information from the rule is used). However, our collaborating experts have ranked the relative efficacy of antimicrobials on a scale from 1 to 10. The number reflects such factors as whether the drug is bacteriostatic or bacteriocidal or its tendency to cause allergic sensitization. Since gentamicin has a higher relative efficacy than either colistin or polymyxin, it is the first drug considered for *Pseudomonas* infections (unless known sensitivity information or previous drug experience indicates that an alternate choice is preferable).

Once MYCIN has selected the apparent best drug for each item in the Set of Indications, it checks to see if one of the drugs is also useful for one or more of the other indications. For example, if the first-choice drug for

[5]*Ed. note:* Amikacin and tobramycin were not yet available in 1974 when this rule was written. The knowledge base was later updated with the new drug information.

Item 1 is the second-choice drug for Item 2 and if the second-choice drug for Item 2 is almost as strongly supported as the first-choice drug, Item 1's first-choice drug also becomes Item 2's first-choice drug. This strategy permits MYCIN to attempt to minimize the number of drugs to be recommended.

A similar strategy is used to avoid giving two drugs of the same drug class. For example, MYCIN knows that if the first choice for one item is penicillin and the first choice for another is ampicillin, then the ampicillin may be given for both indications (because ampicillin covers essentially all organisms sensitive to penicillin).

In the ideal case MYCIN will find a single drug that effectively covers for all the items in the Set of Indications. But even if each item remains associated with a different drug, a screening stage to look for contraindications is required. This rule-based process is described in the next subsection. It should be stressed, however, that the manipulation of drug lists described above is algorithmic; i.e., it is coded in LISP functions that are called from the action clause of the goal rule. There is considerable "knowledge" in this process. Since rule-based knowledge provides the foundation of MYCIN's ability to explain its decisions, it would be desirable eventually to remove this therapy selection method from functions and place it in decision rules.[6]

Rule-Based Screening for Contraindications

Unlike the complex list manipulations described in the preceding subsection, criteria for ruling out drugs under consideration may be effectively placed in rules. The rules in MYCIN for this purpose are termed ORDERRULES. A sample rule of this type is:

```
IF:   1) The therapy under consideration is tetracycline, and
      2) The age (in years) of the patient is less than 13
THEN:  There is strongly suggestive evidence (.8) that
       tetracycline is not a potential therapy for use
       against the organism
```

In order to use MONITOR and FINDOUT with such rules, we must construct appropriate nodes in the context tree and must be able to characterize them with clinical parameters. The context-type used for this purpose is termed POSSTHER and the parameters are classified as PROPTHER. Thus when MYCIN has selected the apparent best drugs for the items in the Set of Indications, it creates a context corresponding to each of these drugs. POSSTHER contexts occur below CURORGS in the context tree. FINDOUT is then called to trace the relevant clinical parameter,

[6]*Ed. note:* See the next chapter for a discussion of how this was later accomplished.

which collects contraindication information (i.e., this becomes a new goal statement), and the normal recursive mechanism through the MONITOR insures that the proper ORDERRULES are invoked.

ORDERRULES allow a great deal of drug-specific knowledge to be stored. For example, the rule above insures that tetracycline is ruled out in youngsters who still have developing bone and teeth.[7] Similar rules tell MYCIN never to give streptomycin or carbenicillin alone, not to give sulfonamides except in urinary tract infections, and not to give cephalothin, clindamycin, lincomycin, vancomycin, cefazolin, or erythromycin if the patient has meningitis. Other ORDERRULES allow MYCIN to consider the patient's drug allergies, dosage modifications, or ecological considerations (e.g., save gentamicin for *Pseudomonas, Serratia,* and *Hafnia* unless the patient is so sick that you cannot risk using a different aminoglycoside while awaiting lab sensitivity data). Finally, there are rules that suggest appropriate combination therapies (e.g., add carbenicillin to gentamicin for known *Pseudomonas* infections). In considering such rules MYCIN often is forced to ask questions that never arose during the initial portion of the consultation. Thus the physician is asked additional questions during the period after MYCIN has displayed the items in the Set of Indications but before any therapy is actually recommended.

After the presumed first-choice drugs have been exposed to the ORDERRULE screening process, MYCIN checks to see whether any of the drugs is now contraindicated. If so, the drug-ranking process is repeated. New first-choice drugs are then subjected to the ORDERRULES. The process continues until all the first-choice drugs have been instantiated as POSSTHERS. These then become the system's recommendations. Note that this strategy may result in the recommendation of drugs that are only mildly contraindicated so long as they are otherwise strongly favored. The therapy recommendation itself takes the following form:

```
My preferred therapy recommendation is as follows:
  In order to cover for Items <1> <2> <3>:
    Give the following in combination:
      1. PENICILLIN
         Dose: 285,000 UNITS/KG/DAY - IV
      2. GENTAMICIN
         Dose: 1.7 MG/KG Q8H - IV OR IM
         Comments: MODIFY DOSE IN RENAL FAILURE
```

The user may also ask for second, third, and subsequent therapy recommendations until MYCIN is able to suggest no reasonable alternatives. The mechanism for these iterations is merely a repeat of the processes described above but with recommended drugs removed from consideration.

---

[7]*Ed. note:* This rule ignores any statement of the mechanism whereby its conclusion follows from its premise. The lack of underlying "support" knowledge accounts for changes introduced in GUIDON when MYCIN's rules were used for education. See Part Eight for further discussion of this point.

5.5 Mechanisms for Storage of Patient Data

5.5.1 Changing Answers to Questions

If a physician decides he or she wants to change a response to a question that has already been answered, MYCIN must do more than merely redisplay the prompt, accept the user's new answer, and make the appropriate change to the value of the clinical parameter in question. In general, the question was originally asked because the premise of a decision rule referenced the clinical parameter. Thus the original response affected the evaluation of at least one rule, and subsequent pathways in the reasoning network may have been affected as well. It is therefore necessary for MYCIN somehow to return to the state it was in at the time the question was originally asked. Its subsequent actions can then be determined by the corrected user response.

Reversing all decisions made since a question was asked is a complex problem, however. The most difficult task is to determine what portions of a parameter's cumulative CF preceded or followed the question requiring alteration. In fact, the extra data structures needed to permit this kind of backing up are so large and complicated, and would be used so seldom, that it seems preferable simply to restart the consultation from the beginning when the user wants to change one of his or her answers.

Restarting is of course also less than optimal, particularly if it requires that the physician reenter the answers to questions that were correct the first time around. Our desire to make the program acceptable to physicians required that we devise some mechanism for changing answers, but restarting from scratch also had obvious drawbacks regarding user acceptance of the system. We therefore needed a mechanism for restarting MYCIN's reasoning process but avoiding questions that had already been answered correctly. When FINDOUT asks questions, it therefore uses the following three-step algorithm:

1. Before asking the question, check to see if the answer is already stored (in the Patient Data Table—see Step 3 below); if the answer is there, use that value rather than asking the user; otherwise go to Step 2.
2. Ask the question using PROMPT or PROMPT1 as usual.
3. Store the user's response in the dynamic record of facts about the patient, called the Patient Data Table, under the appropriate clinical parameter and context.

The Patient Data Table, then, is a growing record of the user's responses to questions from MYCIN. It is entirely separate from the dynamic data record that is explicitly associated with the nodes in the context tree. Note that the Patient Data Table contains only the text responses of the user—there is no CF information (unless included in the user's response), nor are there data derived from MYCIN's rule-based inferences.

The Patient Data Table and the FINDOUT algorithm make the task of changing answers much simpler. The technique MYCIN uses is the following:

a. Whenever the user wants to change the answer to a previous question, he or she enters CHANGE <numbers>, where <numbers> is a list of the questions whose answers need correction.

b. MYCIN looks up the indicated question numbers in its question record.

c. The user's responses to the indicated questions are removed from the current Patient Data Table.

d. MYCIN reinitializes the system, erasing the entire context tree, including all associated parameters; however it leaves the Patient Data Table intact except for the responses deleted in (c).

e. MYCIN restarts the consultation from the beginning.

This simple mechanism results in a restarting of the Consultation System but does not require that the user enter correct answers a second time. Since the Patient Data Table is saved, Step 1 of the FINDOUT algorithm above will find all the user's responses until the first question requiring alteration is reached. Thus the first question asked the user after he or she gives the CHANGE command is, in fact, the earliest of the questions he or she wants to change. There may be a substantial pause after the CHANGE command while MYCIN reasons through the network to the first question requiring alteration, but a pause is to be preferred over a mechanism requiring reentry of all answers. The implemented technique is entirely general because answers to questions regarding context tree propagation are also stored in the Patient Data Table.

5.5.2 Remembering Patients for Future Reference

When a consultation is complete, the Patient Data Table contains all responses necessary for generating a complete consultation for that patient. It is therefore straightforward to store the Patient Data Table (on disk or tape) so that it may be reloaded in the future. FINDOUT will automatically read responses from the table, rather than ask the user, so a consultation may be run several times on the basis of only a single interactive session.

There are two reasons for storing Patient Data Tables for future reference. One is their usefulness in evaluating changes to MYCIN's knowledge base. The other is the resulting ability to reevaluate patients once new clinical information becomes available.

Evaluating New Rules

New rules may have a large effect on the way a given patient case is handled by MYCIN. For example, a single rule may reference a clinical parameter not previously sought or may lead to an entirely new chain in the reasoning network. It is therefore useful to reload Patient Data Tables and run a new version of MYCIN on old patient cases. A few new questions may be asked (because their responses are not stored in the Patient Data Table). Conclusions regarding organism identities may then be observed, as may the program's therapeutic recommendations. Any changes from the decisions reached during the original run (i.e., when the Patient Data Table was created) must be explained. When a new version of MYCIN evaluates several old Patient Data Tables in this manner, aberrant side effects of new rules may be found. Thus a library of stored patient cases provides a useful mechanism for screening new rules before they become an integral part of MYCIN's knowledge base.

Reevaluating Patient Cases

The second use for stored Patient Data Tables is the reevaluation of patient data once additional laboratory or clinical information becomes available. If a user answers several questions with UNKNOWN during the initial consultation session, MYCIN's advice will of course be based on less than complete information. After storing the Patient Data Table, however, the physician may return for another consultation in a day or so once he or she has more specific information. MYCIN can use the previous Patient Data Table for responses to questions whose answers are still up to date. The user therefore needs to answer only those questions that reference new information. A mechanism for the physician to indicate directly what new data are available has not yet been automated, however.[8]

A related capability to be implemented before MYCIN becomes available in the clinical setting is a SAVE command.[9] If a physician must leave the computer terminal midway through a consultation, this option will save the current Patient Data Table on the disk. When the physician returns to complete the consultation, he or she will reload the patient record and the session will continue from the point at which the SAVE command was entered.

It should be stressed that saving the current Patient Data Table is *not* the same as saving the current state of MYCIN's reasoning. Thus, as we have stated above, changes to MYCIN's rule corpus may result in different advice from the same Patient Data Table.

---

[8]*Ed. note:* A RESTART option was subsequently developed to permit reassessment of cases over time.

[9]*Ed. note:* This option was also subsequently implemented.

5.6 Suggested Improvements to the System

This section summarizes some ideas for improvement of the consultation program described in this chapter. Each of the topics mentioned is the subject of current (1974) efforts by one or more of the researchers associated with the MYCIN project.

5.6.1 Dynamic Ordering of Rules

The order in which rules are invoked by the MONITOR is currently controlled solely by their order on the UPDATED-BY property of the clinical parameter being traced.[10] The order of rules on the UPDATED-BY property is also arbitrary, tending to reflect nothing more than the order in which rules were acquired. Since FINDOUT sends all rules on such lists to the MONITOR and since our certainty factor combining function is commutative, the order of rules is unimportant.

Some rules are much more useful than others in tracing the value of a clinical parameter. For example, a rule with a six-condition premise that infers the value of a parameter with a low CF requires a great deal of work (as many as six calls to FINDOUT) with very little gain. On the other hand, a rule with a large CF and only one or two premise conditions may easily provide strong evidence regarding the value of the parameter in question. It may therefore be wise for FINDOUT to order the rules in the UPDATED-BY list on the basis of both information content (CF) and the work necessary to evaluate the premise. Then if the first few rules are successfully executed by the MONITOR, the CF associated with one of the values of the clinical parameter may be so large that invocation of subsequent rules will require more computational effort than they are worth. If FINDOUT therefore ignores such rules (i.e., does not bother to pass them to the MONITOR), considerable time savings may result. Furthermore, entire reasoning chains will in some cases be avoided, and the number of questions asked the user could accordingly be decreased.[11]

5.6.2 Dynamic Ordering of Conditions Within Rules

The MONITOR diagram in Figure 5-6 reveals that conditions are evaluated strictly in the order in which they occur within the premise of the rule. The order of conditions is therefore important, and the most com-

[10]An exception to this point is the self-referencing rules—see Section 5.2.3.

[11]*Ed. note:* Many of these ideas were later implemented and are briefly mentioned in Chapter 4. For example, *meta-rules* provided a mechanism for encoding strategies to help select the most pertinent rules in a set, and the concept of a *unity path* was implemented to favor chains of rules that reached conclusions with certainty at each step in the chain.

monly referenced clinical parameters should be placed earliest in the premise.

Suppose, however, that in a given consultation the clinical parameter referenced in the fourth condition of a rule has already been traced by FINDOUT because it was referenced in some other rule that the MONITOR has already evaluated. As currently designed, MYCIN checks the first three conditions first, even if the fourth condition is already known to be false. Since the first three conditions may well require calls to FINDOUT, the rule may generate unnecessary questions and expand useless reasoning chains.

The solution to this problem would be to redesign the MONITOR so that it reorders the premise conditions, first evaluating those that reference clinical parameters that have already been traced by FINDOUT. In this way a rule will not cause new questions or additions to the reasoning network if any of its conditions are known to be false at the outset.[12]

5.6.3 Prescreening of Rules

An alternate approach to the problem described in the preceding section would be for FINDOUT to judge the implications of every parameter it traces. Once the value has been determined by the normal mechanism, FINDOUT could use the LOOKAHEAD list for the clinical parameter in order to identify all rules referencing the parameter in their premise conditions. FINDOUT could then evaluate the relevant conditions and mark the rule as failing if the condition turns out to be false. Then, whenever the MONITOR begins to evaluate rules that are invoked by the normal recursive mechanism, it will check to see if the rule has previously been marked as false by FINDOUT. If so, the rule could be quickly ruled out without needing to consider the problem of reordering the premise conditions.

At first glance, the dynamic reordering of premise conditions appears to be a better solution than the one just described. The problem with rule prescreening is that it requires consideration of all rules on the parameter's LOOKAHEAD list, some of which may never actually be invoked during the consultation.[13]

5.6.4 Placing All Knowledge in Rules

Although most of MYCIN's knowledge is placed in decision rules, we have pointed out several examples of knowledge that is not rule-based. The simple lists and knowledge tables may be justified on the basis of efficiency,

---

[12] *Ed. note:* The *preview mechanism* in MYCIN was eventually implemented to deal with this issue.

[13] *Ed. note:* It was for this reason that the idea outlined here was never implemented.

especially since those knowledge structures may be directly accessed by rules.

However, the algorithmic mechanisms for therapy selection are somewhat more bothersome. Although we have managed to put many drug-related decision criteria in the ORDERRULES, the mechanisms for creating the potential therapy lists and for choosing the apparent first-choice drug are programmed explicitly in a series of relatively complex LISP functions. Since MYCIN's ability to explain itself is based on rule retrieval, the system cannot give good descriptions of these drug selection procedures. It is therefore desirable to place more of the drug selection knowledge in rules.

Such efforts should provide a useful basis for evaluating the power of our rule-based formalism. If the goal-oriented control structure we have developed is truly general, one would hope that algorithmic approaches to the construction and ordering of lists could also be placed in decision rule format. We therefore intend to experiment with ways for incorporating the remainder of MYCIN's knowledge into decision rules that are invoked by the standard MONITOR/FINDOUT process.[14]

5.6.5 The Need for a Context Graph

The context tree used by MYCIN is the source of one of the system's primary problems in attempting to simulate the consultation process. Every node in the context tree leads to the uppermost patient node by a single pathway. In reality, however, drugs, patients, organisms, and cultures are not interrelated in this highly structured fashion. For example, drugs are often given to cover for more than one organism. The context tree does not permit a single CURDRUG or PRIORDRUG to be associated with more than a single organism. What we need, therefore, is a network of contexts in the form of a graph rather than a pure tree. The reasons why MYCIN currently needs a tree-structured context network are explained in Section 5.1.2. We have come to recognize that a context graph capability is an important extension of the current system, however, and this will be the subject of future design modifications.[15] When implemented, for example, it will permit a physician to discuss a prior drug only once, even though it may have been given to cover for several prior organisms.

---

[14]*Ed. note:* Rule-based encoding of the therapy selection algorithm was eventually undertaken and is described in the next chapter.

[15]*Ed. note:* This problem was never adequately solved and remains a limitation of the EMYCIN architecture (Part Five). A partial solution was achieved when predicate functions were developed that allowed a specific rule to be applied to all contexts of a given type and to draw inferences in one part of the context tree based on findings elsewhere in the context tree.

6

Details of the Revised Therapy Algorithm

William J. Clancey

A program that is designed to provide sophisticated expert advice must cope with the needs of naive users who may find the advice puzzling or difficult to accept. This chapter describes additions to MYCIN that provide for explanations of its therapy decisions, the lack of which was a shortcoming of the original therapy recommendation code described in Section 5.4 of Chapter 5. It deals with an optimization problem that seeks to provide "coverage" for organisms while minimizing the number of drugs prescribed. There are many factors to consider, such as prior therapies and drug sensitivities, and a person often finds it hard to juggle all of the constraints at once. When the optimal solution is provided by a computer program, its correctness may not be immediately obvious to the user. This motivates our desire to provide an explanation capability to justify the program's results.

The explanation capability derives from two basic programming considerations. First, we have used heuristics that capture what expert physicians consider to be good medical practice. Thus, while the program is not designed to mimic the step-by-step problem-solving behavior of a physician, its chief decision criteria have been provided by expert physicians. It is accordingly plausible that the criteria will make sense to other physicians.

The second consideration is that the program must maintain records of decisions that were made. These are used for explaining what occurred

---

This chapter is an expanded version of a paper originally appearing in *Proceedings of the IJCAI 1977*. Used by permission of International Joint Conferences on Artificial Intelligence, Inc.; copies of the *Proceedings* are available from William Kaufmann, Inc., 95 First Street, Los Altos, CA 94022.

during the optimization process and why the output was not different. While the maintenance of records for explanation purposes is not new (e.g., see Winograd, 1972; Bobrow and Brown, 1975; Scragg, 1975a; 1975b), the means that we use to retrieve them are novel, namely a state transition representation of the algorithm. Our work demonstrates that a cleanly structured algorithm can provide both sophisticated performance and a simple, useful explanation capability.

6.1 The Problem

The main problem of the therapy selector is to prescribe the best drug for each organism thought to be a likely cause of the infection, while minimizing the total number of drugs. These two constraints often conflict: the best prescription for, say, four items may require four different drugs, although for any patient usually no more than two drugs need to be given (or should be, for reasons of drug interaction, toxic side effects, cost, etc.).

The original therapy program lacked a general scheme for relating the local constraints (best drug for each item) to the global constraint (fewest possible number of drugs). As we began to investigate the complexities of therapy selection, it became necessary to patch the program to deal with the special cases we encountered. Before long we were losing track of how any given change would affect the program's output. We found it increasingly difficult to keep records during the program execution for later use in the explanation system; indeed, the logic of the program was too confusing to explain easily. We decided to start over, aiming for a more structured algorithm that would provide sophisticated therapy, and by its very organization would provide simple explanations for a naive user. The question was this: what organization could balance these two, sometimes contradictory, goals?

Because we wanted to formulate judgments that could be provided *by* physicians and would appear familiar *to* them, we decided not to use mathematical methods such as evaluation polynomials or Bayesian analysis. On the other hand, MYCIN's inferential rule representation seemed to be inadequate because of the general algorithmic nature of the problem (i.e., iteration and complex data structures). We turned our attention to separating out the optimization criteria of therapy selection from control information (specifications for iteratively applying the heuristics). As is discussed below, the key improvement was to encode canonically the optimization performed by the inner loop of the algorithm.

6.2 Our Solution

6.2.1 Local and Global Criteria

We found that viewing the optimization problem in terms of local and global criteria provides a fruitful means for structuring the problem. Local criteria are the item-specific factors, such as sensitivity of the organism to preferred drugs, toxicity of drugs, the desire to "reserve" drugs for more serious diseases, and the desire to continue current therapy if possible. Global criteria deal with the entire recommendation; we wished to minimize the number of drugs, prescribing only two drugs if possible to cover for all of the most likely organisms.[1] In addition, there were a few patient factors to consider, such as allergies to antibiotics.

Besides providing for optimal therapy, we wished to provide for an explanation capability that would list simple descriptions of the therapy selection heuristics used by the algorithm, as well as reasons for not making a different recommendation.

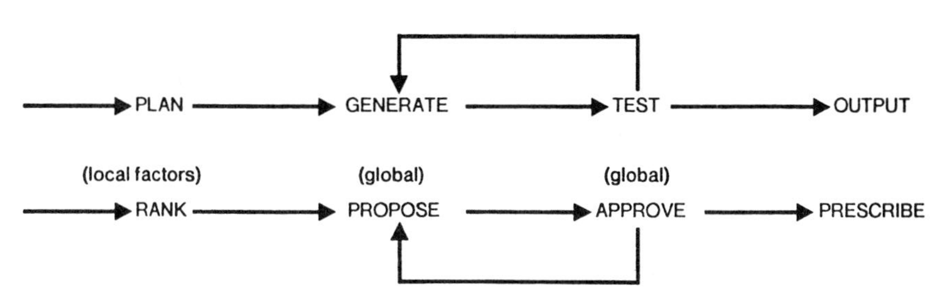

FIGURE 6-1 Therapy selection viewed as a plan-generate-and-test process.

After clearly stating these design goals, we needed an implementation scheme that would bring about the optimization. The key to our solution was the use of a generate-and-test control structure for separately applying the local and global factors. Figure 6-1 shows the steps of the plan-generate-and-test method and, below them, the corresponding steps of our algorithm. Briefly, the steps are

1. plan by ranking the drugs—the local factors are considered here;

[1]Here we realized that we could group the items into those that should definitely be treated ("most likely") and those that could be left out when three or more drugs would be necessary.

	Number of drugs of each rank:		
Instruction	*first*	*second*	*third*
1	1	0	0
2	2	0	0
3	1	1	0
4	1	0	1
.			
.			
.			

FIGURE 6-2 Instructions for the therapy proposer.

2. propose a recommendation and test it, thus dealing with the global factors; and
3. make a final recommendation.

The following sections consider these steps in more detail.

6.2.2 Plan

We start with an initial list of drugs to which each organism is sensitive and sort it by applying production rules for ranking. These reranking rules are applied independently for every organism to be treated. The chief purpose of this sorting process is to incorporate drug sensitivity information for the organisms growing in cultures taken from the patient.[2] Thus we arrive at a patient-specific list of drugs for each organism, reranked and grouped into first, second, and third ranks of choices.

Because this sorting process is a consideration specific to each organism, we refer to it as a local criterion of optimal therapy. We call it (loosely) a planning step because it makes preparations for later steps.

6.2.3 Generate

The second step of the algorithm is to take the ordered drug lists and generate possible recommendations. This is done by a proposer that selects subsets of drugs (a recommendation) from the collection of drugs for all of the organisms to be treated. Selection is directed by a fixed, ordered set of instructions that specify how many drugs to select from each preference group. The first few instructions are listed in Figure 6-2. For example, the

[2]A typical rule might be "If the organism growing from the culture appears to be resistant to the drug, then classify the drug as a third choice."

third instruction tells the proposer to select a drug from each of the first and second ranks. Instructions for one- and two-drug recommendations are taken from a static list; those for recommendations containing three or more drugs are generated from a simple pattern.

It should be clear that the ordering of the instructions ensures that two of the global criteria will be satisfied: prescribing one or two drugs if possible, and selecting the best possible drug(s) for each organism. An instruction therefore serves as a canonical description of a recommendation. Consequently, we can "reduce" alternate subsets of drugs to this form (the number of drugs of each rank) and compare them.

6.2.4 Test

Since all of the drugs for all of the organisms were grouped together for use by the proposer, it is quite possible that a proposed recommendation will not cover all of the most likely organisms. For example, the proposal might have two drugs that are in the first rank for one item but are second or third for other items, or are not even on their lists. Thus the first step of testing is to make sure that all of the most likely items are covered.

The second test ensures that each drug is in a unique drug class. For example, a proposal having both gentamicin and streptomycin would be rejected because these two drugs are aminoglycosides and therefore cause a "redundant" effect.

The last test is for patient-specific contraindications. These rules take into account allergies, age of the patient, pregnancy, etc. These rules are relatively expensive to apply, so they are done last, rather than applying them to each possible drug in the plan step. With this test we have dealt with the last global criterion of therapy selection. The first proposal that satisfies these three tests becomes the therapy advice. The details of drug prescription will not be considered further here; it consists primarily of algorithmic dosage calculation and adjustment in the case of renal failure.

6.2.5 Performance

We have found that the algorithm described above is manageable and performs well. It is straightforward to add new rules for ranking the drugs and for testing the proposals. The canonical instructions are relatively fixed, but it would not be difficult, for example, to provide infection-specific instruction sets. The program has made acceptable recommendations for a library of more than 100 meningitis patients.

6.3 The Explanation Capability

We will now consider how the structure of the algorithm is exploited to produce simple explanations. A sample question about therapy selection is shown in Figure 6-3. The medical decisions that were applied to the drug chloramphenicol are listed as a logical sequence of reasons, which is produced by retrieving and printing traces that were left behind by the program. The trace retrieval program is termed CHRONICLER because its explanations consist of a chronicle of decision events.

```
** WHY DID YOU GIVE CHLORAMPHENICOL FOR E.COLI IN REC-1?

CHLORAMPHENICOL was prescribed for ITEM-2 in RECOMMENDATION-1:

Since
        -- CHLORAMPHENICOL is a treatment of choice for e.coli in meningitis
        -- ITEM-2 is sensitive to CHLORAMPHENICOL
        -- there were no contraindications for it

CHLORAMPHENICOL was prescribed because it was part of the
recommendation that covers for all of the items, using the fewest number
of drugs.
```

FIGURE 6-3 A question concerning why a drug was prescribed. (User's input follows the double asterisks.)

Figure 6-4 shows the general organization of the Explanation System. The traces (discussed below) constitute a dynamic event history. A chronicle of events is printed by using a process transition diagram to selectively retrieve the relevant traces.

Figure 6-5 shows the kind of transition diagram we use to represent the steps of therapy selection. The states roughly correspond to the generate and test steps shown in Figure 6-1. The arrows are labeled as positive (pos) and negative (neg) criteria (i.e., criteria that support or oppose the recommendation of a given drug). These correspond to the medical strategies, e.g., "The drug is on the treatment-of-choice list for the organism (the initial list) and so was considered to cover for the organism." If a drug is prescribed, there must be a sequence of positive criteria leading from the first state to the output state. These are the reasons offered the user as an explanation for prescribing the drug. To make the explanation clearer, the states are reordered into three groups (planning criteria, testing criteria, and generate and output criteria) to conform to the following general scheme:

Since
--<plan criteria>
--<test criteria>

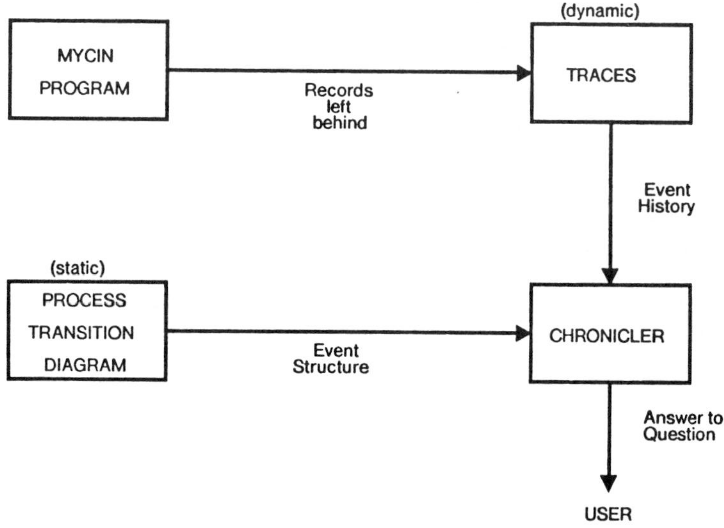

FIGURE 6-4 Organization of the Explanation System.

(therefore)
<generate and output criteria>

On the other hand, if a drug is not prescribed, there must be a negative criterion to explain why it dropped out of contention if it was on the initial list. Failure to prescribe can be caused by either failure to consider the

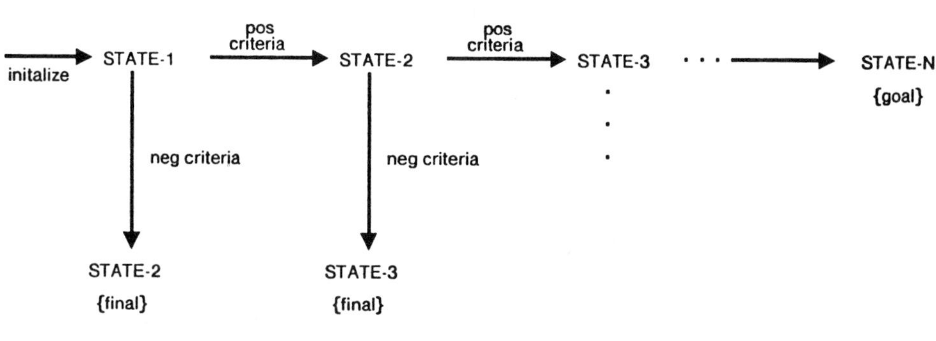

FIGURE 6-5 The state transition diagram.

**** WHY DIDN'T YOU SUGGEST PENICILLIN IN REC-1 FOR STAPH-COAG+?**

PENICILLIN was not prescribed for ITEM-1 in RECOMMENDATION-1:

PENICILLIN was discounted for ITEM-1 because it is NOT DEFINITE that the item is sensitive to this drug. There are other potential therapies under consideration which are much more desirable, viz., current therapies or drugs to which the item is definitely sensitive.

Would you like to see some details? ** **YES**

The drugs to which the staphylococcus-coag-pos is sensitive are: cephalothin (1.0) vancomycin (1.0) gentamycin (1.0) tobramycin (1.0) erythromycin-and-tetracycline (1.0) chloramphenicol-and-erythromycin (1.0) [RULE098 RULE445]

Would you like to know about the history of PENICILLIN in the decision process up to this point? ** **YES**

-- PENICILLIN is a treatment of choice for staphylococcus-coag-pos in meningitis. But as explained above, PENICILLIN was discounted.

FIGURE 6-6 Question concerning why a drug was *not* prescribed.

drug (plan) or failure of a test. A third possibility is that the drug wasn't part of an acceptable recommendation, but was otherwise a plausible choice (when considered alone). In this case, the drug needs to be considered in the context of a full recommendation for the patient.[3] (See Figure 6-9 for an example.)

Figure 6-6 shows an example of a question concerning why a drug was not prescribed. In response to a question of this type, the negative criterion is printed and the user is offered an opportunity to see the positive decisions accrued up to this point. In this example we see that penicillin was not prescribed because it is not definite that the item is sensitive to this drug. That is the negative criterion. The fact that penicillin was a potential treatment of choice permitted its transition to the reranking step.[4] This is shown in Figure 6-7. When MYCIN's rules (as opposed to Interlisp code) are used to make a transition decision, we can provide further details, as shown in Figure 6-6.

For questions involving two drugs, e.g., "Why did you prescribe chloramphenicol instead of penicillin for Item-1?", CHRONICLER is invoked to explain why the rejected drug was not given. Then the user is offered the opportunity to see why the other drug was given.

To summarize, MYCIN leaves behind traces that record the application

[3]Events are recorded as properties of the drugs they involve. The trace includes other contexts such as the item being considered. To deal with iteration, events are of two types: *enduring* and *pass-specific*. Enduring events represent decisions that, once made, are never reconsidered, e.g., the initial ranking of drugs for each organism. Pass-specific events may not figure in the final result; they may indicate computation that failed to produce a solution, e.g., proposing a drug as part of a specific recommendation. Thus traces are accessed by drug name and the context of the computation, including which pass of the generate-and-test process produced the final solution.

[4]Penicillin is given for staph-coag+ *only* if the organism is known to be sensitive to that agent.

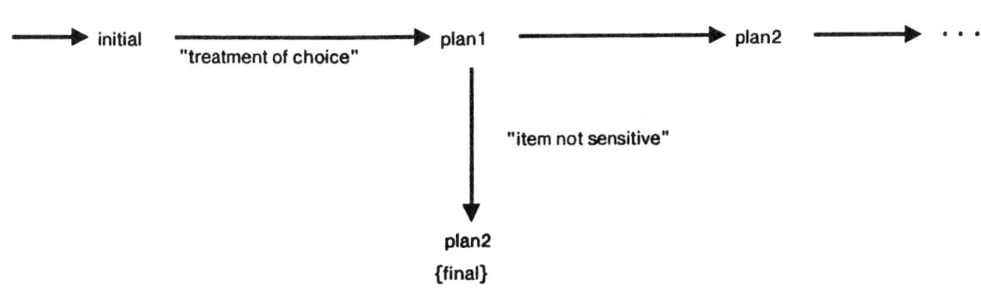

FIGURE 6-7 Trace history for the question shown in Figure 6-6.

of the positive and negative criteria. The Explanation System uses a state transition diagram that represents the steps of the algorithm to retrieve the relevant traces in a logical order.

It is interesting to note that CHRONICLER is described well by Bobrow and Brown's synthesis, contingent knowledge, and analysis (SCA) paradigm for understanding systems (Bobrow and Brown, 1975). Contingent knowledge is a record of program-synthesized observations for later use by an analysis program to answer questions or comment on the observed system. In CHRONICLER the traces and transition diagram constitute the contingent knowledge structure. Synthesis (abstraction of results) is performed by the therapy selector as it classifies the drugs in the various decision steps and records its "observations" in traces. Analysis is performed by CHRONICLER as it "reads" the traces, interpreting them in terms of the state transition diagram. The meteorology question-answering system described by Brown et al. (1973) uses a similar knowledge representation.

6.4 Comparing Alternative Recommendations

The therapy program will print alternative recommendations if asked to do so. This is done by eliminating drugs from contention and rerunning the algorithm. Figure 6-8 shows an example of an alternative recommendation and a comparison of this alternative to the algorithm's first choice. The comparison is made by simply reducing the recommendations to canonical form and then determining their relative ranking in the list of instructions. A recommendation is better than another when it reduces to a better instruction, i.e., when the preference description of its drugs appears earlier in the fixed list of instructions. It is also possible that the comparison

Do you wish to see the next choice therapy?
**** YES**
Which, if any, of the above drugs do you wish eliminated from consideration?
****CHLORAMPHENICOL**

[REC-2] Next best therapy recommendation:
In order to cover for Items <2 3 4>:
Give: GENTAMICIN

In order to cover for Item <1>:
Give: METHICILLIN

RECOMMENDATION-2 is substantially inferior to RECOMMENDATION-1 (because it requires more drugs or drugs that are not as good).

Would you like to see details of this comparison?
**** YES**

Looking at the coverage of the 'most likely' items, we see that:

RECOMMENDATION-1 consists of 1 first choice drug (CHLORAMPHENICOL for ITEM-2 and ITEM-3) and 1 second choice drug (GENTAMICIN for ITEM-3 and ITEM-1)

RECOMMENDATION-2 consists of 1 first choice drug (METHICILLIN for ITEM-1) and 1 third choice drug (GENTAMICIN for ITEM-2 and ITEM-3)

Do you wish to see the next choice therapy?
**** NO**

FIGURE 6-8 Comparing alternative recommendations.

will be a "close call," because one of the recommendations might use better drugs for the most likely organisms but cover for fewer of the less likely organisms. Again, it is the ability to encode output canonically that gives us the ability to make such a direct comparison of alternatives.

6.5 Evaluating a User's Choice of Therapy

The comparison described above is useful to a physician who prefers to give therapy other than MYCIN's first choice and wishes to know if the program truly considers it to be suboptimal therapy. However, it is tedious for the user to request all possible alternatives to be printed, so we offer the user the opportunity to enter his or her own choice of drugs for the organisms that require therapy (Figure 6-9).

Each drug the user suggests for an item is first formed into a standard internal question for CHRONICLER: "Why wasn't <drug> prescribed for <item>?" If there is a negative criterion about this drug for this item in the event history, it is printed and the user is given the option of selecting another drug.

**** WHY DIDN'T YOU GIVE AMPICILLIN-AND-GENTAMICIN FOR E.COLI IN REC-1?**

AMPICILLIN-AND-GENTAMICIN was not prescribed for ITEM-2 in RECOMMENDATION-1:

AMPICILLIN-AND-GENTAMICIN is a plausible choice for e.coli in meningitis, and was not explicitly rejected for use against ITEM-2 in RECOMMENDATION-1. However, the best therapy did not include AMPICILLIN-AND-GENTAMICIN.

If you would like to suggest therapy which includes AMPICILLIN-AND-GENTAMICIN, your regimen will be compared to MYCIN's. Would you like to do this? ** **YES**

For each item in turn, enter the drug you would have prescribed in RECOMMENDATION-1.
In order to minimize the number of drugs in your recommendation, you may not want to prescribe therapy for every item. Items which represent the most likely organisms are indicated with a plus sign (+).

+ ITEM-1 -- the staphylococcus-coag-pos ** **GENTAMICIN**
+ ITEM-2 -- the e.coli ** **AMPICILLIN GENTAMICIN**
+ ITEM-3 -- the klebsiella-pneumoniae ** **GENTAMICIN**
+ ITEM-4 -- the pseudomonas-aeruginose **

[Checking for contraindications . . .]
[Considering AMPICILLIN-AND-GENTAMICIN for use against INFECTION-1 . . .]
[No contraindications found . . .]

[Now comparing your prescription to MYCIN's . . .]

Perhaps you did not realize that one of the drugs you prescribed, GENTAMICIN, will cover for ITEM-4, an item for which you did not prescribe therapy. I have changed your prescription accordingly.

ORGANISMS	Your regimen Drug -- Choice	MYCIN's regimen Drug -- Choice
"most likely"		
ITEM-3	GENTAMICIN -- 3rd	CHLORAMPHENICOL-AND-GENTAMICIN -- 1st
ITEM-2	AMPICILLIN-AND-GENTAMICIN -- 1st	CHLORAMPHENICOL -- 1st
ITEM-1	GENTAMICIN -- 2nd	GENTAMICIN -- 2nd
"less likely"		
ITEM-4	GENTAMICIN -- 2nd	GENTAMICIN -- 2nd

(The desirability of a drug is defined to be its lowest ranking for the items it covers.)

Both prescriptions include fewer than 3 drugs, so we must look at how highly ranked each prescription is for the most likely organism(s).

Your prescription of 1 first choice drug (AMPICILLIN for ITEM-2) and 1 third choice drug (GENTAMICIN for ITEM-3) is not as good as MYCIN's prescription of 1 first choice drug (CHLORAMPHENICOL for ITEM-2 and Item-3) and 1 second choice drug (GENTAMICIN for ITEM-1).

[You may refer to your regimen as RECOMMENDATION-2 in later questions.]

FIGURE 6-9 Evaluating a user's choice of therapy.

Once the user has supplied a set of drugs to cover for all of the most likely organisms, his or her proposal is tested for the criteria of drug class uniqueness and patient-specific factors (described in Section 6.2.4). If the proposal is approved, this recommendation is compared to the program's choice of therapy, just as the program compares its alternatives to its own first-choice recommendation.[5] It is also possible to directly invoke the therapy comparison routine.

6.6 Some Unsolved Problems

There are a number of improvements that could be made to this system. Among the most important to potential users is a more flexible question format. In our experience physicians tend to address short, unspecific questions to the program, e.g., "Why ampicillin?" or "What happened to E. coli?" Processing these questions will require a fairly sophisticated preprocessor that can help the user define such a question more precisely, or at least make some plausible assumptions.

Second, we anticipate the need to explain the heuristics, which now are describable only in a template form.[6] A user might like to know what a "drug sensitivity" is or why a heuristic was not used. Providing simple, fixed-text definitions is easy, but discussing a particular heuristic to the extent of explaining why it was not applicable is well beyond the capabilities of this Explanation System. One possible solution is to represent the heuristics internally in a rulelike form with a set of preconditions in program-readable predicates, like MYCIN's rules. We could then say, for example, that a drug was lowered in rank because its sensitivity was "intermediate," even though it was a current therapy (which would otherwise be reason for continuing to prescribe it). Thus we would be splitting a medical criterion into its logical components. Moreover, human explanations sometimes include hypothetical relations that have important instructional benefit, e.g., "If all of the drugs had been intermediate, then this current therapy would have been given preference." In general, paraphrasing explanations, explaining why an event failed to take place, and relating decisions are difficult because they require some representation of what the heuristics mean. Providing a handle on these underlying concepts is a far cry from a system that can only fill in templates.

Third, it is important to justify the medical heuristics and initial pref-

---

[5]The explanations at this point are more pedagogical than those supplied when the program compares its own alternatives. It seems desirable to phrase comparisons as positively as possible to avoid irritating the user.

[6]That is, each medical heuristic has a string with blanks associated with it, e.g., <drug> "was discounted for" <item> "because it was not *definite* that the item was sensitive to this drug."

erence ranks for drugs. We now provide text annotations that include references and comments about shortcomings and intent.

Finally, we could further develop the tutorial aspects of the Explanation System. Rather than passively answering questions, the Explanation System might endeavor to teach the user about the overall structure and philosophy of the program (upon request!). For example, a user might appreciate the optimality of the results better if he or she understood the separation of factors into local and global considerations. Besides explaining the results of a particular run, an Explanation System might characterize individual decisions in the context of the program's overall design. Parts Six and Eight discuss the issues of explanation and education in more detail.

6.7 Conclusions

We have developed a system that prescribes optimal therapy and is able to provide simple, useful explanations. The system is based on a number of design ideas that are summarized as follows:

1. separate the local and global optimality criteria;
2. apply these criteria in comprehensible steps—a generate-and-test control structure was found to be suitable;
3. justify selected therapies by using canonical descriptions that
   a. juggle several global criteria at once, and
   b. permit direct comparison of alternatives; and
4. exploit the simple control structure by using a state transition diagram to order retrieval of traces.

In addition, the Explanation System has benefited from a few simplifying factors:

1. There are relatively few traces (fewer than 50 drugs to keep track of and fewer than 25 strategies that might be applied).
2. There is a single basic question: Why was (or was not) a particular drug prescribed for a particular organism?

While this therapy selection algorithm may appear straightforward, it is the product of trying to codify an unstructured list of factors presented by physicians. The medical experts did not order these considerations and were not sure how conflicting constraints should be resolved. The framework we imposed, namely, invoking optimality criteria locally and globally within a generate-and-test control structure and describing output canonically, provided a language that enabled us to codify the physicians' judgments, thereby significantly improving the performance and manageability of the program.

Moreover, this well-structured design enables us to print simple explanations of the program's decisions and to compare alternative solutions. We have provided this facility because we want the program to be used intelligently. If a user is confused or disagrees with the optimality criteria, we expect him or her to feel free to reject the results. The explanation system we have provided is intended to encourage thoughtful use of the therapy selection program.

PART THREE

Building a Knowledge Base

7

Knowledge Engineering

From early experience building the DENDRAL system, it was obvious to us that putting domain-specific knowledge into a program was a bottleneck in building knowledge-based systems (Buchanan et al., 1970). In other AI systems of the 1960s and early 1970s, items of knowledge were cast as LISP functions. For example, in the earliest version of DENDRAL the fact that the atomic weight of carbon is 12 was built into a function, called WEIGHT, which returned *12* when called with the argument *C*. The function "knew about" several common chemical elements, but when new elements or new isotopes were encountered, the function had to be changed. Because we wanted to keep our programs "lean" to run in 64K of working memory, we gave our programs only as much knowledge as we thought they would have to know. Thus we often encountered missing items in running new test cases. It was very quickly seen that LISP property lists (data structures) were a superior alternative to LISP code as a way of storing simple facts, so definitions of functions like WEIGHT were changed to retrievals from property lists (using GETPROP's and macros). Defining new objects and properties was trivial in comparison to the overhead of editing functions. This was the beginning of our realization that there is considerable flexibility to be gained by separating domain-specific knowledge from the code that uses that knowledge. This was also our first encounter with the problem that has come to be known as knowledge acquisition (Buchanan et al., 1970).

7.1 The Nature of the Knowledge Acquisition Process

Knowledge acquisition is the transfer and transformation of problem-solving expertise from some knowledge source to a program. There are many

Section 7.1 is largely taken from material originally written for Chapter 5 of *Building Expert Systems* (eds., F. Hayes-Roth, D. Waterman, and D. Lenat). Reading, Mass.: Addison-Wesley, 1983.

sources we might turn to, including human experts, textbooks, data bases, and our own experience. In this section we will concentrate mostly on acquiring knowledge from human experts in an enterprise known as knowledge engineering (Hayes-Roth et al., 1983). These experts are specialists (but not necessarily unique individuals) in a narrow area of knowledge about the world. The expertise that we hope to elucidate is a collection of definitions, relations, specialized facts, algorithms, strategies, and heuristics about the narrow domain area. It is different from general knowledge about the domain and from commonsense knowledge about the world, some of which is also needed by expert systems.

A knowledge base for an expert system is constructed through a process of iterative development. After initial design and prototype implementation, the system grows incrementally both in breadth and depth. While other large software systems are sometimes built by accretion, this style of construction is inescapable for expert systems because the requisite knowledge is impossible to define as one complete block.

One of the key ideas in constructing an expert system is *transparency*—making the system understandable despite the complexity of the task. An expert system needs to be understandable for the following reasons:

- the system matures through incremental improvements, which require thorough understanding of previous versions and of the reasons for good and poor performance on test cases;
- the system improves through criticism from persons who are not (or need not be) familiar with the implementation details;
- the system uses heuristic methods and symbolic reasoning because mathematical algorithms do not exist (or are inefficient) for the problems it solves.

7.1.1 Modes of Knowledge Acquisition

The transfer and transformation required to represent expertise for a program may be automated or partially automated in some special cases. Most of the time a person, called a knowledge engineer, is required to communicate with the expert and the program. The most difficult aspect of knowledge acquisition is the initial one of helping the expert conceptualize and structure the domain knowledge for use in problem solving. Because the knowledge engineer has far less knowledge of the domain than does the expert, by definition, the process of transferring expertise into a program is bound to suffer from communication problems. For example, the vocabulary that the expert uses to talk about the domain with a novice is probably inadequate for high-performance problem solving.

There are several modes of knowledge acquisition for an expert system, which can be seen as variations on the process shown in Figure 7-1.

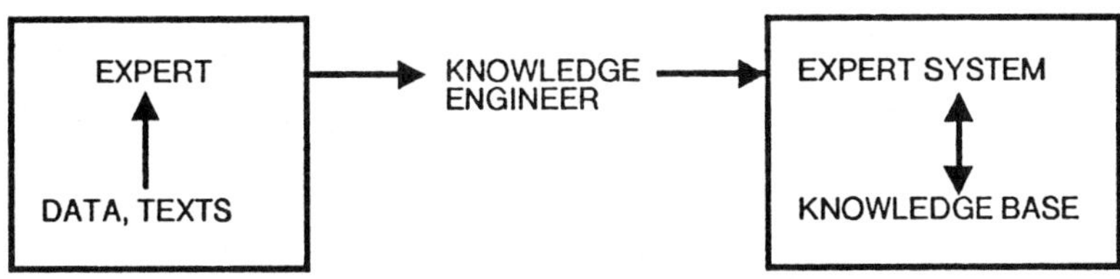

FIGURE 7-1 Important elements in the transfer of expertise. Feedback to the expert about the system's performance on test cases is not shown.

All involve transferring, in one way or another, the expertise needed for high-performance problem solving in a domain from a *source* to a *program*. The source is generally a human expert, but could also be the primary sources from which the expert has learned the material: journal articles (and textbooks) or experimental data. A knowledge engineer translates statements about the domain from the source to the program with more or less assistance from intelligent programs. And there is variability in the extent to which the knowledge base is distinct from the rest of the system.

Handcrafting

Conceptually, the simplest way for a programmer to put knowledge into a program is to code it in. This was the standard mode of building AI programs in the 1950s and 1960s because the main emphasis of most of those systems was demonstrating intelligent behavior for a few problems. AI programmers could be their own experts for many game-playing, puzzle-solving, and mathematics programs. And a few domain specialists became their own AI programmers in order to construct complex systems (Colby, 1981; Hearn, 1971). When the programmer and the specialist are not the same person, however, it is risky to rely on handcrafting to build complex programs embodying large amounts of judgmental knowledge. Generally, it is slow to build and debug such a program, and it is nearly impossible to keep the problem-solving expertise consistent if it grows large by small increments.

Knowledge Engineering

The process of working with an expert to map what he or she knows into a form suitable for an expert system to use has come to be known as *knowledge engineering* (Feigenbaum, 1978; Michie, 1973).

As DENDRAL matured, we began to see patterns in the interactions between the person responsible for the code and the expert responsible for the knowledge. There is a dialogue which, at first, is much like a systems analysis dialogue between analyst and specialist. The relevant concepts are named, and the relations among them made explicit. The knowledge engineer has to become familiar enough with the terminology and structure of the subject area that his or her questions are meaningful and relevant. As the knowledge engineer learns more about the subject matter, and as the specialist learns more about the structure of the knowledge base and the consequences of expressing knowledge in different forms, the process speeds up.

After the initial period of conceptualization, in which most of the framework for talking about the subject matter is laid out, the knowledge structures can be filled in rather rapidly. This period of rapid growth of the knowledge base is then followed by meticulous testing and refinement. Knowledge-engineering *tools* can speed up this process. For example, intelligent editing programs that help keep track of changes and help find inconsistencies can be useful to both the knowledge engineer and the expert. At times, an expert can use the tools independently of the knowledge engineer, thus approaching McCarthy's idea of a program accepting advice from a specialist (McCarthy, 1958). The ARL editor incorporated in EMYCIN (see Chapters 14–16) is a simple tool; the TEIRESIAS debugging system (discussed in Chapter 9) is a more complex tool. Politakis (1982) has recently developed a tool for examining a knowledge base for the EXPERT system (Kulikowski and Weiss, 1982) and suggesting changes, much like the tool for ONCOCIN discussed in Chapter 8.

A recent experiment in knowledge engineering is the ROGET program (Bennett, 1983), a knowledge-based system that aids in the conceptualization of knowledge bases for EMYCIN systems. Its knowledge is part of what a knowledge engineer knows about helping an expert with the initial process of laying out the structure of a new body of knowledge. It carries on a dialogue about the relationships among objects in the new domain, about the goal of the new system, about the evidence available, and about the inferences from evidence to conclusions. Although it knows nothing (initially) about a new knowledge base, it knows something about the structure of other knowledge bases. For example, it knows that evidence can often be divided into "hard" evidence from instruments and laboratory analysis and "soft" evidence from subjective reports and that both are different from identifying features such as gender and race. Much more remains to be done, but ROGET is an important step in codifying the art of knowledge engineering.

Various Forms of "Learning"

For completeness, we mention briefly several other methods of building knowledge-based programs. We have not experimented with these in the context of MYCIN, so we will not dwell on them.

Learning from examples may automate much of the knowledge acquisition process by exploiting large data bases of recorded experience (e.g., hospital records of patients, field service records of machine failures). The conceptualization stage may be bypassed if the terminology of the records is sufficient for problem solving. Induction of new production rules from examples was used by Waterman (1970) in the context of the game of poker and in Meta-DENDRAL (Lindsay et al., 1980) in the context of mass spectrometry. The RX system (Blum, 1982) uses patient records to discover plausible associations.

Other methods of learning are discovery by exploration of new concepts and relations (Lenat, 1983), reading published accounts (Ciesielski, 1980), learning by watching (Waterman, 1978), and learning by analogy (Winston, 1979). See Buchanan et al. (1978) and Barr and Feigenbaum (1982) for reviews of automatic learning methods.

7.2 Knowledge Acquisition in MYCIN

In the MYCIN work we experimented with computer-based tools to acquire knowledge from experts through interactive dialogues. TEIRESIAS, discussed in Chapter 9, is the best-known example. In discussing knowledge acquisition, it is important to remember that there are separate programs under discussion: the expert system, i.e., MYCIN, and the programs that provide help in knowledge acquisition, i.e., TEIRESIAS.

As mentioned above, MYCIN itself was an experiment in keeping medical knowledge separate from the rest of the program. We believed that this would simplify knowledge acquisition, and it does, but not to the extent we had hoped. Because the syntax of the elements carrying knowledge was simplified, however, our focus shifted from the *mechanics* of editing those elements to the *contents* of those knowledge structures. That is, there was an important conceptual shift from thinking of editing data structures to thinking of modifying knowledge structures; we have come to call the latter process *knowledge programming*.

The processes of constructing and editing a knowledge base became interesting subjects of our research. We could see that the communication between expert and program was very slow. So we began investigating computer-based tools that would facilitate the transfer of expertise. In the original version of MYCIN, there were some tools for helping Shortliffe, as knowledge engineer, build and modify the infectious disease knowledge base. No attempt was made to get experts to use the tools directly, although that was clearly a next step. These first tools included a rule language (syntax and parser) that allowed entering a new rule in a quasi-English form. In the example shown in Figure 7-2, the user indicates a desire to enter a new rule by typing NR. He or she is then asked for a rule in English,

```
**NR                                                  [The knowledge engineer starts
The new rule will be called RULE200.                  the rule acquisition routine by
      If:  1-** THE ORGANISM IS A GRAM NEGATIVE ROD   typing NR for New Rule.]
      and  2-** IT IS ANAEROBIC
      and  3-** IT WAS ISOLATED FROM THE BLOOD
      and  4-** YOU THINK THE PORTAL WAS THE GI TRACT
      and  5-**
                                                      [user: carriage return with no
                                                      entry]
      Then: 1-** IT IS PROBABLY A BACTEROIDES
            On a scale of 1 to 10, how much certainty would
            you affix to this conclusion?
            ** 9
      and   2-**
                                                      [user: carriage return with no
                                                      entry]
This is my understanding of your rule:
RULE200

      IF: 1) The site of the culture is blood, and    [Note that the original clause 1
          2) The stain of the organism is gramneg, and  has been expanded to separate
          3) The morphology of the organism is rod, and the two attributes, stain and
          4) The aerobicity of the organism is anaerobic, and morphology.]
          5) The portal of entry of the organism is GI
      THEN: There is strongly suggestive evidence (.9) that the
            organism is bacteroides

Okay? (YES or NO)
** YES
```

FIGURE 7-2 Example of rule acquisition in the original (1974) MYCIN program. (User's input follows double asterisks.)

following the format of other rules in the system. MYCIN translates the rule into its internal LISP representation and then translates it back into English to print out a version of the rule as it has understood the meaning. The user is then asked to approve the rule or modify it. The original system also allowed simple changes to rules in a quick and easy interaction, much as is shown in Figure 7-2 for acquiring a new rule.

This simple model of knowledge acquisition was subsequently expanded, most notably in the work on TEIRESIAS (Chapter 9). Many of the ideas (and lines of LISP code) from TEIRESIAS were incorporated in EMYCIN (Part Five). Contrast Figure 7-2 with the TEIRESIAS example in Section 9.2 and the EMYCIN example in Chapter 14 for snapshots of our ideas on knowledge acquisition. Research on this problem continues.

Two of our initial working hypotheses about knowledge acquisition have had to be qualified. We had assumed that the rules were sufficiently independent of one another that an expert could always write new rules without examining the rest of the knowledge base. Such modularity is desirable because the less interaction there is among rules, the easier and safer it is to modify the rule set. However, we found that some experts are

1. Expert tells knowledge engineer what rules to add or modify.
2. Knowledge engineer makes changes to the knowledge base.
3. Knowledge engineer runs one or more old cases for consistency checking.
4. If any problems with old cases, knowledge engineer discusses them with expert, then goes to Step 1.
5. Expert runs modified system on new case(s) until problems are discovered.
6. If no problems on substantial number of cases, then stops; otherwise, goes to Step 1.

FIGURE 7-3 The major steps of rule writing and refinement after conceptualization.

helped if they see the existing rules that are similar to a new rule under consideration, where similar means either that the *conclusion* mentions the same parameter (but perhaps different values) or that the *premise* clauses mention the same parameters. The desire to compare a proposed rule with similar rules stems largely from the difficulty of assigning CF's to new rules. Comparing other evidence and other conclusions puts the strength of the proposed rule into a partial ordering. For example, evidence *e1* for conclusion *C* could be seen to be stronger than *e2* but weaker than *e3* for the same conclusion. We also assumed, incorrectly, that the control structure and CF propagation method were details that the expert could avoid learning. That is, an expert writing a new rule sometimes needs to understand how the rule will be used and what its effect will be in the overall solution to a problem. These two problems are illustrated in the transcripts of several electronic mail messages reprinted at the end of Chapter 10. The transcripts also reveal much about the vigorous questioning of assumptions that was taking place as rules were being written.

Throughout the development of MYCIN's knowledge base about infectious diseases (once a satisfactory conceptualization for the problem was found), the primary mode of interaction between the knowledge engineer and expert was a recurring cycle as shown in Figure 7-3. Much of the actual time, particularly in the early years, was spent on changes to the code, outside of this loop, in order to get the system to work efficiently (or sometimes to work at all) with new kinds of knowledge suggested by experts. Considerable time was spent with the experts trying to understand their larger perspective on diagnosis and therapy in infectious disease. And some time was spent trying to reconceptualize the program's problem-solving framework. We believed that the time-consuming nature of the six-step loop shown in Figure 7-3 was one of the key problems in building an expert system, although the framework itself was simple and effective. Thus we looked at several ways to improve the expert's and knowledge engineer's efficiency in the loop.

For Step 1 of the loop we created facilities for experts (or other users) to leave comments for the knowledge engineers. We gave them an English-like language for describing new relationships. And we created the explanation facility described in Part Six, so they could understand a faulty line of reasoning well enough to correct the knowledge base. For Step 2, as mentioned, we created tools for the knowledge engineer, to facilitate entry and modification of rules. For Step 3, we created an indexed library of test cases and facilities for running many cases in batch mode overnight. For Step 4, the batch system recorded differences caused by a set of modifications in the advice given on the test cases. The record was then used by the knowledge engineer to assess the detrimental effects, if any, of recent changes to the rules. Some of our concern with human engineering, discussed in Part Eleven, was motivated by Step 5 because we realized the necessity of an expert's "playing with" the system in order to discover its weaknesses.

The TEIRESIAS system discussed in Chapter 9 was the product of an experiment on interactive transfer of expertise. TEIRESIAS was designed to help an expert at Steps 1, 2, and 5. Although the program was never used routinely in its entirety by collaborating infectious disease specialists, we considered the experiment to be highly successful. It showed the power of using a model of the domain-specific knowledge with syntactic editors. It showed that debugging in the context of a specific case is an effective means to focus the expert's attention. TEIRESIAS analyzed a rule set statically to build rule models, which, in turn, were used during the dynamic debugging. It thus "knew what it knew," that is, it had models of the knowledge base. It used the rule models to provide advice about incomplete areas of the knowledge base, to provide suggestions and help during interactive debugging sessions and to provide summary explanations. Much of TEIRESIAS is now embedded in the knowledge acquisition code of EMYCIN.

The rule checker discussed in Chapter 8 was an experiment in static analysis of a rule set, in contrast to TEIRESIAS' dynamic analysis in context. It was not a large project, but it does demonstrate the power of analyzing a rule set for the expert. Its analysis of rules is simpler than TEIRESIAS' static analysis for two reasons: the rules it considers all make conclusions with certainty (i.e., CF = 1); and the clusterings of rules are easier to identify as a result of an extra slot attached to each rule naming the context in which it applies. It analyzes rules for the ONCOCIN system, described in more detail in Chapters 32 and 35.

As we had believed from the start, the kind of analysis performed by the rule checker provides helpful information to the expert writing new rules. To some extent, it is orthogonal to the six-step interactive loop mentioned above, but it might also be seen as Step 2a between entering a set of changes and running test cases. After the expert adds several new rules (through the interactive loop or not), the rule checker will point out logical problems of inconsistency and subsumption and pragmatic problems of redundancy and incompleteness. Any of these is a signal to the expert to examine the subsets of rules in which the rule checker identifies problems. Because this analysis is more systematic than the empirical testing in Steps 3–5 of the six-step loop, it can catch potential problems long before they would manifest themselves in test cases.

Some checking of rules is also done in EMYCIN, as described in the EMYCIN manual (van Melle et al., 1981). As each rule is entered or edited, it is checked for syntactic validity to catch common input errors. By syntactic, we mean issues of rule form—viz., that terms are spelled correctly, values are legal for the parameters with which they are associated, etc.—rather than the actual information (semantic) content (i.e., whether or not the rule "makes sense"). Performing the syntactic checks at acquisition time reduces the likelihood that the consultation program will later fail due to "obvious" errors. This permits the expert to concentrate on debugging logical errors and omissions.

The purely syntactic checks are made by comparing each rule clause with the internal *function template* corresponding to the predicate or action function used in the clause. Using this template, EMYCIN determines whether the argument slots for these functions are correctly filled. For example, each argument requiring a parameter must be assigned a valid parameter (of some context), and any argument requiring a value must be assigned a legal value for the associated parameter. If an unknown parameter is found, the checker tries to correct it with the Interlisp spelling corrector, using a spelling list of all parameters in the system. If that fails, it asks if this is a new (previously unmentioned) parameter. If so, it defines the new parameter and, in a brief diversion, prompts the system builder to describe it. Similar action is also taken if an unrecognized value for a parameter is found.

A limited semantic check is also performed: each new or changed rule is compared with any existing rules that conclude about the same parameter to make sure it does not directly contradict or subsume any of them. A contradiction occurs when two rules with the same set of premise clauses make conflicting conclusions (contradictory values of CF's for the same parameter); subsumption occurs when one rule's premise is a subset of the other's, so that the first rule succeeds whenever the second one does (i.e., the second rule is more specific), and both conclude about the same values. In either case, the interaction is reported to the expert, who may then examine or edit any of the conflicting or redundant rules.

Another experimental system we incorporated into MYCIN was a small body of code that kept statistics on the use of rules and presented the statistical results to the knowledge base builders.[1] It provided another way of analyzing the contents of a knowledge base so potential problems could be examined. It revealed, for example, that some rules never succeeded, even though they were called many times. Even though their con-

---

[1]This code was largely written by Jan Aikins.

clusions were relevant (mentioned a subgoal that was traced), their premise conditions never matched the specific facts of the cases. Sometimes this happens because a rule is covering a very unusual set of circumstances not instantiated in the test cases. Since much expertise resides in such rules, we did not modify them if they were in the knowledge base for that reason. Sometimes, though, the lack of successful invocation of rules indicated a problem. The premises might be too specific, perhaps because of transcription errors in premise clauses, and these did need attention. This experimental system also revealed that some rules *always* succeeded when called, occasionally on cases where they were not supposed to. Although it was a small experiment, it was successful: empirically derived statistics on rule use can provide valuable information to the persons building the knowledge base.

One of the most important questions we have been asking in our work on knowledge acquisition is

> How (or to what extent) can an intelligent system replace a knowledge engineer in helping an expert build a knowledge base?

The experimental systems we have written are encouraging in pointing toward automated assistance (see Chapter 16), but they are far from a definitive solution. We have built tools for the knowledge engineer more readily than for the expert. In retrospect we now believe that we underestimated both the intellectual effort involved in building a good knowledge base and the amount of global information about the expert system that the expert needs to know.

8

Completeness and Consistency in a Rule-Based System

Motoi Suwa, A. Carlisle Scott, and Edward H. Shortliffe

The builders of a knowledge-based expert system must ensure that the system will give its users accurate advice or correct solutions to their problems. The process of verifying that a system is accurate and reliable has two distinct components: checking that the knowledge base is correct, and verifying that the program can interpret and apply this information correctly. The first of these components has been the focus of the research described in this chapter; the second is discussed in Part Ten (Chapters 30 and 31).

Knowledge base debugging, the process of checking that a knowledge base is correct and complete, is one component of the larger problem of knowledge acquisition. This process involves testing and refining the system's knowledge in order to discover and correct a variety of errors that can arise during the process of transferring expertise from a human expert to a computer system. In this chapter, we discuss some common problems in knowledge acquisition and debugging and describe an automated assistant for checking the completeness and consistency of the knowledge base in the ONCOCIN system (discussed in Chapters 32 and 35).

As discussed in Chapters 7 and 9, an expert's knowledge must undergo a number of transformations before it can be used by a computer. First, the person acquires expertise in some domain through study, research, and experience. Next, the expert attempts to formalize this expertise and to express it in the internal representation of an expert system. Finally, the

This chapter is based on an article originally appearing in *The AI Magazine* 3: 16–21 (Autumn 1982).

knowledge, in a machine-readable form, is added to the computer system's knowledge base. Problems can arise at any stage in this process: the expert's knowledge may be incomplete, inconsistent, or even partly erroneous. Alternatively, while the expert's knowledge may be accurate and complete, it may not be adequately transferred to the computer-based representation. The latter problem typically occurs when an expert who does not understand computers works with a knowledge engineer who is unfamiliar with the problem domain; misunderstandings that arise are often unrecognized until performance errors occur. Finally, mistakes in spelling or syntax (made when the knowledge base is entered into the computer) are frequent sources of errors.

The knowledge base is generally constructed through collaboration between experts in the problem domain and knowledge engineers. This difficult and time-consuming task can be facilitated by a program that:

1. checks for inconsistencies and gaps in the knowledge base,
2. helps the experts and knowledge engineers communicate with each other, and
3. provides a clear and understandable display of the knowledge as the system will use it.

In the remainder of this chapter we discuss an experimental program with these capabilities.

8.1 Earlier Work

One goal of the TEIRESIAS program, described in the next chapter, was to provide aids for knowledge base debugging. TEIRESIAS allows an expert to judge whether or not MYCIN's diagnosis is correct, to track down the errors in the knowledge base that led to incorrect conclusions, and to alter, delete, or add rules in order to fix these errors. TEIRESIAS makes no formal assessment of rules at the time they are initially entered into the knowledge base.

In the EMYCIN system for building knowledge-based consultants (Chapter 15), the knowledge acquisition program fixes spelling errors, checks that rules are semantically and syntactically correct, and points out potentially erroneous interactions among rules. In addition, EMYCIN's knowledge base debugging facility includes the following options:

1. a trace of the system's reasoning process during a consultation, available to knowledge engineers familiar with the program's internal representation and control processes;

2. an interactive mechanism for reviewing and correcting the system's conclusions (a generalization of the TEIRESIAS program);
3. an interface to the system's explanation facility to produce automatically, at the end of a consultation, explanations of how the system reached its results; and
4. a verification mechanism, which compares the system's results at the end of a consultation with the stored "correct" results for the case that were saved from a previous interaction with the TEIRESIAS-like option. The comparison includes explanations of why the system made its incorrect conclusions and why it did not make the correct ones.

8.2 Systematic Checking of a Knowledge Base

The knowledge base debugging tools mentioned above allow a system builder to identify problems with the system's knowledge base by observing errors in its performance on test cases. While thorough testing is an essential part of verifying the consistency and completeness of a knowledge base, it is rarely possible to guarantee that a knowledge base is completely debugged, even after hundreds of test runs on sample test cases. TEIRESIAS was designed to aid in debugging an extensive rule set in a fully functional system. EMYCIN was designed to allow incremental building of a knowledge base and running consultations with only a skeletal knowledge base. However, EMYCIN assumes that the task of building a system is simply to encode and add the knowledge.

In contrast, building a new expert system typically starts with the selection of knowledge representation formalisms and the design of a program to use the knowledge. Only when this has been done is it possible to encode the knowledge and write the program. The system may not be ready to run tests, even on simple cases, until much of the knowledge base is encoded. Regardless of how an expert system is developed, its developers can profit from a systematic check on the knowledge base without gathering extensive data for test runs, even before the full reasoning mechanism is functioning. This can be accomplished by a program that checks a knowledge base for completeness and consistency during the system's development.

8.2.1 Logical Checks for Consistency

When knowledge is represented in production rules, inconsistencies in the knowledge base appear as:

- *Conflict:* two rules succeed in the same situation but with conflicting results.
- *Redundancy:* two rules succeed in the same situation and have the same results.
- *Subsumption:* two rules have the same results, but one contains additional restrictions on the situations in which it will succeed. Whenever the more restrictive rule succeeds, the less restrictive rule also succeeds, resulting in redundancy.

Conflict, redundancy, and subsumption are defined above as logical conditions. These conditions can be detected if the syntax allows one to examine two rules and determine if situations exist in which both can succeed and whether the results of applying the two rules are identical, conflicting, or unrelated.

8.2.2 Logical Checks for Completeness

Incompleteness of the knowledge base is the result of:

- *Missing rules:* a situation exists in which a particular inference is required, but there is no rule that succeeds in that situation and produces the desired conclusion.

Missing rules can be detected logically if it is possible to enumerate all circumstances in which a given decision should be made or a given action should be taken.

8.2.3 Pragmatic Considerations

It is often pragmatic conditions, not purely logical ones, that determine whether or not there are inconsistencies in a knowledge base. The semantics of the domain may modify syntactic analysis. Of the three types of inconsistency described above, only conflict is guaranteed to be a true error.

In practice, logical redundancy may not cause problems. In a system where the first successful rule is the only one to succeed, a problem will arise only if one of two redundant rules is revised or deleted while the other is left unchanged. On the other hand, in a system using a scoring mechanism, such as the certainty factors in EMYCIN systems, redundant rules cause the same evidence to be counted twice, leading to erroneous increases in the weight of their conclusions.

In a set of rules that accumulate evidence for a particular hypothesis, one rule that subsumes another may cause an error by causing the same evidence to be counted twice. Alternatively, the expert might have purposely written the rules so that the more restrictive one adds a little more weight to the conclusion made by the less restrictive one.

An exhaustive syntactic approach for identifying missing rules would assume that there should be a rule that applies in each situation defined by all possible combinations of domain variables. Some of these combinations, however, are not meaningful. For example, there are no males who are pregnant (by definition) and no infants who are alcoholics (by reason of circumstances). Like checking for consistency, checking for completeness generally requires some knowledge of the problem domain.

Because of these pragmatic considerations, an automated rule checker should display potential errors and allow an expert to indicate which ones represent real problems. It should prompt the expert for domain-specific information to explain why apparent errors are, in fact, acceptable. This information should be represented so that it can be used to make future checking more accurate.

8.3 Rule Checking in ONCOCIN

8.3.1 Brief Description of ONCOCIN

ONCOCIN (see Chapter 35) is a rule-based consultation system to advise physicians at the Stanford Medical Center cancer clinic on the management of patients who are on experimental treatment protocols. These protocols serve to ensure that data from patients on various treatment regimens can be compared in order to evaluate the success of therapy and to assess the relative effectiveness of alternative regimens. A protocol specifies when the patient should visit the clinic, what chemotherapy and/or radiation therapy the patient should receive on each visit, when laboratory tests should be performed, and under what circumstances and in what ways the recommended course of therapy should be modified.

As in MYCIN, a rule in ONCOCIN has an *action* part that concludes a *value* for some *parameter* on the basis of values of other parameters in the rule's *condition* part. Currently, however, all parameter values can be determined with certainty; there is no need to use weighted belief measures. When a rule succeeds, its action parameter becomes *known* so no other rules with the same action parameter will be tried.

In contrast to MYCIN, rules in ONCOCIN specify the *context* in which they apply. Examples of ONCOCIN contexts are drugs, chemotherapies (i.e., drug combinations), and protocols. A rule that determines the dose of a drug may be specific to the drug alone or to both the drug and the chemotherapy. In the latter case, the context of the rule would be the list of pairs of drug and chemotherapy for which the rule is valid. At any time during a consultation, the *current context* represents the particular drug, chemotherapy, and protocol currently under consideration.

In order to determine the value of a parameter, the system tries rules that conclude about that parameter and that apply in the current context. For example, Rule 75 shown below is invoked to determine the value of the parameter current attenuated dose. The condition will be checked only when the current context is a drug in the chemotherapy MOPP or a drug in the chemotherapy PAVE. Clause 1 of the condition gives a reason to attenuate (lessen) the doses of drugs, and clause 2 mentions a reason not to attenuate more than 75%.

RULE 75

[*action parameter*]	(a)	To determine the current attenuated dose
[*context*]	(b)	for all drugs in MOPP, or for all drugs in PAVE:
[*condition*]	IF:	1) This is the start of the first cycle after a cycle was aborted, and
		2) The blood counts do not warrant dose attenuation
[*action*]	THEN:	Conclude that the current attenuated dose is 75 percent of the previous dose

Certain rules for determining the value of a parameter serve special functions. Some give a "definitional" value in the specified context. These are called *initial rules* and are tried first. Other rules provide a (possibly context-dependent) "default" or "usual" value in the event that no other rule succeeds. These are called *default rules* and are applied last. Rules that do not serve either of these special functions are called *normal rules*. Concluding a parameter's value consists of trying, in order, three groups of rules: initial, normal, then default. A rule's *classification* tells which of these three groups it belongs to.[1]

[1]Internally in LISP, the context, condition, action, and classification are properties of an atom naming the rule. The internal form of Rule 75 is

```
RULE075

CONTEXT:         ((MOPP DRUG)(PAVE DRUG))
CONDITION:       (AND ($IS POST.ABORT 1)
                      ($IS NORMALCOUNTS YES))
ACTION:          (CONCLUDEVALUE ATTENDOSE (PERCENTOF 75 PREVIOUSDOSE))
CLASSIFICATION:  NORMAL
```

As in MYCIN, the LISP functions that are used in conditions or actions in ONCOCIN have *templates* indicating what role their arguments play. For example, both $IS and CONCLUDEVALUE take a parameter as their first argument and a value of that parameter as their second argument. Each function also has a *descriptor* representing its meaning. For example, the descriptor of $IS shows that the function will succeed when the parameter value of its first argument is equal to its second argument.

8.3.2 Overview of the Rule-Checking Program

A rule's context and condition together describe the situations in which it applies. The templates and descriptors of rule functions make it possible to determine the combination of values of condition parameters that will cause a rule to succeed. The rule's context property shows the context(s) in which the rule applies. The contexts and conditions of two rules can therefore be examined to determine if there are situations in which both can succeed. If so, and if the rules conclude different values for the same parameter, they are in conflict. If they conclude the same thing, except that one contains extra condition clauses, then one subsumes the other.

These definitions of inconsistencies simplify the task of checking the knowledge base. The rules can be partitioned into disjoint sets, each of which concludes about the same parameter in the same context. The resulting rule sets can be checked independently. To check a set of rules, the program:

1. finds all parameters used in the conditions of these rules;
2. makes a table, displaying all possible combinations of condition parameter values and the corresponding values that will be concluded for the action parameters (see Figure 8-1);[2] and
3. checks the tables for conflict, redundancy, subsumption, and missing rules; then displays the table with a summary of any potential errors that were found. The rule checker assumes that there should be a rule for each possible combination of values of condition parameters; it hypothesizes missing rules on this assumption (see Figure 8-2).[3]

ONCOCIN's rule checker *dynamically* examines a rule set to determine which condition parameters are currently used to conclude a given action parameter. These parameters determine what columns should appear in the table for the rule set. The program does *not* expect that each of the parameters should be used in every rule in the set (as illustrated by Rule 76 in the example of the next subsection). In contrast, TEIRESIAS (see next chapter) examined the "nearly complete" MYCIN knowledge base and built *static* rule models showing (among other things) which condition parameters were used (in the existing knowledge base) to conclude a given action parameter. When a new rule was added to MYCIN, it was compared

---

[2]Because a parameter's value is always known with certainty and the possible values are mutually exclusive, the different combinations of condition parameter values are disjoint. If a rule corresponding to one combination succeeds, rules corresponding to other combinations in the same table will fail. This would not be true in an EMYCIN consultation system in which the values of some parameters can be concluded with less than complete certainty. In such cases, the combinations in a given table would not necessarily be disjoint.

[3]We plan to add a mechanism to acquire information about the meanings of parameters and the relationships among them and to use this information to omit semantically impossible combinations from subsequent tables.

Rule set: 667 600 82 80 69 67 76

Context: the drug cytoxan in the chemotherapy CVP

Action parameter: the current attenuated dose

Condition parameters:
NORMALCOUNTS—the blood counts do not warrant dose attenuation
CYCLE—the current chemotherapy cycle number
SIGXRT—the number of cycles since significant radiation

Abbreviations in the *Value* column:
V_1—the previous dose advanced by 50 mg/m^2
V_2—250 mg/m^2 attenuated by the minimum count attenuation
V_3—the minimum of 250 mg/m^2 and the previous dose
V_4—the minimum of 250 mg/m^2 and the previous dose attenuated by the minimum count attenuation.

Evaluation	*Rule*	*Value*	*NORMALCOUNTS*	*CYCLE*	*SIGXRT*	*Combination*
	80	250mg/m^2	YES	1	1	C_1
	76 (D)	V_1	YES	(1)	(1)	C_1
R	667	V_2	NO	1	1	C_2
R	67	V_2	NO	1	1	C_2
	76 (D)	V_1	YES	(1)	(OTHER)	C_3
M	—		NO	1	OTHER	C_4
	82	V_3	YES	OTHER	1	C_5
	76 (D)	V_1	YES	(OTHER)	(1)	C_5
C	600	V_3	NO	OTHER	1	C_6
C	69	V_4	NO	OTHER	1	C_6
	76 (D)	V_1	YES	(OTHER)	(OTHER)	C_7
M	—		NO	OTHER	OTHER	C_8

Summary of Comparison

Conflict exists in combination(s): C_6 (RULE600 RULE069)
Redundancy exists in combination(s): C_2 (RULE667 RULE067)
Missing rules are in combination(s): C_4, C_8

Notes

Evaluation: M—missing; C—conflict; R—redundant

Rules: Default rules are indicated by (D).

Values of condition parameters: A value in parentheses indicates that the parameter is not explicitly used in the rule, but the rule will succeed when the parameter has the indicated value.

FIGURE 8-1 An example of output from ONCOCIN's rule-checking program.

Missing rule corresponding to combination C_4:

To determine the current attenuated dose for Cytoxan in CVP
IF: 1) The blood counts do warrant dose attenuation,
2) The current chemotherapy cycle number is 1, and
3) This is not the start of the first cycle after significant radiation
THEN: Conclude that the current attenuated dose is . . .

FIGURE 8-2 Proposed missing rule (English translation). Note that no value is given for the action parameter; this could be filled in by the system builder if the rule looked appropriate for addition to the knowledge base.

with the rule model for its action parameter. TEIRESIAS proposed *missing clauses* if some condition parameters in the model did not appear in the new rule.

8.3.3 An Example

ONCOCIN's rule-checking program can check the entire rule base, or can interface with the system's knowledge acquisition program and check only those rules affected by recent changes to the knowledge base. This latter mode is illustrated by the example in Figure 8-1. Here the system builder is trying to determine if the recent addition of one rule and deletion of another have introduced errors.

The rules checked in the example conclude the current attenuated dose for the drug cytoxan in the chemotherapy named CVP. There are three condition parameters commonly used in those rules. Of these, NORMALCOUNTS takes YES or NO as its value. CYCLE and SIGXRT take integer values. The only value of CYCLE or SIGXRT that was mentioned explicitly in any rule is 1; therefore, the table has rows for values 1 and OTHER (i.e., other than 1).

The table shows that Rule 80 concludes that the attenuated dose should have a value of 250 milligrams per square meter when the blood counts do not warrant dose attenuation (NORMALCOUNTS = YES), the chemotherapy cycle number is 1 (CYCLE = 1), and this is the first cycle after significant radiation (SIGXRT = 1). This combination of values of the condition parameters is labeled C_1.

Rule 76, shown next in Figure 8-1, can succeed in the same situation (C_1) as Rule 80, but it concludes a different dose. These rules do not conflict, however, because Rule 76 is a default rule, which will be invoked only if all normal rules (including Rule 80) fail. Note that NORMALCOUNTS is the only condition parameter that appears explicitly in Rule 76, as indicated by the parentheses around the values of the other two

Rule set: 33 24

Context: the drug DTIC in the chemotherapy ABVD

Action parameter: the dose attenuation due to low WBC

Default value: 100

Evaluation	*Rule*	*Value (percentage)*	*WBC (in thousands)*	*Combination*
			0 1.5 2 3 5	
	33	25	. . . . *** 0	C_1
	24	50	. . . . ***0 . . .	C_2

Summary of Comparison
No problems were found.

Notes
Asterisks appear beneath values included by the rule.
Zeros appear beneath upper and lower bounds that are not included.
(e.g., Rule 33 applies when $1.5 \leq \text{WBC} < 2.0$)

FIGURE 8-3 A table of rules with ranges of numerical values.

parameters. Rule 76 will succeed in all combinations that include NORMALCOUNTS = YES (namely C_1, C_3, C_5, and C_7).

Rules 667 and 67 are redundant (marked R) because both use combination C_2 to conclude the value labeled V_2 (250 mg/m^2 attenuated by the minimum count attenuation).

Rule 600 is in conflict with Rule 69 (both marked C) because both use combination C_6 but conclude different values (and both are categorized as normal rules).

No rules exist for combinations C_4 and C_8, so the program hypothesizes that rules are missing.

The system builder can enter ONCOCIN's knowledge acquisition program to correct any of the errors found by the rule checker. A missing rule can be displayed in either LISP or English (Figure 8-2) and then added to the system's knowledge base after the expert has provided a value for its action parameter.

If a summary table is too big to display, it is divided into a number of subtables by assigning constant values to some of the condition parameters. If the conditions involve ranges of numeric values, the table will display these ranges graphically as illustrated in Figure 8-3.

8.4 Effects of the Rule-Checking Program

The rule-checking program described in this chapter was developed at the same time that ONCOCIN's knowledge base was being built. During this time, periodic runs of the rule checker suggested missing rules that had been overlooked by the oncology expert. They also detected conflicting and redundant rules, generally because a rule had the incorrect context and therefore appeared in the wrong table.

A number of inconsistencies in the use of domain concepts were revealed by the rule checker. For example, on one occasion the program proposed a missing rule for a meaningless combination of condition parameter values. In discussing the domain knowledge that expressed the interrelationship among the values, it became clear that a number of individual yes/no valued parameters could be represented more logically as different values for the same parameter.

The knowledge engineers and oncology experts alike have found the rule checker's tabular display of rule sets much easier to interpret than a rule-by-rule display. Having tabular summaries of related rules has facilitated the task of modifying the knowledge base. Although the program described assists a knowledge engineer in ensuring the consistency and completeness of the rule set in the ONCOCIN system, its design is general, so it can be adapted to other rule-based systems.

9

Interactive Transfer of Expertise

Randall Davis

Whereas much early work in artificial intelligence was devoted to the search for a single, powerful, domain-independent problem-solving methodology [e.g., GPS (Newell and Simon, 1972)], subsequent efforts have stressed the use of large stores of domain-specific knowledge as a basis for high performance. The knowledge base for this sort of program [e.g., DENDRAL (Feigenbaum et al., 1971), MACSYMA (Moses, 1971)] is often assembled by hand, an ongoing task that may involve several person-years of effort. A key element in constructing a knowledge base is the transfer of expertise from a human expert to the program. Since the domain expert often knows nothing about programming, the interaction between the expert and the performance program usually requires the mediation of a human programmer.

We have sought to create a program that could supply much the same sort of assistance as that provided by the programmer in this transfer of expertise. The result is a system called TEIRESIAS[1] (Davis, 1976; 1978; Davis et al., 1977), a large Interlisp program designed to offer assistance in the interactive transfer of knowledge from a human expert to the knowledge base of a high-performance program (Figure 9-1). Information flow from right to left is labeled *explanation*. This is the process by which TEIRESIAS clarifies for the expert the source of the performance program's results and motivations for its actions. This is a prerequisite to knowledge acquisition, since the expert must first discover what the performance pro-

This chapter originally appeared in *Artificial Intelligence* 12: 121–157 (1979). It has been shortened and edited.

[1]The program is named for the blind seer in *Oedipus the King*, since the program, like the prophet, has a form of "higher-order" knowledge.

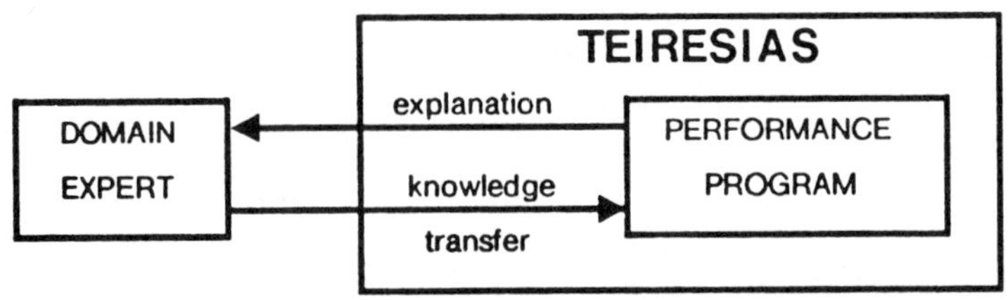

FIGURE 9-1 Interaction between the expert and the performance program is facilitated by TEIRESIAS.

gram already knows and how it used that knowledge. Information flow from left to right is labeled *knowledge transfer*. This is the process by which the expert adds to or modifies the store of domain-specific knowledge in the performance program.

Work on TEIRESIAS has had two general goals. We have attempted first to develop a set of tools for knowledge base construction and maintenance and to abstract from them a methodology applicable to a range of systems. The second, more general goal has been the development of an intelligent assistant. This task involves confronting many of the traditional problems of AI and has resulted in the exploration of a number of solutions, reviewed below.

This chapter describes a number of the key ideas in the development of TEIRESIAS and discusses their implementation in the context of a specific task (acquisition of new inference rules[2]) for a specific rule-based performance program. While the discussion deals with a specific task, system, and knowledge representation, several of the main ideas are applicable to more general issues concerning the creation of intelligent programs.

9.1 Meta-Level Knowledge

A central theme that runs through this chapter (and is discussed more fully in Part Nine) is the concept of *meta-level knowledge,* or knowledge about knowledge. This takes several different forms, but can be summed up generally by saying that a program can "know what it knows." That is, not only can a program use its knowledge directly, but it may also be able to examine it, abstract it, reason about it, and direct its application.

To see in general terms how this might be accomplished, recall that

[2]Acquisition of new conceptual primitives from which rules are built is discussed by Davis (1978), while the design and implementation of the explanation capability suggested in Figure 9-1 is discussed in Part Six.

one of the principal problems of AI is the question of representation of knowledge about the world, for which numerous techniques have been developed. One way to view what we have done is to imagine turning this in on itself, using some of these same techniques to describe the program itself. The resulting system contains both *object-level* representations, which describe the external world, and *meta-level* representations, which describe the internal world of representations. As the discussion of rule models in Sections 9.6 and 9.7 will make clear, such a system has a number of interesting capabilities.

9.2 Perspective on Knowledge Acquisition

We view the interaction between the domain expert and the performance program as *interactive transfer of expertise.* We see it in terms of a teacher who continually challenges a student with new problems to solve and carefully observes the student's performance. The teacher may interrupt to request a justification of some particular step the student has taken in solving the problem or may challenge the final result. This process may uncover a fault in the student's knowledge of the subject (the debugging phase) and result in the transfer of information to correct it (the knowledge acquisition phase). Other approaches to knowledge acquisition can be compared to this by considering their relative positions along two dimensions: (i) the sophistication of their debugging facilities, and (ii) the independence of their knowledge acquisition mechanism.

The *simplest* sort of debugging tool is characterized by programs like DDT, used to debug assembly language programs. The tool is totally passive (in the sense that it operates only in response to user commands), is low-level (since it operates at the level of machine or assembly language), and knows nothing about the application domain of the program. Debuggers like BAIL (Reiser, 1975) and Interlisp's break package (Teitelman, 1974) are a step up from this since they function at the level of programming languages such as SAIL and Interlisp. The explanation capabilities in TEIRESIAS, in particular the HOW and WHY commands (see Part Six for examples), represent another step, since they function at the level of the control structure of the application program. The guided debugging that TEIRESIAS can also provide (illustrated in Section 9.5) represents yet another step, since here the debugger is taking the initiative and has enough built-in knowledge about the control structure that it can track down the error. Finally, at the most sophisticated level are knowledge-rich debuggers like the one described by Brown and Burton (1978). Here the program is active, high-level, informed about the application domain, and capable of independently localizing and characterizing bugs.

By *independence* of the knowledge acquisition mechanism, we mean the degree of human cooperation necessary. Much work on knowledge acquisition has emphasized a highly autonomous mode of operation. There is, for example, a large body of work aimed at inducing the appropriate generalizations from a set of test data; see, for example, Buchanan and Mitchell (1978) and Hayes-Roth and McDermott (1977). In these efforts user interaction is limited to presenting the program with the data and perhaps providing a brief description of the domain in the form of values for a few key parameters; the program then functions independently. Winston's work on concept formation (Winston, 1970) relied somewhat more heavily on user interaction. There the teacher was responsible for providing an appropriate sequence of examples (and nonexamples) of a concept. In describing our work, we have used the phrase "interactive transfer of expertise" to indicate that we view knowledge acquisition as information transfer from an expert to a program. TEIRESIAS does not attempt to derive new knowledge on its own, but rather tries to "listen" as attentively as possible, commenting appropriately to help the expert augment the knowledge base. It thus requires strong cooperation from the expert.

There is an important assumption involved in the attempt to establish this sort of communication: we are assuming that it is possible to distinguish between the *problem-solving paradigm* and the *expertise* or, equivalently, that control structure and representation in the performance program can be considered separately from the content of its knowledge base. The basic control structure(s) and representations are assumed to be established and debugged, and the fundamental approach to the problem is assumed to be acceptable. The question of *how* knowledge is to be encoded and used is settled by the selection of one or more of the available representations and control structures. The expert's task is to enlarge *what* it is the program knows.

There is a corollary assumption, too, in the belief that the control structures and knowledge representations can be made sufficiently comprehensible to the expert that he or she can (a) understand the system's behavior in terms of them and (b) use them to codify his or her own knowledge. This ensures that the expert understands system performance well enough to know what to correct, and can then express the required knowledge, i.e., can "think" in those terms. Thus part of the task of establishing the link shown in Figure 9-1 involves insulating the expert from the details of implementation, by establishing a discourse at a level high enough that he or she does not have to program in LISP.

9.3 Design of the Performance Program

Figure 9-2 shows the major elements of the performance program that TEIRESIAS is designed to help construct. Although the performance program described here is MYCIN, the context within which TEIRESIAS was

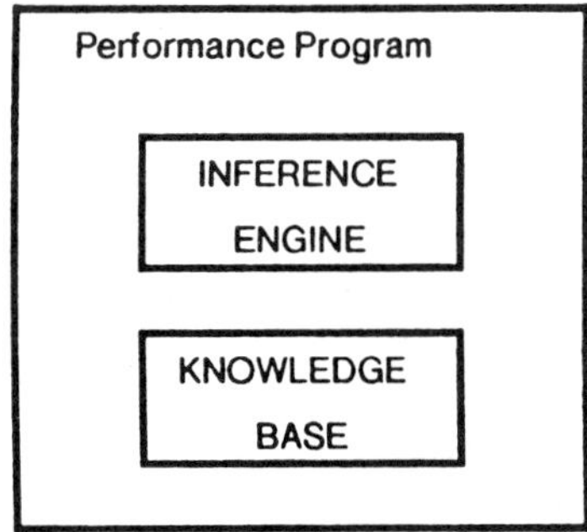

FIGURE 9-2 Architecture of the performance program.

actually developed, many of the features of TEIRESIAS have been incorporated in EMYCIN (see Chapter 15) and are independent of any domain. The *knowledge base* is the program's store of task-specific knowledge that makes possible high performance. The *inference engine* is an interpreter that uses the knowledge base to solve the problem at hand. The main point of interest in this very simple design is the explicit division between these two parts of the program. This design is in keeping with the assumption noted above that the expert's task is to augment the knowledge base of a program whose control structure (inference engine) is assumed to be both appropriate and debugged.

Two important advantages accrue from keeping this division as strict as possible. First, if all of the control structure information has been kept in the inference engine, then we can engage the domain expert in a discussion of the knowledge base alone rather than of questions of programming and control structures. Second, if all of the task-specific knowledge has been kept in the knowledge base, then it is possible to remove the current knowledge base, "plug in" another, and obtain a performance program for a new task (see Part Five). The explicit division thus offers a degree of domain-independence. It does not mean, however, that the inference engine and knowledge base are totally independent: knowledge base content is strongly influenced by the control paradigm used in the inference engine. It is this unavoidable interaction that motivates the important assumption, noted in Section 9.2, that the control structure and knowledge representation are comprehensible to the expert, at least at the conceptual level.

An example of the program in action is shown in Section 9.5. The program interviews the user, requesting various pieces of information that are relevant to selecting the most appropriate antibiotic therapy, then prints its recommendations. In the remainder of this chapter the user will be an expert running MYCIN in order to challenge it, offering it a difficult case and observing and correcting its performance.

We have noted earlier that the expert must have at least a high-level understanding of the operation of the inference engine and the manner of knowledge representation in order to be able to express new knowledge for the performance program. An example of a rule, with brief explanations of the terms premise, Boolean combination, conclusion, and certainty factor, suffices to allow understanding of the representation of knowledge. An equally brief explanation of backward chaining and the conservative strategy of exhaustive evidence gathering suffices to allow understanding of the inference engine. As mentioned in Section 9.2, we are assuming that the expert can understand these concepts without having to deal with details of implementation. Note as well that TEIRESIAS' basic design and the notion of interactive transfer of expertise do not depend on this particular control structure, only on the (nontrivial) assumption that an equally comprehensible explanation can be found for whatever control structure is actually used in the inference engine.

9.4 A Word About Natural Language

Natural language has not been a major focus of this work, and for the most part we have used the simplest techniques that would support the level of performance required. For instance, all questions and responses from TEIRESIAS are either preformed or manufactured by filling in templates with appropriate words (as evidenced by the occasional appearance of ungrammatical phrases like "a organism"). Where answers are free text (rather than multiple choice), the system relies primarily on the keyword- and template-oriented techniques described in Chapter 18. There is no parser in the system, in part to minimize processing time and in part because users often give ungrammatical responses.

9.5 Example of TEIRESIAS in Operation

In the interaction shown in Figure 9-3, the expert is challenging MYCIN with a particular case, observing the program's performance, and then making the necessary correction to the knowledge base. The bug encountered here was created by deleting an existing rule from the knowledge base and removing all references to it. The expert then repairs the bug by tracking down the source of the problem and teaching the system the "new" rule. The deleted rule was chosen in order to display a large number of TEIRESIAS's capabilities in a single example. It is special in no other sense, however, and offers a real trace of the system in action.

In the trace, computer output is in mixed upper and lower case, user responses follow a double asterisk and are in bold upper case, and commentary is indented, italicized, and enclosed in parentheses. The example is also divided into five phases for later reference.

(MYCIN has been provided with details of a case and has just concluded likely causes of the infection.)

My therapy recommendation will be based on the following probable infection(s) and potential causative organism(s):

INFECTION-1 is PRIMARY-BACTEREMIA
<Item 1> E.COLI [ORGANISM-1]
<Item 2> PSEUDOMONAS-AERUGINOSA [ORGANISM-1]

Are all these identities correct?
++** **N**

(The expert disagrees with the results and will indicate to TEIRESIAS the identities that he thinks should have resulted.)

(PHASE I: TRACKING DOWN THE BUG)

Are there any identities missing?
++** **Y**

Which one(s)?
++** **KLEBSIELLA-PNEUMONIAE PROTEUS-NON-MIRABILIS**

Are there any identities that shouldn't have appeared?
++** **PSEUDOMONAS-AERUGINOSA**

Do you want to
1] track down the problem yourself, or
2] allow me to guide the debugging, or
3] ignore it for now and fix it another time?

Type 1, 2 or 3
++** **2**

We'll start with the PSEUDOMONAS-AERUGINOSA first.

(This time, TEIRESIAS will guide the process. It applies the heuristic of starting with an identity that appeared incorrectly.)

The following rules were used in deducing that the identity of ORGANISM-1 is pseudomonas-aeruginosa.

RULE184

Since [1.1] the category of ORGANISM-1 is not known
[1.2] the gram stain of ORGANISM-1 is gramneg
[1.3] the morphology of ORGANISM-1 is rod

FIGURE 9-3 TEIRESIAS example.

[1.4] the aerobicity of ORGANISM-1 is facultative
There is weakly suggestive evidence (.3) that the identity of ORGANISM-1 is pseudomonas-aeruginosa

Is this rule correct?
++** **Y**

Should its premise have failed for this case?
++** **Y**

Which clause of the premise should have been false? [give #]
++** **1**

No conclusions were reached concerning the category of ORGANISM-1
Should it have been possible to conclude a category?
++** **Y**

Which one?
++** **ENTEROBACTERIACEAE**

There were no rules successfully invoked in the attempt to deduce that the category of ORGANISM-1 is enterobacteriaceae.

The following (potentially applicable) rules were *not* executed because the starred [**] clause failed:

RULE116

IF:
1) the identity of ORGANISM-1 is not known
** 2) the gram stain of ORGANISM-1 is not known **
3) the morphology of ORGANISM-1 is not known
4) the site of CULTURE-1 is csf
5) the infection is meningitis
6) the age (in years) of the patient is less than or equal to .17

THEN: There is weakly suggestive evidence (.3) that the category of ORGANISM-1 is enterobacteriaceae

RULE050

IF:
1) the morphology of ORGANISM-1 is rod
2) the gram stain of ORGANISM-1 is gramneg
3) the aerobicity of ORGANISM-1 is facultative
** 4) the infection with ORGANISM-1 was acquired while the patient was hospitalized **

THEN: There is evidence that the category of ORGANISM-1 is enterobacteriaceae

Are all these rules correct?
++** **Y**

Should any of them have been successfully invoked?
++** **N**

(This would be the case if one of the starred premise clauses was false because it had been "stepped on" by yet another rule further back in the chain.)

Is there a rule missing?
++** **Y**

FIGURE 9-3 continued

Ok, then I need a rule that would allow me to deduce that the category of ORGANISM-1 is enterobacteriaceae.
Would you like to give me such a rule now?
++** **Y**

Good . . .

(To review briefly: The expert is tracking down the reason why MYCIN incorrectly concluded that the identity was pseudomonas-aeruginosa. Pseudomonas-aeruginosa appeared because Rule 184 executed successfully. This occurred in part because category was unknown. Category was unknown because all rules to conclude it (50 and 116) failed. Since the expert believes all existing rules are correct, the knowledge base must lack a rule that will conclude about category; in particular, that the category is enterobacteriaceae. This will cause category to be known, inhibiting Rule 184, fixing at least this first problem, the incorrect conclusion about pseudomonas-aeruginosa.

Note how sharply focused the issue has become, for both the expert and TEIRESIAS, as a result of the large amount of contextual information available. The doctor is not being asked to "discuss bacteremia"; instead, the system can at this point say: "I need a rule that would allow me to deduce that the category of ORGANISM-1 is enterobacteriaceae." And it must be a rule which is invocable in the context of this patient. This focus makes it easier for the expert to specify a rule that may never have been explicitly stated or recognized as such. This can be an important advantage in any domain where the knowledge is not yet fully formalized.

The contextual information is useful for TEIRESIAS as well. It provides a number of expectations about the content of the rule that are useful both in understanding what the expert types in and in checking the new rule to make sure that it does indeed solve the problem at hand. Details of this process are explained below.

The trace continues with the expert typing in the rule . . .)

(PHASE II: INTERPRETING THE RULE)

The new rule will be called **RULE383**

```
     If:        1 - THE PATIENT'S INFECTION IS PRIMARY-BACTEREMIA
          and   2 - THE SITE IS ONE OF THE STERILE SITES
          and   3 -
   Then:        1 - THERE IS EVIDENCE (.8) THAT THE CATEGORY IS ENTEROBACTERIACEAE
          and   2 -
```

This may take a few moments . . .

(Generally, it takes on the order of 10 to 30 seconds of cpu time.)

This is my understanding of your rule:

RULE383

IF:
1) Primary-bacteremia is an associated infection for which therapy would cover, and
2) The infection with the organism was acquired while the patient was hospitalized, and
3) The culture was taken from a sterile source, and
4) The organism is not normally found at this site

THEN: There is strongly suggestive evidence (.8) that the category of the organism is enterobacteriaceae

(PHASE III: MODIFYING THE INTERPRETATION)

(TEIRESIAS' initial interpretation of the natural language is incorrect (recall that the example was chosen in part for this reason). In the system's first attempt to understand the rule, each line of the original text has been interpreted as two clauses. This results primarily from the word-by-word approach to meaning. For instance, despite the obvious grammatical simplicity of the first line of text, the system used two connotations of the word "infection" to generate the first two clauses. In the second line of text the word "sterile" was responsible for clause 3, and the word "sites" used as the basis for clause 4. The details of this process are explained below, where it will become clear that while the translation is wrong, it is not unreasonable given the simple natural language facilities.

Nor is it unreasonable that TEIRESIAS has turned each line of English into more than one premise clause. The expert is not restricted to typing the English equivalent of a single premise clause on each line. If he were, rather than typing "the organism is a gram-negative aerobic rod," he would have to type three lines.

We will see later that while TEIRESIAS' interpretations are incorrect, they are all "reasonable" and "consistent," in light of the system's somewhat primitive approach to natural language. The rest of the example shows that even when the initial guesses are incorrect, straightening things out may be very easy.)

Okay? (Yes or No)
++** **N**

(The expert indicates that there is a problem with the interpretation and uses the system's rule editor to specify the changes needed.)

Change premise?
++** **Y**

What clause should be changed in premise?
(type HELP for list of commands)
++** **CHANGE 1**

Suppose (1) were changed to read-
1 - The infection is primary-bacteremia
Would that be ok?
++** **Y**

(Several simple heuristics are invoked to select the next most likely interpretation, based on the English source of this clause and the set of interpretations already rejected. In this case, the second choice is correct.)

Then you'll probably want to delete:

2) The infection with the organism was acquired while the patient was hospitalized

Correct?
++** **Y**

(TEIRESIAS enforces consistency constraints on its interpretation of the English text. One of these constraints indicates that if the new interpretation of clause 1 is correct, then clause 2 must have arisen spuriously. That is, the system realizes it cannot get both the new version of clause 1 and the old clause 2 from the same line of text, and indicates this to the expert.)

FIGURE 9-3 continued

Anything else?
++** **D 3**
clause(s) 3 deleted.

(Realizing that there was another spurious clause, the expert deletes clause 3, but then has second thoughts about the one he chose, so he checks, using the ? command.)

Anything else?
++** **?**
1 - the infection is primary-bacteremia
and 2 - <deleted>
and 3 - <deleted>
and 4 - the organism is not normally found at this site

(He then discovers that he has typed the wrong number, undoes the damage, and deletes the one initially intended. All commands can be abbreviated to a single letter.)

Anything else?
++** **U 3**
clause(s) 3 undeleted.

Anything else?
++** **D 4**
clause(s) 4 deleted.

(There is one last correction to be made for which TEIRESIAS suggests the wording . . .)

Anything else?
++** **C 3**
Suppose (3) were changed to read-
3 - The site of the culture is one of: those sites that are normally sterile

Would that be ok?
++** **Y**

Anything else?
++** **?**
1 - the infection is primary-bacteremia
and 2 - <deleted>
and 3 - the site of the culture is one of: those sites that are normally sterile
and 4 - <deleted>

++** **OK**

(. . . and at last he's happy with the rule.)

Change action?
++** **N**

This is my understanding of your rule:

RULE383
IF: 1) The infection is primary-bacteremia, and
2) The site of the culture is one of: those sites that are normally sterile
THEN: There is strongly suggestive evidence (.8) that the category of the organism is enterobacteriaceae

Okay? (Yes or No)
++** **Y**

(This is the classic test of comprehension: the original English text has been turned into a rule coded in LISP; the LISP is then translated back into English for approval. Compare the results with the expert's original input.

Now that the expert is satisfied that the system understands the rule as he has entered it, TEIRESIAS checks several more things about the rule.)

(PHASE IV: SECOND-GUESSING)

I hate to criticize, Dr. Davis, but did you know that most rules about what the category of a organism might be, that mention -

the site of a culture
the infection

Also mention -

[A] - the portal of entry of a organism

Shall I try to write a clause to account for [A]?
++** **Y**

(The mechanism that makes possible this sort of second-guessing by TEIRESIAS is explained in detail below. Briefly, the system maintains a model of the knowledge base. In checking to see how this new piece of information "fits into" that model, it discovers that its expectations have been only partially met. It indicates to the expert what expectations were left unfulfilled and asks if it should attempt to fill in the missing parts.)

How about-

[A] The portal of entry of the organism is GI

Ok?
++** **Y**

(The expert agreed to the inclusion of a clause about the portal of entry; this determines which attribute to use. TEIRESIAS examines its model of the knowledge base to see which predicate function is likely to be the right one; the model evidently suggested the function SAME. Finally, in order to fix the original bug, it must be possible to invoke the new rule for this patient. Since, in the original consultation, the expert responded that the portal of entry was the GI tract, this is a plausible guess for the value to use. This demonstrates another benefit of the "knowledge acquisition in context" methodology mentioned in Chapter 7.)

Also, most rules about what the category of a organism may be
Also conclude about -

[A] - the identity of a organism

Shall I try to write a clause to account for [A]?

FIGURE 9-3 continued

++** **N**

(The system noticed another unfulfilled expectation concerning the action part of the rule, but the expert always has the option of overriding the system's suggestions, and does so.)

The rule now reads:

RULE383

IF: 1) The infection is primary-bacteremia, and
2) The site of the culture is one of: those sites that are normally sterile, and
3) The portal of entry of the organism is GI
THEN: There is strongly suggestive evidence (.8) that the category of the organism is enterobacteriaceae

(Now that both the expert and TEIRESIAS are satisfied with the rule, there is a bit of bookkeeping to do. First, the new rule is checked by the system (behind the scenes) to be sure that there is nothing obviously wrong with it—for instance, one of the tests ensures that premise clauses are not contradictory. Had this been the case, the system would have noticed it at this point and the user would have been given the option of returning to the rule editor to fix the problem. There are several other things the system checks at this point, but this rule passes all the tests, and hence there is no indication of any problem.)

(PHASE V: FINAL CHECKOUT, BOOKKEEPING, RERUNNING THE CONSULTATION)

Please describe briefly why you added (or changed) this rule. Type an empty line when done.

++** **THE SYSTEM FAILED TO REALIZE IT COULD CONCLUDE**
++** **CATEGORY, AND THIS ALLOWED RULE184 TO INCORRECTLY**
++** **CONCLUDE IDENTITY**
++**

(Over the years of MYCIN development, the experts associated with the project have occasionally looked in astonishment at a rule which, though it had been around for some time, seemed, superficially at least, to make very little sense. The question then arises as to why that rule was added to the knowledge base. To avoid this problem, the expert is required to explain why he wrote or changed the rule.

There are also a number of other bookkeeping-type chores that are being attended to here, again, behind the scenes. TEIRESIAS takes care of tagging the rule with information that will simplify keeping track of the large, and constantly changing, body of rules. We will see in a moment how that information is accessed.)

RULE383 has now been added to the knowledge base.

I will now rerun the consultation to check the effectiveness of your new rule. Get comfortable, since this may take a bit.

Also, new questions may be asked as a result of this new rule. If a question is printed, please answer it with reference to this current patient.

(TEIRESIAS now invokes the performance program as a subprocess to make sure the bug is fixed, and to test for any other side effects. Since MYCIN has saved all the answers from the initial consultation, the

process is fairly inexpensive. The expert is warned about new questions because his new rule may mention an attribute that was not previously traced, or it may indirectly cause the tracing of one. While there are some cases in which it is possible to compute the incremental effect on a given consultation of adding a single new rule to the knowledge base, these are rare enough that in the long run it is computationally cheaper to simply rerun the consultation.)

```
18-DEC-75 16:30:46
----------PATIENT-281----------
   ----------INFECTION-1----------
      -----------CULTURE-1-----------
         -----------ORGANISM-1----------
```

(The answers to all questions were available internally, so the performance program asks nothing new. The context names are printed to let the expert follow the progress of the consultation.)

My therapy recommendation will be based on the following probable
infection(s) and potential causative organism(s):

INFECTION-1 is PRIMARY-BACTEREMIA
<Item 1> E. COLI [ORGANISM-1]
<Item 2> KLEBSIELLA-PNEUMONIAE [ORGANISM-1]
<Item 3> PROTEUS-NON-MIRABILIS [ORGANISM-1]

Well, it appears that things are straightened out.

(The new conclusions are the ones the expert indicated earlier as the correct answers. This does not go unnoticed by TEIRESIAS, which, as before, interrupts the consultation at this point to check the validity of the answers produced.)

Are all these values correct now?
++** **Y**

(As always, TEIRESIAS gives the expert the last word, and waits for approval before proceeding.)

Good, then the problem's been fixed.
. . . continuing with therapy selection now.

(At this point TEIRESIAS allows the performance program subprocess to continue with the normal therapy-selection phase. This has been omitted here for brevity.

The reader may be wondering why three errors disappeared with the addition of one rule. Once the new rule permitted the category of the organism to be concluded, not only did Rule 184 fail, but a second rule that had previously failed was now successfully invoked. This rule used the category of the organism to conclude that klebsiella-pneumoniae and proteus-non-mirabilis were likely identities.

All of the bookkeeping that was done is accessible via the INFOrmation command added to the question-answering facility of the performance program. This gives the expert the background for any rule in the system.)

** INFO 383

was written by Dr. Davis

on December 18, 1975

FIGURE 9-3 continued

for the following reason:

THE SYSTEM FAILED TO REALIZE IT COULD CONCLUDE CATEGORY, AND THIS ALLOWED RULE184 TO INCORRECTLY CONCLUDE IDENTITY.

for patient [281]

[who was described as follows:
CLASSIC CASE OF GRAM NEGATIVE ROD INFECTION FOR A PATIENT WITH A NON-NOSOCOMIAL DISEASE]

FIGURE 9-3 continued

9.6 How It All Works

9.6.1 Overview of the Main Ideas

Before reviewing the trace in more detail, we describe the ideas that make possible the capabilities displayed. This subsection serves primarily to name and briefly sketch each in turn; the details are supplied in subsequent subsections reviewing the example. [See Davis (1976) for more details.]

Knowledge Acquisition in Context

Performance programs of the sort TEIRESIAS helps create will typically find their greatest utility in domains where there are no unifying laws on which to base algorithmic methods. In such domains there is instead a collection of informal knowledge based on accumulated experience. This means an expert specifying a new rule may be codifying a piece of knowledge that has never previously been isolated and expressed as such. Since this is difficult, anything that can be done to ease the task will prove very useful.

In response, we have emphasized knowledge acquisition in the context of a shortcoming in the knowledge base. To illustrate the utility of this approach, consider the difference between asking the expert:

What should I know about the patient?

and saying to him:

> Here is an example in which you say the performance program made a mistake. Here is all the knowledge the program used, here are all the facts of the case, and here is how it reached its conclusions. Now,

what is it that you know and the system doesn't that allows you to avoid making that same mistake?

Note how much more focused the second question is and how much easier it is to answer.

Building Expectations

The focusing provided by the context is also an important aid to TEIRESIAS. In particular, it permits the system to build up a set of expectations concerning the knowledge to be acquired, facilitating knowledge transfer and making possible several useful features illustrated in the trace and described below.

Model-Based Understanding

Model-based understanding suggests that some aspects of understanding can be viewed as a process of matching: the entity to be understood is matched against a collection of prototypes, or models, and the most appropriate model is selected. This sets the framework in which further interpretation takes place. While this view is not new, TEIRESIAS employs a novel application of it, since the system has a model of the knowledge it is likely to be acquiring from the expert.

Giving a Program a Model of Its Own Knowledge

We will see that the combination of TEIRESIAS and the performance program amounts to a system that has a picture of its own knowledge. That is, it not only knows something about a particular domain but also in a primitive sense knows what it knows and employs that model of its knowledge in several ways.

Learning as a Process of Comparison

We do not view learning as simply the addition of information to an existing base of knowledge, but instead take it to include various forms of comparison of the new information with the old. This of course has its corollary in human behavior: a student will quickly point out discrepancies between newly taught material and his or her current stock of information. TEIRESIAS has a similar, though very primitive, capability: it compares new information supplied by the expert with the existing knowledge base, points out inconsistencies, and suggests possible remedies.

Learning by Experience

One of the long-recognized potential weaknesses of any model-based system is dependence on a fixed set of models, since the scope of the program's "understanding" of the world is constrained by the number and types of models it has. As will become clear, the models TEIRESIAS employs are not handcrafted and static, but are instead formed and continually revised as a by-product of its experience in interacting with the expert.

9.6.2 Phase I: Tracking Down the Bug

To provide the debugging facility shown in the dialogue of Section 9.5, TEIRESIAS maintains a detailed record of the actions of the performance program during the consultation and then interprets this record on the basis of an exhaustive analysis of the performance program's control structure. This presents the expert with a comprehensible task because (a) the backward-chaining technique used by the performance program is straightforward and intuitive, even to a nonprogrammer, and (b) the rules are designed to encode knowledge at a reasonably high conceptual level. As a result, even though TEIRESIAS is running through an exhaustive case analysis of the preceding consultation, the expert is presented with a task of debugging *reasoning* rather than *code.*

The availability of an algorithmic debugging process is also an important factor in encouraging the expert to be as precise as possible in making responses. Note that at each point in tracking down the error the expert must either approve of the rules invoked and the conclusions made or indicate which one was in error and supply the correction. This approach is extremely useful in domains where knowledge has not yet been formalized and where the traditional reductionist approach of dissecting reasoning down to observational primitives is not yet well established.[3]

TEIRESIAS further encourages precise comments by keeping the debugging process sharply focused. For instance, when it became clear that there was a problem with the inability to deduce the category, the system first asked which category it should have been. It then displayed only those rules appropriate to that answer, rather than all the rules concerning that topic that were tried.

Finally, consider the extensive amount of contextual information that is now available. The expert has been presented with a detailed example

[3]The debugging process does allow the expert to indicate that the performance program's results are incorrect, but he or she cannot find an error in the reasoning. This choice is offered only as a last resort and is intended to deal with situations where there may be a bug in the underlying control structure of the performance program (contrary to our assumption in Section 9.2).

of the performance program in action, has available all of the facts of the case, and has seen how the relevant knowledge has been applied. This makes it much easier for him or her to specify the particular chunk of knowledge that may be missing. This contextual information will prove very useful for TEIRESIAS as well. It is clear, for instance, what the *effect* of invoking the new rule must be (as TEIRESIAS indicates, it must be a rule that will deduce that the category should be *Enterobacteriaceae*), and it is also clear what the *circumstances* of its invocation must be (the rule must be invocable for the case under consideration, or it won't repair the bug). Both of these pieces of information are especially useful in Phase II and Phase V.

9.6.3 Phase II: Interpreting the Rule

As is traditional, "understanding" the expert's natural language version of the rule is viewed in terms of converting it to an internal representation and then retranslating that into English for the expert's approval. In this case the internal representation is the Interlisp form of the rule, so the process is also a simple type of code generation.

There were a number of reasons for rejecting a standard natural language understanding approach to this problem. First, as noted, understanding natural language is well known to be a difficult problem and was not a central focus of this research. Second, our experience suggested that experts frequently sacrifice precise grammar in favor of the compactness available in the technical language of the domain. As a result, approaches that were strongly grammar-based might not fare well. Finally, technical language often contains a fairly high percentage of unambiguous words, so a simpler approach that includes reliance on keyword analysis has a good chance of performing adequately.

As will become clear, our approach to analyzing the expert's new rule is based on both simple keyword spotting and predictions TEIRESIAS is able to make about the likely content of the rule. Code generation is accomplished via a form of template completion that is similar in some respects to template completion processes that have been used in generating natural language. Details of all these processes are given below.

Models and Model-Based Understanding

To set the stage for reviewing the details of the interpretation process, we digress for a moment to consider the idea of models and model-based understanding, and then to explore their application in TEIRESIAS. In the most general terms, a *model* can be seen as a *compact, high-level description of structure, organization, or content* that may be used both *to provide a framework for lower-level processing* and *to express expectations about the world.* One early, particularly graphic example of this idea can be found in the work on computer vision by Falk (1970). The task there was understanding block-world scenes; the goal was to determine the identity, location, and orientation of each block in a scene containing one or more blocks selected from a known set of possibilities. The key element of this work of interest to us here is the use of a set of *prototypes* for the blocks, prototypes that resembled wire frame models. Although such a description oversimplifies, part of the operation of Falk's system can be described in terms of two phases. The system first performed a preliminary pass to detect possible edge points in the scene and attempted to fit a block model to each collection of edges. The model chosen was then used in the second phase as a guide to further processing. If, for instance, the model accounted for all but one of the lines in a region, this suggested that the extra line might be spurious. If the model fit well except for some line missing from the scene, that was a good hint that a line had been overlooked and indicated as well where to go looking for it.

We can imagine one further refinement in the interpretation process, though it was not a part of Falk's system, and explain it in these same terms. Imagine that the system had available some *a priori* hints about what blocks might be found in the next scene. One way to express those hints would be to bias the matching process. That is, in the attempt to match a model against the data, the system might (depending on the strength of the hint) try the indicated models first, make a greater attempt to effect a match with one of them, or even restrict the set of possibilities to just those contained in the hint.

Note that in this system (i) the models supply a compact, high-level description of structure (the structure of each block), (ii) the description is used to guide lower-level processing (processing of the array of digitized intensity values), (iii) expectations can be expressed by a biasing or restriction on the set of models used, and (iv) "understanding" is viewed in terms of a matching and selection process (matching models against the data and selecting one that fits).

Rule Models

Now, recall our original task of interpreting the expert's natural language version of the rule, and view it in the terms described above. As in the computer vision example, there is a signal to be processed (the text), it is noisy (words can be ambiguous), and there is context available (from the debugging process) that can supply some hints about the likely content of the signal. To complete the analogy, we need a model that can (a) capture the structure, organization, or content of the expert's reasoning, (b) guide the interpretation process, and (c) express expectations about the likely content of the new rule.

Where might we get such a thing? There are interesting regularities

EXAMPLES—the subset of rules this model describes
DESCRIPTION—characterization of a typical member of this subset
- characterization of the premise
- characterization of the action

MORE GENERAL—pointers to models describing more general subsets of rules
MORE SPECIFIC—pointers to models describing more specific subsets of rules

FIGURE 9-4 Rule model structure.

in the knowledge base that might supply what we need. Not surprisingly, rules about a single topic tend to have characteristics in common—there are ways of reasoning about a given topic. From these regularities we have constructed *rule models*. These are abstract descriptions of subsets of rules, built from empirical generalizations about those rules and used to characterize a typical member of the subset.

Rule models are composed of four parts as shown in Figure 9-4. They contain, first, a list of EXAMPLES, the subset of rules from which this model was constructed. Next, a DESCRIPTION characterizes a typical member of the subset. Since we are dealing in this case with rules composed of premise-action pairs, the DESCRIPTION currently implemented contains individual characterizations of a typical premise and a typical action. Then, since the current representation scheme used in those rules is based on associative triples, we have chosen to implement those characterizations by indicating (a) which attributes typically appear in the premise (or action) of a rule in this subset and (b) correlations of attributes appearing in the premise (or action).[4] Note that the central idea is the concept of *characterizing a typical member of the subset.* Naturally, that characterization will look different for subsets of rules, procedures, theorems, or any other representation. But the main idea of characterization is widely applicable and not restricted to any particular representational formalism.

The two remaining parts of the rule model are pointers to models describing more general and more specific subsets of rules. The set of models is organized into a number of tree structures, each of the general form shown in Figure 9-5. At the root of each tree is the model made from all the rules that conclude about the attribute (i.e., the CATEGORY model), below this are two models dealing with all affirmative and all negative rules (e.g., the CATEGORY IS model). Below this are models dealing with rules that affirm or deny specific values of the attribute. These models are not handcrafted by the expert. They are instead assembled by TEIRESIAS on the basis of the current contents of the knowledge base, in what amounts to a simple statistical form of concept formation. The combination of TEIRESIAS and the performance program thus presents a system that has a model of its own knowledge, one it forms itself.

[4]Both (a) and (b) are constructed via simple thresholding operations.

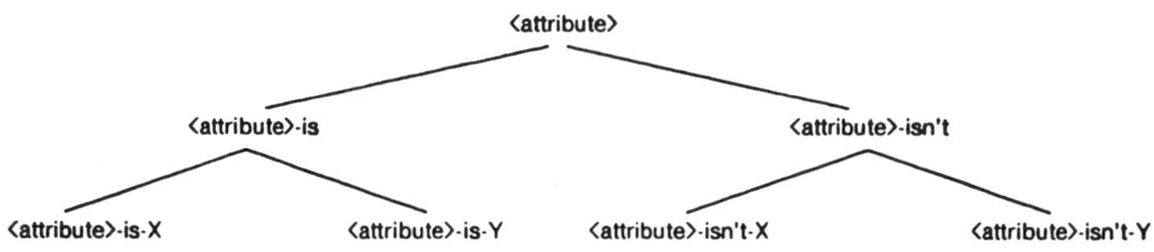

FIGURE 9-5 Organization of the rule models.

The rule models are the primary example of meta-level knowledge used in knowledge aquisition (for discussion of other forms, see Chapter 28). This form of knowledge and its generation by the system itself have several interesting implications illustrated in later sections.

Figure 9-6 shows a rule model; this is the one used by TEIRESIAS in the interaction shown earlier. (Since not all of the details of implementation are relevant here, this discussion will omit some.) As indicated above, there is a list of the rules from which this model was constructed, descriptions characterizing the premise and the action, and pointers to more specific and more general models. Each characterization in the description is shown

```
CATEGORY-IS

EXAMPLES    ((RULE116 .33)
             (RULE050 .78)
             (RULE037 .80)
             (RULE095 .90)
             (RULE152 1.0)
             (RULE140 1.0))

PREMISE     ((GRAM SAME NOTSAME 3.83)
             (MORPH SAME NOTSAME 3.83)
             ((GRAM SAME) (MORPH SAME) 3.83)
             ((MORPH SAME) (GRAM SAME) 3.83)
             ((AIR SAME) (NOSOCOMIAL NOTSAME SAME) (MORPH SAME)
                        (GRAM SAME) 1.50)
             ((NOSOCOMIAL NOTSAME SAME) (AIR SAME) (MORPH SAME)
                        (GRAM SAME) 1.50)
             ((INFECTION SAME) (SITE MEMBF SAME) 1.23)
             ((SITE MEMBF SAME) (INFECTION SAME) (PORTAL SAME)
                        1.23))

ACTION      ((CATEGORY CONCLUDE 4.73)
             (IDENT CONCLUDE 4.05)
             ((CATEGORY CONCLUDE) (IDENT CONCLUDE) 4.73))

MORE-GENL   (CATEGORY-MOD)

MORE-SPEC   NIL
```

FIGURE 9-6 Rule model for rules concluding affirmatively about CATEGORY.

split into its two parts, one concerning the presence of individual attributes and the other describing correlations. The first item in the premise description, for instance, indicates that most rules reaching conclusions about the category mention the attribute GRAM (for gram stain) in their premises; when they do mention it, they typically use the predicate functions SAME and NOTSAME; and the "strength," or reliability, of this piece of advice is 3.83 [see Davis (1976) for precise definitions of the quoted terms].

Correlations are shown as several lists of attribute-predicate pairs. The fourth item in the premise description, for example, indicates that when the attribute gram stain (GRAM) appears in the premise of a rule in this subset, the attribute morphology (MORPH) typically appears as well. As before, the predicate functions are those frequently associated with the attributes, and the number is an indication of reliability.

Choosing a Model

It was noted earlier that tracking down the bug in the knowledge base provides useful context and, among other things, serves to set up TEIRESIAS's expectations about the sort of rule it is about to receive. As suggested, these expectations are expressed by restricting the set of models that will be considered for use in guiding the interpretation. At this point TEIRESIAS chooses a model that expresses what it knows thus far about the kind of rule to expect, and in the current example it expects a rule that will deduce that the category should be *Enterobacteriaceae.*

Since there is not necessarily a rule model for every characterization, the system chooses the closest one. This is done by starting at the top of the tree of models and descending until either reaching a model of the desired type or encountering a leaf of the tree. In this case the process descends to the second level (the CATEGORY-IS model), notices that there is no model for CATEGORY-IS-ENTEROBACTERIACEAE at the next level, and settles for the former.[5]

Using the Rule Model: Guiding the Natural Language Interpretation

TEIRESIAS uses the rule models in two different ways in the acquisition process. The first is as a guide in understanding the text typed by the expert, as is described here. The second is as a means of allowing TEI-

[5]This technique is used in several places throughout the knowledge transfer process, and in general supplies the model that best matches the current requirements, by accommodating varying levels of specificity in the stated expectations. If, for instance, the system had known only that it expected a rule that concluded about category, it would have selected the first node in the model tree without further search. TEIRESIAS also has techniques for checking that the appropriate model has been chosen and can advise the expert if a discrepancy appears. See Davis (1976) for an example.

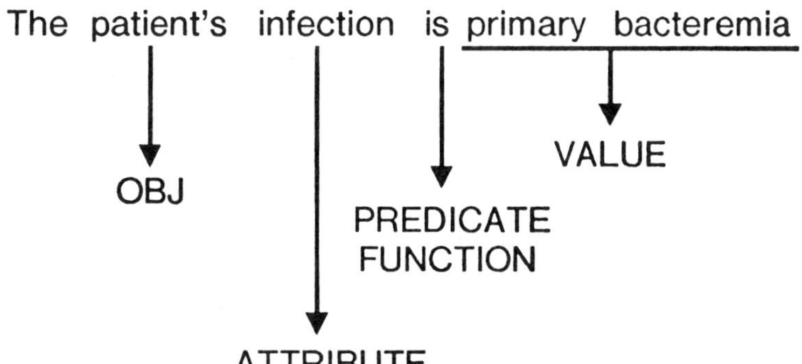

(a) Connotations found in the new rule.

Function	*Template*
SAME	(OBJ ATTRIBUTE VALUE)

(b) Template for the predicate function SAME.

1) (SAME CNTXT TREAT-ALSO PRIMARY-BACTEREMIA)
"Primary bacteremia is an associated infection for which therapy should cover."

2) (SAME CNTXT INFECTION PRIMARY-BACTEREMIA)
"The infection is primary bacteremia."

(c) Two choices for the resulting code (with translations).

FIGURE 9-7 Use of rule models to guide the understanding of a new rule.

RESIAS to see whether the new rule "fits into" its current model of the knowledge base in Phase IV.

To see how the rule models are used to guide the interpretation of the text of the new rule in the example, consider the first line of text typed by the expert in the new rule, Rule 383 (THE PATIENT'S INFECTION IS PRIMARY-BACTEREMIA). Each word is first reduced to a canonical form by a process that can recognize plural endings and that has access to a dictionary of synonyms (see Chapter 18). We then consider the possible connotations that each word may have (Figure 9-7a). Here connotation means the word might be referring to one or more of the conceptual primitives from which rules are built (i.e., it might refer to a predicate function, attribute, object, or value). One set of connotations is shown.[6]

Code generation is accomplished via a fill-in-the-blank mechanism. Associated with each predicate function is a *template* (see Chapter 5), a list structure that resembles a simplified procedure declaration and gives the

[6]The connotations of a word are determined by a number of pointers associated with it, which are in turn derived from the English phrases associated with each of the primitives.

order and generic type of each argument to a call of that function (Figure 9-7b). Associated with each of the primitives that make up a template (e.g., ATTRIBUTE, VALUE) is a procedure capable of scanning the list of connotations to find an item of the appropriate type to fill in that blank. The whole process is begun by checking the list of connotations for the predicate function implicated most strongly (in this case, SAME), retrieving the template for that function, and allowing it to scan the connotations and "fill itself in" using the procedures associated with the primitives. The set of connotations in Figure 9-7a produces the LISP code in Figure 9-7c. The ATTRIBUTE routine finds two choices for the attribute name, TREAT-ALSO and INFECTION, based on associations of the word infection with the phrases used to mention those attributes. The VALUE routine finds an appropriate value (PRIMARY-BACTEREMIA), the OBJect routine finds the corresponding object type (PATIENT) (but following the convention noted earlier, returns the variable name CNTXT to be used in the actual code).

There are several points to note here. First, the first interpretation in Figure 9-7c is incorrect (the system has been misled by the use of the word infection in the English phrase associated with TREAT-ALSO); we'll see in a moment how it is corrected. Second, several plausible (syntactically valid) interpretations are usually available from each line of text, and TEIRESIAS generates all of them. Each is assigned a score (the *text score*) indicating how likely it is, based on how strongly it was implicated by the text. Finally, we have not yet used the rule models, and it is at this point that they are employed.

We can view the DESCRIPTION part of the rule model selected earlier as a set of predictions about the likely content of the new rule. In these terms the next step is to see how well each interpretation fulfills those predictions. Note, for example, that the last line of the premise description in Figure 9-6 "predicts" that a rule about category of organism will contain the attribute PORTAL and the third clause of Rule 383 fulfills this prediction. Each interpretation is scored (employing the "strength of advice" number in the rule model) according to how many predictions it fulfills, yielding the *prediction satisfaction score.* This score is then combined with the text score to indicate the most likely interpretation. Because more weight is given to the prediction satisfaction score, the system tends to "hear what it expects to hear."

Rule Interpretation: Sources of Performance

While our approach to natural language is very simple, the overall performance of the interpretation process is adequate. The problem is made easier, of course, by the fact that we are dealing with a small amount of text in a restricted context and written in a semiformal technical language, rather than with large amounts of text in unrestricted dialogue written in unconstrained English. Even so, the problem of interpretation is substantial. TEIRESIAS' performance is based on the application of the ideas noted above (Section 9.6.1), notably the ideas of building expectations and model-based understanding. Its performance is also based on the use of two additional techniques: the intersection of data-driven and model-driven processing, and the use of multiple sources of knowledge.

First, the interpretation process proceeds in what has been called the *recognition mode*: it is the intersection of a bottom-up (data-directed) process (the interpretations suggested by the connotations of the text) with a top-down (goal-directed) process (the expectations set up by the choice of a rule model). Each process contributes to the end result, but it is the combination of them that is effective. This intersection of two processing modes is important when the interpretation techniques are as simple as those employed here, but the idea is more generally applicable as well. Even with more powerful interpretation techniques, neither data-directed nor goal-directed processing is in general capable of eliminating all ambiguity and finding the correct answer. By moving from both directions, top-down and bottom-up, we make use of all available sources of information, resulting in a far more focused search for the answer. This technique is applicable across a range of different interpretation problems, including those of text, vision, and speech.

Second, in either direction of processing, TEIRESIAS uses a number of different sources of knowledge. In the bottom-up direction, for example, distinct information about the appropriate interpretation of the text comes from (a) the connotations of individual words (interpretation of each piece of data), (b) the function template (structure for the whole interpretation), and (c) internal consistency constraints (interactions between data points), as well as several other sources [see Davis (1976) for the full list]. Any one of these knowledge sources alone will not perform very well, but acting in concert they are much more effective [a principle developed extensively in the HEARSAY system (Reddy et al., 1973)].

The notion of program-generated expectations is also an important source of power, since the selection of a particular rule model supplies the focus for the top-down part of the processing. Finally, the idea of model-based understanding offers an effective way of using the information in the rule model to effect the top-down processing.

Thus our relatively simple techniques supply adequate power because of the synergistic effect of multiple, independent sources of knowledge, because of the focusing and guiding effect of intersecting data-directed and goal-directed processing, and because of the effective mechanism for interpretation supplied by the idea of model-based understanding.

9.6.4 Phase III: Modifying the Interpretation

TEIRESIAS has a simple rule editor that allows the expert to modify existing rules or (as in our example) to indicate changes to the system's attempts to understand a new rule.[7] The editor has a number of simple heuristics built into it to make the rule modification process as effective as possible. In dealing with requests to change a particular clause of a new rule, for instance, the system reevaluates the alternative interpretations, taking into account the rejected interpretation (trying to learn from its mistakes) and making the smallest change possible (using the heuristic that the original clause was probably close to correct). In our example, this succeeds in choosing the correct clause next (the second choice shown in Figure 9-7c).

There are also various forms of consistency checking available. One obvious but effective constraint is to ensure that each word of the text is interpreted in only one way. In the trace shown earlier, for instance, accepting the new interpretation of clause 1 means clause 2 must be spurious, since it attempts to use the word infection in a different sense.

9.6.5 Phase IV: Second-Guessing, Another Use of the Rule Models

After the expert indicates that TEIRESIAS has correctly understood what he or she has written, the system checks to see if *it* is satisfied with the content of the rule. The idea is to use the rule model to see how well this new rule "fits into" the system's model of its knowledge; i.e., does it "look like" a typical rule of the sort expected?

In the current implementation, an incomplete match between the new rule and the rule model triggers a response from TEIRESIAS. Recall the last line of the premise description in the rule model of Figure 9-6:

```
((SITE MEMBF SAME) (INFECTION SAME) (PORTAL SAME) 1.23))
```

This indicates that when the culture SITE for the patient appears in the premise of a rule of this sort, then INFECTION type and organism PORTAL of entry typically appear as well. Note that the new rule in the example has the first two of these, but is missing the last, and the system points this out.

If the expert agrees to the inclusion of a new clause, TEIRESIAS attempts to create it. Since in this case the agreed-on topic for the clause was the portal of entry of the organism, this must be the attribute to use. The rule model suggests which predicate function to use (SAME, since that is the one paired with PORTAL in the relevant line of the rule model), and the template for this function is retrieved. It is filled out in the usual way, except that TEIRESIAS checks the record of the consultation when seeking items to fill in the template blanks. In this case only a value is still missing. Note that since the expert indicated that the portal of entry was

[7] Much of the editor has subsequently been incorporated into EMYCIN—see Chapter 15.

GI, TEIRESIAS uses this as the value for PORTAL. The result is a plausible guess, since it ensures that the rule will in fact work for the current case (note this further use of the debugging in context idea). It is not necessarily correct, of course, since the desired clause may be more general, but it is at least a plausible attempt.

It should be noted that there is nothing in this concept of second-guessing that is specific to the rule models as they are currently designed, or indeed to associative triples or rules as a knowledge representation. The fundamental point (as mentioned above) is testing to see how the new knowledge "fits into" the system's current model of its knowledge. At this point the system might perform any kind of check, for violations of any established prejudices about what the new chunk of knowledge should look like. Additional kinds of checks of rules might concern the strength of the inference, number of clauses in the premise, etc. In general, this second-guessing process can involve any characteristic that the system may have "noticed" about the particular knowledge representation in use.

Note also that this use of the rule model for second-guessing is quite different from the first use mentioned—guiding the understanding of English. Earlier we were concerned about interpreting text and determining what the expert actually said; here the task is to see what the expert plausibly *should have* said. Since, in assembling the rule models, TEIRESIAS may have noticed regularities in the reasoning about the domain that may not yet have occurred to the expert, the system's suggestions may conceivably be substantive and useful.

Finally, all this is in turn an instance of the more general notion of using meta-level knowledge in the process of knowledge acquisition: TEIRESIAS does not simply accept the new rule and add it to the knowledge base; it instead uses the rule model to evaluate the new knowledge in light of its current knowledge base. In a very simple way, learning is effected as a process of examining the relationships between what is already known and the new information being taught.

9.6.6 Phase V: Final Checkout, Bookkeeping, Rerunning the Consultation

When both the expert and TEIRESIAS are satisfied, there is one final sequence of tests to be performed, reflecting once again the benefit of knowledge acquisition in context. At this point TEIRESIAS examines several things about the rule, attempting to make sure that it will in fact fix the problem uncovered. In this case, for instance, the action of the new rule should be a conclusion about category, the category mentioned should be *Enterobacteriaceae,* and the conclusion should be affirmative. The premise should not contain any clauses that are sure to fail in the context in which the rule will be invoked. All these are potential sources of error that would make it obvious that the rule will not fix the bug.

There are also a number of straightforward bookkeeping tasks to be performed, including hooking the new rule into the knowledge base so that it is retrieved and invoked appropriately (in this case it gets added to the list of rules that conclude about category),[8] and tagging it with information that will make it easier to maintain the large and constantly changing body of rules (e.g., the name of the rule author, date of creation, author's justification for adding the rule, a pointer to the consultation that prompted its creation).

At this point, the system also performs any necessary recomputation of rule models. The operation is very fast, since it is clear from the action part of the rule which models may need to be recomputed, and the EXAMPLES part of the model then supplies the names of the other relevant rules. TEIRESIAS then reruns the performance program as a subprocess, and checks the results to see if all of the problems have been repaired.

9.7 Other Uses for the Rule Models

Two other uses have been developed for the rule models, which demonstrate capabilities made possible by meta-level knowledge.

9.7.1 "Knowing What You Know"

As described in Part Six, MYCIN has the ability to answer simple natural language questions about the knowledge base. In response to a question such as "How do you determine the identity of an organism causing an infection?" MYCIN would originally have printed the relevant rules. But a rule model, as a generalization of an entire class of rules, answers the question, too. Figure 9-8 shows one example of MYCIN's capabilities after rule models had been added. By simply "reading" the rule model to the user, TEIRESIAS can supply an overview of the knowledge in the relevant rules. This suggests the structure of global trends in the knowledge of the expert who assembled the knowledge base, and thus helps to make clear the overall approach of the system to a given topic.

---

[8]Note that these tests require the ability to dissect and partially evaluate the rule. The same function template that is used as a pattern for constructing rules is also used as a guide in this dissection and partial evaluation process.

```
** HOW DO YOU DECIDE THAT AN ORGANISM IS PSEUDOMONAS
AERUGINOSA?

Rules which conclude that the identity of the organism is
pseudomonas-aeruginosa generally use one or more of the following pieces
of information:
                the site of the culture
                the gram stain of the organism
                the morphology of the organism
Furthermore, the following relationships hold:
                The gram stain of the organism and the morphology of the
                organism tend to appear together in these rules.
RULE184, RULE116, RULE047, RULE085, and RULE040 conclude that the
                identity of the organism is pseudomonas-aeruginosa.
Which of these do you wish to see?
**
```

FIGURE 9-8 "Knowing what you know."

9.7.2 "Knowing What You Don't Know"

Another use of the models demonstrates that, in a primitive fashion, they give TEIRESIAS a model of what it *doesn't* know. There are models in the current system made from between 2 (the defined minimum) and 35 rules. We have defined a metric to measure the *strength* of a model, based on both the total number of rules from which the model was constructed and the strength of the inference of each of those rules. The entire model set is kept ordered from weakest to strongest, giving the system some indication of its likely competence on a range of subjects. In a very primitive way, it thus gains knowledge of where it is ignorant.

This makes possible a new option for the expert. Instead of adding a rule to fix a bug, the expert can ask the system what it would like to learn. (See Figure 9-9.) The system cycles through the rule models in order, indicating the weakest topics first. This is, of course, a first-order solution to the problem of giving the system an indication of its areas of ignorance. A better solution would supply an indication of how much the system knows about a subject, compared with how much there is to know. There surely are subjects for which three or four rules exhaust the available knowledge, while for others a hundred or more rules may not suffice. The issue is related to work described by Carbonell and Collins (1973) on closed versus open sets. That paper offers some interesting strategies for allowing a program to decide when it is ignorant and how it might reason in the face of the inability to store every fact about a given topic.

There appear to be no easy ways to deduce the incompleteness of the knowledge base using only the information stored in it. It is not valid to say, for instance, that there ought to be even a single rule for every attribute (how could a patient's name be deduced?). Nor is there a well-defined set of attributes for which no rules are likely to exist. Nor is it clear what sort

```
--** WHAT WOULD YOU LIKE TO KNOW?
Answer
   -Y for yes
   -N for no, or
   -Q to quit this.
There are only two rules for concluding that the identity of an
organism might be enterococcus. Would you like to give me a
rule for that?
++** N
There are only 2 rules for concluding that an infection might
be infective-endocarditis. Would you like to offer a rule for
that?
++** Y
The new rule will be called RULE384
   If (1)
```

FIGURE 9-9 "Knowing what you don't know."

of information would allow the incompleteness to be deduced. The issue is a significant one, since a good solution to the problem would not only give TEIRESIAS a better grasp of where the performance program was weak but also provide several important capabilities to the performance program itself. It would, for example, permit the use of the "if it were true I would know" heuristic of Carbonell and Collins (1973). Roughly restated, this says "If I know a great deal about subject *S*, and fact *F* concerns an important aspect of *S*, then if I don't already know that *F* is true, it's probably false." Thus in certain circumstances a lack of knowledge about the truth of a statement can plausibly be used as evidence suggesting that the statement is false. This is another useful form of meta-level knowledge.

9.8 Assumptions and Limitations

The work reported here can be evaluated with respect to both the utility of its approach to knowledge acquisition and its success in implementing that approach.

9.8.1 The Approach

As noted, our approach involves knowledge transfer that is interactive, that is set in the context of a shortcoming in the knowledge base, and that transfers a single rule at a time. Each of these has implications about TEIRESIAS's range of applicability.

Interactive knowledge transfer seems best suited to task domains involving problem solving that is entirely or primarily a high-level cognitive task, with a number of distinct, specifiable principles. Consultations in medicine or financial investments seem to be appropriate domains, but the approach would not seem well suited to those parts of, say, speech understanding or scene recognition in which low-level signal processing plays a significant role.

The transfer of expertise approach presents a useful technique for task domains that do not permit the use of programs (like those noted in Section 9.2) that autonomously induce new knowledge from test data. The autonomous mode may most commonly be inapplicable because the data for a domain simply don't exist yet. In quantitative domains [such as mass spectrum analysis (Buchanan and Feigenbaum, 1978)] or synthesized ("toy") domains [such as the line drawings in Hayes-Roth and McDermott (1977)], a large body of data points is easily assembled. This is not currently true for many domains; consequently induction techniques cannot be used. In such cases interactive transfer of expertise offers a useful alternative.[9]

Knowledge acquisition in context appears to offer useful guidance wherever knowledge of the domain is as yet ill-specified. The context of the interaction need not be a shortcoming in the knowledge base uncovered during a consultation, however, as it was here. Our recent experience suggests that an effective context is also provided by examining certain subsets of rules in the knowledge base and using them as a framework for specifying additional rules. The overall concept is limited, however, to systems that already have at least some minimal amount of information in their knowledge bases. Prior to this, there may be insufficient information to provide any context for the acquisition process.

Finally, the rule-at-a-time approach is a limiting factor. The example given earlier works well, of course, because the bug was manufactured by removing a single rule. In general, acquiring a single rule at a time seems well suited to the later stages of knowledge base construction, in which bugs may indeed be caused by the absence of one or a few rules. We need not be as lucky as in the example, in which one rule repaired three bugs; the approach will also work if three independent bugs arise in a consultation. But early in knowledge base construction, when large subareas of a domain are not yet specified, it appears more useful to deal with groups of rules or, more generally, with larger segments of the basic task [as in Waterman (1978)].

In general then, the interactive transfer of expertise approach seems well suited to the later stages of knowledge base construction for systems performing high-level tasks, and offers a useful technique for domains where extensive sets of data points are not available.

---

[9]Where the autonomous induction technique can be used, it offers the interesting advantage that the knowledge we expect the system to acquire need not be specified ahead of time, indeed not even known. Induction programs are in theory capable of inducing new information (i.e., information unknown to their author) from their set of examples. Clearly, the interactive transfer of expertise approach requires that the expert know and be able to specify precisely what it is the program is to learn.

9.8.2 The Program

Several difficult problems remained unsolved in the final implementation of the program. There is, for instance, the weakness of the technique of natural language understanding. There is also an issue with the technique used to generate the rule models. Model generation could be made more effective even without using a different approach to concept formation. Although an early design criterion suggested keeping the models transparent to the expert, making the process interactive would allow the expert to evaluate new patterns as they were discovered by TEIRESIAS. This might make it possible to distinguish accidental correlations from valid interrelations and might increase the utility and sophistication of TEIRESIAS's second-guessing ability. Alternatively, more sophisticated concept formation techniques might be borrowed from existing work.

There is also a potential problem in the way the models are used. Their effectiveness both in guiding the parsing of the new rule and in second-guessing its content is dependent on the assumption that the present knowledge base is both correct and a good basis for predicting the content of future rules. Either of these can at times be false, and the system may then tend to continue stubbornly down the wrong path.

There is also the difficult problem of determining the impact of any new or changed rule on the rest of the knowledge base, as discussed in Chapter 8, which we have considered only briefly. One difficulty (avoided in the work described in Chapter 8) involves establishing a formal definition of inconsistency for inexact logics, such as CF's (see Chapter 11), since, except for obvious cases (e.g., two identical rules with different strengths), it is not clear what constitutes an inconsistency. Once the definition is established, we would also require routines capable of uncovering them in a large knowledge base. This can be attacked by using an incremental approach (i.e., by checking every rule as it is added, the knowledge base is kept consistent and each consistency check is a smaller task), but the problem is substantial.

9.9 Conclusions

Each of the ideas reviewed above offers some contribution toward achieving the two goals set out at the beginning of this chapter: the development of a methodology of knowledge base construction via transfer of expertise, and the creation of an intelligent assistant to aid in knowledge acquisition. These ideas provide a set of tools and ideas to aid in the construction of knowledge-based programs and represent some new empirical techniques of knowledge engineering. Their contribution here may arise from their potential utility as case studies in the development of a methodology for this discipline.

Knowledge acquisition in the context of a shortcoming in the knowledge base, for instance, has proved to be a useful technique for achieving transfer of expertise, offering advantages to both the expert and TEIRESIAS. It offers the expert a framework for the explication of a new chunk of domain knowledge. By providing a specific example of the performance program's operation and forcing the expert to be specific in his or her criticism, it encourages the formalization of previously implicit knowledge. It also enables TEIRESIAS to form a number of expectations about the knowledge it is going to acquire and makes possible several checks on the content of that knowledge to ensure that it would in fact fix the bug. In addition, because the system has a *model of its own knowledge,* it is able to determine whether a newly added piece of knowledge "fits into" its existing knowledge base.

A second contribution of the ideas reviewed above lies in their ability to support a number of intelligent actions on the part of the assistant. While those actions have been demonstrated for a single task and system, it should be clear that none of the underlying ideas are limited to this particular task or to associative triples or rules as a knowledge representation. The foundation for many of these ideas is the concept of meta-level knowledge, which has made possible a program with a limited form of introspection.

The idea of *model-based understanding,* for instance, found a novel application in the fact that TEIRESIAS has a model of the knowledge base and uses this to guide acquisition by interpreting the model as predictions about the information it expects to receive.

The idea of *biasing the set of models* to be considered offers a specific mechanism for the general notion of *program-generated expectations* and makes possible an assistant whose understanding of the dialogue is more effective.

TEIRESIAS is able to second-guess the expert with respect to the content of the new knowledge by using its models to *see how well the new piece of knowledge "fits into" what it already knows.* An incomplete match between the new knowledge and the system's model of its knowledge prompts it to make a suggestion to the expert. With this approach, learning becomes more than simply adding the new information to the knowledge base; TEIRESIAS examines as well the relationship between the new and existing knowledge.

The concept of meta-level knowledge makes possible *multiple uses of the knowledge in the system:* information in the knowledge base is not only used directly (during the consultation) but also examined and abstracted to form the rule models.

TEIRESIAS also represents a synthesis of the ideas of model-based understanding and learning by experience. Although both of these have been developed independently in previous AI research, their combination produces a novel sort of feedback loop (Figure 9-10). Rule acquisition relies on the set of rule models to effect the model-based understanding process. This results in the addition of a new rule to the knowledge base, which in turn prompts the recomputation of the relevant rule model(s).[10]

This loop has a number of interesting implications. First, performance on the acquisition of the next rule may be better because the system's "picture" of its knowledge base has improved—the rule models are now computed from a larger set of instances, and their generalizations are more likely to be valid. Second, since the relevant rule models are recomputed each time a change is made to the knowledge base, the picture they supply is kept constantly up to date, and they will at all times be an accurate reflection of the shifting patterns in the knowledge base. This is true as well for the trees into which the rule models are organized: they too grow (and shrink) to reflect the changes in the knowledge base.

Finally, and perhaps most interesting, the models are not handcrafted by the system architect or specified by the expert. They are instead formed by the system itself, and formed as a result of its experience in acquiring rules from the expert. Thus, despite its reliance on a set of models as a basis for understanding, TEIRESIAS's abilities are not restricted by the existing set of models. As its store of knowledge grows, old models can become more accurate, new models will be formed, and the system's stock of knowledge about its knowledge will continue to expand. This appears to be a novel capability for a model-based system.

---

[10]The models are recomputed when any change is made to the knowledge base, including rule deletion or modification, as well as addition.

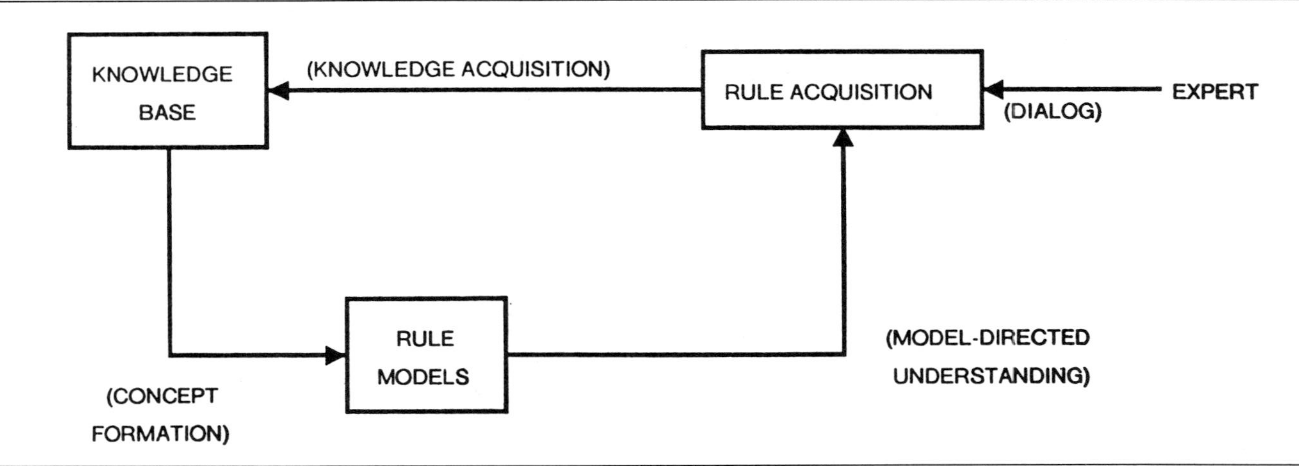

FIGURE 9-10 Model-directed understanding and learning by experience combine to produce a useful feedback loop.

PART FOUR

Reasoning Under Uncertainty

10

Uncertainty and Evidential Support

As we began developing the first few rules for MYCIN, it became clear that the rules we were obtaining from our collaborating experts differed from DENDRAL's situation-action rules in an important way—the inferences described were often uncertain. Cohen and Axline used words such as "suggests" or "lends credence to" in describing the effect of a set of observations on the corresponding conclusion. It seemed clear that we needed to handle probabilistic statements in our rules and to develop a mechanism for gathering evidence for and against a hypothesis when two or more relevant rules were successfully executed.

It is interesting to speculate on why this problem did not arise in the DENDRAL domain. In retrospect, we suspect it is related to the inherent complexity of biological as opposed to artificial systems. In the case of DENDRAL we viewed our task as hypothesis generation guided by rule-based constraints. The rules were uniformly categorical (nonprobabilistic) and were nested in such a way as to assure that contradictory evidence was never an issue.[1] In MYCIN, however, an overall strategy for nesting categorical rules never emerged; the problem was simply too ill-structured. It was possible to tease out individual inference rules from the experts working with us, but the program was expected to select relevant rules during a consultation and to accumulate probabilistic evidence regarding the competing hypotheses.

In response to these observations we changed the evolving system in two ways. First, we modified the rule structure to permit a conclusion to be drawn with varying degrees of certainty or belief. Our initial intent was to represent uncertainty with probabilistic weights on a 0-to-1 scale. Second, we modified the data structures for storing information. Rather than simply recording attribute-object-value triples, we added a fourth element to represent the extent to which a specific value was believed to be true. This meant that the attribute of an object could be associated with multiple competing values, each associated with its own certainty weight.

---

[1]In the model of mass spectrometry used by DENDRAL, the statistical nature of events is largely ignored in favor of binary decisions about occurrence or nonoccurrence of events.

It was logical to turn to probability theory in our initial efforts to define the meaning of these certainty values. Bayes' Rule (or Bayes' Theorem) the traditional evidence-combining technique used in most medical diagnosis programs, provided a model for how the weights could be manipulated if they were interpreted as probabilities. For reasons that are discussed in detail in the next chapter, we were gradually led to consider other interpretations of the numerical weights and to reject a purely probabilistic interpretation of their meaning.

Shortliffe was encouraged by Buchanan, as well as by Professors Patrick Suppes and Byron Brown, who were on his thesis committee, to attempt to formalize the numerical weights rather than to define and combine them in a purely *ad hoc* fashion. There ensued many months of reading the literature of statistics and the philosophy of science, focusing on the theory of confirmation and attempting to understand the psychological issues underlying the assignment of certainty weights. Chapter 11, originally published in 1975, summarizes the formal model that ultimately emerged from these studies. The concept of certainty factors (CF's) was implemented and tested in MYCIN and became a central element of other EMYCIN systems that have been developed in the ensuing years.

Another source of uncertainty in a knowledge base is the imprecision in language. Even though the vocabulary of medicine is technical, it is not without ambiguity. For example, one question asks whether the dosage of a drug given previously was "adequate." Rules use the answers given in response to such questions with the assumption that the user and the expert who wrote the rules agree on the meanings of such terms. What do we do to help satisfy this assumption? Rule writers are encouraged to anticipate the ambiguities when formulating their questions. They write the English forms of the TRANS and PROMPT values. Also, they can supply further clarification in the REPROMPT value, which is printed when the user types a question mark. MYCIN (and EMYCIN) provides facilities for experts to clarify their use of terms, but cannot guarantee the elimination of ambiguity.[2]

10.1 Analyses of the CF Model

Although the motives behind the CF model were largely pragmatic and we justified the underlying assumptions by emphasizing the system's excellent performance (see, for example, Chapter 31), several theoretical ob-

[2]Fuzzy logic (Zadeh, 1978) quantifies the degree to which imprecise concepts are satisfied, thus adding another level of detail to the reasoning. For our purposes, it is sufficient to ask the user whether a concept, such as "adequateness," is satisfied—where an appropriate response may be "Yes (0.7)." In fuzzy logic, a possibility distribution for the user's understanding of the concept "adequate" would be matched against a corresponding distribution for the rule writer's understanding. We believe this is an unnecessary layer of detail for the precision we want to achieve (or feel is justified by the precision of the information).

jections to the model were subsequently raised. Professor Suppes had been particularly influential in urging Shortliffe to relate CF's to the rules of conventional probability theory,[3] and the resulting definitions of MB's and MD's did help us develop an intuitive sense of what our certainty measures might mean. However, the probabilistic definitions also permitted formal analyses of the underlying assumptions in the combining functions and of limitations in the applicability of the definitions themselves.

For example, as we note in Chapter 11, the source of confusion between $\mathrm{CF}(h,e)$ and $P(h|e)$ becomes clear when one sees that, for small values of the prior probabilities $P(h)$, $\mathrm{CF}(h,e) \approx P(h|e)$. Our effort to ignore prior probabilities was largely defended by observing that, in the absence of all information, priors for a large number of competing hypotheses are uniformly small. For parameters such as organism identity, which is the major diagnostic decision that MYCIN must address, the assumption of small priors is reasonable. The same model is used, however, to deal with *all* uncertain parameters in the system, including yes-no parameters for which the prior probability of one of the values is necessarily greater than or equal to 0.5.

The significance of the 0.2 threshold used by many of MYCIN's predicates (see Chapter 5) was also a source of puzzlement to many observers of the CF model. This discontinuity in the evaluation function is not an intrinsic part of the CF theory (and is ignored in Chapter 11) but was added as a heuristic for pruning the reasoning network.[4] If *any* small positive CF were accepted in evaluating the premise of a rule, without a threshold, two undesirable results would occur:

1. Very weak evidence favoring a condition early in the rule premise would be "accepted" and would lead to consideration of subsequent conditions, possibly with resulting backward-chained reasoning. It is wasteful to pursue these conditions, possibly with generation of additional questions to the user, if the evidence favoring the rule's premise cannot exceed 0.2 (recall that $AND uses min in calculating the TALLY—see Chapters 5 and 11 for further details).
2. Even if low-yield backward chaining did not occur, the rule would still have limited impact on the value of the current subgoal since the TALLY for the rule premise would be less than 0.2.

---

[3]Suppes pressed us early on to state whether we were trying to model how expert physicians *do* think or how they *ought to* think. We argued that we were doing neither. Although we were of course influenced by information regarding the relevant cognitive processes of experts [see, for example, the recent books by Elstein et al. (1978) and Kahneman et al. (1982)], our goals were oriented much more toward the development of a high-performance computer program. Thus we sought to show that the CF model allowed MYCIN to reach good decisions comparable to those of experts and intelligible both to experts and to the intended user community of practicing physicians.

[4]Duda et al. (1976) have examined this discontinuity and the relationship of CF's to their Bayesian updating model used in the PROSPECTOR system.

Thus the 0.2 threshold was added for pragmatic reasons and should not be viewed as central to the CF model itself. In later years questions arose as to whether the value of the threshold should be controlled dynamically by the individual rules or by meta-rules (rather than being permanently bound to 0.2), but this feature was never implemented.

Another important limitation of MYCIN's control scheme was noted in the mid-1970s but was never changed (although it would have been easy to do so). The problem results from the requirement that the premise of a rule be a conjunction of conditionals with disjunctions handled by multiple rules. As described in Chapter 5, A V B V C → D was handled by defining three rules: A → D, B → D, and C → D. If all rules permitted conclusions with certainty, the three rules would indeed be equivalent to a single disjunctive rule with certain inference (CF = 1). However, with CF's less than unity, all three rules might succeed for a given case, and then each rule would contribute incremental evidence in favor of D. This evidence would be accumulated using the CF combining function, that is, $CF_{COMBINE}$, and might be very different from the CF that the expert would have given if asked to assign a weight to the single disjunctive rule. This problem could have been handled by changing the rule monitor to allow disjunctions in a rule premise, but the change was never implemented because a clear need never arose.

The rule interpreter does not allow rules to be written whose primary connective is disjunction ($OR). We have encouraged splitting primary disjunctions into separate rules for this reason. Thus

[1] ($OR ABC) → D

would be written as three separate rules:

[2] A → D
[3] B → D
[4] C → D

Conceptually this is simple and straightforward. In some cases, however, the disjuncts are better understood as a set, and [1] would be a clearer expression than [2], [3], and [4]. In these cases, Carli Scott has pointed out that [1] can be rewritten as a primary conjunction wih only one clause:

[5] ($AND ($OR A B C)) → D

This uncovers a limitation on the CF model, however. While [5] should give the same results as [2], [3], and [4] together, the resulting CF's on conclusion D will differ. The reason is that in [5] the CF on the rule will be multiplied by the MAX of the CF's of the disjunction A, B, or C, while in [2], [3], and [4] the cumulative CF associated with D will be the result of combining three products according to the combining function.[5]

[5]It is possible to force them to give the same result by adjusting the CF's either on [5] or on [2], [3] and [4]. We would not expect a rule writer to do this, however, nor would we think the difference would matter much in practice.

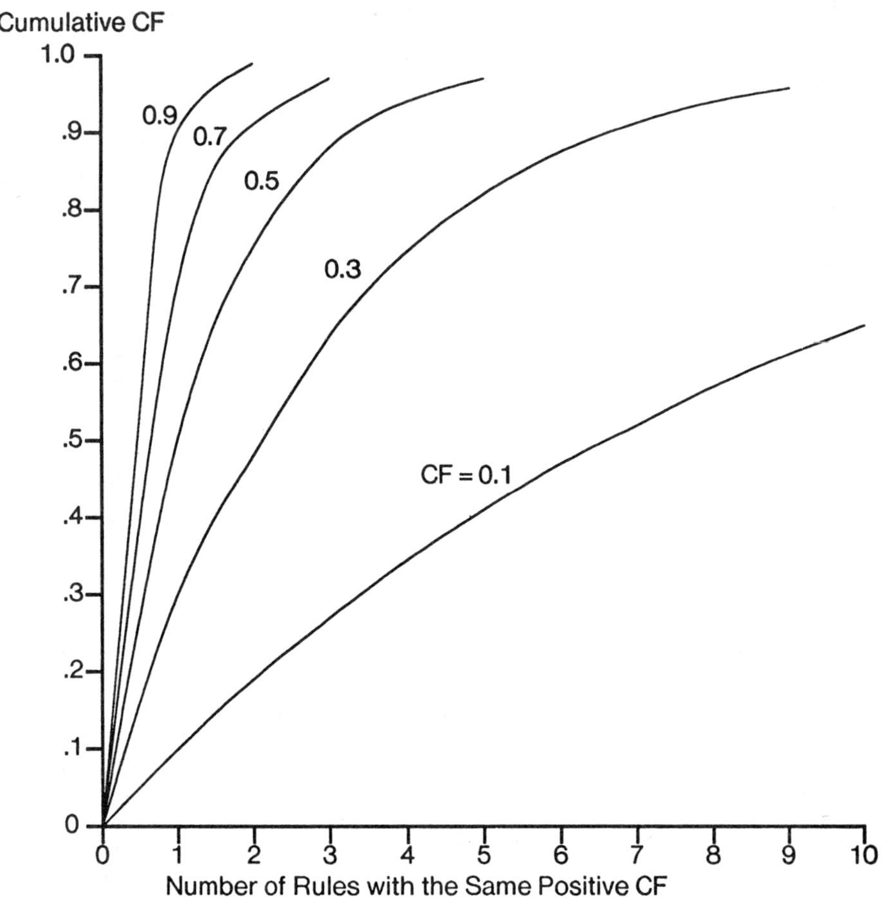

FIGURE 10-1 Family of curves showing how rapidly MYCIN's CF combining function converges for rules with the same CF.

Another limitation for some problems is the rapidity with which CF's converge on the asymptote 1. This is easily seen by plotting the family of curves relating the number of rules with a given CF, all providing evidence for a hypothesis, to the resulting CF associated with the hypothesis.[6] The result of plotting these curves (Figure 10-1) is that $CF_{COMBINE}$ is seen to converge rapidly on 1 no matter how small the CF's of the individual rules are. For some problem areas, therefore, the combining function needs to be revised. For example, damping factors of various sorts could be devised

[6]This was first pointed out to us by Mitch Model, who was investigating the use of the CF model in the context of the HASP/SIAP program (Nii et al., 1982).

(but were not) that would remedy this problem in ways that are meaningful for various domains. In MYCIN's domain of infectious diseases, however, this potential problem never became serious. In PROSPECTOR this problem does not arise because there is no finite upper limit to the likelihood ratios used.

As we were continuing to learn about the CF model and its implications, other investigators, faced with similar problems in building medical consultation systems, were analyzing the general issues of inexact inference (Szolovits and Pauker, 1978) and were in some cases examining shortcomings and strengths of CF's. Later, Schefe analyzed CF's and fuzzy set theory (Schefe, 1980). Dr. Barclay Adams, a member of the research staff at the Laboratory of Computer Science, Massachusetts General Hospital, responded to our description of the MYCIN model with a formal analysis of its assumptions and limitations (Adams, 1976), included in this book as Chapter 12. The observations there nicely specify the assumptions that are necessary if the CF's in MYCIN's rules are interpreted in accordance with the probabilistic definitions from Chapter 11. Adams correctly notes that there may be domains where the limitations of the CF model, despite their minimal impact on MYCIN's performance, would seriously constrain the model's applicability and success. For example, if MYCIN had required a single best diagnosis, rather than a clustering of leading hypotheses, there would be reason to doubt the model's ability to select the best hypothesis on the basis of a maximal CF.

Even before the Adams paper appeared in print, many of the same limitations were being noted within the MYCIN project. For example, in January of 1976 Shortliffe prepared an extensive internal memo that made several of the same observations cited by Adams.[7] He was aided in these analyses by Dana Ludwig, a medical student who studied the CF model in detail as a summer research project. The Shortliffe memo outlined five alternate CF models and argued for careful consideration of one that would require the use of *a priori* probabilities of hypotheses in addition to the conventional CF's on rules. The proposed model was never implemented, however, partly due to time constraints but largely because MYCIN's decision-making performance was proving to be excellent despite the theoretical limitations of CF's. Some of us felt that a one-number calculus was preferable in this domain to a more theoretically sound calculus that requires experts to supply estimates of two or more quantities per rule. It is interesting to note, however, that the proposals developed bore several similarities to the subjective Bayesian model developed at about the same time for SRI's PROSPECTOR system (Duda et al., 1976). The CF model has been used successfully in several EMYCIN systems (see Part Five) and in the IRIS system (Trigoboff, 1978) developed at Rutgers University for diagnosing glaucomas.

[7]This is the file CF.MEMO referred to by Clancey in the exchange of electronic messages at the end of this chapter.

There is an additional element of uncertainty in rules that is also bound up in the CF's. Besides capturing some measure of increased probability associated with the conclusion after the premises are known and some measure of the utility associated with the conclusion, the CF also includes some measure of how "flaky" the rule is. That is, a CF of 0.2 can indicate that the probability increases by 20% (rather precisely) or that the rule writer felt there was a positive association between premises and conclusion but was only 20% certain of it. Some rule writers would be able to quantify their degree of doubt about the CF's (e.g., "I am about 90% certain that this strength of association is 0.5"), but there is no provision in our CF model for doing so. In most cases where increased precision is possible, rule writers would have prior and posterior probabilities and would not need a one-number calculus.

Despite the shortcomings of the CF model, it must be recognized that the issues we were addressing reflected a somewhat groping effort to cope with the limitations of probability theory. It has therefore been with considerable interest that we have discovered in recent years the work of Dempster and Shafer. Shafer's book, *The Mathematical Theory of Evidence,* appeared in 1976 and proposed solutions to many of the same problems being considered in the MYCIN work. Several aspects of the CF model appear as special cases of their theory. Interestingly, Bayesian statistics is another special case. Our recent attempt to understand the Dempster-Shafer model and its relevance to MYCIN is described in Chapter 13. This work, the most recent in the book, was largely done by Jean Gordon, a mathematician who recently joined our group when she came to Stanford as a medical student. Because of new insights regarding the topics underlying CF's and the relationships to probabilistic reasoning, we have chosen to include that analysis in this volume even though we have not implemented the ideas in the program.

10.2 Evolution of the CF Model

Although the model described in Chapter 11 has persisted to the present for the MYCIN program, and for other EMYCIN systems (see Part Five), a few revisions and additional observations have been made in the intervening years. The only major change has been a redefinition of the combining function by Bill van Melle. This was undertaken for two reasons:

1. the potential for a single piece of negative evidence to overwhelm several pieces of positive evidence (or vice versa); and
2. the computational expense of storing both MB's and MD's (rather than cumulative CF's) in order to maintain commutativity.

The second of these points is discussed briefly in Chapter 11, but the first may require clarification. Consider, for example, eight or nine rules all supporting a single hypothesis with CF's in the range 0.4 to 0.8. Then the asymptotic behavior of the cumulative MB would result in a value of about 0.999. Suppose now that a single disconfirming rule were to succeed with CF = 0.8. Then the net support for the hypothesis would be

$$\text{CF} = \text{MB} - \text{MD} = 0.999 - 0.8 = 0.199$$

This behavior was counterintuitive and occasionally led MYCIN to reach incorrect inferences, especially in situations where the final CF after tracing became less than 0.2. This would drop the final belief below the established threshold. Hence a single piece of negative evidence could overwhelm and negate the combined evidence of *any number* of supporting rules.

As a result, we changed both the definition of a CF and the corresponding combining function to soften the effect:

$$\text{CF} = \frac{\text{MB} - \text{MD}}{1 - \min(\text{MB},\text{MD})}$$

$$\text{CF}_{\text{COMBINE}}(X,Y) = \begin{cases} X + Y(1 - X) & X, Y \text{ both} > 0 \\ \dfrac{X + Y}{1 - \min(|X|, |Y|)} & \text{one of } X, Y < 0 \\ -\text{CF}_{\text{COMBINE}}(-X,-Y) & X, Y \text{ both} < 0 \end{cases}$$

Note that the definition of CF is unchanged for any single piece of evidence (where either MD or MB is zero by definition) and that the combining function is unchanged when both CF's are the same sign. It is only when combining two CF's of opposite sign that any change occurs. The reader will note, for example, that

$$\text{CF}_{\text{COMBINE}}(0.999,-0.80) = 0.199/0.2 = 0.99$$

whereas

$$\text{CF}_{\text{COMBINE}}(0.55,-0.5) = 0.05/0.5 = 0.1$$

In addition, the change in $\text{CF}_{\text{COMBINE}}$ preserved commutativity without the need to partition evidence into positive and negative weights for later combination. Thus, rather than storing both MB and MD for each hypothesis, MYCIN simply stores the current cumulative CF value and combines it with new evidence as it becomes available. Beginning in approximately 1977 these changes were incorporated into all EMYCIN systems.

10.3 Assessing the CF Model

Even before the change in the combining function was effected, we had observed generally excellent decision-making performance by the program and therefore questioned just how sensitive MYCIN's decisions were to the CF's on rules or to the model for evidence accumulation. Bill Clancey (then a student on the project) undertook an analysis of the CF's and the sensitivity of MYCIN's behavior to those values. The following discussion is based in large part on his analysis and the resulting data.

The CF's in rules reflect two kinds of knowledge. In some cases, such as a rule that correlates the cause of meningitis with the age of the patient, the CF's are statistical and are derived from published studies on the incidence of disease. However, most CF's represent a mixture of probabilistic and cost/benefit reasoning. One criticism of MYCIN's rules has been that utility considerations (in the decision analytic sense) are never made explicit but are "buried" in a rule's CF. For example, the rule that suggests treating for *Pseudomonas* in a burned patient is leaving out several other organisms that can also cause infection in that situation. However, *Pseudomonas* is a particularly aggressive organism that often causes fatal infections and yet is resistant to most common antibiotics. Thus its "weight" is enhanced by rules to ensure that it is adequately considered when reaching therapy decisions.[8] Szolovits and Pauker (1978) have also provided an excellent discussion of the issues complicating the combination of decision analytic concepts and categorical reasoning in medical problems.

Figure 10-2 is a bar graph showing how frequently various CF values occur in MYCIN's rules. All but about 60 of the 500 rules in the most recent version of the system have CF's.[9] The cross-hatched portion of each bar shows the frequency of CF's in the 1975 version of MYCIN, when there were only 200 rules dealing with bacteremia. The open portion of each bar refers to the CF's of incremental rules since that time, most of which deal with meningitis. The overall pattern is about the same, although the more recent system has proportionally more small positive CF's. This makes sense because the newer rules often deal with softer data (clinical evidence) in contrast to the rules for bacteremia, which generally interpret

[8]Self-referencing rules, described in Chapter 5, were often used to deal with such utility considerations. As mentioned in Chapter 3, they allowed dangerous organisms, initially suggested with only minimal certainty, to be reconsidered and further confirmed by special evidence. For example: *if* you are already considering *Pseudomonas and* the patient has ecthyma gangrenosum skin lesions, *then* there is even greater importance to the conclusion that the pathogen is *Pseudomonas.*

[9]The rules without CF's do not associate evidence with hypotheses but make numerical computations or save a text string to be printed later. Note also that some rules, particularly tabular rules, make many conclusions and thus account for the fact that there are more CF's than rules.

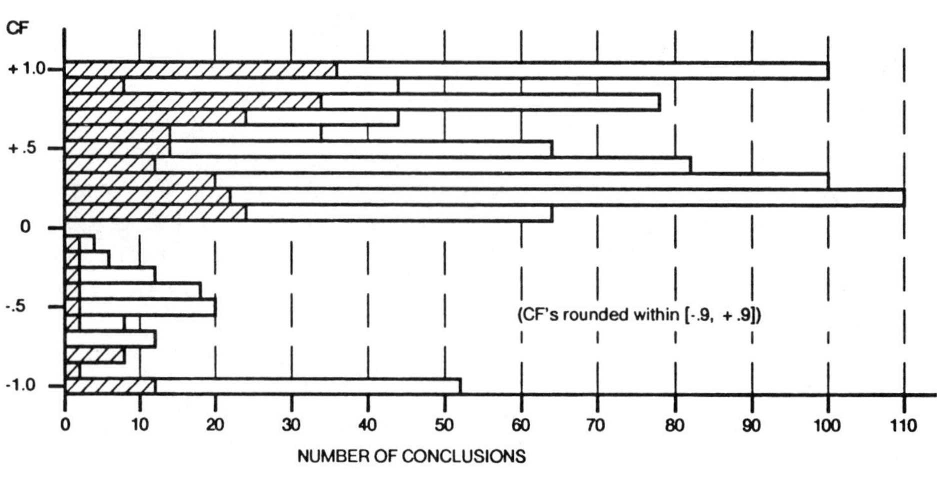

FIGURE 10-2 Frequency of CF's in MYCIN's rules. Cross-hatched bars indicate frequencies for the 1975 version of MYCIN. Open bars show frequencies since then.

more concrete laboratory results. The bimodal distribution with peaks at 0.8 and 0.2 (ignoring for a moment those rules, often definitional, that reach conclusions with certainty) suggests that experts tend to focus on strong associations (+0.8, a number that might seem less binding than 0.9) and many weak associations (+0.2, the minimum CF that will allow the inferred parameter to exceed the threshold for partial belief). In contrast there are relatively few rules with negative CF's. We suspect this reflects the natural tendency to state evidence in a positive way.

Analysis of MYCIN's reasoning networks suggests that the program should not be very sensitive to changes in rule CF's. This conclusion is based on two observations about how CF's are actually used in the program. First, inference chains are short, and premises often pass a TALLY of 1.0 to the conclusion (see Chapter 5), so the effect of multiplying CF's from one step in the chain to the next is minimal. Second, conclusions are frequently made by only a single rule, thereby avoiding the use of $CF_{COMBINE}$ for all but a few key parameters. Observe that the first effect deals with combination of CF's from goal to goal (by passing a value from a rule premise to the conclusion) and the second deals with combination of evidence for a single goal.

Intrigued by observations such as those outlined above, Clancey enlisted the assistance of Greg Cooper, and in 1979 they undertook an experiment to determine quantitatively how sensitive MYCIN is to changes in rule CF's. The ten cases used in the formal evaluation of the meningitis rule set (see Chapter 31) were used for this study. The cases were run in batch mode using systematic variations of the CF's in MYCIN's rules. For

Number of intervals	*Number of cases (out of 10)* *Same organisms and therapy*	*Different organisms*	*Different organisms and therapy*
10	9	1	0
5	7	3	0
4	8	2	1
3	5	5	1
2	1	9	3

FIGURE 10-3 Results of CF sensitivity experiment.

each run, rules were modified by mapping the existing rule CF's onto a new, coarser scale. The original CF scale has 1000 intervals from 0 to 1000.[10] Trials were run using ten, five, four, three, and two intervals. Thus, when there are five intervals, all rule CF's are mapped onto 0, 200, 400, 600, 800, and 1000, rounding as necessary. When there are two intervals, only the numbers 0, 500, and 1000 are used.

CF's were combined using the usual combining function (the revised version that was in use by 1979). Thus intermediate conclusions mapped onto arbitrary numbers from 0 to 1000. Clustering the final organism list was done in the normal way (cutting off at the largest gap). Finally, negative CF's were treated analogously, for example, mapping onto 0, −333, −666, and −1000 when there were three intervals.

In examining results, we are interested primarily in three possible outcomes: (1) no change to the item list (and hence no change in therapy); (2) different organisms, but the same therapy; and (3) new therapy (and therefore different organisms). Figure 10-3 summarizes the data from the ten cases run with five different CF scales.

Degradation of performance was only pronounced when the number of intervals was changed to three (all rule CF's mapped onto 0, 333, 666, and 1000). But even here five of the ten cases had the same organism list and therapy. It wasn't until CF's were changed to 0, 500, and 1000 that a dramatic change occurred; and even with nine new organism lists, we find that seven of the ten cases had the same therapy. The fact that the organism list did not change radically indicates that MYCIN's rule set is not "fine-tuned" and does not need to be. The rules use CF's that can be modified by ± 0.2, showing that there are few deliberate (or necessary) interactions in the choice of CF's. The observed stability of therapy despite changing organism lists probably results because a single drug will cover for many organisms, a property of the domain.

---

[10]CF's are handled internally on a 0 to 1000 scale to avoid floating-point arithmetic, which is more expensive in Interlisp than is integer arithmetic.

10.4 Additional Uses of Certainty Factors

By the early 1980s, when much of our research was focusing on issues other than EMYCIN systems, we still often found CF's to be useful computational devices. One such example was the work of Jerry Wallis, described in detail in Chapter 20. His research modeled causal chains with rules and used CF's to represent the uncertainty in the causal links. Because his system reasoned both from effects to causes and from causes to effects, techniques were needed to prevent fruitless searching of an entire connected subgraph of the network. To provide a method for search termination, the concept of a subthreshold path was defined, i.e., a path of reasoning whose product of CF's can be shown to be below the threshold used to reject a hypothesis as unknown. For example, if there is a linear reasoning path of four rules (R1, R2, R3, and R4) where A can be asked of the user and E is the goal that initiated a line of backward-chained reasoning:

then if B were known with certainty, E would be known only with a CF of $(0.4)(0.7)(0.7) = 0.19$. This is less than the conventional cutoff of 0.2 used in EMYCIN systems, so the line of reasoning from B to E would be considered a subthreshold path. There is no need to invoke rule R1 and ask question A in an effort to conclude B because the result cannot affect the final value for the variable E. If the product of CF's is tabulated during the backward-chaining process, the accumulated value provides a method for limiting the search space that needs to be investigated.

In a branched reasoning tree this becomes slightly more complex. Normally, when a rule is used to conclude a value with a particular CF, that number is stored with the parameter's value in case it is later needed by other rules. In the example above, termination of the search from E back to A (due to the subthreshold condition at B) would have left the value at C "unknown" and might have left a CF of 0 stored at that node. Suppose, though, that another rule, R5, later needed the value of C because of consideration of goal F:

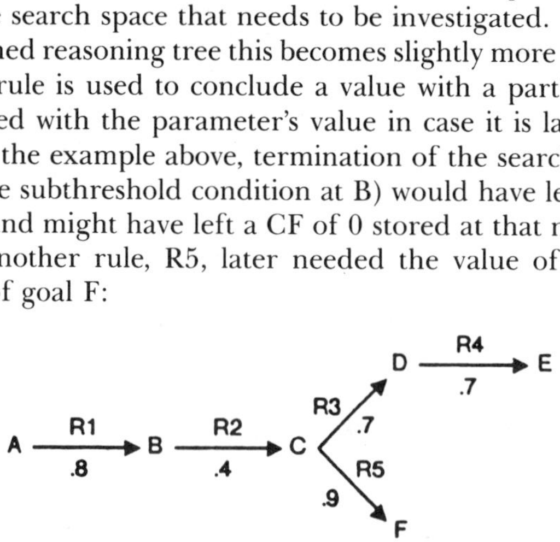

It would be inappropriate to use the unknown value of C stored from the previous inference process, for now it would be appropriate to back-chain further using R1 (the higher CF of 0.9 associated with R5, compared to the composite CF of 0.49 associated with the chaining of rules R3 and R4, keeps the path to A from being subthreshold this time). Thus, if one wants to use previous results only if they are appropriate, it is necessary to store the "vigor" with which a value was investigated along with its CF. Wallis proposed that this be computed by multiplying the CF's from the goal (in this case E) through the value in question. Then, when a node is investigated for a second time via an alternate reasoning chain, this measure of vigor, or *investigation strength,* can be used to determine whether to investigate the node further. If the stored investigation strength is greater than the investigation strength of the new reasoning chain, the old value can be used. Otherwise the backward-chaining process must be repeated over a larger portion of the search space.

Although there is further complexity in these ideas developed by Wallis, the brief discussion here shows some of the ways in which concepts drawn from the CF model have been broadened in other settings. Despite the theoretical limitations discussed above and in the subsequent chapters, these concepts have provided an extremely useful tool for dealing with issues of inexact inference in the expert systems that we have developed.

10.5 An Electronic Exchange Regarding CF's

We close this chapter with a series of informal electronic mail messages that were exchanged by some members of our research group in 1976 (Carli Scott, Bruce Buchanan, Bill Clancey, Victor Yu, and Jan Aikins). Victor was developing the meningitis rule set at the time and was having frequent problems deciding what CF's to assign to individual rules and how to anticipate the ramifications of any decisions made. The messages are included in their entirety. Not only do they provide insight into the way that our ideas about CF's evolved through a collaborative effort over many years, but they are also representative of the kinds of dialogues that occurred frequently among members of the project. Because many of the ideas in this book evolved through such interchanges, we felt it was appropriate to provide one verbatim transcript of a typical discussion. The ideas expressed were fresh at the time and not fully worked out, so the messages (and Clancey's closing memo) should be seen as examples of project style rather than as an exposition of the "last word" on the topics discussed.

Date: 26 Feb 1976
From: Scott
Subject: Summary of discussion
To: MYCIN gang

This is a summary of what I think came out of yesterday's meeting. Please read it and send me comments, objections, etc.

1) Victor [Yu] has assigned certainty factors to his rules based on the relative strengths of the evidence in these rules. While trying to find a numerical scale that would work as he wanted it to with the system's 0.2 cutoff and combining functions, he had to adjust certainty factors of various rules. Now that this scale has been established, however, he assigns certainty factors using this scale, and does NOT adjust certainty factors of rules if he doesn't like the system's performance. Furthermore, he does NO combinatorial analysis before determining what CF to use; he is satisfied that using the scale he has devised, the system's combining function, and the 0.2 cutoff, the program will arrive at the right results for any combination of factors, and if it doesn't, he looks for missing information to add.

2) Assuming that the parameters IDENT and COVERFOR are disambiguated in Victor's set of rules, Ted [Shortliffe] believes the CF's that Victor uses in his rules, and approves of the idea of using a cutoff for COVERFOR since this is what we've been doing with bacteremia (since it is a binary decision, a cutoff makes sense for COVERFOR). Furthermore, this is quite similar to what clinicians do: they accumulate lots of small bits of clinical evidence, then decide if the total is enough to make them cover for a particular organism—independent of what the microbiological evidence suggests.

3) Bruce [Buchanan] and BC [Bill Clancey] still object to Victor's CF's because they seem too precise (since he is working in the 0 to 0.2 range). My claim is that he really isn't making numbers more precise, the difference in CF's from one strength to the next is 0.05 (i.e., the classes of rules he has are assigned CF's 0.05, 0.1, 0.15, 0.2, 0.25, . . .). This is no finer a distinction than we've had in the past—we have rules with CF 0.2, 0.25, 0.3, 0.35. I don't see why the smaller absolute values of the CF's Victor uses makes much difference; the rules have much smaller strengths than any rules we've had before, so they should have smaller CF's.

4) There seems to be concern because Victor believes in his CF's, and relies on them to combine in the right way. In the past, we never dealt with this type of accumulation of small bits of information that would combine to give either enough total info or not (though I believe CF's were designed to handle just such combinations). Since Victor has defined guidelines on deciding how strong the evidence must be in order for a rule to be assigned a certain CF, and since he has tested these guidelines within the framework of MYCIN's combining functions, he believes that it all works as it should. Furthermore, he believes that he can define these "points of reference" so that future medical people can add rules, using the same guideline that Victor has used, and they should fit into the system and work fine with his rules.

5) I am satisfied with what Victor is doing, and would like to try Ted's suggestion of separating COVERFOR from IDENT in Victor's system. I believe the result of this would be that the program would continue to perform very well on meningitis patients, and Ted, Victor, (I believe) Larry [Fagan],

and I would all be happy with the results. I think points (3) and (4) above sum up other people's objections that might remain. If this is so, what are suggestions from people who still aren't happy with the model? Is everyone satisfied with everything now? Are there more objections that I missed? Have I completely misunderstood something? Have I completely misunderstood everything? Please let me know what you think so we can start to work out problems that might remain.

Carli

Date: 27 Feb 1976
From: Buchanan
To: MYCIN gang

Carli,

Thanks for your summary—it appears to be correct in almost every detail. I would like you to try separating COVERFOR and IDENT as soon as possible since that is needed for bacteremia anyway and is a help in clarifying the conceptual basis on which the program makes a recommendation. I also think that everyone will be happy with the results, especially me if it brings the knowledge bases into a common framework.

My concern is I would also like you to begin working on the rerepresentation of the context tree to help us with time relations and the infection-organism link. As Ted described it, you and he have pretty well worked things out. Because it is necessary for the FOREACH[11] mechanism and is desirable for many other reasons, I would like us not to delay it. Do you see problems with this?

As I tried to say yesterday, my reservations with the meningitis system stem from my uneasiness with the CF model, which we all know needs improving (which Pacquerette [a visiting student from France] was starting, but won't finish). I don't want Victor to become dependent on a particular mechanism for combining CF's—because we hope the mechanism will be improved soon. I have no doubt that the rules work well now, and I don't disagree at all with the need for firm reference points for the CF's.

As soon as COVERFOR and IDENT are separate, could you try the meningitis patients again, enlisting whatever help you need? Then we'll be able to decide whether that meets all our specs. After that we can be working on the context tree and time problems while Victor continues development on the medical side. I foresee no difficulty in mapping the CF's from existing rules (meningitis as well as bacteremia) into whatever numbers are appropriate for a new CF model when we have one—with firm reference points if at all possible.

Bruce

PS: I think a reference point for defining how strongly suggestive some evidence is for a conclusion is easier when almost all conclusions are about identities of organisms that should be treated for. In bacteremia the rules conclude about so many different things that it is harder—but no less desir-

---

[11]FOREACH is a quantification primitive in rules.

able—to be precise about what "weakly suggestive" and "strongly suggestive" mean.

Date: 27 Feb 1976
From: Clancey
To: MYCIN gang

Your summarization of the meeting was excellent. Here I will go into more detail about the problem with Victor's choice of certainty factors.

Your claim that Victor's preciseness in selecting CF's is not different from the distinctions made in the past ignores my wariness about the RANGE in which he is being precise. Your examples (0.25, 0.3, 0.35) are greater than 0.2, the range in which I showed that the current system is insensitive to even large variation of the CF's chosen. (That is, a change in the range of ± 0.2 does not affect system performance (rule invocation and success), as long as the numbers are > 0.2.) The area in which Victor is working which is bothersome is <0.2 (your examples: 0.05, 0.1, 0.15, 0.2). What Bruce was saying, I believe, was that accumulation of evidence in this area is going to affect very much the invocation and success of rules. It is in this range that CHANGES to the CF of a rule for purposes of adjusting system performance violate the principle of a rule being a modular, independent chunk of knowledge.

Now, first, Victor tells us that he does not make these adjustments.Rather, he is assigning numbers according to a consistent scale about belief which he has devised in his subdomain. I am very pleased to hear this, and am in full agreement with his claim that such a scale is necessary and should be defined for ALL rules in MYCIN.

What remains disturbing is the certainty factor model itself. Here we have no sure intuition about the performance meaning of 0.05 as opposed to 0.1, yet we are assigning them as if they were significantly different from one another. It is clear to everyone working on the CF model, I believe, that we need a combining function that will make use of these numerical representations of subjective distinctions. For example, I would expect a good model to take as many pieces of 0.1 evidence as Victor deems significant, i.e., makes a condition (parameter value) "true," and bumps the conglomeration above 0.2. The problem here is that I DO NOT expect Victor or anyone to be able to assign facts a weighting that is independent of the entire context. That is, the 0.1 that comes from Rule 371 for CATEGORY FUNGUS may combine (in Victor's mind) with the conclusion in Rule 372 of the same value to give a feeling of the CATEGORY ACTUALLY BEING FUNGUS >0.2, so SAME succeeds. But perhaps the same CF value combination coming from Rule 385 DOES NOT make for belief in the conclusion (NOT >0.2). It seems entirely conceivable in my mind that Victor would find some combination of rule successes to be completely nonsensical. So, he would not know what to make of it at all, and would almost certainly not make the same conclusions as he would if he looked at each set of premise clauses independently.

I am saying here that rules that break observations into many small parts, resulting in CF's <0.2 intended to combine to form an accumulated observation, ignore the total perspective, which says, "Hey, wait a minute, these 6 clauses can't appear together: why was she given corticosteroids if she has

XX? This doesn't mean FUNGUS to me; no, I want to know why that prescription was made." This same criticism does not apply with the same force to many rules with CF >0.2 because they bring together a "more significant set of facts." They do this by capturing (often disjoint) pictures of the world that in themselves MAKE SENSE. I do not at all understand how a rule can be written that can at once stand on its own and yet NOT be significant truth (i.e., believable observation, tangible conclusion). It is my suspicion that Victor has not built a system in which EVIDENCE combines plausibly, but rather a system in which independent rules SUCCEED TOGETHER to make a conclusion that could be expressed as a single rule, and WOULD have to be expressed that way to have a CF > 0.2.

Now, Victor has said that he could have combined these rules to give a body of rules in which these same small observations appear together, thus yielding larger CF's. However, he believes that this would result in far more rules (to allow for the cross product of occurrences), and he would not be sure that he had covered all of the possible cases. Well, certainly, with respect to the latter, we can tell him if the larger set covers all of the various combinations. The question of having far more rules is, I suppose, a valid concern. But at least then we could feel sure that only the PLAUSIBLE observations had been combined.

To summarize, we talk about accumulating "lots of small bits of clinical evidence," but I do not understand how a bit of EVIDENCE could be NOTKNOWN (the definition of CF <=0.2). To me, evidence gathered by a rule should be an all-or-nothing thing—if something more is needed to make the parameter KNOWN [i.e., CF > 0.2], then I expect that there is something to be made explicit in the rule. This is the only way in which I can interpret the notion of a discrete cutoff at 0.2. Above that point I know something; below it I know nothing (NOTKNOWN). The only plausible explanation I have for Victor's small CF's is that they are like tags that record an observation. It would make me much happier to see each of these CF's changed to NOTICEDP, with definite (= 1) CF's. Then these parameters could be combined with evidence garnered from lab rules.

I would be happy to hear other opinions about the 0.2 cutoff and its meaning for rule CF's.

Bill

Date: 28 Feb 1976
From: Aikins
Subject: On Wednesday's meeting
To: MYCIN gang

There are three things that I feel we should consider in our discussions that have not yet been mentioned. The first is a concern about knowledge acquisition. I feel that whatever we decide, the MYCIN acquisition module should be designed so that a recognized medical expert could, without too much difficulty, add a new rule or other piece of knowledge to the MYCIN data base. I wonder if a doctor in Boston would be able to add a meningitis rule to MYCIN without hurting the performance of Victor's system. I got the impression that Victor's system was somewhat fragile in this regard. I doubt that he would want to give up the ability to easily add medical knowledge to MYCIN. I fear that we would be doing just that. (This problem includes the question of maintaining rule modularity.)

My second concern is that even if we can define fairly well what we mean by 0.7, 0.5, anything above 0.2, 0.2, etc., it seems that the next problem will be to define 0.25, 0.225, 0.175, 0.5, etc. We could continue this defining of CF's in smaller and smaller intervals forever. However, I doubt that medical science is exact enough for us to be able to do this.

This brings us to my third concern. In my recent meeting with Dr. Ken Vosti [a professor in Stanford's Division of Infectious Diseases], he stated a problem, already familiar to most of us, that even if we could reach agreement among the infectious disease experts at Stanford as to the "right" CF's to put on our rules, the infectious disease experts on the East Coast and other places would probably not agree with us. Now let's take this one step further. Say we are able to assign fairly straightforward meanings to our CF's. Now we have the problem of a doctor in some other part of the country who doesn't want to use MYCIN because our CF's don't agree with what he would use. In other words, by defining our CF's at all rigorously, we're inviting disagreement. So, concerns two and three are saying that we can never define each number on the 0 to 1.0 scale, and if we could, that might not be such a good idea anyway.

I have no solutions to offer at this time, but I hope everyone will keep these concerns in mind. I feel that CF's are designed to give doctors who read and write the rules a certain "commonsense referent" as to how valid the rule might be. If CF's become more important than that, I fear we will use too much of our medical expertise in deciding on the "right" CF for each rule, time that could be used to add more medical knowledge to the MYCIN data base.

Jan

Date: 29 Feb 1976
From: Yu
Subject: On Wed. meeting and Clancey
To: Clancey, Scott
cc: MYCIN gang

Bill,

1. Why is the system insensitive to CF? Certainly, this is not true for the meningitis rules.

2. Your point about plausible situations is a good one, and deserves further amplification and discussion. The reason I have "separated" the number of premises that in the bacteremia rules would have been combined is that I believe they are independent premises. I don't believe I ever said the reason for separating them is to avoid having too many rules; the reason for separating them is to cover a number of subtle clinical situations that would otherwise not have been considered. More on this later.

3. Finally, I should add that the 0.2 cutoff was selected because it is the one being used for SIGNIFICANCE and I thought it would best mesh with the current system. I must admit that I am surprised at the furor it has

evoked; if you wish to use some other cutoff, that's fine with me—the CF's could be easily adjusted.

4. I didn't understand a few of the points you raised, so I look forward to the next meeting.

Finally, I should say that the system that I have proposed is not meant in any way to replace the current bacteremia rules; it was merely a simple, practical way to handle meningitis. I did not feel the approach used in bacteremia was precise enough to handle meningitis.

Victor

Date: 29 Feb 1976
From: Yu
Subject: On Wed. meeting and Aikins
To: Aikins, Scott
cc: MYCIN gang

Jan,

1. You state that we are giving up the ability to "easily" add rules to MYCIN. Certainly, it is currently "easy" to add new rules to MYCIN; however, it is not so "easy" to rationalize, justify, and analyze these new rules. Furthermore, it becomes "difficult" when the system starts giving incorrect therapy after these new rules have been added.
2. I believe a doctor in Boston would have an "easier" task of adding new meningitis rules, as compared to bacteremia rules. He now has some reference points and definite guidelines on how a rule should be written. Again, the rule is more likely to be compatible with the existing system, since the new rule is written along the same guidelines and same philosophy. This is not the case with the bacteremia rules where it is likely and even probable that any new rule written by a non-MYCIN person could cause the system to malfunction.
3. I have not attempted to specifically define every increment between CF's.
4. I need not remind all of us that we are dealing directly with human lives. If another M.D. on the East Coast disagrees with our CF's and has data (be it strong or weak) as the basis for his disagreement, then we had better know about it. I claim that one of the advantages of specific criteria for CF's is that this "invites disagreement" (or to put it another way—critical analysis of the rules by non-MYCIN experts is possible).
5. What is this mystical "commonsense referent" that you have mentioned? (Likewise, Ted has stated that physicians would PROBABLY agree fairly closely on the CF's currently in MYCIN. If this is true, then my arguments for preciseness are invalid and unnecessary.)
6. Your last point concerning using too much time and effort on the CF question, when we could be adding more medical knowledge—I will merely refer you to Matthew: Chapter 7, verses 24–27.

Cheers,
Victor

Date: 1 Mar 1976
From: Clancey
Subject: More about certainty factors and a reply to your message
To: Yu
cc: MYCIN gang

Thanks for commenting on my remarks on CF's. I am well aware that my observations suffered from vagueness. As you might expect, this was just a first-shot approach to issues that have been bothering me. I am now preparing a paper that discusses rule modularity. I believe that you will find that it clarifies my arguments from last week. Briefly, I see now that the problem is not so much with the CF's you have proposed, but is instead a general issue concerning all rules.

As for the furor, as far as I am concerned, your rules have the precise property I predicted last August would not occur, namely, small CF's. What will come of this discussion, I believe, is primarily a better understanding of rules. More on this later in the week.

I will now briefly reply to your numbered remarks:

1. You will notice that I said the system was insensitive to variations in CF>0.2 in so far as rule success and invocation are concerned. This excludes calculations that use CF's in percentage cutoffs. Do you have other sensitivities in mind?
2. It was Larry who told me that you wanted to form a large rule set from the combinations of these rules. Perhaps this was only the gist of a side argument that centered on allowing for all cases. I look forward to hearing about these "subtle clinical situations that would otherwise not be covered."
3. I have no problem with the 0.2 cutoff, per se.

Bill

---

3 March 1976
From: Clancey
Subject: Modularity of rules
To: Yu
cc: MYCIN gang

I have completed a write-up of my understanding of what we mean by rule independence. I consider this useful as a tutorial to those who perhaps have not fully appreciated the significance of the constraint P(e1 & e2| h) = P(e1|h)*P(e2|h), which is discussed in several of Ted's write-ups on the relation of CF's to probabilities.

For those of you for whom this is old hat by now, I would appreciate it if you would peruse my memo and let me know if I've got it straight.

I've expanded the discussion of plausibility of rule interaction here also. This appears to be an issue worth pursuing.

The memo is CF.MODULAR on my directory. It is about 3 pages long.

Bill Clancey

<CLANCEY>CF.MODULAR.1

I. Introduction

This memo arose from my desire to understand rule CF's of less than the 0.2 threshold. How could such a rule be evidence of something? Does a rule having a CF less than 0.2 pose any problems to the process of combining certainty factors? What does it mean to say that a rule is modular? Must a rule satisfy some property relating to its certainty factor to be considered modular?

After thinking out all of these problems for myself, I re-examined our publications in the light of my new understanding. Alas! The ideas discussed below have long been known and were simply overlooked or undervalued by me. Indeed, I suspect that most of us have to some degree failed to appreciate Ted's thesis, from which I will be quoting below.

II. What Is Modularity?

The following is a restatement of one requirement for rule independence. As Ted discusses in CF.MEMO, it is a necessary assumption for our combining functions to be consistent with probability theory, namely: P(e1 & e2|h) = P(e1|h)*P(e2|h), and the same for ~h (e=premise and h= action of rule).

Let {Ri} be a subset of the UPDATED-BY rules for some parameter P, all of which mention the same value for P in the conclusion, namely VALUEP, though perhaps with different certainty factors. (If P is a yes-no parameter, then this set contains all of the UPDATED-BY rules.) Now let P! be the power set of R, and for every element of P!, let PREMi designate the union of the premises of all rules Rj in the power set element i.

Now for every PREMi that is logically consistent (no subset of premises is unsatisfiable), it must be the case that the CF applied to the new rule PREMi→VALUEP is given by the combining function applied over all rule CF's in the power set element. If so, we can say that these original rules are independent logically and so can contribute evidence incrementally, regardless of the pattern of succession or failure of the set.

This is a requirement for rule modularity. It can also be shown [working from assumption 9 of the memo: P(e1 & e2) = P(e1)*P(e2)] that premises must be independent "for ALL rules dealing with a clinical parameter regardless of the value specified (e.g., all rules that conclude anything about the identity of an organism). This assumption is generally avoided by Bayesians. I have not examined our rules closely with this assumption in mind, but I suspect we may discover several examples of nonindependent PREMISES" (Shortliffe, CF.MEMO). This is a generalization of the above restriction, which I believe is more intuitive.

It is worth reviewing at this time some of the related restrictions on rules and CF's mentioned in Ted's thesis.

A. Given mutually exclusive hypotheses hi for an observation e, the sum of their CF's, CF(hi,e), must not exceed 1. (From CF.MEMO, page 7: "We often find that this rule is broken.")

B. "We must insist that dependent pieces of evidence be grouped into single rather than multiple rules."

C. "The rule acquisition procedure requires a screening process to see if the new rule improperly interacts with other rules in the knowledge base."

Some of the consistency checks Ted discusses are subsumption and rule contradictions.

III. Understanding Modularity

I did not fully appreciate these problems, even after several readings over the past year, until I worked out an example containing nonindependent rules.

Example: Consider the following rules having CF's that I believe to be valid. The rules would be used in a consultation system for deciding whether or not to carry an umbrella.

Rule A: If the weatherman said that there is a 20% chance of rain today, then I expect it to rain today (0.1).

Rule B: If it is summer, then I expect it to rain today (−0.9).

Rule C: If there are many clouds, then I expect it to rain today (0.1).

Now let these rules succeed in various combinations:

Power set element	*Computed CF*	*Preferred CF*	*Evaluation*
A & B & C	−0.71	0.5	wrong
A & B	−0.8	0.21	wrong
A & C	−0.19	?	okay
B & C	−0.8	?	wrong

These rules are not modular—the combined CF does not correspond to what I believe when I form the combination of the premises in my mind. Specifically, I give far more weight to clouds and weatherman's prediction of rain in the summer (when I expect neither) than in the winter (when clouds and 20% chance are common).

Using Webster's definition of belief, "the degree of mental acceptance of an idea or conclusion," I think that it would be fair to say that I DO NOT believe the conclusion of "rain today," given premises A, C, A & C, or B & C. As far as MYCIN's operation is concerned, this corresponds to a CF<0.2. The CF combining function has not worked above because my rules are not independent. (It is also possible for independent rules to combine improperly because the combining function is wrong—more on this later.)

Looking again at the rules I wrote above, I feel that Rule A in particular is a bad rule. It takes a mere fragment of an argument and tries to draw a conclusion. Now admittedly we know something, given that 20% was predicted, but we are being logically naive to think that this fact alone is worth isolating. It depends radically on other information for its usefulness. Moreover, the context in which it is true will radically determine the conclusion we draw from it. We saw above that in summer I am far more inclined to give it weight than in winter. The only thing I AM willing to say given just this clause is that it probably won't be fair (0.3). (Like Wittgenstein, I ask myself, "What do I know now?")

IV. Implications for 0.2 Rules

I see now that the problem I was anticipating in my earlier message will hold if the rules are not modular. My fear was that a rule having a CF<0.2 was more likely to have a premise that was incomplete than was a rule of CF>0.2. I understand now that a 0.2 rule, like any other rule, is acceptable if there is no known argument that involves its premise with that of another rule, other than one that simply adds the evidence together incrementally according to the combining function. A new argument that is built from the evidence mentioned in the other rules is proof that the individual rules are not modular. (Subsumption is an explicit form of this.) Thus, Victor's claim that he wants to allow for all combinations MUST rest on the inherent independence of his premise sets. Again, no conclusion whatsoever should be drawn from the coincidence of any combination of premise sets, other than that arrived at by the CF combining function. Moreover, every conclusion collected incrementally by the combining function must be one Victor would reach with the same strength, given that union of premise clauses (cf., B & C above). In fact, I am willing to believe now that a rule having a CF<0.2 is perhaps MORE likely to be independent because it wouldn't have been given such a small CF unless the author saw it as minimally useful. That is, it stands on its own as a very weak observation having no other inferential value (I am still wary of calling it "evidence"). If it had a higher CF, it would almost certainly be useful in combination with other observations. Based on Victor's decision to separate meningitis clinical and lab rules, I conclude that doctors do not have the ability to relate the two. Is this correct? I believe that Ted has also questioned Victor's rules in this respect.

V. Plausibility

The problem of plausible combination of rules is difficult to anticipate because it is precisely the unanticipated coincidence of rule success that we are most likely to find objectionable. Suppose that we do find two rules D and E that we can't imagine ever succeeding at the same time, yet there is no logical reason for this not to occur (i.e., the rules are not mutually exclusive; not always easy to determine since all rules that cause these rules to be invoked must be examined). In this case we should try to define a new parameter that explains the connection between these two parameters, which we do not as yet understand. (A method of theory formation: ask yourself "What would I think if these two pieces of evidence were true?" Perhaps the actions are in conflict—why? Perhaps the premises never appear together (usually aren't both true)—why not? Do this for the power set of all evidence under consideration.)

VI. What Does This Say About MYCIN's Rule Set?

(1) They must be disjoint (mutually exclusive) within an UPDATED-BY subset, or (2) the parameters in the premises of rules that succeed together must be logically noninteracting. This means that there must be nothing significant about their coincidence. Their contribution separately must be the same as an inference that considers them together. [In pseudochemical terms, the rule CF is a measure of (logical) force, which binds together the clauses of the premise in a single rule.]

Taking my example, I should rewrite the rules and form a new set including A & B & C and A & B. Rules A and C are incomplete. They say nothing here because they say something when a context is added. Leaving them separate led to a nonsensical result (B & C), which CF theory claims should make sense. This is an example of where plausibility of rule interaction must be made at rule acquisition time. Indeed, I believe now that unless we require our rules to be disjoint within an UPDATED-BY set, it will be very difficult to say whether or not a rule is modular. For too long I have assumed that because a rule looks like a discrete object it is necessarily modular. I have assumed that it is sufficient to have a CF combining function that models adequately the process of incrementally collecting evidence, forgetting that this evidence MUST be discrete for the function to be valid. Otherwise, a FUNCTION is replacing a logical argument, which a rule unifying the premises would represent.

VII. Making Rules Modular

It remains to detect if MYCIN's rules are modular. We must look for premises that are still "charged" with inference potential, as measured relative to clauses in other rules. Victor has said that his rules are modular (at least the ones having CF<0.2). If so, there is no problem, though we should be wary about the 0.05/0.15 distinctions. (How is it that "evidence" that is too weak to yield an acceptable conclusion nevertheless is definite enough to be put in one of three CF categories: 0.05, 0.10 and 0.15?)

One method for detecting rule modularity is as follows. Given, for example, three rules A, B, and C, where B and C have the same CF (all three mention VALUEP), then if A & B and A & C are determined to have different certainty factors (where & denotes the process of combining the rules into a single rule), then the rules A, B, and C aren't modular.

On the other hand, given two rules A and B known to be modular (our knowledge of the domain cannot yield an argument that combines the premises), then A & B must have a CF given by the combining function (obviously true for disjoint rules). This gives us a way for evaluating a combining function.

11

A Model of Inexact Reasoning in Medicine

Edward H. Shortliffe and Bruce G. Buchanan

Inexact reasoning is common in the sciences. It is characterized by such phrases as "the art of good guessing," the "softer aspects of physics" (or chemistry, or any other science), and "good scientific judgment." By definition, inexact reasoning defies analysis as applications of sets of inference rules that are expressed in the predicate logic. Yet it need not defy all analysis. In this chapter we examine a model of inexact reasoning applied to a subdomain of medicine. Helmer and Rescher (1960) assert that the traditional concept of "exact" versus "inexact" science, with the social sciences accounting for the second class, has relied on a false distinction usually reflecting the presence or absence of mathematical notation. They point out that only a small portion of natural science can be termed exact—areas such as pure mathematics and subfields of physics in which some of the exactness "has even been put to the ultimate test of formal axiomatization." In several areas of applied natural science, on the other hand, decisions, predictions, and explanations are made only after exact procedures are mingled with unformalized expertise. The general awareness regarding these observations is reflected in the common references to the "artistic" components in the "science of medicine."

During the years since computers were first introduced into the medical arena, researchers have sought to develop techniques for modeling clinical decision making. Such efforts have had a dual motivation. Not only has their potential clinical significance been apparent, but the design of such programs has required an analytical approach to medical reasoning, which has in turn led to distillation of decision criteria that in some cases

This chapter is a shortened and edited version of a paper appearing in *Mathematical Biosciences* 23: 351–379 (1975).

had never been explicitly stated. It is both fascinating and educational for experts to reflect on the inference rules that they use when providing clinical consultations.

Several programs have successfully modeled the diagnostic process. Many of these have relied on statistical decision theory as reflected in the use of Bayes' Theorem for manipulation of conditional probabilities. Use of the theorem, however, requires either large amounts of valid background data or numerous approximations and assumptions. The success of Gorry and Barnett's early work (Gorry and Barnett, 1968) and of a similar study by Warner and coworkers using the same data (Warner et al., 1964) depended to a large extent on the availability of good data regarding several hundred individuals with congenital heart disease.

Although conditional probability provides useful results in areas of medical decision making such as those we have mentioned, vast portions of medical experience suffer from having so few data and so much imperfect knowledge that a rigorous probabilistic analysis, the ideal standard by which to judge the rationality of a physician's decisions, is not possible. It is nevertheless instructive to examine models for the less formal aspects of decision making. Physicians seem to use an ill-defined mechanism for reaching decisions despite a lack of formal knowledge regarding the interrelationships of all the variables that they are considering. This mechanism is often adequate, in well-trained or experienced individuals, to lead to sound conclusions on the basis of a limited set of observations.[1]

The purpose of this chapter is to examine the nature of such nonprobabilistic and unformalized reasoning processes and to propose a model by means of which such incomplete "artistic" knowledge might be quantified. We have developed this model in response to the needs of a computer program that will permit the opinions of experts to become more generally available to nonexperts. The model is, in effect, an approximation to conditional probability. Although conceived with medical decision making in mind, it is potentially applicable to any problem area in which real-world knowledge must be combined with expertise before an informed opinion can be obtained to explain observations or to suggest a course of action.

We begin with a brief discussion of Bayes' Theorem as it has been utilized by other workers in this field. The theorem will serve as a focus for discussion of the clinical problems that we would like to solve by using computer models. The potential applicability of the proposed decision model is then introduced in the context of the MYCIN system. Once the problem has been defined in this fashion, the criteria and numerical characteristics of a quantification scheme will be proposed. We conclude with a discussion of how the model is used by MYCIN when it offers opinions to physicians regarding antimicrobial therapy selection.

---

[1]Intuition may also lead to unsound conclusions, as noted by Schwartz et al. (1973).

11.1 Formulation of the Problem

The medical diagnostic problem can be viewed as the assignment of probabilities to specific diagnoses after analyzing all relevant data. If the sum of the relevant data (or evidence) is represented by e, and d_i is the ith diagnosis (or "disease") under consideration, then $P(d_i|e)$ is the conditional probability that the patient has disease i in light of the evidence e. Diagnostic programs have traditionally sought to find a set of evidence that allows $P(d_i|e)$ to exceed some threshold, say 0.95, for one of the possible diagnoses. Under these circumstances the second-ranked diagnosis is sufficiently less likely (<0.05) that the user is content to accept disease i as the diagnosis requiring therapeutic attention.[2]

Bayes' Theorem is useful in these applications because it allows $P(d_i|e)$ to be calculated from the component conditional probabilities:

$$P(d_i|e) = \frac{P(d_i)\ P(e|d_i)}{\Sigma\ P(d_j)\ P(e|d_j)}$$

In this representation of the theorem, d_i is one of n disjoint diagnoses, $P(d_i)$ is simply the *a priori* probability that the patient has disease i before any evidence has been gathered, and $P(e|d_i)$ is the probability that a patient will have the complex of symptoms and signs represented by e, given that he or she has disease d_i.

We have so far ignored the complex problem of identifying the "relevant" data that should be gathered in order to diagnose the patient's disease. Evidence is actually acquired piece by piece, the necessary additional data being identified on the basis of the likely diagnoses at any given time. Diagnostic programs that mimic the process of analyzing evidence incrementally often use a modified version of Bayes' Theorem that is appropriate for sequential diagnosis (Gorry and Barnett, 1968):

> Let e_1 be the set of all observations to date, and s_1 be some new piece of data. Furthermore, let e be the new set of observations once s_1 has been added to e_1. Then:
>
> $$P(d_i|e) = \frac{P(s_1|d_i\ \&\ e_1)\ P(d_i|e_1)}{\Sigma\ P(s_1|d_j\ \&\ e_1)\ P(d_j|e_1)}$$

The successful programs that use Bayes' Theorem in this form require huge amounts of statistical data, not only $P(s_k|d_j)$ for each of the pieces of

[2]Several programs have also included utility considerations in their analyses. For example, an unlikely but lethal disease that responds well to treatment may merit therapeutic attention because $P(d_i|e)$ is nonzero (although very small).

data, s_k, in e, but also the interrelationships of the s_k within each disease d_j.[3] The congenital heart disease programs (Gorry and Barnett, 1968; Warner et al., 1964) were able to acquire all the necessary conditional probabilities from a survey of several hundred patients with confirmed diagnoses and thus had nonjudgmental data on which to base their Bayesian analyses.

Edwards (1972, pp. 139–140) has summarized the kinds of problems that can arise when an attempt is made to gather the kinds of data needed for rigorous analysis:

> My friends who are expert about medical records tell me that to attempt to dig out from even the most sophisticated hospital's records the frequency of association between any particular symptom and any particular diagnosis is next to impossible—and when I raise the question of complexes of symptoms, they stop speaking to me. For another thing, doctors keep telling me that diseases change, that this year's flu is different from last year's flu, so that symptom-disease records extending far back in time are of very limited usefulness. Moreover, the observation of symptoms is well-supplied with error, and the diagnosis of diseases is even more so; both kinds of errors will ordinarily be frozen permanently into symptom-disease statistics. Finally, even if diseases didn't change, doctors would. The usefulness of disease categories is so much a function of available treatments that these categories themselves change as treatments change—a fact hard to incorporate into symptom-disease statistics.
>
> All these arguments against symptom-disease statistics are perhaps somewhat overstated. Where such statistics can be obtained and believed, obviously they should be used. But I argue that usually they cannot be obtained, and even in those instances where they have been obtained, they may not deserve belief.

An alternative to exhaustive data collection is to use the knowledge that an expert has about the disease—partly based on experience and partly on general principles—to reason about diagnoses. In the case of this judgmental knowledge acquired from experts, the conditional probabilities and their complex interrelationships cannot be acquired in an exhaustive manner. Opinions can be sought and attempts made to quantify them, but the extent to which the resulting numbers can be manipulated as probabilities is not clear. We shall explain this last point more fully as we proceed. First, let us examine some of the reasons that it might be desirable to construct a model that allows us to avoid the inherent problems of explicitly relating the conditional probabilities to one another.

A conditional probability statement is, in effect, a statement of a decision criterion or rule. For example, the expression $P(d_i|s_k)=x$ can be read as a statement that there is a $100x\%$ chance that a patient observed to have symptom s_k has disease d_i. Stated in rule form, it would be

[3]For example, although s_1 and s_2 are independent over all diseases, it may be true that s_1 and s_2 are closely linked for patients with disease d_i. Thus relationships must be known within *each* of the d_j; overall relationships are not sufficient.

IF: The patient has sign or symptom s_k
THEN: Conclude that he has disease d_i with probability x

We shall often refer to statements of conditional probability as decision rules or decision criteria in the diagnostic context. The value of x for such rules may not be obvious (e.g., "y strongly suggests that z is true" is difficult to quantify), but an expert may be able to offer an estimate of this number based on clinical experience and general knowledge, even when such numbers are not readily available otherwise.

A large set of such rules obtained from textbooks and experts would clearly contain a large amount of medical knowledge. It is conceivable that a computer program could be designed to consider all such general rules and to generate a final probability of each d_i based on data regarding a specific patient. Bayes' Theorem would only be appropriate for such a program, however, if values for $P(s_1|d_i)$ and $P(s_1|d_i \text{ \& } s_2)$ could be obtained. As has been noted, these requirements become unworkable, even if the subjective probabilities of experts are used, in cases where a large number of diagnoses (hypotheses) must be considered. The first requires acquiring the inverse of every rule, and the second requires obtaining explicit statements regarding the interrelationships of all rules in the system.

In short, we would like to devise an approximate method that allows us to compute a value for $P(d_i|e)$ solely in terms of $P(d_i|s_k)$, where e is the composite of all the observed s_k. Such a technique will not be exact, but since the conditional probabilities reflect judgmental (and thus highly subjective) knowledge, a rigorous application of Bayes' Theorem will not necessarily produce accurate cumulative probabilities either. Instead, we look for ways to handle decision rules as discrete packets of knowledge and for a quantification scheme that permits accumulation of evidence in a manner that adequately reflects the reasoning process of an expert using the same or similar rules.

11.2 MYCIN's Rule-Based Approach

As has been discussed, MYCIN's principal task is to determine the likely identity of pathogens in patients with infections and to assist in the selection of a therapeutic regimen appropriate for treating the organisms under consideration. We have explained how MYCIN models the consultation process, utilizing judgmental knowledge acquired from experts in conjunction with certain statistical data that are available from the clinical microbiology laboratory and from patient records.

It is useful to consider the advantages provided by a rule-based system for computer use of judgmental knowledge. It should be emphasized that we see these advantages as being sufficiently strong in certain environments that we have devised an alternative and approximate approach that parallels the results available using Bayes' Theorem. We do not argue against the use of Bayes' Theorem in those medical environments in which sufficient data are available to permit its adequate use.

The advantages of rule-based systems for diagnostic consultations include:

1. the use of general knowledge (from textbooks or experts) for consideration of a specific patient (even well-indexed books may be difficult for a nonexpert to use when considering a patient whose problem is not quite the same as those of patients discussed in the text);
2. the use of judgmental knowledge for consideration of very small classes of patients with rare diseases about which good statistical data are not available;
3. ease of modification (since the rules are not explicitly related to one another and there need be no prestructured decision tree for such a system, rule modifications and the addition of new rules need not require complex considerations regarding interactions with the remainder of the system's knowledge);
4. facilitated search for potential inconsistencies and contradictions in the knowledge base (criteria stored explicitly in packets such as rules can be searched and compared without major difficulty);
5. straightforward mechanisms for explaining decisions to a user by identifying and communicating the relevant rules;
6. an augmented instructional capability (a system user may be educated regarding system knowledge in a selective fashion; i.e., only those portions of the decision process that are puzzling need be examined).

We shall use the following rule for illustrative purposes throughout this chapter:

```
IF:   1) The stain of the organism is gram positive, and
      2) The morphology of the organism is coccus, and
      3) The growth conformation of the organism is chains
THEN:    There is suggestive evidence (.7) that the identity
         of the organism is streptococcus
```

This rule reflects our collaborating expert's belief that gram-positive cocci growing in chains are apt to be streptococci. When asked to weight his belief in this conclusion,[4] he indicated a 70% belief that the conclusion was valid. Translated to the notation of conditional probability, this rule seems

[4]In the English-language version of the rules, the program uses phrases such as "suggestive evidence," as in the above example. However, the numbers following these terms, indicating degrees of certainty, are all that is used in the model. The English phrases are not given by the expert and then quantified; they are, in effect, "canned-phrases" used only for translating rules into English representations. The prompt used for acquiring the certainty measure from the expert is as follows: "On a scale of 1 to 10, how much certainty do you affix to this conclusion?"

to say $P(h_1|s_1 \,\&\, s_2 \,\&\, s_3)=0.7$ where h_1 is the hypothesis that the organism is a *Streptococcus*, s_1 is the observation that the organism is gram-positive, s_2 that it is a coccus, and s_3 that it grows in chains. Questioning of the expert gradually reveals, however, that despite the apparent similarity to a statement regarding a conditional probability, the number 0.7 differs significantly from a probability. The expert may well agree that $P(h_1|s_1 \,\&\, s_2 \,\&\, s_3)=0.7$, but he becomes uneasy when he attempts to follow the logical conclusion that therefore $P(\neg h_1|s_1 \,\&\, s_2 \,\&\, s_3)=0.3$. He claims that the three observations are evidence (to degree 0.7) *in favor* of the conclusion that the organism is a *Streptococcus* and should not be construed as evidence (to degree 0.3) *against Streptococcus*. We shall refer to this problem as Paradox 1 and return to it later in the exposition, after the interpretation of the 0.7 in the rule above has been introduced.

It is tempting to conclude that the expert is irrational if he is unwilling to follow the implications of his probabilistic statements to their logical conclusions. Another interpretation, however, is that the numbers he has given should not be construed as probabilities at all, that they are judgmental measures that reflect a level of *belief*. The nature of such numbers and the very existence of such concepts have interested philosophers of science for the last half-century. We shall therefore digress temporarily to examine some of these theoretical issues. We then proceed to a detailed presentation of the quantitative model we propose. In the last section of this chapter, we shall show how the model has been implemented for ongoing use by the MYCIN program.

11.3 Philosophical Background

The familiar P-function[5] of traditional probability theory is a straightforward concept from elementary statistics. However, because of imperfect knowledge and the dependence of decisions on individual judgments, the P-function no longer seems entirely appropriate for modeling some of the decision processes in medical diagnosis. This problem with the P-function has been well recognized and has generated several philosophical treatises

[5]The P-function may be defined in a variety of ways. Emanuel Parzen (1960) suggests a set-theoretical definition: Given a random situation, which is described by a sample description space s, probability is a function P that to every event e assigns a nonnegative real number, denoted by $P(e)$ and called the probability of the event e. The probability function must satisfy three axioms:

Axiom 1: $P(e) \geq 0$ for every event e;
Axiom 2: $P(s) = 1$ for the certain element s;
Axiom 3: $P(e \cup f) = P(e) + P(f)$ if $ef = 0$ or, in words, the probability of the union of two mutually exclusive events is the sum of their probabilities.

during the last 30 years. One difficulty with these analyses is that they are, in general, more theoretical than practical in orientation. They have characterized the problem well but have offered few quantitative or theoretical techniques that lend themselves to computer simulation of related reasoning processes. It is useful to examine these writings, however, in order to avoid recognized pitfalls.

This section therefore summarizes some of the theory that should be considered when analyzing the decision problem that we have described. We discuss several interpretations of probability itself, the theory on which Bayes' Theorem relies. The difficulties met when trying to use the *P*-function during the modeling of medical decision making are reiterated. Then we discuss the theory of confirmation, an approach to the interpretation of evidence. Our discussion argues that confirmation provides a natural environment in which to model certain aspects of medical reasoning. We then briefly summarize some other approaches to the problem, each of which has arisen in response to the inadequacies of applied probability. Although each of these alternate approaches is potentially useful in the problem area that concerns us, we have chosen to develop a quantification scheme based on the concept of confirmation.

11.3.1 Probability

Swinburne (1973) provides a useful classification of the theories of probability proposed over the last 200 years. The first of these, the Classical Theory of Probability, asserts that if the probability of an event is said to be P, then "there are integers m and n such that $P = m/n$ . . . such that n exclusive and exhaustive alternatives must occur, m of which constitute the occurrence of s." This theory, like the second and third to be described, is called "statistical probability" by Swinburne. These interpretations are typified by statements of the form "the probability of an A being a B is P."

The second probability theory cited by Swinburne, the Propensity Theory, asserts that probability propositions "make claims" about a propensity or "would-be" or tendency in things. If an atom is said to have a probability of 0.9 of disintegrating within the next minute, a statement has been made about its propensity to do so.

The Frequency Theory is based on the familiar claim that propositions about probability are propositions about proportions or relative frequencies as observed in the past. This interpretation provides the basis for the statistical data collection used by most of the Bayesian diagnostic programs.

Harré (1970) observes that statistical probability seems to differ syntactically from the sense of probability used in inference problems such as medical diagnosis. He points out that the traditional concept of probability refers to what is likely to turn out to be true (in the future), whereas the other variety of probability examines what has already turned out to be true but cannot be determined directly. Although these two kinds of problems may be approached on the basis of identical observations, the occurrence or nonoccurrence of future events is subject to the probabilistic analysis of statistics, whereas the verification of a belief, hypothesis, or conjecture concerning a truth in the present requires a "process" of analysis commonly referred to as *confirmation*. This distinction on the basis of tense may seem somewhat artificial at first, but it does serve a useful purpose as we attempt to develop a framework for analysis of the diagnosis problem.

Swinburne also discusses two more theories of probability, each of which bears more direct relation to the problem at hand. One is the Subjective Theory originally put forward by Ramsey (1931) and developed in particular by Savage (1974) and de Finetti (1972). In their view, statements of probability regarding an event are propositions regarding people's actual belief in the occurrence (present or future) of the event in question. Although this approach fails as an explanation of statistical probability (where beliefs that may be irrational have no bearing on the calculated probability of, say, a six being rolled on the next toss of a die), it is alluring for our purposes because it attempts to recognize the dependence of decisions, in certain problem areas, on both the weight of evidence and its interpretation as based on the expertise (beliefs) of the individual making the decision. In fact, de Finetti (1972, p. 4) has stated part of our problem explicitly:

> On many occasions decision-makers make use of expert opinion. Such opinions cannot possibly take the form of advice bearing directly on the decision; .... Occasionally, [the expert] is required to state a probability, but it is not easy to find a convenient form in which he can express it.

Furthermore, the goals of the subjective probabilists seem very similar to those which we have also delineated (de Finetti, 1972, p. 144):

> We hold it to be chimerical for anyone to arrive at beliefs, opinions, or determinations without the intervention of his personal judgment. We strive to make such judgments as dispassionate, reflective, and wise as possible by a doctrine which shows where and how they intervene and lays bare possible inconsistencies among judgments.

One way to acquire the subjective probabilities of experts is suggested by Savage and described by a geological analyst as follows (Grayson, 1960, p. 256):

> The simplest [way] is to ask the geologist. . . . The geologist looks at the evidence, thinks, and then gives a figure such as 1 in 5 or 50-50. Admittedly this is difficult. . . . Thus, several ways have been proposed to help the geologist make his probability estimate explicit. . . . The leading proponent of personal [i.e., subjective] probabilities, Savage, proposes what seems to be the most workable method. One can, namely, ask the person not how he feels

> but what he would do in such and such a situation. Accordingly, a geologist would be confronted with a choice-making situation.

There is one principal problem to be faced, however, in attempting to adopt the subjectivist model for our computer program—namely, the subjectivists' criticism of those who avoid a Bayesian approach. Subjectivists assert that the conditional and initial probabilities needed for use of Bayes' Theorem may simply be acquired by asking the opinion of an expert. We must reject this approach when the number of decision criteria becomes large, however, because it would require that experts be asked to quantify an unmanageably large number of interrelationships.[6]

A final point to be made regarding subjectivist theory is that the probabilities so obtained are meant to be utilized by the *P*-function of statistical probability so that inconsistencies among the judgments offered by the experts may be discovered. Despite apparently irrational beliefs that may be revealed in this way ("irrational" here means that the subjective probabilities are inconsistent with the axioms of the *P*-function), the expert opinions provide useful criteria, which may lead to sound decisions if it is accepted that the numbers offered are not necessarily probabilities in the traditional sense. It is our assertion that a new quantitative system should therefore be devised in order to utilize the experts' criteria effectively.

Let us return now to the fifth and final category in Swinburne's list of probability theories (Swinburne, 1973). This is the Logical Theory, which gained its classical exposition in J. M. Keynes' *A Treatise on Probability* (1962). Since that time, its most notable proponent has been Rudolf Carnap. In the Logical Theory, probability is said to be a logical relation between statements of evidence and hypotheses. Carnap describes this and the frequency interpretation of probability as follows (Carnap, 1950, p. 19):

> (i) Probability_1 is the degree of confirmation of a hypothesis *h* with respect to an evidence statement *e*; e.g., an observational report. This is a logical semantical concept. A sentence about this concept is based, not on observation of facts, but on logical analysis. . . .
>
> (ii) Probability_2 is the relative frequency (in the long run) of one property of events or things with respect to another. A sentence about this concept is factual, empirical.

In order to avoid confusion regarding which concept of probability is being discussed, the term *probability* will hereafter be reserved for probability_2, i.e., the *P*-function of statistical probability. Probability_1, or epistemic probability as Swinburne (1973) describes it, will be called *degree of confirmation* in keeping with Carnap's terminology.

---

[6]It would also complicate the addition of new decision criteria since they would no longer be modular and would thus require itemization of all possible interactions with preexisting criteria.

11.3.2 Confirmation

Carnap's interpretation of confirmation rests upon strict logical entailment. Several authors, however, have viewed the subject in a broader context, such as our application requires. For example, just as the observation of a black raven would logically "confirm" the hypothesis that "all ravens are black" (where "confirm" means "lends credence to"), we also want the fact that an organism is gram-positive to "confirm" the hypothesis that it is a *Streptococcus*, even though the conclusion is based on world knowledge and not on logical analysis.

Carnap (1950) makes a useful distinction among three forms of confirmation, which we should consider when trying to characterize the needs of our decision model. He calls these classificatory, comparative, and quantitative uses of the concept of confirmation. These are easily understood by example:

a. classificatory: "the evidence e confirms the hypothesis h"
b. comparative: "e_1 confirms h more strongly than e_2 confirms h" or "e confirms h_1 more strongly than e confirms h_2"
c. quantitative: "e confirms h with strength x"

In MYCIN's task domain, we need to use a semiquantitative approach in order to reach a comparative goal. Thus, although our individual decision criteria might be quantitative (e.g., "gram-positive suggests *Streptococcus* with strength 0.1"), the effort is merely aimed at singling out two or three identities of organisms that are approximately equally likely and that are "comparatively" much more likely than any others. There is no need to quote a number that reflects the consulting expert's degree of certainty regarding his or her decisions.

When quantitative uses of confirmation are discussed, the degree of confirmation of hypothesis h on the basis of evidence e is written as $C[h,e]$. This form roughly parallels the familiar P-function notation for conditional probability, $P(h|e)$. Carnap has addressed the question of whether it is reasonable to quantify degree of confirmation (Carnap, 1950). He notes that, although the concept is familiar to us all, we attempt to use it for comparisons of relative likelihood rather than in a strict numerical sense. In his classic work on the subject, however, he suggested that we all know how to use confirmation as a quantitative concept in contexts such as "predictions of results of games of chance [where] we can determine which numerical value [others] implicitly attribute to probability$_1$, even if they do not state it explicitly, by observing their reactions to betting proposals." The reason for our reliance on the opinions of experts is reflected in his observation that individuals with experience are inclined to offer theoretical arguments to defend their viewpoint regarding a hypothesis; "this shows that they regard probability$_1$ as an objective concept." However, he was willing to admit the subjective nature of such concepts some years later when, in discussing the nature of inductive reasoning, he wrote (Carnap, 1962, p. 317):

> I would think that inductive reasoning should lead, not to acceptance or rejection [of a proposition], but to the assignment of a number to the proposition, viz., its value (credibility value) .... This rational subjective probability ... is sufficient for determining first the rational subjective value of any act, and then a rational decision.

As mentioned above, quantifying confirmation and then manipulating the numbers as though they were probabilities quickly leads to apparent inconsistencies or paradoxes. Carl Hempel presented an early analysis of confirmation (Hempel, 1965), pointing out as we have that $C[h,e]$ is a very different concept from $P(h|e)$. His famous Paradox of the Ravens was presented early in his discussion of the logic of confirmation. Let h_1 be the statement that "all ravens are black" and h_2 the statement that "all nonblack things are nonravens." Clearly h_1 is logically equivalent to h_2. If one were to draw an analogy with conditional probability, it might at first seem valid, therefore, to assert that $C[h_1,e]=C[h_2,e]$ for all e. However, it appears counterintuitive to state that the observation of a green vase supports h_1, even though the observation does seem to support h_2. $C[h,e]$ is therefore different from $P(h|e)$ for it seems somehow wrong that an observation of a vase could logically support an assertion about ravens.

Another characteristic of a quantitative approach to confirmation that distinguishes the concept from probability was well-recognized by Carnap (1950) and discussed by Barker (1957) and Harré (1970). They note that it is counterintuitive to suggest that the confirmation of the negation of a hypothesis is equal to one minus the confirmation of the hypothesis, i.e., $C[h,e]$ is not $1 - C[\neg h,e]$. The streptococcal decision rule asserted that a gram-positive coccus growing in chains is a *Streptococcus* with a measure of support specified as 7 out of 10. This translates to $C[h,e]=0.7$ where h is "the organism is a *Streptococcus*" and e is the information that "the organism is a gram-positive coccus growing in chains." As discussed above, an expert does not necessarily believe that $C[\neg h,e]=0.3$. The evidence is said to be *supportive* of the contention that the organism is a *Streptococcus* and can therefore hardly also support the contention that the organism is *not* a *Streptococcus*.

Since we believe that $C[h,e]$ does not equal $1 - C[\neg h,e]$, we recognize that disconfirmation is somehow separate from confirmation and must be dealt with differently. As Harré (1970) puts it, "we need an independently introduced *D*-function, for disconfirmation, because, as we have already noticed, to confirm something to ever so slight a degree is not to disconfirm it at all, since the favorable evidence for some hypothesis gives no support whatever to the contrary supposition in many cases." Our decision model must therefore reflect this distinction between confirmation and disconfirmation (i.e., confirmatory and disconfirmatory evidence).

The logic of confirmation has several other curious properties that have puzzled philosophers of science (Salmon, 1973). Salmon's earlier analysis on the confirmation of scientific hypotheses (Salmon, 1966) led to the conclusion that the structure of such procedures is best expressed by Bayes' Theorem and a frequency interpretation of probability. Such an assertion is appealing because, as Salmon expresses the point, "it is through this interpretation, I believe, that we can keep our natural sciences empirical and objective." However, our model is not offered as a solution to the theoretical issues with which Salmon is centrally concerned. We have had to abandon Bayes' Theorem and the P-function simply because there are large areas of expert knowledge and intuition that, although amenable in theory to the frequency analysis of statistical probability, defy rigorous analysis because of insufficient data and, in a practical sense, because experts resist expressing their reasoning processes in coherent probabilistic terms.

11.3.3 Other Approaches

There are additional approaches to this problem area that bear mentioning, even though they are peripheral to confirmation and probability as we have described them. One is the *theory of fuzzy sets* first proposed by Zadeh (1965) and further developed by Goguen (1968). The theory attempts to analyze and explain an ancient paradox paraphrased by Goguen as follows:

> If you add one stone to a small heap, it remains small. A heap containing one stone is small. Therefore (by induction) every heap is small.

The term *fuzzy set* refers to the analogy with set theory whereby, for example, the set of tall people contains all 7-foot individuals but may or may not contain a man who is 5 feet 10 inches tall. The "tallness" of a man in that height range is subject to interpretation; i.e., the edge of the set is fuzzy. Thus, membership in a set is not binary-valued (true or false) but is expressed along a continuum from 0 to 1, where 0 means "not in the set," 1 means "in the set," and 0.5 means "equally likely to be in or out of the set." These numbers hint of statistical probability in much the same way that degrees of confirmation do. However, like confirmation, the theory of fuzzy sets leads to results that defy numerical manipulation in accordance with the axioms of the P-function. Although an analogy between our diagnostic problem and fuzzy set theory can be made, the statement of diagnostic decision criteria in terms of set membership does not appear to be a natural concept for the experts who must formulate our rules. Furthermore, the quantification of Zadeh's "linguistic variables" and the mechanisms for combining them are as yet poorly defined. Fuzzy sets have therefore been mentioned here primarily as an example of another semistatistical field in which classic probability theory fails.

There is also a large body of literature discussing the *theory of choice*, an approach to decision making that has been reviewed by Luce and Suppes (1965). The theory deals with the way in which personal preferences and the possible outcomes of an action are considered by an individual who must select among several alternatives. Tversky describes an approach based on "elimination by aspects" (Tversky, 1972), a method by which alternatives are ruled out on the basis of either their undesirable characteristics (aspects) or the desirable characteristics they lack. The theory thus combines preference (utility) with a probabilistic approach. Shackle suggests a similar approach (Shackle, 1952; 1955), but utilizes different terminology and focuses on the field of economics. He describes "expectation" as the act of "creating imaginary situations, of associating them with named future dates, and of assigning to each of the hypotheses thus formed a place on a scale measuring the degree of belief that a specified course of action on our own part will make this hypothesis come true" (Shackle, 1952). Selections among alternatives are made not only on the basis of likely outcomes but also on the basis of uncertainty regarding expected outcomes (hence his term the "logic of surprise").

Note that the theory of choice differs significantly from confirmation theory in that the former considers selection among mutually exclusive actions on the basis of their potential (future) outcomes and personal preferences regarding those outcomes, whereas confirmation considers selection among mutually exclusive hypotheses on the basis of evidence observed and interpreted in the present. Confirmation does not involve personal utilities, although, as we have noted, interpretation of evidence may differ widely on the basis of personal experience and knowledge. Thus we would argue that the theory of choice might be appropriately applied to the selection of therapy once a diagnosis is known, a problem area in which personal preferences regarding possible outcomes clearly play an important role, but that the formation of the diagnosis itself more closely parallels the kind of decision task that engendered the theory of confirmation.

We return, then, to confirmation theory as the most useful way to think about the medical decision-making problem that we have described. Swinburne suggests several criteria for choosing among the various confirmation theories that have been proposed (Swinburne, 1970), but his reasons are based more on theoretical considerations than on the pragmatics of our real-world application. We will therefore propose a technique that, although it draws closely on the theory of confirmation described above, is based on desiderata derived intuitively from the problem at hand and not from a formal list of acceptability criteria.

11.4 The Proposed Model of Evidential Strength

This section introduces our quantification scheme for modeling inexact medical reasoning. It begins by defining the notation that we use and describing the terminology. A formal definition of the quantification function is then presented. The remainder of the section discusses the characteristics of the defined functions.

Although the proposed model has several similarities to a confirmation function such as those mentioned above, we shall introduce new terms for the measurement of evidential strength. This convention will allow us to clarify from the outset that we seek only to devise a system that captures enough of the flavor of confirmation theory that it can be used for accomplishing our computer-based task. We have chosen *belief* and *disbelief* as our units of measurement, but these terms should not be confused with their formalisms from epistemology. The need for two measures was introduced above in our discussion of a disconfirmation measure as an adjunct to a measure for degree of confirmation. The notation will be as follows:

- $MB[h,e] = x$ means "the measure of increased belief in the hypothesis h, based on the evidence e, is x"
- $MD[h,e] = y$ means "the measure of increased disbelief in the hypothesis h, based on the evidence e, is y"

The evidence e need not be an observed event, but may be a hypothesis (itself subject to confirmation). Thus one may write $MB[h_1,h_2]$ to indicate the measure of increased belief in the hypothesis h_1 given that the hypothesis h_2 is true. Similarly $MD[h_1,h_2]$ is the measure of increased disbelief in hypothesis h_1 if hypothesis h_2 is true.

To illustrate in the context of the sample rule from MYCIN, consider e = "the organism is a gram-positive coccus growing in chains" and h = "the organism is a *Streptococcus*." Then $MB[h,e] = 0.7$ according to the sample rule given us by the expert. The relationship of the number 0.7 to probability will be explained as we proceed. For now, let us simply state that the number 0.7 reflects the extent to which the expert's belief that h is true is increased by the knowledge that e is true. On the other hand, $MD[h,e] = 0$ for this example; i.e., the expert has no reason to increase his or her disbelief in h on the basis of e.

In accordance with subjective probability theory, it may be argued that the expert's personal probability $P(h)$ reflects his or her belief in h at any given time. Thus $1 - P(h)$ can be viewed as an estimate of the expert's disbelief regarding the truth of h. If $P(h|e)$ is greater than $P(h)$, the observation of e increases the expert's belief in h while decreasing his or her disbelief regarding the truth of h. In fact, the proportionate decrease in disbelief is given by the following ratio:

$$\frac{P(h|e) - P(h)}{1 - P(h)}$$

This ratio is called the measure of increased belief in h resulting from the observation of e, i.e., $MB[h,e]$.

Suppose, on the other hand, that $P(h|e)$ were less than $P(h)$. Then the observation of e would decrease the expert's belief in h while increasing his or her disbelief regarding the truth of h. The proportionate decrease in belief in this case is given by the following ratio:

$$\frac{P(h) - P(h|e)}{P(h)}$$

We call this ratio the measure of increased disbelief in h resulting from the observation of e, i.e., $MD[h,e]$.

To summarize these results in words, we consider the measure of increased belief, $MB[h,e]$, to be the proportionate decrease in disbelief regarding the hypothesis h that results from the observation e. Similarly, the measure of increased disbelief, $MD[h,e]$, is the proportionate decrease in belief regarding the hypothesis h that results from the observation e, where belief is estimated by $P(h)$ at any given time and disbelief is estimated by $1 - P(h)$. These definitions correspond closely to the intuitive concepts of confirmation and disconfirmation that we have discussed above. Note that since one piece of evidence cannot both favor and disfavor a single hypothesis, when $MB[h,e] > 0$, $MD[h,e] = 0$, and when $MD[h,e] > 0$, $MB[h,e] = 0$. Furthermore, when $P(h|e) = P(h)$, the evidence is independent of the hypothesis (neither confirms nor disconfirms) and $MB[h,e] = MD[h,e] = 0$.

The above definitions may now be specified formally in terms of conditional and *a priori* probabilities:

$$MB[h,e] = \begin{cases} 1 & \text{if } P(h) = 1 \\ \dfrac{\max[P(h|e),P(h)] - P(h)}{\max[1,0] - P(h)} & \text{otherwise} \end{cases}$$

$$MD[h,e] = \begin{cases} 1 & \text{if } P(h) = 0 \\ \dfrac{\min[P(h|e),P(h)] - P(h)}{\min[1,0] - P(h)} & \text{otherwise} \end{cases}$$

Examination of these expressions will reveal that they are identical to the definitions introduced above. The formal definition is introduced, however, to demonstrate the symmetry between the two measures. In addition, we define a third measure, termed a *certainty factor* (CF), that combines the MB and MD in accordance with the following definition:

$$CF[h,e] = MB[h,e] - MD[h,e]$$

The certainty factor is an artifact for combining degrees of belief and disbelief into a single number. Such a number is needed in order to facilitate comparisons of the evidential strength of competing hypotheses. The use of this composite number will be described below in greater detail. The following observations help to clarify the characteristics of the three measures that we have defined (MB, MD, CF):

Characteristics of the Belief Measures

1. Range of degrees:

a. $0 \leq MB[h,e] \leq 1$

b. $0 \leq MD[h,e] \leq 1$

c. $-1 \leq CF[h,e] \leq +1$

2. Evidential strength and mutually exclusive hypotheses:
If h is shown to be certain $[P(h|e) = 1]$:

a. $MB[h,e] = \dfrac{1 - P(h)}{1 - P(h)} = 1$

b. $MD[h,e] = 0$

c. $CF[h,e] = 1$

If the negation of h is shown to be certain $[P(\neg h|e) = 1]$:

a. $MB[h,e] = 0$

b. $MD[h,e] = \dfrac{0 - P(h)}{0 - P(h)} = 1$

c. $CF[h,e] = -1$

Note that this gives $MB[\neg h,e] = 1$ if and only if $MD[h,e] = 1$ in accordance with the definitions of MB and MD above. Furthermore, the number 1 represents absolute belief (or disbelief) for MB (or MD).Thus if $MB[h_1,e] = 1$ and h_1 and h_2 are mutually exclusive, $MD[h_2,e] = 1$.[7]

---

[7]There is a special case of Characteristic 2 that should be mentioned. This is the case of logical truth or falsity where $P(h|e) = 1$ or $P(h|e) = 0$, regardless of e. Popper has also suggested a quantification scheme for confirmation (Popper, 1959) in which he uses $-1 \leq C[h,e] \leq +1$, defining his limits as:

$$-1 = C[\neg h,h] \leq C[h,e] \leq C[h,h] = +1$$

This proposal led one observer (Harré, 1970) to assert that Popper's numbering scheme "obliges one to identify the truth of a self-contradiction with the falsity of a disconfirmed general hypothesis and the truth of a tautology with the confirmation of a confirmed existential hypothesis, both of which are not only question begging but absurd." As we shall demonstrate, we avoid Popper's problem by introducing mechanisms for approaching certainty asymptotically as items of confirmatory evidence are discovered.

3. Lack of evidence:

a. $MB[h,e] = 0$ if h is not confirmed by e (i.e., e and h are independent or e disconfirms h)

b. $MD[h,e] = 0$ if h is not disconfirmed by e (i.e., e and h are independent or e confirms h)

c. $CF[h,e] = 0$ if e neither confirms nor disconfirms h (i.e., e and h are independent)

We are now in a position to examine Paradox 1, the expert's concern that although evidence may support a hypothesis with degree x, it does not support the negation of the hypothesis with degree $1 - x$. In terms of our proposed model, this reduces to the assertion that, when e confirms h:

$$CF[h,e] + CF[\neg h,e] \neq 1$$

This intuitive impression is verified by the following analysis for e confirming h:

$$\begin{aligned} CF[\neg h,e] &= MB[\neg h,e] - MD[\neg h,e] \\ &= 0 - \frac{P(\neg h|e) - P(\neg h)}{-P(\neg h)} \\ &= \frac{[1 - P(h|e)] - [1 - P(h)]}{1 - P(h)} = \frac{P(h) - P(h|e)}{1 - P(h)} \\ CF[h,e] &= MB[h,e] - MD[h,e] \\ &= \frac{P(h|e) - P(h)}{1 - P(h)} - 0 \end{aligned}$$

Thus

$$\begin{aligned} CF[h,e] + CF[\neg h,e] &= \frac{P(h|e) - P(h)}{1 - P(h)} + \frac{P(h) - P(h|e)}{1 - P(h)} \\ &= 0 \end{aligned}$$

Clearly, this result occurs because (for any h and any e) $MB[h,e] = MD[\neg h,e]$. This conclusion is intuitively appealing since it states that evidence that supports a hypothesis disfavors the negation of the hypothesis to an equal extent.

We noted earlier that experts are often willing to state degrees of belief in terms of conditional probabilities but they refuse to follow the assertions to their logical conclusions (e.g., Paradox 1 above). It is perhaps revealing to note, therefore, that when the *a priori* belief in a hypothesis is small (i.e.,

$P(h)$ is close to zero), the CF of a hypothesis confirmed by evidence is approximately equal to its conditional probability on that evidence:

$$\text{CF}[h,e] = \text{MB}[h,e] - \text{MD}[h,e] = \frac{P(h|e) - P(h)}{1 - P(h)} - 0 \approx P(h|e)$$

whereas, as shown above, $\text{CF}[\neg h,e] = -P(h|e)$ in this case. This observation suggests that confirmation, to the extent that it is adequately represented by CF's, is close to conditional probability (in certain cases), although it still defies analysis as a probability measure.

We believe, then, that the proposed model is a plausible representation for the numbers an expert gives when asked to quantify the strength of his or her judgmental rules. The expert gives a positive number ($\text{CF} > 0$) if the hypothesis is confirmed by observed evidence, suggests a negative number ($\text{CF} < 0$) if the evidence lends credence to the negation of the hypothesis, and says there is no evidence at all ($\text{CF} = 0$) if the observation is independent of the hypothesis under consideration. The CF combines knowledge of both $P(h)$ and $P(h|e)$. Since the expert often has trouble stating $P(h)$ and $P(h|e)$ in quantitative terms, there is reason to believe that a CF that weights both the numbers into a single measure is actually a more natural intuitive concept (e.g., "I don't know what the probability is that all ravens are black, but I *do* know that every time you show me an additional black raven my belief is increased by x that all ravens are black.").

If we therefore accept CF's rather than probabilities from experts, it is natural to ask under what conditions the physician's behavior based on CF's is irrational.[8] We know from probability theory, for example, that if there are n mutually exclusive hypotheses h_i, at least one of which must be true, then $\Sigma^n P(h_i|e) = 1$ for all e. In the case of certainty factors, we can also show that there are limits on the sums of CF's of mutually exclusive hypotheses. Judgmental rules acquired from experts must respect these limits or else the rules will reflect irrational quantitative assignments.

Sums of CF's of mutually exclusive hypotheses have two limits—a lower limit for disconfirmed hypotheses and an upper limit for confirmed hypotheses. The lower limit is the obvious value that results because $\text{CF}[h,e] \geqslant -1$ and because more than one hypothesis may have $\text{CF} = -1$. Note first that a single piece of evidence may absolutely disconfirm several of the competing hypotheses. For example, if there are n colors in the universe and C_i is the ith color, then ARC_i may be used as an informal notation to denote the hypothesis that all ravens have color C_i. If we add the hypothesis ARC_0 that some ravens have different colors from others, we know $\Sigma_0^n P(\text{ARC}_i) = 1$. Consider now the observation e that there is a raven of color C_n. This single observation allows us to conclude that $\text{CF}[\text{ARC}_i,e] = -1$ for $1 \leqslant i \leqslant n - 1$. Thus, since these $n - 1$ hypotheses

[8]We assert that behavior is irrational if actions taken or decisions made contradict the result that would be obtained under a probabilistic analysis of the behavior.

are absolutely disconfirmed by the observation e, Σ_1^{n-1} CF[ARC$_i$,e] = $-(n - 1)$. This analysis leads to the general statement that, if k mutually exclusive hypotheses h_i are disconfirmed by an observation e:

$$\Sigma_1^k \text{ CF}[h_i,e] \geqslant -k \text{ [for } h_i \text{ disconfirmed by } e]$$

In the colored raven example, the observation of a raven with color C_n still left two hypotheses in contention, namely ARC$_n$ and ARC$_0$. What, then, are CF[ARC$_n$,e], CF[ARC$_0$,e], and the sum of CF[ARC$_n$,e] and CF[ARC$_0$,e]? It can be shown that, if k mutually exclusive hypotheses h_i are confirmed by an observation e, the sum of their CF's does not have an upper limit of k but rather:

$$\Sigma^k \text{ CF}[h_i,e] \leqslant 1 \text{ [for } h_i \text{ confirmed by } e]$$

In fact, Σ^k CF[h_i,e] is *equal* to 1 if and only if $k = 1$ *and* e implies h_1 with certainty, but the sum can get arbitrarily close to 1 for small k and large n. The analyses that lead to these conclusions are available elsewhere (Shortliffe, 1974).

The last result allows us to analyze critically new decision rules given by experts. Suppose, for example, we are given the following rules: CF[h_1,e] = 0.7 and CF[h_2,e] = 0.4, where h_1 is "the organism is a *Streptococcus*," h_2 is "the organism is a *Staphylococcus*," and e is "the organism is a gram-positive coccus growing in chains." Since h_1 and h_2 are mutually exclusive, the observation that Σ CF[h_i,e] > 1 tells us that the suggested certainty factors are inappropriate. The expert must either adjust the weightings, or we must normalize them so that their sum does not exceed 1. Because behavior based on these rules would be irrational, we must change the rules.

11.5 The Model as an Approximation Technique

Certainty factors provide a useful way to think about confirmation and the quantification of degrees of belief. However, we have not yet described how the CF model can be usefully applied to the medical diagnosis problem. The remainder of this chapter will explain conventions that we have introduced in order to use the certainty factor model. Our starting assumption is that the numbers given us by experts who are asked to quantify their degree of belief in decision criteria are adequate approximations to the numbers that would be calculated in accordance with the definitions of MB and MD if the requisite probabilities were known.

When we discussed Bayes' Theorem earlier, we explained that we would like to devise a method that allows us to approximate the value for $P(d_i|e)$ solely from the $P(d_i|s_k)$, where d_i is the ith possible diagnosis, s_k is the

kth clinical observation, and e is the composite of all the observed s_k. This goal can be rephrased in terms of certainty factors as follows:

> Suppose that MB$[d_i,s_k]$ is known for each s_k, MD$[d_i,s_k]$ is known for each s_k, and e represents the conjunction of all the s_k. Then our goal is to calculate CF$[d_i,e]$ from the MB's and MD's known for the individual s_k's.

Suppose that $e = s_1 \,\&\, s_2$ and that e confirms d_i. Then:

$$\text{CF}[d_i,e] = \text{MB}[d_i,e] - 0 = \frac{P(d_i|e) - P(d_i)}{1 - P(d_i)}$$

$$= \frac{P(d_i|s_1 \,\&\, s_2) - P(d_i)}{1 - P(d_i)}$$

There is no exact representation of CF$[d_i,s_1 \,\&\, s_2]$ purely in terms of CF$[d_i,s_1]$ and CF$[d_i,s_2]$; the relationship of s_1 to s_2, within d_i and all other diagnoses, needs to be known in order to calculate $P(d_i|s_1 \,\&\, s_2)$. Furthermore, the CF scheme adds one complexity not present with Bayes' Theorem because we are forced to keep MB's and MD's isolated from one another. Suppose s_1 confirms d_i (MB > 0) but s_2 disconfirms d_i (MD > 0). Then consider CF$[d_i,s_1 \,\&\, s_2]$. In this case, CF$[d_i,s_1 \,\&\, s_2]$ must reflect both the disconfirming nature of s_2 and the confirming nature of s_1. Although these measures are reflected in the component CF's (it is intuitive in this case, for example, that CF$[d_i,s_2] \leq$ CF$[d_i,s_1 \,\&\, s_2] \leq$ CF$[d_i,s_1]$), we shall demonstrate that it is important to handle component MB's and MD's separately in order to preserve commutativity (see Item 3 of the list of defining criteria below). We have therefore developed an approximation technique for handling the net evidential strength of incrementally acquired observations. The combining convention must satisfy the following criteria (where $e+$ represents all confirming evidence acquired to date, and $e-$ represents all disconfirming evidence acquired to date):

Defining Criteria

1. Limits:

a. MB$[h,e+]$ increases toward 1 as confirming evidence is found, equaling 1 if and only if a piece of evidence logically implies h with certainty

b. MD$[h,e-]$ increases toward 1 as disconfirming evidence is found, equaling 1 if and only if a piece of evidence logically implies $\neg h$ with certainty

c. CF$[h,e-] \leq$ CF$[h,e- \,\&\, e+] \leq$ CF$[h,e+]$

These criteria reflect our desire to have the measure of belief approach certainty asymptotically as partially confirming evidence is acquired, and to have the measure of disbelief approach certainty asymptotically as partially disconfirming evidence is acquired.

2. Absolute confirmation or disconfirmation:

a. If MB$[h,e+] = 1$, then MD$[h,e-] = 0$ regardless of the disconfirming evidence in $e-$; i.e., CF$[h,e+] = 1$

b. If MD$[h,e-] = 1$, then MB$[h,e+] = 0$ regardless of the confirming evidence in $e+$; i.e., CF$[h,e-] = -1$

c. The case where MB$[h,e+]$ = MD$[h,e-] = 1$ is contradictory and hence the CF is undefined

3. Commutativity:

If s_1 & s_2 indicates an ordered observation of evidence, first s_1 and then s_2:

a. MB$[h,s_1$ & $s_2]$ = MB$[h,s_2$ & $s_1]$

b. MD$[h,s_1$ & $s_2]$ = MD$[h,s_2$ & $s_1]$

c. CF$[h,s_1$ & $s_2]$ = CF$[h,s_2$ & $s_1]$

The order in which pieces of evidence are discovered should not affect the level of belief or disbelief in a hypothesis. These criteria assure that the order of discovery will not matter.

4. Missing information:

If $s_?$ denotes a piece of potential evidence, the truth or falsity of which is unknown:

a. MB$[h,s_1$ & $s_?]$ = MB$[h,s_1]$

b. MD$[h,s_1$ & $s_?]$ = MD$[h,s_1]$

c. CF$[h,s_1$ & $s_?]$ = CF$[h,s_1]$

The decision model should function by simply disregarding rules of the form CF$[h,s_?] = x$ if the truth or falsity of $s_?$ cannot be determined.

A number of observations follow from these criteria. For example, Items 1 and 2 indicate that the MB of a hypothesis never decreases unless its MD goes to 1. Similarly, the MD never decreases unless the MB goes to 1. As evidence is acquired sequentially, both the MB and MD may become nonzero. Thus CF = MB − MD is an important indicator of the *net* belief in a hypothesis in light of current evidence. Furthermore, a certainty factor of zero may indicate either the absence of both confirming and disconfirming evidence (MB = MD = 0) or the observation of pieces of evidence that are equally confirming and disconfirming (MB = MD, where each is nonzero). Negative CF's indicate that there is more reason to disbelieve the hypothesis than to believe it. Positive CF's indicate that the hypothesis is more strongly confirmed than disconfirmed.

It is important also to note that, if $e = e+ \ \& \ e-$, then CF$[h,e]$ represents the certainty factor for a complex new rule that could be given us by an expert. CF$[h,e]$, however, would be a highly specific rule customized for the few patients satisfying *all* the conditions specified in $e+$ and $e-$. Since the expert gives us only the component rules, we seek to devise a mechanism whereby a calculated cumulative CF$[h,e]$, based on MB$[h,e+]$ and MD$[h,e-]$, gives a number close to the CF$[h,e]$ that would be calculated if all the necessary conditional probabilities were known.

The first of the following four combining functions satisfies the criteria that we have outlined. The other three functions are necessary conventions for implementation of the model.

Combining Functions

1. Incrementally acquired evidence:

$$\mathrm{MB}[h,s_1 \ \& \ s_2] = \begin{cases} 0 & \text{if } \mathrm{MD}[h,s_1 \ \& \ s_2] = 1 \\ \mathrm{MB}[h,s_1] + \mathrm{MB}[h,s_2](1 - \mathrm{MB}[h,s_1]) & \text{otherwise} \end{cases}$$

$$\mathrm{MD}[h,s_1 \ \& \ s_2] = \begin{cases} 0 & \text{if } \mathrm{MB}[h,s_1 \ \& \ s_2] = 1 \\ \mathrm{MD}[h,s_1] + \mathrm{MD}[h,s_2](1 - \mathrm{MD}[h,s_1]) & \text{otherwise} \end{cases}$$

2. Conjunctions of hypotheses:

$$\mathrm{MB}[h_1 \ \& \ h_2,e] = \min(\mathrm{MB}[h_1,e], \mathrm{MB}[h_2,e])$$

$$\mathrm{MD}[h_1 \ \& \ h_2,e] = \max(\mathrm{MD}[h_1,e], \mathrm{MD}[h_2,e])$$

3. Disjunctions of hypotheses:

$$\mathrm{MB}[h_1 \text{ or } h_2,e] = \max(\mathrm{MB}[h_1,e], \mathrm{MB}[h_2,e])$$

$$\mathrm{MD}[h_1 \text{ or } h_2,e] = \min(\mathrm{MD}[h_1,e], \mathrm{MD}[h_2,e])$$

4. Strength of evidence:

If the truth or falsity of a piece of evidence s_1 is not known with certainty, but a CF (based on prior evidence e) is known reflecting the degree of belief in s_1, then if MB$'[h,s_1]$ and MD$'[h,s_1]$ are the degrees of belief and disbelief in h when s_1 is known to be true with certainty (i.e., these are the decision rules acquired from the expert) then the actual degrees of belief and disbelief are given by:

$$\mathrm{MB}[h,s_1] = \mathrm{MB}'[h,s_1] \cdot \max(0, \mathrm{CF}[s_1,e])$$

$$\mathrm{MD}[h,s_1] = \mathrm{MD}'[h,s_1] \cdot \max(0, \mathrm{CF}[s_1,e])$$

This criterion relates to our previous statement that evidence in favor of a hypothesis may itself be a hypothesis subject to confirmation. Suppose, for instance, you are in a darkened room when testing the generalization that all ravens are black. Then the observation of a raven that you think is black, but that may be navy blue or purple, is less strong evidence in favor of the hypothesis that all ravens are black than if the sampled raven were known with certainty to be black. Here the hypothesis being tested is "*all* ravens are black," and the evidence is itself a hypothesis, namely the uncertain observation "*this* raven is black."

Combining Function 1 simply states that, since an MB (or MD) represents a proportionate decrease in disbelief (or belief), the MB (or MD) of a newly acquired piece of evidence should be applied proportionately to the disbelief (or belief) still remaining. Combining Function 2a indicates that the measure of belief in the conjunction of two hypotheses is only as good as the belief in the hypothesis that is believed less strongly, whereas Combining Function 2b indicates that the measure of disbelief in such a conjunction is as strong as the disbelief in the most strongly disconfirmed. Combining Function 3 yields complementary results for disjunctions of hypotheses. The corresponding CF's are merely calculated using the definition CF = MB − MD. Readers are left to satisfy themselves that Combining Function 1 satisfies the defining criteria.[9]

Combining Functions 2 and 3 are needed in the use of Combining Function 4. Consider, for example, a rule such as:

$$\mathrm{CF}'[h,s_1 \;\&\; s_2 \;\&\; (s_3 \text{ or } s_4)] = x$$

Then, by Combining Function 4:

$$\begin{aligned}\mathrm{CF}[h,s_1 \;\&\; s_2 \;\&\; (s_3 \text{ or } s_4)] &= x \cdot \max(0,\mathrm{CF}[s_1 \;\&\; s_2 \;\&\; (s_3 \text{ or } s_4),e]) \\ &= x \cdot \max(0,\mathrm{MB}[s_1 \;\&\; s_2 \;\&\; (s_3 \text{ or } s_4),e] \\ &\qquad - \mathrm{MD}[s_1 \;\&\; s_2 \;\&\; (s_3 \text{ or } s_4),e])\end{aligned}$$

[9]Note that $\mathrm{MB}[h,s_?] = \mathrm{MD}[h,s_?] = 0$ when examining Criterion 4.

Thus we use Combining Functions 2 and 3 to calculate:

$$\begin{aligned} \mathrm{MB}[s_1 \,\&\, s_2 \,\&\, (s_3 \text{ or } s_4),e] &= \min(\mathrm{MB}[s_1,e], \mathrm{MB}[s_2,e], \mathrm{MB}[s_3 \text{ or } s_4,e]) \\ &= \min(\mathrm{MB}[s_1,e], \mathrm{MB}[s_2,e], \\ &\qquad \max(\mathrm{MB}[s_3,e], \mathrm{MB}[s_4,e])) \end{aligned}$$

MD[s_1 & s_2 & (s_3 or s_4),e] is calculated similarly.

An analysis of Combining Function 1 in light of the probabilistic definitions of MB and MD does not prove to be particularly enlightening. The assumptions implicit in this function include more than an acceptance of the independence of s_1 and s_2. The function was conceived purely on intuitive grounds in that it satisfied the four defining criteria listed. However, some obvious problems are present. For example, the function always causes the MB or MD to increase, regardless of the relationship between new and prior evidence. Yet Salmon has discussed an example from subparticle physics (Salmon, 1973) in which either of two observations taken alone confirms a given hypothesis, but their conjunction disproves the hypothesis absolutely! Our model assumes the absence of such aberrant situations in the field of application for which it is designed. The problem of formulating a more general quantitative system for measuring confirmation is well recognized and referred to by Harré (1970): "The syntax of confirmation has nothing to do with the logic of probability in the numerical sense, and it seems very doubtful if any single, general notion of confirmation can be found which can be used in all or even most scientific contexts." Although we have suggested that perhaps there *is* a numerical relationship between confirmation and probability, we agree that the challenge for a confirmation quantification scheme is to demonstrate its usefulness within a given context, preferably without sacrificing human intuition regarding what the quantitative nature of confirmation should be.

Our challenge with Combining Function 1, then, is to demonstrate that it is a close enough approximation for our purposes. We have attempted to do so in two ways. First, we have implemented the function as part of the MYCIN system (Section 11.6) and have demonstrated that the technique models the conclusions of the expert from whom the rules were acquired. Second, we have written a program that allows us to compare CF's computed both from simulated real data and by using Combining Function 1. Our notation for the following discussion will be as follows:

CF*[h,e] = the computed CF using the definition of CF from Section 11.4 (i.e., "perfect knowledge" since $P(h|e)$ and $P(h)$ are known)

CF[h,e] = the computed CF using Combining Function 1 and the known MB's and MD's for each s_k where e is the composite of the s_k's (i.e., $P(h|e)$ not known, but $P(h|s_k)$ and $P(h)$ known for calculation of MB[h,s_k] and MD[h,s_k])

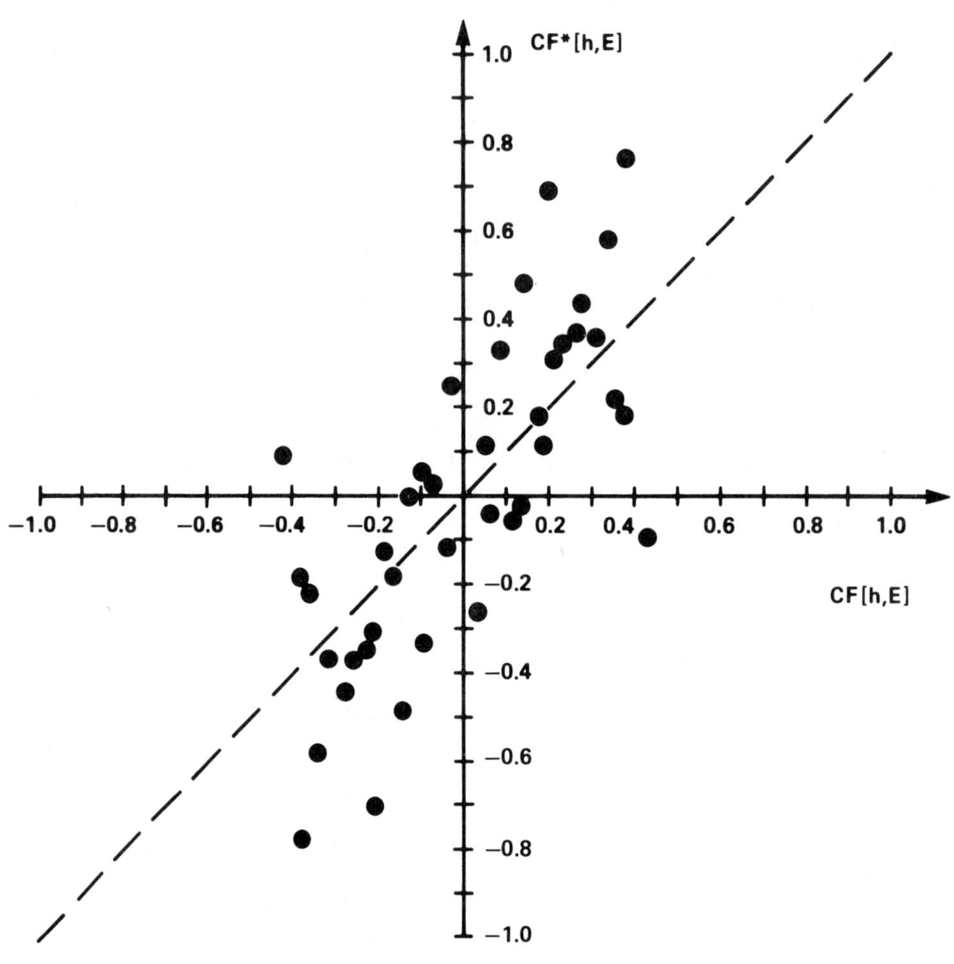

FIGURE 11-1 Chart demonstrating the degree of agreement between CF and CF* for a sample data base. CF is an approximation of CF*. The terms are defined in the text.

The program was run on sample data simulating several hundred patients. The question to be asked was whether CF[*h,e*] is a good approximation to CF*[*h,e*]. Figure 11-1 is a graph summarizing our results. For the vast majority of cases, the approximation does not produce a CF[*h,e*] radically different from the true CF*[*h,e*]. In general, the discrepancy is greatest when Combining Function 1 has been applied several times (i.e., several pieces of evidence have been combined). The most aberrant points, however, are those that represent cases in which pieces of evidence were strongly interrelated for the hypothesis under consideration (termed *con-*

ditional nonindependence). This result is expected because it reflects precisely the issue that makes it difficult to use Bayes' Theorem for our purposes.

Thus we should emphasize that we have not avoided many of the problems inherent with the use of Bayes' Theorem in its exact form. We have introduced a new quantification scheme, which, although it makes many assumptions similar to those made by subjective Bayesian analysis, permits us to use criteria as rules and to manipulate them to the advantages described earlier. In particular, the quantification scheme allows us to consider confirmation separately from probability and thus to overcome some of the inherent problems that accompany an attempt to put judgmental knowledge into a probabilistic format. Just as Bayesians who use their theory wisely must insist that events be chosen so that they are independent (unless the requisite conditional probabilities are known), we must insist that dependent pieces of evidence be grouped into single rather than multiple rules. As Edwards (1972) has pointed out, a similar strategy must be used by Bayesians who are unable to acquire all the necessary data:

> An approximation technique is the one now most commonly used. It is simply to combine conditionally non-independent symptoms into one grand symptom, and obtain [quantitative] estimates for that larger more complex symptom.

The system therefore becomes unworkable for applications in which large numbers of observations must be grouped in the premise of a single rule in order to ensure independence of the decision criteria. In addition, we must recognize logical subsumption when examining or acquiring rules and thus avoid counting evidence more than once. For example, if s_1 implies s_2, then $CF[h,s_1 \& s_2] = CF[h,s_1]$ regardless of the value of $CF[h,s_2]$. Function 1 does not "know" this. Rules must therefore be acquired and utilized with care. The justification for our approach therefore rests not with a claim of improving on Bayes' Theorem but rather with the development of a mechanism whereby judgmental knowledge can be efficiently represented and utilized for the modeling of medical decision making, especially in contexts where (a) statistical data are lacking, (b) inverse probabilities are not known, and (c) conditional independence can be assumed in most cases.

11.6 MYCIN's Use of the Model

Formal quantification of the probabilities associated with medical decision making can become so frustrating that some investigators have looked for ways to dispense with probabilistic information altogether (Ledley, 1973). Diagnosis is not a deterministic process, however, and we believe that it should be possible to develop a quantification technique that approximates probability and Bayesian analysis and that is appropriate for use in those cases where formal analysis is difficult to achieve. The certainty factor model that we have introduced is such a scheme. The MYCIN program uses certainty factors to accumulate evidence and to decide on likely identities for organisms causing disease in patients with bacterial infections. A therapeutic regimen is then determined—one that is appropriate to cover for the organisms requiring therapy.

MYCIN remembers the alternate hypotheses that are confirmed or disconfirmed by the rules for inferring an organism's identity. With each hypothesis is stored its MB and MD, both of which are initially zero. When a rule for inferring identity is found to be true for the patient under consideration, the action portion of the rule allows either the MB or the MD of the relevant hypothesis to be updated using Combining Function 1. When all applicable rules have been executed, the final CF may be calculated, for each hypothesis, using the definition CF = MB − MD. These alternate hypotheses may then be compared on the basis of their cumulative certainty factors. Hypotheses that are most highly confirmed thus become the basis of the program's therapeutic recommendation.

Suppose, for example, that the hypothesis h_1 that the organism is a *Streptococcus* has been confirmed by a single rule with a CF = 0.3. Then, if e represents all evidence to date, $\text{MB}[h_1,e] = 0.3$ and $\text{MD}[h_1,e] = 0$. If a new rule is now encountered that has CF = 0.2 in support of h_1, and if e is updated to include the evidence in the premise of the rule, we now have $\text{MB}[h_1,e] = 0.44$ and $\text{MD}[h_1,e] = 0$. Suppose a final rule is encountered for which CF = −0.1. Then if e is once again updated to include all current evidence, we use Function 1 to obtain $\text{MB}[h_1,e] = 0.44$ and $\text{MD}[h_1,e] = 0.1$. If no further system knowledge allows conclusions to be made regarding the possibility that the organism is a *Streptococcus*, we calculate a final result, $\text{CF}[h_1,e] = 0.44 - 0.1 = 0.34$. This number becomes the basis for comparison between h_1 and all the other possible hypotheses regarding the identity of the organism.

It should be emphasized that this same mechanism is used for evaluating *all* knowledge about the patient, not just the identity of pathogens. When a user answers a system-generated question, the associated certainty factor is assumed to be +1 unless he or she explicitly modifies the response with a CF (multiplied by ten) enclosed in parentheses. Thus, for example, the following interaction might occur (MYCIN's question is in lower-case letters):

```
14) Did the organism grow in clumps, chains, or pairs?
** CHAINS (6) PAIRS (3) CLUMPS (−8)
```

This capability allows the system automatically to incorporate the user's uncertainties into its decision processes. A rule that referenced the growth conformation of the organism would in this case find:

$$\begin{array}{llll} \text{MB[chains},e] & = 0.6 & \text{MD[chains},e] & = 0 \\ \text{MB[pairs},e] & = 0.3 & \text{MD[pairs},e] & = 0 \\ \text{MB[clumps},e] & = 0 & \text{MD[clumps},e] & = 0.8 \end{array}$$

Consider, then, the sample rule:

$$\text{CF}[h_1,s_1 \ \& \ s_2 \ \& \ s_3] = 0.7$$

where h_1 is the hypothesis that the organism is a *Streptococcus*, s_1 is the observation that the organism is gram-positive, s_2 that it is a coccus, and s_3 that it grows in chains. Suppose gram stain and morphology were known to the user with certainty, so that MYCIN has recorded:

$$\text{CF}[s_1,e] = 1 \qquad \text{CF}[s_2,e] = 1$$

In the case above, however, MYCIN would find that

$$\text{CF[chains},e] = \text{CF}[s_3,e] = 0.6 - 0 = 0.6$$

Thus it is no longer appropriate to use the rule in question with its full confirmatory strength of 0.7. That CF was assigned by the expert on the assumption that all three conditions in the premise would be true with certainty. The modified CF is calculated using Combining Function 4:

$$\begin{aligned} \text{CF}[h_1,s_1 \ \& \ s_2 \ \& \ s_3] &= \text{MB}[h_1,s_1 \ \& \ s_2 \ \& \ s_3] - \text{MD}[h_1,s_1 \ \& \ s_2 \ \& \ s_3] \\ &= 0.7 \cdot \max(0, \text{CF}[s_1 \ \& \ s_2 \ \& \ s_3,e]) - 0 \end{aligned}$$

Calculating CF[s_1 & s_2 & s_3,e] using Combining Function 2 gives:

$$\begin{aligned} \text{CF}[h_1,s_1 \ \& \ s_2 \ \& \ s_3] &= (0.7)\ (0.6) - 0 \\ &= 0.42 - 0 \end{aligned}$$

i.e.,

$$\text{MB}[h_1,s_1 \ \& \ s_2 \ \& \ s_3] = 0.42$$

and

$$\text{MD}[h_1,s_1 \ \& \ s_2 \ \& \ s_3] = 0$$

Thus the strength of the rule is reduced to reflect the uncertainty regarding s_3. Combining Function 1 is now used to combine 0.42 (i.e., MB[h_1,s_1 & s_2 & s_3]) with the previous MB for the hypothesis that the organism is a *Streptococcus*.

We have shown that the numbers thus calculated are approximations at best. Hence it is not justifiable simply to accept as correct the hypothesis with the highest CF after all relevant rules have been tried. Therapy is therefore chosen to cover for all identities of organisms that account for a sufficiently high proportion of the possible hypotheses on the basis of their

CF's. This is accomplished by ordering them from highest to lowest and selecting all those on the list until the sum of their CF's exceeds z (where z is equal to 0.9 times the sum of the CF's for *all* confirmed hypotheses). This *ad hoc* technique therefore uses a semiquantitative approach in order to attain a comparative goal.

Finally, it should be noted that our definition of CF's allows us to validate those of our rules for which frequency data become available. This would become increasingly important if the program becomes a working tool in the clinical setting where it can actually be used to gather the statistical data needed for its own validation. Otherwise, validation necessarily involves the comments of recognized infectious disease experts who are asked to evaluate the program's decisions and advice. Evaluations of MYCIN have shown that the program can give advice similar to that suggested by infectious disease experts (see Part Ten). Studies such as these have allowed us to gain confidence that the certainty factor approach is robust enough for use in a decision-making domain such as antimicrobial selection.

12

Probabilistic Reasoning and Certainty Factors

J. Barclay Adams

The development of automated assistance for medical diagnosis and decision making is an area of both theoretical and practical interest. Of methods for utilizing evidence to select diagnoses or decisions, probability theory has the firmest appeal. Probability theory in the form of Bayes' Theorem has been used by a number of workers (Ross, 1972). Notable among recent developments are those of de Dombal and coworkers (de Dombal, 1973; de Dombal et al., 1974; 1975) and Pipberger and coworkers (Pipberger et al., 1975). The usefulness of Bayes' Theorem is limited by practical difficulties, principally the lack of data adequate to estimate accurately the *a priori* and conditional probabilities used in the theorem. One attempt to mitigate this problem has been to assume statistical independence among various pieces of evidence. How seriously this approximation affects results is often unclear, and correction mechanisms have been explored (Ross, 1972; Norusis and Jacquez, 1975a; 1975b). Even the independence assumption requires an unmanageable number of estimates of probabilities for most applications with realistic complexity. To circumvent this problem, some have tried to elicit estimates of probabilities directly from experienced physicians (Gorry, 1973; Ginsberg, 1971; Gustafson et al., 1971), while others have turned from the use of Bayes' Theorem and probability theory to the use of discriminant analysis (Ross, 1972) and nonprobabilistic methods (Scheinok and Rinaldo, 1971; Cumberbatch and Heaps, 1973; Cumberbatch et al., 1974; Glesser and Collen, 1972).

Shortliffe and Buchanan (1975) have offered a model of inexact reasoning in medicine used in the MYCIN system (Chapter 11). Their model

---

This chapter is a shortened and edited version of a paper appearing in *Mathematical Biosciences* 32: 177–186 (1976).

uses estimates provided by expert physicians that reflect the tendency of a piece of evidence to prove or disprove a given hypothesis. Because of the highly promising nature of the MYCIN system, this model deserves examination. Shortliffe and Buchanan conceived their system purely on intuitive grounds and assert that it is an alternative to probability theory. I shall show below that a substantial part of this model can be derived from and is equivalent to probability theory with the assumption of statistical independence. In Section 12.1 I first review a simple probability model and discuss some of its limitations.

12.1 A Simple Probability Model

Consider a finite population of n members. Members of the population may possess one or more of several properties that define subpopulations or sets. Properties of interest might be e_1 or e_2, which might be evidence for or against a disease, and h, a certain disease state or other hypothesis about an individual. The number of individuals with a certain property, say e, will be denoted $n(e)$, and the number with both of two properties e_1 and e_2 will be denoted $n(e_1 \,\&\, e_2)$. Probabilities are taken as ratios of numbers of individuals. From the observation that:

$$\frac{n(e \,\&\, h)}{n(e)} \cdot \frac{n}{n(h)} = \frac{n(e \,\&\, h)}{n(h)} \cdot \frac{n}{n(e)}$$

a convenient form of Bayes' Theorem follows immediately:

$$\frac{P(h|e)}{P(h)} = \frac{P(e|h)}{P(e)}$$

Now consider the case in which two pieces of evidence e_1 and e_2 bear on a hypothesis or disease state h. Let us make the assumptions that these pieces of evidence are independent both in the population as a whole and in the subpopulation with h; that is:

$$\frac{n(e_1 \,\&\, e_2)}{n} = \frac{n(e_1)}{n} \cdot \frac{n(e_2)}{n} \tag{1}$$

and

$$\frac{n(e_1 \,\&\, e_2 \,\&\, h)}{n(h)} = \frac{n(e_1 \,\&\, h)}{n(h)} \cdot \frac{n(e_2 \,\&\, h)}{n(h)} \tag{2}$$

or

$$P(e_1 \;\&\; e_2) = P(e_1)P(e_2) \tag{3}$$

and

$$P(e_1 \;\&\; e_2|h) = P(e_1|h)P(e_2|h) \tag{4}$$

With these the right-hand side of Bayes' Theorem becomes

$$\frac{P(e_1 \;\&\; e_2|h)}{P(e_1 \;\&\; e_2)} = \frac{P(e_1|h)}{P(e_1)} \cdot \frac{P(e_2|h)}{P(e_2)} \tag{5}$$

and, because of this factoring, the right-hand side is computationally simple.

Now, because of the dearth of empirical data to estimate probabilities, suppose we were to ask experts to estimate the probabilities subjectively. We could ask for estimates of the ratios $P(e_i|h)/P(e_i)$ and $P(h)$, and from these compute $P(h|e_i \;\&\; e_2 \;\&\; \ldots \;\&\; e_n)$. The ratios $P(e_i|h)/P(e_i)$ must be in the range $[0,1/P(h)]$. Most physicians are not accustomed to thinking of diseases and evidence in terms of probability ratios. They would more willingly attempt to quantitate their intuition by first deciding whether a piece of evidence tends to prove or disprove a hypothesis and then assigning a parameter on a scale of 0 to 10 as a measure of the weight or strength of the evidence. One way to translate this parameterization into an "estimate" of a probability ratio is the following. Divide the intuitive parameter by 10, yielding a new parameter, which for evidence favoring the hypothesis will be called MB, the physician's measure of belief, and for evidence against the hypothesis will be called MD, the physician's measure of disbelief. Both MB and MD are in the range [0,1] and have the value 0 when the evidence has no bearing on the hypothesis. The value 1 for MB[h,e] means that all individuals with e have h. The value 1 for MD[h,e] means that no individual with e has h. From these physician-estimated parameters we derive the corresponding probability ratios in the following way. For evidence against the hypothesis we simply take

$$\frac{P(e|h)}{P(e)} = 1 - \text{MD}[h,e] \tag{6}$$

For evidence favoring the hypothesis we use a similar construct by taking the evidence as against the negation of the hypothesis, i.e., by considering the subpopulation of individuals who do not have h, denoted $\neg h$. So we construct the ratio of probabilities using MB:

$$\frac{P(e|\neg h)}{P(e)} = 1 - \text{MB}[h,e] \tag{7}$$

Now, to continue the parallel, we write Bayes' Theorem for two pieces of evidence favoring a hypothesis:

$$\frac{P(\neg h|e_1 \,\&\, e_2)}{P(\neg h)} = \frac{P(e_1 \,\&\, e_2|\neg h)P(e_1 \,\&\, e_2)}{P(e_1 \,\&\, e_2)} \tag{8}$$

with

$$\frac{P(e_1 \,\&\, e_2|h)}{P(e_1 \,\&\, e_2)} = \frac{P(e_1|\neg h)}{P(e_1)} \cdot \frac{P(e_2|\neg h)}{P(e_2)} \tag{9}$$

where, for the last equality, independence of e_1 and e_2 in $\neg h$ is assumed. By using the identities

$$P(h) + P(\neg h) = 1 \tag{10}$$

$$P(h|e) + P(\neg h|e) = 1 \tag{11}$$

one then has a computationally simple way of serially adjusting the probability of a hypothesis with new evidence against the hypothesis:

$$P(h|e'') = \frac{P(e_i|h)}{P(e_i)} \cdot P(h|e') \tag{12}$$

or new evidence favoring the hypothesis:

$$P(h|e'') = 1 - \frac{P(e_i|\neg h)}{P(e_i)} \cdot [1 - P(h|e')] \tag{13}$$

where e_i is the new evidence, e'' is the total evidence after the introduction of e_i, and e' is the evidence before the new evidence is introduced [note that $P(h|e') = P(h)$ before any evidence is introduced]. Alternatively, one could combine all elements of evidence against a hypothesis simply by using independence as in Equation (5) and separately combine all elements of evidence favoring a hypothesis by using Equation (9), and then use Equations (12) and (13) once.

The attractive computational simplicity of this scheme is vitiated by the restrictive nature of the independence assumptions made in deriving it. The MB's and MD's for different pieces of evidence cannot be chosen arbitrarily and independently. This can be clearly seen in the following simple theorem. If e_1 and e_2 are independent both in the whole population and in the subpopulation with property h, then

$$P(h|e_1)P(h|e_2) = P(h|e_1 \,\&\, e_2)P(h) \tag{14}$$

This follows from dividing Equation (2) by Equation (1). The nature of restrictions placed on the probabilities can be seen from the limiting case in which all members of e_1 are in h. In that case, $P(h|e_1) = P(h|e_1 \ \& \ e_2) = 1$, so $P(h|e_2) = P(h)$; that is, if some piece of evidence is absolutely diagnostic of an illness, then any evidence that is independent can have no diagnostic value. This special case of the theorem was noted in a paper of Warner et al. (1961). Restrictions this forces on the MB's can be further demonstrated by the following example. We write Bayes' Theorem with the independence assumption as follows:

$$\frac{P(e_1|h)}{P(e_1)} \cdot \frac{P(e_2|h)}{P(e_2)} = \frac{P(h|e_1 \ \& \ e_2)}{P(h)} \tag{15}$$

Consider the case of two pieces of evidence that favor the hypothesis. Using Equations (6), (10), and (11), one can express $P(e|h)/P(e)$ in terms of MB as follows:

$$\frac{P(e|h)}{P(e)} = 1 + \left(\frac{1}{P(h)} - 1\right)\text{MB}[h,e] \tag{16}$$

Using this form and the fact that $P(h|e_1 \ \& \ e_2) \leqslant 1$, we get from Equation (15)

$$\left\{1 + \left(\frac{1}{P(h)} - 1\right)\text{MB}[h,e_1]\right\}\left\{1 + \left(\frac{1}{P(h)}\right)\text{MB}[h,e_2]\right\} \leqslant \frac{1}{P(h)} \tag{17}$$

This is not satisfied for all values of the MB's; e.g., if $P(h) = 1/11$ and $\text{MB}[h,e_1] = 0.7$, then we must choose the narrow range $\text{MB}[h,e_2] \leqslant 0.035$ to satisfy the inequality. Most workers in this field assume that elements of evidence are statistically independent only within each of a complete set of mutually exclusive subpopulations and not in the population as a whole; thus the properties of (14) and (15) do not hold. Occasionally, writers have implicitly made the stronger assumption of independence in the whole space (Slovic et al., 1971).

12.2 The MYCIN Model

The model developed by Shortliffe and Buchanan is in part equivalent to that in Section 12.1. They introduce quantities MB[h,e] and MD[h,e], which are identical to those we have defined above (and were the reason for selecting our choice of parameterization). They postulate rules for combining MB$[h,e_1]$ with MB$[h,e_2]$ to yield MB$[h,e_1 \& e_2]$ and similar rules for MD. With one exception discussed below, these rules need not be postulated because they are equivalent to, and can be derived from, the method of combining probability ratios under the assumption of independence used in the previous section. For example, the rule for MD's is derived as follows by using Equation (5):

$$1 - \mathrm{MD}[h,e_1 \ \& \ e_2] = \frac{P(e_1 \ \& \ e_2|h)}{P(e_1 \ \& \ e_2)} = \frac{P(e_1|h)}{P(e_1)} \cdot \frac{P(e_2|h)}{P(e_2)} \tag{18}$$

or

$$1 - \mathrm{MD}[h,e_1 \ \& \ e_2] = (1 - \mathrm{MD}[h,e_1])(1 - \mathrm{MD}[h,e_2]) \tag{19}$$

which is an algebraic rearrangement of the rule postulated in their paper. A similar construct holds for MB. The exceptional case in the MYCIN model is one in which a piece of evidence proves a hypothesis (all with e_1 have h). As noted in the previous section, this case excludes the possibility of other independent diagnostically meaningful evidence. In the MYCIN model, if e proves h, then one sets MD equal to zero for the combined evidence. A similar assumption is introduced for the case that evidence disproves a hypothesis. To maintain internal consistency the MB's and MD's must be subject to the restrictions discussed in Section 12.1. This important fact is not noted in the work of Shortliffe and Buchanan.

Two other properties are assumed for the MB's and MD's by Shortliffe and Buchanan. The extent or importance of the use of these assumptions in the employment of their model is not clear, but does not seem great. One concerns the conjunction of hypotheses h_1 and h_2, for which they assume

$$\mathrm{MB}[h_1 \ \& \ h_2,e] = \min(\mathrm{MB}[h_1,e],\mathrm{MB}[h_2,e]) \tag{20}$$

$$\mathrm{MD}[h_1 \ \& \ h_2,e] = \max(\mathrm{MD}[h_1,e],\mathrm{MD}[h_2,e]) \tag{21}$$

Unstated are strong restrictive assumptions about the relationship of h_1 and h_2. As an extreme example, suppose that h_1 and h_2 are mutually exclusive; then the conjunction h_1 & h_2 is false (has probability zero) no matter what the evidence, and the assumptions on the conjunction of hypotheses would be unreasonable. In the context of the probability model of Section 12.1, one can derive a relationship

$$\frac{P(h_1 \ \& \ h_2|e)}{P(h_1 \ \& \ h_2)} = \frac{P(h_1|e)}{P(h_1)} \cdot \frac{P(h_2|e)}{P(h_2)} \tag{22}$$

only by making strong assumptions on the independence of h_1 and h_2.

A pair of further assumptions made by Shortliffe and Buchanan concerns the disjunction of two hypotheses, denoted $h_1 \vee h_2$. These are

$$\mathrm{MB}[h_1 \vee h_2,e] = \max(\mathrm{MB}[h_1,e],\mathrm{MB}[h_2,e]) \quad (23)$$

$$\mathrm{MD}[h_1 \vee h_2,e] = \min(\mathrm{MD}[h_1,e],\mathrm{MD}[h_2,e]) \quad (24)$$

Again these contain unstated assumptions about the relationship of h_1 and h_2. If, for example, h_1 and h_2 are mutually exclusive and each has a probability of being true, then the disjunction $h_1 \vee h_2$ should be more likely or probable or confirmed than either h_1 or h_2. Expressions for $P(e|h_1 \vee h_2)/P(e)$ can be derived in probability theory, but they have no compact or perspicuous form.

The MYCIN model combines separately all evidence favoring a hypothesis to give $\mathrm{MB}[h,e_f]$, where $e_f = e_{f1}$ & e_{f2} & . . . & e_{fn}, the intersection of all elements of evidence favoring hypothesis h. Similarly, all elements against a hypothesis are combined to give $\mathrm{MD}[h,e_a]$. By Bayes' Theorem these provide measures of $P(h|e_f)/P(h)$ and $P(h|e_a)/P(h)$. These could be combined using the probability theory outlined in Section 12.1 to give $P(h|e_f \,\&\, e_a)/P(h)$, an estimate of the change of the probability due to the evidence. However, it is at this point that the MYCIN model departs from standard probability theory. Shortliffe and Buchanan combine the MB with the MD by defining a certainty factor to be

$$\mathrm{CF}[h,e_f \,\&\, e_a] = \mathrm{MB}[h,e_f] - \mathrm{MD}[h,e_a] \quad (25)$$

The certainty factor is used in two ways. One is to rank hypotheses to select those for further action. The other is as a weighting factor for the credibility of a hypothesis h, which is supposed by an intermediate hypothesis i, which in turn is supported by evidence e. The appropriateness of CF for each of these roles will be examined.

One of the uses of CF is to rank hypotheses. Because $\mathrm{CF}[h,e]$ does not correspond to the probability of h given e, it is not difficult to give examples in which, of two hypotheses, the one with the lower probability would have the higher certainty factor, or CF. For example, consider two hypotheses h_1 and h_2 and some body of evidence e that tends to confirm both hypotheses. Suppose that the *a priori* probabilities were such that $P(h_1) \gg P(h_2)$ and $P(h_1|e) > P(h_2|e)$; it is possible that $\mathrm{CF}[h_1,e] < \mathrm{CF}[h_2,e]$. For example, if $P(h_1) = 0.8$, $P(h_2) = 0.2$, $P(h_1|e) = 0.9$, $P(h_2|e) = 0.8$, then $\mathrm{CF}[h_1,e] = 0.5$ and $\mathrm{CF}[h_2,e] = 0.75$. This failure to rank according to probabilities is an undesirable feature of CF. It would be possible to avoid it if it were assumed that all *a priori* probabilities were equal.

The weighting role for CF is suggested by the intuitive notion that in a chain of reasoning, if e implies i with probability $P(i|e)$, and i, if true, implies h with probability $P(h|i)$, then

$$P(h|e) = P(h|i)P(i|e) \quad (26)$$

This is not true in general; however, a set of assumptions can be identified under which it will be true. Suppose the population with property h is contained in the set with i, and the set with i is contained in the set with e. This may be expressed as

$$n(h \,\&\, i) = n(h) \qquad n(i \,\&\, e) = n(i) \qquad n(h \,\&\, e) = n(h) \tag{27}$$

These allow us to write

$$\frac{n(h \,\&\, e)}{n(e)} = \frac{n(h \,\&\, i)}{n(i)} \cdot \frac{n(i \,\&\, e)}{n} \tag{28}$$

which is the desired result in numerical form. The proposal of Shortliffe and Buchanan, which may be written as

$$\text{MB}[h,e] = \text{MB}[h,i]\max(0, \text{CF}[i,e]) \tag{29}$$

$$\text{MD}[h,e] = \text{MD}[h,i]\max(0, \text{CF}[i,e]) \tag{30}$$

is not true in general under the assumptions of (27) or any other natural set, as may be demonstrated by substitution into these relationships of the definitions of MB, MD, and CF.

12.3 Conclusions

The simple model of Section 12.1 is attractive because it is computationally simple and apparently lends itself to convenient estimation of parameters by experts. The weakness of the system is the inobvious interdependence restriction placed on the estimation of parameters by the assumptions of independence. The MYCIN model is equivalent in part to the simple probability model presented and suffers from the same subtle restrictions on parameter estimation if it is to remain internally consistent.

The ultimate measure of success in models of medical reasoning of this sort, which attempt to mimic physicians, is the closeness of their approach to perfect imitation of experts in the field. The empirical success of MYCIN using the model of Shortliffe and Buchanan stands in spite of theoretical objections of the types discussed in the preceding sections. It is probable that the model does not founder on the difficulties pointed out because in actual use the chains of reasoning are short and the hypotheses simple. However, there are many fields in which, because of its shortcomings, this model could not enjoy comparable success.

The fact that in trying to create an alternative to probability theory or reasoning Shortliffe and Buchanan duplicated the use of standard theory demonstrates the difficulty of creating a useful and internally consistent system that is not isomorphic to a portion of probability theory. In proposing such a system, a careful delineation of its relationship to conventional probability theory can contribute to an understanding and clear exposition of its assumptions and approximations. It thereby allows tests of whether these are satisfied in the proposed field of use.

13

The Dempster-Shafer Theory of Evidence

Jean Gordon and Edward H. Shortliffe

The drawbacks of pure probabilistic methods and of the certainty factor model have led us in recent years to consider alternate approaches. Particularly appealing is the mathematical theory of evidence developed by Arthur Dempster. We are convinced it merits careful study and interpretation in the context of expert systems. This theory was first set forth by Dempster in the 1960s and subsequently extended by Glenn Shafer. In 1976, the year after the first description of CF's appeared, Shafer published *A Mathematical Theory of Evidence* (Shafer, 1976). Its relevance to the issues addressed in the CF model was not immediately recognized, but recently researchers have begun to investigate applications of the theory to expert systems (Barnett, 1981; Friedman, 1981; Garvey et al., 1981).

We believe that the advantage of the Dempster-Shafer theory over previous approaches is its ability to model the narrowing of the hypothesis set with the accumulation of evidence, a process that characterizes diagnostic reasoning in medicine and expert reasoning in general. An expert uses evidence that, instead of bearing on a single hypothesis in the original hypothesis set, often bears on a larger subset of this set. The functions and combining rule of the Dempster-Shafer theory are well suited to represent this type of evidence and its aggregation.

For example, in the search for the identity of an infecting organism, a smear showing gram-negative organisms narrows the hypothesis set of all possible organisms to a proper subset. This subset can also be thought of as a new hypothesis: the organism is one of the gram-negative organisms. However, this piece of evidence gives no information concerning the relative likelihoods of the organisms in the subset. Bayesians might assume equal priors and distribute the weight of this evidence equally among the gram-negative organisms, but, as Shafer points out, they would thus fail to distinguish between uncertainty, or lack of knowledge, and equal certainty. Because he attributes belief to subsets, as well as to individual elements of the hypothesis set, we believe that Shafer more accurately reflects the evidence-gathering process.

A second distinct piece of evidence, such as morphology of the organism, narrows the original hypothesis set to a different subset. How does the Dempster-Shafer theory pool these two pieces of evidence? Each is represented by a belief function, and two belief functions are merged via a combination rule to yield a new function. The combination rule, like the Bayesian and CF combining functions, is independent of the order in which evidence is gathered and requires that the hypotheses under consideration be mutually exclusive and exhaustive. In fact, the Dempster-Shafer combination rule includes the Bayesian and CF functions as special cases.

Another consequence of the generality of the Dempster-Shafer belief functions is avoidance of the Bayesian restriction that commitment of belief to a hypothesis implies commitment of the remaining belief to its negation, i.e., that $P(h) = 1 - P(\neg h)$. The concept that, in many situations, evidence partially in favor of a hypothesis should not be construed as evidence partially against the same hypothesis (i.e., in favor of its negation) was one of the desiderata in the development of the CF model, as discussed in Chapter 11. As in the CF model, the beliefs in each hypothesis in the original set need not sum to 1 but may sum to a number less than or equal to 1; some of the belief can be allotted to subsets of the original hypothesis set.

Thus the Dempster-Shafer model includes many of the features of the CF model but is based on a firm mathematical foundation. This is a clear advantage over the *ad hoc* nature of CF's. In the next sections, we motivate the exposition of the theory with a medical example and then discuss the relevance of the theory to MYCIN.

13.1 Basics of the Dempster-Shafer Theory

13.1.1 A Simple Example of Medical Reasoning

Suppose a physician is considering a case of cholestatic jaundice for which there is a diagnostic hypothesis set of hepatitis (hep), cirrhosis (cirr), gallstone (gall) and pancreatic cancer (pan). There are, of course, more than four causes of jaundice, but we have simplified the example here for illustrative purposes. In the Dempster-Shafer theory, this set is called a *frame of discernment,* denoted Θ. As noted earlier, the hypotheses in Θ are assumed mutually exclusive and exhaustive.

One piece of evidence considered by the physician might support the diagnosis of intrahepatic cholestasis, which is defined for this example as

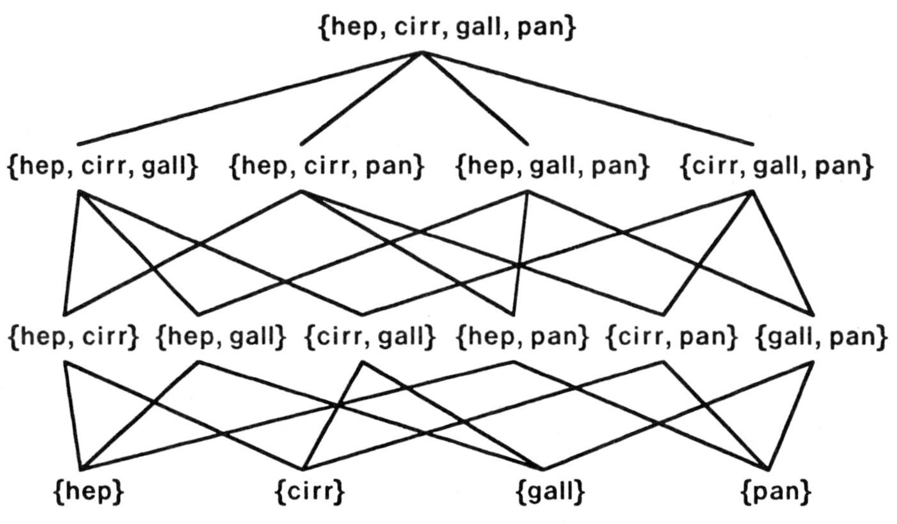

FIGURE 13-1 The subsets of the set of causes of cholestasis.

the two-element subset of Θ {hep, cirr}, also represented by the hypothesis HEP-OR-CIRR. Similarly, the hypothesis extrahepatic cholestasis corresponds to {gall, pan}. Evidence confirming intrahepatic cholestasis to some degree will cause the physician to allot a proportional amount of belief to that subset.

A new piece of evidence might help the physician exclude hepatitis to some degree. Evidence disconfirming hepatitis (HEP) is equivalent to evidence confirming the hypothesis NOT-HEP, which corresponds to the hypothesis CIRR-OR-GALL-OR-PAN or the subset {cirr, gall, pan}. Thus evidence disconfirming hepatitis to some degree will cause the physician to allot a proportional amount of belief to this three-element subset.

As illustrated above, a subset of hypotheses in Θ gives rise to a new hypothesis, which is equivalent to the disjunction of the hypotheses in the subset. Each hypothesis in Θ corresponds to a one-element subset (called a *singleton*). By considering all possible subsets of Θ, denoted 2^Θ, the set of hypotheses to which belief can be allotted is enlarged. Henceforth, we use the term *hypothesis* in this enlarged sense to denote any subset of the original hypotheses in Θ.

A pictorial representation of 2^Θ is given in Figure 13-1. Note that a set of size n has 2^n subsets. (The empty set, ∅, is one of these subsets, but corresponds to a hypothesis known to be false and is not shown in Figure 13-1.

In a given domain, only some subsets in 2^Θ will be of diagnostic interest. Evidence often bears on certain disease categories as well as on specific disease entities. In the case of cholestatic jaundice, evidence available to

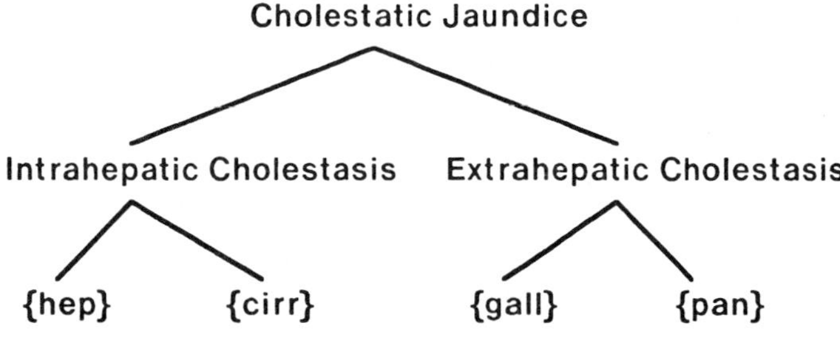

FIGURE 13-2 The subsets of clinical interest in cholestatic jaundice.

the physician tends to support either intrahepatic cholestasis, extrahepatic cholestasis, or the singleton hypotheses. The tree of Figure 13-1 can thus be pruned to that of Figure 13-2, which summarizes the hierarchical relations of clinical interest. In at least one medical artificial intelligence system, the causes of jaundice have been usefully structured in this way for the diagnostic task (Chandrasekharan et al., 1979).

13.1.2 Basic Probability Assignments

The Dempster-Shafer theory uses a number in the range [0,1] to indicate belief in a hypothesis given a piece of evidence. This number is the degree to which the evidence supports the hypothesis. Recall that evidence against a hypothesis is regarded as evidence for the negation of the hypothesis. Thus, unlike the CF model, the Dempster-Shafer model avoids the use of negative numbers.

The impact of each distinct piece of evidence on the subsets of Θ is represented by a function called a *basic probability assignment* (bpa). A bpa is a generalization of the traditional probability density function; the latter assigns a number in the range [0,1] to every singleton of Θ such that the numbers sum to 1. Using 2^Θ, the enlarged domain of all subsets of Θ, a bpa denoted m assigns a number in [0,1] to every subset of Θ such that the numbers sum to 1. (By definition, the number 0 must be assigned to the empty set, since this set corresponds to a false hypothesis. It is false because the hypotheses in Θ are assumed exhaustive.) Thus m allows assignment of a quantity of belief to every element in the tree of Figure 13-1, not just to those elements on the bottom row, as is the case for a probability density function.

The quantity $m(A)$ is a measure of that portion of the total belief committed exactly to A, where A is an element of 2^Θ and the total belief is 1. This portion of belief cannot be further subdivided among the subsets of A and does not include portions of belief committed to subsets of A. Since belief in a subset certainly entails belief in subsets containing that subset (i.e., nodes "higher" in the network of Figure 13-1), it would be useful to define a function that computes a total amount of belief in A. This quantity would include not only belief committed exactly to A but belief committed to all subsets of A. Such a function, called a *belief function*, is defined in the next section.

The quantity $m(\Theta)$ is a measure of that portion of the total belief that remains unassigned after commitment of belief to various proper subsets of Θ. For example, evidence favoring a single subset A need not say anything about belief in the other subsets. If $m(A)=s$ and m assigns no belief to other subsets of Θ, then $m(\Theta)=1 - s$. Thus the remaining belief is assigned to Θ and not to the negation of the hypothesis (equivalent to A^c, the set-theoretic complement of A), as would be required in the Bayesian model.

Examples

Example 1. Suppose that there is no evidence concerning the specific diagnosis in a patient with known cholestatic jaundice. The bpa representing ignorance, called the vacuous bpa, assigns 1 to $\Theta=\{$hep, cirr, gall, pan$\}$ and 0 to every other subset of Θ. Bayesians might attempt to represent ignorance by a function assigning 0.25 to each singleton, assuming no prior information. As remarked before, such a function would imply more information given by the evidence than is truly the case.

Example 2. Suppose that the evidence supports, or confirms, the diagnosis of intrahepatic cholestasis to the degree 0.6, but does not support a choice between cirrhosis and hepatitis. The remaining belief, $1 - 0.6 = 0.4$, is assigned to Θ. The hypothesis corresponding to Θ is known to be true under the assumption of exhaustiveness. Bayesians would assign the remaining belief to extrahepatic cholestasis, the negation of intrahepatic cholestasis. Such an assignment would be an example of Paradox 1, discussed in Chapter 11. Thus $m(\{$hep, cirr$\})=0.6$, $m(\Theta) = m(\{$hep, cirr, gall, pan$\}) = 0.4$, and the value of m for every other subset of Θ is 0.

Example 3. Suppose that the evidence disconfirms the diagnosis of hepatitis to the degree 0.7. This is equivalent to confirming that of NOT-HEP to the degree 0.7. Thus $m(\{$cirr, gall, pan$\})=0.7$, $m(\Theta)=0.3$, and the value of m for every other subset of Θ is 0.

Example 4. Suppose that the evidence confirms the diagnosis of hepatitis to the degree 0.8. Then $m(\{$hep$\})=0.8$, $m(\Theta)=0.2$, and m is 0 elsewhere.

13.1.3 Belief Functions

A belief function, denoted Bel, corresponding to a specific bpa, m, assigns to every subset A of Θ the sum of the beliefs committed exactly to every subset of A by m. For example,

$$\begin{aligned}\text{Bel}(\{\text{hep, cirr, pan}\}) = {} & m(\{\text{hep, cirr, pan}\}) + m(\{\text{hep, cirr}\}) \\ & + m(\{\text{hep, pan}\}) + m(\{\text{cirr, pan}\}) \\ & + m(\{\text{hep}\}) + m(\{\text{cirr}\}) + m(\{\text{pan}\})\end{aligned}$$

Thus, Bel(A) is a measure of the total amount of belief in A and not of the amount committed precisely to A by the evidence giving rise to m.

Referring to Figure 13-1, Bel and m are equal for singletons, but Bel(A), where A is any other subset of Θ, is the sum of the values of m for every subset in the subtree formed by using A as the root. Bel(Θ) is always equal to 1 since Bel(Θ) is the sum of the values of m for every subset of Θ. This sum must be 1 by definition of a bpa. Clearly, the total amount of belief in Θ should be equal to the total amount of belief, 1, since the singletons are exhaustive.

To illustrate, the belief function corresponding to the bpa of Example 2 is given by Bel(Θ) = 1, Bel(A) = 0.6, where A is any proper subset of Θ containing {hep, cirr}, and the value of Bel for every other subset of Θ is 0.

13.1.4 Combination of Belief Functions

As discussed in Chapter 11, the evidence-gathering process in medical diagnosis requires a method for combining the support for a hypothesis, or for its negation, based on multiple, accumulated observations. The Dempster-Shafer model also recognizes this requirement and provides a formal proposal for its management. Given two belief functions, based on two observations, but with the same frame of discernment, Dempster's combination rule, shown below, computes a new belief function that represents the impact of the combined evidence.

Concerning the validity of this rule, Shafer (1976) writes that although he can provide "no conclusive *a priori* argument, . . . it does seem to reflect the pooling of evidence." In the special case of a frame of discernment containing two elements, Dempster's rule can be found in Johann Heinrich Lambert's book, *Neues Organon*, published in 1764. In another special case where the two bpa's give support to exactly one and the same hypothesis, the rule reduces to that found in the MYCIN CF model and in *Ars Conjectandi*, the work of the mathematician Jakob Bernoulli in 1713.

The Dempster combination rule differs from the MYCIN combining function in the pooling of evidence supporting mutually exclusive hypotheses. For example, evidence supporting hepatitis reduces belief in each of the singleton hypotheses—CIRR, GALL, and PAN—and in any disjunction not containing HEP, e.g., CIRR-OR-GALL-OR-PAN, NOT-HEP, CIRR-OR-PAN, etc. As we discuss later, if the Dempster-Shafer model were adapted for use in MYCIN, each new piece of evidence would have a wider impact on other hypotheses than it does in the CF model. The Dempster combination rule also gives rise to a very different result regarding belief in a hypothesis when confirming and disconfirming evidence is pooled.

Let Bel_1 and Bel_2 and m_1 and m_2 denote two belief functions and their respective bpa's. Dempster's rule computes a new bpa, denoted $m_1 \oplus m_2$, which represents the combined effect of m_1 and m_2. The corresponding belief function, denoted $\text{Bel}_1 \oplus \text{Bel}_2$, is then easily computed from $m_1 \oplus m_2$ by the definition of a belief function.

If we sum all products of the form $m_1(X)m_2(Y)$, where X and Y run over all subsets of Θ, the result is 1 by elementary algebra and the definition of a bpa:

$$\sum m_1(X)m_2(Y) = \sum m_1(X) \sum m_2(Y) = 1 \times 1 = 1 \tag{1}$$

The bpa representing the combination of m_1 and m_2 apportions this number 1, the total amount of belief, among the subsets of Θ by assigning $m_1(X)m_2(Y)$ to the intersection of X and Y. Note that there are typically several different subsets of Θ whose intersection equals that of X and Y. Thus, for every subset A of Θ, Dempster's rule defines $m_1 \oplus m_2(A)$ to be the sum of all products of the form $m_1(X)m_2(Y)$, where X and Y run over all subsets whose intersection is A. The commutativity of multiplication ensures that the rule yields the same value regardless of the order in which the functions are combined. This is an important property since evidence aggregation should be independent of the order of its gathering. The following two examples illustrate the combination rule.

Example 5. As in Examples 2 and 3, suppose that for a given patient one observation supports intrahepatic cholestasis to degree 0.6 (m_1) whereas another disconfirms hepatitis (i.e., confirms {cirr, gall, pan}) to degree 0.7 (m_2). Then our net belief based on both observations is given by $m_1 \oplus m_2$. For computational purposes, an "intersection tableau" with values of m_1 and m_2 along the rows and columns, respectively, is a helpful device. Only nonzero values of m_1 and m_2 need be considered, since if $m_1(X)$ and/or $m_2(Y)$ is 0, then the product $m_1(X)m_2(Y)$ contributes 0 to $m_1 \oplus m_2(A)$, where A is the intersection of X and Y. Entry i,j in the tableau is the intersection of the subsets in row i and column j. Clearly, some of these entries may be the same subset. The product of the bpa values is in parentheses next to the subset. The value of $m_1 \oplus m_2(A)$ is computed by summing all products in the tableau adjacent to A.

		m_2 {cirr, gall, pan} (0.7)	Θ (0.3)
m_1	{hep, cirr} (0.6)	{cirr} (0.42)	{hep, cirr} (0.18)
	Θ (0.4)	{cirr, gall, pan} (0.28)	Θ (0.12)

In this example, a subset appears only once in the tableau and $m_1 \oplus m_2$ is easily computed:

$$m_1 \oplus m_2(\{\text{cirr}\}) = 0.42$$

$$m_1 \oplus m_2(\{\text{hep, cirr}\}) = 0.18$$

$$m_1 \oplus m_2(\{\text{cirr, gall, pan}\}) = 0.28$$

$$m_1 \oplus m_2(\Theta) = 0.12$$

$m_1 \oplus m_2$ is 0 for all other subsets of Θ

Since $\text{Bel}_1 \oplus \text{Bel}_2$ is fairly complex, we give only a few sample values:

$$\begin{aligned} \text{Bel}_1 \oplus \text{Bel}_2(\{\text{hep, cirr}\}) &= m_1 \oplus m_2(\{\text{hep, cirr}\}) + m_1 \oplus m_2(\{\text{hep}\}) \\ &\quad + m_1 \oplus m_2(\{\text{cirr}\}) \\ &= 0.18 + 0 + 0.42 \\ &= 0.60 \end{aligned}$$

$$\begin{aligned} \text{Bel}_1 \oplus \text{Bel}_2(\{\text{cirr, gall, pan}\}) &= m_1 \oplus m_2(\{\text{cirr, gall, pan}\}) \\ &\quad + m_1 \oplus m_2(\{\text{cirr, gall}\}) \\ &\quad + m_1 \oplus m_2(\{\text{cirr, pan}\}) \\ &\quad + m_1 \oplus m_2(\{\text{gall, pan}\}) + m_1 \oplus m_2(\{\text{cirr}\}) \\ &\quad + m_1 \oplus m_2(\{\text{gall}\}) + m_1 \oplus m_2(\{\text{pan}\}) \\ &= 0.28 + 0 + 0 + 0 + 0.42 + 0 + 0 \\ &= 0.70 \end{aligned}$$

$$\text{Bel}_1 \oplus \text{Bel}_2(\{\text{hep, cirr, pan}\}) = \text{Bel}_1 \oplus \text{Bel}_2(\{\text{hep, cirr}\}) = 0.60$$

since

$$m_1 \oplus m_2(\{\text{hep, cirr, pan}\}) = m_1 \oplus m_2(\{\text{hep, pan}\}) = m_1 \oplus m_2(\{\text{cirr, pan}\}) = 0$$

In this example, the reader should note that $m_1 \oplus m_2$ satisfies the definition of a bpa: $\Sigma\, m_1 \oplus m_2(X) = 1$, where X runs over all subsets of Θ and $m_1 \oplus m_2(\varnothing) = 0$. Equation (1) shows that the first condition in the definition is always fulfilled. However, the second condition is problematic in cases where the "intersection tableau" contains null entries. This situation did not occur in Example 5 because every two sets with nonzero bpa values always had at least one element in common. In general, nonzero products of the form $m_1(X)m_2(Y)$ may be assigned when X and Y have an empty intersection.

Dempster deals with this problem by normalizing the assigned values so that $m_1 \oplus m_2(\varnothing) = 0$ and all values of the new bpa lie between 0 and 1. This is accomplished by defining κ as the sum of all nonzero values assigned to $\varnothing$ in a given case ($\kappa = 0$ in Example 5). Dempster then assigns 0 to $m_1 \oplus m_2(\varnothing)$ and divides all other values of $m_1 \oplus m_2$ by $1 - \kappa$.[1]

Example 6. Suppose now that, for the same patient as in Example 5, a third observation (m_3) confirms the diagnosis of hepatitis to the degree 0.8 (cf. Example 4). We now need to compute $m_3 \oplus m_4$, where $m_4 = m_1 + m_2$ of Example 5.

		$m_4 = m_1 \oplus m_2$			
		{cirr} (0.42)	{hep, cirr} (0.18)	{cirr, gall, pan} (0.28)	Θ (0.12)
m_3	{hep} (0.8)	$\varnothing$ (0.336)	{hep} (0.144)	$\varnothing$ (0.224)	{hep} (0.096)
	Θ (0.2)	{cirr} (0.084)	{hep, cirr} (0.036)	{cirr, gall, pan} (0.056)	Θ (0.024)

In this example, there are two null entries in the tableau, one assigned the value 0.336 and the other 0.224. Thus

$$\kappa = 0.336 + 0.224 = 0.56 \text{ and } 1 - \kappa = 0.44$$

$$m_3 \oplus m_4(\{\text{hep}\}) = (0.144 + 0.096)/0.44 = 0.545$$

$$m_3 \oplus m_4(\{\text{cirr}\}) = 0.084/0.44 = 0.191$$

$$m_3 \oplus m_4(\{\text{hep, cirr}\}) = 0.036/0.44 = 0.082$$

$$m_3 \oplus m_4(\{\text{cirr, gall, pan}\}) = 0.056/0.44 = 0.127$$

$$m_3 \oplus m_4(\Theta) = 0.024/0.44 = 0.055$$

$$m_3 \oplus m_4 \text{ is 0 for all other subsets of } \Theta$$

Note that $\Sigma m_3 \oplus m_4(X) = 1$, as is required by the definition of a bpa.

13.1.5 Belief Intervals

After all bpa's with the same frame of discernment have been combined and the belief function Bel defined by this new bpa has been computed, how should the information given by Bel be used? Bel(A) gives the total

[1] Note that the revised values will still sum to 1 and hence satisfy that condition in the definition of a bpa. If $a + b + c = 1$ then $(a+b)/(1-c) = 1$ and $a/(1-c) + b/(1-c) = 1$.

amount of belief committed to the subset A after all evidence bearing on A has been pooled. However, the function Bel contains additional information about A, namely, $\text{Bel}(A^c)$, the extent to which the evidence supports the negation of A, i.e., A^c. The quantity $1-\text{Bel}(A^c)$ expresses the plausibility of A, i.e., the extent to which the evidence allows one to fail to doubt A.

The information contained in Bel concerning a given subset A may be conveniently expressed by the interval

$$[\text{Bel}(A)\ \ 1-\text{Bel}(A^c)]$$

It is not difficult to see that the right endpoint is always greater than the left: $1-\text{Bel}(A^c) \geqslant \text{Bel}(A)$ or, equivalently, $\text{Bel}(A) + \text{Bel}(A^c) \leqslant 1$. Since $\text{Bel}(A)$ and $\text{Bel}(A^c)$ are the sum of all values of m for subsets of A and A^c, respectively, and since A and A^c have no subsets in common, $\text{Bel}(A) + \text{Bel}(A^c) \leqslant \Sigma m(X) = 1$ where X ranges over all subsets of Θ.

In the Bayesian situation, in which $\text{Bel}(A) + \text{Bel}(A^c) = 1$, the two endpoints of the belief interval are equal and the width of the interval $1 - \text{Bel}(A^c) - \text{Bel}(A)$ is 0. In the Dempster-Shafer model, however, the width is usually not 0 and is a measure of the belief that, although not committed to A, is also not committed to A^c. It is easily seen that the width is the sum of belief committed exactly to subsets of Θ that intersect A but that are not subsets of A. If A is a singleton, all such subsets are supersets of A, but this is not true for a nonsingleton A. To illustrate, let $A=\{\text{hep}\}$:

$$\begin{aligned}1 - \text{Bel}(A^c) - \text{Bel}(A) &= 1 - \text{Bel}(\{\text{cirr, gall, pan}\}) - \text{Bel}(\{\text{hep}\})\\ &= 1 - [m(\{\text{cirr, gall, pan}\}) + m(\{\text{cirr, gall}\})\\ &\quad + m(\{\text{cirr, pan}\}) + m(\{\text{gall, pan}\}) + m(\{\text{cirr}\})\\ &\quad + m(\{\text{gall}\}) + m(\{\text{pan}\})] - m(\{\text{hep}\})\\ &= m(\{\text{hep, cirr}\}) + m(\{\text{hep, gall}\})\\ &\quad + m(\{\text{hep, pan}\}) + m(\{\text{hep, cirr, gall}\})\\ &\quad + m(\{\text{hep, cirr, pan}\})\\ &\quad + m(\{\text{hep, gall, pan}\}) + m(\Theta)\end{aligned}$$

Belief committed to a superset of {hep} might, on further refinement of the evidence, result in belief committed to {hep}. Thus the width of the belief interval is a measure of that portion of the total belief, 1, that could be added to that commited to {hep} by a physician willing to ignore all but the disconfirming effects of the evidence.

The width of a belief interval can also be regarded as the amount of uncertainty with respect to a hypothesis, given the evidence. It is belief that is committed by the evidence to neither the hypothesis nor the negation of the hypothesis. The vacuous belief function results in width 1 for all belief intervals, and Bayesian functions result in width 0. Most evidence leads to belief functions with intervals of varying widths, where the widths are numbers between 0 and 1.

13.2 The Dempster-Shafer Theory and MYCIN

MYCIN is well suited for implementation of the Dempster-Shafer theory. First, mutual exclusivity of singletons in a frame of discernment is satisfied by the sets of hypotheses in MYCIN constituting the frames of discernment (single-valued parameters; see Chapter 5). This condition may be a stumbling block to the model's implementation in other expert systems where mutual exclusivity cannot be assumed. Second, the belief functions that represent evidence in MYCIN are of a particularly simple form and thus reduce the combination rule to an easily managed computational scheme. Third, the variables and functions already used to define CF's can be adapted and modified for belief function values. These features will now be discussed and illustrated with examples from MYCIN. It should be noted that we have not yet implemented the model in MYCIN.

13.2.1 Frames of Discernment in MYCIN

How should the frames of discernment in MYCIN be chosen? Shafer (1976, p. 36) points out:

> It should not be thought that the possibilities that comprise Θ will be determined and meaningful independently of our knowledge. Quite to the contrary: Θ will acquire its meaning from what we know or think we know; the distinctions that it embodies will be embedded within the matrix of our language and its associated conceptual structures and will depend on those structures for whatever accuracy and meaningfulness they possess.

The "conceptual structures" in MYCIN are the associative triples found in the conclusions of the rules, which have the form (object attribute value).[2] Such a triple gives rise to a singleton hypothesis of the form "the attribute of object is value." A frame of discernment would then consist of all triples with the same object and attribute. Thus the number of triples, or hypotheses in Θ, will equal the number of possible values that the object may assume for the attribute in question. The theory requires that these values be mutually exclusive, as they are for single-valued parameters in MYCIN.

For example, one frame of discernment is generated by the set of all triples of the form (*Organism-1 Identity X*), where *X* ranges over all possible identities of organisms known to MYCIN—*Klebsiella, E. coli, Pseudomonas,* etc. Another frame is generated by replacing *Organism-1* with *Organism-2*. A third frame is the set of all triples of the form (*Organism-1 Morphology*

[2]Also referred to as (context parameter value); see Chapter 5.

X), where *X* ranges over all known morphologies—coccus, rod, bacillus, etc.[3]

Although it is true that a patient may be infected by more than one organism, organisms are represented as separate contexts in MYCIN (not as separate values of the same parameter). Thus MYCIN's representation scheme is particularly well suited to the mutual exclusivity demand of the Dempster-Shafer theory. Many other expert systems meet this demand less easily. Consider, for example, how the theory might be applicable in a system that gathers and pools evidence concerning the identity of a patient's disease. Then there is often the problem of multiple, coexistent diseases; i.e., the hypotheses in the frame of discernment may not be mutually exclusive. One way to overcome this difficulty is to choose Θ to be the set of all subsets of all possible diseases. The computational implications of this choice are harrowing, since if there are 600 possible diseases (the approximate scope of the INTERNIST knowledge base), then

$$|\Theta| = 2^{600} \qquad \text{and} \qquad |2^{\Theta}| = 2^{2^{600}}$$

However, since the evidence may actually focus on a small subset of 2^{Θ}, the computations need not be intractable. A second, more reasonable alternative would be to apply the Dempster-Shafer theory after partitioning the set of diseases into groups of mutually exclusive diseases and considering each group as a separate frame of discernment. The latter approach would be similar to that used in INTERNIST-1 (Miller et al., 1982), where scoring and comparison of hypotheses are undertaken only after a special partitioning algorithm has separated evoked hypotheses into subsets of mutually exclusive diagnoses.

13.2.2 Rules as Belief Functions

In the most general situation, a given piece of evidence supports many of the subsets of Θ, each to varying degrees. The simplest situation is that in which the evidence supports only one subset to a certain degree and the remaining belief is assigned to Θ. Because of the modular way in which knowledge is captured and encoded in MYCIN, this latter situation applies in the case of MYCIN rules.

If the premises confirm the conclusion of a rule with degree *s*, where *s* is above threshold value, then the rule's effect on belief in the subsets of

[3]The objection may be raised that in some cases all triples with the same object and attribute are not mutually exclusive. For example, both (Patient-1 Allergy Penicillin) and (Patient-1 Allergy Ampicillin) may be true. In MYCIN, however, these triples tend not to have partial degrees of belief associated with them; they are usually true-false propositions ascertained by simple questioning of the user by the system. Thus it is seldom necessary to combine evidence regarding these multi-valued parameters (see Chapter 5), and these hypotheses need not be treated by the Dempster-Shafer theory.

Θ can be represented by a bpa. This bpa assigns s to the singleton corresponding to the hypothesis in the conclusion of the rule, call it A, and assigns $1-s$ to Θ. In the language of MYCIN, the CF associated with this conclusion is s. If the premise disconfirms the conclusion with degree s, then the bpa assigns s to the subset corresponding to the negation of the conclusion, A^c, and assigns $1-s$ to Θ. The CF associated with this conclusion is $-s$. Thus, we are arguing that the CF's associated with rules in MYCIN and other EMYCIN systems can be viewed as bpa's in the Dempster-Shafer sense and need not be changed in order to implement and test the Dempster-Shafer model.

13.2.3 Types of Evidence Combination in MYCIN

The revised quantification scheme we propose for modeling inexact inference in MYCIN is the replacement of the previous CF combining function with the Dempster combination rule applied to belief functions arising from the triggering of domain rules. The combination of such functions is computationally simple, especially when compared to that of two general belief functions.

To illustrate, we consider a frame of discernment, Θ, consisting of all associative triples of the form (Organism-1 Identity X), where X ranges over all identities of organisms known to MYCIN. The triggering of two rules affecting belief in these triples can be categorized in one of the three following ways.

Category 1. Two rules are both confirming or both disconfirming of the same triple, or conclusion. For example, both rules confirm *Pseudomonas* (Pseu), one to degree 0.4 and the other to degree 0.7. The effect of triggering the rules is represented by bpa's m_1 and m_2, where $m_1(\{\text{Pseu}\})=0.4$, $m_1(\Theta)=0.6$, and $m_2(\{\text{Pseu}\})=0.7$, $m_2(\Theta)=0.3$. The combined effect on belief is given by $m_1 \oplus m_2$, computed using the following tableau:

		m_2	
		{Pseu} (0.7)	Θ (0.3)
m_1	{Pseu} (0.4)	{Pseu} (0.28)	{Pseu} (0.12)
	Θ (0.6)	{Pseu} (0.42)	Θ (0.18)

Note that $\kappa=0$ in this example, so no normalization is required (i.e., $1-\kappa=1$).

$$m_1 \oplus m_2(\{\text{Pseu}\}) = 0.28 + 0.12 + 0.42 = 0.82$$

$$m_1 \oplus m_2(\Theta) = 0.18$$

Note that $m_1 \oplus m_2$ is a bpa that, like m_1 and m_2, assigns some belief to a certain subset of Θ, {Pseu}, and the remaining belief to Θ. For two confirming rules, the subset is a singleton; for disconfirming rules, the subset is a set of size $n-1$, where n is the size of Θ.

This category demonstrates that the original MYCIN CF combining function is a special case of the Dempster function (MYCIN would also combine 0.4 and 0.7 to get 0.82). From earlier definitions, it can easily be shown, using the Dempster-Shafer model to derive a new bpa corresponding to the combination of two CF's of the same sign, that

$$\begin{aligned} m_1 \oplus m_2(A) &= s_1 s_2 + s_1(1-s_2) + s_2(1-s_1) \text{ where } s_i = m_i(A),\ i=1, 2 \\ &= s_1 + s_2(1-s_1) \\ &= s_2 + s_1(1-s_2) \\ &= 1 - (1-s_1)(1-s_2) \\ &= 1 - m_1 \oplus m_2(\Theta) \end{aligned}$$

Category 2. One rule is confirming and the other disconfirming of the same singleton hypothesis. For example, one rule confirms {Pseu} to degree 0.4, and the other disconfirms {Pseu} to degree 0.8. The effect of triggering these two rules is represented by bpa's m_1 and m_3, where m_1 is defined in the example from Category 1 and $m_3(\{\text{Pseu}\}^c) = 0.8$, $m_3(\Theta) = 0.2$. The combined effect on belief is given by $m_1 \oplus m_3$.

		m_3	
		{Pseu}^{c} (0.8)	Θ(0.2)
m_1	{Pseu} (0.4)	$\varnothing$ (0.32)	{Pseu} (0.08)
	Θ (0.6)	{Pseu}^{c} (0.48)	Θ (0.12)

Here $\kappa = 0.32$ and $1-\kappa = 0.68$.

$$m_1 \oplus m_3(\{\text{Pseu}\}) = 0.08/0.68 = 0.118$$

$$m_1 \oplus m_3(\{\text{Pseu}\}^c) = 0.48/0.68 = 0.706$$

$$m_1 \oplus m_3(\Theta) = 0.12/0.68 = 0.176$$

$m_1 \oplus m_3$ is 0 for all other subsets of Θ

Given m_1 above, the belief interval of {Pseu} is initially $[\text{Bel}_1(\{\text{Pseu}\})\ \ 1-\text{Bel}_1(\{\text{Pseu}\}^c)] = [0.4\ \ 1]$. After combination with m_3, it becomes $[0.118\ \ 0.294]$. Similarly, given m_3 alone, the belief interval of {Pseu} is $[0\ \ 0.2]$. After combination with m_1, it becomes $[0.118\ \ 0.294]$.

As is illustrated in this category of evidence aggregation, an essential aspect of the Dempster combination rule is the reducing effect of evidence supporting a subset of Θ on belief in subsets disjoint from this subset. Thus evidence confirming $\{\text{Pseu}\}^c$ will reduce the effect of evidence confirming {Pseu}; in this case the degree of support for {Pseu}, 0.4, is reduced to 0.118. Conversely, evidence confirming {Pseu} will reduce the effect of evidence confirming $\{\text{Pseu}\}^c$; 0.8 is reduced to 0.706. These two effects are reflected in the modification of the belief interval of {Pseu} from [0.4 1] to [0.118 0.294], where $0.294 = 1 - \text{Bel}(\{\text{Pseu}\}^c) = 1 - 0.706$.

If $A=\{\text{Pseu}\}$, $s_1=m_1(A)$, and $s_3=m_3(A^c)$, we can examine this modification of belief quantitatively:

$$m_1 \oplus m_3(A) = s_1(1-s_3)/(1-s_1s_3) \text{ where } \kappa = s_1s_3$$

$$m_1 \oplus m_3(A^c) = s_3(1-s_1)/(1-s_1s_3)$$

$$m_1 \oplus m_3(\Theta) = (1-s_1)(1-s_3)/(1-s_1s_3)$$

Thus s_1 is multiplied by the factor $(1-s_3)/(1-s_1s_3)$, and s_3 is multiplied by $(1-s_1)/(1-s_1s_3)$. Each of these factors is less than or equal to 1.[4] Thus combination of confirming and disconfirming evidence reduces the support provided by each before combination.

Consider the application of the MYCIN CF combining function to this situation. If CF_p is the positive (confirming) CF for {Pseu} and CF_n is the negative (disconfirming) CF:[5]

$$\begin{aligned} \text{CF}_{\text{COMBINE}}[\text{CF}_p,\text{CF}_n] &= (\text{CF}_p + \text{CF}_n)/(1 - \min\{|\text{CF}_p|,|\text{CF}_n|\}) \\ &= (s_1 - s_3)/(1 - \min\{s_1,s_3\}) \\ &= (0.4 - 0.8)/(1 - 0.4) \\ &= -0.667 \end{aligned}$$

When this CF is translated into the language of Dempster-Shafer, the result of the MYCIN combining function is belief in {Pseu} and $\{\text{Pseu}\}^c$ to the degrees 0 and 0.667, respectively. The larger disconfirming evidence of 0.8 essentially negates the smaller confirming evidence of 0.4. The confirming evidence reduces the effect of the disconfirming from 0.8 to 0.667.

By examining $\text{CF}_{\text{COMBINE}}$, it is easily seen that its application to CF's of the opposite sign results in a CF whose sign is that of the CF of greater magnitude. Thus support for A and A^c is combined into reduced support for one or the other. In contrast, the Dempster function results in reduced support for *both* A and A^c. The Dempster function seems to us a more realistic reflection of the competing effects of conflicting pieces of evidence.

Looking more closely at the value of 0.667 computed by the MYCIN function, we observe that its magnitude is less than that of the correspond-

---

[4] $s_1s_3 \leq s_i$ implies $1-s_1s_3 \geq 1-s_i$ implies $(1-s_i)/(1-s_1s_3) \leq 1$ for $i=1, 3$.

[5] See Section 10.2 for a discussion of this modified version of the original CF combining function, which was defined and defended in Chapter 11.

ing value of 0.706 computed by the Dempster function. It can be shown that the MYCIN function always results in greater reductions. To summarize, if s_1 and s_3 represent support for A and A^c, respectively, with $s_1 \geqslant s_3$, and if s_1' and s_3' represent support after Dempster combination, then the MYCIN function results in support for only A, where this support is less than s_1'. Similarly, if $s_3 \geqslant s_1$, the MYCIN function results in support for only A^c, where the magnitude of this support is less than s_3'.

The difference in the two approaches is most evident in the case of aggregation of two pieces of evidence, one confirming A to degree s and the other disconfirming A to the same degree. MYCIN's function yields $\text{CF}=0$, whereas the Dempster rule yields belief of $s(1-s)/(1-s^2)=s/(1+s)$ in each of A and A^c. These results are clearly very different, and again the Dempster rule seems preferable on the grounds that the effect of confirming and disconfirming evidence of the same weight should be different from that of no evidence at all.

We now examine the effect on belief of combination of two pieces of evidence supporting mutually exclusive singleton hypotheses. The MYCIN combining function results in no effect and differs most significantly from the Dempster rule in this case.

Category 3. The rules involve different hypotheses in the same frame of discernment. For example, one rule confirms {Pseu} to degree 0.4, and the other disconfirms {Strep} to degree 0.7. The triggering of the second rule gives rise to m_4 defined by $m_4(\{\text{Strep}\}^c)=0.7$, $m_4(\Theta)=0.3$. The combined effect on belief is given by $m_1 \oplus m_4$.

		m_4	
		{Strep}^{c} (0.7)	Θ (0.3)
m_1	{Pseu} (0.4)	{Pseu} (0.28)	{Pseu} (0.12)
	Θ (0.6)	{Strep}^{c} (0.42)	Θ (0.18)

In this case, $\kappa=0$.

$$m_1 \oplus m_4(\{\text{Pseu}\}) = 0.28 + 0.12 = 0.40$$

$$m_1 \oplus m_4(\{\text{Strep}\}^c) = 0.42$$

$$m_1 \oplus m_4(\Theta) = 0.18$$

$m_1 \oplus m_4$ is 0 for all other subsets of Θ

$$\text{Bel}_1 \oplus \text{Bel}_4(\{\text{Pseu}\}) = 0.40$$

$$\begin{aligned}\text{Bel}_1 \oplus \text{Bel}_4(\{\text{Strep}\}^c) &= m_1 \oplus m_4(\{\text{Strep}\}^c) + m_1 \oplus m_4(\{\text{Pseu}\}) \\ &= 0.42 + 0.40 \\ &= 0.82\end{aligned}$$

$$\text{Bel}_1 \oplus \text{Bel}_4(\{\text{Pseu}\}^c) = \text{Bel}_1 \oplus \text{Bel}_4(\{\text{Strep}\}) = 0$$

Before combination, the belief intervals for {Pseu} and $\{\text{Strep}\}^c$ are [0.4 1] and [0.7 1], respectively. After combination, they are [0.4 1] and [0.82 1], respectively. Note that evidence confirming {Pseu} has also confirmed $\{\text{Strep}\}^c$, a superset of {Pseu}, but that evidence confirming $\{\text{Strep}\}^c$ has had no effect on belief in {Pseu}, a subset of $\{\text{Strep}\}^c$.

13.2.4 Evidence Combination Scheme

We now propose an implementation in MYCIN of the Dempster-Shafer method, which minimizes computational complexity. Barnett (1981) claims that direct translation of the theory, without attention to the order in which the belief functions representing rules are combined, results in exponential increases in the time for computations. This is due to the need to enumerate all subsets or supersets of a given set. Barnett's scheme reduces the computations to linear time by combining the functions in a simplifying order. We outline his scheme adapted to MYCIN.

Step 1. For each triple (i.e., singleton hypothesis), combine all bpa's representing rules confirming that value of the parameter. If $s_1, s_2, \ldots, s_k$ represent different degrees of support derived from the triggering of k rules confirming a given singleton, then the combined support is

$$1 - (1 - s_1)(1 - s_2) \ldots (1 - s_k)$$

(Refer to Category 1 combinations above if this is not obvious.) Similarly, for each singleton, combine all bpa's representing rules disconfirming that singleton. Thus all evidence confirming a singleton is pooled and represented by a bpa, and all evidence disconfirming the singleton (confirming the hypothesis corresponding to the set complement of the singleton) is pooled and represented by another bpa. We thus have $2n$ bpa's, where n is the size of Θ. These functions all have the same form as the original functions. This step is identical to the original approach for gathering confirming and disconfirming evidence into MB's and MD's, respectively.

Step 2. For each triple, combine the two bpa's computed in Step 1. Such a computation is a Category 2 combination and has been illustrated. We now have n bpa's, which are denoted $\text{Evi}_1, \text{Evi}_2, \ldots, \text{Evi}_n$.

Step 3. Combine the bpa's computed in Step 2 in one computation, using formulae developed by Barnett (1981), to obtain a final belief function Bel. A belief interval for each singleton hypothesis can then be computed. The form of the required computation is shown here without proof. See Barnett (1981) for a complete derivation.

Let $\{i\}$ represent the ith of n singleton hypotheses in Θ and let

$$\text{Evi}_i(\{i\}) = p_i$$

$$\text{Evi}_i(\{i\}^c) = c_i$$

$$\text{Evi}_i(\Theta) = r_i$$

Since $p_i + c_i + r_i = 1$, $r_i = 1 - p_i - c_i$. Let $d_i = c_i + r_i$. Then it can be shown that the function Bel resulting from combination of $\text{Evi}_1, \ldots, \text{Evi}_n$ is given by

$$\text{Bel}(\{i\}) = \text{K}[p_i \prod_{j \neq i} d_j + r_i \prod_{j \neq i} c_j]$$

For a subset A of Θ with $|A| > 1$,

$$\text{Bel}(A) = \text{K}([\prod_{\text{all } j} d_j] [\Sigma_{j \in A} p_i/d_j] + [\Pi_{j \notin A} c_j] [\Pi_{j \in A} d_j] - \prod_{\text{all } j} c_j)$$

where

$$\text{K}^{-1} = [\prod_{\text{all } j} d_j] [1 + \sum_{\text{all } j} p_j/d_j] - \prod_{\text{all } j} c_j$$

as long as $p_j \neq 1$ for all j.

An Example

The complex formulation for combining belief functions shown above is computationally straightforward for limited numbers of competing hypotheses such as are routinely encountered in medical domains. As we noted earlier, the INTERNIST program (Miller et al., 1982) partitions its extensive set of possible diagnoses into a limited subset of likely diseases that could be seen as the current frame of discernment. There are likely to be knowledge-based heuristics that can limit the search space in other domains and thereby make calculations of a composite belief function tenable.

Example 7. Consider, for example, the net effect of the following set of rules regarding the diagnosis of the infecting organism. Assume that all other rules failed and that the final conclusion about the beliefs in competing hypotheses will be based on the following successful rules:

R1: disconfirms {Pseu} to the degree 0.6
R2: disconfirms {Pseu} to the degree 0.2
R3: confirms {Strep} to the degree 0.4
R4: disconfirms {Staph} to the degree 0.8
R5: confirms {Strep} to the degree 0.3
R6: disconfirms {Pseu} to the degree 0.5

R7: confirms {Pseu} to the degree 0.3
R8: confirms {Staph} to the degree 0.7

Note, here, that Θ = {Staph, Strep, Pseu} and that for this example we are making the implicit assumption that the patient has an infection with one of these organisms.

Step 1. Considering first confirming and then disconfirming evidence for each organism, we obtain:

{Pseu} confirmed to the degree $s_1 = 0.3$, disconfirmed to the degree $s_1' = 1 - (1 - 0.6)(1 - 0.2)(1 - 0.5) = 0.84$

{Staph} confirmed to the degree $s_2 = 0.7$, disconfirmed to the degree $s_2' = 0.8$

{Strep} confirmed to the degree $s_3 = 1 - (1 - 0.4)(1 - 0.3) = 0.58$, disconfirmed to the degree $s_3' = 0$

Step 2. Combining the confirming and disconfirming evidence for each organism, we obtain:

$$\text{Evi}_1(\{\text{Pseu}\}) = \frac{0.3(1 - 0.84)}{1 - (0.3)(0.84)} = 0.064 = p_1$$

$$\text{Evi}_1(\{\text{Pseu}\}^c) = \frac{0.84(1 - 0.3)}{1 - (0.3)(0.84)} = 0.786 = c_1$$

Thus $r_1 = 0.15$ and $d_1 = 0.786 + 0.15 = 0.936$.

$$\text{Evi}_2(\{\text{Staph}\}) = \frac{0.7(1 - 0.08)}{1 - (0.7)(0.8)} = 0.318 = p_2$$

$$\text{Evi}_2(\{\text{Staph}\}^c) = \frac{0.8(1 - 0.07)}{1 - (0.7)(0.8)} = 0.545 = c_2$$

Thus $r_2 = 0.137$ and $d_2 = 0.545 + 0.137 = 0.682$.

$$\text{Evi}_3(\{\text{Strep}\}) = 0.58 = p_3$$

$$\text{Evi}_3(\{\text{Strep}\}^c) = 0 = c_3$$

Thus $r_3 = 0.42$ and $d_3 = 0.42$.

Step 3. Assessing the effects of belief in the various organisms on each other, we obtain:

$$
\begin{aligned}
K^{-1} &= d_1 d_2 d_3(1 + p_1/d_1 + p_2/d_2 + p_3/d_3) - c_1 c_2 c_3 \\
&= (0.936)(0.682)(0.42)(1 + 0.064/0.936 + 0.318/0.682 \\
&\qquad + 0.58/0.42) - (0.786)(0.545)(0) \\
&= 0.268(1 + 0.068 + 0.466 + 1.38) \\
&= 0.781 \\
K &= 1.28
\end{aligned}
$$

$$
\begin{aligned}
\text{Bel}(\{\text{Pseu}\}) &= K(p_1 d_2 d_3 + r_1 c_2 c_3) \\
&= 1.28((0.064)(0.682)(0.42) + (0.15)(0.545)0) \\
&= 0.023
\end{aligned}
$$

$$
\begin{aligned}
\text{Bel}(\{\text{Staph}\}) &= K(p_2 d_1 d_3 + r_2 c_1 c_3) \\
&= 1.28((0.318)(0.936)(0.42) + (1.137)(0.786)0) \\
&= 0.160
\end{aligned}
$$

$$
\begin{aligned}
\text{Bel}(\{\text{Strep}\}) &= K(p_3 d_1 d_2 + r_3 c_1 c_2) \\
&= 1.28((0.58)(0.936)(0.682) + (0.42)(0.786)(0.545))
\end{aligned}
$$

$$
\begin{aligned}
\text{Bel}(\{\text{Pseu}\}^c) &= K(d_1 d_2 d_3(p_2/d_2 + p_3/d_3) + c_1 d_2 d_3 - c_1 c_2 c_3) \\
&= 1.28(0.268(0.466 + 1.381) + (0.786)(0.682)(0.42)) \\
&= 0.922
\end{aligned}
$$

$$
\begin{aligned}
\text{Bel}(\{\text{Staph}\}^c) &= K(d_1 d_2 d_3(p_1/d_1 + p_3/d_3) + c_2 d_1 d_3 - 0) \\
&= 1.28(0.268(0.068 + 1.381) + (0.545)(0.936)(0.42)) \\
&= 0.771
\end{aligned}
$$

$$
\begin{aligned}
\text{Bel}(\{\text{Strep}\}^c) &= K(d_1 d_2 d_3(p_1/d_1 + p_2/d_2) + c_3 d_1 d_2 - 0) \\
&= 1.28(0.268(0.068 + 0.466) + 0) \\
&= 0.184
\end{aligned}
$$

The final belief intervals are therefore:

Pseu: [0.023 0.078] Staph: [0.160 0.229] Strep: [0.704 0.816]

13.3 Conclusion

The Dempster-Shafer theory is particularly appealing in its potential for handling evidence bearing on categories of diseases as well as on specific disease entities. It facilitates the aggregation of evidence gathered at varying levels of detail or specificity. Thus collaborating experts could specify rules that refer to semantic concepts at whatever level in the domain hierarchy is most natural and appropriate. They would not be limited to the most specific level—the singleton hypotheses of their frame of discernment—but would be free to use more unifying concepts.

In a system in which all evidence either confirms or disconfirms singleton hypotheses, the combination of evidence via the Dempster scheme is computationally simple if ordered appropriately. Due to its present rule format, MYCIN provides an excellent setting in which to implement the theory. Claims by others that MYCIN is ill-suited to this implementation due to failure to satisfy the mutual exclusivity requirement (Barnett, 1981) reflect a misunderstanding of the program's representation and control mechanisms. Multiple diseases are handled by instantiating each as a separate context; within a given context, the requirements of single-valued parameters maintain mutual exclusivity.

In retrospect, however, we recognize that the hierarchical relationships that exist in the MYCIN domain are not adequately represented. For example, evidence suggesting *Enterobacteriaceae* (a family of gram-negative rods) could have explicitly stated that relationship rather than depending on rules in which an observation supported a list of gram-negative organisms with varying CF's based more on guesswork than on solid data. The evidence really supported the higher-level concept, *Enterobacteriaceae*, and further breakdown may have been unrealistic. In actual practice, decisions about treatment are often made on the basis of high-level categories rather than specific organism identities (e.g., "I'm pretty sure this is an enteric organism, and would therefore treat with an aminoglycoside and a cephalosporin, but I have no idea which of the enteric organisms is causing the disease").

If the MYCIN knowledge base were restructured in a hierarchical fashion so as to allow reasoning about unifying high-level concepts as well as about the competing singleton hypotheses, then the computations of the Dempster-Shafer theory would increase exponentially in complexity. The challenge is therefore to make these computations tractable, either by a modification of the theory or by restricting the evidence domain in a reasonable way. Further work should be directed to this end.

PART FIVE

Generalizing MYCIN

14

Use of the MYCIN Inference Engine

One of the reasons for undertaking the original MYCIN experiment was to test the hypothesis that domain-specific knowledge could successfully be kept separate from the inference procedures. We felt we had done just that in the original implementation; specifically, we believed that knowledge of a new domain, when encoded in rules, could be substituted for MYCIN's knowledge of infectious diseases and that no changes to the inference procedures were required to produce MYCIN-like consultations. In the fall of 1974 Bill van Melle began to investigate our claim seriously. He wrote (van Melle, 1974):

> The MYCIN program for infectious disease diagnosis claims to be general. One ought to be able to take out the clinical knowledge and plug in knowledge about some other domain. The domain we had in mind was the diagnosis of failures in machines. We had available a 1975 *Pontiac Service Manual,* containing a wealth of diagnostic information, mostly in decision tree form, with branching on the results of specific mechanical tests. Since MYCIN's rule base can be viewed as an implicit decision tree, with judgments based on laboratory test results, it at least seemed plausible that rules could be written to represent these diagnostic procedures. Because of the need to understand a system in order to write rules for diagnosing it, a fairly simple system, the horn circuit, was selected for investigation.

After some consideration, van Melle decided that the problem required only a degenerate context tree, with "the horn" as the only context, and that all relevant rules in the Pontiac manual could be written as definitional rules with no uncertainty. Two rules of his fifteen-rule system are shown in Figure 14-1.

Much of MYCIN's elaborate mechanism for gathering and weighing evidence was unnecessary for this simple problem. Nevertheless, the project provided support for our belief that MYCIN's diagnostic procedures

RULE002

IF: 1) The horn is inoperative is a symptom of the horn, and
2) The relay does click when the horn button is depressed, and
3) The test lamp does not light when one end is grounded and the other connected to the green wire terminal of the relay while the horn button is depressed

THEN: It is definite (1.0) that a diagnosis of the horn is replace the relay

[HORNRULES]

RULE003

IF: 1) The horn is inoperative is a symptom of the horn, and
2) The relay does not click when the horn button is depressed, and
3) The test lamp does light when one end is grounded and the other is touched to the black wire terminal of the relay

THEN: It is definite (1.0) that there is an open between the black wire terminal of the relay and ground

[HORNRULES]

FIGURE 14-1 English versions of two rules from the first nonmedical knowledge base for EMYCIN.

were general enough to allow substitutions of new knowledge bases.[1] As a result, we began the project described in Chapter 15, under the name EMYCIN.[2] In Chapter 16 we describe two applications of EMYCIN and discuss the extent to which building those two systems was easier because of the framework provided. Remember, too, that the MYCIN system itself was successfully reimplemented as another instantiation of EMYCIN.

The flexibility needed by MYCIN to extend or modify its knowledge base was exploited in EMYCIN. Neither the syntax of rules nor the basic ideas underlying the context tree and inference mechanism were changed. The main components of an EMYCIN consultation system are described in Chapter 5, specifically for the original MYCIN program. These are as follows:

---

[1]It also revealed several places in the code where shortcuts had been taken in keeping medical knowledge separate. For example, the term *organism* was used in the code occasionally as being synonymous with *cause*.

[2]We are indebted to Joshua Lederberg for suggesting the phrase Essential MYCIN, i.e, MYCIN stripped of its domain knowledge. EMYCIN is written in Interlisp, a programming environment for a particular dialect of the LISP language, and runs on a DEC PDP-10 or -20 under the TENEX or TOPS20 operating systems. The current implementation of EMYCIN uses about 45K words of resident memory and an additional 80K of swapped code space. The version of Interlisp in which it is embedded occupies about 130K of resident memory, leaving approximately 80K free for the domain knowledge base and the dynamic data structures built up during a consultation. A manual detailing the operation of the system for the prospective system designer is available (van Melle et al., 1981).

Contexts	Objects of interest, organized hierarchically in a tree, called the context tree
Parameters	The attributes of objects about which the system reasons
Rules	Associations among object-attribute-value triples

While these concepts were generalized and access to them made simpler, they are much the same in EMYCIN as they were in the original system.

The major conceptual shift in generalizing MYCIN to EMYCIN was to focus primarily on the persons who build new systems rather than on the persons who use them. Much of the interface to users remains unchanged. The interface to system builders, however, became easier and more transparent. We were attempting to reduce the time it takes to create an expert system by reducing the effort of a knowledge engineer in helping an expert. As discussed in Chapter 16, we believe the experiment was successful in this respect.

Much of the TEIRESIAS system (discussed in Chapter 9) has been incorporated in EMYCIN. Thus the debugging facilities are very similar. In addition, EMYCIN allows rules to be entered in the Abbreviated Rule Language, called ARL, that simplifies the expression of new relations. For example, the rule premise

```
($AND (SAME CNTXT SITE BLOOD)
      (GREATERP* (VAL1 CNTXT SICKDEGREE) 2)
      ($OR (NOTSAME CNTXT BURNED)
           (LESSERQ* (PLUS (VAL1 CNTXT NUMCULS)
                           (VAL1 CNTXT NUMPOS))
                     3)))
```

might have been entered as either

```
(SITE = BLOOD AND
SICKDEGREE > 2 AND
~BURNED OR NUMCULS + NUMPOS LE 3)
```

or

```
(SITE = BLOOD, SICKDEGREE > 2, ~BURNED OR NUMCULS + NUMPOS LE 3)
```

In the sample EMYCIN dialogue shown in Figure 14-2, EMYCIN can be seen to ask about contexts, parameters, and rules for a hypothetical consultation system about business problems. EMYCIN keeps track of the properties, such as TRANS (for the appropriate English translation of the concept name), and does the bookkeeping necessary to create a new knowledge base. Then it helps the user debug the knowledge base in the context of sample cases.

@<**EMYCIN**>**EMYCIN** *[Run EMYCIN from the appropriate directory.]*

EMYCIN 12-Dec-80 . . .

Do you wish to create a new knowledge base? **Yes**
Enter a word or phrase to describe your domain, i.e. fill in the blank in
"this program performs a ---- consultation". (e.g.
infectious disease, structural analysis).
**** business problem**
Enter a one-word name for the root of your context tree, the central "object" with which the consultation is concerned (e.g. PATIENT, STRUCTURE):
**** COMPANY** *[The "root" of the context tree]*
Please enter a word or phrase as "translation" of COMPANY:
** company--Okay? **Yes** *[EMYCIN makes the obvious suggestion, we accept it. The translation might have been fancier, say "municipal agency."]*

And the plural form is:
** companys--Okay? **No** *[EMYCIN doesn't know some spelling rules.]*
**** companies** *[So spell it right.]*
Parameter group: COMPANY-PARMS--Okay? **Yes**
COMPANY
PRINTID: COMPANY--Okay? **Yes** *[i.e., there will be a COMPANY-1, COMPANY-2, in consultations]*
Enter a list of parameters which will always be asked to the user when a COMPANY is created:
COMPANY
INTIALDATA: **(CNAME PROBLEM EMPLOYEES)**
And now a list of parameters to infer whenever a COMPANY is created:
COMPANY
GOALS: **(TOOLS)**
Do you want the program to automatically display the values concluded for some or all of the GOALS? **Yes**
[Automatically print the values of TOOLS at end of each consultation.]
Now please define each of the parameters listed above. Each is a member of COMPANY-PARMS.
What kind of parm is CNAME--Yes/No, Singlevalued, Multivalued, or Ask-All? **Singlevalued**
CNAME
EXPECT: **ANY**
CNAME
TRANS: **(THE NAME OF *)**
CNAME
PROMPT: **(WHAT COMPANY IS HAVING A PROBLEM?)**

What kind of parm is PROBLEM--Yes/No, Singlevalued, Multivalued, or Ask-All? **Singlevalued**
PROBLEM
EXPECT: **(PAYROLL INVENTORY)**
PROBLEM
TRANS: **(THE TYPE OF PROBLEM)**

FIGURE 14-2 Sample dialogue with EMYCIN to create a new consultation program for business problems. (User's input is in boldface, and <cr> indicates that the user typed a carriage return. Comments are in italics.) [This sample is taken from *The EMYCIN Manual* (van Melle et al., 1981).]

PROBLEM
PROMPT: **(IS THE PROBLEM WITH PAYROLL OR INVENTORY?)**

What kind of parm is EMPLOYEES--Yes/No, Singlevalued, Multivalued, Ask-All? **Singlevalued**
EMPLOYEES
EXPECT: **POSNUMB**
EMPLOYEES
UNITS: <**cr**> *[<cr> here gives the property a value of NIL.]*
EMPLOYEES
RANGE: <**cr**>
EMPLOYEES
TRANS: **(THE NUMBER OF EMPLOYEES OF *)**
EMPLOYEES
PROMPT: **(HOW MANY PEOPLE DOES * EMPLOY?)**

What kind of parm is TOOLS--Yes/No, Singlevalued, Multivalued, or Ask-All? **Multivalued**
TOOLS
LEGALVALS: **TEXT** *[Values produced by CONCLUDETEXT, the results to be printed.]*

TOOLS
TRANS: **(THE TOOLS TO USE IN SOLVING THE PROBLEM)**

Okay, now back to COMPANY . . . *[Now that we've defined those parms, finish defining the context type.]*

COMPANY
SYN: (((CNAME) (CNAME)))--Yes, No, or Edit? **Yes** *[The company name (CNAME) will be used to translate a COMPANY.]*
Creating rule group COMPANYRULES to apply to COMPANY contexts . . .

. . Autosave . .
Please give a one-word identifier for your knowledge base files:
**** BUSINESS**
<EMYCIN>CHANGES.BUSINESS;1
Are there any descendants of COMPANY in the context tree? **No**

Rules, Parms, Go, etc.? **Rules**
Author of any new rules, if not yourself: <**cr**>
Will you be entering any of the rule information properties? **No** *[This is asked upon the first entrance to the rule editor.]*

Rule# or NEW: **NEW** *[Now enter rules to deduce each of the GOALS defined above; in this case, just TOOLS.]*

RULE001
PREMISE: **(PROBLEM = PAYROLL AND EMPLOYEES > 1000)**
RULE001
ACTION: **(TOOLS = "a large computer")**

Translate, No further change, or prop name: **TRANSLATE**

RULE001

[This rule applies to companies, and is tried in order to find out about the tools to use in solving the problem]

If: 1) The type of problem is payroll, and
2) The number of employees of the company is greater than 1000
Then: It is definite (1.0) that the following is one of the tools to use in solving the problem: a large computer

Translate, No further change, or prop name: <**cr**>

Rule# or NEW: <**cr**> *[Finished entering rules.]*

Rules, Parms, Go, etc.? **Save** *[Save the knowledge base.]*
<EMYCIN>CHANGES.BUSINESS;2
Rules, Parms, Go, etc.? **Go** *[Run a consultation to test the knowledge base.]*

Special options (type ? for help):
** <**cr**> *[No options needed.]*

20-Oct-79 14:16:48

--------COMPANY-1--------
1) What company is having a problem?
** **IBM**
2) Is the problem with payroll or inventory?
** **PAYROLL**
3) What is the number of employees of ibm?
** **10000000**
Conclusions: the tools to use in solving the problem are as follows: a large computer.

Enter Debug/review, Rules, Parms, Go, etc.? **Parameters**

Parameter name: **cname**
Property: **PROPERNOUN**
CNAME
PROPERNOUN: **T**
Property: <**cr**>

[A small parameter change—we noted that ibm was not capitalized. Setting the PROPERNOUN property will fix the problem.]

Parameter name: <**cr**> *[Finished entering parameters.]*

Rules, Parms, Go, etc.? **Save** *[Save these changes to the knowledge base.]*

<EMYCIN>CHANGES.BUSINESS;3

Rules, Parms, Go, etc.? **Quit**
@
.
.
.

[Sometime later...]

@<**EMYCIN**>**EMYCIN**
EMYCIN 12-DEC-80

Hi.

Should I load <EMYCIN>CHANGES.BUSINESS;3? **Yes**
File created 25-Sep-81 10:49:24
CHANGESCOMS

FIGURE 14-2 continued

(<EMYCIN>CHANGES.BUSINESS;3)

Do you want to enter Rules, Parms, Go, etc. (? for help)? **New consultation**
[confirm] <**cr**>
Special options (type ? for help):
** <**cr**>

23-Feb-91 10:28:37

--------COMPANY-1--------
1) What company is having a problem?
**** STANFORD**
2) Is the problem with payroll or inventory?
**** INVENTORY**
3) How many people does Stanford employ?
**** 10000**

I was unable to make any conclusion about the tools to use in solving the problem.

[No rules have yet been entered for making conclusions about inventory problems.]

Enter Debug/review phase, or other option (? for help)? **Quit**

FIGURE 14-2 continued

15

EMYCIN: A Knowledge Engineer's Tool for Constructing Rule-Based Expert Systems

William van Melle, Edward H. Shortliffe, and Bruce G. Buchanan

Much current work in artificial intelligence focuses on computer programs that aid scientists with complex reasoning tasks. Recent work has indicated that one key to the creation of intelligent systems is the incorporation of large amounts of task-specific knowledge. Building knowledge-based, or expert, systems from scratch can be very time-consuming, however. This suggests the need for general tools to aid in the construction of knowledge-based systems.

This chapter describes an effective domain-independent framework for constructing one class of expert programs: rule-based consultants. The system, called EMYCIN, is based on the domain-independent core of the MYCIN program. We have reimplemented MYCIN as one of the consultation systems that run under EMYCIN.

15.1 The Task

EMYCIN is used to construct a *consultation program,* by which we mean a program that offers advice on problems within its domain of expertise. The consultation program elicits information relevant to the case by asking

---

This chapter is a shortened and edited version of a paper appearing in *Pergamon-Infotech state of the art report on machine intelligence,* pp. 249–263. Maidenhead, Berkshire, U.K.: Infotech Ltd., 1981.

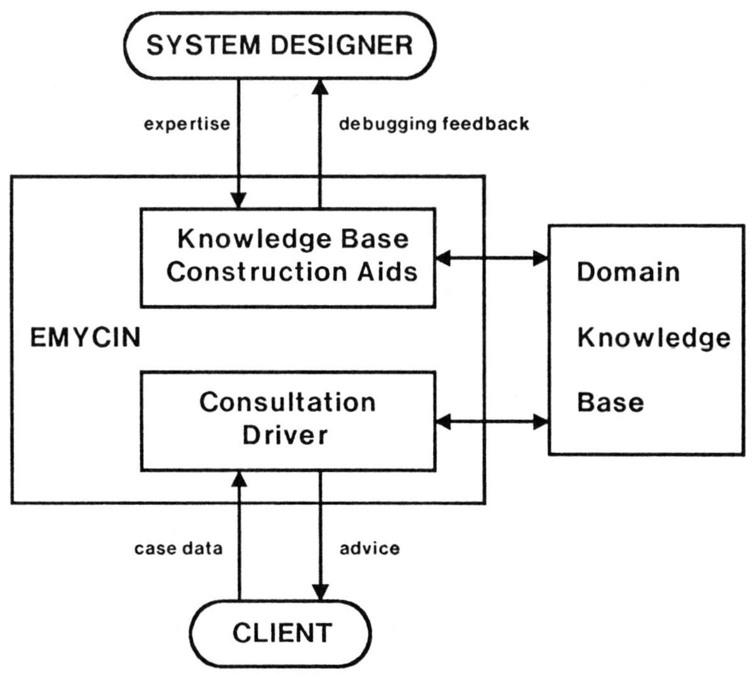

FIGURE 15-1 The major roles of EMYCIN: acquiring a knowledge base from the system designer, and interpreting that knowledge base to provide advice to a client.

questions. It then applies its knowledge to the specific facts of the case and informs the user of its conclusions. The user is free to ask the program questions about its reasoning in order to better understand or validate the advice given.

There are really two "users" of EMYCIN, as depicted in Figure 15-1. The *system designer,* or *expert,* interacts with EMYCIN to produce a *knowledge base* for the domain. EMYCIN then interprets this knowledge base to provide advice to the *client,* or *consultation user.* Thus the combination of EMYCIN and a specific knowledge base of domain expertise is a new *consultation program.* Some instances of such consultation programs are described below.

15.2 Background

Some of the earliest work in artificial intelligence attempted to create generalized problem solvers. Programs such as GPS (Newell and Simon, 1972) and theorem provers (Nilsson, 1971), for instance, were inspired by the apparent generality of human intelligence and motivated by the desire to develop a single program applicable to many problems. While this early work demonstrated the utility of many general-purpose techniques (such as problem decomposition into subgoals and heuristic search in its many forms), these techniques alone did not offer sufficient power for high performance in complex domains.

Recent work has instead focused on the incorporation of large amounts of task-specific knowledge in what have been called *knowledge-based systems.* Such systems have emphasized high performance based on the accumulation of large amounts of knowledge about a single domain rather than on nonspecific problem-solving power. Some examples to date include efforts at symbolic manipulation of algebraic expressions (Moses, 1971), chemical inference (Lindsay et al., 1980), and medical consultations (Pople, 1977; Shortliffe, 1976). Although these systems display an expert level of performance, each is powerful in only a very narrow domain. In addition, assembling the knowledge base and constructing a working program for such domains is a difficult, continuous task that has often extended over several years. However, because MYCIN included in its design the goal of keeping the domain knowledge well separated from the program that manipulates the knowledge, the basic rule methodology provided a foundation for a more general rule-based system.

With the development of EMYCIN we have now come full circle to GPS's philosophy of separating the deductive mechanism from the problem-specific knowledge; however, EMYCIN's extensive user facilities make it a much more accessible environment for producing expert systems than were the earlier programs.[1] Like MYCIN's, EMYCIN's representation of facts is in attribute-object-value triples, with an associated certainty factor. Facts are associated in *production rules.* Rules of the same form are shown throughout this book. Figures 16-2 and 16-5 in the next chapter show rules from two different consultation systems constructed in EMYCIN.

15.2.1 Application of Rules—The Rule Interpreter

The control structure is primarily MYCIN's goal-directed backward chaining of rules. At any given time, EMYCIN is working toward the goal of establishing the value of some parameter of a context; this operation is termed *tracing* the parameter. To this end, the system retrieves the (precomputed) list of rules whose conclusions bear on the goal. SACON's Rule 50 (see Figures 15-2 and 16-2) would be one of several rules retrieved in an attempt to determine the stress of a substructure. Then for each rule

[1]Even so, it is still not an appropriate tool for building certain kinds of application systems because some of its power comes from the specificity of the rule-based representation and backward-chaining inference structure. See Section 15.5 for a discussion of these limitations.

in the list, EMYCIN evaluates the premise; if true, it makes the conclusion indicated in the action. The order of the rules in the list is assumed to be arbitrary, and all the rules are applied unless one of them succeeds and concludes the value of the parameter with certainty (in which case the remaining rules are superfluous).

This control structure was also designed to be able to deal gracefully with incomplete information. If the user is unable to supply some piece of data, the rules that need the data will fail and make no conclusions. The system will thus make conclusions, if possible, based on less information. Similarly, if the system has inadequate rules (or none at all) for concluding some parameter, it may ask the user for the value. When too many items of information are missing, of course, the system will be unable to offer sound advice.

15.2.2 More on the Rule Representation

There are many advantages to having rules as the primary representation of knowledge. Since each rule is intended to be a single "chunk" of information, the knowledge base is inherently modular, making it relatively easy to update. Individual rules can be added, deleted, or modified without drastically affecting the overall performance of the system. The rules are also a convenient unit for explanation purposes, since a single step in the reasoning process can be meaningfully explained by citing the English translation of the rule used.

While the syntax of rules permits the use of any LISP functions as matching predicates in the premises of rules, or as special action functions in the conclusions of rules, there is a small set of standard functions that are most frequently used. The system contains information about the use of these predicates and functions in the form of function *templates*. For example, the predicate SAME is described as follows:

(a) *function template:* (SAME CNTXT PARM VALUE)
(b) *sample function call:* (SAME CNTXT SITE BLOOD)

The system can use these templates to "read" its own rules. For example, the template shown here contains the standard symbols CNTXT, PARM, and VALUE, indicating the components of the associative triple that SAME tests. If clause (b) above appears in the premise of a given rule, the system can determine that the rule needs to know the site of the culture and, in particular, that it tests whether the culture site is (i.e., is the same as) blood. When asked to display rules that are relevant to blood cultures, the system will know that this rule should be selected. The most common matching predicates and conclusion functions are those used in MYCIN (see Chapter 5): SAME, NOTSAME, KNOWN, NOTKNOWN, DEFINITE, NOTDEFINITE, etc.

15.2.3 Explanation Capability

As will be described in Part Six, EMYCIN's *explanation program* allows the user of a consultation program to interrogate the system's knowledge, either to find out about inferences made (or not made) during a particular consultation or to examine the static knowledge base in general, independently of any specific consultation.

During the consultation, EMYCIN can offer explanations of the current, past, and likely future lines of reasoning. If the motivation for any question that the program asks is unclear, the client may temporarily put off answering and instead inquire why the information is needed. Since each question is asked in an attempt to evaluate some rule, a first approximation to an explanation is simply to display the rule currently under consideration. The program can also explain what reasoning led to the current point and what use might later be made of the information being requested. This is made possible by examining records left by the rule interpreter and by reading the rules in the knowledge base to determine which are relevant. This form of explanation requires no language understanding by the program; it is invoked by simple commands from the client (WHY and HOW).

Another form of explanation is available via the *Question-Answering (QA) Module,* which is automatically invoked after the consultation has ended, and which can also be entered during the consultation to answer questions other than those handled by the specialized WHY and HOW commands mentioned above. The QA Module accepts simple English-language questions (a) dealing with any conclusion drawn during the consultation, or (b) about the domain in general. Explanations are again based on the rules; they should be comprehensible to anyone familiar with the domain, even if that person is not familiar with the intricacies of the EMYCIN system. The questions are parsed by pattern matching and keyword look-up, using a dictionary that defines the vocabulary of the domain. EMYCIN automatically constructs the dictionary from the English phrases used in defining the contexts and parameters of the domain; the system designer may refine this preliminary dictionary to add synonyms or to fine-tune QA's parsing.

15.3 The System-Building Environment

The system designer's principal task is entering and debugging a knowledge base, viz., the rules and the object-attribute structures on which they operate. The level at which the dialogue between system and expert takes place is an important consideration for speed and efficiency of acquisition.

```
IF:  Composition = (LISTOF METALS) and
     Error < 5 and
     Nd-stress > .5 and
     Cycles > 10000
THEN:  Ss-stress = fatigue
```

FIGURE 15-2 Example of ARL format for SACON's Rule 50.

The knowledge base must eventually reside in the internal LISP format that the system manipulates to run the consultation and to answer questions. At the very basic level, one could imagine a programmer using the LISP editor to create the necessary data structures totally by hand;[2] here the entire translation from the expert's conceptual rule to LISP data structures is performed by the programmer. At the other extreme, the expert would enter rules in English, with the entire burden of understanding placed on the program.

The actual means used in EMYCIN is at a point between these extremes. Entering rules at the base LISP level is too error-prone, and requires greater facility with LISP on the part of the system designer than is desirable. On the other hand, understanding English rules is far too difficult for a program, especially in a new domain where the vocabulary has not even been identified and organized for the program's use. (Just recognizing new parameters in free English text is a major obstacle.[3]) EMYCIN instead provides a terse, stylized, but easily understood, language for writing rules and a high-level knowledge base editor for the knowledge structures in the system. The knowledge base editor performs extensive checks to catch common input errors, such as misspellings, and handles all necessary bookkeeping chores. This allows the system builder to try out new ideas quickly and thereby to get some idea of the feasibility of any particular formulation of the domain knowledge into rules.

15.3.1 Entering Rules

The Abbreviated Rule Language (ARL) constitutes an intermediate form between English and pure LISP. ARL is a simplified ALGOL-like language that uses the names of the parameters and their values as operands; the operators correspond to EMYCIN predicates. For example, SACON's Rule 50 could have been entered or printed as shown in Figure 15-2.

ARL resembles a shorthand form derived from an *ad hoc* notation that we have seen several of our domain experts use to sketch out sets of rules.

[2]This is the way the extensive knowledge base for the initial MYCIN system was originally created.

[3]The task of building an assistant for designers of new EMYCIN systems is the subject of current research by James Bennett (Bennett, 1983). The name of the program is ROGET.

The parameter names are simply the labels that the expert uses in defining the parameters of the domain. Thus they are familiar to the expert. The conciseness of ARL makes it much easier to enter than English or LISP, which is an important consideration when entering a large body of rules.

Rule Checking

As each rule is entered or edited, it is checked for syntactic validity to catch common input errors. By syntactic, we mean issues of rule form—whether terms are spelled correctly, values are legal for the parameters with which they are associated, etc.—rather than the actual information content (i.e., semantic considerations as to whether the rule "makes sense"). Performing the syntactic check at acquisition time reduces the likelihood that the consultation program will fail due to "obvious" errors, thus freeing the expert to concentrate on debugging logical errors and omissions. These issues are also discussed in Chapter 8.

EMYCIN's purely syntactic check is made by comparing each clause with the corresponding function template and seeing that, for example, each PARM slot is filled by a valid parameter and that its VALUE slot holds a legal value for the parameter. If an unknown parameter is found, the checker tries to correct it with the Interlisp spelling corrector, using a spelling list of all parameters in the system. If that fails, it asks if this is a new (previously unmentioned) parameter. If so, it defines the new parameter and, in a brief diversion, prompts the system builder to describe it. Similar action is also taken if an illegal value for a parameter is found.

A limited semantic check is also performed: each new or changed rule is compared with any existing rules that conclude about the same parameter to make sure it does not directly contradict or subsume any of them. A contradiction occurs when two rules with the same set of premise clauses make conflicting conclusions (contradictory values or CF's for the same parameter); subsumption occurs when one rule's premise is a subset of another's, so that the first rule succeeds whenever the second one does (i.e., the second rule is more specific), and both conclude about the same values. In either case, the interaction is reported to the expert, who may then examine or edit any of the offending rules.

15.3.2 Describing Parameters

Information characterizing the parameters and contexts of the domain is stored as *properties* of each context or parameter being described. When a new entity is defined, the acquisition routines automatically prompt for the properties that are always needed (e.g., EXPECT, the list of values expected for this parameter); the designer may also enter optional properties (those needed to support special EMYCIN features). The properties are all checked for validity, in a fashion similar to that employed by the rule checker.

15.3.3 System Maintenance

While the system designer builds up the domain knowledge base as described above, EMYCIN automatically keeps track of the changes that have been made (new or changed rules, parameters, etc.). The accumulated changes can be saved on a file by the system builder either explicitly with a simple command or automatically by the system every *n* changes (the frequency of automatic saving can be set by the system builder). When EMYCIN is started in a subsequent session, the system looks for this file of changes and loads it in to restore the knowledge base to its previous state.

15.3.4 Human Engineering

Although the discussion so far has concentrated on the acquisition of the knowledge base, it is also important that the resulting consultation program be pleasing in appearance to the user. EMYCIN's existing human-engineering features relieve the system builder of many of the tedious cosmetic concerns of producing a usable program. Since the main mode of interaction between the consultation program and the client is in the program's questions and explanations, most of the features concentrate on making that interface as comfortable as possible. A main feature in this category that has already been described is the explanation program—the client can readily find out why a question is being asked, or how the program arrived at its conclusions. The designer can also control, by optionally specifying the PROMPT property for each parameter that is asked for, the manner in which questions are phrased. More detail can be specified, for example, than would appear in a simple prompt generated by the system from the parameter's translation.

EMYCIN supplies a uniform input facility that allows the normal input-editing functions—character, word, and line deletions—and on display terminals allows more elegant editing capabilities (insertion or deletion in the middle of the line, for example) in the style of screen-oriented text editors. It performs spelling correction and TENEX-style completion[4] from a list of possible answers; most commonly this list is the list of legal

[4]After the user types ESCAPE or ALTMODE, EMYCIN fills out the rest of the phrase if the part the user has typed is unambiguous. For example, when EMYCIN expects the name of an organism, PSEU is unambiguous for PSEUDOMONAS-AERUGINOSA. Thus the automatic completion of input can save considerable effort and frustration.

values for the parameter being asked about, as supplied by the system designer.

In most places where EMYCIN prompts for input, the client may type a question mark to obtain help concerning the options available. When the program asks for the value of a parameter, EMYCIN can provide simple help by listing the legal answers to the question. The system designer can also include more substantial help by giving rephrasings of or elaborations on the original question; these are simply entered via the data base editor as an additional property of the parameter in question. This capability provides for both streamlined questions for experienced clients and more detailed explanations of what is being requested for those who are new to the consultation program.

15.3.5 Debugging the Knowledge Base

There is more to building a knowledge base than just entering rules and associated data structures. Any errors or omissions in the initial knowledge base must be corrected in the debugging process. In EMYCIN the principal method of debugging is to run sample consultations; i.e., the expert plays the role of a client seeking advice from the system and checks that the correct conclusions are made. As the expert discovers errors, he or she uses the knowledge acquisition facilities described above to modify existing rules or add new ones.

Although the explanation program was designed to allow the consultation user to view the program's reasoning, it is also a helpful high-level debugging aid for the system designer. Without having to resort to LISP-level manipulations, it is possible to examine any inferences that were made, find out why others failed, and thereby locate errors or omissions in the knowledge base. The TEIRESIAS program developed the WHY/HOW capability used in EMYCIN for this very task (see Chapter 9).

EMYCIN provides a debugger based on a portion of the TEIRESIAS program. The debugger actively guides the expert through the program's reasoning chain and locates faulty (or missing) rules. It starts with a conclusion that the expert has indicated is incorrect and follows the inference chain back to locate the error.

The rule interpreter also has a debugging mode, in which it prints out assorted information about what it is doing: which rules it tries, which ones succeed (and what conclusions they make), which ones fail (and for what reason), etc. If the printout indicates that a rule succeeded that should have failed, or vice versa, the expert can interrupt immediately, rather than waiting for the end of the consultation to do the more formal TEIRESIAS-style review.

In either case, once the problem is corrected, the expert can then restart and try again, with the consultation automatically replayed using the new or modified rules.

Case Library

EMYCIN has facilities for maintaining a library of sample cases. These can be used for testing a complete system, or for debugging a growing one. The answers given by the consultation user to all the questions asked during the consultation are simply stored away, indexed by their context and parameter. When a library case is rerun, answers to questions that were previously asked are looked up and automatically supplied; any new questions resulting from changes in the rule base are asked in the normal fashion. This makes it easy to check the performance of a new set of rules on a "standard" case. It is especially useful during an intensive debugging session, since the expert can make changes to the knowledge base and, with a minimum of extra typing, test those changes—effectively reducing the "turnaround time" between modifying a rule and receiving consultation feedback.

The BATCH Program

A problem common to most large systems is that new knowledge entered to fix one set of problems often introduces new bugs, affecting cases that once ran successfully. To simplify the task of keeping the knowledge base consistent with cases that are known to be correctly solved, EMYCIN's BATCH program permits the system designer to run any or all cases in the library in background mode. BATCH reports the occurrence of any changes in the results of the consultation and invokes the QA Module to explain why the changes occurred. Of course, the system builder must first indicate to the system which parameters represent the results or the most important intermediate steps by which the correctness of the consultation is to be judged. The use of the BATCH program could be viewed as a form of additional semantic checking to supplement the checking routinely performed at the time of rule acquisition.

15.3.6 The Rule Compiler

To improve efficiency in a running consultation program, EMYCIN provides a *rule compiler* that transforms the system's production rules into a decision tree, eliminating the redundant computation inherent in a rule interpreter. The rule compiler then compiles the resulting tree into machine code. The consultation program can thereby use an efficient deductive mechanism for running the actual consultation, while the flexible rule format remains available for acquisition, explanation, and debugging. For details about the rule compiler see van Melle (1980).

15.4 Applications

Several consultation systems have been written using EMYCIN. The original MYCIN program provides advice on diagnosis and therapy for infectious diseases. MYCIN is now implemented in EMYCIN, but its knowledge base was largely constructed before EMYCIN was developed as a separate system. SACON and CLOT (described in Chapter 16), PUFF (Aikins et al., 1983), HEADMED (Heiser et al., 1978), LITHO (Bonnet, 1981), DART (Bennett and Hollander, 1981), BLUEBOX (Mulsant and Servan-Schreiber, 1983), and several other demonstration systems have been successfully built in EMYCIN. All have clearly shown the power of starting with a well-developed framework and concentrating on the knowledge base. For example, to bring the SACON program to its present level of performance, about two person-months of the experts' time were required to explicate their task as consultants and to formulate the knowledge base, and about the same amount of time was required to implement and test the rules in a preliminary version of EMYCIN. CLOT was constructed as a joint effort by an experienced EMYCIN programmer and a collaborating medical student. Following approximately ten hours of discussion about the contents of the knowledge base, they entered and debugged in another ten hours a preliminary knowledge base of some 60 rules using EMYCIN. Both knowledge bases would need considerable refinement before the programs would be ready for general use. The important point, however, is that starting with a framework like EMYCIN allows system builders to focus quickly on the expertise necessary for high performance because the underlying framework is ready to accept it.

15.5 Range of Applicability

EMYCIN is designed to help build and run programs that provide consultative advice. The resulting consultation system takes as input a body of measurements or other information pertinent to a case and produces as output some form of recommendation or analysis of the case. The framework seems well suited for many diagnostic or analytic problems, notably some classes of fault diagnosis, where several input measurements (symptoms, laboratory tests) are available and the solution space of possible diagnoses can be enumerated. It is less well suited for "formation" problems, where the task is to piece together existing structures according to specified constraints to generate a solution.

EMYCIN was not designed to be a general-purpose representation language. It is thus wholly unsuited for some problems. The limitations derive largely from the fact that EMYCIN has chosen one basic, readily understood representation for the knowledge in a domain: production rules that are applied by a backward-chaining control structure and that operate on data in the form of associative triples. The representation, at least as implemented in EMYCIN, is unsuitable for problems of constraint satisfaction, or those requiring iterative techniques.[5] Among other classes of problems that EMYCIN does not attempt to handle are simulation tasks and tasks involving planning with stepwise refinement. One useful heuristic in thinking about the suitability of EMYCIN for a problem is that the consultation system should work with a "snapshot" of information about a case. Good advice should not depend on analyzing a continued stream of data over a time interval.

Even those domains that have been successfully implemented have demonstrated some of the inadequacies of EMYCIN. In addition to representational difficulties, other problems noted have been the lack of user control over the consultation dialogue (e.g., the order of questions) and the amount of time a user must spend supplying information. These limitations are discussed further in subsequent chapters.

[5]The VM program (Chapter 22), however, has shown that production rules can be used to provide advice in a dynamic setting where iterative monitoring is required. Greatly influenced by EMYCIN design issues, VM deals with the management of patients receiving assisted ventilation after cardiac surgery.

16

Experience Using EMYCIN

James S. Bennett and Robert S. Engelmore

The development of expert systems is plagued with a well-known and crucial bottleneck: in order for these systems to perform at all the domain-specific knowledge must be engineered into a form that can be embedded in the program. Advances in understanding and overcoming this knowledge acquisition bottleneck rest on an analysis of both the process and the product of our current, rather informal interactions with experts. To this end the purpose and structure of two quite dissimilar rule-based systems are reviewed. Both systems were constructed using the EMYCIN system after interviewing an expert. The first, SACON (Bennett et al., 1978), is meant to assist an engineer in selecting a method to perform a structural analysis; the second, CLOT (Bennett and Goldman, 1980), is meant to assist a physician in determining the presence of a blood clotting disorder.

The presentation of the details of these two systems is meant to accomplish two functions. The first is to provide an indication of the scope and content of these rule-based systems. The reader need not have any knowledge of the specific application domain; the chapter will present the major steps and types of inferences drawn by these consultants. This conceptual framework, what we term the *inference structure,* forms the basis for the expert's organization of the domain expertise and, hence, the basis for successful acquisition of the knowledge base and its continued maintenance. The second purpose of this chapter is to indicate the general form and function of these inference structures.

We first present the motivations and major concepts of both the SACON and CLOT systems. A final section then summarizes a number of observations about the knowledge acquisition process and the applicability of EMYCIN to these tasks. This chapter thus shows how the knowledge acquisition ideas from Chapter 9 and the EMYCIN framework from Chapter 15 have been used in domains other than infectious disease.

This chapter is a shortened and edited version of a paper appearing in *Pergamon-Infotech state of the art report on machine intelligence.* Maidenhead, Berkshire, U.K.: Infotech Ltd., 1981.

16.1 SACON: A Consultant for Structural Analysis

SACON (Structural Analysis CONsultant) was developed to advise nonexpert engineers in the use of a general-purpose computer program for structural analysis. The automated consultant was constructed using the EMYCIN system. Through a substitution of structural engineering knowledge for the medical knowledge, the program was converted easily from the domain of infectious diseases to the domain of structural analysis.

The purpose of a SACON consultation is to provide advice to a structural engineer regarding the use of a structural analysis program called MARC (MARC Corporation, 1976). The MARC program uses finite-element analysis techniques to simulate the mechanical behavior of objects, for example, the metal fatigue of an airplane wing. Engineers typically know *what* they want the MARC program to do—e.g., examine the behavior of a specific structure under expected loading conditions—but do not know *how* the simulation program should be set up to do it. The MARC program offers a large (and, to the novice, bewildering) choice of analysis methods, material properties, and geometries that may be used to model the structure of interest. From these options the user must learn to select an appropriate subset of methods that will simulate the correct physical behavior, preserve the desired accuracy, and minimize the (typically large) computational cost. A year of experience with the program is required to learn how to use all of MARC's options proficiently. The goal of the automated consultant is to bridge this "what-to-how" gap, by recommending an analysis strategy. This advice can then be used to direct the MARC user in the choice of specific input data—e.g., numerical methods and material properties. Typical structures that can be analyzed by both SACON and MARC include aircraft wings, reactor pressure vessels, rocket motor casings, bridges, and buildings.

16.1.1 The SACON Knowledge Base

The objective of a SACON consultation is to identify an *analysis strategy* for a particular structural analysis problem. The engineer can then implement this strategy, using the MARC program, to simulate the behavior of the structure. This section introduces the mathematical and physical concepts used by the consultant when characterizing the structure and recommending an analysis strategy.

An analysis strategy consists of an *analysis class* and a number of associated *analysis recommendations.* Analysis classes characterize the complexity of modeling the structure and the ability to analyze the material behaviors of the structure. Currently, 36 analysis classes are considered;

among them are Nonlinear Geometry Crack Growth, Nonlinear Geometry Stress Margin, Bifurcation, Material Instability, Inelastic Stiffness Degradation, Linear Analysis, and No Analysis. The analysis recommendations advise the engineer on specific features of the MARC program that should be activated when performing the actual structural analysis. (The example consultation in Figure 16-3 concludes with nine such recommendations.)

To determine the appropriate analysis strategy, SACON infers the critical material stress and deflection behaviors of a structure under a number of loading conditions. Among the material stress behaviors inferred by SACON are Yielding Collapse, Cracking Potential, Fatigue, and Material Instabilities; material deflection behaviors inferred by SACON are Excessive Deflection, Flexibility Changes, Incremental Strain Failure, Buckling, and Load Path Bifurcation.

Using SACON, the engineer decomposes the structure into one or more *substructures* and provides the data describing the materials, the general geometries, and the boundary conditions for each of these substructures. A substructure is a geometrically contiguous region of the structure composed of a single material, such as high-strength aluminum or structural steel, and having a specified set of kinematic boundary conditions. A structure may be subdivided by the structural engineer in a number of different ways; the decomposition is chosen that best reveals the worst-case material behaviors of the structure.

For each substructure, SACON estimates a numeric *total loading* from one or more *loadings*. Each loading applied to a substructure represents one of the typical mechanical forces on the substructure during its working life. Loadings might, for example, include loadings experienced during various maneuvers, such as braking and banking for planes, or, for buildings, loadings caused by natural phenomena, such as earthquakes and windstorms. Each loading is in turn composed of a number of point or distributed *load components*.

Given the descriptions of the component substructures and the descriptions of the loadings applied to each substructure, the consultant estimates stresses and deflections for each substructure using a number of simple *mathematical models*. The behaviors of the complete structure are found by determining the sum of the peak relative stress and deflection behaviors of all the substructures. Based on these peak responses (essentially the worst-case behaviors exhibited by the structure), its knowledge of available analysis types, and the tolerable analysis error, SACON recommends an analysis strategy. Figure 16-1 illustrates the basic types of inferences drawn by SACON during a consultation.

Judgmental knowledge for the domain, and about the structural analysis task in particular, is represented in EMYCIN in the form of production rules. An example of a rule, which provides the transition from simple numeric estimates of stress magnitudes to symbolic characterizations of stress behaviors for a substructure, is illustrated in Figure 16-2.

One major feature of EMYCIN that was not used in this task was the

Analysis Strategy of the Structure
↑
Worst-Case Stress and Deflection
Behaviors of the Structure
↑
Symbolic Stress and Deflection
Behaviors of Each Substructure
↑
Composite Numeric Stress and Deflection
Estimations of Each Loading
↑
Numeric Stress and Deflection
Magnitudes of Each Load Component

FIGURE 16-1 Inference structure during a SACON consultation. The user specifies loading and substructure descriptions that the system uses to infer material behaviors and, finally, an analysis strategy.

certainty factor mechanism—i.e., the ability to draw inferences using uncertain knowledge. The present consultation strategy and the associated mathematical models were designed to estimate extreme loading conditions, from which SACON concludes the appropriate analysis class. Consequently, by using a conservative model, the rules, though inexact, are sufficiently accurate for predicting response bounds with certainty.

The existing knowledge base is able to select from among 36 nonlinear analysis strategies. If nonlinear analysis is not indicated by the response estimates, the consultation recommends linear analysis. In addition, if relative stress and displacement estimates are low (less than 5% of critical values), the consultation indicates that no analysis is required. The knowledge base consists of 170 rules and about 140 consultation parameters. A

RULE050

IF: 1) The material composing the sub-structure is one of: the metals, and
2) The analysis error (in percent) that is tolerable is between 5 and 30, and
3) The non-dimensional stress of the sub-structure is greater than .9, and
4) The number of cycles the loading is to be applied is between 1000 and 10000
THEN: It is definite (1.0) that fatigue is one of the stress behavior phenomena in the sub-structure

```
PREMISE:  ($AND (SAME CNTXT MATERIAL (LISTOF METALS))
                (BETWEEN* CNTXT ERROR 5 30)
                (GREATER* CNTXT ND-STRESS .9)
                (BETWEEN* CNTXT CYCLES 1000 10000))
ACTION:   (CONCLUDE CNTXT SS-STRESS FATIGUE TALLY 1.0)
```

FIGURE 16-2 A sample rule from SACON, showing both the English and LISP forms.

typical consultation (2 substructures, 3 loadings, 3 load components) requires about 25 minutes in an interactive session.

The transcript in Figure 16-3 illustrates SACON's interactions with an engineer and SACON's recommendation of an analysis strategy. The engineer's responses to questions follow the prompt (**) and are printed in bold capitals.

July 26, 1978 10:54AM in <SACON>MARC.SAV;80709 by SACON>

Hello Dr. Melosh,

This consultation concerns the 747 wing. The purpose of the consultation is to demonstrate the general features of a structural analysis consultation on a simple problem. Thus the consultation involves only one substructure: The total wing.

26-Jul-78 10:54:44
[consultation of 13-Jul-78 1:55PM].
--------STRUCTURE-28--------
1) What is the name of STRUCTURE-28?
** **BOEING 747 WING**
2) Assuming that your characterization of the boeing 747 wing in terms of its geometry, material characteristics, and boundary conditions are accurate, how much error (in percent) is tolerable for the analysis?
** **10**
3) Do you want to examine the responses of the boeing 747 wing, to evaluate its instability, or both?
** **EXAMINE-RESPONSES**
4) Does the boeing 747 wing have any time dependent terms in its equations of equilibrium?
** **NO**
5) Is heating or cooling of interest in determining structure responses?
** **NO**
6) Have you decomposed the boeing 747 wing into a number of potential sub-structures which are relevant to this analysis?
** **YES**

--------SUB-STRUCTURE-1--------
7) What is the name of SUB-STRUCTURE-1?
** **TOTAL WING**
8) What is the material composing most of the total wing (SUB-STRUCTURE-1)?
** **HIGH-STRENGTH-ALUMINUM**
9) Enter the average longest dimension of the total wing (SUB-STRUCTURE-1) in inches (or <number> CMS):
** **1420**
10) Enter the weight of the total wing (SUB-STRUCTURE-1) in pounds (or <number> KGS):
** **46000**
11) Is the total wing (SUB-STRUCTURE-1) thin-walled or solid?
** **THIN-WALLED**
12) What is the configuration of support for the total wing (SUB-STRUCTURE-1)?
** **ONE-SIDE**
13) Is the total wing (SUB-STRUCTURE-1) to be modelled as a 1, 2, or 3 dimensional system?
** **2**
14) Would you describe the construction of the total wing (SUB-STRUCTURE-1) to be truss and/or frame elements (NETWORK), sheets and/or blocks of material (CONTINUUM), or a combination of both?
** **CONTINUUM**
15) Is the overall geometry of the total wing (SUB-STRUCTURE-1) curved or planar?
** **PLANAR**

FIGURE 16-3 A SACON consultation.

The first loading applied to the total wing (SUB-STRUCTURE-1) will be called:

--------LOADING-1--------
16) What is the name of LOADING-1?
** **FLIGHT**
17) Enter the number of loading cycles to be applied:
** **20000**
The first load component associated with LOADING-1 will be called:

--------LOAD-COMPONENT-1--------
18) Would you describe LOAD-COMPONENT-1 as being DISTRIBUTED over most of the sub-structure or as acting at a POINT of the sub-structure?
** **DISTRIBUTED**
19) Which surface of the sub-structure does LOAD-COMPONENT-1 act NORMAL to? (If more than one surface, you should consider the loading as two or more component loadings)
** **WIDTH-LENGTH**
20) Enter the average wall thickness of the total wing (SUB-STRUCTURE-1) in inches (or <number> CMS):
** **.31**
21) Enter the average depth of the total wing (SUB-STRUCTURE-1) in inches (or <number> CMS):
** **41**
22) Enter the magnitude of the distributed load (in psi):
** **1**
23) Are there any other load components associated with LOADING-1?
** **NO**
24) Are there any other loading conditions associated with the total wing (SUB-STRUCTURE-1)?
** **NO**
25) Are there any other sub-structures of the boeing 747 wing relevant to this analysis?
** **NO**
26) Do the supports of the boeing 747 wing involve Coulomb friction, nonlinear springs, and/or gapping?
** **NO**

The following analysis classes are relevant to the analysis of your structure:
1) general-inelastic

The following recommendations apply to this case:

Activate incremental stress—incremental strain analysis.

Model nonlinear stress-strain relation of the material.

Solution will be based on a mix of gradient and Newton methods.

Logic to scan peak stress at each step and evaluate fatigue integrity should be used.

Logic to scan stresses, smooth, and compare with allowable stresses (with appropriate safety factors) should be used.

Logic to scan deflections, calculate relative values, and compare with code limits, should be called upon.

Cumulative strain damage should be calculated.

Analysis should include two or more load cycles (if cyclic) with extrapolation for strain accumulation.

Shakedown extrapolation logic should be used.

A single cycle of loading is sufficient for the analysis.

Do you wish advice on another structure?
** **NO**

16.2 CLOT: A Consultant for Bleeding Disorders

In a different, and in some ways more standard, application of EMYCIN, we have recently developed a prototype of a consultant called CLOT, which advises physicians on the presence and types of disorders of the human coagulation system. CLOT was constructed by augmenting the EMYCIN system with domain-specific knowledge about bleeding disorders encoded as production rules. Section 16.3 describes the general structure of the CLOT knowledge base.

Our primary intent in constructing CLOT was to explore knowledge acquisition techniques that might be useful during the initial phases of knowledge base specification. Thus we sought to determine the primary inference structures and preliminary medical concepts that a consultant might require. We acquired the initial medical expertise for CLOT from a third-year medical student within a brief amount of time. This expertise has not yet been refined by an acknowledged expert physician. We conjecture that with these structures now in place the arduous task of detailing the knowledge required for truly expert performance can proceed at a more rapid pace. However, we have not had the opportunity to test this conjecture (cf. Mulsant and Servan-Schreiber, 1984).

16.3 The CLOT Knowledge Base

The primary objective of a CLOT consultation is to identify the presence and type of bleeding defect in a patient. If a defect is diagnosed, the consultant attempts to refine its diagnosis by identifying the specific conditions or syndromes in the patient and their plausible causes. These refined diagnoses can then be used by the physician to evaluate the patient's clinical status and to suggest possible therapies. At present, CLOT makes no attempt to recommend such therapies. This section briefly introduces the physiological basis and inference structure used by the consultant when characterizing the bleeding defect of the patient.

There are two major types of bleeding disorders, corresponding to defects in the two component subsystems of the human coagulation system. The first subsystem, termed the platelet-vascular system, is composed of the blood vessels and a component of the blood, the platelets. Upon sustaining an injury, the blood vessels constrict, reducing the flow of blood to the injured area. This vasoconstriction in turn activates the platelets, causing them to adhere to one another and form a simple, temporary "plug," or thrombus. This thrombus is at last reinforced by fibrin, a protein resulting from a complex, multienzyme pathway, the second component subsystem of the coagulation system. Fibrin converts the initial platelet plug into the more permanent clot with which most people are familiar. A defect in either the platelet-vascular or the coagulation (enzymatic) subsystem can cause prolonged and uncontrollable bleeds. For example, the familiar "bleeder's" disease (hemophilia) is the result of a missing or altered enzyme in the coagulation system, which inhibits the formation of fibrin and hence of the final clot.

CLOT was designed to be used eventually by a physician attending a patient with a potential bleeding problem. The system assumes that the physician has access to the necessary laboratory tests and the patient's medical history. CLOT attempts to diagnose the bleeding defect by identifying which of the two coagulation subsystems might be defective. This inference is based first on clinical evidence and then, independently, on the laboratory findings. Finally, if these independent conclusions are mutually consistent, an overall estimation of the defect is deduced and reported.

The consultation begins with the collection of standard demographic data about the patient (name, age, sex, and race) followed by a review of the clinical, qualitative evidence for a bleeding disorder. The physician is asked to describe an episode of bleeding in terms of its location, whether its onset was immediate or prolonged, and whether the physician feels the amount of bleeding was disproportionate for its type. Other factors such as the spontaneity of the bleeding, its response to applied pressure, and its persistence (duration) are also requested. These data are supplemented with facts from the patient's background and medical history to provide an estimate of the significance of the episode. These factors are then used to provide suggestive, but not definitive, evidence for the presence of a bleeding defect. This suggestive, rather than diagnostic, expertise was encoded using EMYCIN's certainty factor mechanism. Each rule mentions a key clinical parameter whose presence or absence contributes to the final, overall certainty of a particular bleeding disorder. (See Figure 16-4.)

The clinical description of the bleeding episode is followed by a report of the coagulation-screen test results. These six standard, quantitative measurements made of the patient's blood sample are used to determine if the blood clots abnormally. If the patient's blood does clot abnormally, CLOT attempts to infer what segment of the enzymatic pathway might be impaired and what platelet dysfunction might be present.

Finally, if clinical and laboratory evidence independently produce a mutually consistent estimation of the defect type, the case data and the intermediate inferences about the significance and possible causes of the bleed combine to produce a refined diagnosis for the patient. Currently, for patients experiencing a significant bleed, these conclusions include specific enzyme deficiencies, von Willebrand's syndrome, Kallikrein defects, thrombocytopenia, and thrombocytosis.

RULE025

IF: 1) Bleeding-history is one of the reasons for this consultation,
2) There is an episode of significant bleeding in the patient,
3) Coagulation-defect is one of the bleeding disorders in the patient,
4) The defective coagulation pathway of the patient is intrinsic, and
5) There are not factors which interfere with the patient's normal bleeding

THEN: It is definite (1.0) that the following is one of the bleeding diagnoses of the patient: The patient has one or more of the following conditions: Hemophilia A, von Willebrand's syndrome, an IX, XI, or XII deficiency, or a high molecular weight Kallikrein defect.

```
PREMISE: ($AND (SAME CNTXT REASON BLEEDING-HISTORY)
               (SAME CNTXT SIGBLD)
               (SAME CNTXT FINALDEF COAGULATION-DEFECT)
               (SAME CNTXT DEFPATH INTRINSIC)
               (NOTSAME CNTXT INTERFERENCE))
ACTION: (CONCLUDETEXT CNTXT DX (TEXT DXHEMOPHILIA) TALLY 1000)
```

FIGURE 16-4 A sample rule from CLOT. RULE025 partly determines the final diagnosis.

Figure 16-5 indicates the major inferences drawn by CLOT during a consultation.

The current knowledge base is able to select from among 13 refined diagnoses and can indicate that the patient is a normal bleeder. CLOT is also able to detect possibly false negative test results due to various interfering factors such as recent exercise, pregnancy, presence of chronic illnesses, and the patient's use of drugs known to alter the clotting process. The knowledge base consists of 63 rules and 50 consultation parameters. A typical consultation requires about five minutes of interaction. A sample consultation is shown in Figure 16-6. The transcript in Figure 16-6 illustrates CLOT's interactions with a physician about a patient and CLOT's final diagnosis. The physician's responses follow the prompt (**) and are printed in bold capitals.

Final Diagnosis

↑

Final, Consistent Estimation
of the Bleeding Defect

↑

Estimation of Enzymatic and Platelet
Defects on the Basis of the Coagulation Battery

↑

Initial Estimation of Bleeding Defect Type
Based on Clinical Evidence

FIGURE 16-5 Inference structure during a CLOT consultation.

--------PATIENT-110--------
1) Name:
** **Pt110**
2) Age:
** **90 YEARS**
3) Sex:
** **FEMALE**
4) Race:
** **CAUCASIAN**
5) Please indicate your reason(s) for requesting this consultation:
** **BLEEDING-HISTORY**
6) What type of bleeding describes Pt110's most recent episode of bleeding?
** **HEMARTHROSIS**
7) Is there a history of a genetic bleeding disorder in Pt110's family?
** **YES**
8) Was the onset of the bleed immediate or delayed?
** **DELAYED**
9) BT:
** **5 MINUTES**
10) PT:
** **13**
11) PTT:
** **50**
12) TT:
** **15**
13) FSF:
** **NORMAL**
14) Has Pt110 recently exercised?
** **NO**
15) Is Pt110 currently receiving any of the following drugs: ASA, Heparin, Coumarin, oral-contraceptives, Ephedrine, Epinephrine, ADH?
** **NO**
16) Is Pt110 diagnosed as having cirrhosis, collagen disease, cancer, or any chronic disease?
** **NO**

Conclusions: the blood disorders of Pt110 are as follows:
COAGULATION-DEFECT (.97)
Conclusions: the statements about the consistency of the case data and CLOT's interpretation are as follows:

Both clinical and lab data are internally consistent and there is overall, consistent interpretation of the blood disorder.

Conclusions: the bleeding diagnoses of Pt110 are as follows:

The patient has one or more of the following conditions:

Hemophilia A, von Willebrand's syndrome, an IX, XI, or XII deficiency, or a high molecular weight Kallikrein defect. (.97)

FIGURE 16-6 Transcript of a CLOT consultation.

16.4 EMYCIN as a Knowledge Representation Vehicle

We did not find the representation formalism of EMYCIN to be a hindrance to either the formulation of the knowledge by the expert or its eventual implementation in either program. In fact, the simplicity of using and explaining both EMYCIN's rule-based formalism and its backward-chaining control structure actually facilitated the rapid development of the knowledge base during the early stages of the consultant's design. Moreover, the control structure, like the rule-based formalism, seemed to impose a salutary discipline on the expert during the formulation of the knowledge base.

The development of SACON was a major test of the domain-independence of the EMYCIN system. Previous applications using EMYCIN had been primarily medical, with the consultations focusing on the diagnosis and prescription of therapy for a patient. Structural analysis, with its emphasis on structures and loadings, allowed us to detect the small number of places where this medical bias had unduly influenced the system design, notably in the text strings used for prompting and giving advice.

Both the MARC expert and the medical student found that their knowledge was easily cast into the rule-based formalism and that the existing predicate functions and context-tree mechanism provided sufficient expressive power to capture the task of advising their respective clients. The existing interactive facilities for performing explanation, question answering, and consultation were found to be well developed and were used directly by our application. None of these features required any significant reprogramming.

EMYCIN provides many tools to aid the knowledge engineer during the process of embedding the expertise into the system. During the construction of CLOT we found that the knowledge acquisition tools in EMYCIN had substantially improved since the construction of SACON. These facilities now perform a large amount of useful checking and default specification when specifying an initial knowledge base. In particular, a new facility had been implemented that provides assistance during the specification of the context tree. This facility eliminates a substantial amount of user effort by setting up the multitude of data structures for each context and ensuring their mutual consistency. Furthermore, the facility for acquiring clinical parameters of a context now performs a significant amount of prompting and value checking on the basis of a simple parameter classification scheme; we found these facilities very useful.

We made extensive use of the ARL (Abbreviated Rule Language) facility when acquiring the rules for CLOT. Designed to capitalize on the stereotypically terse expression of rule clauses by experts, ARL reduces the amount of typing time and, again, ensures that the correct forms are used when specifying both the antecedent and consequent parts of a rule. For example, when specifying the CLOT rule shown in Figure 16-4, the medical student engaged in the interaction shown in Figure 16-7. The user's input follows a colon or a question mark.

In addition to ARL, EMYCIN's rule-subsumption checker also proved very useful during the specification of larger rule sets in the system. This checker analyzes each new rule for possible syntactic subsumptions, or equivalences with the premise clauses of the other rules. We found that,

```
Enter Parms, Rules, Save changes, or Go? Rules

Rule number of NEW: NEW
RULE025
PREMISE: (REASON = BLEEDING, SIGBLD, FINALDEF = COAGULATION,
         DEFPATH = INTRINSIC ~ INTERFERENCE)
RULE025
ACTION: (DX = DXHEMOPHILIA)
BLEEDING → BLEEDING-HISTORY? Yes
COAGULATION → COAGULATION-DEFECT? Yes
Translate, No further changes, or prop name:
```

FIGURE 16-7 Interaction with EMYCIN, using the Abbreviated Rule Language (ARL) to specify the CLOT rule shown in Figure 16-4.

for the larger rule sets, the checker detected these inconsistencies, due to either typing mistakes or actual errors in the rule base logic, and provided a graceful method for dealing with them. Together these facilities contributed to the ease and remarkable rapidity of construction of this consultant. For further details on the design and operation of these aids, see van Melle (1980).

16.5 Observations About Knowledge Acquisition

To bring the SACON program to its present level of performance, we estimate that two person-months of the expert's time were required to explicate the consultation task and formulate the knowledge base, and about the same amount of time was required to implement and test the rules. This estimate does not include the time devoted to meetings, problem formulation, demonstrations, and report writing. For the first 170 rules in the knowledge base, we estimate the average time for formulating and implementing a rule was about four hours. The marginal time for a new rule is about two hours.[1]

The construction of CLOT required approximately three days, divided as follows. The first day was spent discussing the major medical concepts, clinical setting, and diagnostic strategies that were appropriate for this consultant. At the end of this period, the major subtasks of the consultant had been sketched, and a large portion of the clinical parameters the consultant would request of the physician had been mentioned. The following

[1]These estimates represent a simple average that held during the initial construction of these projects. They do not reflect the wide variation in the amount of effort spent defining rules versus the other knowledge base development tasks that occurred over that time period.

two days were spent detailing aspects of the parameters and rules that the EMYCIN system required (i.e., specifying expected values, allowable ranges on numeric parameters, question formats, etc.) and entering these details into the system itself. We may approximate the average cost of formulating and implementing a rule in such a system based on the number of person-hours spent in construction versus the number of rules specified. CLOT required about 60 person-hours to specify 60 rules yielding a rate of 1 person-hour per rule. The marginal cost for a new rule is expected to be similar.

Our experience explicating these rule bases provided an opportunity to make some observations about the process of knowledge acquisition for consultation systems. Although these observations were made with respect to the development of SACON and CLOT, other knowledge-based consultation systems have demonstrated similar processes and interactions.

Our principal observation is that the knowledge acquisition process is composed of three major phases. These phases are characterized strongly by the types of interaction that occur between expert and knowledge engineer and by the type of knowledge that is being explicated and transferred between the participants during these interactions. At present only a small fraction of these interactions can be held directly with the knowledge-based system itself (Davis, 1976; 1977), and research continues to expand the knowledge acquisition expertise of these systems.

16.5.1 The Beginning Phase

The beginning phase of the knowledge formalization process is characterized by the expert's ignorance of knowledge-based systems and unfamiliarity with the process of explicitly describing exactly what he or she knows and does. At the same time, the knowledge engineers are notably ignorant about the application domain and clumsily seek, by analogy, to characterize the possible consultation tasks that could be performed (i.e., "Well, in MYCIN we did this . . . . ").

During the initial weeks of effort, the domain expert learns what tools are available for representing the knowledge, and the knowledge engineer becomes familiar with the important concepts of the domain. During this period, the two formulate a taxonomy of the potential consultation areas for the application of the domain and the types of advice that could be given. Typically, a small fragment of the complete spectrum of consultation tasks is selected to be developed during the following phases of the knowledge acquisition effort. For example, the MYCIN project began by limiting the domain of expertise to the diagnosis and prescription of therapy for bacteremia (blood infections); SACON is currently restricted to determining analysis strategies for structures exhibiting nonlinear, nonthermal, time-independent material behaviors.

Having decided on the subdomain that is to be developed and the type of advice that is to be tendered, the team next identifies the major factors (parameters) and reasoning steps (rules) that will be used to characterize the object of the consultation (be it patient or airplane wing) and to recommend any advice. This forms the inference structure of the consultant.

16.5.2 The Middle Phase

After this initial conceptual groundwork is laid, work proceeds to detailing the reasoning chains and developing the major rule sets in the system. During the development of these rule sets, the amount of domain vocabulary, expressed as contexts, parameters, and values, increases substantially. Enough knowledge is explicated during this middle phase to advise a large number of common cases.

While developing these systems, we profited by "hand-simulating" any proposed rules and parameter additions. In particular, major advances in building the structural analysis knowledge base came when the knowledge engineer would "play EMYCIN" with the expert. During the sessions the knowledge engineer would prompt the expert for tasks that needed to be performed. By simulating the backward-chaining manner of EMYCIN, we asked, as was necessary, for rules to infer the parameter values, "fired" these rules, and thus defined a large amount of the parameter, object, and rule space used during the present consultations. This process of simulating the EMYCIN system also helped the expert learn how the program worked in detail, which in turn helped him develop more rules and parameters.

16.5.3 The Final Phase

Finally, when the knowledge base is substantially complete, the system designers concentrate on *debugging* the existing rule base. This process typically involves the addition of single rules to handle obscure cases and might involve the introduction of new parameters. However, the major structure of the knowledge base remains intact (at least for this subdomain), and interactions with the expert involve relatively small changes. (Chapters 8 and 9 describe debugging and refining a knowledge base that is nearly complete.)

The initial development of the knowledge base is greatly facilitated when the knowledge engineering team elicits a well-specified consultation goal for the system as well as an inference structure such as that depicted in Figure 16-1. Without these conceptual structures to give direction to the knowledge explication process, a confused and unusable web of facts typically issues from the expert. We speculate that the value of these organizational structures is not restricted to the production system methodology. They seem to be employed whenever human experts attempt to formalize their knowledge in any representation formalism, be it production rules, predicate calculus, frames, etc. Indeed, when difficulties arise in building a usable knowledge base, we suspect that the trouble is as likely to come from a poor choice of inference structure as from the choice of any particular representation scheme.

The inference structure is a form of *meta-knowledge,* i.e., knowledge about the structure and use of the domain expertise (see Part Nine). Our experience shows that this meta-knowledge should be elicited and discussed early in the knowledge acquisition process, in order to insure that a sufficient knowledge base is acquired to complete a line of reasoning, and to reduce the time and cost of system development. Also, Chapter 29 discusses the need to explain such meta-level knowledge.

Making the inference structure an explicit part of the program would assist the explanation, tutoring, and further acquisition of the knowledge base. Several researchers, including Swartout (1981) and Clancey (1979b), have employed portions of the inference structure to guide both the design and tutoring of a knowledge-based system. The success of this work supports the hypothesis that the inference structure will play a critical role in the development of new knowledge-based consultation systems.

PART SIX

Explaining the Reasoning

17

Explanation as a Topic of AI Research

In describing MYCIN's design considerations in Chapter 3, we pointed out that an ability of the program to explain its reasoning and defend its advice was an early major performance goal. It would be misleading, however, to suggest that explanation was a primary focus in the original conception. As was true for many elements of the system, the concept of system transparency evolved gradually during the early years. In reflecting on that period, we now find it impossible to recall exactly when the idea was first articulated. The SCHOLAR program (Carbonell, 1970a) was our working model of an interactive system, and we were trying to develop ways to use that model for both training and consultation. Thus, with hindsight, we can say that the issue of making knowledge understandable was in our model, although it was not explicitly recognized at first as a research issue of importance.

17.1 The Early Explanation Work

When the first journal article on MYCIN appeared in 1973 (Shortliffe et al., 1973), it included examples of the program's first rudimentary explanation capabilities. The basic representation and control strategies were relatively well developed at that time, and it was therefore true that any time the program asked a question some domain rule under consideration had generated the inquiry. To aid with system debugging, Shortliffe had added a RULE command that asked MYCIN to display (in LISP) the rule currently under consideration. At the weekly research meetings it was acknowledged that if the rules were displayed in English, rather than in LISP, they would provide a partial justification of the question for the user and thereby be useful to a physician obtaining a consultation. We then devised the translation mechanism (described in Chapter 5), assigning the TRANS property to all clinical parameters, predicate functions, and other key data structures used in rules. Thus, when a user typed "RULE" in response to a question from MYCIN, a translation of the current rule was displayed as an explanation. This was the extent of MYCIN's explanation capability when the 1973 paper was prepared.

At approximately the same time as that first article appeared, Gorry published a paper that influenced us greatly (Gorry, 1973). In retrospect, we believe that this is a landmark essay in the evolution of medical AI. In it he reviewed the experience of the M.I.T. group in developing a program that used decision analysis techniques to give advice regarding the diagnosis of acute renal failure (Gorry et al., 1973). Despite the successful decision-making performance of that program, he was concerned by its obvious limitations (p. 50):

> Decision analysis is a useful tool when the problem has been reduced to a small, well-defined task of action selection. [However,] it cannot be the sole basis of a program to assist clinicians in an area such as renal disease.

He proceeded to describe the M.I.T. group's nascent work on an AI system that used "experimental knowledge" as the basis for understanding renal diseases[1] and expressed excitement about the potential of the symbolic reasoning techniques he had recently discovered (p. 50):

> The new technology [AI] . . . has greatly facilitated the development [of the prototype system] and it seems likely that a much improved program can be implemented. The real question is whether sufficient improvement can be realized to make the program useful. At present, we cannot answer the question, but I can indicate the chief problem areas to be explored: [concept identification, language development, and explanation].

We will not dwell here on his discussion of the first two items, but regarding the third (p. 51):

> ..If experts are to use and improve the program directly, then it must be able to explain the reasons for its actions. Furthermore, this explanation must be in terms that the physician can understand. The steps in a deduction and the facts employed must be identified for the expert so that he can correct one or more of them if necessary. As a corollary, the user must be able to find out easily what the program knows about a particular subject.

Gorry's discussion immediately struck a sympathetic chord for us in our own work. The need for explanation to provide transparency and to encourage acceptance by physicians seemed immediately intuitive, not only for expert system builders (as Gorry discussed) but also for the eventual

[1]This program later became the Present Illness Program (Pauker et al., 1976).

end-users of consultation systems.[2] Our early RULE command, however, did not meet the criteria for explanation outlined by Gorry above.

During the next two years, the development of explanation facilities for MYCIN became a major focus of the research effort. Randy Davis had joined the project by this time, and his work on the TEIRESIAS program, which would become his thesis, started by expanding the simple RULE command and language translation features that Shortliffe had developed. Davis changed the RULE command to WHY and implemented a history tree (see Chapter 18) that enabled the user to examine the entire reasoning chain upward to the topmost goal by asking WHY several times in succession. He also developed the HOW feature, which permitted the user to descend alternate branches of the reasoning network. By the time the second journal article appeared in 1975 (Shortliffe et al., 1975), explanation and early knowledge acquisition work were the major topics of the exposition.[3]

In addition to the RULE command, Shortliffe developed a scheme enabling the user to ask free-text questions at the end of a session after MYCIN had given its advice. He was influenced in this work by Dr. Ken Colby, then at Stanford and actively involved in the development of the PARRY program (Colby et al., 1974). Shortliffe was not interested in undertaking cutting-edge research in natural language understanding (he had taken Roger Schank's course at Stanford in computational linguistics and realized it would be unrealistic to tackle the problem exhaustively for a limited portion of his own dissertation work). He was therefore convinced by Colby's suggestion to exploit existing methods, such as keyword search, and to take advantage of the limited vocabulary used in the domain of infectious diseases. The resulting early version of MYCIN's question-answering system was described in a chapter of his dissertation (Shortliffe, 1974).

When Carli Scott first joined the project, she was completing a master's degree in computer science and needed a project to satisfy her final requirements. She was assigned the task of refining and expanding the question-answering (QA) capability in the program. Not only did this work complete her M.S. requirements, but she continued to devote much of her time to explanation during her next few years with the project. She was assisted in this work by Bill Clancey, then a Ph.D. candidate in computer science, who joined us at about the same time. MYCIN's explanation capability was tied to its rule-based representation scheme, so Clancey was particularly interested in how the therapy algorithm might be transferred from LISP code into rules so that it could be made accessible to the explanation routines. His work in this area is the subject of Chapter 6 in this volume.

---

[2]Almost ten years later we undertook a formal study (described in Chapter 34) that confirmed this early intuition. A survey of 200 physicians revealed that high-quality explanation capabilities were the most important requirement for an acceptable clinical consultation system.

[3]This simple model of explanations still has considerable appeal. See Clark and McCabe (1982) for a discussion of implementing WHY and HOW in PROLOG, for example.

By late 1976 the explanation features of the system had become highly polished, and Scott, Clancey, Davis, and Shortliffe collaborated on a paper that appeared in the *American Journal of Computational Linguistics* in 1977. That paper is included here as Chapter 18. It describes MYCIN's explanation capabilities in some detail. Although most of the early work described in that chapter stressed the need to provide explanations to *users*, we have also seen the value such capabilities have for *system builders*. As mentioned in Chapters 9 and 20, system builders—both experts and knowledge engineers—find explanations to be valuable debugging aids. The features described in Chapter 18 were incorporated into EMYCIN and exist there relatively unchanged to the present.

17.1.1 Explaining the Pharmacokinetic Dosing Model

By the mid-1970s much of the project time was being spent on knowledge base refinement and enhancement. Because we needed assistance from someone with a good knowledge of the antimicrobial agents in use, we sought the involvement of a clinical pharmacist. Sharon Bennett, a recent pharmacy graduate who had taken a clinical internship at the Palo Alto Veterans Administration Hospital affiliated with Stanford, joined the project and played a key role in knowledge base development during the mid- to late-1970s. Among the innovations she brought to the group was an eagerness to heighten MYCIN's utility by making it an expert at dosage adjustment as well as drug selection. She and Carli Scott worked together closely to identify the aspects of pharmacokinetic modeling that could be captured in rules and to identify the elements that were so mathematical in nature that they required encoding in special-purpose functions. By this time, however, the need for explanation capabilities had become so obvious to the project's members that even this specialized code was adapted so that explanations could be provided. A paper describing the features, including a brief discussion of explanation of dosing, was prepared for the *American Journal of Hospital Pharmacy* and is included here as Chapter 19. We include the paper here not only because it demonstrates the special-purpose explanation features that were developed, but also because it shows the way in which mathematical modeling techniques were integrated into a large system that was otherwise dependent on AI representation methods.

17.2 Recent Research in Explanation

Even after research on MYCIN terminated, the development of high-performance explanation capabilities for expert systems remained a major focus of our work. Several small projects and a few doctoral dissertations have dealt with the issue. This level of interest developed out of the MYCIN experience and a small group seminar series held in 1979 and 1980. Several examples of inadequate responses by MYCIN (to questions asked by users) were examined in an effort to define the reasons for suboptimal performance. One large area of problems related to MYCIN's lack of *support knowledge,* the underlying mechanistic or associational links that explain why the action portion of a rule follows logically from its premise. This limitation is particularly severe in a teaching setting where it is incorrect to assume that the system user will already know most rules in the system and merely needs to be reminded of their content. Articulation of these points was largely due to Bill Clancey's work, and they are a central element of his analysis of MYCIN's knowledge base in Chapter 29.

Other sources of MYCIN's explanation errors were its failure to deal with the context in which a question was asked (i.e., it had no sense of dialogue, so each question required full specification of the points of interest without reference to earlier exchanges) and a misinterpretation of the user's intent in asking a question. We were able to identify examples of simple questions that could mean four or five different things depending on what the user knows, the information currently available about the patient under consideration, or the content of earlier discussions. These issues are inevitably intertwined with problems of natural language understanding, and they reflect back on the second of Gorry's three concerns (language development) mentioned earlier in this chapter.

Partly as a result of work on the problem of student modeling by Bill Clancey and Bob London in the context of GUIDON, we were especially interested in how modeling the user's knowledge might be used to guide the generation of explanations. Jerry Wallis began working on this problem in 1980 and developed a prototype system that emphasized causal reasoning chains. The system associated measures of *complexity* with both rules and concepts and measures of *importance* with concepts. These reasoning chains then guided the generation of explanations in accordance with a user's level of expertise and the reasoning details that were desired. Chapter 20 describes that experimental system and defines additional research topics of ongoing interest.

Our research group continues to explore solutions to the problems of explanation in expert systems. John Kunz has developed a program called AI/MM (Kunz, 1983), which combines simple mathematical models, physiologic principles, and AI representation techniques to analyze abnormalities in fluids and electrolyte balance. The resulting system can use causal links and general laws of nature to explain physiologic observations by reasoning from first principles. The program generates English text to explain these observations.

Greg Cooper has developed a system, known as NESTOR, that critiques diagnostic hypotheses in the area of calcium metabolism. In order to critique a user's hypotheses, his system utilizes powerful explanation capabilities. Similarly, the work of Curt Langlotz, who has adapted ONCOCIN to critique a physician's therapy plan (see Chapter 32), requires the program to explain the basis for any disagreements that occur. Langlotz has developed a technique known as hierarchical plan analysis (Langlotz and Shortliffe, 1983), which controls the comparison of two therapy plans and guides the resulting explanatory interaction. Langlotz is also pursuing a new line of investigation that we did not consider feasible during the MYCIN era: the use of graphics capabilities to facilitate explanations and to minimize the need for either typing or natural language understanding. Professional workstations and graphics languages have recently reduced the cost of high-resolution graphics systems (and the cost of programming them) enough that we expect considerably more work in this area.

Bill Clancey's NEOMYCIN research (Clancey and Letsinger, 1981), mentioned briefly in Chapter 21 and developed partially in response to his analysis of MYCIN in Chapter 29, also has provided a fertile arena for explanation research. Diane Warner Hasling has worked with Clancey to develop an explanation feature for NEOMYCIN (Hasling et al., 1983) similar to the HOW's and WHY's of MYCIN (Chapter 18). Because NEOMYCIN is largely guided by domain-independent meta-rules, however, useful explanations cannot be generated simply by translating rules into English. NEOMYCIN is raising provocative questions about how strategic knowledge should be capsulized and instantiated in the domain for explanation purposes.

Finally, we should mention the work of Randy Teach, an educational psychologist who became fascinated by the problem of explanation, in part because of the dearth of published information on the subject. Teach joined the project in 1980, discovered the issue while working on the survey of physicians' attitudes toward computer-based consultants reported in Chapter 34, and undertook a rather complex psychological experiment in an attempt to understand how physicians explain their reasoning to one another (Teach, 1984). We mention the work because it reflects the way in which the legacy of MYCIN has broadened to involve a diverse group of investigators from several disciplines. We believe that explanation continues to provide a particularly challenging set of issues for researchers from computer science, education, psychology, linguistics, philosophy, and the domains of potential application.

17.3 Current Perspective

We believe now that there are several overlapping reasons for wanting an expert system to explain its reasoning. These are

- understanding
- debugging

- education
- acceptance
- persuasion

Understanding the contents of the knowledge base and the line of reasoning is a major goal of work on explanation. Both the system builder and the user need to understand the knowledge in the system in order to maintain it and use it effectively. The system can sometimes take the initiative to inform users of its line of reasoning, such as when MYCIN prints intermediate conclusions about the type of infection or the likely identities of organisms causing a problem. More often, however, we think of a system providing explanations in response to specific requests.

The debugging rationale is important, especially because knowledge bases are built incrementally. As mentioned, this was one of Shortliffe's original motivations for displaying the rule under consideration. This line of research continues in work to provide monitoring tools within programming environments so that a system builder can watch what a system is doing while it is running. Mitch Model's Ph.D. research (Model, 1979) used MYCIN as one example for the monitoring tools he designed. His work shows the power of describing a reasoning system's activities along several different dimensions and the power of displaying those activities in different windows on a display screen.

Education is another important reason to provide insights into a knowledge base. Users who feel they learn something by interacting with an expert system are likely to use it again. As discussed in Part Eight, educating users can become as complex as providing good advice. In any case, making the knowledge base and line of reasoning understandable is a necessary step in educating users. This line of research continues in Clancey's work on NEOMYCIN (Clancey and Letsinger, 1981).

Acceptance and persuasion are closely linked. Part of making an expert system acceptable is convincing potential users and managers that its conclusions are reasonable. That is, if they understand how a system reaches conclusions on several test cases and believe that process is reasonable, they will be more likely to trust its conclusions on new cases. For the same reason, it is also important to show that the system is responsive to differences between cases.

Persuading users that a system's conclusions are correct also requires the same kind of window into the knowledge base and line of reasoning. When using a consultant program, a person is expected to understand the conclusions (and the basis for them) well enough to accept responsibility for acting on them. In medicine, for example, physicians have a moral and legal responsibility for the consequences of their actions, so they must understand why—and sometimes be persuaded that—a consultant's recommendations are appropriate.

18

Methods for Generating Explanations

A. Carlisle Scott, William J. Clancey, Randall Davis, and Edward H. Shortliffe

A computer program that models an expert in a given domain is more likely to be accepted by experts in that domain, and by nonexperts seeking its advice, if the system can explain its actions. This chapter discusses the general characteristics of explanation capabilities for rule-based systems: what types of explanations they should be able to give, what types of knowledge they will need in order to give these explanations, and how this knowledge might be organized (Figure 18-1). The explanation facility in MYCIN is discussed to illustrate how the various problems can be approached.

A consultative rule-based system need not be a psychological model, imitating a human's reasoning process. The important point is that the system and a human expert use the same (or similar) knowledge about the domain to arrive at the same (or similar) answers to a given problem. The system's *knowledge base* contains the domain-specific knowledge of an expert as well as facts about a particular problem under consideration. When a rule is used, its actions make changes to the internal data base, which contains the system's *decisions* or *deductions*.

The process of trying rules and taking actions can be compared to reasoning, and explanations require displays of how the rules use the information provided by the user to make various intermediate deductions and finally to arrive at the answer. If the information contained in these rules adequately shows why an action was taken (without getting into programming details), an explanation can simply entail printing each rule or its free-text translation.

This chapter is a revised version of a paper originally appearing in *American Journal of Computational Linguistics,* Microfiche 62, 1977.

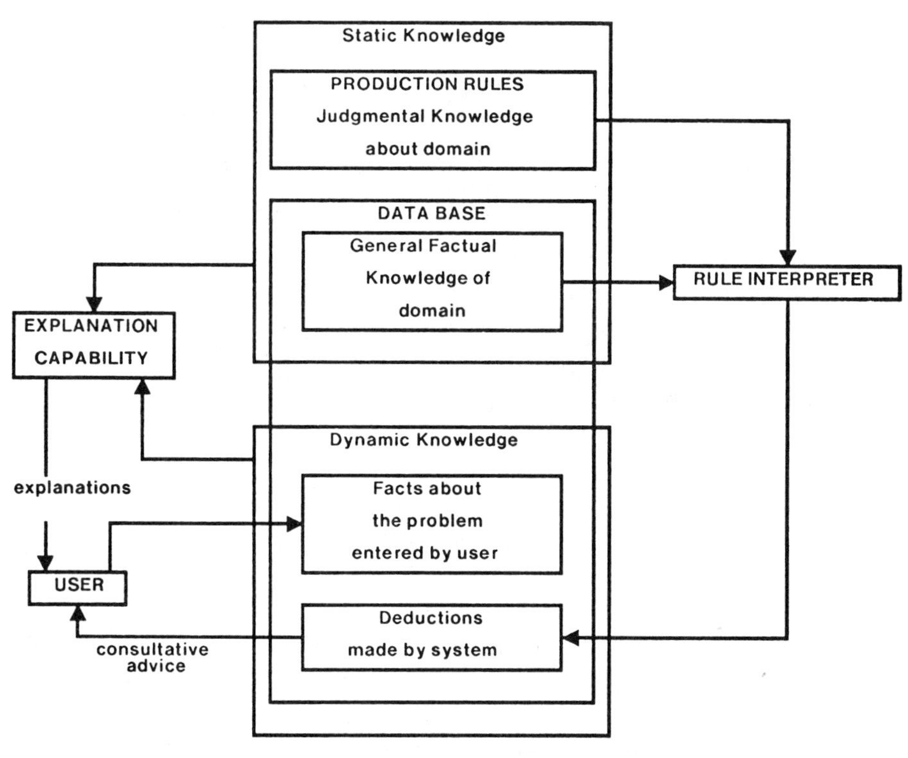

FIGURE 18-1 A rule-based consultation system with explanation capability. The three components of a rule-based system (a rule interpreter, a set of production rules, and a data base) are augmented by an explanation capability. The data base is made up of general facts about the system's domain of expertise, facts that the user enters about a specific problem, and deductions made about the problem by the system's rules. These deductions form the basis of the system's consultative advice. The explanation capability makes use of the system's knowledge base to give the user explanations. This knowledge base is made up of static domain-specific knowledge (both factual and judgmental) and dynamic knowledge specific to a particular problem.

Performance Characteristics of an Explanation Capability

The purpose of an explanation capability (EC) is to give the user access to as much of the system's knowledge as possible. Ideally, it should be easy for a user to get a complete, understandable answer to any sort of question about the system's knowledge and operation—both in general terms and with reference to a particular consultation. This implies three major goals in the development of an explanation capability:

1. It is important to ensure that the EC can handle questions about all relevant aspects of the system's knowledge and actions. It should be capable of giving several basic types of explanation, for example,

   - how it made a certain decision
   - how it used a piece of information
   - what decision it made about some subproblem
   - why it did not use a certain piece of information
   - why it failed to make a certain decision
   - why it required a certain piece of information
   - why it did not require a certain piece of information
   - how it will find out a certain piece of information (while the consultation is in progress)
   - what the system is currently doing (while the consultation is in progress)

2. It is important to enable the user to get an explanation that answers the question completely and comprehensively.
3. Finally, it is also necessary to make the EC easy to use. A novice should be able to use the EC without first spending a large amount of time learning how to request explanations.

We will distinguish two functions for an EC: the reasoning status checker (RSC) to be used during the consultation, and the general question answerer (GQA) to be used during the consultation or after the system has printed its results. An RSC answers questions asked during a consultation about the status of the system's reasoning process. A few simple commands often suffice to handle the questions that the RSC is expected to answer. A GQA answers questions about the current state of the system's knowledge base, including both static domain knowledge and facts accumulated during the consultation. It must recognize a wide range of question types about many aspects of the system's knowledge. For this reason, a few simple commands that are easy to learn but still cover all the possible questions that might be asked may be difficult to define. Consequently, natural language processing may be important for a useful GQA.

In an interactive consultation, the system periodically requests information about the problem. This offers the user an opportunity to request explanations while the consultation is in progress. In noninteractive consultations, the user has no opportunity to interact with the system until after it has printed its conclusions. Unless there is a mechanism for interrupting the reasoning process and asking questions, the EC for such a

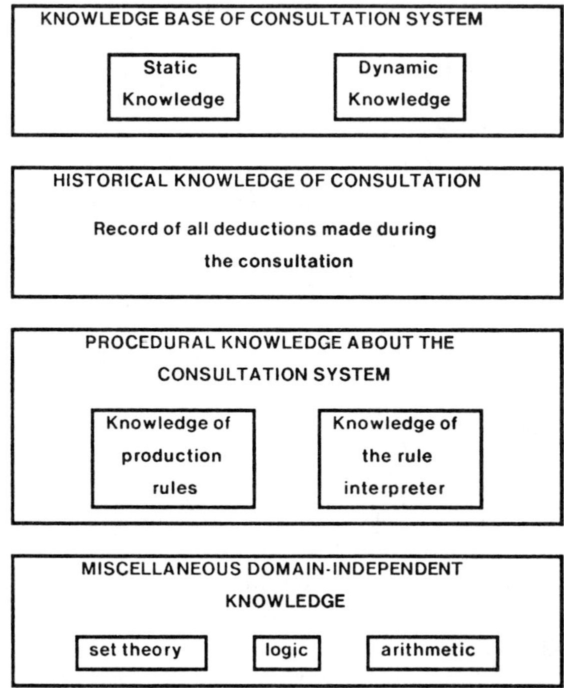

FIGURE 18-2 Knowledge requirements for an explanation capability (EC). Access to the consultation system's knowledge base is a prerequisite for adequate performance of the EC. Other types of knowledge may be added to the system to enable the EC to answer a wider range of questions.

system will be limited to questions about the system's final knowledge state. It will have no RSC.

An EC must know what is in the system's knowledge base and how it is organized (Figure 18-2). In order to give explanations of the system's actions, an EC also needs to understand how the system's rule interpreter works: when rules will be tried, how they can fail, and what causes the interpreter to try one rule but not another. This general "schema" for how or why certain rules are used, together with a comprehensive record of the specific actions taken during a particular consultation, can be used as a basis for explaining the results of that consultation.

An RSC will need a record of what the system has done in order to explain how it arrived at the current step. General knowledge of how the rule interpreter works is necessary to explain where the current step will lead. The ability to understand individual rules is necessary to the extent that the content of a rule may explain why it was necessary to use that rule or may affect which rules will be tried in the future.

A GQA will need more information about the system since the scope of its explanations is much broader. It must know how the system stores knowledge about its area of expertise (the static knowledge with which it starts each consultation), how it stores facts gathered during a particular consultation (its dynamic knowledge), and how the dynamic knowledge was obtained or inferred. Thus the GQA must have access to all the information that the RSC uses: a detailed record of the consultation, an understanding of the rule interpreter, and the ability to understand rules.

18.1 Design Considerations

To complement the preceding discussion of an EC, we must describe relevant design considerations for the parent consultation system. This discussion is not meant to define the "correct" way of representing or organizing knowledge, but rather to mention factors that should be taken into account when deciding what representation or organization will be best for a developing system.

The first step is to decide what basic types of questions the system should be able to answer. This will have a direct influence on how the EC is implemented. It is important, however, to make the initial design flexible enough to accommodate possible future additions; if the basic forms are sufficiently diverse, limited natural language understanding may be necessary, depending on the level of performance expected of the EC.

The format and organization of the consultation system's knowledge base will also affect the design of an EC because both static and dynamic knowledge must be readily accessible. The more disorganized the knowledge base, the more difficult will be the task of the EC because more complicated routines will be needed to access the desired information. Similarly, when the ordering of events is important, the dynamic record must reflect that ordering as well as the reasons why each event occurred.

The EC often needs to understand the underlying semantics of individual rules. This requirement can be met by having the system's knowledge base include a description of what each rule means, encoded in a form that is of use to the EC. If the format of the system's rules is highly stylized and well defined, however, it is possible instead to implement a mechanism for "reading" the rules and describing their meaning in natural language. This can be achieved through a high-level description of the individual components of the rules, one that tells what each element means. If the rule set consists of a large number of rules, and they are composed entirely of a relatively small number of primitive elements, this second approach has the advantage that less information needs to be stored—a description of each of the primitive components, as opposed to a description of each rule. When new rules are added to the system, the first approach requires that descriptions of these rules must be added. With the second approach, provided that the new rules are constructed from the standard rule components, no additional descriptive information is needed.

As well as understanding rules in the knowledge base, an EC must also be able to "read" the interpreter or have access to some stored description of how the interpreter works. A third option is to build knowledge of how the interpreter works directly into the EC; the information need not be stated explicitly but can be used implicitly by the programmer in writing the actual EC code. The EC can then function as a set of "specialists," each capable of giving a single type of explanation.

Finally, the GQA generally must be able to make deductions from facts in the knowledge base. If logic is needed only to determine the answers to questions of a certain type, it may be possible to build the necessary deductions into the specialist for answering that type of question. On the other hand, the GQA will often need to be expanded to do more than simply give explanations of the system's actions or query its data base—it will be expected to answer questions involving inferences (e.g., to check for equality or set membership, to make arithmetical comparisons, or to make logical deductions). Information of this type can often be embodied in a new kind of specialist that deals with logical deduction or comparison.

18.2 An Example—MYCIN

MYCIN's domain of expertise, its mechanisms for knowledge representation, and its inference mechanisms have been discussed in detail earlier in this book. We will not repeat those points here except to emphasize issues that relate directly to this discussion.

18.2.1 Organization of Knowledge in MYCIN

As we have discussed, an EC must have access to all components of the system's knowledge base. MYCIN's knowledge base consists of static medical knowledge plus dynamic knowledge about a specific consultation. Static knowledge is further classified as *factual* or *judgmental*. Factual knowledge consists of facts that are medically valid, by definition and with certainty, independent of the particular case. Judgmental knowledge, on the other hand, is composed of the rules acquired from experts. Although this knowledge is also assumed to be medically valid, the indicated inferences are often drawn with less than complete certainty and are seldom definitional. The conventions for storing both dynamic and static knowledge, including attribute-object-value triples, tables, lists, and rules themselves, are described in detail in Chapter 5.

Knowledge of Rule Structure

Each of MYCIN's rules is composed of a small number of conceptual primitives drawn from a library of 60 such primitives that make up the language in which rules are written. This design has facilitated the implementation of a mechanism for translating rules into English (described in Chaper 5). Each primitive function has a *template* (Chapter 9) with blanks to be filled in using translations of the function's arguments. A large part of MYCIN's explanation capability depends on this ability to translate rules into a form that the user can understand.

In order to understand rules, the system's various specialists use a small amount of knowledge about rules in general, together with descriptions or templates of each of the rule components. As an example, the following rule (shown in LISP and its English translation) is composed of the units $AND, SAME, and CONCLUDE:

```
RULE009

PREMISE:  ($AND (SAME CNTXT GRAM GRAMNEG)
                (SAME CNTXT MORPH COCCUS))
ACTION:   (CONCLUDE CNTXT IDENTITY NEISSERIA TALLY 800)

IF:  1) The gram stain of the organism is gramneg, and
     2) The morphology of the organism is coccus
THEN:  There is strongly suggestive evidence (.8) that the identity
       of the organism is Neisseria
```

When the rule is used, the LISP atom CNTXT is bound to some object, the context to which the rule is applied; see Chapter 5. The template for CONCLUDE is shown below. This describes each of the arguments to the function: first, an object (context); second, an attribute (clinical parameter); third, a value for this parameter; fourth, the tally, or degree of certainty, of the premise; and last, the certainty factor, a measure of how strong our belief in this conclusion would be if the premise of the rule were definitely true.

Template for CONCLUDE: (CNTXT PARM VALU TALLY CF)

Having a small number of rule components also facilitates examination of rules to see which might be applicable to the explanation at hand. MYCIN's knowledge of rules, therefore, takes the form of a general mechanism for "reading" them. On the other hand, no attempt has been made to read the code of the rule interpreter. Procedural knowledge about the interpreter is embodied in "specialists," each capable of answering a single type of question. Each specialist knows how the relevant part of the control structure works and what pieces of knowledge it uses.

To understand how a specialist might use a template such as that shown above, consider an explanation that involves finding all rules that can conclude that the identity of an organism is *Neisseria*. The appropriate specialist would start with those rules used by the system to conclude values for the parameter IDENTITY. Using templates of the various action functions that appear in each of these rules, the specialist picks out only those (like Rule 009) that have NEISSERIA in their VALU slot.

This also illustrates the sort of knowledge that can be built into a specialist. The specialist knows that the control structure uses stored lists telling which rules can be used to determine the value of each parameter. Furthermore, it knows that it is necessary to look only at the rules' actions since it is the action that *concludes* facts, while the premise *uses* facts.

The History Tree

Many of the EC's specialists need a record of the interaction with the user. This record is built during the consultation and is organized into a tree structure called the *history tree*, which reflects MYCIN's goal-directed approach. Each node in the tree represents a goal and contains information about how the system tried to accomplish this goal (by asking the user or by trying rules). Associated with each rule is a record of whether or not the rule succeeded, and if not, why it failed. If evaluating the premise of a rule causes the system to trace a new parameter, thereby setting up a new subgoal, the node for this subgoal is the offspring of the node containing the rule that caused the tracing. Figure 18-3 shows part of a representative history tree. In this example, Rule 003 caused the tracing of the parameter CATEGORY, which is used in the premise of this rule.

Other Domain-Independent Knowledge

MYCIN's question-answering ability is limited to describing the system's actions and explaining what facts the system knows. The system also has capabilities for the use of specialized logic. For example, to explain why a particular decision was *not* made, MYCIN recognizes that a reasonable response is to explain what *prevented* the system from using rules that *would have made* that decision. For situations such as this, the necessary logic is built into the appropriate specialist; there is no general representation of knowledge about logic, arithmetic, or set theory. To find out if ORGANISM-1 and ORGANISM-2 have the same identity, for example, it is necessary for the user to ask separately for the identity of each organism, then to compare the answers to these questions.

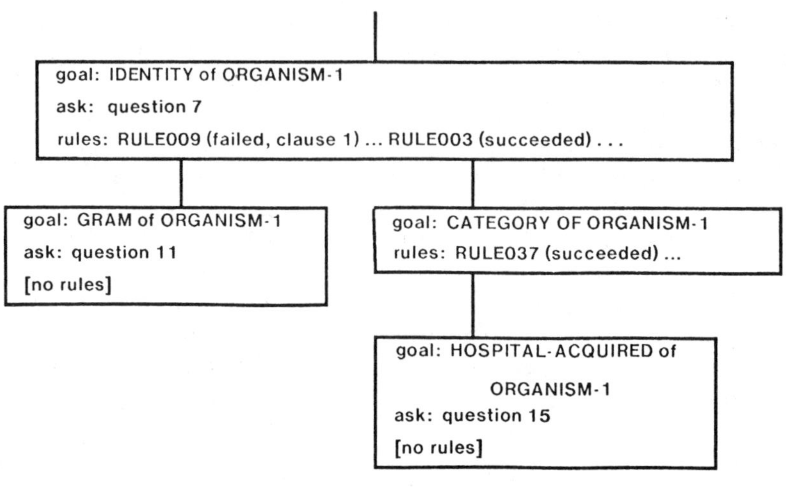

FIGURE 18-3 Portion of a history tree. (Rule 009 is shown in the text; see Figure 18-4 for Rule 003 and Rule 037.)

18.2.2 Scope of MYCIN's Explanation Capability (EC)

Because we wish to allow the user to see how MYCIN makes all its decisions, we have tried to anticipate all types of questions a user might ask and to make every part of the system's knowledge base and reasoning process accessible. The EC consists of several specialists, each capable of giving one type of explanation. These specialists are grouped into three sets: one for explaining what the system is doing at a given time, one for answering questions about the system's static knowledge base, and one for answering questions about the dynamic knowledge base. The first set forms MYCIN's reasoning status checker; the second and third together make up the system's general question answerer.

MYCIN's Reasoning Status Checker (RSC)

Whenever MYCIN asks a question, the user is allowed to examine the current reasoning chain by asking WHY the piece of information being sought by the system is important. As explained above, the system asks a question in order to find out about its current goal. Consider the partial history tree shown in Figure 18-3. HOSPITAL-ACQUIRED is one subgoal, CATEGORY is another at the next level up, and Rule 037 links them. The "reason" for asking if the infection was hospital-acquired, then, is the program's use of Rule 037 in an effort to determine the value of the higher subgoal CATEGORY. The answer to WHY at this point is thus a lucid display of the goals and the rules linking them. Since any WHY could

```
                    [preceded by the first 14 questions in the consultation]

15) Is the patient's illness with ORGANISM-1 a hospital-acquired infection?
** WHY
[i.e. WHY is it important to determine whether or not the infection with
        ORGANISM-1 was acquired while the patient was hospitalized?]
[1.0] This will aid in determining the category of ORGANISM-1.
        It has already been established that
                [1.1] the gram stain of ORGANISM-1 is gramneg, and
                [1.2] the morphology of ORGANISM-1 is rod, and
                [1.3] the aerobicity of ORGANISM-1 is facultative
        Therefore, if
                [1.4] the infection with ORGANISM-1 was not acquired while the
                        patient was hospitalized
        then
                there is strongly suggestive evidence (.8) that the category of
                        ORGANISM-1 is enterobacteriaceae
        ALSO: there is weakly suggestive evidence (.1) that the identity of
                        ORGANISM-1 is pseudomonas-aeruginosa
        [RULE037]
** WHY
[i.e. WHY is it important to determine the category of ORGANISM-1?]
[2.0]. . . in order to determine the identity of ORGANISM-1.
      It has already been established that
              [2.1] this blood culture was taken from a sterile source
      Therefore, if
              [2.2] this current organism and at least one of the list of members
                      associated with the category of the organism agree with
                      respect to the following properties: air conformation
      then
              There is strongly suggestive evidence (.9) that each of them is the
                      identity of ORGANISM-1
        [RULE003]
** HOW 1.3
[i.e. HOW was it established that the aerobicity of ORGANISM-1 is
        facultative?]
The following were used:
[3.1] RULE027 indicated there is strongly suggestive evidence (.8) that the
        aerobicity of ORGANISM-1 is facultative
[3.2] RULE027 indicated there is weakly suggestive evidence (.2) that the
        aerobicity of ORGANISM-1 is anaerobic
Since this gave a cumulative CF of (.8) for facultative, and (.2) for
        anaerobic, it has been established that the aerobicity of ORGANISM-1
        is facultative
** HOW 1.1
[i.e. HOW was it established that the gram stain of ORGANISM-1 is gramneg?]
You said so [question 11].
```

FIGURE 18-4 MYCIN's reasoning status checker (user entries follow the double asterisks).

potentially have several interpretations, and we wanted to avoid extensive natural language processing in this component of MYCIN's EC, MYCIN first restates its understanding of the meaning of the user's WHY (Figure 18-4). The higher goal is then presented, followed by the rule. The clauses in the premise of the rule are divided into those already established and those yet to be determined. Finally, since rules may have multiple conclu-

```
IS BLOOD A STERILE SITE?
WHAT ARE THE NONSTERILE SITES?
WHAT ORGANISMS ARE LIKELY TO BE FOUND IN THE THROAT?
IS BACTEROIDES AEROBIC?
WHAT METHODS OF COLLECTING SPUTUM CULTURES DO YOU CONSIDER?
WHAT DOSAGE OF STREPTOMYCIN DO YOU GENERALLY RECOMMEND?
HOW DO YOU DECIDE THAT AN ORGANISM MIGHT BE STREPTOCOCCUS?
WHY DO YOU ASK WHETHER THE PATIENT HAS A FEVER OF UNKNOWN ORIGIN?
WHAT DRUGS WOULD YOU CONSIDER TO TREAT E.COLI?
HOW DO YOU USE THE SITE OF THE CULTURE TO DECIDE AN ORGANISM'S IDENTITY?
```

FIGURE 18-5 Sample questions about MYCIN's static knowledge.

sions about different clinical parameters, the relevant conclusion is presented first and all others follow.

As Figure 18-4 illustrates, additional links in the reasoning chain can be examined by repeating the WHY command. For any of the subgoals mentioned in answer to a WHY, the user may ask HOW this goal was (or will be) achieved. MYCIN's reasoning status checker is described in more detail by Shortliffe et al. (1975) and Davis et al. (1977).

MYCIN's General Question Answerer (GQA)

The question-answering part of the system has natural language routines for analyzing the user's input. The system recognizes questions phrased in a number of ways, thereby making the question-answering facility easier to use. Questions about the static knowledge base may deal with judgmental knowledge (e.g., rules used to conclude a certain piece of information) or they may ask about factual knowledge (e.g., entries in tables and lists). Some questions about static knowledge are shown in Figure 18-5.

Perhaps the more important part of the question-answering system is its ability to answer questions about a particular consultation. While some users may be interested in checking the extent of MYCIN's static knowledge, most questions will ask for a justification of, or for the rationale behind, particular decisions that were made during the consultation. Listed in Figure 18-6 are the types of questions about dynamic knowledge that can be handled at present. A few examples of each type are given. The slot <cntxt> indicates some context that was discussed in the consultation; <parm> is some clinical parameter of this context; <rule> is one of the system's decision rules. Before a question can be answered, it must be classified as belonging to one of these groups. As Figure 18-6 illustrates, each question type may be asked in a variety of ways, some specifying the parameter's value, some phrased in the negative, and so forth. MYCIN's natural language processor must classify the questions, then determine what specific clinical parameters, rules, etc., are being referenced.

1. What is <parm> of <cntxt>?

   TO WHAT CLASS DOES ORGANISM-1 BELONG?
   IS ORGANISM-1 CORYNEBACTERIUM-NON-DIPHTHERIAE?

2. How do you know the value of <parm> of <cntxt>?

   HOW DO YOU KNOW THAT CULTURE-1 WAS FROM A STERILE SOURCE?
   DID YOU CONSIDER THAT ORGANISM-1 MIGHT BE A BACTEROIDES?
   WHY DON'T YOU THINK THAT THE SITE OF CULTURE-1 IS URINE?
   WHY DID YOU RULE OUT STREPTOCOCCUS AS A POSSIBILITY FOR ORGANISM-1?

3. How did you use <parm> of <cntxt>?

   DID YOU CONSIDER THE FACT THAT PATIENT-1 IS A COMPROMISED HOST?
   HOW DID YOU USE THE AEROBICITY OF ORGANISM-1?

4. Why didn't you find out about <parm> of <cntxt>?

   DID YOU FIND OUT ABOUT THE CBC ASSOCIATED WITH CULTURE-1?
   WHY DIDN'T YOU NEED TO KNOW WHETHER ORGANISM-1 IS A CONTAMINANT?

5. What did <rule> tell you about <cntxt>?

   HOW WAS RULE 178 HELPFUL WHEN YOU WERE CONSIDERING ORGANISM-1?
   DID RULE 116 TELL YOU ANYTHING ABOUT INFECTION-1?
   WHY DIDN'T YOU USE RULE 189 FOR ORGANISM-2?

FIGURE 18-6 Types of questions about a consultation, with examples.

18.2.3 Understanding the Question

The main emphasis in the development of MYCIN has been the creation of a system that can provide sound diagnostic and therapeutic advice in the field of infectious diseases. The explanation system was included in the system's original design in order to make the consultation program's decisions acceptable, justifiable, and instructive. Since the question-answering facility was not the primary focus of the research, it is not designed to be a sophisticated natural language understander. Instead, it uses crude techniques, relying strongly on the very specific vocabulary of the domain, to "understand" what information is being requested (Figure 18-7).

The analysis of a question is broken into three phases (Steps 1–3 of Figure 18-7): the first creates a list of *terminal,* or root, *words;* the second determines what type of question is being asked (see the classification of questions above); and the last determines what particular parameters, lists, etc., are relevant to the question. In the first and third steps, the system dictionary is important. The dictionary contains approximately 1400 words that are commonly used in the domain of infectious diseases. It includes all words that are acceptable values for a parameter, common synonyms

1. The question is reduced to a list of terminal words.
2. Pattern matching classifies the question as a rule-retrieval question, and divides it into a premise part and an action part.
3. Dictionary properties of the terminal words are used to determine which parameters (and their values) are relevant to each part of the question. These vocabulary clues are listed in the form (<parm> (<values>) weight) where weight is used by the scoring mechanism to determine which parameters should be eliminated from consideration.
4. After selecting only the most strongly indicated parameters, the final translation tells what rules can answer the question: there are no restrictions on the premise, and the action must contain the parameter CONTAMINANT with any value.
5. The answer consists of finding all rules that meet these restrictions, and printing those that the user wants to see.

FIGURE 18-7 Major steps in understanding a question, finding rules, and printing an answer. See Figure 18-8 for an example.

of these words, and words used elsewhere by the system in describing the parameter (e.g., when translating a rule into English or requesting the value of the parameter).

We now briefly describe how MYCIN achieves each of the five tasks outlined in Figure 18-7. An example analysis is shown in Figure 18-8.

Step 1: Reducing the Question to Terminal Words

Each word in the dictionary has a synonym pointer to its terminal word (terminal words point to themselves). For the purpose of analyzing the question, a nonterminal word is considered to be equivalent to its (terminal) synonym. Terminal words have associated with them a set of properties or descriptors (Table 18-1) that are useful in determining the meaning of a question that uses a terminal word or one of its synonyms. A given word may be modified by more than one of these properties.

The first three properties of terminal words are actually inverse pointers, generated automatically from attributes of the clinical parameters. Specifically, a word receives the "acceptable value" pointer to a clinical parameter (Property 1 in Table 18-1) if it appears in the parameter's list of acceptable values—a list that is used during the consultation to check the user's response to a request for the parameter's value (see EXPECT attribute, Chapter 5).

Also, each clinical parameter, list, and table has an associated list of keywords that are commonly used when talking about that parameter, list, or table. These words are divided according to how sure we can be that a doctor is referring to this parameter, list, or table when the particular word

```
**WHEN DO YOU DECIDE THAT AN ORGANISM IS A CONTAMINANT?

[1] Terminal words:          WHEN DO YOU CONCLUDE THAT A ORGANISM IS A CONTAMINANT

[2] Question type:           Rule retrieval
    Premise part:            (WHEN DO YOU CONCLUDE)
    Action part:             (THAT A ORGANISM IS A CONTAMINANT)

[3] vocab. clues:            (WHENINFECT (ANY) 1) (WHENSTOP (ANY) 1)
       (Premise)             (WHENSTART (ANY) 1) (DURATION (ANY) 1)
    vocab. clues:            (CONTAMINANT (ANY) 4) (FORM (ANY) 1)
       (Action)              (SAMEBUG (ANY) 1) (COVERFOR (ANY) 1)

[4] Final translation:
       Premise: ANY
       Action: (CONTAMINANT ANY)

[5] The rules listed below conclude about:
       whether the organism is a contaminant
    6, 31, 351, 39, 41, 42, 44, 347, 49, 106
    Which do you wish to see?
       ** 6

    RULE006

    IF:  1) The culture was taken from a sterile source, and
         2) It is definite that the identity of the organism
            is one of: staphylococcus-coag-neg bacillus-
            subtilis corynebacterium-non-diphtheriae
    THEN:  There is strongly suggestive evidence (.8)
           that the organism is a contaminant
```

FIGURE 18-8 Sample of MYCIN's analysis of a general question. (User input follows the double asterisks. Steps 1 through 4 are usually not shown to the user. See Figure 18-7 for a description of what is occurring in each of the five steps.)

TABLE 18-1 Properties of Terminal Words

1. The word is an acceptable value for some clinical parameter(s).
2. The word *always* implicates a certain clinical parameter, system list, or table (e.g., the word "identity" always implicates the parameter IDENTITY, which means the identity of an organism).
3. The word *might* implicate a certain parameter, system list, or table (e.g., the word "positive" might implicate the parameter NUMPOS, which means the number of positive cultures in a series).
4. The word is part of a phrase that can be thought of as a single word (examples of such phrases are "transtracheal aspiration," "how long," and "not sterile").

is used in a question. It is from this list that terminal words' "implication" pointers (Properties 2 and 3 in Table 18-1) are generated.

During the first phase of parsing, each word in the original text is replaced by its terminal word. For words not found in the dictionary, the system uses Winograd's root-extraction algorithm (Winograd, 1972) to see if the word's lexical root is in the dictionary (e.g., the root of "decision" is "decide"). If so, the word is replaced by the terminal word for its root. Words still unrecognized after root extraction are left unchanged.

The resulting list of terminal and unrecognized words is then passed to a function that recognizes phrases. Using Property 4 (Table 18-1), the function identifies a phrase and replaces it with a single synonymous terminal word (whose dictionary properties may be important in determining the meaning of the question).

Step 2: Classifying the Question

The next step is to classify the question so that the program can tell which specialist should answer it. Since all questions about the consultation must be about some specific context, the system requires that the name of the context (e.g., ORGANISM-1) be stated explicitly. This provides an easy mechanism to separate general questions about the knowledge base from questions about a particular consultation.

Further classification is done through a pattern-matching approach similar to that used by Colby et al. (1974). The list of words created by the first phase is tested against a number of patterns (about 50 at present). Each pattern has a list of actions to be taken if the pattern is matched. These actions set flags that indicate what type of question was asked. In the case of questions about judgmental knowledge (called *rule-retrieval questions*), pattern matching also divides the question into the part referring to the rule's premise and the part referring to its action. For example, in "How do you decide that an organism is streptococcus?" there is no premise part, and the action part is "an organism is streptococcus"; in "Do you ever use the site of the culture to determine an organism's identity?" the premise part is "the site of the culture" and the action part is "an organism's identity."

Steps 3 and 4: Determining What Pieces of Knowledge Are Relevant

The classification of a question guides its further analysis. Each question type has an associated template with blanks to be filled in from the question. The different blanks and the techniques for filling them in are listed in Table 18-2. With the question correctly classified, the general question

TABLE 18-2 Mechanisms for Analyzing a Question

Slot	*Analysis cues for filling a slot*
<cntxt>	The context must be mentioned by name, e.g., ORGANISM-2.
<rule>	Either a rule's name (RULE047) will be mentioned or the word "rule" will appear, together with the rule's number (47).
<value>	One of the terminal words in the question has a dictionary property indicating that it is a legal value for the parameter (Property 1, Table 18-1), e.g., THROAT is a legal value for the parameter SITE.
<parm>	All of the words in the list are examined to see if they implicate any clinical parameters. Strong implications come from words with properties showing that the word is an acceptable value of the parameter, or that the word *always* implicates that parameter (Properties 1 and 2, Table 18-1). Weak implications come from words with properties showing that they *might* implicate the parameter (Property 3, Table 18-1). The system uses an empirical scoring mechanism for picking out only the most likely parameters. Associated with certain parameters are words or patterns that *must* appear in the question in order for the parameter to be implicated. This scheme allows the system to distinguish among related parameters that may be implicated by the same keywords in the first pass. For example, the word "PMN" implicates parameters CSFPOLY (the percent of PMN's in the CSF) and PMN (the percent of PMN's in the complete blood count). These are distinguished by requiring that the word "CSF" be present in a question in order for CSFPOLY to be implicated.
<list>	System lists are indicated in a manner similar to that for parameters, except that scoring is not done. Lists, like parameters, may have associated patterns that must be present in the question. Furthermore, lists have properties telling which other system lists are their subsets. If a question implicates both a list and a subset of that list, the more general (larger) list is discarded. As an example, the question "Which drugs are aminoglycosides?" implicates two lists: the list of all drugs, and the list of drugs that are aminoglycosides. The system only considers the more specific list of aminoglycosides when answering the question.
<table>	Tables are indicated in a manner similar to that for lists except that an entry in the table must also be present in the question. For example, the word "organism" may indicate two tables: one containing a classification of organisms, and the other containing normal flora of various portals. The question "What organisms are considered to be subtypes of *Pseudomonas*?" will correctly implicate the former table, and "What are the organisms likely to be found in the throat?" will implicate the latter, because PSEUDOMONAS is in the first table and THROAT is in the second.

answerer can tell which specialist should answer it. Filling in all blanks in the template gives the specialist all the information needed to find the answer.

Step 5: Answering the Question

Corresponding to each question type, there are a number of possible answer templates. For example, for questions of the form "How do you know the value of <parm> of <cntxt>?" two of the answer templates are

> I used <rule> to conclude that <parm> of <cntxt> is <value>. This gave a cumulative CF of <certainty factor>. The last question asked before the conclusion was made was <question number>.
>
> In answer to question <question number> you said that <parm> of <cntxt> is <value>.

The specialist for answering questions of a given type has to check the history tree or the system's knowledge base in order to determine which of the answer templates is appropriate for a particular question. Some blanks in the answer template are filled in by the same items as are used to fill blanks in the question template. The remainder are filled by the specialist with the information that answers the question. In the above example, the slots <parm>, <cntxt>, and possibly <value> would be filled in from the question, and the other slots would be filled from the history tree.

18.2.4 Questions About MYCIN's Static Knowledge

General questions about MYCIN's factual knowledge (Figure 18-9) are the easiest to answer. The specialist that provides answers to such questions must look up the desired information in the system's static knowledge base. Generally, an answer consists of simply displaying this information. The most processing occurs when checking the retrieved information against some item in the question for equality or set membership.

As was discussed in the previous section, the specialist that answers questions about judgmental knowledge is more complicated (Figure 18-8). Answering such questions (Figure 18-10) involves built-in knowledge about the rule set, plus the ability to "read" the rules. By the time the question has been analyzed, the specialist knows which parameters must appear in the premise and which must appear in the action of any rule that answers the question. Values may be specified for any of the parameters. To answer the question, the rule-retrieval specialist must first find every rule whose

****IS BLOOD A STERILE SITE?**
Yes. Blood is one of those sites that are normally sterile.

**** WHAT ARE THE NONSTERILE SITES?**
Those sites that are normally nonsterile are: CERVIX,
CUTANEOUS-ULCER, LOCHIA, NOSE, SKIN, STOOL, THROAT, URETHRA,
VAGINA.

**** WHAT ORGANISMS ARE LIKELY TO BE FOUND IN THE THROAT?**
The likely pathogens associated with throat are: STREPTOCOCCUS-
PNEUMONIAE, STREPTOCOCCUS-GROUP-A, NEISSERIA-MENINGITIDIS.

**** IS BACTEROIDES AEROBIC?**
No, the aerobicity of bacteroides is anaerobic.

**** WHAT DOSAGE OF STREPTOMYCIN DO YOU GENERALLY RECOMMEND?**
The suggested dosage and route of streptomycin is 7.5 mg/kg
q12h IM (or IV).

**** HOW DO YOU TREAT MENINGOCOCCAL BACTEREMIA?**
For treatment of NEISSERIA-MENINGITIDIS in PRIMARY-BACTEREMIA
Select therapy from among the following drugs (ranked according
to relative efficacy, assuming uniform sensitivity):

PENICILLIN	(.91)
AMPICILLIN	(.9)
SULFISOXAZOLE	(.8)
CHLORAMPHENICOL	(.7)
ERYTHROMYCIN	(.5)
TETRACYCLINE	(.4)

FIGURE 18-9 Questions about factual knowledge.

premise and action satisfy these constraints. It accordingly needs to know that there are two special lists associated with each parameter: one containing every rule that uses the parameter in its premise, and the other containing every rule that concludes about the parameter in its action (LOOKAHEAD and UPDATED-BY, see Chapter 5). Using these lists for the various parameters mentioned in the question, the specialist can find those rules that might answer the question. If no values were specified, the job is done and the relevant rules can be displayed without further analysis; otherwise, it is necessary to read each of the rules in the list and to eliminate those that do not mention the correct values for the parameter.

The rule-retrieval specialist also makes use of a piece of MYCIN's knowledge discussed in Chapter 9. The system contains models of its own knowledge (called *rule models*), which are used primarily during acquisition of new medical knowledge from an expert (Davis, 1976). These models, however, can be put to many uses—one is to explain general patterns in decision making. The rule models are abstract descriptions of subsets of rules and are generated automatically by reading the rules. For example, the model for IDENT IS PSEUDOMONAS tells what features are common to the majority of rules that conclude that the identity of an organism is *Pseudomonas*.

If a model exists describing the rules about which the question is ask-

```
** WHY DO YOU ASK WHETHER THE PATIENT HAS A FEVER OF UNKNOWN
   ORIGIN?
The rules listed below use:
        whether the patient has a true fever of unknown origin

RULE180

IF:  1) The site of the culture is blood, and
     2) The number of cultures in the series including the
        culture is greater than or equal to 1, and
     3) The number of cultures in this series which were
        positive for the organism is less than or equal to 1,
        and
     4) The patient has a true fever of unknown origin, and
     5) Cardiac-surgery is a relevant item from the history of
        the patient
Then: There is suggestive evidence (.6) that the infection is
      infective-endocarditis

** WHAT DOES GU MANIPULATION TELL YOU ABOUT THE IDENTITY OF AN
   ORGANISM?
The rules listed below use:
        whether the patient has had a genito-urinary manipulative
            procedure
to conclude about:
        the identity of the organism
156, 163, 190
Which do you wish to see?
        ** 156

RULE156

IF:  1) The site of the culture is blood, and
     2) The gram stain of the organism is gramneg, and
     3) The morphology of the organism is rod, and
     4) The portal of entry of the organism is urine, and
     5) The patient has not had a genito-urinary manipulative
        procedure, and
     6) Cystitis is not a problem for which the patient has
        been treated
THEN: There is suggestive evidence (.6) that the identity of
      the organism is e.coli
```

FIGURE 18-10 Rule-retrieval questions.

ing, the rule-retrieval specialist incorporates this model's information into its answer (Figure 18-11). Thus the question-answering facility is able to give some information about strategies for achieving some of the system's goals, as well as giving the individual rules that use the strategies.

18.2.5 Consultation-Specific Questions

Some of the simplest questions about a specific consultation are those that inquire about the value of a particular parameter (Figure 18-12). The specialist that answers these questions must know how to retrieve this in-

```
** HOW DO YOU DECIDE THAT AN ORGANISM MIGHT BE
   PSEUDOMONAS AERUGINOSA?
   Rules which conclude that the identity of the organism is
   pseudomonas-aeruginosa generally use one or more of the
   following pieces of information:
          the site of the culture
          the gram stain of the organism
          the morphology of the organism
   Furthermore, the following relationships hold:
   The gram stain of the organism, and the morphology of the
          organism tend to appear together in these rules.
   RULE184, RULE116, RULE047, RULE085, RULE040 conclude that
          the identity of the organism is pseudomonas-aeruginosa.
          Which of these do you wish to see?
          ** 184

   RULE184

   IF:  1) The category of the organism is not known, and
        2) The gram stain of the organism is gramneg, and
        3) The morphology of the organism is rod, and
        4) The aerobicity of the organism is facul
 THEN:  There is weakly suggestive evidence (.1) that the
        identity of the organism is pseudomonas-aeruginosa
```

FIGURE 18-11 Response that uses rule models.

formation. In some cases it will also be necessary to make comparisons to see if a value specified in the question is one of the values that was inferred for that parameter.

Answering other types of consultation-specific questions involves the use of knowledge about the control structure:

- how the system acquires information,
- why the system tries to find out about parameters,
- how information is used once it is acquired,
- what causes a rule to be tried, and
- what causes a rule to fail.

```
** TO WHAT CLASS DOES ORGANISM-1 BELONG?
The category of ORGANISM-1 is enterobacteriaceae (.9)

** IS ORGANISM-1 A STREPTOCOCCUS?
No.
The identity of ORGANISM-1 is e.coli (.74) bacteroides (.7)
       klebsiella-pneumoniae (.4) pseudomonas-aeruginosa (.22)
       enterobacter (.21) proteus-non-mirabilis (.19) serratia (.03)
       salmonella (.02)
```

FIGURE 18-12 Questions about a parameter's value.

**** HOW DO YOU KNOW THAT CULTURE-1 WAS FROM A STERILE SOURCE?**
I used rule189 to conclude that this blood culture was taken from
a sterile source. This gave a cumulative CF of (1.0). The
last question asked before the conclusion was made was 7.

**** DID YOU CONSIDER BACTEROIDES AS A POSSIBILITY FOR ORGANISM-1?**
Yes. I used rule095 to conclude that the identity of ORGANISM-1
is bacteroides. This gave a cumulative CF of (.7). The
last question asked before the conclusion was made was 20.

**** HOW DO YOU KNOW THAT ORGANISM-1 IS E.COLI?**
The following rules made conclusions about whether the identity
of ORGANISM-1 is e.coli

	cumulative certainty		last question asked
Rule	Yes	No	before conclusion was made
RULE021	(.47)		20
RULE084	(.55)		22
RULE003	(.74)		24

In answer to question 9 you said that the identity of ORGANISM-1
is e.coli (.3)

FIGURE 18-13 Questions regarding how a conclusion was made.

The specialist for answering questions like "How do you know the value of <parm> of <cntxt>?" knows that the value of a parameter can come from two sources: it can be deduced by rules, or the user can give it in response to a question. The history tree will show which (possibly both) of these sources provided the particular information mentioned in the question (Figure 18-13).

If the question is phrased in the negative, it is necessary first to find all the ways the conclusion *could* have been made (this is a simple task of rule retrieval), then to explain why it *wasn't* made in this consultation (Figure 18-14). The specialist for answering these questions must know what situations can prevent conclusions from being made. The second question in Figure 18-14 illustrates how the answer to one question might cause another question to be asked.

The specialist for answering questions of the form "How did you use <parm> of <cntxt>?" needs to know not only how to find the specific rules that might use a parameter, but also how a parameter can cause a rule to fail and how one parameter can prevent another from being used. The history tree can be checked to see which of the relevant rules used the parameter, which failed because of the parameter, and which failed for some other reason, preventing the parameter from being used (Figure 18-15).

For questions of the form "Why didn't you find out about <parm> of <cntxt>?" general knowledge of MYCIN's control structure tells the conditions under which it would have been necessary to find out some piece of information. The record of the consultation can be used to de-

**** WHY DID YOU RULE OUT STREPTOCOCCUS AS A POSSIBILITY FOR ORGANISM-1?**

The following rules could have been used to determine that the
identity of ORGANISM-1 is streptococcus: RULE033. However,
none of these succeeded in the context of ORGANISM-1.
If you would like an explanation for why any of these
rules failed, please enter their numbers:
**** 33**

Clause 2 of RULE033 ["the morphology of the organism is coccus"]
was already known to be false for ORGANISM-1, so the rule
was never tried.

**** WHY DON'T YOU THINK THAT THE MORPHOLOGY OF ORGANISM-1 IS COCCUS?**

It is definite that the morphology of ORGANISM-1 is rod. Knowing
this with certainty rules out all other values for the
morphology of ORGANISM-1, including coccus.

FIGURE 18-14 Questions regarding why a conclusion was not made.

**** HOW DID YOU USE THE AEROBICITY OF ORGANISM-1?**

The aerobicity of ORGANISM-1 was used in the following rules:
RULE003, RULE005, RULE084.
The aerobicity of ORGANISM-1 caused the following rules to fail:
RULE035, RULE051, RULE052, RULE053, RULE111.
The aerobicity of ORGANISM-1 also would have been used in:
RULE037, RULE050, RULE058, RULE086, RULE110, RULE184,
RULE203, RULE204, RULE205. However, none of these
succeeded in the context of ORGANISM-1. If you would
like an explanation for why any of these rules failed,
please enter their numbers:
**** 37**

RULE037 was tried in the context of ORGANISM-1, but it failed
due to clause 1 ["the category of the organism is not
known"].

**** DID YOU CONSIDER THE FACT THAT PATIENT-1 IS NOT A COMPROMISED HOST?**

The fact that Fred Jones is not a compromised host caused the
following rules to fail: RULE085, RULE106.
The fact that Fred Jones is not a compromised host also would
have been used in: RULE109. However, none of these
succeeded in the context of PATIENT-1. If you would
like an explanation for why any of these rules failed,
please enter their numbers:
**** NONE**

FIGURE 18-15 Questions regarding how information was used.

termine why these conditions never arose for the particular parameter in question (Figure 18-16). Figure 18-16 also illustrates that MYCIN's general question answerer allows a user to get as much information as is desired. The first answer given was not really complete in itself, but it led the user to ask another question to get more information. Then another question was asked to determine why clause 1 of Rule 159 was false. The answers to the first two questions both mentioned rules, which could be printed if the user wanted to examine them. The special command PR (Print Rule) is for the user's convenience. It requires no natural language processing and thus can be understood and answered immediately ("What is Rule 109?" or "Print Rule 109" also would be understood).

In questions that ask about the application of a rule to a context there are three possibilities: the rule told us something about the context; the rule failed when applied to that context; or the rule was never tried in that context. The history tree tells which of these is the case. Furthermore, if a rule succeeded, there is a record of all the conclusions it made, and if it failed, the reason for failure is recorded. As Figure 18-17 illustrates, rules are only applicable in certain contexts. If the rule could not apply to the context mentioned in the question but might be relevant when applied to some other context (which is an ancestor or descendent in the context tree), then the question is answered as if it had mentioned the relevant context.

There are interactions among the different types of questions, but they weren't mentioned earlier for the sake of clarity. Sometimes a question may indicate an incorrect assumption about the state of MYCIN's knowledge. For example, a question could be "Why don't you think that ORGANISM-1 is *E. coli*?" when, in fact, the system has concluded that the organism *is E. coli*. To answer this question, the explanation system would explain how it *did* make such a decision, despite the phrasing of the question. Similarly, when asked how the system used (or concluded about) some parameter that was never traced, the system explains why it didn't need to find out about the parameter, regardless of how the question was phrased.

18.3 Conclusions

Consultation systems form a class of artificial intelligence programs that can provide useful solutions to real-world problems. The utility of such systems, however, depends on their acceptability to human users. One feature that can increase their acceptability is a mechanism whereby they can explain or justify their advice.

The development of an explanation mechanism for a consultation system is very much related to the problems of representing knowledge and of making use of different sources of knowledge. Since the use of inference rules provides a unified way to represent modular pieces of knowledge,

**** DID YOU FIND OUT ABOUT THE CBC ASSOCIATED WITH CULTURE-1?**
During the preceding consultation, I never had reason to try to find out whether the results of the CBC from the time period of this blood culture are available. It would have been necessary to know this information in order to use any of the following: RULE109. However, none of these succeeded in the context of this blood culture. If you would like an explanation for why any of these rules failed, please enter their numbers:
**** 109**
RULE109 would be relevant to this blood culture when applied to: ORGANISM-1.
I never had reason to try to apply RULE109 to ORGANISM-1. I would have needed to use RULE109 in order to find out whether ORGANISM-1 is a contaminant. However, during the preceding consultation, I never had reason to try to find out whether ORGANISM-1 is a contaminant.

**** WHY DIDN'T YOU NEED TO KNOW WHETHER ORGANISM-1 IS A CONTAMINANT?**
During the preceding consultation, I never had reason to try to find out whether ORGANISM-1 is a contaminant. It would have been necessary to know this information in order to use any of the following: RULE006, RULE007, RULE106, RULE108, RULE109, RULE159. However, none of these succeeded in the context of ORGANISM-1. If you would like an explanation for why any of these rules failed, please enter their numbers:
**** 159**
RULE159 was tried in the context of ORGANISM-1, but it failed due to clause 1 ["it is suspected that the identity of the organism is corynebacterium-non-diphtheriae"]

**** IS ORGANISM-1 CORYNEBACTERIUM-NON-DIPHTHERIAE?**
No. The identity of ORGANISM-1 is e.coli (.74) bacteroides (.7) klebsiella-pneumoniae (.4) pseudomonas-aeruginosa (.22) enterobacter (.21) proteus-non-mirabilis (.19) serratia (.03) salmonella (.02)

**** PR 109**
RULE109
IF: 1) The culture was taken from a sterile source, and
2) It is not known whether the organism is a contaminant, and
3) The patient is not a compromised host, and
4) The patient was febrile due to the infection, and
5) The results of the CBC from the time period of the culture are available, and
6) A - The white count from the CBC is greater than 10.5, or
B - The percent of PMN's in the CBC at the time the culture was obtained is greater than 78, or
C - The percent of WBC's which were bands in the CBC at the time the culture was obtained is greater than 10
THEN: There is strongly suggestive evidence (.8) that the organism is not a contaminant

FIGURE 18-16 Questions about why a parameter was not traced.

**** DID RULE 116 TELL YOU ANYTHING ABOUT INFECTION-1?**
RULE116 would be relevant to the primary-bacteremia when applied
to: ORGANISM-1.
Clause 5 of RULE116 ["the infection is meningitis"] was already
known to be false for ORGANISM-1, so the rule was never tried.

**** HOW WAS RULE 178 HELPFUL WHEN YOU WERE CONSIDERING ORGANISM-1?**
RULE178 would be relevant to ORGANISM-1 when applied to:
CULTURE-1.
I never had reason to try to apply RULE178 to this blood culture.
I would have needed to use RULE178 in order to find out
whether this blood culture was taken from a sterile source.
However, I was already certain that this blood culture was
taken from a sterile source.

**** WHAT DID RULE 295 TELL YOU ABOUT ORGANISM-1?**
I used RULE295 to conclude that the identity of ORGANISM-1 is
hemophilus-influenzae. This gave a cumulative CF of (.25).
The last question asked before the conclusion was made
was 36.

**** WHY DIDN'T YOU USE RULE 112 TO FIND OUT ABOUT ORGANISM-1?**
RULE112 was not executed because it would have caused circular
reasoning when applied to ORGANISM-1. Would you like to
see the chain of rules and parameters which makes up this
circle?
**** YES**
I wanted to know about the identity of ORGANISM-1 because I
try to find out the identity of the organism for all
current organisms of the patient.
To find out about the identity of ORGANISM-1, I tried to use
RULE021. Before I could use RULE021, I needed to know about
a prior organism with possibly the same identity as
ORGANISM-1.
To find out about a prior organism with possibly the same
identity as ORGANISM-1, I tried to use RULE005. Before I
could use RULE005, I needed to know about the aerobicity of
ORGANISM-1.
To find out about the aerobicity of ORGANISM-1, I tried to use
RULE031. Before I could use RULE031, I needed to know about
the category of ORGANISM-1.
To find out about the category of ORGANISM-1, I tried to use
RULE112. Before I could use RULE112, I needed to know about
the identity of ORGANISM-1.
But this is the unknown parameter I sought originally.

FIGURE 18-17 Questions regarding the application of rules.

the task of designing an explanation capability is simplified for rule-based consultation systems. The example of MYCIN shows how this can be done and illustrates further that a system designed for a single domain with a small, technical vocabulary can give comprehensive answers to a wide range of questions without sophisticated natural language processing.

19

Specialized Explanations for Dosage Selection

Sharon Wraith Bennett and A. Carlisle Scott

In this chapter we describe specialized routines that MYCIN uses to evaluate and explain appropriate drug dosing. The processes that the program uses in its selection of antimicrobials and subsequent dosage calculations have been refined to take into account a variety of patient- and drug-specific factors. Originally, all dosage recommendations were based on normal adult doses. However, it was soon recognized that the program needed to be able to recommend optimal therapy by considering information about the patient, such as age and renal function, as well as pharmacokinetic variables of the drugs. The addition of an ability to customize doses expanded the capabilities of the consultation program.

Earlier chapters have described the way in which MYCIN uses clinical and laboratory data to establish the presence of an infection and the likely identity of the infecting organism(s). If positive laboratory identification is not available, MYCIN ranks possible pathogens in order of likelihood. Antimicrobials are then chosen to treat effectively all likely organisms. In order to select drugs to which the organisms are usually sensitive, MYCIN uses susceptibility data from the Stanford bacteriology laboratory. The program also considers the fact that the patient's previous antimicrobial treatment may influence an organism's susceptibility. MYCIN disfavors a drug that the patient is receiving at the time a positive culture was obtained.

Drug-specific factors are then considered before therapy is chosen. Some drugs, such as many of the cephalosporins, are not recommended for patients with meningitis because they do not adequately cross the blood-

This chapter is an abridged version of a paper, some of which was originally presented by Sharon Wraith Bennett at the 12th Annual Midyear Clinical Meeting of the American Society of Hospital Pharmacists, Atlanta, Georgia, December 8, 1977, and which appeared in *American Journal of Hospital Pharmacy* 37: 523–529 (1980).

brain barrier and may lead to the development of resistance (Fisher et al., 1975). One antimicrobial may be selected over another, similar drug because it causes fewer or less severe side effects. For example, nafcillin is generally preferred over methicillin for treatment of staphylococcal infections because of the reported interstitial nephritis associated with methicillin (Ditlove et al., 1977). MYCIN'S knowledge base therefore requires continual updating with new indications or adverse reactions as they are reported in the medical literature.

Several patient-specific factors may further limit the list of acceptable antimicrobials. Tetracycline, for example, is not recommended for children (Conchie et al., 1970) or pregnant (Anthony, 1970) or breast-feeding (O'Brien, 1974) women. Also, prior adverse reactions to antimicrobials must be considered by the program.

19.1 Customizing Doses

Efficacious treatment of infectious diseases begins with selection of an antimicrobial; however, it is likely that the patient will not be cured unless the dose and the route of administration of the drug are appropriate. MYCIN takes into account the site of the infection, the age of the patient, and the patient's renal status in determining the dosage regimen for each drug.

Consider, for example, the importance of patient age in therapy planning. The half-life of some drugs may be longer in neonates than in adults because of the immaturity of the former's microsomal enzyme system and kidneys (Weiss et al., 1960). Therefore, the doses of these drugs, in mg/kg amounts, should be lower in the neonates than in the adults. On the other hand, some antimicrobials, such as gentamicin, may require a higher relative dose in children than in the adults, possibly because of a larger volume of distribution (Siber et al., 1975). MYCIN therefore uses different calculations when appropriate for determining doses for neonates, infants, children, and adults.

Most antimicrobials are fully or partially excreted by the kidneys; for this reason, it is necessary to consider the patient's renal function in order to determine a safe and effective regimen. The program uses the patient's creatinine clearance as an indicator of the degree of renal impairment. Doses are adjusted in patients over six months of age if the creatinine clearance falls below 80 ml/min/1.73 m^2 and if more than 15% of the drug is excreted unchanged in the urine. In children between one week and six months of age, the dose is changed if the creatinine clearance is less than 60ml/min/1.73 m^2. A creatinine clearance of 30ml/min/1.73 m^2 indicates

```
.
.
.
47) Does John Jones have a clinically significant allergic reaction to any antimicrobial agent?
** NO
48) Do you have reason to suspect that John Jones may have impaired renal function?
** YES
49) What is the most recent creatinine clearance in ml/min which you feel is a true representation of John Jones's
    renal function?
** UNKNOWN
50) What is the most recent serum creatinine of John Jones (in mg/100ml)?
** 1.9
51) What is the previous serum creatinine of John Jones (in mg/100ml)?
** 1.8
52) Number of days between John Jones two most recent serum creatinines:
** 2
53) John Jones's weight in kilograms (or <number> POUNDS):
** 70
54) John Jones's height in centimeters (or <number> INCHES):
** 175
Estimated body surface area is 1.9 sq. meters.
Dosage adjustments will be based on the calculated creatinine
        clearance of 42.7 ml/min/1.73 sq. meters (adjusted to
        average body surface area).
.
.
.
```

FIGURE 19-1 The patient's creatinine clearance is used as an indicator of the degree of renal function. When the creatinine clearance is not known, it is estimated from the age, sex, weight, and serum creatinine of the patient and adjusted to average body surface area before the dose is calculated.

renal impairment in infants[1] between one day and one week old (Edelmann and Barnett, 1971). Because of the passage of maternal creatinine into the infant serum at birth, no estimate of renal function is attempted if the newborn is less than one day old. For infants younger than six months, MYCIN warns the user of the large degree of possible error in the estimated doses because of the changing renal function and a poor relationship between glomerular filtration rate and body surface area (Rubin et al., 1949).

When the creatinine clearance of an adult patient is not known, it is estimated from the age, sex, weight, and serum creatinine (Jelliffe and Jelliffe, 1972) (Figure 19-1). For children less than 12 years of age, the height and serum creatinine are used to estimate the creatinine clearance (Schwartz et al., 1976). If two consecutive serum creatinines indicate rap-

[1]The creatinine clearance in infants is less than in adults because of decreased glomerular membrane permeability, smaller glomerular filtering surface, lower perfusion pressure, and lower renal plasma flow.

```
[REC-1] My preferred therapy recommendation is:
Give the following in combination:
        1) CHLORAMPHENICOL
           Give: 1.75g (17.6 ml) q6h IV [calculated on basis of 25 mg/kg]
        2) GENTAMICIN
           After a loading dose of: 112 mg (2.8 ml, 80mg/2ml ampule) IV
                 [calculated on basis of 1.6 mg/kg],
           give: 70 mg (1.8 ml, 80mg/2ml ampule) q8h IV [calculated on
                 basis of 1.0 mg/kg] plus consider giving 5 mg q24h
                 Intrathecal
           Or, after a loading dose of: 140 mg (3.6 ml, 80mg/2ml ampule)
                 IV [calculated on basis of 2.0 mg/kg],
           give: 119 mg (3.0 ml, 80mg/2ml ampule) q14h IV [calculated on
                 basis of 1.7 mg/kg] plus consider giving 5 mg q24h
                 Intrathecal
                    [normal dose is 1.7 mg/kg q8h IV]
Would you like to enter a new dosing interval?
** YES
Please enter the number of hours.
** 12
           After a loading dose of: 133 mg (3.4 ml, 80mg/2ml ampule) IV
                 [calculated on basis of 1.9 mg/kg],
           give: 105 mg (2.6 ml, 80mg/2ml ampule) q12h IV [calculated on
                 basis of 1.4 mg/kg] plus consider giving 5 mg q24h
                 Intrathecal
```

FIGURE 19-2 MYCIN provides three different dosage regimens for each antimicrobial whose dose must be adjusted in renal failure. One method changes the dose, another alters the interval, and the third calculates a new dose given any interval.

idly changing renal function, a warning is printed, which recommends repeating the assessment of the degree of impairment before an accurate dosage regimen can be determined. The creatinine clearance is adjusted to average body surface area (Boyd, 1935) before the program calculates a dose (Figure 19-2). If the creatinine clearance indicates renal failure, MYCIN calculates doses based on the first-order pharmacokinetic properties of the antimicrobials (see Figure 19-2) and the patient's creatinine clearance. (A description of the formulas is included in Figure 19-4.)

The program provides three different dosage regimens for each antimicrobial whose dose must be adjusted. One method changes the dose, another alters the dosing interval, while the third calculates a new dose given any interval. This last option allows the physician to select a dosing interval that is convenient for the staff to follow and a dose that is a reasonable volume to administer. A loading dose is calculated for each regimen so that an effective blood level can be reached as soon as possible. The dose is provided in both a mg/kg amount and the number of milliliters, capsules, or tablets required (Figure 19-2).

If a patient's renal function changes during therapy, the physician can obtain a new dosage recommendation without repeating the entire infectious disease consultation. A shortened version of the consultation will recalculate the doses on the basis of the patient's current renal function. The program will request only the information necessary for determining the new doses, such as the most recent creatinine clearance (or serum creatinine).

19.2 Selection of Dosage Regimen

Although it is widely debated which dosage regimen is best, it is generally recognized that the blood level of antimicrobials used to treat bacteremias should exceed the minimum inhibitory concentration (MIC) while remaining below toxic levels. The health professional must decide between allowing the drug level to fluctuate above and below the MIC and consistently maintaining the drug level above the MIC through more frequent dosing. This decision is based on a variety of factors including the organism identity and the drug under consideration. To aid the prescriber in selecting the most appropriate regimen, MYCIN generates a graph for each regimen showing the predicted steady-state blood levels over time (Figure 19-3) (Gibaldi and Perrier, 1975). The MIC of the organism and the toxic level of the drug (when they are available) are also included on the graph. The graph provides a rough estimate of the blood levels and the time of peak concentration in the patient. It is provided to improve the initial selection of a dosage regimen, not to replace the measurement of blood levels. Monitoring blood levels whenever they are available is strongly recommended.

19.3 Explanation of Recommendations

At the conclusion of the consultation, the physician can ask MYCIN simple questions to obtain assurance that the diagnosis and treatment are reasonable. These questions may refer to the current consultation or they may be general, regarding any of the system's knowledge. The program provides a justification for the therapy selection, which includes the reasons for selecting one antimicrobial instead of another. Also available is an explanation of the calculations used to decide on a dose (Figure 19-4). The physician can also ask to see relevant parts of MYCIN'S knowledge base, including justification and literature references (Figure 19-5).

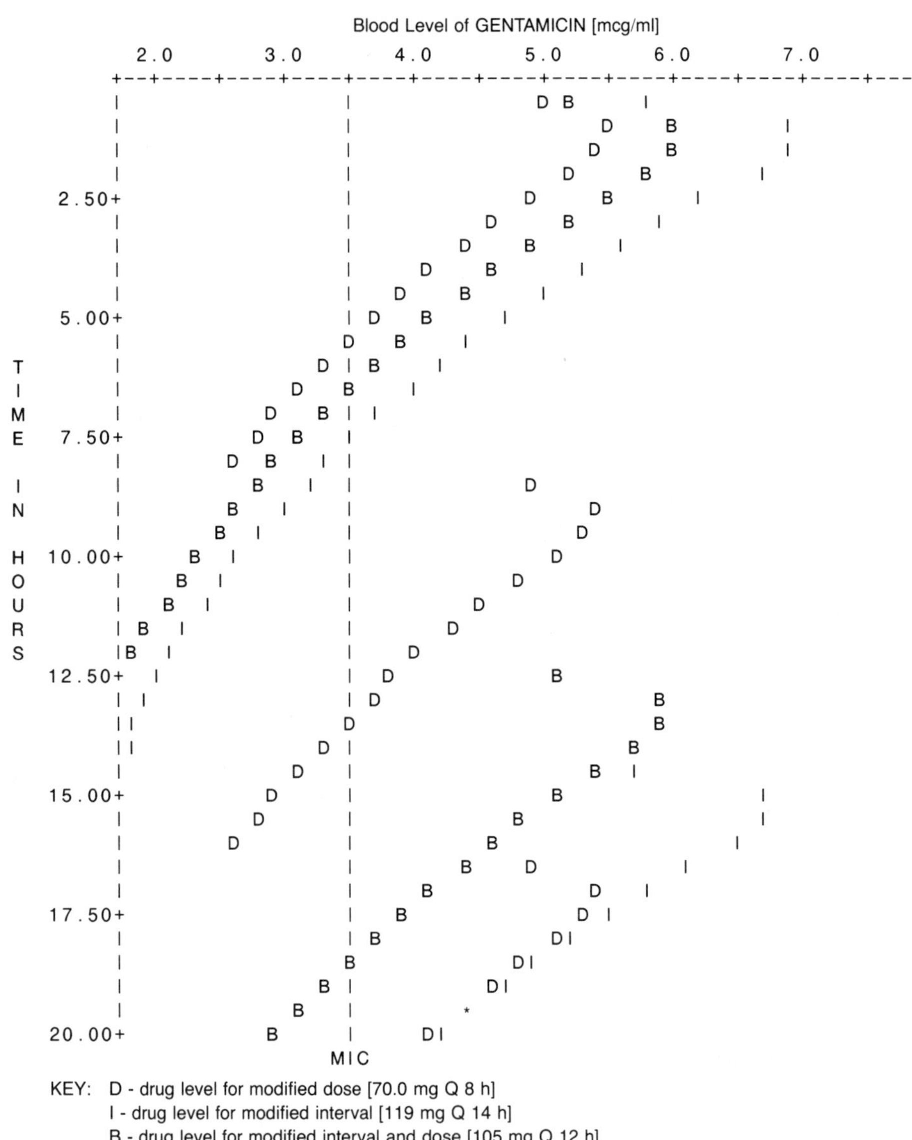

FIGURE 19-3 Graph of blood levels of a drug (gentamicin) over time for different doses and dose intervals. The graph is shown precisely as it is printed by the computer. Note that regimen I, with the longest dosing interval, reaches the highest blood levels episodically but also leaves the patient with blood levels below the MIC for the longest period of time. The somewhat atypical orientation of this graph, designed for terminal output, displays time vertically, blood level horizontally.

**** HOW DID YOU CALCULATE THE DOSE FOR GENTAMICIN?**

When GENTAMICIN is given for MENINGITIS, the recommended dosage is:
if age is > 2 yrs then 1.7 mg/kg q8h IV plus consider giving 5 mg q24h IT,
else 2.3 mg/kg q8h IV plus consider giving 2.5-4 mg/day IT.

The normal dose for John Jones is: 119 mg (3.0 ml, 80mg/2ml ampule) q8h IV [calculated on the basis of 1.7 mg/kg] plus consider giving 5 mg q24h IT

GENTAMICIN is excreted by the kidneys, so its dosage must be modified in renal failure.

The following table shows how the patient's renal function was determined:

Identifier	Value	Definition
SCR1	1.9	the most recent serum creatinine (mg/100ml)
SCR2	1.8	the previous serum creatinine (mg/100ml)
CCr(f)	42.7	estimated creatinine clearance, adjusted for normal body surface area (ml/min/1.73 sq. meters)
CCr(n)	100	the average normal creatinine clearance for John Jones's age group
CCr(min)	80	the minimum normal creatinine clearance for John Jones's age group

Since CCr(f) < CCr(min), John Jones has renal impairment.

To modify the dosage of GENTAMICIN, the following pharmacokinetic parameters were used:

Identifier	Value	Definition
a	.007	the fraction hourly loss of a drug due to non-renal processes
b	.0022	the slope of the plot of the elimination rate constant of a drug versus the patient's creatinine clearance
Q	.57	the drug's elimination rate fraction: elimination rate of the drug as a fraction of the drug's "normal" elimination rate.

Q was calculated using the formula:

$$Q = [a + b * CCr(f)] / [a + b * CCr(n)]$$

My first dosage recommendation decreased the amount of GENTAMICIN and left the dosing interval unchanged. The new amount was calculated by multiplying the old amount by Q.
The second recommendation increased the dosing interval and left the amount of GENTAMICIN unchanged. The new interval was calculated by dividing the old interval by Q.

FIGURE 19-4 The physician can ask MYCIN questions to obtain assurance that the diagnosis, treatment, and dose are reasonable.

19.4 Summary and Conclusions

MYCIN is able to customize therapy recommendations by using its knowledge base in conjunction with patient-specific information. The large knowledge base contains facts about organism susceptibilities to drugs, ep-

```
** HOW DO YOU DETERMINE BODY SURFACE AREA?
RULE104

[This rule applies to any patient, and is tried in order to find out
        about the patient's estimated body surface area]

IF:  1) The weight of the patient is known, and
     2) The height of the patient is known
THEN:   Use Boyd's algorithm to calculate body surface area from
        weight and height [Boyd, E. The Growth of the Surface
        Area of the Human Body, 1935, pp 1-133.]
Author: Wraith
Justification: A comparative evaluation with statistical analysis of
        the Boyd method with the DuBois formula demonstrated that the
        Boyd formula is more accurate for abnormal body types.
        [Sendray J. et al., Determination of human body surface area from
        height and weight, Applied Physiology, 7(1):1-12, July 1954.]
```

FIGURE 19-5 The person obtaining a MYCIN consultation can see the decision rules that the program uses, including justification and literature references.

idemiology of infectious diseases, and pharmacokinetics and toxicity of various antimicrobials. This knowledge enables the program to determine appropriate treatment specific to a patient's age, renal function, and prior drug reactions. MYCIN'S explanation capability allows the user to analyze the process by which the program arrived at a therapy recommendation. This capability may also play an educational role by reminding the physician of critical factors to consider when prescribing therapy for other patients.

Increasing evidence of inappropriate antimicrobial therapy indicates a need for assistance in the expanding area of infectious disease therapy selection (Neu and Howrey, 1975). There is a recognized need for continuing education as well as for computational assistance with dosage adjustments in renal failure. This is not surprising when one recognizes all of the factors that must be considered in a therapy decision. One response to the problem of antimicrobial misuse is to increase the availability of consultations with infectious diseases experts. A consultation not only provides assistance in determining the appropriate therapy for the patient under consideration but also is an educational experience for the physician requesting it. Computer-based consultation programs such as MYCIN can provide medical professionals with clinical advice and educational information when human consultants are not available.

20

Customized Explanations Using Causal Knowledge

Jerold W. Wallis and Edward H. Shortliffe

Developers of expert systems have increasingly recognized the importance of explanation capabilities to the acceptance of their programs; such capabilities are also critical in medical consultation system development (Gorry, 1973; Shortliffe, 1980). Good explanations serve four functions in a consultation system: (1) they provide a method for examining the program's reasoning if errors arise when the system is being built; (2) they assure users that the reasoning is logical, thereby increasing user acceptance of the system; (3) they may persuade users that unexpected advice is appropriate; and (4) they can educate users in areas where users' knowledge may be weak. These diverse roles impose several requirements on the system. For example, the explanations must adequately represent the reasoning processes of the program, and they should allow the user to examine the reasoning history or underlying knowledge at various levels of detail. In addition, although the program's approach to a problem need not be identical to an expert's approach, the program's overall strategy and reasoning steps must be understandable and seem logical, regardless of the user's level of expertise. This means that the system must have the capability to tailor its explanations to the varying needs and characteristics of its users.

In this chapter we describe recent experiments in the design and implementation of a prototype explanation program. Our past work in explanation for consultation systems, described in Chapter 18, dealt primarily with the ability to cite the rules involved in a particular decision. Although MYCIN's responses provide an accurate description of a portion

---

This chapter is based on a paper originally appearing in *Methods of Information in Medicine* 21: 127–136 (July 1982).

```
** DO YOU TREAT PSEUDOMONAS-AERUGINOSA BACTEREMIA WITH CARBENICILLIN?
   Yes, for treatment of PSEUDOMONAS-AERUGINOSA in BACTEREMIA, the drugs
   of choice (ranked by relative efficacy, assuming sensitivity) are:

   1st choice:
       CARBENICILLIN-AND-TOBRAMYCIN
       CARBENICILLIN-AND-GENTAMICIN
       AMIKACIN-AND-CARBENICILLIN
   2nd choice:
        TOBRAMYCIN
        GENTAMICIN
        AMIKACIN
```

FIGURE 20-1 An example of an interaction with MYCIN's explanation program. Note that the rule for selecting a drug to cover *Pseudomonas aeruginosa* is adequate for allowing MYCIN to reach the correct conclusion but that the underlying reason for combining two drugs is unclear.

of its reasoning, to understand the overall reasoning scheme a user needs to request a display of *all* rules that are used. Additionally, rules such as that shown in the interaction of Figure 20-1 are designed largely for efficiency and therefore frequently omit underlying causal mechanisms that are known to experts but that a novice may need in order to understand a decision. The rule guiding the choice of carbenicillin with an aminoglycoside, for example, does not mention the synergism of the two drugs when combined in the treatment of serious *Pseudomonas aeruginosa* infections. Finally, while MYCIN does have a limited sense of discourse (viz., an ability to modify responses based on the topic under discussion), its explanations are not customized to the questioner's objectives or characteristics.

MYCIN's explanation capabilities were expanded by Clancey in his work on the GUIDON tutorial system (Chapter 26). In order to use MYCIN's knowledge base and patient cases for tutorial purposes, Clancey found it necessary to incorporate knowledge about teaching. This knowledge, expressed as *tutoring rules*, and a four-tiered measure of the baseline knowledge of the student (beginner, advanced, practitioner, or expert), enhanced the ability of a student to learn efficiently from MYCIN's knowledge base. Clancey also noted problems arising from the frequent lack of underlying "support" knowledge, which is needed to explain the relevance and utility of a domain rule (Chapter 29).

More recently, Swartout has developed a system that generates explanations from a record of the development decisions made during the writing of a consultation program to advise on digitalis dosing (Swartout, 1981). The domain expert provides information to a "writer" subprogram, which in turn constructs the advising system. The traces left by the writer, a set of domain principles, and a domain model are utilized to produce explanations. Thus both the knowledge acquisition process and automatic programming techniques are intrinsic to the explanations generated by Swartout's system. Responses to questions are customized for different kinds of users by keeping track of what class is likely to be interested in a given piece of code.

Whereas MYCIN generates explanations that are usually based on a single rule,[1] Weiner has described a system named BLAH (Weiner, 1980) that can summarize an entire reasoning chain in a single explanatory statement. The approach developed for BLAH was based on a series of psycholinguistic studies (Linde, 1978; Linde and Goguen, 1978; Weiner, 1979) that analyzed the ways in which human beings explain decisions, choices, and plans to one another. For example, BLAH structures an explanation so that the differences among alternatives are given before the similarities (a practice that was noted during the analysis of human explanations).

The tasks of interpreting questions and generating explanations are confounded by the problems inherent in natural language understanding and text generation. A consultation program must be able to distinguish general questions from case-specific ones and questions relating to specific reasoning steps from those involving the overall reasoning strategy. As previously mentioned, it is also important to tailor the explanation to the user, giving appropriate supporting causal and empirical relationships. It is to this last task that our recent research has been aimed. We have deferred confronting problems of natural language understanding for the present, concentrating instead on representation and control mechanisms that permit the generation of explanations customized to the knowledge and experience of either physician or student users.

20.1 Design Considerations: The User Model

For a system to produce customized explanations, it must be able to model the user's knowledge and motivation for using the system. At the simplest level, such a model can be represented by a single measure of what the user knows in this domain and how much he or she wants to know (i.e., to what level of detail the user wishes to have things explained). One approach is to record a single rating of a user's *expertise*, similar to the four categories mentioned above for GUIDON. The model could be extended to permit the program to distinguish subareas of a user's expertise in different portions of the knowledge base. For example, the measures could be dynamically updated as the program responds to questions and explains segments

[1]Although MYCIN's WHY command has a limited ability to integrate several rules into a single explanation (Shortliffe et al., 1975), the user wishing a high-level summary must specifically augment the WHY with a number that indicates the level of detail desired. We have found that the feature is therefore seldom used. It would, of course, be preferable if the system "knew" on its own when such a summary is appropriate.

of its knowledge. If the user demonstrates familiarity with one portion of the knowledge base, then he or she probably also knows about related portions (e.g., if physicians are familiar with the detailed biochemistry of one part of the endocrine system, they are likely to know the biochemistry of other parts of the endocrine system as well). This information can be represented in a manner similar to Goldstein's rule pointers, which link analogous rules, rule specializations, and rule refinements (Goldstein, 1978). In addition, the model should ideally incorporate a sense of dialogue to facilitate user interactions. Finally, it must be self-correcting (e.g., if the user unexpectedly requests information on a topic the program had assumed he or she knew, the program should correct its model prior to giving the explanation). In our recent experiments we have concentrated on the ability to give an explanation appropriate to the user's level of knowledge and have deemphasized dialogue and model correction.

20.2 Knowledge Representation

20.2.1 Form of the Conceptual Network

We have found it useful to describe the knowledge representation for our prototype system in terms of a semantic network (Figure 20-2).[2] It is similar to other network representations used in the development of expert systems (Duda et al., 1978b; Weiss et al., 1978) and has also been influenced by Rieger's work on the representation and use of causal relationships (Rieger, 1976). A network provides a particularly rich structure for entering detailed relationships and descriptors in the domain model. *Object nodes* are arranged hierarchically, with links to the possible attributes (*parameters*) associated with each object. The *parameter nodes*, in turn, are linked to the possible *value nodes*, and *rules* are themselves represented as nodes with links that connect them to value nodes. These relationships are summarized in Table 20-1.

The *certainty factor* (CF) associated with each value and rule node (Table 20-1) refers to the belief model developed for the MYCIN system (Chapter 11). The property *ask first/last* controls whether or not the value of a parameter is to be requested from the user before an attempt is made to compute it using inference rules from the knowledge base (see LABDATA, Chapter 5). The *text justification* of a rule is provided when the system builder has decided not to break the reasoning step into further compo-

[2]The descriptive power of a semantic network provides clarity when describing this work. However, other representation techniques used in artificial intelligence research could also have captured the attributes of our prototype system.

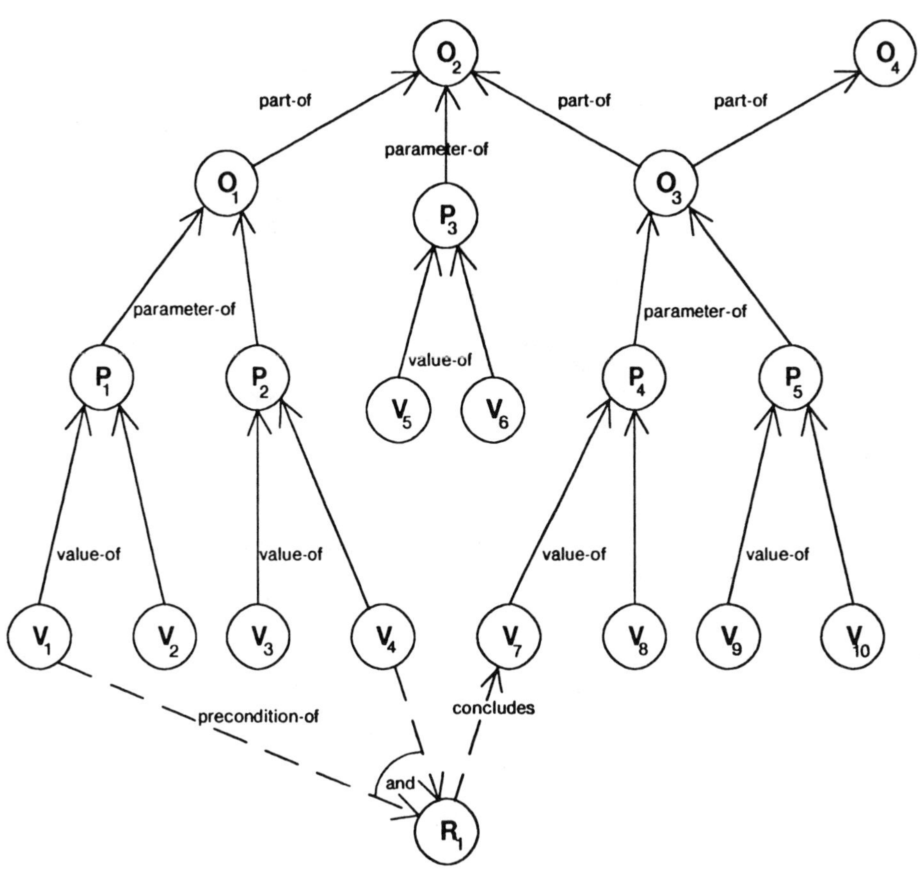

FIGURE 20-2 Sample section of network showing *object*, *parameter*, *value*, and *rule nodes*. Dashed lines indicate the following rule:

IF: PARAMETER-1 of OBJECT-1 is VALUE-1, and
PARAMETER-2 of OBJECT-1 is VALUE-4
THEN: Conclude that PARAMETER-4 of OBJECT-3 is VALUE-7

nent parts but wishes to provide a brief summary of the knowledge underlying that rule. *Complexity*, *importance*, and *rule type* are described in more detail below.

20.2.2 Rules and Their Use

In the network (Figure 20-2) rules connect value nodes with other value nodes. This contrasts with the MYCIN system in which rules are functionally associated with an object-parameter pair and succeed or fail only after

TABLE 20-1

Type of Node	*Static Information (associated with node)*	*Dynamic Information (consultation-specific)*
object node	part-of link (hierarchic) parameter list	
parameter node	object link value-node list default value text definition	
value node	parameter-node link precondition-rule list conclusion-rule list importance complexity ask first/last	contexts for which this value is true certainty factor explanation data ask state
rule node	precondition list (boolean) conclusion certainty factor rule type complexity text justification	explanation data

completion of an exhaustive search for *all* possible values associated with that pair. To make this clear, consider a rule of the following form:

```
IF:    DISEASE-STATE of the LIVER is ALCOHOLIC-CIRRHOSIS
THEN:  It is likely (.7) that the SIZE of ESOPHAGEAL-VEINS is INCREASED
```

When evaluating the premise of this rule to decide whether it applies in a specific case, a MYCIN-like system would attempt to determine the certainty of *all* possible values of the DISEASE-STATE of the LIVER, producing a list of values and their associated certainty factors. Our experimental system, on the other hand, would only investigate rules that could contribute information specifically about ALCOHOLIC-CIRRHOSIS. In either case, however, rules are joined by backward chaining.

Because our system reasons backwards from single values rather than from parameters, it saves time in reasoning in most cases. However, there are occasions when this approach is not sufficient. For example, if a value is concluded with absolute certainty (CF = 1) for a parameter with a mutually exclusive set of values, this necessarily forces the other values to be false (CF = −1). Lines of reasoning that result in conclusions of absolute certainty (i.e., reasoning chains in which all rules make conclusions with

CF = 1) have been termed *unity paths* (see Chapter 3). In cases of mutually exclusive values of parameters, complete investigation of one value requires consideration of any other value that could be reached by a unity path. Thus the representation must allow quick access to such paths.

When reasoning by elimination, similar problems arise if a system focuses on a single value. One needs the ability to conclude a value by ruling out all other possible values for that parameter; this entails a slight modification of the organizational and reasoning scheme. One strategy is to use this elimination method in cases of mutually exclusive options only after the normal backward-chaining process fails (provided that the possibilities represented in the knowledge base are known to span *all* potential values).

20.2.3 Complexity and Importance

The design considerations for adequate explanations require additions to the representation scheme described above. To provide customized explanations, appropriate for different levels of expertise, we have found it useful to associate a measure of *complexity*, both with the inference rules and with the concepts about which they are concluding. Because some concepts are key ideas in a reasoning chain and should be mentioned regardless of their complexity, a measure of *importance* associated with concepts is useful as well. Currently, both measures are specified at the time knowledge is added to the system, but a dynamic modification of these initial values would improve the flexibility of the approach.

Even though complexity and importance are related, one cannot necessarily be predicted from the other. For example, biochemical details of the endocrine system are *complex* but are not *important* to an understanding of endocrine abnormalities, yet the same *complexity* of biochemical detail is *important* for understanding the glycogen storage diseases. A measure of a fact's importance was also used by Carbonell (1970a) in the form of "relevancy tags," supplemented by "distance" in a semantic network, but he did not distinguish between the two concepts discussed here.

20.3 Explanation Capabilities

20.3.1 Tailored Explanations

The measurements of complexity and importance described above facilitate the generation of tailored explanations. Consider a linear causal chain representing a simplified causal mechanism for the existence of kidney stones (Figure 20-3). A sample interaction based on this reasoning chain might be as follows:[3]

Sample Interaction 1:

**EXPERTISE 3 [the user indicates his or her level of expertise on a scale of 1 to 10 where 10 = expert]

**HOW DOES HYPERPARATHYROIDISM CAUSE RENAL STONES?
  Renal stones are caused by hypercalcemia
    Hypercalcemia is caused by hyperparathyroidism

**MORE DETAIL
  Renal stones are caused by increased urinary calcium
    Increased urinary calcium is caused by hypercalcemia
      Hypercalcemia is caused by increased bone breakdown
        Increased bone breakdown is caused by hyperparathyroidism

**EXPERTISE 7 [the user indicates that he or she is more expert here than above]

**HOW DOES HYPERPARATHYROIDISM LEAD TO INCREASED BONE BREAKDOWN?
  Bone breakdown is caused by increased osteoclast activity
    Increased osteoclast activity is caused by increased cyclic-AMP
      Increased cyclic-AMP is caused by hyperparathyroidism

This sample dialogue demonstrates: (1) the user's ability to specify his or her level of expertise, (2) the program's ability to employ the user's expertise to adjust the amount of detail it offers, and (3) the user's option to request more detailed information about the topic under discussion.

Two user-specific variables are used to guide the generation of explanations:[4]

EXPERTISE: A number representing the user's current level of knowledge. As is discussed below, reasoning chains that involve simpler concepts as intermediates are collapsed to avoid the display of information that might be obvious to the user.

DETAIL: A number representing the level of detail desired by the user when receiving explanations (by default a fixed increment added to the EXPERTISE value). A series of steps that is excessively detailed can be collapsed into a single step to avoid flooding the user with information. However, if the user wants more detailed information, he or she can request it.

As shown in Figure 20-3, a measure of complexity is associated with each value node. Whenever an explanation is produced, the concepts in

[3]Our program functions as shown except that the user input requires a constrained format rather than free text. We have simplified that interaction here for illustrative purposes. The program actually has no English interface.

[4]Another variable we have discussed but not implemented is a focusing parameter that would put a ceiling on the number of steps in the chain to trace when formulating an explanation. A highly focused explanation would result in a discussion of only a small part of the reasoning tree. In such cases, it would be appropriate to increase the detail level as well.

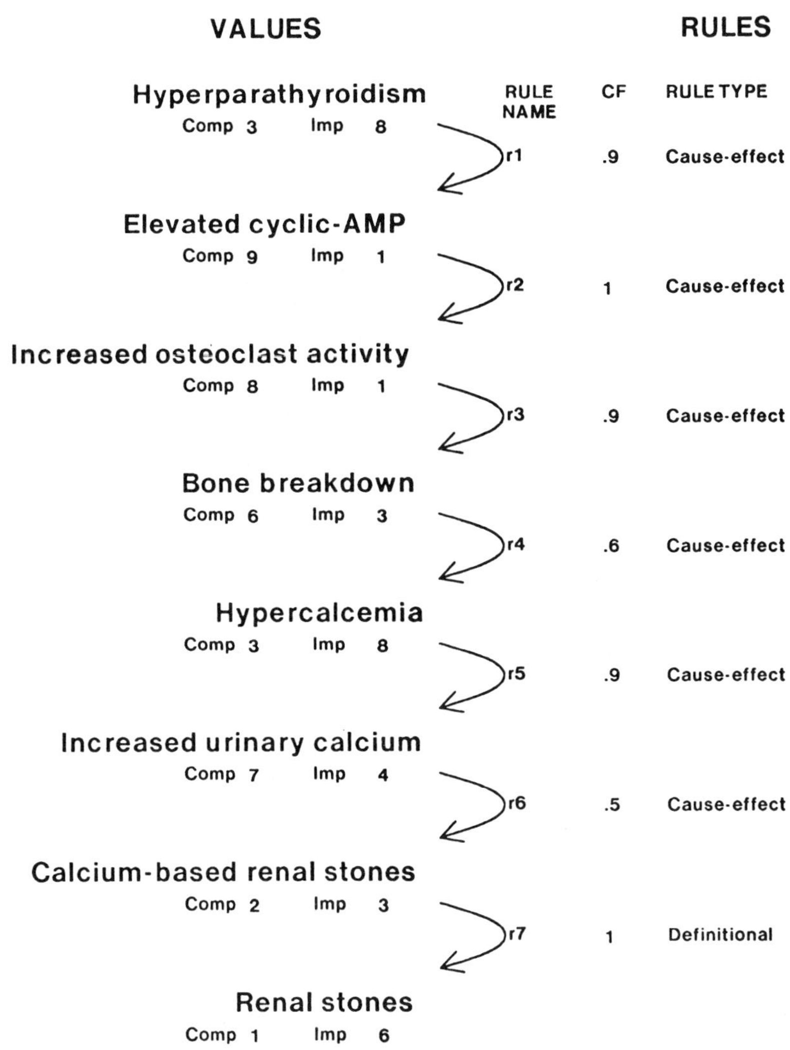

FIGURE 20-3 An example of a small section of a causal knowledge base, with measures of the complexity (Comp) and importance (Imp) given for the value nodes (concepts). This highly simplified causal chain is provided for illustrative purposes only. For example, the effect of parathormone on the kidney (promoting retention of calcium) is not mentioned, but it would have an opposite causal impact on urinary calcium. This reasoning chain is linear (each value has only one cause) and contains only cause-effect and definitional rules. Sample Interactions 1 and 2 (see text) are based on this reasoning chain.

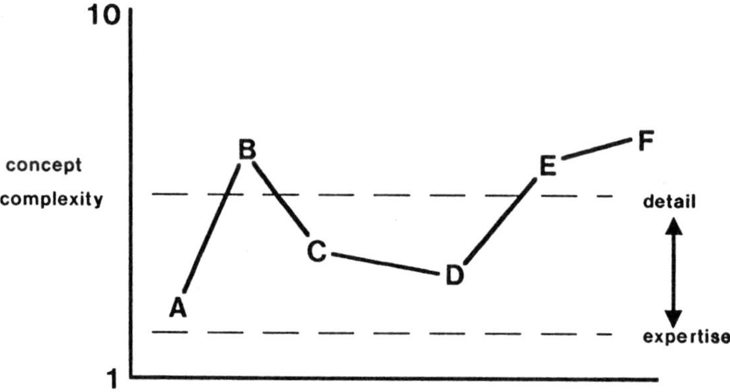

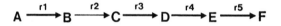

FIGURE 20-4 Diagram showing the determination of which concepts (parameter values) to explain to a user with a given expertise and detail setting. The letters A through F represent the concepts (values of parameters) that are linked by the inference rules r1 through r5. Only those concepts whose complexity falls in the range between the dashed lines (including the lines themselves) will be mentioned in an explanation dialogue. Explanatory rules to bridge the intermediate concepts lying outside this range are generated by the system.

the reasoning chain are selected for exposition on the basis of their complexity; those concepts with complexity lying between the user's expertise level and the calculated detail level are used.[5] Consider, for example, the five-rule reasoning chain linking six concepts shown in Figure 20-4. When intermediate concepts lie outside the desired range (concepts B and E in this case), broader inference statements are generated to bridge the nodes that are appropriate for the discussion (e.g., the statement that A leads to C would be generated in Figure 20-4). Terminal concepts in a chain are always mentioned, even if their complexity lies outside the desired range (as is true for concept F in the example). This approach preserves the

[5]The default value for DETAIL in our system is the EXPERTISE value incremented by 2. When the user requests more detail, the detail measure is incremented by 2 once again. Thus, for the three interchanges in Sample Interaction 1, the expertise-detail ranges are 3–5, 3–7, and 7–9 respectively. Sample Interaction 2 demonstrates how this scheme is modified by the importance measure for a concept.

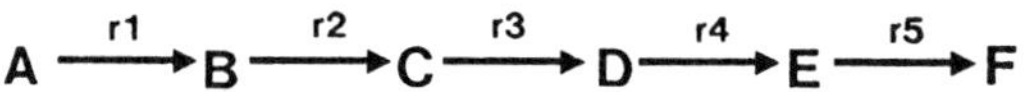

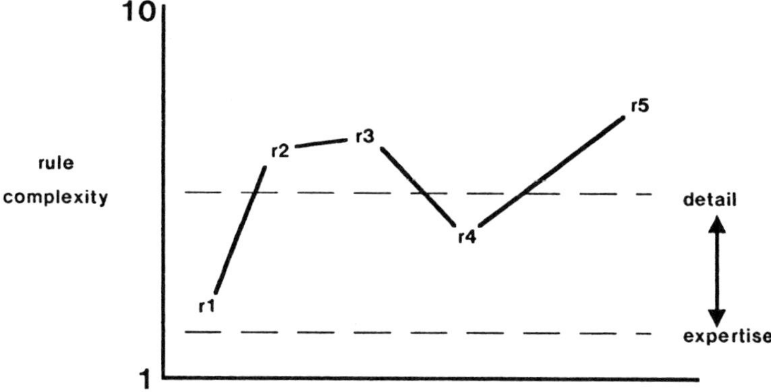

FIGURE 20-5 Diagram showing the determination of which rules to explain further for a user with a given expertise and detail setting. When a rule is mentioned because of the associated concepts, but the rule itself is too complex, further text associated with the rule is displayed.

logical flow of the explanation without introducing concepts of inappropriate complexity.

We have also found it useful to associate a complexity measure with each inference rule to handle circumstances in which simple concepts (low complexity) are linked by a complicated rule (high complexity).[6] This situation typically occurs when a detailed mechanism, one that explains the association between the premise and conclusion of a rule, consists of several intermediate concepts that the system builder has chosen not to encode explicitly.[7] When building a knowledge base, it is always necessary to limit the detail at which mechanisms are outlined, either because the precise mechanisms are unknown or because minute details of mechanisms are not particularly useful for problem solving or explanation. Thus it is useful to add to the knowledge base a brief text justification (Table 20-1) of the mechanism underlying each rule.

Consider, for example, the case in Figure 20-5, which corresponds to

[6]The opposite situation does not occur; rules of low complexity do not link concepts of higher complexity.

[7]Patil has dealt with this problem by explicitly representing causal relationships concerning acid-base disorders at a variety of different levels of detail (Patil et al., 1981).

the reasoning chain represented in Figure 20-4. Although rule r3 links two concepts (C and D) that are within the *complexity-detail range* for the user, the relationship mentioned in rule r3 is itself considered to be outside this range. When generating the explanation for this reasoning chain, the program mentions concepts C and D, and therefore mentions rule r3 despite its complexity measure. Since the rule is considered too complex for the user, however, the additional explanatory text associated with the rule is needed in this case. If the rule had fallen within the complexity-detail range of the user, on the other hand, the text justification for the rule would not have been required.[8]

Further modulation of rule and concept selection is accomplished using the importance measure associated with parameters. A high importance forces the inclusion of a reasoning step in an explanation, thereby overriding the complexity considerations that were shown in Figures 20-4 and 20-5. When the importance level of a concept is two or more points above the expertise of the user, the item is included in the explanation. Consider, for example, the following dialogue, which demonstrates the way in which the importance measure is used:

Sample Interaction 2:

```
**EXPERTISE 6

**HOW DOES HYPERPARATHYROIDISM CAUSE RENAL STONES?
        Renal stones are caused by increased urinary calcium
            Increased urinary calcium is caused by hypercalcemia
                  Hypercalcemia is caused by increased bone breakdown
                      Bone breakdown is caused by increased osteoclast activity
                          Increased osteoclast activity is caused by hyperparathyroidism
```

Note that this example shows a response to the same question asked in Sample Interaction 1. This time, however, the expertise level is 6 rather than 3. Hypercalcemia is therefore mentioned only because its importance level of 8 (see Figure 20-3) is 2 points higher than the expertise of the user; the complexity level of hypercalcemia does not fall within the expertise-detail range of the user and thus would not have been included in the explanation if it were not for its high importance. The other items mentioned are either terminal concepts in the chain (renal stones and hyperparathyroidism) or have a complexity measure lying within the user's expertise-detail range of 6–8.

Many reasoning chains are not as simple as those shown in Figures 20-3, 20-4, and 20-5. When explaining a branched reasoning chain, for example, the explanation system can set aside the branches of the chain and mention them only when it is appropriate to the level of detail required by the user. This feature provides users with an overview of the reasoning process to help them decide whether it is necessary to examine the more detailed steps. This capability is illustrated in the following dialogue, which

[8]An example of this approach is included in Sample Interaction 4 in Section 20.3.2.

involves a patient with hypercalcemia and a possible malignancy who has undergone prolonged bed rest:

Sample Interaction 3:

```
**WHY DOES THE PATIENT HAVE INCREASED SERUM CALCIUM?
        Increased serum calcium is suggested by immobilization and malignancy

**MORE DETAIL
          Increased serum calcium is implied by increased bone breakdown
             Increased bone breakdown is suggested by 2 paths of reasoning:
                Increased bone breakdown is implied by increased osteoclast activity
                   Increased osteoclast activity is implied by prolonged immobilization
                Increased bone breakdown is also implied by malignant bone invasion
```

20.3.2 Types of Rules

Our refinement of the rule types presented by Clancey (Chapter 29) yields five types of rules[9] that are relevant to explanation strategies:

definitional: the conclusion is a restatement of the precondition in different terms

cause-effect: the conclusion follows from the precondition by some mechanism, the details of which may not be known

associational: the conclusion and the precondition are related, but the causal direction (if any) is not known

effect-cause: the presence of certain effects are used to conclude about a cause with some degree of certainty

self-referencing: the current state of knowledge about a value is used to update that value further[10]

The importance of distinguishing between cause-effect and effect-cause rules is shown in Figure 20-6, which considers a simplified network concerning possible fetal Rh incompatibility in a pregnant patient. Reasoning backwards from the goal question "Is there a fetal-problem?" one traverses three steps that lead to the question of whether the parents are Rh incompatible; these three steps use cause-effect and definitional links only. However, in order to use the laboratory data concerning the amniotic fluid to form a conclusion about the presence of fetal hemolysis, effect-cause links must be used.

The sample interactions in Section 20.3.1 employed only cause-effect

[9]Rules considered here deal with domain knowledge, to be distinguished from strategic or meta-level rules (Davis and Buchanan, 1977).

[10]In many cases self-referencing rules can be replaced by strategy rules (e.g., "If you have tried to conclude a value for this parameter and have failed to do so, then use the default value for the parameter").

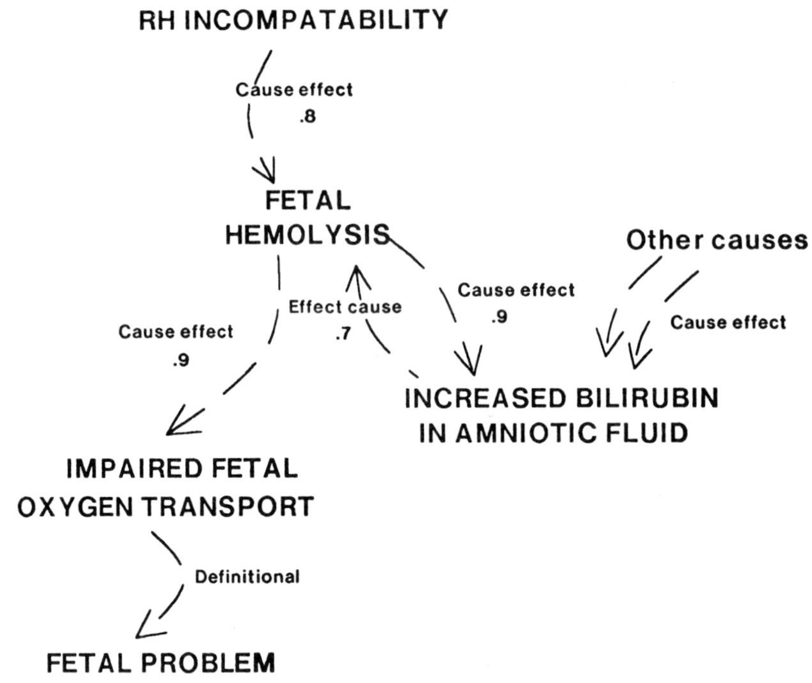

FIGURE 20-6 A simple causal network showing the difference in reasoning between effect-cause and cause-effect rules in the medical setting. The number beside a link indicates the *certainty factor* (CF) associated with the rule. Note that an actual rule network for this domain would be more complex, with representation of intermediate steps, associated medical concepts, default values, and definitions.

and definitional rules. An explanation for an effect-cause rule, on the other hand, requires a discussion of the inverse cause-effect rule (or chain of rules) and a brief mention of other possibilities to explain the certainty measure associated with the rule. As discussed above, the expertise of a user may also require that the program display a text justification for the causal relationships cited in a cause effect rule. Consider, for example, an interaction in which an explanation of the effect-cause rule in Figure 20-6 is produced:

Sample Interaction 4:

> **WHY DO INCREASED BILIRUBIN COMPOUNDS IN THE AMNIOTIC FLUID IMPLY FETAL HEMOLYSIS?
>
> Fetal hemolysis leads to bilirubin compounds in the fetal circulation;

equilibration then takes place between the fetal plasma and the amniotic fluid, leading to increased bilirubin compounds in the amniotic fluid
While the relationship in this direction is nearly certain, the inverse relationship is less certain because of the following other possible causes of increased bilirubin compounds in the amniotic fluid:
Maternal blood in the amniotic fluid from trauma
Maternal blood in the amniotic fluid from prior amniocentesis

The response regarding the equilibration of fetal plasma and amniotic fluid is the stored text justification of the cause-effect rule that leads from "fetal hemolysis" to "increased bilirubin in amniotic fluid." The individual steps could themselves have been represented in causal rules if the system builder had preferred to enter rule-based knowledge about the nature of hemolysis and bilirubin release into the circulation. The second component of the response, on the other hand, is generated from the other cause-effect rules that can lead to "increased bilirubin in amniotic fluid."

The other types of rules require minor modifications of the explanation strategy. Definitional rules are usually omitted for the expert user on the basis of their low complexity and importance values. An explanation of an associational rule indicates the lack of known causal information and describes the degree of association. Self-referencing rules frequently have underlying reasons that are not adequately represented by a causal network; separate support knowledge associated with the rule (Chapter 29), similar to the text justification shown in Sample Interaction 4, may need to be displayed for the user when explaining them.

20.4 Causal Links and Statistical Reasoning

We have focused this discussion on the utility of representing causal knowledge in an expert system. In addition to facilitating the generation of tailored explanations, the use of causal relationships strengthens the reasoning power of a consultation program and can facilitate the acquisition of new knowledge from experts. However, an attempt to reason from causal information faces many of the same problems that have been encountered by those who have used statistical approaches for modeling diagnostic reasoning. It is possible to generate an effect-cause rule, and to suggest its corresponding probability or certainty, only if the information given in the corresponding cause-effect rule is accompanied by additional statistical information. For example, Bayes' Theorem may be used to determine the probability of the ith of k possible "causes" (e.g., diseases), given a specific observation ("effect"):

$$P(\text{cause}_i|\text{effect}) = \frac{P(\text{effect}|\text{cause}_i)\,P(\text{cause}_i)}{\sum_{j=1}^{k} P(\text{cause}_j)\,P(\text{effect}|\text{cause}_j)}$$

This computation of the probability that the *i*th possible cause is present given that the specific effect is observed, $P(\text{cause}_i|\text{effect})$, requires knowledge of the *a priori* frequencies $P(\text{cause}_i)$ for each of the possible causes (cause_1, cause_2 . . . cause_k) of the effect. These data are not usually available for medical problems and are dependent on locale and prescreening of the patient population (Shortliffe et al., 1979; Szolovits and Pauker, 1978). The formula also requires the value of $P(\text{effect}|\text{cause}_j)$ for all cause-effect rules leading to the effect, not just the one for the rule leading from cause_i to the effect. In Figure 20-6, for example, the effect-cause rule leading from "increased bilirubin in amniotic fluid" to "fetal hemolysis" could be derived from the cause-effect rule leading in the opposite direction only if all additional cause-effect rules leading to "increased bilirubin in amniotic fluid" were known (the "other causes" indicated in the figure) and if the relative frequencies of the various possible causes of "increased bilirubin in amniotic fluid" were also available. A more realistic approach is to obtain the inference weighting for the effect-cause rule directly from the expert who is building the knowledge base. Although such subjective estimates are fraught with danger in a purely Bayesian model (Leaper et al., 1972), they appear to be adequate (see Chapter 31) when the numerical weights are supported by a rich semantic structure (Shortliffe et al., 1979).

Similarly, problems are encountered in attempting to produce the inverse of rules that have Boolean preconditions. For example, consider the following rule:

```
IF:    (A and (B or C))
THEN:  Conclude D
```

Here D is known to imply A (with a certainty dependent on the other possible causes of D and their relative frequencies) only if B or C is present. While the inverse rule could be generated using Bayes' Theorem given the *a priori* probabilities, one would not know the certainty to ascribe to cases where *both* B *and* C are present. This problem of conditional independence tends to force assumptions or simplifications when applying Bayes' Theorem. Dependency information can be obtained from data banks or from an expert, but cannot be derived directly from the causal network.

It is instructive to note how the Present Illness Program (PIP) and CADUCEUS, two recent medical reasoning programs, deal with the task of representing both cause-effect and effect-cause information. CADUCEUS (Pople, 1982) has two numbers for each manifestation of disease, an "evoking strength" (the likelihood that an observed manifestation is caused by the disease) and a "frequency" (the likelihood that a patient with a disease will display a given manifestation). These are analogous to the inference weightings on effect-cause rules and cause-effect rules, respectively. However, the first version of the CADUCEUS program (INTERNIST-1) did not allow for combinations of manifestations that give higher (or lower) weighting than the sum of the separate manifestations,[11] nor did it provide a way to explain the inference paths involved (Miller et al., 1982).

PIP (Pauker et al., 1976; Szolovits and Pauker, 1978) handles the implication of diseases by manifestations by using "triggers" for particular disease frames. No weighting is assigned at the time of frame invocation; instead PIP uses a scoring criterion that does not distinguish between cause-effect and effect-cause relationships in assigning a numerical value for a disease frame. While the information needed to explain the program's reasoning is present, the underlying causal information is not.[12]

In our experimental system, the inclusion of both cause-effect rules and effect-cause rules with explicit certainties, along with the ability to group manifestations into rules, allows flexibility in constructing the network. Although causal information taken alone is insufficient for the construction of a comprehensive knowledge base, the causal knowledge can be used to propose effect-cause relationships for modification by the system-builder. It can similarly be used to help generate explanations for such relationships when effect-cause rules are entered.

20.5 Conclusion

We have argued that a need exists for better explanations in medical consultation systems and that this need can be partially met by incorporating a user model and an augmented causal representation of the domain knowledge. The causal network can function as an integral part of the reasoning system and may be used to guide the generation of tailored explanations and the acquisition of new domain knowledge. Causal information is useful but not sufficient for problem solving in most medical domains. However, when it is linked with information regarding the complexity and importance of the concepts and causal links, a powerful tool for explanation emerges.

Our prototype system has been a useful vehicle for studying the techniques we have discussed. Topics for future research include: (1) the development of methods for dynamically determining complexity and importance (based on the semantics of the network rather than on numbers provided by the system builder); (2) the discovery of improved techniques for using the context of a dialogue to guide the formation of an expla-

---

[11]This problem is one of the reasons for the move from INTERNIST-1 to the new approaches used in CADUCEUS (Pople, 1982).

[12]Recently the ABEL program, a descendent of PIP, has focused on detailed modeling of causal relationships (Patil et al., 1981).

nation; (3) the use of linguistic or psychological methods for determining the reason a user has asked a question so that a customized response can be generated; and (4) the development of techniques for managing the various levels of complexity and detail inherent in the mechanistic relationships underlying physiological processes. The recent work of Patil, Szolovits, and Schwartz (1981), who have separated such relationships into multiple levels of detail, has provided a promising approach to the solution of the last of these problems.

PART SEVEN

Using Other Representations

21

Other Representation Frameworks

Representing knowledge in an AI program means choosing a set of conventions for describing objects, relations, and processes in the world. One first chooses a conceptual framework for thinking about the world—symbolically or numerically, statically or dynamically, centered around objects or around processes, and so forth. Then one needs to choose conventions within a given computer language for implementing the concepts. The former is difficult and important; the latter is both less difficult and less important because good programmers can find ways of working with almost any concept within almost any programming language.

In one respect finding a representation for knowledge is like choosing a set of data structures for a program to work with. Tables of data, for example, are often conveniently represented as arrays. But manipulating knowledge structures imposes additional requirements. Because some of an expert's knowledge is inferential, conventions are needed for a program to interpret the structures. And, as we have emphasized, an expert (or knowledge engineer) needs to be able to edit knowledge structures quickly and easily in order to refine the program's knowledge base iteratively. Some programming conventions facilitate editing and interpreting knowledge; others throw up road blocks.

The question of how to represent knowledge for intelligent use by programs is one of two major questions motivating research in AI. (The other major theme over the last 25 years is how to *use* the knowledge for intelligent problem solving.) Although we were not developing new representations in MYCIN, we were experimenting with the power of one representation, modified production rules, for reasoning in a detailed and ill-structured domain, medicine. Chapters 1 and 3 have described much of the historical context of our work with rules. As should be obvious from Chapters 3 through 6, we added many embellishments to the basic production rule representation in order to cope with the demands of the problem and of physicians. We stumbled over many items of medical knowledge that were difficult to encode or use in the simple formalism with which we started. Our choice of rules and fact triples, with CF's, has been explained in Part Two. As summarized at the end of Chapter 3, we were under no illusion that we were creating a "pure" production system. We had taken many liberties with the formalism in order to make it more flexible and understandable. However, we still felt that the stylized condition-action form of knowledge brought many advantages because of its simplicity. For example, creating English translations from the LISP rules and translating stylized English rules into LISP were both somewhat simplified because of the restricted syntax. Similarly, creating explanations of a line of reasoning was simplified as well, because of the simple backward-chaining control structure that links rules together dynamically.

Representing knowledge in procedures was one alternative we were trying hard to avoid. Our experience with DENDRAL and with the therapy algorithm in MYCIN (Chapter 6) showed how inflexible and opaque a set of procedures could be for an expert maintaining a knowledge base. And, as mentioned in previous chapters, we saw that production rules offered some opportunity for making a knowledge base easier to understand and modify.

We were aware of predicate calculus as a possibility for representing MYCIN's knowledge. We were working in a period in AI research when logic and resolution-based theorem provers were being recommended for many problems. We did not seriously entertain the idea of using logic, however, largely because we felt that inexact reasoning was undeveloped in theorem-proving systems.

We had initially experimented with a semantic network representation, as mentioned in Chapter 3. Although we felt we could store medical knowledge in that form, we felt it was difficult to focus a dialogue in which gaps in the knowledge were filled both by inference and by the user's answers to questions. Minsky's paper on frames (Minsky, 1975) did not appear until after this work was well underway. Even so, we were looking for a more structured representation, specifically rules, to build editors and parsers for, to modify and explain, and to reason with in an understandable line of reasoning.

In this part we describe three experiments with alternative representations and control structures in programs called VM, CENTAUR, and WHEEZE. The first two programs were written for Ph.D. requirements, the last as a class project. All are programs that work on medical problems, although in areas outside of infectious diseases. Another experiment with representations is described in Chapter 20 in the context of explanation. There MYCIN's rules are rewritten in an inference net (cf. Duda et al., 1978b) in order to facilitate explaining the inferences at different levels of detail.

The VM program discussed in Chapter 22 was selected by Professor E. Feigenbaum, H. Penny Nii, and Dr. John Osborn and worked on primarily by Larry Fagan for his Ph.D. dissertation. Feigenbaum and Nii had been developing the SU/X program[1] (Nii and Feigenbaum, 1978) for interpretation of multisensor data. Feigenbaum was a friend of Osborn's, knew of Osborn's pioneering work on computer monitoring in intensive care, and saw this as a possible domain in which to explore further the problems in multisensor signal understanding involving signals for which the time course is important to the interpretation. Osborn agreed to be the expert collaborator. Fagan had been working on MYCIN and had contributed to the code as well as to the knowledge base of meningitis rules. (In Feigenbaum's words, Fagan had become "MYCINized.") So it was natural that his initial thinking about the ICU data interpretation problem was in MYCIN's terms. Fagan quickly found, however, that the MYCIN model was not appropriate for a problem of monitoring data continuously over time. MYCIN was much too oriented toward a "snapshot" of data about a patient at a fixed time (although some elements of data in the "snapshot" name historical parameters, such as dates of prior infections). The only obvious mechanism for making MYCIN work with a stream of data in the ICU was to restart the program at frequent time intervals to reason about each new "snapshot" of data gathered during each 2–5 minute time period. This is inelegant and completely misses any sense of continuity or the changing context in which data are being gathered. Thus VM was designed to remedy this deficiency.

The other two programs in Part Seven were designed as alternatives to a rule-based representation, varying the representation of one program, called PUFF. Although desirable, it is difficult in AI to experiment with programs by varying one parameter at a time while holding everything else fixed. Of course, not everything else could remain fixed for such a gross experiment. Both CENTAUR and WHEEZE, discussed in Chapters 23 and 24, were deliberate attempts to alter the representation and control of the PUFF program (while leaving the knowledge base unchanged) in order to examine advantages and disadvantages of alternatives.

PUFF is a program that diagnoses pulmonary (lung) diseases. The problem was suggested to Feigenbaum and Nii by Osborn at the time VM was being formulated, and appeared to be appropriate for a MYCIN-like approach. It was initially programmed using EMYCIN (see Part Five), in collaboration with Drs. R. Fallat and J. Osborn at Pacific Medical Center in San Francisco (Aikins et al., 1983). About 50–60 rules were added to EMYCIN [in a much shorter time than expected (Feigenbaum, 1978)] to interpret the type and severity of pulmonary disorders.[2] The primary data are mostly from an instrument known as a spirometer that measures flows and volumes of patients' inhalation and exhalation. The conlusions are diagnoses that account for the spirometer data, the patient history data, and the physician's observations.

---

[1]Later known as HASP (Nii et al., 1982).

[2]These handled obstructive airways disease. Many other rules were later added to handle other classes of pulmonary disease. The system now contains about 250 rules.

EMYCIN-PUFF	(Aikins and Nii—see Chapter 14)
CENTAUR	(Aikins—see Chapter 23)
WHEEZE	(Smith and Clayton—see Chapter 24)
BASIC-PUFF	(Pacific Medical Center—see Aikins et al., 1983)
AGE-PUFF	(Nii and Aiello—see Aiello and Nii, 1981)

FIGURE 21-1 Five implementations of PUFF.

PUFF has been a convenient vehicle for experimentation because it is a small system. Figure 21-1 lists five different implementations of essentially the same knowledge base.

In developing CENTAUR, Aikins focused on the problem of making control knowledge explicit and understandable. She recognized the awkwardness of explanations of rules or rule clauses that were primarily *controlling* MYCIN's inferences as opposed to *making* substantive inferences. For example, many of the so-called self-referencing rules are awkward to explain:

If A & B & C,
then A

In these rules, one intent of mentioning parameter A in both conclusion and premise is to *screen* the rule and keep it from forcing questions about parameters B and C if there is not already evidence for A. This is largely an issue of control, and the kind of problem that CENTAUR is meant to remedy. The solution is to use frames to represent the context and control information and MYCIN-like rules to represent the substantive medical relations. Thus there is a frame for A to represent the context in which a set of rules should be invoked, one of which would be:

$$B \: \& \: C \rightarrow A$$

This is much more natural to explain than trying to say why, or in what sense, A can be evidence for itself. CENTAUR was demonstrated using the same knowledge as in the EMYCIN version of PUFF (Aikins, 1983).

David Smith and Jan Clayton developed WHEEZE as a further experiment with frames. They asked, in effect, if *all* the knowledge in PUFF could be represented in frames and what benefits would follow from doing so. In a short time (as a one-term class project) they reimplemented PUFF with a frame-based representation. Chapter 24 is a summary of their results.

The version of PUFF written in BASIC (BASIC-PUFF) is a simplified version of the EMYCIN rule interpreter with the medical knowledge built into the code (Aikins et al., 1983). It was redesigned to run efficiently on a PDP-11 in the pulmonary laboratory at Pacific Medical Center. Its knowledge has been more finely tuned than it was in the original version, but is largely the same. BASIC-PUFF is directly coupled to the spirometer in the pulmonary function lab and automatically provides interpretations of the test results. Thus it turns the spirometer into a "smart instrument" instead of simply a data-collecting and recording device. Its interpretations are printed immediately, reviewed by a physician, and inserted into the permanent record with the physician's signature. In the majority of cases, the physician makes no additions or corrections to the conclusions; in some, however, additional notes are made to clarify the program's suggestions. BASIC-PUFF provides one model of technology transfer for expert systems: first implement a prototype with "off-the-shelf" tools such as EMYCIN, then rewrite the system to run efficiently on a small computer.

Another experiment in which the PUFF knowledge base was recast into a different formalism is the AGE-PUFF version (Aiello and Nii, 1981). The intent was to use this small, easily managed knowledge base to experiment with control issues, more specifically to explore the adequacy of the BLACKBOARD model, with event-driven control (Erman et al., 1980). Further experiments with AGE-PUFF are reported by Aiello (1983).

One of the difficulties with a production rule formalism is in representing control information. For example, if we want rules R3, R5, and R7 to be executed in that order, then we have to arrange for the LHS of R7 not to match any current data base until after R3 and R5 have fired. Often this is accomplished by defining a flag that is set when and only when R3 fires and that is checked by R5, and another that is set by R5 and checked by R7, as described in Chapter 2. The authors of MYCIN's rules have only a few means available to influence the system's backward chaining, one of which is to define "dummy" parameters that act as flags. To the best of our knowledge, this was not done in MYCIN (in fact, it was explicitly avoided), but it has been done by others using EMYCIN.

Another means of influencing the control is to order the clauses in premises of rules. This was done much of the time as a way of keeping MYCIN from pursuing minutiae before the more general context that motivates asking about minute details was established. Since MYCIN evaluates the premise clauses from first to last, in order,[3] putting more general, context-setting clauses at the beginning of the premise assures that the more specific clauses will not be asked about, or even considered, unless the context is appropriate. Using the order of premise clauses for this kind of screening permits the system builder to use early clauses to ensure that some parameters are traced first. For example, the predicate KNOWN is often used to cause a parameter to be traced.

Still another means of representing controlling information in the rule-based formalism is via meta-rules, described in Chapter 28. Another

[3]An exception is the preview mechanism described earlier.

similar approach is via strategy rules, as described in Chapter 29. The unity path mechanism (Chapter 3) also affects the order of rule invocation.

ONCOCIN (discussed in Chapters 32 and 35) incorporates many of the ideas from these experiments, most notably the framelike representation of control knowledge and the description of changing contexts over time. It builds on other results presented in this book as well, so its design is described later. ONCOCIN clearly shows the influence of the evolution of our thinking presented in this section.

One piece of recent research not included in this volume is the rerepresentation of MYCIN's knowledge along the lines described in Chapter 29. The new program, called NEOMYCIN (Clancey and Letsinger, 1981), carries much of its medical knowledge in rules. But it also represents (a) the taxonomy of diseases as a separate hierarchy, (b) strategy knowledge as meta-rules, (c) causal knowledge as links in a network, and (d) knowledge about disease processes in the form of frames characterizing location and temporal properties. One main motivation for the reconceptualization was to provide improved underpinnings for the tutorial program described in Chapter 26. Because of the richer knowledge structures in NEOMYCIN, informative explanations can be given regarding the program's diagnostic strategies, as well as the medical rules.

NEOMYCIN, along with other recent work, emphasizes the desirability of augmenting MYCIN's homogeneous set of rules with a classification of types of knowledge and additional knowledge of each type. In MYCIN's rule set, the causal mechanisms, the taxonomic structure of the domain, and the problem-solving strategies are all lumped together. An augmented knowledge base should separate these different types of knowledge to facilitate explanation and maintenance of the knowledge base, and perhaps to enhance performance as well. Causal mechanisms have been represented and used in several domains, including medicine (Patil et al., 1981) and electronics debugging (Davis, 1983). Mathematical models have been merged with symbolic causal models in AI/MM (Kunz, 1983). As a result of this recent work, considerably richer alternatives than MYCIN's homogeneous rule set can be found.

Finally, it should be noted that the chapters in this part describe rather fundamental viewpoints on representation. Within a rule-based or frame-based (or mixed) framework there are still numerous details of representing uncertainty, quantified variables, strategies, temporal sequences, bookkeeping information, and other concepts mentioned throughout the book.

22

Extensions to the Rule-Based Formalism for a Monitoring Task

Lawrence M. Fagan, John C. Kunz, Edward A. Feigenbaum, and John J. Osborn

The Ventilator Manager (VM) program is an experiment in expert system development that builds on our experience with rules in the MYCIN system. VM is designed to interpret on-line quantitative data in the intensive care unit (ICU) of a hospital. After a major cardiovascular operation, a patient often needs mechanical assistance with breathing and is put in the ICU so that many parameters can be monitored. Many of those data are relevant to helping physicians decide whether the patient is having difficulty with the breathing apparatus (the ventilator) or is breathing adequately enough to remove the mechanical assistance. The VM program interprets these data to aid in managing postoperative patients receiving mechanical ventilatory assistance.

VM was strongly influenced by the MYCIN architecture, but the program was redesigned to allow for the description of events that change over time. VM is an extension of a physiologic monitoring system[1] and is designed to perform five specialized tasks in the ICU:

This chapter is a longer and extensively revised version of a paper originally appearing in *Proceedings of the Sixth IJCAI* (1979, pp. 260–262). Used by permission of International Joint Conferences on Artificial Intelligence, Inc.; copies of the *Proceedings* are available from William Kaufmann, Inc., 95 First Street, Los Altos, CA 94022.

[1]VM was developed as a collaborative research project between Stanford University and Pacific Medical Center (PMC) in San Francisco. It was tested with patient information acquired from a physiologic monitoring system implemented in the cardiac surgery ICU at PMC and developed by Dr. John Osborn and his colleagues (Osborn et al., 1969).

1. detect possible errors in measurement,
2. recognize untoward events in the patient/machine system and suggest corrective action,
3. summarize the patient's physiologic status,
4. suggest adjustments to therapy based on the patient's status over time and long-term therapeutic goals, and
5. maintain a set of case-specific expectations and goals for future evaluation by the program.

VM differs from MYCIN in two major respects. It interprets measurements over time, and it uses a state-transition model of intensive care therapies in addition to clinical knowledge about the diagnostic implications of data. Most medical decision-making programs, including MYCIN, have based their advice on the data available at one particular time. In actual practice, the clinician receives additional information from tests and observations over time and reevaluates the diagnosis and prognosis of the patient. Both the progression of the disease and the response to previous therapy are important for assessing the patient's situation.

Data are collected in different therapeutic situations, or *contexts*. In order to interpret the data properly, VM includes a model of the stages that a patient follows from ICU admission through the end of the critical monitoring phase. The correct interpretation of physiologic measurements depends on knowing which stage the patient is in. The goals for intensive care are also stated in terms of these clinical contexts. The program maintains descriptions of the current and optimal ventilatory therapies for any given time. Details of the VM system are given by Fagan (1980).

22.1 The Application

The intensive care unit monitoring system at Pacific Medical Center (Osborn et al., 1969) was designed to aid in the care of patients in the period immediately following cardiac surgery. The basic monitoring system has proven to be useful in caring for patients with marked cardiovascular instability or severe respiratory malfunction (Hilberman et al., 1975). Most of these patients are given breathing assistance with a mechanical ventilator until the immediate effects of anesthesia, surgery, and heart-lung bypass have subsided. The ventilator is essential to survival for many of these patients. Electrocardiogram leads are always attached, and patients usually have indwelling arterial catheters to assure adequate monitoring of blood pressure and to provide for the collection of arterial blood for gas analysis. The ventilator-to-patient airway is monitored to collect respiratory flows, rates, and pressures. Oxygen and carbon dioxide concentrations are also measured. All of these measurements are available at the bedside through the use of specialized computer terminals.

The mechanical ventilator provides total or partial breathing assistance (or ventilation) for seriously ill patients. Most ventilator therapy is with a type of machine that delivers a fixed volume of air with every breath, but a second type of machine delivers air at each breath until a fixed pressure is attained. Both the type and settings of the ventilator are adjusted to match the patient's intrinsic breathing ability. The "volume" mechanical ventilator provides a fixed volume of air under pressure through a tube to the patient. The ventilator can be adjusted to provide breaths at fixed intervals, which is called *controlled mandatory ventilation* (CMV), or in response to sucking by the patient, which is known as *assist mode*. Adjustments to the output volume or the respiration rate of the ventilator are made to ensure an adequate *minute volume* to the patient. When the patient's status improves, the mechanical ventilator is disconnected and replaced by a *T-piece* that connects an oxygen supply with the tube to the patient's lungs. If the patient can demonstrate adequate ventilation, the tube is removed (*extubation*). Often many of these clinical transitions must be repeated until the patient can breathe without assistance.

Three types of problems can occur in managing the patient on the mechanical ventilator:

1. changes in the patient's recovery process, requiring modifications to the life support equipment,
2. malfunctions of the life support equipment, requiring replacement or adjustment of the ventilator, and
3. failures of the patient to respond to therapeutic interventions within the expectations of the clinicians in charge.

22.2 Overview of the Ventilator Manager Program

The complete system (diagrammed in Figure 22-1) includes the patient monitoring sensors in the ICU, the basic monitoring system running on IBM 1800 and PDP-11 computers at the Pacific Medical Center, and the VM measurement interpretation program running on the SUMEX-AIM PDP-10 computer located at Stanford University Medical Center. Patient measurements are collected by the monitoring system for VM at two- or ten-minute intervals. Summary information, suggestions to the clinicians, and requests for additional information are generated at SUMEX for evaluation by research clinicians. The program's outputs are in the form of periodic graphical summaries of the major conclusions of the program and short suggestions for the clinician (as shown in Figures 22-2 and 22-3).

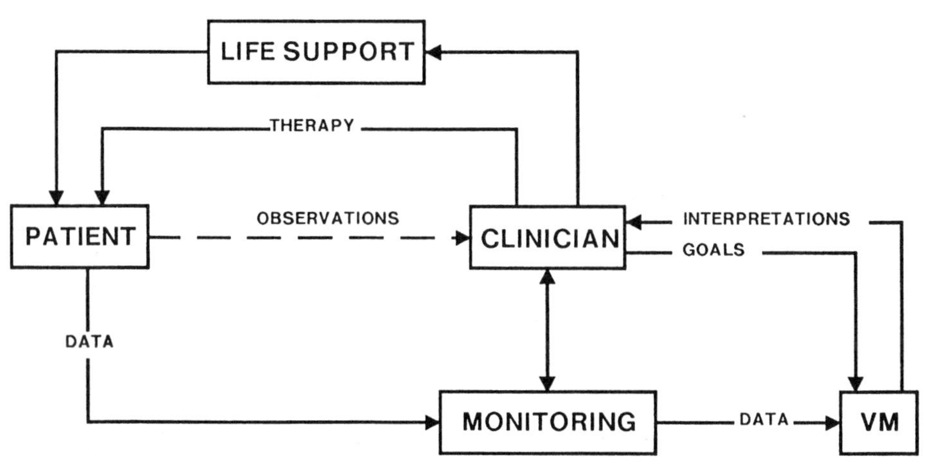

FIGURE 22-1 VM system configuration. Physiological measurements are gathered automatically by the monitoring system and provided to the interpretation program. The summary information and therapeutic suggestions are sent back to the ICU for consideration by clinicians.

Summary generated at time 15:40

All conclusions:

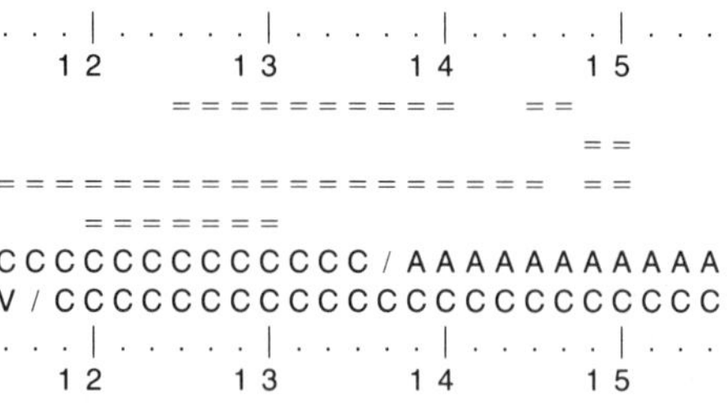

```
                              . . . | . . . . . . | . . . . . . | . . . . . . | . . .
                                   1 2         1 3          1 4          1 5
BRADYCARDIA[PRESENT]                     = = = = = = = = = =     = =
HEMODYNAMICS[STABLE]                                                    = =
HYPERVENTILATION[PRESENT]     = = = = = = = = = = = = = = = = = = = =   = =
HYPOTENSION[PRESENT]                = = = = = = = =
Goal Location                 C C C C C C C C C C C C C / A A A A A A A A A A A
Patient Location              V / C C C C C C C C C C C C C C C C C C C C C C C
                              . . . | . . . . . . | . . . . . . | . . . . . . | . . .
                                   1 2         1 3          1 4          1 5
```

FIGURE 22-2 Summary of conclusions drawn by VM based on four hours of patient data. Current and optimal patient therapy stages are represented by their first letter: V = VOLUME, A = ASSIST, C = controlled mandatory ventilation, / = changing. A double bar (=) is printed for each ten-minute interval in which the conclusion on the left is made.

```
.. 1640..
** SUGGEST CONSIDER PLACING PATIENT ON T-PIECE IF
** PA02 > 70 ON FI02 <= .4                    [measure of blood gas status]
** PATIENT AWAKE AND TRIGGERING VENTILATOR
** ECG IS STABLE

.. 1650 .... 1700 .... 1710 .... 1720 .... 1730 .... 1740 .... 1750 ..
.. 1800 ..
** HYPERVENTILATION
** PATIENT HYPERVENTILATING.
** SUGGEST REDUCING EFFECTIVE ALVEOLAR VENTILATION.
** TO REDUCE ALVEOLAR VENTILATION, REDUCE TIDAL VOLUME,
** REDUCE RESPIRATION RATE, OR
** INCREASE DISTAL DEAD SPACE TUBING VOLUME

.. 1810 ..
** SYSTEM ASSUMES PATIENT STARTING T-PIECE

.. 1813 .... 1815 .... 1817 ..
** HYPOVENTILATION

.. 1819 .... 1822 ..
** HYPOVENTILATION
```

FIGURE 22-3 Trace of program output. Format is ". . <time of day> . ." followed by suggestions for clinicians. Comments are in brackets.

22.2.1 Measurement Interpretation

Knowledge is represented in VM by production rules of the form shown in Figure 22-4.

The historical relations in the premise of a rule cause the program to check values of parameters for a period of time; e.g., HYPERVENTILATION is PRESENT for more than ten minutes. *Conclusions* made in the action part of the rule assert that a parameter has had a particular value during the time instance when the rule was examined. *Suggestions* are text statements, printed out for clinicians, that state important conclusions and a possible list of remedies. *Expectations* assert that specific measurements

```
IF:    Historical relations about one or more parameters hold

THEN:  1) Make a conclusion based on these facts;
       2) Make appropriate suggestions to clinicians; and
       3) Create new expectations about the
          future values of parameters.
```

FIGURE 22-4 Format for rules in VM. Not every rule's action part includes conclusions, suggestions, and expectations.

should be within the specified ranges at some point in the future. Thus a rule examines the current and historical data to interpret what is happening at the present and to predict events in the future.

Additional information associated with each rule includes the symbolic name (e.g., STABLE-HEMODYNAMICS), the rule group (e.g., rules about instrument faults), the main concept (definition) of the rule, and all of the therapeutic states in which it makes sense to apply the rule. The list of states is used to focus the program on the set of rules that are applicable at a particular point in time. Figure 22-5 shows a sample rule for determining hemodynamic stability (i.e., a measure of the overall status of the cardiovascular system).[2]

STATUS RULE: STABLE-HEMODYNAMICS
DEFINITION: Defines stable hemodynamics based on blood pressures and heart rate
APPLIES TO: patients on VOLUME, CMV, ASSIST, T-PIECE
COMMENT: Look at mean arterial pressure for changes in blood pressure and systolic blood pressure for maximum pressures.
IF
  HEART RATE is ACCEPTABLE
  PULSE RATE does NOT CHANGE by 20 beats/minute in 15 minutes
  MEAN ARTERIAL PRESSURE is ACCEPTABLE
  MEAN ARTERIAL PRESSURE does NOT CHANGE by 15 torr in 15 minutes
  SYSTOLIC BLOOD PRESSURE is ACCEPTABLE
THEN
  The HEMODYNAMICS are STABLE

FIGURE 22-5 Sample VM rule.

The VM knowledge base includes rules to support five reasoning steps that are evaluated at the start of each new time segment:

1. characterize measured data as reasonable or spurious;
2. determine the therapeutic state of the patient (currently the mode of ventilation);
3. adjust expectations of future values of measured variables when the patient state changes;
4. check physiological status, including cardiac rate, hemodynamics, ventilation, and oxygenation; and
5. check compliance with long-term therapeutic goals.

Each reasoning step is associated with a collection of rules, and each rule is classified by the type of conclusions made in its action portion; e.g., all rules that determine the validity of the data are classed together.

---

[2]The complete rule set, from which this rule was selected, is included in the dissertation by Fagan (1980), which is available from University Microfilms, #AAD80-24651.

22.2.2 Treating Measurement Ranges Symbolically

Most of the rules represent the measurement values symbolically, using the terms ACCEPTABLE or IDEAL to characterize the appropriate ranges. The actual meaning of ACCEPTABLE changes as the patient moves from state to state, but the statement of the relation between physiological measurements remains constant. For example, the rule shown in Figure 22-5 checks to see if the patient's heart rate is ACCEPTABLE. In the different clinical states, or stages of mechanical assistance, the definition of ACCEPTABLE changes. Immediately after cardiac surgery a patient's heart rate is not expected to be in the same range as it is when he or she is moved out of the ICU. Mentioning the symbolic value ACCEPTABLE in a rule, rather than the state-dependent numerical range, thus reduces the number of rules needed to describe the diagnostic situation.

The meaning of the symbolic range is determined by other rules that establish expectations about the values of measured data. For example, when a patient is taken off the ventilator, the upper limit of acceptability for the expired carbon dioxide measurement is raised. (Physiologically, a patient will not be able to exhale all the CO_2 produced by his or her system, and so CO_2 will accumulate.) The actual numeric calculation of EXPIRED pCO2 HIGH in the premise of any rule will change when the context switches (removal from ventilatory support), but the statement of the rules remains the same. A sample rule that creates these expectations is shown in Figure 22-6.

22.2.3 Therapy Rules

Therapy rules can be divided into two classes: the long-term therapy assessment (e.g., when to put the patient on the T-piece), and the determination of response to a clinical problem, such as hyperventilation or hypertension. The two rules shown in Figure 22-7, for selecting T-piece therapy and for responding to a hyperventilation problem, demonstrate several key factors in the design of the rule base:

- use of a hierarchy of physiological states,
- use of the program's determination of patient's clinical state,
- generation of conditional suggestions.

The abstracted hierarchy of states, such as hemodynamic stability, is important because it makes the rules more understandable. Since the definition of stability changes with transition to different clinical stages, as described above, rules about stability are clearer if they mention the concept rather than the context-specific definition. It is important for the program to determine what state the patient is in, since the program is

```
INITIALIZING RULE: INITIALIZE-CMV
DEFINITION: Initialize expectations for
            patients on controlled mandatory
            ventilation (CMV) therapy
APPLIES TO: all patients on CMV
IF ONE OF:
    PATIENT TRANSITIONED FROM VOLUME TO CMV
    PATIENT TRANSITIONED FROM ASSIST TO CMV
THEN EXPECT THE FOLLOWING
```

		[...	acceptable	range ...	]	
			[... ideal	...]		
	very low	low	min	max	high	very high
MEAN PRESSURE	60	75	80	95	110	120
HEART RATE		60			110	
EXPIRED pCO2	22	28	30	35	42	50
...						

FIGURE 22-6 Portion of an initializing rule. This type of rule establishes initial expectations of acceptable and ideal ranges of variables after state changes. Not all ranges are defined for each measurement. EXPIRED pCO2 is a measure of the percentage of carbon dioxide in expired air measured at the mouth.

designed to avoid interrupting the activities in the ICU to ask questions of the physicians or nurses. Its design is thus different from the design of a one-shot consultation system such as MYCIN. A physician will change the mode of assistance from CMV (where the machine does all the work of breathing) to ASSIST (where the machine responds to a patient's attempts to breathe). The VM program has to know that this transition is normal and to determine when it occurs in order to avoid drawing inappropriate conclusions. The advice that VM offers is often conditional. Unlike other consultation programs such as MYCIN, VM attempts to avoid a dialogue with the clinician. When the appropriateness of a suggestion depends on facts not known to VM, it creates a conditional suggestion. The clinician can check those additional facts and make an independent determination of the appropriateness of the suggestion.

22.2.4 Selecting Optimal Therapy

The stages of ventilatory therapy are represented in VM by a finite state graph (see Figure 22-8). The boxed nodes of the graph represent the values associated with the parameters "PatientLocation," specifying the current state, and "GoalLocation," specifying alternative therapies. The arcs of the graph represent transition rules and therapy rules. Thus goals are expressed as "moves" away from the current therapeutic setting, and each

```
THERAPY-RULE: THERAPY.A-T
DEFINITION: DEFINES READINESS TO TRANSITION FROM ASSIST MODE TO T-PIECE
COMMENT: If patient has stable hemodynamics, ventilation is acceptable, and patient has been
         awake and alert enough to interact with the ventilator for a period of time then transition
         to T-piece is indicated.
APPLIES TO: ASSIST
IF
  HEMODYNAMICS ARE STABLE
  HYPOVENTILATION NOT PRESENT
  RESPIRATION RATE ACCEPTABLE
  PATIENT IN ASSIST FOR > 30 MINUTES
THEN
  THE GOAL IS FOR THE PATIENT TO BE ON THE T-PIECE
  SUGGEST CONSIDER PLACING PATIENT ON T-PIECE IF
    Pa02 > 70 on FI02 <= 0.4
    PATIENT AWAKE AND TRIGGERING VENTILATOR
    ECG IS STABLE

THERAPY-RULE: THERAPY.VENTILATOR-ADJUSTMENT-FOR-HYPERVENTILATION
DEFINITION: MANAGE HYPERVENTILATION
APPLIES TO: VOLUME ASSIST CMV
IF
  HYPERVENTILATION PRESENT for > 8 minutes
  COMMENT wait a short while to see if hyperventilation persists
  V02 not low
THEN
  SUGGEST PATIENT HYPERVENTILATING.
    SUGGEST REDUCING EFFECTIVE ALVEOLAR VENTILATION.
    TO REDUCE ALVEOLAR VENTILATION, REDUCE TV BY 15%, REDUCE RR, OR
      INCREASE DISTAL DEAD SPACE TUBING VOLUME
```

FIGURE 22-7 Two therapy rules. The first (THERAPY.A-T) suggests a T-piece trial; the second resolves a hyperventilation problem.

possible move corresponds to a decision rule. The overall clinical goal, of course, is to make the patient self-sufficient, specifically, to remove the mechanical breathing assistance (extubate) as soon as is practical for each patient. The knowledge base is linked to the graph through the APPLIES TO statement specified in the introductory portion of each rule.

The mechanism for deriving and representing therapy decisions in VM takes into account the relationship between VM's suggestions and actual therapy changes. Computer-generated suggestions about therapy changes are decoupled from actual changes due to: (1) additional information to the clinician suggesting modification to or disagreement with VM's suggestion; (2) sociologic factors that delay the implementation of the therapy decisions (e.g., T-piece trials have been delayed due to concern about disturbing a patient in the next bed); or (3) variation of criteria among clinicians for making therapy decisions. Because of the discrepancy between computer-generated goals and actual therapy, VM cannot assume that the patient is actually in the stage that the program has determined

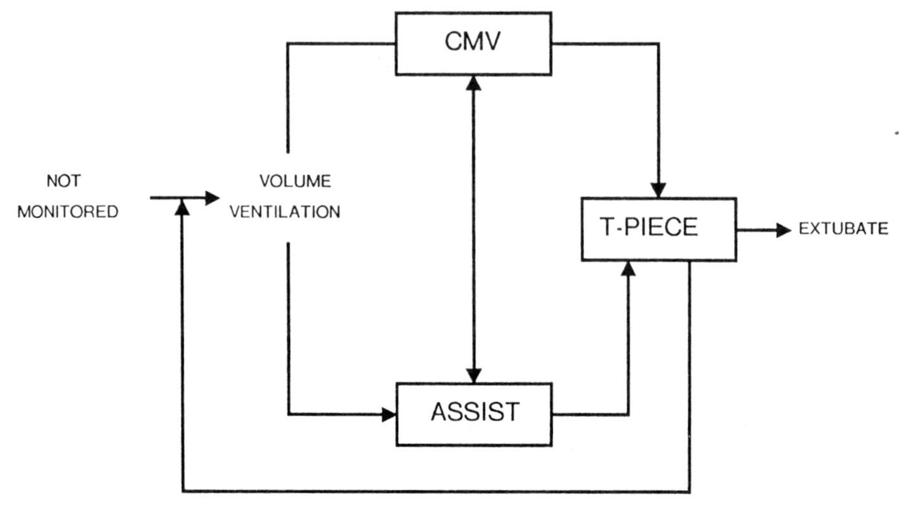

FIGURE 22-8 Therapy state graph.

is optimal. Transition rules in VM allow the program to notice changes in a patient's state. They reset the description of the context, then, so that the data will be interpreted correctly. However, when the therapy rules are evaluated, the program may determine that the previous state is still more appropriate.

Two models can be created for representing the period of time between the suggestion of therapy (a new goal) and its implementation. The first model is that therapy goals are the same as last stated, unless explicitly changed. It assumes that once a new therapeutic goal is established, the goal should persist until either the therapy is initiated or the goal is negated by a rule. This model is based on the common clinical practice of continuing recently initiated therapy even if the situation has changed. This clinical practice, which might be termed *hysteresis*,[3] is used to avoid frequent changes in treatment strategy—i.e., avoid oscillation in the decision-making process. While clinicians acknowledge this behavior, they find it hard to verbalize rules for rescinding previous therapy goals. This hysteresis has also been evident in the formulation of some of the therapy rules. The rule that suggests a switch from assist mode to T-piece is stated in terms of ACCEPTABLE limits; the rule for aborting T-piece trials (back to assist mode or CMV) is stated in terms of VERY HIGH or VERY LOW limits. This leaves a "grey area" between the two decision points and precludes fluctuating between decisions.

[3]Hysteresis is "a lag of effect when the forces acting on a body are changed" (*Webster's New World Dictionary*, 1976).

The second model for representing therapeutic goals requires that the appropriate goal be asserted each time the rule set is evaluated. If no therapy rules succeed in setting a new goal, the goal is asserted to be the current therapy. This scheme ignores the apparent practices of clinicians, but represents a more "conservative" approach that is consistent with the rule-writing strategy used by our experts. This model is potentially sensitive to minor perturbations in the patient measurements, but such sensitivity implies that a borderline therapy decision was originally made.

22.3 Details of VM

22.3.1 Parameters

The knowledge in VM is based on relationships among the various parameters of the patient, such as respiration rate, sex, and hyperventilation. The program assigns values to each of these parameters as it applies its knowledge to the patient data: the respiration rate is high, the sex of the patient is male, and hyperventilation is present. In a changing domain, the values associated with each parameter may vary with time, for example, "hyperventilation was present for one-half hour, starting two hours ago." Not all parameters have the same propensity to change over time; a classification is given in Figure 22-9.

Parameters are represented internally by using the property list notation of LISP. The property list contains both static elements (e.g., the list of rules that use the parameter in the premise) and dynamic elements (e.g., the time when the parameter was last updated). The static elements are input when the parameter is described or calculated from the contents of the rule set. The dynamic elements are computed as the program interprets patient data. Figure 22-10 lists the properties associated with parameters (although not every parameter has every property).

Figure 22-11 shows a "snapshot" of the parameters RR (respiration rate) and HEMODYNAMICS taken after 120 minutes of data have been processed. Associated with values assigned to parameters (e.g., RR LOW or HEMODYNAMICS STABLE) are lists of intervals when those conclusions were made. Each interval is calculated in terms of the elapsed time since patient data first became available. Thus, in the example, the hemodynamics were stable from 2–8 minutes into the program, momentarily at 82 minutes, and in the interval of 99–110 minutes of elapsed time.

The properties USED-IN, CONCLUDED-IN, and EXPECTED-IN are used to specify how the parameters are formed into a network of rules. These pointers can be used to guide various strategies for examining the rules—e.g., find and evaluate each rule that uses respiration rate or each rule that concludes hemodynamic status.

Constant

Examples: surgery type, sex
Input: once
Reliability: value is good until replaced

Continuous

Examples: heart rate, blood pressure
Input: at regular intervals (6–20 times/hour)
Reliability: presumed good unless input data are missing or artifactual

Volunteered

Examples: temperature, blood gases
Input: at irregular intervals (2–10 times/day)
Reliability: good for a period of time, possibly a function of the current situation

Deduced

Examples: hyperventilation, hemodynamic status
Input: calculated whenever new data are available
Reliability: a function of the reliability of each of the component parameters.

FIGURE 22-9 Classification of parameters.

The UPDATED-AT and GOOD-FOR properties are used to determine the status of the parameter over time, when it was last given a value and the time period during which a conclusion made about this parameter can reasonably be used for making future conclusions. The GOOD-FOR property can also be a pointer to a context-dependent rule.

DEFINITION: free form text describing the parameter
USED-IN: a list of the names of rules that use this parameter to make conclusions
CONCLUDED IN: names of rules where this parameter is concluded
EXPECTED-IN: names of rules where expectations about this parameter are made
GOOD-FOR: length of time that a measurement can be assumed to be valid; if missing, then must be recomputed, input if possible, or assumed unknown
UPDATED-AT: the last time any conclusion was made about this parameter

FIGURE 22-10 Properties associated with parameters.

```
RR
--
  DEFINITION:  (RESPIRATION RATE)
  USED-IN:  (TRANSITION.V-CMV TRANSITION.V-A TRANSITION.A-CMV
             TRANSITION.CMV-A STATUS.BREATHING-EFFORT/T THERAPY.A-CMV
             THERAPY.A-T THERAPY.T-V ABNORMAL-EC02)
  EXPECTED-IN:  (INITIALIZE.V INITIALIZE.CMV INITIALIZE.V-RETURN
                 INITIALIZE.A INITIALIZE.T-PIECE)
  GOOD-FOR:  15                [information is good for 15 minutes]
  UPDATED-AT:  82              [last updated at 82 minutes after start]
  LOW:  ((72 . 82) (52 . 59))  [concluded to be LOW from 52–59 minutes and 72–82
                                minutes after start]


HEMODYNAMICS
------------
  DEFINITION:  (HEMODYNAMICS)
  CONCLUDED-IN:  (STATUS.STABLE-HEMODYN/V,A,CMV)
  USED-IN:  (THERAPY.CMV-A THERAPY.A-T THERAPY.T-PIECE-TO-EXTUBATE)
  GOOD-FOR:  NIL               [this is a derived parameter so reliability is based on
                                other parameters]
  UPDATED-AT:  110             [last updated at 110 minutes after start]
  STABLE:  ((99 . 110) (82 . 82) (2 . 8))
```

FIGURE 22-11 "Snapshot" of parameters RR (respiration rate) and HEMODYNAMICS after 120 minutes of elapsed time.

22.3.2 Measurements

Over 30 measurements are provided to VM every 2 to 10 minutes.[4] The interval is dependent on the situation; shorter intervals are used at critical times as specified by the clinician at the bedside. It is not appropriate to store this information using the interval notation above, since most measurements change with every new collection of data. Predefined intervals, e.g., respiration rate from 5–10, 10–15, and 15–20 breaths/minute, could be used to classify the data, but meaningful ranges change with time. Instead, symbolic ranges such as HIGH and LOW are calculated from the measurements as appropriate. A large quantity of data is presented to the program, in contrast to typical knowledge-based medical systems. About 5000 measurement values per patient are collected each day (30 measurements per collection with 6–8 data collections/hour). Patients are monitored from a few hours to a few weeks, with the average about 1.5 days. While this amount of information could be stored in a large-scale program such as VM, only the most recent information is used to make conclusions. The program stores in memory about one hour's worth of data, independent of the time interval between measurement collections (the remainder

[4]Clinicians can select the default sample rate: fast (2 minutes) or slow (10 minutes). An extra data sample can be taken immediately on request.

of the data are available on secondary storage). Technically, this storage is accomplished by maintaining a queue of arrays that contain the entire collection of measurements that vary over time. The length of the queue is adjusted to maintain an hour's worth of data. Schematically, the measurement storage might be represented as follows:

Elapsed time	69	59	58	...	09
Respiration rate	9	9	10	...	9
Systolic blood pressure	141	154	153	...	150
.					
.					
.					
Clock time	1230 [*current time*]	1220	1219	...	1130

Throwing away old measurements does not limit the ability of the program to utilize historical data. The *conclusions* based on the original data, which are stored much more compactly, are maintained throughout the patient run. Thus the numerical measurement values are replaced by symbolic abstractions over time.

One current limitation is the program's inability to reevaluate past conclusions, especially when measurements are taken but are not reported until some time later. One example of this is the interpretation of blood gas measurements. It takes about 20–30 minutes for the laboratory to process blood gas samples, but by that time the context may have changed. The program cannot then back up to the time that the blood gases were taken and proceed forward in time, reevaluating the intervening measurements in light of the new data. The resolution of conflicts between expectations and actual events may also require modification of old conclusions. This is especially true when forthcoming events are used to imply that an alternative cause provides a better explanation of observed phenomena.

22.3.3 Rules

Rules used in VM have a fixed structure. The premise of a rule is constructed from the conjunction or disjunction of a set of clauses. Each clause checks relationships about one or more of the parameters known to the program. Each of these relationships, such as "the respiration rate is between an upper and lower limit," will be tested to determine if the premise is satisfied. If the clauses are combined conjunctively and each clause is true, or combined disjunctively and at least one clause is true, then the rule is said to "succeed." As explained in Section 22.3.6 on uncertainty in VM, no probabilistic weighting scheme is currently used in the rule evaluation (although the mechanism is built into the program).

When a rule succeeds, the action part of the rule is activated. The action portion of each rule is divided into three sections: conclusions (or interpretations), suggestions, and expectations. The only requirement is that at least one statement (of any of the three types) is made in the action part of the rule. The first section of the action of the rule is composed of the conclusions that can be drawn from the premise of the rule. These conclusions (in the form of a parameter assuming a value) are asserted by the program to exist at the current time and are stored away for producing summaries and to provide new facts for use by other rules. When the same conclusion is also asserted in the most recent time when data are available to the program, then the new conclusion is considered a *continuation* of the old one. The time interval associated with the conclusion is then extended to include the current time. This extension presumes that the time period between successive conclusions is short enough that continuity can be asserted.

The second section of the action is a list of suggestions that are printed for the clinician. Each suggestion is a text string to be printed that summarizes the conclusions made by the rule.[5] Often this list of suggestions includes additional factors to check that cannot be verified by the program—e.g., the alertness of the patient. By presenting the suggestions as conditional statements, the need to interact with the user to determine the current situation is minimized. The disadvantage of this method is that the program maintains a more nebulous view of the patient's situation, unless it can be ascertained later that one of the suggestions was carried out.

The last section of the action part of the rule is the generation of new expectations about the ranges of measurements for the future. Expectations are created to help the program interpret future data. For example, when a patient is first moved from assist mode to the T-piece, many parameters can be expected to change drastically because of the stress as well as the altered mode of breathing. When the measurements are taken, then, the program is able to interpret them correctly. New upper and lower bounds are defined for the acceptable range of values for heart rate, for example, for the duration of time specified. The duration might be specified in minutes or in terms of a context (e.g., "while the patient is on the T-piece").

MYCIN does not place any constraints on the types of conclusions made in the action part of the rule, although most rules use the CONCLUDE function in their right-hand sides. For example, MYCIN calls a program to compute the optimal therapy as an action part of a rule (Chapter 6). The basic motivation behind imposing some structure on rules was to act as a mnemonic device during rule acquisition. The same advantage is found in framelike systems with explicit component names—e.g., CAUSED-BY, MUST-HAVE, and TRIGGERS in the Present Illness Program (Szolovits and Pauker, 1978).

---

[5]Not every conclusion has a corresponding suggestion, particularly when the conclusion denotes a "normal" status—e.g., hemodynamic stability.

A rule is represented internally by a property list with a fixed set of properties attached to the name of the rule:

RULEGROUP	Defines type or class of the rule; in this case, the rules that deduce the status of the patient
DEFINITION	Free text that defines the main idea of the rule
COMMENT	The collected comments from the external form of the rule
NODE	All of the contexts for which this rule makes sense (currently limited to the values associated with the patient's therapeutic setting)
EVAL	Specifies the methods of evaluation; ALL OF for conjunction, ONE OF for disjunction, X% for requirement of a fixed percentage of verified premise clauses
ORIGLHS	A copy of the external notation of the premise of the rule, used in explanations and tracing
FILELOCATION	The description of the location on a file of the original text of the rule
M	The translated premise of the rule, a list of calls to premise functions (M stands for match)
I	The list of interpretations (conclusions) to be made
S	The list of suggestions to be printed out
E	The list of expectations to be made

The actual processing of a rule is carried out by a series of functions that test conditions, make interpretations, make suggestions, or create expectations. Each of these functions has a well-defined semantic interpretation and provides the primitives for encoding the knowledge base.

The translation between an external format, e.g., RESPIRATION RATE > 30, and the corresponding internal format, (MCOMP RR > 30), is made by the same parsing program used in EMYCIN.[6] The MCOMP function is given a parameter name (RR), a relation (less than, greater than, or equal to), and a number with which to compare it. The execution of the MCOMP function returns a numerical representation of TRUE, FALSE or UNKNOWN, based on the current value of respiration rate. Figure 22-12 demonstrates the external and internal representations of a typical rule.

22.3.4 Premise Functions

One goal of the VM implementation is to create a simple set of premise functions that are able to test for conditions across time. Many of the static premise functions have been adapted from the MYCIN program; e.g.,

[6]The parsing program was written by James Bennett, based on work by Hendrix (1977).

```
STATUS RULE:   STATUS. STABLE-HEMODYNAMICS
DEFINITION:   Defines stable hemodynamics based
         on blood pressures and heart rate
APPLIES TO:   patients on VOLUME, CMV, ASSIST,
         T-PIECE
COMMENT:   Look at mean arterial pressure for
         changes in blood pressure and systolic
         blood pressure for maximum pressures.
IF
  HEART RATE is ACCEPTABLE
  PULSE RATE does NOT CHANGE by 20 beats/minute
         in 15 minutes
  MEAN ARTERIAL PRESSURE is ACCEPTABLE
  MEAN ARTERIAL PRESSURE does NOT CHANGE by 15
         torr in 15 minutes
  SYSTOLIC BLOOD PRESSURE is ACCEPTABLE
THEN
  The HEMODYNAMICS are STABLE


RULEGROUP:   STATUS-RULE
DEFINITION:   ((DEFINES STABLE HEMODYNAMICS BASED)
               (ON BLOOD PRESSURES AND HEART RATE))
COMMENT:   ((LOOK AT MEAN ARTERIAL PRESSURE FOR)
             (CHANGES IN BLOOD PRESSURE AND SYSTOLIC)
             (BLOOD PRESSURE FOR MAXIMUM PRESSURES))
NODE:   (VOLUME CMV ASSIST T-PIECE)
EVAL:   (ALL OF)
ORIGLHS:   ((HEART RATE IS ACCEPTABLE)
            (PULSE RATE DOES NOT CHANGE BY 20 BEATS/MINUTE IN 15
              MINUTES)
            (MEAN ARTERIAL PRESSURE IS ACCEPTABLE)
            (MEAN ARTERIAL PRESSURE DOES NOT CHANGE BY 15 TORR
              IN 15 MINUTES)
            (SYSTOLIC BLOOD PRESSURE IS ACCEPTABLE))
FILELOCATION:   (<Puff/VM>VM.RULES;18 12538 13143)
M:   ((MSIMP HR ACCEPTABLE NIL)
      (FLUCT PR CHANGE 20 (0.0 15) NOT)
      (MSIMP MAP ACCEPTABLE NIL)
      (FLUCT MAP CHANGE 15 (0.0 15) NOT)
      (MSIMP SYS ACCEPTABLE NIL))
I:   ((INTERP HEMODYNAMICS = STABLE NIL))
```

FIGURE 22-12 External and internal representations for a rule in VM.

MCOMP encompasses the functions of GREATERP, LESSP, numeric EQUAL, and their negations in MYCIN. Most of the functions listed below test the value of a parameter within a time interval and return TRUE, FALSE or UNKNOWN. As mentioned earlier, they reference concepts, such as HIGH value or STABLE value, that are defined by rules at each stage. Each function is composed of the following program steps: (a) find out the value of the parameter mentioned in the time period mentioned (otherwise, use the current time), (b) make the appropriate tests, and (c) negate the answer, if required. Table 22-1 lists the premise functions.

TABLE 22-1

Class	*Function*	*Format*	*Example*	*Action*
Testing measurement values	FLUCT	FLUCT [parameter, direction, amount, time-range, negation]	THE MEAN ARTERIAL PRESSURE DOES NOT CHANGE BY 15 TORR IN 15 MINUTES	Calculates slopes or ranges from the table of measurements; direction can be rises, drops, or changes
	STABILITY	STABILITY [parameter, time-range, negation]	RESPIRATION RATE IS NOT STABLE FOR 20 MINUTES	Calculates the stability of the measurement by comparing the distance between the average and the maximum and minimum values over the time range
	MSIMP	MSIMP [parameter, relation, negation]	RESPIRATION RATE IS NOT HIGH	Compares the current value of a parameter with one of the expectation types; relation can be very low, low, abnormally low, acceptable, high, very high, or abnormally high
	MCOMP	MCOMP [parameter, relation, compared to, negation]	HEART RATE IS NOT >150 HEART RATE IS < THE IDEAL-MINIMUM EXPECTATION LIMIT	Compares the current value of the parameter with a numeric cutoff or a symbolic range; relation can be greater than, less than or equal to; compared-to can be any number, ideal-minimum, ideal-maximum, very low, etc.
	BETWEEN	BETWEEN [parameter, lower-limit, upper-limit, negation]	PULSE RATE IS NOT BETWEEN 40 AND 60 BEATS/MINUTE	Compares the current value of the parameter with a numeric range

Testing derived conclusions	TIMEEXP	TIMEEXP [parameter, value, relation, time-range, negation]	PATIENT IS ON CMV FOR GREATER THAN 30 MINUTES	Checks that the parameter has had a value for the specified period of time; the time range may be in the past, e.g., 20 to 40 minutes ago; relation can be greater than, less than, or equal to
	TRANSITION	TRANSITION [parameter, from-node, to-node]	PATIENT TRANSITIONED FROM ASSIST MODE TO THE T-PIECE	Checks for state changes; parameter is usually PATIENT or GOAL; from-node and to-node are equipment configurations, e.g., ASSIST MODE.
Interpretation	INTERP	INTERP [parameter, value, negation]	THERE IS HYPERVENTILATION	Makes conclusions; updates property list of parameter to show changes
Suggestion	SUGGEST	SUGGEST [arbitrary-text]	SUGGEST PUTTING THE PATIENT ON THE T-PIECE IF PATIENT IS AWAKE	Prints suggestion when rule succeeds
Expectation	EXPECT	EXPECT [parameter, limit-type, limit, expectation-type, time-range]	THE ACCEPTABLE RANGE FOR SYSTOLIC BLOOD PRESSURES IS 110-150 (while the patient is on volume ventilation)	Sets up one of three levels of expectations: for all time, for the duration of the current context, or for a fixed interval; limit-type can be upper limit, lower limit, range, or table; expectation-type can be default, context, or timed
Miscellaneous	EQUATION	EQUATION [variables, equation]	FN(TIDAL VOLUME, WEIGHT): TIDAL VOLUME > 3 * WEIGHT	Evaluates equation and returns Boolean value
	EXECUTE	EXECUTE [rule-group]	EXECUTE STATUS-RULES	Evaluates each of the rules in the named group according to the method specified in Section 22.3.5

22.3.5 Control Structure

A simple control structure is used to apply the knowledge base to the patient data. This method starts by the execution of the goal rule, which in turn evaluates a set of rules corresponding to each level of abstraction in order: first, data validation, followed by context checking and expectation setting, determination of physiological status, and finally, therapeutic response, if necessary. From the group of rules at each level of reasoning, each rule is selected in turn. The current context as determined by the program is compared against the list of applicable contexts for each rule (the NODE property). The premise portions of acceptable rules are examined. If the parameter mentioned in a premise clause has not yet been fully evaluated, an indexing scheme is used to select the rules within this rule set that can make that conclusion. Using this method avoids the necessity of putting the rules in a specific order. The rule is added to a list of "used" rules, and the next unexamined rule is studied. The list of evaluated rules is erased each time the rule set is evaluated. When a rule succeeds, the action part of the rule is used to make interpretations, print suggestions, and set expectations.

Most rules attempt to explain the interpretation of measurements that have "violated" their expectations. Thus, for the portion of the rules that mention an "out-of-range" measurement value in their premise or that are based on the conclusions of these rules, the following strategy could be used: compare all measurements against the current expectations, and forward chain only those measurements with values that require explanation. This method is not useful when the rule specifies that several normal measurements imply a normal situation, e.g., determining hemodynamic stability. These "normal" rules would have to be separated and forward- or backward-chained as appropriate.

22.3.6 Uncertainty in VM

Although the MYCIN certainty factor mechanism (Chapter 11) is incorporated into the VM structure, it has not been used. Most of the representation of uncertainty has been encoded symbolically in the contents of each rule. Rules conclude that measurement values can be spurious (under specified conditions), and the interpreter prohibits using such aberrant values for further inferences. Any value associated with a measured parameter that was concluded too long ago is considered to be unknown and, therefore, no longer useful in the reasoning mechanism. This is meant to be a first approximation to our intuition that confidence in an interpretation decays over time unless it is reinforced by new observations.

Uncertainty has been implicitly incorporated in the VM knowledge base in the formulation of some rules. In order to make conclusions with a higher level of certainty, premise clauses were added to rules that correlated strongly with existing premise clauses—e.g., using both mean and systolic blood pressures. The choice of measurement ranges in several therapy rules also took into account the element of uncertainty. Although the experts wanted four or five parameters within the IDEAL limit prior to suggesting the transition to the next optimal therapy state, they often used the ACCEPTABLE limits. In fact, it would be unlikely that all measurements would simultaneously fall into IDEAL range. Therefore, incorporating these "grey areas" into the definition of the symbolic ranges was appropriate. There are at least two possible explanations for the lack of certainty factors in VM rule base: (1) on the wards, it is only worthwhile to make an inference if one strongly believes and can support the conclusion; and (2) the measurements available from the monitoring system were chosen because of their high correlation with patients' conditions.

As mentioned elsewhere, the PUFF and SACON systems also did not use the certainty factor mechanism. The main goal of these systems was to classify or categorize a small number of conclusions as opposed to making fine distinctions between competing hypotheses. This view of uncertainty is consistent with the intuitions of other researchers in the field (Szolovits and Pauker, 1978, p. 142):

> If possible, a carefully chosen categorical reasoning mechanism which is based on some simple model of the problem domain should be used for decision making. Many such mechanisms may interact in a large diagnostic system, with each being limited to its small subdomain. . . . When the complex problems need to be addressed—which treatment should be selected, how much of the drug should be given, etc.—then causal or probabilistic models are necessary. The essential key to their correct use is that they must be applied in a limited problem domain where their assumptions can be accepted with confidence. Thus, it is the role of categorical methods to discover what the central problem is and to limit it as strongly as possible; only then are probabilistic techniques appropriate for its solution.

22.3.7 Representation of Expectations in VM

Representing expectations about the course of patient measurements is a major design issue in VM. In the ICU situation, most of the expectations are about the typical ranges (bounds) associated with each physiological measurement. Interpreting the relationship between measurement values and their expectations is complicated particularly at the discontinuities caused by setting numeric boundaries. For example, on a scale of possible blood pressure values ranging from 50 to 150, how much difference can there be between measurement values of 119 and 121, in spite of some boundary at 120? However, the practice of setting specific limits and then treating values symbolically (e.g., TOO HIGH) appears to be a common educational and clinical technique. The ill effects on decision making of

Symbolic value	*Interpretation*
IDEAL	The desired level or range of a measurement
ACCEPTABLE	The limits of acceptable values beyond which corrective action is necessary—bounds are high and low (similar for rate)
VERY UNACCEPTABLE	Limit at which data are extremely out of range—e.g., on which the definition of severe hypotension is based
IMPOSSIBLE	Outside the limits that are physiologically possible

FIGURE 22-13 Representing expectations using symbolic bounds.

setting specific limits are minimized by the practice of using multiple measurements in coming to specific conclusions. One alternative to using symbolic ranges would be to express values as a percentage of some predefined norm. This has the same problems as discrete numeric values, however, when the percentage is used to draw conclusions. When it was important clinically to differentiate how much an expectation was exceeded, the notion of alternate ranges (e.g., VERY HIGH) was utilized. For the physiological parameters, several types of bounds on expectations have been established, as shown in Figure 22-13. In VM these limits are not static; they are adapted to the patient situation. Currently, the majority of the expectation changes are associated with changes in ventilator support. These expectations are established on recognition of the changes in therapy and remain in effect until another therapy context is recognized. A more global type of expectation can be specified that persists for the entire time patient data are collected. A third type of expectation type corresponds to a perturbation, or local disturbance in the patient's situation. An example of this is the suctioning maneuver where a vacuum device is put in the patient's airway. This disturbance has a characteristic effect on almost every measurement but only persists for a short period of time, usually 10–15 minutes. After this time, the patient's state is similar to what it was in the period just preceding the suction maneuver. It is possible to build a hierarchy out of these expectation types based on their expected duration; i.e., assume the global expectation unless a specific contextual expectation is set, provided a local perturbation has not recently taken place.

Knowledge about the patient could be used to "customize" the expectation limits for the individual patient. The first possibility is the use of historical information to establish *a priori* expectations based on type of surgery, age, length of time on the heart/lung machine, and presurgical pulmonary and hemodynamic status. The second type of customization could be based on the observation that patient measurements tend to run within tighter bands than the *a priori* expectations. The third type of expectation based on transient events can be used to adjust for the effects of temporary intervention by clinicians. This requires expert knowledge about the side effects of each intervention and about the variation between different classes of patients to these temporary changes.

22.3.8 Summary Reports

Summary reports are also provided at fixed intervals of time, established at the beginning of the program. Summaries include: (1) a description of current conclusions (e.g., PATIENT HYPERVENTILATING FOR 45 MINUTES); (2) a graph with time on one axis (up to six hours) and recent conclusions on the other; and (3) a similar graph with time versus measurements that are beyond the expected limits. (Figure 22-2 shows a portion of a sample summary report.)

The summary report is based on several lists generated by the program. The first list is composed of parameter-value pairs concluded by the program. This list is extended by the INTERP function called from the action portion of rules. The second list includes pairs of measurement types and symbolic ranges (e.g., RESPIRATION RATE—HIGH). This list is augmented during the process of comparing measurement values to expected ranges. These lists are built up from the start of the program and are not reset during new time intervals. The graphs are created by sorting the lists alphabetically, and then collecting the time intervals associated with each parameter-value pair. The conclusion and expectation graphs cover the period from six hours ago until the current time, with a double bar (=) plotted for each ten-minute period that the conclusion was made.

The number of items in each graph is controlled by the number of currently active pathophysiological conclusions subject to a static list of parameters and values that are omitted (for example, some intermediate conclusions are not plotted). When the rule base is extended into other problem areas of ICU data interpretation, new sets of rules may have to be created to select which of the current conclusions should be graphed.

The graph of "violated" expectations presents a concise display of the combination of measurements that are simultaneously out of range. Most of these conclusions have been fed into rules that determine the status of the patient. Patterns that occur often, but fail to trigger rules about the status of the patient, become candidates for the development of new rules.

22.4 Summary and Conclusions

VM uses a simple data-directed interpreter to apply a knowledge base of rules to data about patients in an intensive care unit. These rules are arranged according to a set of levels ranging from measurement validation to therapy planning, and are currently formulated as a categorical system. Interactive facilities exist to examine the evaluation of rules while VM is monitoring data from a patient, and to input additional test results to the system for interpretation.

22.4.1 Representing Knowledge About Dynamic Clinical Settings

In VM we have begun to experiment with mechanisms for providing MYCIN-like systems with the ability to represent the dynamic nature of the diagnosis and therapy process. As mentioned in the introduction, MYCIN was designed to produce therapeutic decisions for one critical moment in a patient's hospital course. This was extended with a "restart mechanism" that allows for selectively updating those parameters that might change in the interval between consultations. MYCIN can start a new consultation with the updated information, but the results of the original consultation are lost. In VM, three requirements are necessary to support the processing of new time frames: (1) examining the values of historical data and conclusions, (2) determining the validity of those data, and (3) combining new conclusions with previous conclusions.

New premise functions, which define the relationships about parameters that can be tested when a rule is checked for validity, were created to examine the historical data. Premise functions used in MYCIN include tests to see if: (a) any value has been determined for a parameter, (b) the value associated with a parameter is in a particular numerical range, or (c) there is a particular value associated with a parameter. VM includes a series of time-related premise functions. One function examines trends in input data over time—e.g., THE MEAN ARTERIAL PRESSURE DOES NOT RISE BY 15 TORR IN 15 MINUTES. A second function determines the stability of a series of measurements, by examining the variation of measurements over a specific time period. Other functions examine previously deduced conclusions, as in THE PATIENT HAS BEEN ON THE T-PIECE FOR GREATER THAN 30 MINUTES or THE PATIENT HAS NEVER BEEN ON THE T-PIECE. Functions also exist for determining changes in the state of the patient—e.g., THE PATIENT HAS TRANSITIONED FROM ASSIST MODE TO THE T-PIECE. When VM is required to check if a parameter has a particular value, it must also check to see if the value is "recent" enough to be useful.

The notion that data are reliable for only a given period of time is also used in the representation of conclusions made by the program. When the same conclusion is made in contiguous time periods (two successive evaluations of the rule set), then the conclusions are coalesced. The result is a series of intervals that specify when a parameter assumed a particular value. In the MYCIN system this information is stored as several different parameters. For example, the period when a drug was given is represented by a pair of parameters corresponding to the starting and ending times of administration. In MYCIN, if a drug was again started and stopped, a new entity—DRUG-2—would have to be created. The effect of the VM representation is to aggregate individual conclusions into *states* whose persistence denotes a meaningful interpretation of the status of the patient.

22.4.2 Building a Symbolic Model

A sequence of states recognized by the program represents a segmentation of a time line. Specifying the possible sequences of states in a dynamic setting constitutes a symbolic model of that setting. The VM knowledge base contains a model of the stages involved in ventilatory therapies. This model is used in three ways by the program: (1) to limit the number of rules examined by the program, (2) to provide a basis for comparing actual therapy with potential therapies, and (3) to provide the basis for the adjustment of expectations used to interpret the incoming data.

Attached to each rule in VM is a list of the clinical situations in which the rule makes sense. When rules are selected for evaluation, this list is examined to determine if the rule is applicable. This provides a convenient filter to increase the speed of the program. A set of rules is used to specify the conditions for suggesting alternative therapeutic contexts. Since these rules are examined every few minutes, they serve both to suggest when the patient's condition has changed sufficiently for an adjustment in ventilatory therapy and to provide commentary concerning clinical maneuvers that have been performed but are not consistent with the embedded knowledge for making therapeutic decisions. The model also provides mechanisms for defining expectations about reasonable values for the measured data. Much of the knowledge in VM is stated in terms of these expectations, and they can be varied in response to changes in the patient's situation.

22.4.3 Comparison of MYCIN and VM Design Goals

MYCIN was designed to serve on a hospital ward as an expert consultant for antimicrobial therapy selection. A typical interaction might take place after the patient has been diagnosed and preliminary cultures have been drawn but before very much microbiological data are available. In critical situations, a tentative decision about therapy must often be made on partial information about cultures. In return for assistance, the clinician is asked to provide answers to questions during a consultation.

The intensive care unit is quite different from the static situation addressed by MYCIN, however. Continuous monitoring and evaluation of the patient's status are required. The problem is one of making therapeutic adjustments, many of which are minor, such as adjusting the respiratory rate on the ventilator, over a long period of time. The main reasons for using VM are to monitor status or to investigate an unusual event. The program must therefore be able to interpret measurements with minimal human participation. When an interaction does take place, e.g., when an unexpected event is noted, the program must be concise in its warning. VM's environment differs from MYCIN's in that natural language is an unlikely mode of communication.

This difference in the timing and style of the user-machine interaction has considerable impact on system design. For example, the VM system must be able to:

1. reach effective decisions on the presumption that input from a clinician will be brief,
2. use historical data to determine a clinical situation,
3. provide advice at any point during the patient's hospital stay,
4. follow up on the outcomes of previous therapeutic decisions, and
5. summarize conclusions made over time.

A consultation program should also be able to model the changing medical environment so that the program can interpret the available data in context. Areas such as that of infectious disease require an assessment of clinical problems in a variety of changing clinical situations, e.g., "patients who are severely ill but lack culture results," "patients after culture data are available," "patients after partial or complete therapy," or "patients with acquired superinfection."

It is also necessary that VM contain knowledge that can be used to follow a case over a period of time. This is complicated by the fact that the user of the system may not follow the therapy recommended. VM then has to determine what actions were taken and adjust its knowledge of the patient accordingly. Also, if the patient does not react as expected to the given therapy, then the program has to determine what alternative therapeutic steps may be required.

During the implementation of the VM program, we observed many types of clinical behavior that represent a challenge to symbolic modeling. One such behavior is the reluctance of clinicians to change therapies frequently. After a patient meets the criteria for switching from therapy A to therapy B, e.g., assist mode to T-piece, clinicians tend to allow the patient's status to drop below optimal criteria before returning to therapy A. This was represented in the knowledge base by pairs of therapy selection rules (A to B, B to A) with a grey zone between the two criteria. For example, ACCEPTABLE limits might be used to suggest going from therapy A to therapy B, whereas VERY HIGH or VERY LOW limits would be used for going from B to A. If the same limit were used for going in each direction, a small fluctuation of one measurement near a cutoff value would provide very erratic therapy suggestions. A more robust approach makes decisions in such situations based on the length of time a patient has been in a given state and on the patient's previous therapy or therapies.

The VM program has been used as a test-bed to investigate methods for increasing the capabilities of symbolic processing approaches by extending the production rule methodology. The main area of investigation has been in the representation of knowledge about dynamic clinical settings. There are two components of representing a situation that changes over time: (1) providing the mechanism for accessing and evaluating data in each new time frame, and (2) building a symbolic model to represent the ongoing processes and transitions in the medical environment.

23

A Representation Scheme Using Both Frames and Rules

Janice S. Aikins

Much of artificial intelligence research has focused on determining the appropriate knowledge representations to use in order to achieve high performance from knowledge-based systems. The principal hypothesis being explored in this chapter is that there are many advantages to a system that uses both framelike structures and rules to solve problems in knowledge-intensive domains. These advantages can be grouped into two broad categories: those dealing with the knowledge base representation itself, and those dealing with the system's reasoning and performance. In order to test this hypothesis, a knowledge representation was designed that uses a combination of frames and rules in a data structure called a *prototype*. The domain chosen was that of pulmonary physiology. The task was to interpret a set of pulmonary function test results, producing a set of interpretation statements and a diagnosis of pulmonary disease in the patient.[1] Initially, a MYCIN-like production rule system called PUFF (Kunz et al., 1978) was written to perform pulmonary function test interpretations. Problems with the production rule formalism in PUFF and similar rule-based systems motivated the creation of a prototype-directed system, called CENTAUR. See Aikins (1980; 1983) for more detailed discussions of this system.

CENTAUR uses prototypes that characterize the typical features of each pulmonary disease. Each feature is called a component of the pro-

This chapter is based on a technical memo (HPP-79-10) from the Heuristic Programming Project, Department of Computer Science, Stanford University. Used with permission.

[1]It should be noted, however, that the methodology used is not domain-specific; the task that was chosen is not important for the comparisons made between various knowledge representation schemes.

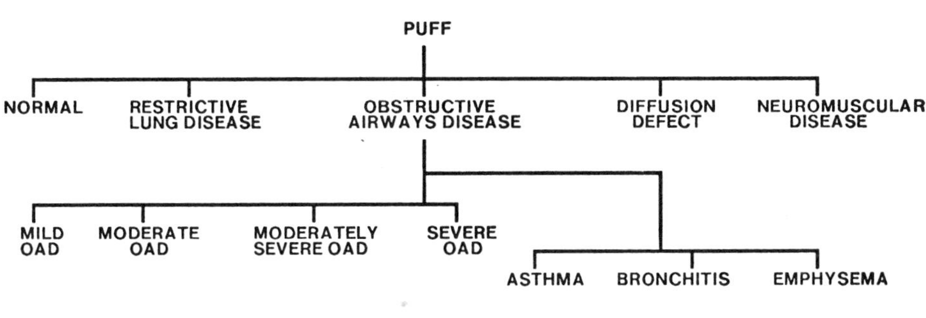

FIGURE 23-1 A portion of the prototype network.

totype. Associated with each component are rules used to deduce a value for the component. The prototypes focus the search for new information by guiding the invocation of the rules and eliciting the most relevant information from the user. These prototypes are linked together in a network in which the links specify the relationships between the prototypes. For example, the obstructive airways disease prototype is linked to the asthma prototype with a SUBTYPE link, because asthma is a subtype of obstructive airways disease (see Figure 23-1).

This chapter discusses the problems of a purely rule-based system and the advantages afforded by using a combination of rules and frames in the prototype-directed system. A complementary piece of research (Aikins, 1979), not discussed here, deals with the problems of a frame-based system. Previous research efforts have discussed systems using frames [see, for example, Minsky (1975) and Pauker and Szolovits (1977)] and systems using a pure rule-based approach to representation (Chapter 2). Still other systems have used alternate knowledge representations to perform large knowledge-based problem-solving tasks. For example, INTERNIST (Pople, 1977) represents its knowledge using a framelike association of diseases with manifestations. Each manifestation, in turn, is associated with the list of diseases in which the manifestation is known to occur. In PROSPECTOR (Duda et al., 1978a), the framelike data structures have been replaced by a semantic network. Few researchers, however, have used both frames and production rules or have attempted to draw comparisons between these knowledge representation methodologies. CENTAUR offers an appropriate mechanism with which to experiment with these representation issues.

This paper presents an example of the CENTAUR system performing an interpretation of a set of pulmonary function test results and focuses on CENTAUR's knowledge representation and control structure. In addition, some advantages of the prototype-directed system over the rule-based approach for this problem are suggested.

23.1 The CENTAUR System

CENTAUR is a consultation system that produces an interpretation of data and a diagnosis based on a set of test results. The inputs to the system are the pulmonary function test results and a set of patient data including the patient's name, sex, age, and a referral diagnosis. The output consists of both a set of interpretation statements that serve to explain or comment on the pulmonary function test results and a final diagnosis of pulmonary disease in the patient.

CENTAUR uses a hypothesis-directed approach to problem solving where the hypotheses are represented by the prototypes. The goal of the system is to confirm that one or more of the prototypes in the prototype network match the data in an actual case. The final set of confirmed prototypes is the system's solution for classifying the data in that case. The prototypes represent the various pulmonary diseases, their severity, and their subtypes, with the result that the set of confirmed prototypes represents the diagnosis of pulmonary disease in the patient.

The system begins by accepting the test and patient data. Data entered in the system suggest or "trigger" one or more of the prototypes. The triggered prototypes are placed on a hypothesis list and are ordered according to how closely they match the data. The prototype that matches the data most closely is selected to be the current prototype, the system's current best hypothesis about how to classify the data in the case.

In the example in Figure 23-2, the prototype that represents a pulmonary function consultation (PUFF) has been selected as the initial current prototype.[2] Initial data are requested and the user's responses (in boldface and following the asterisks) are recorded. The system attempts to fill in values for the components of a prototype, which may cause rules to be invoked, or, if no rules are associated with a component, the system will ask the user for the value. When all of the prototype components have values, the system decides whether the given data values are sufficiently close to those expected for the prototype to confirm that the prototype matches the data.[3] Another prototype is then selected as the current pro-

[2]Just as the pulmonary disease prototypes represent typical ranges of values for the pulmonary function tests for patients with that disease, the pulmonary function prototype states some of the typical features of a pulmonary function consultation. For example, for any pulmonary function consultation, an initial set of test and patient data is required, and both a final interpretation and pulmonary diagnosis are generated. Similarly, the prototype network of the CENTAUR system includes a prototype called MYCIN, which states typical features of a MYCIN infectious disease consultation. Above both of these prototypes is a third prototype, CONSULTATION, which states some domain-independent features of any consultation. For example, the CONSULTATION prototype contains a component called STRATEGY, which allows the user to specify whether a confirmation strategy (to confirm the most likely hypothesis) or an elimination strategy (to disprove the least likely hypothesis) is desired.

[3]The system maintains a confirmed list of prototypes that have been shown to match the data in the case and a disproved list of prototypes that have been proved not to match the data.

totype, and the process repeats. The system moves through the prototype network confirming or disproving disease prototypes. The attempt to match data and prototypes continues until each datum has been explained by some confirmed prototype or until the system has concluded that it cannot account for any more of the data. A portion of the prototype network for the pulmonary function application is given in Figure 23-1. Details of the knowledge representation and control structure for the CENTAUR system are given in Section 23.2 and Section 23.3.

Figure 23-2 is an example of an interpretation of a set of pulmonary function test results for one patient. Comments are in italics. Many additional lines of trace are printed to show what CENTAUR is doing between questions.

---

*CENTAUR
14-Jan-79 13:54:07

CURRENT PROTOTYPE: PUFF

The current hypothesis is that an interpretation of the pulmonary function tests is desired.

[Control slot of PUFF prototype being executed ...]

--------PATIENT-7446--------

(The initial data given by the user.)

1) Patient's identifying number:
** **9007**
2) referral diagnosis:
** **ASTHMA**
[Trigger for ASTHMA and CM 900]

Prototype ASTHMA is triggered by the value ASTHMA for the referral diagnosis. The certainty measure (CM) indicates on a numerical scale the degree of certainty with which the prototype is indicated by the data.)

3) RV/RV-predicted:
** **261**
4) TLC(body box)observed/predicted:
** **139**
5) FVC/FVC-predicted:
** **81**
[Trigger for Normal and CM 500]

(The questioning continues and other prototypes are triggered by the data values.)

FIGURE 23-2 An example of the interpretation of a set of patient test results. Debugging information (not routinely provided) is shown to help demonstrate the process of prototype invocation. (Key: ALS = amyotrophic lateral sclerosis; FEV1 = forced expiratory volume at one minute; FVC = forced vital capacity; MMF = maximal midexpiratory flow; OAD = obstructive airways disease; RDX = referral diagnosis; RLD = restrictive lung disease; RV = residual volume; TLC = total lung capacity.)

6) FEV1/FVC ratio:
** **40**
7) the DLCO/DLCO-predicted:
** **117**
[Trigger for NORMAL and CM 700]
8) Change in FEV1 post-dilation - pre-dilation:
** **31**
9) MMF/MMF-predicted:
** **12**
[Trigger for OAD and CM 900]
10) The slope (F50-obs-F25-obs)/FVC-obs:
** **9**
[Trigger for OAD and CM 900]

TRIGGERED PROTOTYPES
PROTOTYPE: ASTHMA, CM: 900, REASON: RDX was ASTHMA
PROTOTYPE: NORMAL, CM: 500, REASON: FVC was 81
PROTOTYPE: NORMAL, CM: 700, REASON: DLCO was 117
PROTOTYPE: OAD, CM: 900, REASON: MMF was 12
PROTOTYPE: OAD, CM: 900, REASON: F5025 was 9

(A list of the prototypes that have been triggered is given. The CM and the value that caused the trigger are also listed.)

Confirmed List: PUFF

It is confirmed that an interpretation of the pulmonary function tests is desired.

(The primary purpose of the pulmonary function prototype is to acquire the initial data from the user. It has no components and is thus confirmed when it has completed its task.)

MoreSpecific Prototypes chosen: NORMAL OAD

(Although there are five possible, more specific disease prototypes for PUFF, only the two that were triggered by the initial data are selected as possibilities to pursue.)

[New prototypes being filled in ... NORMAL OAD]

(These prototypes are filled in with the data values that are already known in the case.)

! Surprise Value ! 261 for RV in NORMAL, CM: 700
! Surprise Value ! 139 for TLC in NORMAL, CM: 400
! Surprise Value ! 40 for FEV1/FVC in NORMAL, CM: -166
! Surprise Value ! 12 for MMF in NORMAL, CM: -499
! Surprise Value ! 9 for F5025 in NORMAL, CM: -699

(Any data values that are not consistent with the values expected for that disease prototype are noted as surprise values, and the CM for that prototype is lowered. In this case, five of the data values are not consistent with the NORMAL pulmonary function prototype.)

Hypothesis List: (OAD 990) (NORMAL -699)

(The hypothesis list of triggered prototypes is then ordered according to the CM of the prototypes and a new current prototype is chosen.)

CURRENT PROTOTYPE: OAD

The current hypothesis is that there is an interpretation of Obstructive Airways Disease.

Components of OAD chosen to trace: F25 D-RV/TLC

FIGURE 23-2 continued

(In order to instantiate the OAD prototype, two more components must have values. These are asked of the user if there are no rules associated with the components that can be used to deduce their values.)

11) The flow F25:
** **UNKNOWN**
12) RV/TLC Observed-Predicted:
** **25**

Confirmed List: OAD PUFF

It is confirmed that there is an interpretation of Obstructive Airways Disease.

(The OAD prototype is confirmed. Control information associated with the prototype specifies that the degree of OAD should be determined next, followed by the subtype of OAD.)

MoreSpecific Prototypes chosen: MILD-OAD MODERATE-OAD
MODERATELY-SEVERE-OAD SEVERE-OAD

(No degree prototypes were triggered by the data values, so all of them are selected as possible hypotheses to be filled in along with the data values in the case.)

[New prototypes being filled in ... MILD-OAD MODERATE-OAD
MODERATELY-SEVERE-OAD SEVERE-OAD]
...

(More surprise values are noted, and the hypothesis list is ordered, leading to a current prototype of SEVERE-OAD.)

CURRENT PROTOTYPE: SEVERE-OAD

The current hypothesis is that there is an interpretation of Severe Obstructive Airways Disease.

Components of SEVERE-OAD chosen to trace: FEV1

13) FEV1:
** **42**

(The consultation continues with new components being asked and classified.)

Confirmed List: SEVERE-OAD OAD PUFF

It is confirmed that there is an interpretation of Severe
Obstructive Airways Disease.

MoreSpecific Prototypes chosen: ASTHMA

Hypothesis List: (ASTHMA 900)

(Next the subtypes of OAD are explored. ASTHMA is chosen from three possible subtypes because it was triggered by the initial data.)

CURRENT PROTOTYPE: ASTHMA

The current hypothesis is that there is an interpretation of Asthma.

Components of ASTHMA chosen to trace: DEG-REV

14) The change in resistance pre-dilation - post-dilation:
** **20**

Confirmed List: ASTHMA SEVERE-OAD OAD PUFF

It is confirmed that there is an interpretation of Asthma.

[Facts marked Accounted For by ASTHMA, SEVERE-OAD, OAD]

(There are no further degrees or subtypes to be explored for this case. Thus data values that can be accounted for by one of the confirmed prototypes are marked. If there are data values remaining that cannot be accounted for by the confirmed prototypes, the system will attempt to determine if there are multiple diseases in the patient.)

[Action slot of OAD prototype being executed ...]

(At this point the system begins executing any actions associated with the confirmed prototypes. There are no actions for ASTHMA or SEVERE-OAD, so the OAD action is the first to be executed.)

OAD Action Clause
Display the findings about the diagnosis of obstructive airways disease
Conclusions: the findings about the diagnosis of obstructive airways disease are as follows:
Elevated lung volumes indicate overinflation.
The RV/TLC ratio is increased, suggesting a SEVERE degree of air trapping.
Forced Vital Capacity is normal but the FEV1/FVC ratio is reduced, suggesting airway obstruction of a SEVERE degree.
Low mid-expiratory flow is consistent with severe airway obstruction.
Obstruction is indicated by curvature of the flow-volume loop which is of SEVERE degree.
Reversibility of airway obstruction is confirmed by improvement in airway resistance following bronchodilation.

[Action slot of PUFF prototype being executed ...]

PUFF Action Clause
Display the conclusion statements about this interpretation
Conclusions: the conclusion statements about this interpretation are as follows:
Smoking probably exacerbates the severity of the patient's airway obstruction.
Discontinuation of smoking should help relieve the symptoms.
Good response to bronchodilators is consistent with an asthmatic condition, and their continued use is indicated.

PUFF Action Clause
Display the summary statements about this interpretation
Conclusions: the summary statements about this interpretation are as follows:

SEVERE Obstructive Airways Disease, Subtype ASTHMA

Do you wish advice on another patient?
** **NO**

FIGURE 23-2 continued

23.2 Knowledge Representation in CENTAUR

Knowledge is represented in CENTAUR by both rules and prototypes. Each prototype contains two kinds of information: domain-specific *components* that express the substantive characteristics of each prototype, and domain-independent *slots* that specify information used in running the system. Each component may, in turn, have slots of information associated with it, including a RULES slot that links the component to rules that determine values of the component. Thus the outline of a prototype can be viewed as shown in Figure 23-3.

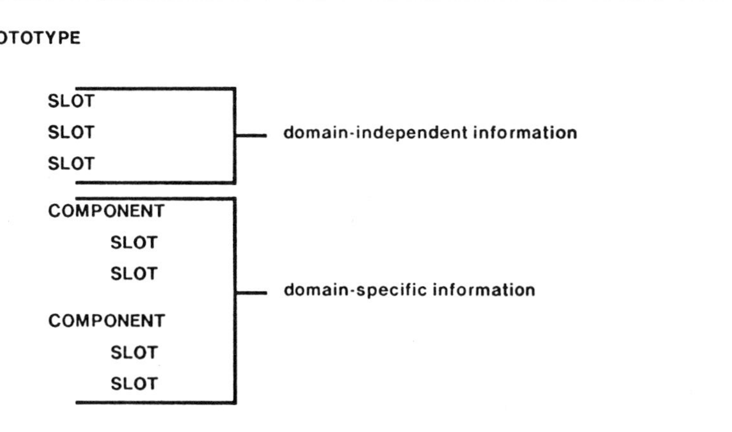

FIGURE 23-3 Prototype outline.

The rules consist of one or more premise clauses followed by one or more action clauses. An example is given in Figure 23-4.[4] In general, the premise clauses specify a set of value ranges for some of a prototype's components, and the action clauses make conclusions about the values of other components. Besides these static data structures, there are also data structures that give information about the actual data values obtained during the consultation. These are called *facts* and are discussed in Section 23.2.3.

23.2.1 Prototypes and Components

Most of CENTAUR's prototypes represent the characteristic features of some pulmonary disease. For example, there is a prototype for obstructive airways disease (OAD), a portion of which is shown in Figure 23-5. In the

[4]As in MYCIN, the rule is stored internally in the Interlisp form shown; the English translation is generated from that.

```
RULE013
------
   PREMISE:        ($AND ($OR ($AND (LESSP* (VAL1 CNTXT MMF)
                                            20)
                                    (GREATERP* (VAL1 CNTXT FVC)
                              ($AND (LESSP* (VAL1 CNTXT MMF)
                                            15)
                                    (LESSP* (VAL1 CNTXT FVC)
                                            80)]
   ACTION:         (DO-ALL (CONCLUDE CNTXT DEG<-MMF SEVERE TALLY 900)
                           (CONCLUDETEXT CNTXT FINDINGS<-OAD (TEXT $MMF)
                                         TALLY 1000))
```

RULE013

[This rule applies to any patient, and is tried in order to find out about the degree of obstructive airways disease as indicated by the MMF or the findings about the diagnosis of obstructive airways disease.]

If: 1) A: The MMF/MMF-predicted ratio is less than 20, and
  B: The FVC/FVC-predicted ratio is greater than 80, or
 2) A: The MMF/MMF-predicted ratio is less than 15, and
  B: The FVC/FVC-predicted ratio is less than 80

Then: 1) There is strongly suggestive evidence (.9) that the degree of obstructive airways disease as indicated by the MMF is severe, and
 2) It is definite (1.0) that the following is one of the findings about the diagnosis of obstructive airways disease: Low midexpiratory flow is consistent with severe airway obstruction.

FIGURE 23-4 A sample rule in CENTAUR in both Interlisp and English versions.

OAD prototype, there are components for many of the pulmonary function tests that are useful in characterizing a patient with OAD; two of these are shown in the figure. For example, the total lung capacity of a patient with OAD is typically higher than that of a person with normal pulmonary function. Thus there is a component, TOTAL LUNG CAPACITY, with a range of *plausible values* that are characteristic of a person with OAD.

In addition to a set of plausible values, that is, values consistent with the hypothesis represented by the prototype, the components may have additional information associated with them. (The ways in which this information is used are discussed in Section 23.3.) There may be one or more *possible error values,* that is, values that are inconsistent with the prototype or that might have been specified by the expert to check what he or she considers to be a measurement error. Generally, both a reason for the error and a possible fix for the error are specified. For example, the expert may specify that one of the pulmonary function tests be repeated to ensure accuracy. A component may also have a *default value.* Thus all of the components in a disease prototype, with their default values, form a picture of the typical patient with the disease. Finally, each component has an *importance measure* (from 0 to 5) that indicates the relative importance of a particular component in characterizing the disease.

In addition to the domain-specific components, each prototype con-

PROTOTYPE GENERAL INFORMATION	Obstructive Airways Disease (OAD)
--Bookkeeping Information	Author: Aikins Date: 27-OCT-78 Source: Dr. Fallat
--Pointers to other prototypes (link prototype)	Pointers: (degree MILD-OAD) (degree MODERATE-OAD) ... (subtype ASTHMA) ...
--English phrases	Hypothesis: "There is an interpretation of OAD."
COMPONENTS Plausible Values Default Value Possible Error Values Rules Importance of value to this prototype . . .	TOTAL LUNG CAPACITY Plausible Values: >100 Importance: 4 REVERSIBILITY Rules: 19,21,22,25 Importance: 0 (value not considered)
CONTROL INFORMATION	Deduce the degree of OAD Deduce the subtype of OAD Deduce any findings associated with OAD
ACTION INFORMATION	Print the findings associated with OAD

FIGURE 23-5 A sample prototype showing possible slots on the left and values of those slots for OAD on the right.

tains slots for general information associated with it. This includes bookkeeping information (name of the prototype, its author, date on which the prototype was created, and source for the information contained there) and English phrases used in communicating with the user. There are also pointers to other prototypes in the prototype network, which are useful, for example, when either more general disease categories or more specific subtypes of disease are indicated. Some control information is represented explicitly in slots associated with the prototype (Section 23.3). This information includes what to do in order to confirm the prototype and what to do when the prototype has been confirmed or disproved. Each prototype also has associated with it a *certainty measure* (from -1000 to 1000) that indicates how certain the system is that the prototype matches the data in each case.

23.2.2 Rules

The CENTAUR knowledge base also includes rules, which are grouped into four sets according to their functions. They refer to values for components in their premise clauses and make conclusions about values of components in their action clauses. An example of one of the rules is given in Figure 23-4. The RULES slot associated with a component contains a list of all rules that make a conclusion about that component. These may be applied when a value is needed for the component.[5]

Many of the rules are classified as *patient rules,* rules dealing with the patient. Besides the patient rules, there are three other sets of rules. Those rules whose actions make summary statements about the results of the pulmonary function tests are classified as *summary rules;* rules that refer to values of components in their premises and suggest general disease categories in their actions are classified as *triggering rules.* These are used to "trigger" or suggest the disease prototypes. Those rules that are used in a second stage of processing, after the system has formulated lists of confirmed and disproved prototypes are called *refinement rules;* they are used to refine a preliminary diagnosis, producing a final diagnosis about pulmonary disease in the patient. The refinement rules constitute a further set of domain expertise; they test the system's tentative conclusions, which may result in a modification of these conclusions. For example, if two diseases can account for a given pulmonary function test result and both have been confirmed in that case, a refinement rule may determine which disease process should account for the test result in the final interpretation.

23.2.3 Facts

In CENTAUR, each piece of case-specific data that has been acquired either initially from the patient's pulmonary function test results or later during the interpretation process is called a *fact.* Each fact has six fields of information associated with it. When a fact is first introduced into the system, its name, value, and certainty factor[6] fields are instantiated. For example, if the user specifies that the total lung capacity of the patient is 126 with a certainty factor of 0.8, then a fact is created:

```
NAME: Total Lung Capacity
VALUE: 126
CERTAINTY FACTOR: .8
```

The fourth field associated with the fact indicates where it was obtained: from the user (this includes the initial pulmonary function test results), from the rules, or as a default value associated with a prototype component. Thus, in the fact about total lung capacity, the fourth field would have the value USER.

The fifth field of each fact becomes instantiated once fact values are classified as being plausible values, possible error values, or surprise values

[5]If no rules are associated with the component, the user will be asked for the value. If the user responds UNKNOWN and the component has a default value, that value will be used.

[6]The certainty factor is just MYCIN's CF—a number ranging from −1 to 1 that indicates the importance of the given value.

for a given prototype. Surprise values are all of those values that are neither plausible values nor possible error values. They indicate facts that cannot be accounted for by the hypothesis represented by the prototype. In the fact about total lung capacity, the fifth field might contain the classification (PV OAD) and (SV NORMAL) meaning that the value of 126 for the total lung capacity of a patient would be a plausible value if the patient had obstructive airways disease, but would be a surprise value if the patient were considered to have normal pulmonary function.

The last field associated with a fact indicates which confirmed prototypes can account for the given value. When a prototype is confirmed, all of the facts that correspond to components in the prototype and whose values are plausible values for the component are said to be "accounted for" by that prototype. When the OAD prototype is confirmed, for a patient with total lung capacity of 126, for example, the last field of the sample fact for total lung capacity would be filled in with the prototype name OAD.

23.3 Control Structure for CENTAUR

The control information used by CENTAUR is contained either in slots that are associated with the individual prototypes or in a simple interpreter. Some control strategies are specific to an individual prototype and need to be associated with it, while more general system control information is more efficiently expressed in the interpreter.

Basically, the interpreter attempts to match one or more of the prototypes with the data in an actual case. At any one time there is one current prototype that the system is attempting to match to the facts of the case. Attempting a match for this prototype entails finding values for the prototype components, i.e., instantiating the prototype. The exact method to be used in instantiating the prototype depends on the individual prototype and is expressed in one of the prototype control slots.

When all of the facts have been accounted for by some confirmed prototype, or when no prototype can account for a known fact,[7] the system has completed the hypothesis-formation stage. The confirmed list of prototypes then represents the system's hypothesis about how to classify the facts. At this point, additional knowledge may be applied before generating the final pulmonary function interpretation and diagnosis. Some of this knowledge is represented in the refinement rules associated with the confirmed prototypes. Further information may be sought from the user at

[7]This statement oversimplifies the actual matching criteria used by the system. Some tolerance for a mismatch between known fact values and plausible values in the prototype is allowed.

this stage. For example, further lab tests may be suggested or additional test results may be required before a final diagnosis is given.

The result of executing the refinement rules is a final set of confirmed prototypes and a list of all facts with an indication of which prototypes account for which facts. The system then executes the clauses specified in the action slot of each confirmed prototype. Typically, these clauses express a clean-up chore such as executing summary rules associated with the prototype[8] or printing interpretation statements. The action slot of the PUFF prototype itself causes the final interpretation and pulmonary diagnosis to be printed.

23.3.1 Prototype Control Slots

Four of the slots associated with a prototype contain clauses that are executed by the system at specific times to control the consultation. Each clause expresses some action to be taken by the system at different stages: (a) in order to instantiate the prototype (CONTROL slot), (b) upon confirmation of the prototype (IF-CONFIRMED slot), (c) in the event that a prototype is disproved (IF-DISPROVED slot), and (d) in a clean-up phase after the system processing has been completed (ACTION slot).

When a prototype is first selected as the current prototype, the system executes the clauses in the CONTROL slot of that prototype. The information in this slot indicates how to proceed in order to instantiate the prototype, usually specifying what data should be acquired and in what order they should be acquired. Therefore, executing these clauses will cause values to be obtained for the prototype components. The CONTROL slot can be thought of as a rule whose implicit premise is "if this prototype is selected as the current prototype" and whose action is the given set of clauses. If no CONTROL slot is associated with a prototype, the interpreter will attempt to fill in values for the prototype components in order according to their importance measures.

When all of the clauses in the CONTROL slot have been executed and the prototype has been instantiated, a decision is made as to whether the prototype should be confirmed as matching the facts of the case.[9] The system then checks either the IF-CONFIRMED slot or the IF-DISPROVED slot to determine what should be done next. These slots can be viewed as rules whose implicit premise is either "if this prototype is confirmed as matching the data" or "if this prototype is proved not to match the data." The appropriate actions are then indicated in the set of clauses contained in the slot.

---

[8]Recall that the premise of a summary rule typically checks the values for one or more parameters and that the action generates an appropriate summarizing statement.

[9]It would be possible to associate such a confirmation criterion with each individual prototype, but this has not been found to be necessary for the pulmonary diagnosis problem. Instead, the system uses a general algorithm, applicable to all of the prototypes, that checks the values of the components and their importance measures to determine if the prototype should be marked as confirmed.

The fourth slot specifying clauses to be executed is the ACTION slot. The implicit premise in this slot is "if the system has completed its selection of confirmed prototypes and this prototype is confirmed." Thus the clauses in the ACTION slot are the last ones to generate summary statements or print data interpretations.

23.4 Advantages of the Prototype-Directed Approach

One question addressed by this research is this: in what ways are both frames and rules superior to either alone? Comparisons can be drawn between purely rule-based systems, such as PUFF, at one end of the spectrum and purely frame-based systems at the other. This section states some of the advantages of the prototype-directed approach used in CENTAUR for the pulmonary function interpretation task, as compared to the purely rule-based approach used in PUFF. The next chapter discusses a purely frame-based approach to the same problem. These advantages can be grouped into two broad categories: those dealing with knowledge base representation, and those dealing with reasoning and performance.

23.4.1 Knowledge Representation

Specific advantages of using prototypes in the pulmonary function domain include the following:

A. *Rules attached to prototypes are used to represent only medical expertise, not computational information.* In the PUFF system, there are rules that guide computation by controlling the invocation of other rules. This feature can be very confusing to the medical experts since they do not know which rules are intended to represent medical expertise and which rules serve a necessary computational function. For example, a PUFF rule necessary to determine whether there is obstructive airways disease (OAD) in the patient is

> If an attempt has been made to deduce the degree of OAD, and an attempt has been made to deduce the subtype of OAD, and an attempt has been made to deduce the findings about OAD, then there is an interpretation of potential OAD.

This rule expresses some of the control structure of the system, namely, that when there is an interpretation of OAD, then the degree, subtype, and findings associated with the OAD should be determined. The rule is confusing because it implies that finding out the degree, subtype, and findings leads to an interpretation of OAD—which might be misinterpreted as medical expertise. In fact, this rule is executed for every case and causes all of the other OAD rules to be invoked, even when no OAD is present.

In CENTAUR, rules that guide computation have been removed from the rule base, leaving a less confusing, more uniform rule base, where each rule represents some "chunk" of medical expertise. Computation is now guided by the prototypes. For example, the CONTROL slot represents information dealing with how to instantiate the prototype. For the OAD prototype, this CONTROL slot specifies that deducing the degree, subtype, and findings of obstructive airways disease are the steps to take in instantiating that prototype.

B. *Prototypes represent more clearly some of the medical expertise formerly contained in rules.* In some cases, medical expertise that has been represented in the production rules is more clearly represented in the prototype. Consider, for example, the following PUFF rule:

> If the degree for OAD is NONE, and the degree for OAD by the MMF is greater than or equal to MILD, then the degree for the OAD is MILD.

The medical expertise expressed in this rule is not apparent. In order to understand this rule, it is necessary to see it as one part of a group of several other rules, all of which together help to determine the degree of obstructive airways disease in the patient. The first clause of the rule, "If the degree for OAD is NONE," is partly a description of the medical context, indicating that the degree of OAD has not been established. However, it is also control information in that it requires that the degree for OAD be determined, which, in turn, invokes the other rules. Yet part of the motivation for using rules is that each rule should be a single "chunk" of knowledge, understandable in its own right. Further, what is really being said in this rule is that in determining the degree of OAD in the patient, there are several pulmonary function measurements to be considered, but, of these, the MMF measurement should be given somewhat more weight. In CENTAUR, this fact is represented explicitly in the OAD prototype by giving the MMF component an importance measure higher than those of the other measurement components.

C. *Knowledge is represented explicitly by prototypes.* As was indicated in paragraphs A and B above, making knowledge explicit is one of the advantages of the prototype representation. Not only is knowledge about how to instantiate the prototype represented explicitly, but knowledge about what to do if the prototype is confirmed or disproved, as well as what are appropriate clean-up actions to perform for the prototype, e.g., printing findings or summarizing data, is also represented. Other information, such as the importance measure to assign to one of the prototype components when matching prototypes to data, is also made explicit. All of this specifies to those working with the knowledge base precisely what information is represented and what role that information plays in the computation.

D. *Additional knowledge is represented by prototypes.* By adding a set of disease prototypes, some new knowledge about pulmonary disease can be represented. In MYCIN additional knowledge can be added as properties of *rules,* but it is difficult to add new knowledge about diseases. For example, plausible ranges of values for each of the pulmonary function tests for each disease, as well as the relative importance of each measurement in a particular disease prototype, can be listed.

23.4.2 Reasoning and Performance of the System

A second category of advantages deals with the way the system reasons about the problem. This is evident in part by watching the performance of the system, that is, the questions that are asked and the order in which information is acquired. Some of the advantages of a prototype-directed system are the following:

E. *Consultation flow follows the physician's reasoning.* The consultation begins with specific test results suggesting or "triggering" some of the prototypes. The prototypes serve as tentative hypotheses about how to classify the data in a given case. They also guide further inquiry. As new information is acquired, these hypotheses are revised, or, in CENTAUR's terms, prototypes are confirmed or disproved and new prototypes may then be suggested. The process of medical problem solving has been discussed by many researchers [e.g., Elstein et al. (1978)], and it is widely felt that this sequence of suggesting hypotheses, acquiring further information, and then revising the hypotheses is, in fact, the problem-solving process used by most physicians. Thus there is increased conceptual clarity, in that the user can understand what the program is doing. Other advantages that accrue from this approach include: (a) the knowledge base is easier to modify and extend, and (b) the system can offer the user a more intelligible explanation of its performance during the consultation. Giving the system the ability to explain its knowledge and performance has been a primary design goal of the present research efforts. Since the prototype-directed system reasons in a manner more like a human user, its behavior seems more natural and transparent and thus is more likely to be accepted by physicians.

F. *The order in which questions are asked can be controlled.* In a rule-based system such as PUFF, questions are asked of the user as rules are invoked that contain clauses referring to information that is not yet known. The designers of PUFF, or any EMYCIN system, control the order in which the questions are asked only by writing rules to enforce some order. As has been discussed, this procedure results in a potentially confusing rule base where some rules represent medical expertise and others guide computation. In the prototype-directed system, the expert specifies the order in which information is to be acquired for each prototype in the CONTROL slot. Thus control information is labeled explicitly as such, and the rule base remains uniformly a body of medical expertise. The expert can also specify what information must be acquired and what information is optional, using the importance measure associated with each component.[10]

G. *Only relevant questions are asked.* Another advantage of CENTAUR over the rule-based version of PUFF is that only those hypotheses suggested by the initial data are explored. For example, if the total lung capacity (TLC) for the patient is 70, then CENTAUR would begin exploring the possibility of restrictive lung disease (RLD) because a low TLC would trigger the RLD prototype.[11] In the PUFF program, the first disease tried is always OAD, so the PUFF program would begin asking questions dealing with OAD. These questions would seem irrelevant considering the data, and, indeed, if there were no data to indicate OAD, such questions would not be asked by CENTAUR.

H. *Inconsistent information is indicated.* During a consultation, it is also possible to point out inconsistent or possibly erroneous data as they are entered, so that a technician can repeat a test immediately or at least decide if it is worth the time to continue analyzing the case. This feature is invoked when possible error values are detected for a component of a prototype, or when no prototype can be determined to account for a given value.[12]

23.5 Summary

CENTAUR was designed in response to problems that occurred while using a purely rule-based system. The CENTAUR system offers an appropriate environment in which to experiment with knowledge representation issues such as determining what knowledge is most easily represented in rules and what is most easily represented in frames. In summary, much research remains to be done on this and associated knowledge representation issues. This present research is one attempt to make explicit the art of choosing the knowledge representation in AI by drawing comparisons between various approaches and by identifying the reasons for selecting one fundamental approach over another.

[10]Optional information is indicated by assigning a component an importance measure of 0.

[11]A low TLC is consistent with a hypothesis of RLD; a high TLC is consistent with OAD.

[12]It is also possible that there is an overly restricted range of plausible values for a prototype component, in which case the user may extend the range to encompass the indicated value.

24

Another Look at Frames

David E. Smith and Jan E. Clayton

The success of MYCIN-like systems has demonstrated that for many diagnostic tasks expert behavior can be successfully captured in simple goal-directed production systems. However, even for this class of problems, difficulties have arisen with both the representation and control mechanisms. One such system, PUFF (Kunz et al., 1978), has established a creditable record in the domain of pulmonary function diagnosis. The representation problems in PUFF are manifest in a number of rules that have awkward premises and conclusions. The control problems are somewhat more severe. Physicians have criticized PUFF on the grounds that it asks questions that do not follow a logical line of reasoning and that it does not notice data that are atypical or erroneous for the determined diagnosis.

In the CENTAUR system, described in Chapter 23, an attempt was made to correct representational deficiencies by using prototypes (frames) to characterize some of the system's knowledge. A more complex control scheme was also introduced. It made use of *triggering rules* for suggesting and ordering system goals, and included an additional attention-focusing mechanism by using frames as an index into the set of relevant rules.

In an attempt to carry the work of Aikins one step further, we have constructed an experimental system for pulmonary function diagnosis, called WHEEZE. Our objectives were to provide a uniform declarative representation for the domain knowledge and to permit additional control flexibility beyond that offered by PUFF or CENTAUR. To achieve the first of these objectives, all of PUFF's rules have been translated into a frame representation (discussed in Section 24.1). The second objective, control flexibility, is achieved by using an agenda-based control scheme (discussed

This chapter is an expanded version of a paper originally appearing in *Proceedings of the First National Conference on Artificial Intelligence*, Stanford, Calif., August 1980, pp. 154–156. Used with permission of the American Association for Artificial Intelligence.

in Section 24.2). New goals for the agenda are suggested by the success or failure of other goals on the agenda. In the final section, results and the possibilities of generalization are discussed.

24.1 Representation

24.1.1 The Language

We have chosen to use a representation language called RLL (Greiner and Lenat, 1980). The language is *frame-based,* where a frame consists of a set of *slots,* or attributes. We did not rely on the special features of RLL in any fundamental way. Any of the multitude of frame-based languages would have served equally well.

24.1.2 Vocabulary

In our knowledge base, there are three different kinds of frames that contain domain-specific diagnostic knowledge and knowledge about the case: assertion frames, patient frames, and patient datum frames.

Assertion Frames

The majority of the diagnostic knowledge is captured in a set of frames called *assertions.* Most assertions in the knowledge base are about the physiological state of the patient, e.g., "the patient's total lung capacity is high." But there are other types of assertions as well, such as "the total lung capacity measurement is erroneous." The organization of an assertion frame is shown in Figure 24-1.

An assertion may be related to other assertions in the knowledge base in several ways as shown in Figure 24-1. The substantiating evidence for an assertion is specified in the Manifestation slot for the assertion. This slot can be thought of as a set of links to secondary assertions that contribute to the confirmation of the assertion in question. It has been necessary to allow a considerable richness of combinations of manifestations for an assertion; consequently, each entry in the slot may be an individual manifestation or a simple function of individual manifestations, such as OneOf, TwoOf, TwoOrMoreOf, SomeOf, etc. Associated with each manifestation link is a number indicating the *importance* of the link in suggesting belief or disbelief in the assertion. The ManifestationOf slot is the inverse

Isa	Assertion
Description	<commentary>
Manifestation	<a list of assertions on which this assertion depends>
ManifestationOf	<a list of assertions that this assertion is a manifestation of—the inverse of the Manifestation slot>
Certainty	<a number between − 1000 and 1000 that indicates to what degree the assertion is believed, if its manifestations are believed>
SuggestiveOf	<related assertions that are worth investigating if this assertion is believed>
ComplementaryTo	<related assertions that are worth investigating if this assertion is not believed>
CategorizationOf	<the patient datum that this assertion is concerned with>
CategoryCriterion	<the allowed range of the patient datum corresponding to this assertion>
DegreeOfBelief	<a number between − 1000 and 1000 that indicates to what degree the assertion is believed>
Findings	<text to be reported to the user if this assertion is believed>

FIGURE 24-1 Organization of an assertion frame.

of the Manifestation slot; i.e., it contains a list of the assertions that have that assertion as a manifestation.

The Certainty slot, in WHEEZE, is an indicator of how likely an assertion is, given that its manifestations are believed. If the manifestations are strong indicators of the assertion, the Certainty slot will have a high value. The Certainty slot is a property of the knowledge rather than a statement about a particular consultation.

When an assertion is directly related to a patient datum, it is termed a *categorization* of that patient datum. This relationship is specified by the CategorizationOf and CategoryCriterion slots of the assertion. CategorizationOf indicates which patient datum the assertion depends on, while CategoryCriterion specifies the range in which the value must be for the assertion to be verified. For example, the assertion "the patient's TLC is greater than 110" (TLC stands for total lung capacity) would be a categorization of the TLC value with the category criterion being value>110.

The relationship may also be used in the reverse manner. A high-level datum such as SeverityOfDisease could be defined as one of a disjoint set of assertions being true (MildDisease, ModerateDisease, etc.), in which case the categorization relationship might be used to determine the datum from the assertions.

Each assertion has a DegreeOfBelief slot associated with it indicating to what degree the assertion is believed to be true in that particular consultation. The value of this slot can be any integer between −1000 and 1000, where 1000 indicates complete faith and −1000 means total denial of the assertion. It may also take on the value Unknown, indicating that the knowledge needed to determine the degree of belief of the assertion is not known. Note that there is a distinction made between a degree of belief that has not yet been investigated, a degree of belief that has been investigated but cannot be determined due to insufficient evidence (degree of belief Unknown) and a degree of belief that indicates equal positive and negative evidence (DegreeOfBelief = 0).

Unlike the Certainty slot, the DegreeOfBelief is determined by the system during the consultation. For an assertion that has only the categorization relationship (no manifestations), the DegreeOfBelief depends only on the Certainty of the assertion and on the patient datum being in the specified range. For assertions *with* manifestations, the DegreeOfBelief of the assertion can be a general function of the Certainty of the assertion, the DegreeOfBelief of each of its manifestations, and the importance attributed to each manifestation. The function used in MYCIN and PUFF is a simple thresholding mechanism, where, if the minimum of the antecedents is above some threshold (generally 200), the DegreeOfBelief is effectively set to the certainty factor. Importance measures provide additional flexibility by permitting the antecedents of a rule to be weighted. Several different combination mechanisms have been considered:

1. Sum the products of the DegreeOfBelief slots and the importance factors for each manifestation, then use a thresholding mechanism.
2. Sum the products of the DegreeOfBelief slots and the importance factors for each manifestation, then multiply this by the certainty factor.
3. Threshold the minimum of the DegreeOfBelief/importance ratios for the manifestations.

There are two assertion slots that indicate related assertions worth pursuing when an assertion is confirmed or denied. The SuggestiveOf slot contains a list of assertions to investigate if the current assertion is confirmed. Conversely, the ComplementaryTo slot is a list of assertions that should be pursued if the current assertion is denied. These slots function like the "triggering" rules in CENTAUR since they suggest goals to investigate.

The Findings slot of an assertion contains text that should be printed out if the assertion is confirmed. In PUFF, this text was contained in the conclusion portions of rules.

Isa	Patient
Age	<the patient's age>
Sex	<the patient's sex>
PackYearsSmoked	<the number of cigarette-smoking years specified in number of packs per day times number of years of smoking>
TLC	<the value of the total lung capacity for the patient>
RDX	<the referral diagnosis>
ConfirmedAssertions	<assertions that have already been confirmed for this patient>
DeniedAssertions	<assertions that have a DegreeOfBelief less than 0>
Agenda	<a pointer to an agenda frame containing assertions worth pursuing>

FIGURE 24-2 Organization of a patient frame.

Patient Frames

Information about the patient is kept in a frame named after that patient. In general, it contains slots for all of the patient data and for the state of the consultation. As shown in Figure 24-2, the majority of the slots in the patient frame contain the values of test data, derived data, or more general facts about the patient. Most of these values are entered directly by the physician; however, there are data that are derived or calculated from other values. The slots in the patient frame do not contain any information about obtaining the value for that slot. Instead, that information is kept in the corresponding patient datum frame (discussed below). The ConfirmedAssertions and DeniedAssertions slots keep track of the assertions that have already been tested. The Agenda slot contains a pointer to the agenda frame for the patient. It is important to note that the patient frame does not contain any heuristic knowledge about the system. Its only purpose is to hold current information about the patient.

Patient Datum Frames

In addition to patient and assertion frames, there are frames in the knowledge base for each type of patient datum (as shown in Figure 24-3). These frames indicate how a datum is obtained (whether it is requested from the physician or derived from other data), what a typical value for the datum

Isa	PatientDatum
Description	<commentary on this specific datum>
ToGetValue	<how to get the value of this datum if it is not known>
Categorization	<the set of assertions that are categorizations of this datum>
TypicalValue	<the value of this datum expected for a normal patient>

FIGURE 24-3 Organization of a patient datum frame.

might be, and what categories the value may be placed in. When the value of a patient datum is requested and not yet known, the frame for that patient datum is consulted and the information about how to obtain that datum is applied. This information takes the form of a procedure in the ToGetValue slot of the frame.

For a given patient datum, there may be many low-level assertions that are categorizations of the datum. These are specified by the Categorization slot. For example, the Categorization slot of TLC (total lung capacity) might contain the assertions TLC=80to100, TLC=100to120, TLC<80, and TLC>120, indicating that there are four major categories of the values. Thus the patient datum contains heuristic knowledge about how the datum is derived and how it relates to assertions in the network.

24.1.3 Translation

The process of translating a PUFF rule into a WHEEZE assertion consists of several steps. First, an assertion must be created embodying the conclusion and findings of the rule. Next, assertions corresponding to each of the antecedents of the rule must be constructed (if they are not already present) and added to the Manifestation slot of the assertion. If a manifestation is a categorization of some patient datum, then the CategorizationOf and CategoryCriterion slots for that manifestation must be filled in accordingly, and the frame describing that patient datum must be created.

Figure 24-4 is an example of how a particular PUFF rule was translated into our representation. The conclusion of the rule corresponds to the assertion and findings. The antecedents became the manifestations of the assertion. Quite often the manifesting assertions are not already present in the knowledge base and must be created. For example, the assertion frame RDX-Asthma (meaning "referral diagnosis of asthma") had to be added to the knowledge base when the RefractoryAsthma frame was created, since it is one of the manifestations of RefractoryAsthma. The patient

PUFF Rule 42

If: 1) There are postbronchodilation test results, and

2) The degree of reversibility of airway obstruction of the patient is less than or equal to slight, and

3) Asthma is one of the referral diagnoses of the patient

Then: It is definite (1000) that the following is one of the conclusion statements about this interpretation: The poor response to bronchodilators is an indication of an asthmatic condition in a refractory state.

REFRACTORY-ASTHMA

Isa	PhysiologicalState
Manifestation	(OAD BronchodilationTestResults RDX-Asthma (*OneOf OADReversibility-None OADReversibility-Slight))
Certainty	1000
DegreeOfBelief	
Findings	The poor response to bronchodilators is an indication of an asthmatic condition in a refractory state.
ComplementaryTo	((RefractoryAsthma-None 5))

FIGURE 24-4 PUFF rule and corresponding WHEEZE frame for refractory asthma.

datum RDX (referral diagnosis) also had to be added, since RDX-Asthma was specified as a categorization of RDX. Most of the other rules in the system were translated in an analogous fashion.

While there is not a one-to-one mapping between the representations we have used and the rules in PUFF, we can imagine automating the process. The most difficult problem in conversion is to create meaningful and consistent names for the assertions in the knowledge base. In most cases we used some combination of keywords in the conclusion of the rule we were mapping into the assertion (as in Figure 24-4).

24.2 Control Structure

Depth-first, goal-directed search is often used in production systems because questions asked by the system are focused on specific topics. Thus the system appears to follow a coherent line of reasoning, more closely mimicking that of human diagnosticians. There are, however, many widely recognized limitations. No mechanism is provided for dynamically select-

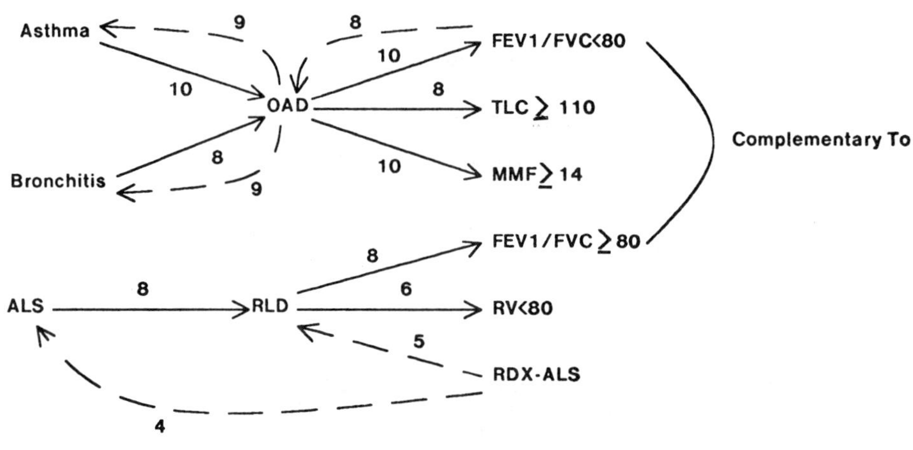

FIGURE 24-5 A simplified portion of the WHEEZE knowledge base. The solid lines indicate Manifestation links (e.g., OAD is a manifestation of Asthma); the dashed lines represent SuggestiveOf links. The numbers represent the corresponding importance and SuggestiveOf values of the links. (Key: ALS = amyotrophic lateral sclerosis; FEV1 = forced expiratory volume at one minute; FVC = forced vital capacity; MMF = maximal midexpiratory flow; OAD = obstructive airways disease; RDX = referral diagnosis; RLD = restrictive lung disease; RV = residual volume; TLC = total lung capacity.)

ing or ordering the initial set of goals. Consequently, the system may explore many "red herrings" and ask irrelevant questions before encountering a good hypothesis. In addition, a startling piece of evidence (strongly suggesting a different hypothesis) cannot cause suspension of the current investigation and pursuit of the alternative.

For the assertion network in Figure 24-5, a depth-first, goal-directed system like PUFF would start with the goals Asthma, Bronchitis, and ALS (amyotrophic lateral sclerosis) and work backwards in a goal-directed fashion toward OAD (obstructive airways disease) and RLD (restrictive lung disease) and then toward FEV1/FVC<80, MMF≥14, etc. In contrast, the CENTAUR system would make use of triggering rules to allow primitive data (e.g., RDX-ALS and FEV1/FVC<80) to suggest whether ALS and OAD were worth investigating and the order in which to investigate them. It would then proceed in a goal-directed fashion to try to verify those goals.

Expert diagnosticians use more than simple goal-directed reasoning. They seem to work by alternately constructing and verifying hypotheses, corresponding to a mix of data- and goal-directed search. They expect expert systems to reason in an analogous manner. It is therefore necessary that the system designer have some control over the reasoning behavior of the system. These intuitions, and the work on triggering described in Chapter 23, have led us to adopt a control mechanism that permits a combination of backward chaining and forward (data-driven) exploration together with any search strategy ranging from pure depth-first to pure breadth-first search. This control structure is implemented by using an agenda, with each suggested assertion being placed on the agenda according to some specified priority. The control strategy is as follows:

1. Examine the top assertion on the agenda.
2. If its subassertions (manifestations) are known, the relative belief of the assertion is determined. If confirmed, any assertions of which it is suggestive are placed on the agenda according to the specified measure of suggestivity. If denied, complementary assertions are placed on the agenda according to their measures of suggestivity.
3. If it cannot be immediately verified or rejected, then its unknown manifestations are placed on the agenda according to their measures of importance and the agenda level of the original assertion.

By varying the importance factors, SuggestiveOf values, and the initial items placed on the agenda, numerous control strategies are possible. For example, if high-level goals are placed on the agenda initially and subgoals are always placed at the top of the agenda, depth-first, goal-directed behavior will result. Alternatively, if low-level data are placed on the agenda initially and assertions suggested by these data assertions are always placed below them on the agenda, breadth-first, data-driven behavior will result. More commonly, what is desired is a mixture of the two, in which assertions suggest others as being likely and goal-directed verification is employed to investigate the likely assertions. The example below illustrates how this can be done.

In the knowledge base of Figure 24-5, suppose that RDX-ALS is confirmed, suggesting RLD to the agenda at level 5 and ALS at level 4. RLD is then examined, and since its manifestations are unknown, they are placed at the specified level on the agenda. The agenda now contains FEV1/FVC≥80 at level 8, RV<80 and RLD at level 5, and ALS at level 4. FEV1/FVC≥80 is therefore selected. Suppose that it is found to be false. Its complementary assertion (FEV1/FVC<80) is placed at level 8 on the agenda and is immediately investigated. It is, of course, true, causing OAD to be placed at level 8 on the agenda. The diagnosis proceeds by investigating the manifestations of OAD; and, if OAD is confirmed, Asthma and Bronchitis are investigated.

Although many subtleties have been glossed over in this example, it is important to note that:

1. The manipulation of SuggestiveOf and importance values can change the order in which assertions are examined, therefore changing the

order in which questions are asked and results are printed out. (In the example, FEV1/FVC was asked for before RV.)

2. Surprise values (data contrary to the hypothesis currently being investigated) may suggest goals to the agenda that are high enough to cause suspension of the current investigation. (The surprise FEV1/FVC value caused suspension of the RLD investigation in favor of the OAD investigation. If the suggestivity of the link from FEV1/FVC<80 to OAD were not as high, this would not have occurred.)
3. Low-level data assertions cause the suggestion of high-level goals, thus selecting and ordering goals to avoid irrelevant questions. (In the example, RLD and ALS were suggested and ordered by the low-level assertion RDX-ALS.)

24.3 Conclusions

It is no surprise that WHEEZE exhibits the same diagnostic behavior as its predecessors, PUFF and CENTAUR, on a standard set of ten patient test cases. The three systems are also roughly comparable in efficiency. WHEEZE and CENTAUR are somewhat slower than PUFF, but this may be misleading, since little effort has been expended on optimizing either of these systems.

The frame representation described in Section 24.1 has proved entirely adequate for capturing the domain knowledge of both PUFF and CENTAUR. In some cases, several rules were collapsed into a single assertion frame. In other cases, intermediate assertions, corresponding to common groups of clauses in rule premises, were added to the knowledge base. This had the effect of simplifying other assertion frames. The combination of representation and control structure also eliminated the need for many awkward interdependent rules and eliminated the need for screening clauses in others.

There are several less tangible effects of using a frame representation. Our purely subjective view is that a uniform, declarative representation is often more perspicuous. As an example, all of the interconnections between assertions about disease states are made explicit by the Manifestation and ManifestationOf slots. As a result, it is easier to find all other assertions related to a given assertion. This in turn makes it somewhat easier to understand and predict the control flow of the system.

Since the agenda-based control mechanism includes backward-chaining and goal-triggering capabilities, it has also proved adequate for capturing the control flow of PUFF and CENTAUR. In addition, the flexibility of agenda-based control was used to advantage. Suggestiveness and importance factors were used to change the order in which questions were asked and conclusions printed out. They were also used to eliminate the need to order carefully sets of antecedent assertions.

There is evidence that mixed goal-directed and data-directed control models human diagnostic behavior much more closely than either pure goal-directed or data-directed search (Elstein et al., 1978). The diagnostic process is one of looking at available symptoms, allowing them to suggest higher-level hypotheses, and then setting out to prove or disprove those hypotheses, all the while recognizing hypotheses that might be suggested by symptoms appearing in the verification process. Pauker and Szolovits (1977) have noted that a physician will go to great lengths to explain data inconsistent with a partially verified hypothesis before abandoning it. This type of behavior is not altogether inconsistent with the strategy we have employed, albeit for a different reason. The combination of a partially verified hypothesis and data inconsistent with it may be enough to boost an assertion that would explain the inconsistent data "above" an alternative hypothesis on the agenda. Oddly enough, some of this behavior seems to be a natural consequence of the control structure we have employed.

24.3.1 Generalizing

There is no reason to suppose that the representation and control mechanisms used in WHEEZE could not be used to advantage in other diagnostic production systems. A system similar to EMYCIN (Chapter 15), having both knowledge acquisition and explanation capabilities, could certainly be based on frames and agenda-based control. It also seems likely that an analogue of the EMYCIN rule compiler could be developed to take portions of an assertion network and produce efficient LISP code that would perform identically to the agenda-based control scheme operating on the assertion network.

A second class of extensions that becomes possible with a frame-based system is the addition of other kinds of knowledge not essential to the diagnostic process. For example, in the development of GUIDON (Chapter 26) Clancey noted that a substantial proportion of the domain knowledge had been compiled out of the rules used by most high-performance systems. Within our framework there is no reason why this information could not be added while still maintaining high performance. Such additional information might also be useful for enhanced explanation of system behavior.

24.3.2 Some Outstanding Questions

In the discussion above, claims were made about the perspicuity of the frame representation and about the flexibility of the agenda-based control mechanism. Of course, the acid test would be to see how well domain experts could adapt to the representation and to see whether or not they would become facile at tailoring control flow.

A second question that we pondered is this: how would WHEEZE be different if we had started with a basic frame system and the agenda-based control mechanism and worked with an expert to help build up the system from scratch? It is entirely possible that the backward-chaining production system paradigm had a significant effect on the vocabulary and knowledge that make up both PUFF and CENTAUR. In other words, the medium may have influenced the "message."

To a large extent, we have only paraphrased PUFF's rules in a different representational medium. This paraphrase may not be the most natural way to do diagnosis in the new architecture. Unfortunately, we do not have sufficient expertise in pulmonary function diagnosis to consider radical reformulations of the domain knowledge. For this reason, it would be interesting to see a new diagnostic system developed using the basic architecture we have proposed.

PART EIGHT

Tutoring

25

Intelligent Computer-Aided Instruction

The idea of directly teaching students "how to think" goes back at least to Polya (1957), if not to Socrates, but it reached a new stage of development in Papert's laboratory (Papert, 1970). In the LOGO lab, young students were taught AI concepts such as hierarchical decomposition, opening up a new dimension by which they could take apart a problem and reason about its solution. In part, Polya's heuristics have seemed vague and too general, too hard to follow in real problems (Newell, 1983). But progress in AI programming, particularly expert system design, has suggested a vocabulary of *structural concepts* that we now see must be conveyed along with the heuristics to make them intelligible (see Chapter 29).

Developing in parallel with Papert's educational experiments and capitalizing even more directly on AI technology, programs called *intelligent tutoring systems* (ITS) were constructed in the 1970s. In contrast with the computer-aided instruction (CAI) programs of the 1960s, these programs used new AI formalisms to separate out the subject matter they teach from the programs that control interactions with students. This is called intelligent computer-aided instruction (ICAI). This approach has several advantages: it becomes possible to keep records of what the student knows; the logic of teaching can be generalized and applied to multiple problems in multiple problem domains; and a model of student knowledge can be inferred from student behavior and used as a basis for tutoring. The well-known milestones in ITS research include:

- interacting with the student in a mixed-initiative dialogue[1] (Carbonell, 1970b) and tutoring by the Socratic method (Collins, 1976)

Parts of this chapter are taken from the final report to the Office of Naval Research for the first period of GUIDON research (1979–1982). That report appeared as a technical memo (HPP-82-2) written by William J. Clancey and Bruce G. Buchanan from the Heuristic Programming Project, Department of Computer Science, Stanford University.

[1]In a mixed-initiative dialogue between a student and a program, either party can initiate questions and expect reasonable responses from the other party. This contrasts sharply with drill and practice programs or MYCIN's dialogue, in which users cannot volunteer information or direct the program's reasoning.

- evaluating student hypotheses for consistency with measurements taken (Brown et al., 1975)
- enumerating bugs in causal reasoning (Stevens et al., 1978)
- interpreting student behavior in terms of expert knowledge ("overlay model") (Burton, 1979; Carr and Goldstein, 1977; Clancey, 1979b)
- codifying discourse procedures for teaching (Clancey, 1979c)
- constructing models of incorrect plans or procedures (Genesereth, 1981; Brown and Burton, 1978)
- relating incorrect procedures to a generative theory (Brown and Van-Lehn, 1980)

The record of ITS research reveals a few recurring questions:

1. *Nature of expertise:* What is the knowledge we want to teach a student?
2. *Modeling:* How can we determine what the student knows?
3. *Tutoring:* How can we improve the student's performance?

Almost invariably, researchers have backed off from initially focusing on the last question—"How shall we teach?"—to reconsider the second question, that of building a model of the student's knowledge. This follows from the assumption that student errors are not random but reflect misconceptions about the procedure to be followed or facts in the problem domain and that the best teaching strategy is to address directly the student's misconceptions.

In order to extend the research in building models of misconceptions in well-understood domains such as subtraction to more complex domains such as physics, medicine, and electronic troubleshooting, we need a sounder understanding of the nature of knowledge and expertise. Comparison studies of experts and novices (Chi et al., 1980; Feltovich et al., 1980; Lesgold, 1983) reveal that how the expert structures a problem, the very concepts he or she uses for thinking about the problem, distinguishes an expert's reasoning from a student's often formal, bottom-up approach. These studies suggest that we might directly convey to the student the kinds of quick associations, patterns, and reasoning strategies that experts build up tediously over long exposure to many kinds of problems—the kind of knowledge that tends not to be written down in basic textbooks.

It is with this premise—that we will be better teachers by better understanding expertise—that research on expert systems becomes of keen interest to the educator. These *knowledge-based programs* contain within them a large number of facts and rulelike associations for solving problems in restricted domains of medicine, science, and engineering. While these programs were developed originally just for the sake of building systems that could solve difficult problems, they have special interest to research in cognitive science as simulation models that can be used as a "laboratory workbench" for experimenting with knowledge structures and control strategies. By altering the "program as a model," one can test hypotheses about human performance [for example, see Johnson et al. (1981)].

Another natural application for expert systems in education is to use them as the "knowledge foundation" for an intelligent tutoring system. Brown pioneered this technology in the SOPHIE3 system (Brown et al., 1974), which took a student through the paces of debugging a circuit. Brown, Collins (1978), and Goldstein (1978) pioneered the use of production rules to express knowledge about how to interact with a student and how to interpret his or her behavior. The first tutor built on top of a complex expert system was GUIDON (Clancey, 1979a), using MYCIN's 450 production rules and tables for teaching medical diagnosis by the case method. GUIDON's teaching expertise is represented cleanly and independently of the domain rules; it has been demonstrated for both medical and engineering domains.[2]

25.1 Tutoring from MYCIN's Knowledge Base

Early in the course of building MYCIN, we observed that a program with enough medical knowledge for consulting had high potential for educating physicians and medical students. Physicians who seek advice from a consultant—human or machine—do so because they are uncertain whether or not they are ignoring important possibilities or making conclusions that are correct. Along with confirmation and advice, a consultant provides reasons, answers questions, and cites related issues. The educational component of a computer-based consultant was too obvious for us to ignore.

MYCIN's *conclusions* alone would not help a physician understand the medical context of the case he or she presents to the program. But the *dialogue* with MYCIN already begins to illuminate what are the key factors for reaching those conclusions. Because MYCIN asks whether or not the patient has been burned, for example, a physician is reminded that this factor is relevant in this context. This is very passive instruction, however, and does not approach the Socratic dialogue we expect from good teachers.

MYCIN's *explanation capabilities* were introduced to give a physician an opportunity to examine parts of the dialogue he or she found puzzling. When the program asks whether or not the patient has burns, the user can inquire why that information is relevant. As described in Part Six, answers to such inquiries elucidate MYCIN's line of reasoning on the case at hand and thus provide brief instructional interchanges in the course of a consultation. Similarly, the *question-answering capabilities* give a physician

---

[2]In GUIDON teaching knowledge is treated as a form of expertise. That is, GUIDON has a knowledge base of teaching rules that is distinct from MYCIN's knowledge base of infectious disease rules.

instructional access to the static knowledge base. Although we now understand better the difference between MYCIN's explanation capabilities and an active tutor, we enthusiastically wrote in 1974 (Shortliffe, 1974, pp. 230–231):

> As . . . emphasized throughout this report, an ability to instruct the user was an important consideration during the design of MYCIN. We believe it is possible to learn a great deal simply by asking MYCIN for consultative advice and taking advantage of the program's explanation capabilities. It is quite likely, in fact, that medical students in their clinical years will comprise a large percentage of MYCIN's regular users.

We were also aware of the need to make an instructional program more active, as others in AI were doing. In 1974 we noted (Shortliffe, 1974, p. 231):

> It would be possible . . . to adapt MYCIN so that its emphasis became primarily educational rather than consultative. This could be accomplished in a number of ways. In one scenario, MYCIN would present a sample patient to a student. The program would then judge the student's ability to ask important questions and to reach valid conclusions regarding both the identity of the organism(s) and the most appropriate therapeutic regimen. By comparing the student's questions and decisions to its own, MYCIN could infer inadequacies in the user's knowledge and enter into a tutorial discourse customized for the student. . . . We have no plans to pursue this application in the near future.

It was within this intellectual context that Clancey began asking about the adequacy of MYCIN's knowledge base for education. We initially believed that the rules and tables MYCIN used for diagnosing causes of infections would be a sufficient instructional base for an ICAI program. We felt that the only missing intelligence was pedagogical knowledge: how to carry on a mixed-initiative dialogue, how to select and present information, how to build and use a model of the student, and so on. Clancey began work on a tutorial program, called GUIDON, within two years after the material quoted above was written. The initial model of interaction between MYCIN and GUIDON is shown schematically in Figure 25-1.

GUIDON was first conceived as an extension of the explanation system of the MYCIN consultation program. This previous research provided the building blocks for a teaching program:

- modular representation of knowledge in production rules
- English translation of the internal rule representation
- a developed "history trace" facility for recording reasoning steps
- representation in the system of the grammar of its rules, so they can be parsed and reasoned about by the system itself
- an explanation subsystem with a well-developed vocabulary for the log-

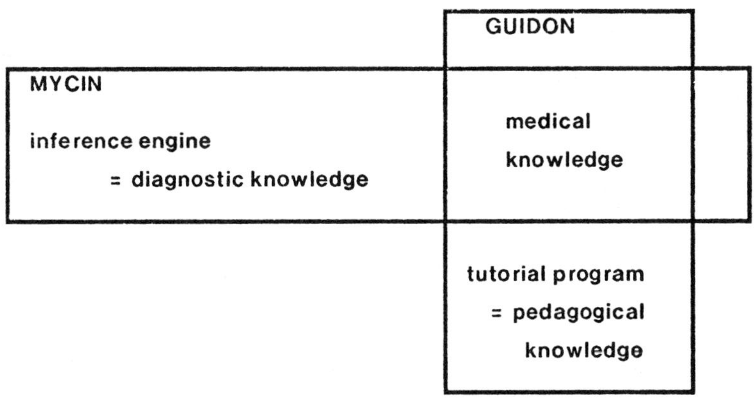

FIGURE 25-1 Model of interaction between MYCIN and GUIDON.

ical kinds of questions that can be asked about MYCIN's reasoning ("Why didn't you ask X?" or "How did you use X to conclude about Y?")

With this foundation, we constructed a tutoring program that would take MYCIN's solution to a problem, analyze it, and use it as the basis for a dialogue with a student trying to solve the same problem. About two hundred tutoring rules were developed, organized into "discourse procedures" for carrying on the dialogue (offering advice, deciding whether and how to interrupt, etc.) (Clancey, 1979b). Student modeling rules were used to interpret a student's partial problem solutions in terms of MYCIN's knowledge, and the resulting model was used to decide how much to tell the student and when to test his or her understanding.

Our 1978 proposal to the Office of Naval Research (ONR) for GUIDON research outlined investigation of both problem-solving and teaching strategies. With the program so well developed, it was expected that early experimentation could be done with alternative teaching approaches. However, during preliminary discussions with other researchers in this field, a key question was repeatedly raised. To paraphrase John Brown (August 2, 1978, at Stanford University):

> What is the nature of the expertise to be transmitted by this system [GUIDON]? You are not just unfolding a chain of inferences; there is also glue or a model of process. . . . What makes a rule click?

Following this lead, we began to concentrate on the nature of the expertise to be taught. GUIDON's interactions were studied, particularly the kind of feedback it was able to provide in response to incorrect partial solutions. The inability of the program to provide strategical guidance—

advice about what to do next—revealed that the "glue" that was missing had something to do with the system of rules as a whole. With over 400 rules to learn, there had to be some kind of underlying logic that made them fit together; the idea of teaching a set of weakly structured rules was now seriously in question. Significantly, this issue had not arisen in the years of developing MYCIN but was now apparently critical for teaching, and probably had important implications for MYCIN's explanation and knowledge acquisition capabilities as well.

It soon became clear that GUIDON needed to know more than MYCIN knows about diagnosis. MYCIN's route from goal to specific questions is not the only acceptable line of reasoning or strategy for gathering evidence. The order in which MYCIN asks for test results, for example, is often arbitrary. Thus a student is not necessarily wrong if he or she deviates from that order. Moreover, MYCIN's explicit knowledge about medicine is often less complete than what a tutor needs to convey to a student. It is associational knowledge and does not represent causal relationships explicitly. The causal models have been "compiled into" the associations. Thus MYCIN cannot justify an inference from A to B in terms of a causal chain, $A \rightarrow A_1 \rightarrow A_2 \rightarrow B$. A student, therefore, is left with an incomplete, and easily forgotten, model of the disease process. These two major shortcomings are discussed at length in Chapters 26 and 29.

25.2 Recent Work

Complementing the studies of differences between experts and novices, as well as our own work at Stanford on systems that explain their reasoning, our recent work has shown that expert systems must represent knowledge in a special way if it is to be used for teaching (Chapter 29). First, *the program must convey organizations and approaches that are useful to the student;* this argues for a knowledge base that reflects ways of thinking used by people (the hypothesis formation approach). Second, *various kinds of knowledge must be separated out and made explicit so reasoning steps can be carefully articulated*—the expert's associations must be decomposed into structural and strategic components. Under our current contract with ONR, such an expert system, called NEOMYCIN, has been constructed (Clancey and Letsinger, 1981). It is being readied for use with students through both active development of its knowledge base and construction of modeling programs that will use it as a basis for interpreting student behavior.

The ultimate goal of our work in the past few years has been to use NEOMYCIN for directly teaching diagnostic problem solving to students. Students will have the usual classroom background but will be exposed in this tutoring system to a way of thinking about and organizing their textbook knowledge that is usually taught only informally in apprenticeship settings. That is, we are beginning to capture in an expert system what we deem to be the essential knowledge that separates the expert from the novice and teaching it to the novice in practice sessions in which its value for getting a handle on difficult, confusing problems will be readily apparent. Empirical studies are a key part of this research.

We view our work as the logical "next step" in knowledge-based tutoring. Just as representing expert knowledge in a simulation program provides a vehicle for testing hypotheses about how people reason, using this knowledge in a tutoring system will enable us to see how the knowledge might be explained and recognized in student behavior. The experience with the first version of GUIDON, as detailed further in Chapter 26, illustrates how the tutoring framework provides a "forcing function" that requires us to clarify what we want to teach and how we want to teach it.

During 1979–1980 a study was undertaken to determine how an expert remembered MYCIN's rules (the "model of process" glue) and how he or she remembered *to use them.* This study utilized several common AI methods for knowledge acquisition but built upon them significantly through the development of an epistemological framework for characterizing kinds of knowledge, detailed in Chapter 29. The expert's explanations were characterized in terms of: strategy, structure, inference rule, and support. With this kind of framework, discussions with the expert were more easily focused, and experiments were devised for filling in the gaps in what we were told.

By the end of 1980, we had formulated and implemented a new, comprehensive psychological model of medical diagnosis (Clancey and Letsinger, 1981) based on extensive discussions with Dr. Tim Beckett. NEOMYCIN is a consultation program in which MYCIN's rules are reconfigured according to our epistemological framework. That is, the knowledge representation separates out the inference rules (simple associations among data and hypotheses) from the structural and strategic knowledge: *we separate out what a heuristic is from when it is to be applied.* Moreover, the strategies and structure we have chosen model how an expert reasons. We have attempted to capture the expert's forward-directed inferences, "diagnostic task structure," and the types of focusing strategies he or she uses. This explicit formulation of diagnostic strategy in the form of meta-rules is exactly the material that our original proposal only mentioned as a hopeful aside. Recently, we have been fine-tuning NEOMYCIN, investigating its applicability to other domains, and exploiting it as the foundation of a student model.

25.3 Multiple Uses of the Same Knowledge

From a slightly different perspective, we were also interested in exploring the question of whether or not one knowledge base could be used for multiple purposes. From the DENDRAL and MYCIN experiences, we

Predictive Rule for DENDRAL:

IF the molecular structure contains the subgraph

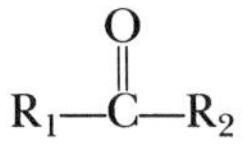

$$R_1—\overset{\overset{\displaystyle O}{\|}}{C}—R_2$$ (where R_1 and R_2 represent any substructures)

THEN predict that the molecule will fragment in the mass spectrometer at either side of the carbon atom, retaining the positive charge on the C=O group.

Corresponding Interpretive Rule for DENDRAL:

IF the mass spectrum shows data points at masses x_1 and x_2 such that the sum of x_1 and x_2 is the molecular weight plus 28 mass units (the overlapping C=O group) and at least one of the two peaks is high (because the fragmentation is favorable)

THEN infer that the molecular structure contains the subgraph

$$R_1—\overset{\overset{\displaystyle O}{\|}}{C}—R_2$$

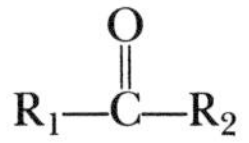

where the masses of R_1 and R_2 are just $(x_1 - 28)$ and $(x_2 - 28)$.

FIGURE 25-2 Two forms of the same knowledge in DENDRAL.

were painfully aware of how difficult it is for experts to build a single knowledge base capable of supporting high performance in reasoning. Yet there are many related reasoning tasks in any domain for which one knowledge base would be important. We had been troubled, for example, by the fact that DENDRAL's predictive rules of mass spectrometry had to be recast to serve as interpretive rules.[3] Prediction is from cause to effect; interpretation depends on inferences from effects to causes. An example from DENDRAL is shown in Figure 25-2. When we began working on MYCIN, we were thus already sensitized to the issue of avoiding the work of recasting MYCIN's interpretive rules in a form suitable for teaching or other purposes.

The GUIDON program discussed in the next chapter has at least three important facets. First, GUIDON can be seen as an expert system in its own right. Its expertise is in pedagogy, but it obviously needs a knowledge base of medicine to teach from as well as a knowledge base about pedagogy. Second, we had hoped that GUIDON would help us understand the problem of transfer of expertise. We believe there is some symmetry between GUIDON's transferring medical knowledge to a student and an expert's

[3]We experimented with two ways of using predictive rules for interpretation in DENDRAL: (a) generate the interpretive rules automatically from the predictive model (Delfino et al., 1970), and (b) simulate the behavior of a skeletal structure under all plausible substitutions of substructures for the unnamed radicals in order to infer the structure and location of substituents around the skeleton (Smith et al., 1972).

transferring his or her medical knowledge to MYCIN. We need to do much more work here. And third, because professional educators cannot yet provide a firm set of pedagogical rules and heuristics, GUIDON can also be seen as a laboratory for experimenting with alternative teaching strategies. In all three of these areas, the possibilities are exciting because of the newness of the territory and frightening because of the expanse of uncharted waters.

26

Use of MYCIN's Rules for Tutoring

William J. Clancey

How can we make the expertise of knowledge-based programs accessible to students? Knowledge-based programs (Davis et al., 1977; Lenat, 1976; Pople, 1977; Goldstein and Roberts, 1977) achieve high performance by interpreting a specialized set of facts and domain relations in the context of particular problems. These knowledge bases are generally built by interviewing human experts to extract the knowledge they use to solve problems in their area of expertise. However, it is not clear that the organization and level of abstraction of this performance knowledge is suitable for use in a tutorial program.

A principal feature of MYCIN's formalism is the separation of the knowledge base from the interpreter for applying it. This makes the knowledge accessible for multiple uses, including explanation of reasoning (Davis, 1976) and tutoring. In this chapter we explore the use of MYCIN's knowledge base as the foundation of a tutorial system called GUIDON. The goal of this project is to study the problem of transferring the expertise of MYCIN-like systems to students. An important result of this study is that although MYCIN-like rule-based expert systems constitute a good basis for tutorial programs, they are not sufficient in themselves for making knowledge accessible to students.

In GUIDON we have augmented the performance knowledge of rules by adding two other levels: a *support level* to justify individual rules, and an *abstraction level* to organize rules into patterns (see Section 26.3.3). The GUIDON system also contains teaching expertise that is represented explicitly and that is independent of the contents of the knowledge base. This

This chapter is a shortened version of an article originally appearing in *International Journal of Man-Machine Studies* 11: 25–49 (1979).

is expertise for carrying on a tutorial dialogue intended to present the domain knowledge to a student in an organized way, over a number of sessions. Section 26.2 describes design considerations for this tutorial dialogue, given the structure of the knowledge in MYCIN-like problem areas (described in Section 26.1).

GUIDON is designed to transfer the expertise of MYCIN-like programs in an efficient, comprehensible way. In doing this, we overlap several areas of research in intelligent computer-aided instruction (ICAI), including means for structuring and planning a dialogue, generating teaching material, constructing and verifying a model of what the student knows, and explaining expert reasoning.

The nature of MYCIN-like knowledge bases makes it reasonable to experiment with various teaching strategies. The representation of teaching expertise in GUIDON is intended to provide a flexible framework for such experimentation (Section 26.3). To illustrate the use of this framework in the first version of GUIDON, we present in this chapter two sample interactions and describe the domain knowledge and teaching strategies used by the program (Section 26.4 and Section 26.5). The sample interactions and rule listings were generated by the implemented program.

26.1 Description of the Knowledge Base

MYCIN's knowledge base of infectious diseases that we use for tutoring has been built over four years through interactions with physicians. It currently contains approximately 450 rules. In addition, there are several hundred facts and relations stored in tables, which are referenced by the rules. In this chapter, each precondition is called a *subgoal.* If all of the subgoals in the premise can be achieved (shown to be true), then a conclusion can be made about the goal in the action.

The tutoring system we are developing will also work with problems and rules in another domain, assuming some parallels between the structure of the knowledge in the new domain and the structure of the existing medical knowledge. Thus GUIDON is a multiple-domain tutorial program. The overall configuration of this system is shown in Figure 26-1. One advantage of this system is that a fixed set of teaching strategies can be tried in different domains, affording an important perspective on their generality. This method of integrating domain and teaching expertise is quite distinct from the design of early frame-oriented computer-aided instruction (CAI) systems. For example, in the tutor for infectious diseases by Feurzeig et al. (1964), medical and teaching expertise were "compiled" together into the branching structure of the frames (dialogue/content situations). In GUIDON, domain and teaching expertise are decoupled and stated explicitly.

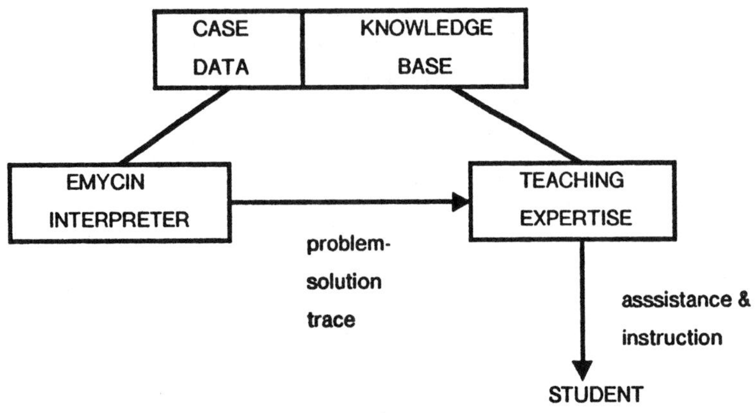

FIGURE 26-1 Modules for a multiple-domain tutorial system.

26.2 Development of a Tutorial Program Based on MYCIN-like Systems

In addition to the domain knowledge of the expert program, a tutorial program requires expertise about teaching, such as the ability to tailor the presentation of domain knowledge to a student's competence and interests (Brown and Goldstein, 1977). The GUIDON program, with its teaching expertise and augmented domain knowledge, is designed to be an active, intelligent agent that helps make the knowledge of MYCIN-like programs accessible to students.

With the original MYCIN system, it was clear that even rudimentary explanations of the system's reasoning could provide some instruction to users. For example, one can ask why case data are being sought by the program and how goals will be (were) achieved. However, we believe that this is an inefficient way for a student to learn the contents of the knowledge base. The MYCIN program is only a passive "teacher": it is necessary for the student to ask an exhaustive series of questions in order to discover all of the reasoning paths considered by the program. Moreover, the MYCIN program contains no model of the user, so program-generated explanations are never tailored to his or her competence or interests. On the other hand, GUIDON acts as an agent that keeps track of the knowledge that has been presented to the student in previous sessions and looks for opportunities to deepen and broaden the student's knowledge of MYCIN's expertise. GUIDON's teaching expertise includes capabilities to measure a student's competence and to use this measure as a basis for selecting knowledge to present. Some of the basic questions involved in converting a rule-based expert program into a tutorial program are:

- What kind of dialogue might be suitable for teaching the knowledge of MYCIN-like consultation systems?
- What strategies for teaching will be useful?
- Will these strategies be independent of the knowledge base content?
- How will they be represented?
- What additions to the performance knowledge of MYCIN-like systems might be useful in a tutorial program?

As the first step in approaching these questions, the following sections discuss some of the basic ways in which MYCIN's domain and formalism have influenced design considerations for GUIDON. Section 26.2.1 describes the nature of the dialogue we have chosen for tutorial sessions. Section 26.2.2 discusses the nature of MYCIN's performance knowledge and argues for including additional domain knowledge in the tutorial program. Sections 26.2.3 and 26.2.4 argue that the uncertainty of MYCIN's knowledge and the size of its knowledge base make it desirable to have a framework for experimenting with teaching strategies. This framework is presented in Section 26.3.

26.2.1 A Goal-Directed Case Dialogue

In a GUIDON tutorial session, a student plays the role of a physician consultant. A sick patient (the *case*) is described to the student in general terms: age, sex, race, and lab reports about cultures taken at the site of the infection. The student is expected to ask for other information that might be relevant to this case. For example, did the patient become infected while hospitalized? Did the patient ever live in the San Joaquin Valley? GUIDON compares the student's questions to those asked by MYCIN and critiques the student's line of reasoning. When the student draws hypotheses from the evidence collected, GUIDON compares these conclusions to those that MYCIN reached, given the same information about the patient. We refer to this dialogue between the student and GUIDON as a *case dialogue*. Because GUIDON attempts to transfer expertise to students exclusively through case dialogues, we call it a *case method tutor*.

GUIDON's purpose is to broaden the student's knowledge by pointing out inappropriate lines of reasoning and suggesting approaches the student did not consider. An important assumption is that the student has a suitable background for solving the case; he or she knows the vocabulary and the general form of the diagnostic task. The criterion for having learned MYCIN's problem-solving methods is therefore straightforward: when presented with novel, difficult cases, does the student seek relevant data and draw appropriate conclusions?

Helping the student solve the case is greatly aided by placing constraints on the case dialogue. A *goal-directed dialogue* is a discussion of the rules applied to achieve specific goals. In general, the topics of this dialogue are precisely those "goals" that are concluded by MYCIN rules.[1] During the dialogue, only one goal at a time is considered; data that cannot be used in rules to achieve this goal are "irrelevant." This is a strong constraint on the student's process of asking questions and making hypotheses. A goal-directed dialogue helps the tutor to follow the student as he or she solves the problem, increasing the chance that timely assistance can be provided.[2]

Our design of GUIDON has also been influenced by consideration of the expected sophistication of the students using it. We assume the students are well motivated and capable of a serious, mixed-initiative dialogue. Various features (not all described in this paper) make the program flexible, so that students can use their judgment to control the depth and detail of the discussion. These features include the capability to request:

- descriptions of all data relevant to a particular goal
- a subgoal tree for a goal
- a quiz or hint relevant to the current goal
- a concise summary of all evidence already discussed for a goal
- discussion of a goal (of the student's choice)
- conclusion of a discussion, with GUIDON finishing the collection of evidence for the goal and indicating conclusions that the student might have drawn

26.2.2 Single Form of Expertise

The problem of multiple forms of expertise has been important in ICAI research. For example, when mechanistic reasoning is involved, qualitative and quantitative forms of expertise may be useful to solve the problem (Brown et al., 1976). De Kleer has found that strategies for debugging an electronic circuit are "radically different" depending on whether one does local mathematical analysis or uses a higher-level, functional analysis of components (Brown et al., 1975). One might argue that a tutor for electronics should also be ready to recognize and generate arguments on both of these levels.[3]

For all practical purposes, GUIDON does not need to be concerned about multiple forms of expertise. This is primarily because reasoning in

[1]A typical sequence of (nested) goals is as follows: (a) reach a diagnosis, (b) determine which organisms might be causing the infection, (c) determine the type of infection, (d) determine if the infection has been partially treated, etc.

[2]Sleeman uses a similar approach for allowing a student to explore algorithms (Sleeman, 1977).

[3]See Carr and Goldstein (1977) for a related discussion.

infectious disease problem solving is based on judgments about empirical information, rather than on arguments based on causal mechanisms (Weiss et al., 1978). MYCIN's judgments are "cookbook" responses that address the data directly, as opposed to attempting to explain it in terms of physiological mechanisms. Moreover, the expertise to solve a MYCIN case on this level of abstraction constitutes a "closed" world (Carbonell and Collins, 1973): all of the objects, attributes, and values that are relevant to the solution of a case are determined by a MYCIN consultation that is performed before a tutorial session begins.[4]

Even though MYCIN's domain makes it possible for cases to be solved without recourse to the level of physiological mechanisms, a student may find it useful to know this support knowledge that lies behind the rules. Section 26.3.3 describes the domain knowledge we have added to MYCIN's performance knowledge in developing GUIDON.

26.2.3 Weak Model of Inquiry

Even though the MYCIN world can be considered to be closed, there is no strong model for ordering the collection of evidence.[5] Medical problem solving is still an art. While there are some conventions to ensure that all routine data are collected, physicians have no agreed-upon basis for numerically optimizing the decision of what to do next.[6] During a tutoring session, it is not only difficult to tell a student what is the "next best" piece of evidence to gather but also difficult to decide what to say about the evidence-gathering strategy. For example, when offering assistance, should the tutor suggest the domain rule that most confirms the evidence already collected or a rule that contradicts this evidence?[7]

26.2.4 Large Number of Rules

MYCIN provides to GUIDON an AND/OR tree of goals (the OR nodes) and rules (the AND nodes) that were pursued during consultation on a case. This tree constitutes a trace of the application of the knowledge base

[4]There is always the possibility that a student may present an exotic case to GUIDON that is beyond its expertise. While MYCIN has been designed to detect simple instances of this (i.e., evidence of an infection other than bacteremia or meningitis), we decided to restrict GUIDON tutorials to the physician-approved cases in the library (currently over 100 cases).

[5]In the WUMPUS program (Carr and Goldstein, 1977), for example, it is possible to rank each legal move (analogous to seeking case data in MYCIN) and so rate the student according to "rejected inferior moves" and "missed superior moves." The same analysis is possible in the WEST program (Burton, 1979).

[6]See, for example, Sprosty (1963).

[7]MYCIN's rules are not based on Bayesian probabilities, so it is not possible to use optimization techniques like those developed by Hartley et al. (1972). Arguments against using Bayes' Theorem in expert systems can be found in Chapter 11.

to the given case.[8] Many of the 450 rules are not tried because they conclude about goals that do not need to be pursued to solve the case. Hundreds of others fail to apply because one or more preconditions are not satisfied. Finally, 20% of the rules typically make conclusions that contribute varying degrees of belief about the goals pursued.

Thus MYCIN's interpreter provides the tutorial program with much information about the case solution (see Figure 26-1). It is not clear how to present this to a student. What should the tutor do when the student pursues a goal that MYCIN did not pursue? (Interrupt? Wait until the student realizes that the goal contributes no useful information?) Which dead-end search paths pursued by MYCIN should the tutor expect the student to consider? For many goals there are too many rules to discuss with the student; how is the tutor to decide which to present and which to omit? What techniques can be used to produce coherent plans for guiding the discussion through lines of reasoning used by the program? One solution is to have a framework that allows guiding the dialogue in different ways. The rest of this paper shows how GUIDON has been given this flexibility by viewing it as a discourse program.

26.3 A Framework for a Case Method Tutorial Program

One purpose of this tutorial project is to provide a framework for testing teaching methods. Therefore, we have chosen an implementation that makes it possible to vary the strategies that the tutor uses for guiding the dialogue. Using methods similar to those used in knowledge-based programs, we have formalized the tutorial program in rules and procedures that codify expertise for carrying on a case dialogue.

This section is a relatively abstract discussion of the kinds of knowledge needed to guide a discourse and the representation of that knowledge. The reader may find it useful to consider the sample dialogues in Figures 26-6 and 26-7 before proceeding.

[8]Before a tutorial session, GUIDON scans each rule used by MYCIN and compiles a list of all subgoals that needed to be achieved before the premise of the rule could be evaluated. In the case of a rule that failed to apply, GUIDON determines all preconditions of the premise that are false. By doing this, GUIDON's knowledge of the case is independent of the order in which questions were asked and rules were applied by MYCIN, so topics can be easily changed and the depth of discussion controlled flexibly by both GUIDON and the student. This process of automatically generating a solution trace for any case can be contrasted with SOPHIE's single, fixed, simulated circuit (Brown et al., 1976).

26.3.1 Discourse Knowledge

Our implementation of GUIDON's dialogue capabilities makes use of knowledge obtained from studies of discourse in AI (Bobrow et al., 1977; Bruce, 1975; Deutsch, 1974; Winograd, 1977). To quote Bruce (1975, emphasis added):

> [It is] . . . useful to have a model of how social interactions typically fit together, and thus a model of discourse structure. Such a model can be viewed as a heuristic which suggests likely *action sequences.* . . . There are places in a discourse where questions make sense, others where explanations are expected. [These paradigms] . . . facilitate generation and subsequent understanding.

Based on Winograd's analysis of discourse (Winograd, 1977), it appears desirable for a case method tutor to have the following forms of knowledge for carrying on a dialogue:

- Knowledge about *dialogue patterns.* Faught (1977) mentions two types of patterns: interpretation patterns (to understand a speaker), and action patterns (to generate utterances). GUIDON uses action patterns represented as *discourse procedures* for directing and focusing the case dialogue. These are the *action sequences* mentioned by Bruce. They are invoked by tutoring rules, discussed in Section 26.3.2.[9]
- Forms of *domain knowledge* for carrying on a specific dialogue. Section 26.3.3 surveys the augmented domain knowledge available to GUIDON.
- Knowledge of the *communication situation.* This includes the tutorial program's understanding of the student's intentions and knowledge, as well as the tutor's intentions for carrying on the dialogue. These components are represented in GUIDON by an *overlay student model* (in which the student's knowledge is viewed as a subset of the expert program's), a *lesson plan* (a plan of topics to be discussed, created by the tutor for each case), and a *focus record* (to keep track of factors in which the student has shown interest recently) (Section 26.3.4). Knowledge of the communication situation controls the use of dialogue patterns.

The following sections give details about these forms of knowledge.

---

[9]Because of the constraints a goal-directed dialogue imposes on the student, we have not found it necessary to use interpretation patterns at this time. They might be useful to follow the student's reasoning in a dialogue that is not goal-directed.

26.3.2 Dialogue Patterns: Discourse Procedures and Tutoring Rules

The sequences of actions in discourse procedures serve as an ordered list of options—types of remarks for the program to consider making. For example, the procedure for discussing a domain rule (hereafter, d-rule) includes a step that indicates to "consider mentioning d-rules related to the one just discussed." Thus a discourse procedure step specifies in a schematic form *when* a type of remark might be appropriate. *Whether* to take the option (e.g., is there an "interesting" d-rule to mention?) and *what* to say exactly (the discourse pattern for mentioning the d-rule) will be dynamically determined by tutoring rules (hereafter, t-rules) whose preconditions refer to the student model, case lesson plan, and focus record (hereafter referred to jointly as the communication model).

T-rules are generally invoked as a *packet* to achieve some tutorial goal.[10] T-rule packets are of two types:

1. *T-rules for accumulating belief.* Updating the communication model and determining how "interesting" a topic is are two examples.[11] Generally, a packet of t-rules of this type is applied exhaustively.
2. *T-rules for selecting a discourse procedure to follow.* Generally, a packet of this type stops trying t-rules when the first one succeeds. The form of t-rules of this type is shown in Figure 26-2. Knowledge referenced in the premise part of a t-rule of this type is described in subsequent sections. The action part of these t-rules consists of stylized code, just like the steps of a discourse procedure.[12] A step may invoke:
   a. a packet of t-rules, e.g., to select a question format for presenting a given d-rule
   b. a discourse procedure, e.g., to discuss sequentially each precondition of a d-rule
   c. a primitive function, e.g., to accept a question from the student, perform bookkeeping, etc.

Below is an outline of the t-rules currently implemented in GUIDON. Except where noted, examples of these t-rules are presented in discussions of the sample tutorial dialogues in this chapter.

---

[10]Packets are implemented as stylized Interlisp procedures. This should be contrasted with the interpreter used by the expert program that invokes d-rules directly, indexing them according to the goal that needs to be determined.

[11]GUIDON uses MYCIN's certainty factors (Chapter 11) for representing the program's belief in an assertion.

[12]Discourse procedure steps also contain control information (e.g., for iteration) that is not important to this discussion.

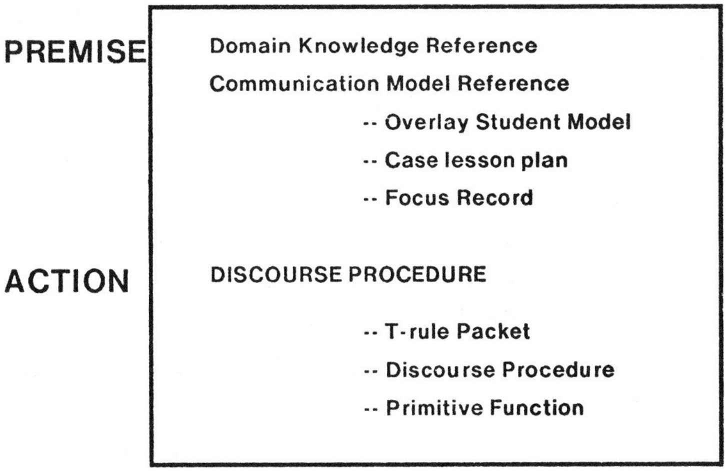

PREMISE	Domain Knowledge Reference Communication Model Reference -- Overlay Student Model -- Case lesson plan -- Focus Record
ACTION	DISCOURSE PROCEDURE -- T-rule Packet -- Discourse Procedure -- Primitive Function

FIGURE 26-2 Form of a tutorial rule for selecting a discourse procedure.

1. T-rules for selecting discourse patterns
   a. guiding discussion of a d-rule
   b. responding to a student hypothesis
   c. choosing question formats
2. T-rules for choosing domain knowledge
   a. providing orientation for pursuing new goals (not demonstrated in this paper)
   b. measuring interestingness of d-rules
3. T-rules for maintaining the communication model
   a. updating the overlay model when d-rules fire
   b. updating the overlay model during hypothesis evaluation
   c. creating a lesson plan (not implemented)

All t-rules are translated by a program directly from the Interlisp source code, using an extension of the technique used for translating MYCIN's rules. This accounts for some of the stilted prose in the examples that follow.

I. META-LEVEL ABSTRACTIONS:	rule models rule schemata	
II. PERFORMANCE:	rules lists and tables	
III. SUPPORT:	definitions mechanism descriptions justifications literature references	

FIGURE 26-3 Organization of domain knowledge into three tiers.

26.3.3 Augmented Representation of Domain Knowledge

The representation of domain knowledge available to GUIDON can be organized in three tiers, as shown in Figure 26-3. Subsequent subsections briefly describe the components of each tier, starting with the middle one.

Performance Tier

The performance knowledge consists of all the rules and tables used by MYCIN to make goal-directed conclusions about the initial case data. The output of the consultation is passed to the tutor: an extensive AND/OR tree of traces showing which rules were applied, their conclusions, and the case data required to apply them. GUIDON fills in this tree by determining which subgoals appear in the rules. In Figure 26-4 COVERFOR signifies the goal to determine which organisms should be "covered" by a therapy recommendation; d-rule 578, shown in Figure 26-5, concludes about this goal; BURNED is a subgoal of this rule.

Tutorial rules make frequent reference to this data structure in order to guide the dialogue. For example, the response to the request for help shown in Figure 26-6 (line 17) is based first of all on the rules that were used by MYCIN for the current goal. Similarly, the t-rules for supplying the case data requested by the student check to see if MYCIN asked for the same information, e.g., the WBC (white blood count) in the sample

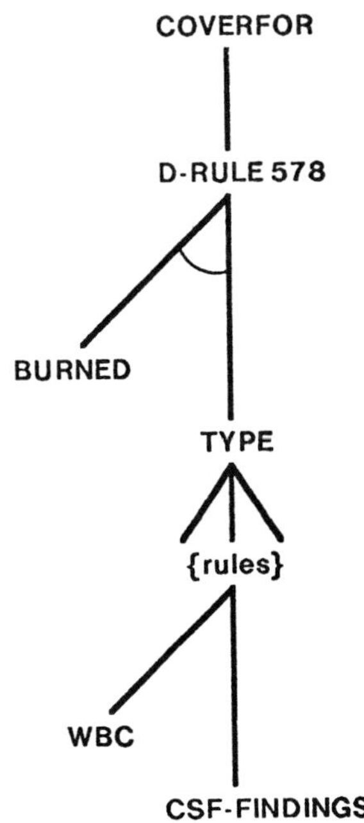

FIGURE 26-4 The portion of the AND/OR tree of goals and rules created by the expert program that is relevant to the dialogue shown in Figure 26-6. Figure 26-5 shows the contents of d-rule 578.

dialogue of Figure 26-6.[13] Associated documentation for d-rule 578 is also shown in Figure 26-5.

Support Tier

The support tier of the knowledge base consists of annotations to the rules and the factors used by them.[14] For example, there are "canned-text" descriptions of every laboratory test in the MYCIN domain, including, for instance, remarks about how the test should be performed. Mechanism descriptions provided by the domain expert are used to provide some explanation of a rule beyond the canned text of the justification. For the infectious disease domain of MYCIN, they indicate how a given factor leads

[13]Other possibilities include: the question is not relevant to the current goal; the case data can be deduced by definition from other known data; or a d-rule indicates that the requested data are not relevant to this case.

[14]Rule justifications, author, and edit date were first proposed by Davis (1976) as knowledge base maintenance records.

Abstraction Level

RULE-SCHEMA: MENINGITIS.COVERFOR.CLINICAL
RULE-MODEL: COVERFOR-IS-MODEL
KEY-FACTOR: BURNED
DUAL: D-RULE577

Performance Level

D-RULE578

IF: 1) The infection which requires therapy is meningitis, and
2) Organisms were not seen on the stain of the culture, and
3) The type of the infection is bacterial, and
4) The patient has been seriously burned
THEN: There is suggestive evidence (.5) that pseudomonas-aeruginosa is one of the organisms (other than those seen on cultures or smears) which might be causing the infection

UPDATES: COVERFOR
USES: (TREATINF ORGSEEN TYPE BURNED)

Support Level

MECHANISM-FRAME: BODY-INFRACTION.WOUNDS
JUSTIFICATION: "For a very brief period of time after a severe burn the surface of the wound is sterile. Shortly thereafter, the area becomes colonized by a mixed flora in which gram-positive organisms predominate. By the 3rd post-burn day this bacterial population becomes dominated by gram-negative organisms. By the 5th day these organisms have invaded tissue well beneath the surface of the burn. The organisms most commonly isolated from burn patients are Pseudomonas, Klebsiella-Enterobacter, Staph., etc. Infection with Pseudomonas is frequently fatal."
LITERATURE: MacMillan BG: Ecology of Bacteria Colonizing the Burned Patient Given Topical and System Gentamicin Therapy: a five-year study, J Infect Dis 124:278-286, 1971.
AUTHOR: Dr. Victor Yu
LAST-CHANGE: Sept. 8, 1976

FIGURE 26-5 Domain rule 578 and its associated documentation. (All information is provided by a domain expert, except for the key factor, which is computed by the tutor from the rule schema and contents of the particular rule. See third subsection of Section 26.3.3.)

to a particular infection with particular organisms by stating the origin of the organism and the favorable conditions for its growth at the site of the infection. Thus the frame associated with the factor "a seriously burned patient" shows that the organisms originate in the air and grow in the exposed tissue of a burn, resulting in a frequently fatal infection.

Abstraction Tier

The abstraction tier of the knowledge base represents patterns in the performance knowledge. For example, a rule schema is a description of a *kind* of rule: a pattern of preconditions that appears in the premise, the goal concluded, and the context of its application. The schema and a canned-text annotation of its significance are formalized in the MYCIN knowledge base by a physician expert. This schema is used by the tutor to "subtract off" the rule preconditions common to all rules of the type, leaving behind the factors that are specific to this particular rule, i.e., the *key factors* of this rule. Thus the key factor of d-rule 578 (see Figure 26-5), the fact that the patient has been seriously burned, was determined by removing the "contextual" information of the name of the infection, whether organisms were seen, and the type of the infection. (Examples of the use of key factors occur throughout the hypothesis evaluation example in Figure 26-7, particularly lines 4–9.)

Rule models (Davis, 1976) are program-generated patterns that represent the typical clusters of factors in the expert's rules. Unlike rule schemata, rule models do not necessarily correspond to domain concepts, although they do represent factors that tend to appear together in domain arguments (rules). For example, the gram stain of an organism and its morphology tend to appear together in rules for determining the identity of an organism. Because rule models capture the factors that most commonly appear in rules for pursuing a goal, they are valuable as a form of orientation for naive students.

Use of Meta-Knowledge in Tutorial Rules

Meta-knowledge of the representation and application of d-rules plays an important role in t-rules. For example, in the dialogue excerpt shown in Figure 26-6 GUIDON uses function templates[15] to "read" d-rule 578 and discovers that the type of the infection is a subgoal that needs to be completed before the d-rule can be applied. This capability to examine the domain knowledge and reason about its use enables GUIDON to make multiple use of any given production rule during the tutorial session. Here are some uses we have implemented:

- examine the rule (if it was tried in the consultation) and determine what subgoals needed to be achieved before it could be applied; if the rule failed to apply, determine all possible ways this could be determined (perhaps more than one precondition is false)
- examine the state of application of the rule during a tutorial interaction (what more needs to be done before it can be applied?) and choose an appropriate method of presentation
- generate different questions for the student
- use the rule (and variations of it) to understand a student's hypothesis
- summarize arguments using the rule by extracting the key point it addresses

[15]A function's template "indicates the order and generic type of the arguments in a typical call of that function" (see Chapter 28).

The ability to use domain knowledge in multiple ways is an important feature of a "generative" tutor like GUIDON.[16] Flexible use of knowledge permits us to write a variety of tutoring rules that select and present teaching material in multiple ways. This is important because we want to use the MYCIN/GUIDON system for experimenting with teaching strategies.

26.3.4 Components of the Communication Model

The components of the communication model are

1. an overlay student model,
2. a case lesson plan, and
3. a focus record.

The Overlay Student Model

The d-rules that were fired during the consultation associated with the given case are run in a forward direction as the student is given case data.[17] In this way, GUIDON knows at every moment what the expert program would conclude based on the evidence available to the student. We make use of knowledge about the history and competence of the student to form hypotheses about which of the expert's conclusions are probably known to the student. This has been termed an *overlay model* of the student by Goldstein, because the student's knowledge is modeled in terms of a subset and simple variations of the expert rule base (Goldstein, 1977). Our work was originally motivated by the structural model used in the WEST system (Burton and Brown, 1982).

Special t-rules for updating the overlay model are invoked whenever the expert program successfully applies a d-rule. These t-rules must decide whether the student has reached the same conclusion. This decision is based on:

- the inherent complexity of the d-rule (e.g., some rules are trivial definitions, others have involved iterations),
- whether the tutor believes that the student knows how to achieve the subgoals that appear in the d-rule (factors that require the application of rules),
- background of the student (e.g, year of medical school, intern, etc.), and
- evidence gathered in previous interactions with the student.

---

[16]Generative CAI programs select and transform domain knowledge in order to generate individualized teaching material. See Koffman and Blount (1973) for discussion.

[17]This is one application of the problem solution trace. The structure of this trace permits the program to repetitively reconsider d-rules (indexing them by the case data referenced in the premise part), without the high cost of reinterpreting premises from scratch.

These considerations are analogous to those used by Carr and Goldstein for the WUMPUS tutor (Carr and Goldstein, 1977).

The Case Lesson Plan

Before a human tutor discusses a case with a student, he or she has an idea of what should be discussed, given the constraints of time and the student's interests and capabilities. Similarly, in later versions of GUIDON a lesson plan will be generated before each case session.[18] We'd like the lesson plan to give GUIDON a global sense about the value of discussing particular topics, especially since the depth of emphasis will impact on the student's understanding of the problem's solution. The lesson plan of the type we are proposing provides consistency and goal-directedness to the tutor's presentations.

The lesson plan will be derived from:

- The student model: where does the student need instruction?
- Professed student interests (perhaps the case was chosen because of features the student wants to know more about)
- Intrinsic importance of topics: what part does this information play in understanding the solution of the problem?
- Extrinsic importance of topics: given the universe of cases, how interesting is this topic? (A datum that is rarely available is probably worth mentioning when it is known, no matter how insignificant the evidence it contributes.)

We believe that these considerations will also be useful for implementing automatic selection of cases from the consultation library.

The Focus Record

The purpose of the focus record is to maintain continuity during the dialogue. It consists of a set of global variables that are set when the student asks about particular goals and values for goals. T-rules reference these variables when selecting d-rules to mention or when motivating a change in the goal being discussed. An example is provided in Section 26.4.1.

---

[18]Goldstein's "syllabus" and BIP's "Curriculum Information Network" are fixed networks that relate skills in terms of their complexities and dependencies. The lesson plan discussed here is a program-generated plan for guiding discussion of a particular problem with a particular student. We believe that a skill network relating MYCIN's rules will be useful for constructing dialogue plans.

26.4 T-Rules for Guiding Discussion of a Goal

In this section we consider an excerpt from a dialogue and some of the discourse procedures and tutoring rules involved. Suppose that a first-year medical student has just read about treatment for burned patients suspected to have a meningitis infection. His microbiology text mentioned several organisms, but it wasn't clear to him how other factors such as the age and degree of sickness of the patient might affect diagnosis of an actual case. GUIDON is available to him, so he decides to ask the program to select a relevant case from the MYCIN library for a tutorial session.

The program begins by invoking the discourse procedure CASE-DISCUSSION. One of the first steps is to choose a case. At this point the student described the case he wanted using keywords ("burned meningitis patient").[19] GUIDON selected the case and set the scene for the student. There is one pending culture from the CSF (cerebral spinal fluid, where meningitis infections occur). In the excerpt in Figure 26-6, the dialogue has reached the subtask of determining the organisms that might be causing the infection.

When the student requested help (line 17), the program had been following the pattern for discussing a goal. The request for help led to the invocation of tutoring rules. The teaching strategy represented by these t-rules is to provide help for a goal by suggesting a d-rule to the student. The discourse procedure that provides help in this context first invokes a packet of t-rules that will choose a d-rule to mention to the student. The second step is to invoke a packet of t-rules that will choose a presentation method.

26.4.1 Choosing a D-Rule to Mention in Order to Provide Help for a Goal

D-rule 578 (Figure 26-5) was chosen because it became the focus of the discussion when the student asked about the relevance of the "burned" factor. That is, when the student asked the question in line 8, a variable was set to indicate that the most recent factor referred to for this goal was "burned" (the focus topic). Then when the packet of t-rules for choosing a d-rule to present was invoked, the following t-rule succeeded:[20]

---

[19]Student input to the GUIDON program is in the form of menu options and simple English phrases that are parsed using keyword analysis and pattern-matching routines developed for MYCIN's question-answering module (see Chapter 18).

[20]T-rule numbers are of the form <procedure number that invokes the rule>.<index of the rule>. Thus t-rule 26.03 is the third rule in discourse procedure number 26.

You should now proceed to ask questions that will enable you to make a hypothesis about the organisms (other than those seen on cultures or smears) which might be causing the infection.

{Initiative is given to the student; he or she may ask for more data, make a hypothesis, or use a special option.}

**** HOW IS THE FACT THAT THE PATIENT IS BURNED RELEVANT?**

{One option is to ask how a piece of data is relevant to the current goal.}

The fact that patient-326 is seriously burned will be used to conclude that pseudomonas-aeruginosa is one of the organisms which might be present (in addition to those seen on cultures or smears) [Rule 578].

**** HELP**

{The HELP option is a request for assistance: the student asks "where do I go from here?"}

Try to determine the type of the infection: bacterial, fungal, viral, or Tb.

{To provide help, GUIDON chose: (1) a rule to discuss (d-rule 578 was chosen because the dialogue just focused on it); and (2) a method of presentation—"tell the student to finish incomplete subgoals mentioned in the rule." Thus, a new topic is set up, "the type of the infection." Initiative is returned to the student. . . . }

**** WHAT IS THE PATIENT'S WBC?**

The white count from the patient's peripheral CBC is 1.9 thousand.

{The tutor observes that this question is relevant to the new topic and provides the requested data. The dialogue continues in this goal-directed manner . . . }

FIGURE 26-6 Sample interaction: gathering data. Input from the student follows double asterisks; annotations appear in italics within curly brackets. Lines are numbered for reference within the text.

T-RULE26.03

IF: The recent context of the dialogue mentioned either a "deeper subgoal" or a factor relevant to the current goal

THEN: Define the focus rule to be the d-rule that mentions this focus topic

This example illustrates how the communication model guides the session by controlling t-rules. Often there is no obvious d-rule to suggest to the student. It is then useful for the tutor to have some measure of the interestingness of a d-rule at this time in the discussion. The t-rules presented below are applied to a set of d-rule candidates, ranking them by how strongly the tutor believes that they are interesting.

Change in Belief Is Interesting

One measure of interest is the contribution the d-rule would make to what is currently known about the goal being discussed. If the d-rule contributes evidence that raises the certainty of the determined value of the goal to more than 0.2, we say that the value of the goal is now significant.[21] This contribution of evidence is especially interesting because it depends on what evidence has already been considered.

As is true for all t-rules, this determination is a heuristic, which will benefit from experimentation. In t-rule 25.01 we have attempted to capture the intuitive notion that, in general, change in belief is interesting: the more drastic the change, the more interesting the effect. The numbers in the conclusion of t-rule 25.01 are certainty factors that indicate our belief in this interestingness.

T-RULE25.01

IF: The effect of applying the d-rule on the current value of the goal has been determined
THEN: The "value interest" of this d-rule depends on the effect of applying the d-rule as follows:
a. if the value contributed is still insignificant then .05
b. if a new insignificant value is contributed then .05
c. if a new significant value is contributed then .50
d. if a significant value is confirmed then .70
e. if a new strongly significant value is contributed then .75
f. if an insignificant value becomes significant then .80
g. if an old value is now insignificant then .85
h. if belief in an old value is strongly contradicted then .90

Use of Special Facts or Relations Is Interesting

In contrast to that in t-rule 25.01, the measure of interest in t-rule 25.06 below is static. We'd like to make sure that the student knows the information in tables used by the expert program, so we give special consideration to a d-rule that references a table.

T-RULE25.06

IF: The d-rule mentions a static table in its premise
THEN: Define the "content interest" to be .50

26.4.2 Guiding Discussion of a D-Rule

Returning to our example, after selecting d-rule 578, the tutor needed to select a method for presenting it. The following t-rule was successfully applied:

---

[21]For example, if the goal is the "organism causing the infection" and the certainty associated with the value "pseudomonas" is 0.3, then this value is significant.

T-RULE2.04

IF: 1) The number of factors appearing in the d-rule which need to be asked by the student is zero, and
2) The number of subgoals remaining to be determined before the d-rule can be applied is equal to 1

THEN: Substep i. Say: subgoal-suggestion
Substep ii. Discuss the goal with the student in a goal-directed mode [Proc001]
Substep iii. Wrap up the discussion of the rule being considered [Proc017]

The premise of this t-rule indicates that all preconditions of the d-rule can be evaluated, save one, and this d-rule precondition requires that other d-rules be considered. The action part of this t-rule is a sequence of actions to be followed, i.e., a discourse pattern. In particular, substep (i) resulted in the program printing "try to determine the type of the infection . . . " (line 22).[22] The discourse procedure invoked by substep (ii) will govern discussion of the type of the infection (in simple terms, a new context is set up for interpreting student questions and use of options). After the type of the infection is discussed (relevant data are collected and hypotheses drawn), the tutor will direct the dialogue to a discussion of the conclusion to be drawn from d-rule 578.

Other methods for suggesting a d-rule are possible and are selected by other t-rules in the packet that contains t-rule 2.04. For example, the program could simply tell the student the conclusion of the d-rule (if the d-rule can be evaluated based on data currently available to the student), or quiz the student about the d-rule, or sequentially discuss each precondition of the d-rule, and so on.

26.5 T-Rules for Responding to a Student's Hypothesis

A student's hypothesis provides the tutor with considerable evidence about the student's knowledge of the d-rules. It is an excellent opportunity for the tutor to update the model of the student's understanding and use that model to make instructive remarks. The chief strategy behind the tutorial remarks illustrated in Figure 26-7 is to state evidence directly, or to use simple true-false questions when the overlay model shows that student is probably ignorant of the rules to apply (lines 10–16), or otherwise to use fill-in and multiple choice questions that are intended to "entrap" the stu-

[22]"Say <label>" designates something the program will "say" to the student. The label is useful for debugging, because every print statement is uniquely labeled.

{After presentation of relevant case data . . . }

**** I THINK THAT THE ORGANISMS PRESENT ARE DIPLOCOCCUS-PNEUMONIAE, PSEUDOMONAS-AERUGINOSA, AND NEISSERIA-MENINGITIDIS.**

Good. The age of the patient gives evidence for concluding that Diplococcus-Pneumoniae might be present (Rule 507). The fact that the patient has been seriously burned is good reason to suspect Pseudomonas-Aeruginosa (Rule 578). Both conclusions apply because the infection which requires therapy is meningitis, no organisms were seen on a gram stain of the culture, and the type of the infection is bacterial.

The age of the patient also leads one to suspect Neisseria-Meningitidis (Rule 507). Do the fact that the infection was acquired while the patient was hospitalized and information about the diseases to which the patient has been exposed support this conclusion?

**** NO**

Right, this would be good reason to rule out Neisseria-Meningitidis (Rule 561).

What facts about this case tell you that the organisms that might be present are: E.Coli and Klebsiella-Pneumoniae?

**** HELP**

{The student was expected to describe each factor with a phrase, one per line. Help is provided by listing all relevant factors for the current goal.}

Choose from:

1. The patient does not have a TB risk factor and the patient's x-ray is not abnormal
2. Otitis-media and Epiglottitis are not among the diagnoses which are consistent with the patient's clinical history
3. The white count from the patient's peripheral CBC is less than 2.5 thousand
4. The infection was acquired while the patient was hospitalized
5. The patient has been seriously burned
6. None of these

**** 1 3 4** *{This question was a form of "entrapment." Notice that the choices all appear in Figure 26-8.}*

You're right about the WBC (Rule 557) and the evidence gained from the fact that the infection was acquired while the patient was hospitalized (Rule 545). However, the fact that the patient does not have a TB risk factor and the patient's x-ray is not abnormal is weak evidence that Mycobacterium-TB is not one of the organisms which might be present (Rule 160).

FIGURE 26-7 Sample interaction continued: hypothesis evaluation.

dent (lines 17–32). "Entrapment," as used here, involves forcing the student to make a choice that will reveal some aspect of his or her understanding.[23] In this example, all choices listed (lines 24–32) actually

[23]Many of GUIDON's question-asking strategies resemble the "Socratic" strategies formalized by Collins (1976), probably because our production rule representation of domain knowledge makes it convenient to think in terms of "relevant factors" for determining the "value of a goal" (terms we share with Collins). However, the relation between factor and goal in MYCIN is not necessarily causal as it is in the network representation used by Collins.

appear in rules applied by MYCIN (see Figure 26-8). When the student wrongly chose number 1 ("no TB risk factor and no abnormal x-ray"), GUIDON indicated how that evidence actually was used by MYCIN.

26.5.1 Updating the Overlay Student Model After a Student Hypothesis

Figure 26-8 illustrates how the overlay model is updated for the hypothesis in line 1 of Figure 26-7. T-rules are invoked to determine how strongly the tutor believes that the student has taken each of the relevant d-rules into account. That is, a packet of t-rules (packet number 6 here) is tried in the context of each d-rule. Those t-rules that succeed will modify the cumulative belief that the given d-rule was considered by the student. T-rule 6.05 succeeded when applied to d-rules 545 and 557. The student mentioned a value (PSEUDOMONAS) that they conclude (clause 1 of the t-rule) but missed others (clause 3). Moreover, the student did not mention values that can *only* be concluded by these d-rules (clause 2), so the overall evidence that these d-rules were considered is weak (−0.70).[24]

T-RULE6.05

IF: 1) The hypothesis does include values that can be concluded by this d-rule, as well as others, and
2) The hypothesis does not include values that can only be concluded by this d-rule, and
3) Values concluded by the d-rule are missing in the hypothesis
THEN: Define the belief that the d-rule was considered to be −.70

After each of the d-rules applied by MYCIN is considered independently, a second pass is made to look for patterns. Two judgmental tutorial rules from this second rule packet are shown below. T-rule 7.01 applied to d-rule 578: of the d-rules that conclude *Pseudomonas,* this is the only one that is believed to have been considered, thus increasing our belief that d-rule 578 was used by the student. T-rule 7.05 applies to d-rules 545 and 561: the factor NOSOCOMIAL appears only in their premises, and they are not believed to have been considered. This is evidence that NOSOCOMIAL was not considered by the student, increasing our belief that each of the d-rules that mention it were not considered.

T-RULE7.01

IF: You believe that this domain rule was considered, it concludes a value present in the student's hypothesis, and no other rule that mentions this value is believed to have been considered
THEN: Modify the cumulative belief that this rule was considered by .40

T-RULE7.05

IF: This domain rule contains a factor that appears in several rules, none of which are believed to have been considered to make the hypothesis
THEN: Modify the cumulative belief that this rule was considered by −.30

---

[24]The certainty factor of −0.70 was chosen by the author. Experience with MYCIN shows that the precise value is not important, but the scale from −1 to 1 should be used consistently.

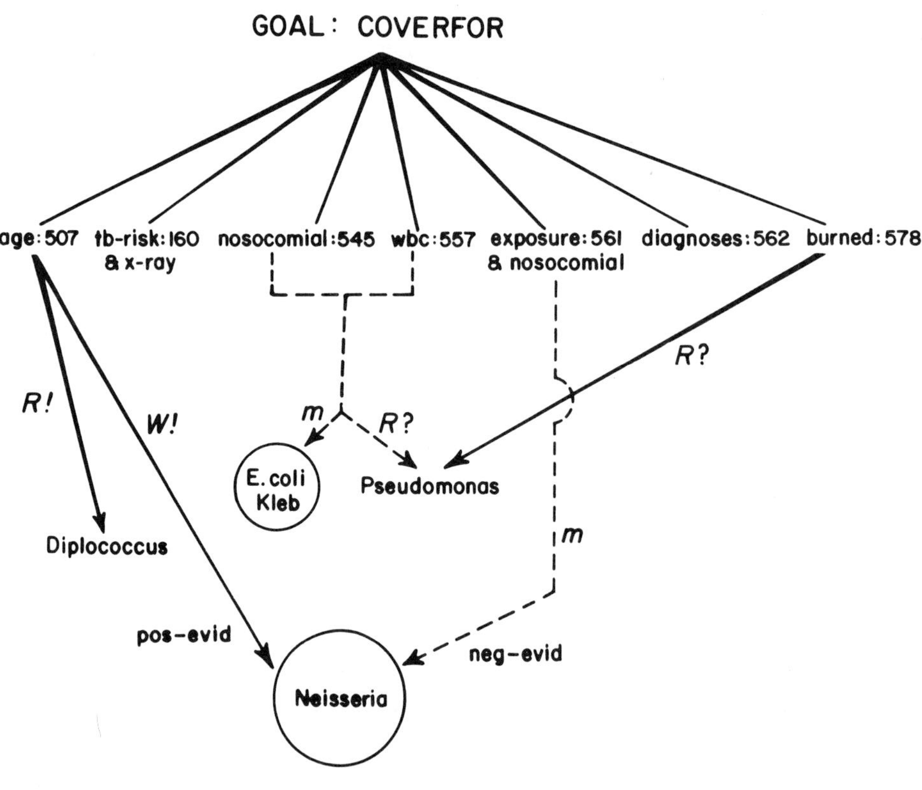

FIGURE 26-8 **Interpreting a student hypothesis in terms of expert rules. Key: D-rules that conclude about organisms to cover for are shown with their key factors (see Figure 26-5). Circled values are missing from the student's hypothesis (e.g., E.coli) or wrongly stated (e.g., Neisseria). Dotted lines lead from rules the student probably did not use. Also, *m* = evidence link that the tutor deduced is unknown to the student; *R* and *W* = links to right and wrong values that the tutor believes are known by the student; *!* = unique link, expert knows of no other evidence at this time; *?* = questionable, tutor isn't certain which evidence was considered by the student. For example, *R?* means that the student stated this value, it is correct, and more than one d rule supplies evidence for it.**

Future improvements to this overlay model will make it possible to recognize student behavior that can be explained by simple variations of the expert's d-rules:

1. *Variation in the premise of a d-rule:* The student is using a d-rule that fails

to apply or applies a successful d-rule prematurely (is misinformed about case data or is confused about the d-rule's premise).

2. *Variation in the action of a d-rule:* The student draws the wrong conclusion (wrong value and/or degree of certainty).

26.5.2 Presentation Methods for D-Rules the Student Did Not Consider

Returning to our example, after updating the overlay model, the tutor needs to deal with discrepancies between the student's hypothesis and what the expert program knows. The following t-rules are from a packet that determines how to present a d-rule that the student evidently did not consider. The tutor applies the first tutorial rule that is appropriate. In our example, t-rule 9.02 generated the question shown in lines 10–14 of Figure 26-7. T-rule 9.03 (a default rule) generated the question shown in lines 17–32.

T-RULE9.01

IF: 1) The d-rule is not on the lesson plan for this case, and
2) Based on the overlay model, the student is ignorant about the d-rule
THEN: Affirm the conclusions made by the d-rule by simply stating the key factors and values to be concluded

T-RULE9.02

IF: The goal currently being discussed is a true/false parameter
THEN: Generate a question about the d-rule using "facts" format in the premise part and "actual value" format in the action part

T-RULE9.03

IF: True
THEN: Generate a question about the d-rule using "fill-in" format in the premise part and "actual value" format in the action part

26.5.3 Choosing Question Formats

When the tutor responds to a hypothesis, the context of the dialogue generally determines which question format is appropriate. However, during other dialogue situations it is not always clear which format to use (e.g., when quizzing the student about a rule that MYCIN has just applied using case data just given to the student). Our strategy is to apply special t-rules to determine which formats are logically valid for a given d-rule, and then to choose randomly from the candidates.

T-rule 3.06 is part of a packet of t-rules that chooses an appropriate format for a question based on a given d-rule. The procedure for formatting a question is to choose templates for the action part and premise part that are compatible with each other and the d-rule itself.

T-RULE3.06

IF: 1) The action part of the question is not "wrong value," and
2) The action part of the question is not "multiple choice," and
3) Not all of the factors in the premise of the d-rule are true/false parameters
THEN: Include "multiple choice" as a possible format for the premise part of the question

T-rule 3.06 says that if the program is going to present a conclusion that differs from that in the d-rule it is quizzing about, it should not state the premise as a multiple choice. Also, it would be nonsensical to state both the premise and action in multiple-choice form. (This would be a matching question—it is treated as another question type.) Clause 3 of this t-rule is necessary because it is nonsensical to make a multiple-choice question when the only choices are true and false.

As can be seen here, the choice of a question type is based on purely logical properties of the rule and interactions among question formats. About 20 question types (combined premise/conclusion formats) are possible in the current implementation.

26.6 Concluding Remarks

We have argued in this chapter that it is desirable to add teaching expertise and other levels of domain knowledge to MYCIN-like expert programs if they are to be used for education. Furthermore, it is advantageous to provide a flexible framework for experimenting with teaching strategies, for we do not know the best methods for presenting MYCIN-like rules to a student.

The framework of the GUIDON program includes knowledge of discourse patterns and the means for determining their applicability. The discourse patterns we have codified into procedures permit GUIDON to carry on a mixed-initiative, goal-directed case method dialogue in multiple domains. These patterns are invoked by tutoring rules, which are in turn controlled by a communication model. The components of this model are a lesson plan (topics the tutor plans to discuss), an overlay model (domain knowledge the tutor believes is being considered by the student), and a focus record (topics recently mentioned in the dialogue). Finally, we observed that meta-knowledge about the representation and use of domain rules made it possible to use these rules in a variety of ways during the dialogue. This is important because GUIDON's capability to reason flexibly about domain knowledge appears to be directly related to its capability to guide the dialogue in multiple, interesting ways.

Furthermore, we have augmented the performance knowledge of MYCIN-like systems by making use of support knowledge and meta-level abstractions in the dialogue. The problem-solving trace provided by the interpreter is augmented by GUIDON to enable it to plan dialogues (by looking ahead to see what knowledge is needed to solve the problem) and to carry on flexible dialogues (by being able to switch the discussion at any time to any portion of the AND/OR solution tree).

Early experience with this program has shown that the tutor must be selective about its choice of topics if the dialogues are not to be overly tedious and complicated. That is, it is desirable for tutorial rules to exert a great deal of control over which discourse options are taken. We believe that it is chiefly in selection of topics and emphasis of discussion that the "intelligence" of this tutor resides.

PART NINE

Augmenting the Rules

27

Additional Knowledge Structures

We have so far described MYCIN largely in terms of its knowledge base and inference mechanism, and specifically in terms of rules and a rule interpreter that allow high-performance problem solving. In Chapters 27 through 29 we describe additional knowledge structures that increase the flexibility and transparency of MYCIN's knowledge base. We refer to many of these as *meta-level knowledge.*

When we speak of meta-level knowledge we mean nothing more than knowledge *about* knowledge. In a computer program it needs to be represented and interpreted in order to be useful, but the main idea is that it can be an explicit, and flexible, element of expertise. For example, meta-level knowledge can help in modifying an existing rule and in integrating the modification into the whole rule set because it provides additional information about the existing rules to the editor.

The ideas for using meta-level knowledge in MYCIN grew out of several projects that Randy Davis was working on in the mid-1970s. In the context of knowledge acquisition, we had found that the simple rule editor needed more knowledge about the structure and contents of the rules and about the representations of objects (contexts). In the context of explanation, we found that the predicates (such as SAME) used in rules could be matched to keywords in questions much more easily if the structure of the predicates were known to MYCIN. And, in the context of controlling MYCIN's inferences, we saw that rules *about* MYCIN's rules could provide an element of control. Davis was working on solutions to these problems and saw that the common thread that bound these different parts of the TEIRESIAS system together was meta-level knowledge.

Our first instances of domain-independent meta-level reasoning were (a) the unity path mechanism, by which MYCIN checks for a chain of inferences known to be true with certainty (CF = 1.0) before evaluating other rules, and (b) the preview mechanism, by which MYCIN looked over the clauses of a rule before exhaustively evaluating them to see if the conjunction of premise clauses was already falsified by virtue of any clause already known to be false (or not "true enough"). In both instances, MYCIN is reasoning *about* its rules before executing them. The important difference between these mechanisms and the meta-knowledge that evolved from work by Davis is that the former are buried in the code of the rule interpreter and thus are not open to examination by other parts of the system, or by the user. After these initial meta-level reasoning techniques were added to the rule interpreter, however, Davis was careful to separate any additional meta-level knowledge structures from the editor, explanation generator, and interpreter, just as we had done with the (object-level) medical knowledge. As a result, the new system (MYCIN plus TEIRESIAS) contains considerably more knowledge about its own knowledge structures than did MYCIN alone. Many of these ideas have subsequently been incorporated into EMYCIN. Chapter 28 provides a summary of the knowledge structures used by TEIRESIAS for knowledge acquisition (see Chapter 9) and control of MYCIN's inferences. This was a line of development that was not anticipated in DENDRAL,[1] and its systematic treatment by Davis in his dissertation was an advance for AI.

Bill Clancey was working on GUIDON at about the same time and was discovering that additional knowledge structures, including meta-level knowledge, were essential for tutoring. TEIRESIAS' knowledge about the form and contents of MYCIN's rules was certainly helpful in constructing GUIDON, but Clancey began focusing more on representing MYCIN's *strategies*. In the course of his research, he also uncovered the importance of two additional kinds of knowledge: knowledge about the *structure* of the domain (and thus about the structure of the rule set), and *support* knowledge that justifies individual rules. Chapter 29 is a careful analysis of these three types of meta-level knowledge that Clancey terms "strategic, structural and support knowledge." This analysis was written in 1981–1982 (and published in 1983) and thus is a recent critique of the structure of MYCIN's knowledge base. We were not unaware of many of the issues raised here, but Clancey provides a coherent framework for thinking about them.

27.1 The Context Tree

In the original (1974) version of MYCIN, several knowledge structures had already been added to the basic rule representation, as discussed in Chapter 5. Most notable among these was the context tree, in which we encoded knowledge about relations among the objects mentioned in rules. The discussion here is taken from the EMYCIN manual (van Melle et al., 1981) and explains this important structure in more detail.

[1]We used the term Meta-DENDRAL to refer to the program that inferred new knowledge for DENDRAL, but we did not have a well-developed concept of knowledge about knowledge.

As described in Chapter 15, an EMYCIN knowledge base is composed of factual knowledge about the domain and production rules that control the consultation interaction and make inferences about a case. Of all the structures the expert must specify for an EMYCIN system, the context tree is perhaps the most important, yet the least discussed. The context tree forms the backbone of the consultant, organizing both the conceptual structure of the knowledge base and the basic flow of the consultation interaction. The tree also indicates the goals for which the consultant will initially attempt to determine values. Since the principles for designing new context trees are poorly understood, this discussion provides examples from various existing EMYCIN systems.

The context tree is composed of at least one, but possibly many, context-types. A context-type corresponds to an actual or conceptual entity in the domain of the consultant, e.g., a patient, an aircraft, or an oil well. Each context-type in the context tree is very much like a record declaration in a traditional programming language. It describes the form of all of its instances created during a case. Thus there are two related but distinct aspects of the context tree mechanism: a static tree of *context-types* and a dynamic tree of *context-instances.* The static tree of types is the structure defined by the expert during system construction and forms the knowledge base "core."

The static tree is used to guide the creation of the dynamic context tree of instances during the consultation. These instances are also organized into a tree that has a form reflecting the structure of the static hierarchy. We distinguish these two structures by referring to them as the static tree and the instance tree. A moderately complex example of each of these types of trees for the SACON system is given in the Figures 27-1 and 27-2. In these and later figures, the links, or relationships, among context-types are labeled to show different uses of the tree.

Each knowledge base has one main, or root, context-type for which there will be a single instance for each consultation. It corresponds to the main subject of the consultation. In MYCIN, for example, the main context-type is PATIENT, and consultation provides advice about disease(s) of the patient. In SACON, the main context-type is STRUCTURE, and a consultation gives advice about performing structural analysis on a structure (such as a bridge or an airplane wing).

Some domains are simple enough that no other context-types are needed. PUFF, for example, needed only attributes of the main context PATIENT. However, other systems, such as MYCIN and SACON, require the ability to discuss multiple objects. In these cases, the context-types are organized into a simple tree structure with the main context at the root. For each context-type that is subordinate to another context-type there is an implicit one-to-many relationship between the instances of each type created during a consultation. Thus, for SACON, there can be many SUBSTRUCTURE instances for the single STRUCTURE instance during a case, and there can be several LOADING instances for each SUBSTRUC-

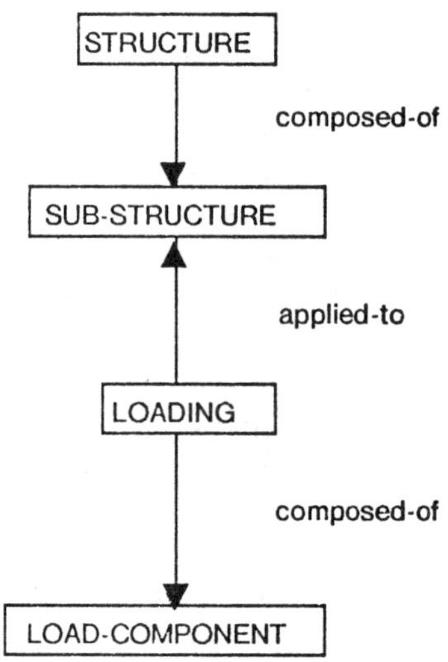

FIGURE 27-1 SACON's static tree of context-types.

TURE instance. It should be noted that, except for the root-type, every possible context-type need not be instantiated during a consultation. In the MYCIN system, for example, the patient may or may not have had any prior drug therapy.

The static tree is the major repository of structural and control information about the consultant. It indicates, in particular, the possible parameters of a context (its PARMGROUP) and the groups of rules that can be applied to instances of a context (its RULETYPES). Hence, the context-types must be defined before one can proceed to acquire rules and parameters, since both of these are defined with respect to the context tree. In addition, the static relationships among the context-types dictate, in large part, the basic mechanism for the propagation of the dynamic tree of instances during a consultation (see Chapter 5).

All of the rules used by the consultant to reason about the domain are written without regard to specific context-instances in an actual consultation. A rule instead refers to parameters of certain context-*types*, and the rule is applied to all the context-instances for which its parameter group is relevant. For example, a rule that concludes about a parameter of a LOADING, say FORCE-BOUND, will be applied to all instances of LOADING, as shown in Figure 27-2 (e.g., LOADING-1, LOADING-2) and may or may not succeed within each instance depending on whether its premise is true in that particular context. In addition, if a rule refers to a specific context-type, its premise can refer to the parameters of any direct ancestors of this context-type. Continuing with our example, the rule premise could refer to parameters of any SUBSTRUCTURE and of the STRUCTURE

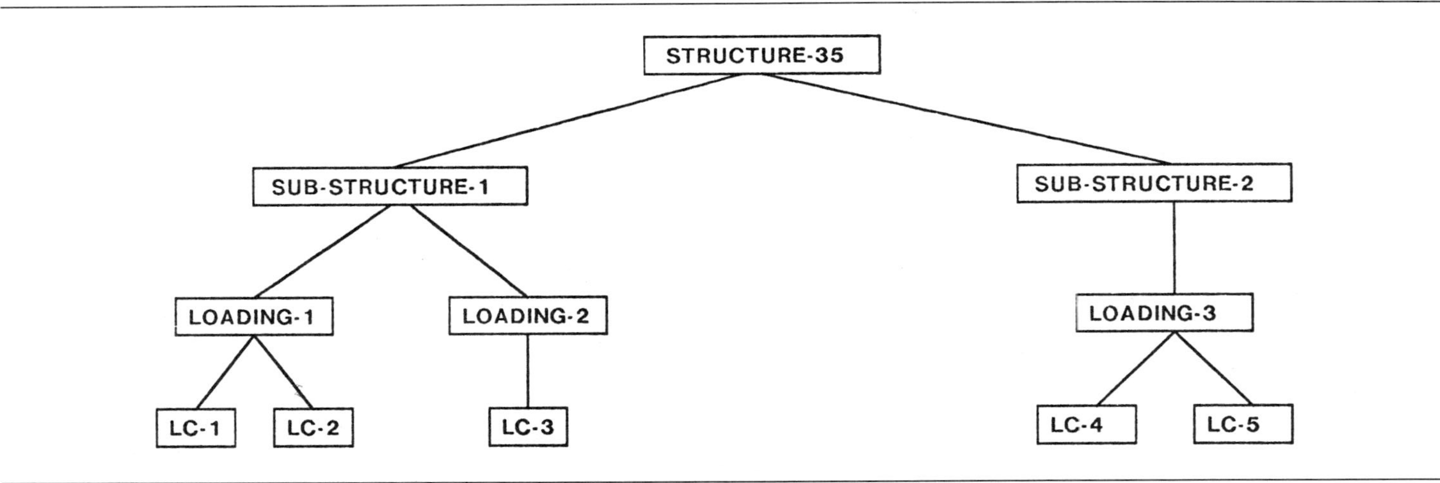

FIGURE 27-2 An instance tree from SACON.

itself. The instance tree organization makes clear which LOADING instances are associated with which SUBSTRUCTURE instance.

If a rule is applied to some context-instance and uses information about context-instances *lower* in the tree, however, an implicit iteration occurs: the rule is applied to each of the lower instances in turn. If the lower context-types have not yet been instantiated, the program digresses to ask about their creation at this time. Thus contexts are instantiated because rules need them,[2] just as parameters are traced when rules need them. In fact, since the goals of the consultation usually consist of finding out something about the root of the tree, the only way that lower context-types are instantiated at all is through the application of rules that use information about lower context-types.

27.1.1 Uses of the Context Tree

There have been a few rather stereotypic uses of the context tree. Although experience to date has by no means exhausted the possible uses, the examples shown here should help readers to understand how an expert and knowledge engineer might select appropriate context-types and organize them in a new domain.

The primary use of additional contexts has been to *structure the data or evidence* to be collected. Thus, in the MYCIN system, the culture contexts describe the tests performed to isolate organisms. Additional information about the patient's current and previous therapies, the cultures, and MYCIN's own estimation of the suspected infections are also represented in the tree. The current context organization for MYCIN is shown in Figure 27-3 and should be contrasted with the sample instance tree of Figure 5-1 (which reflects MYCIN's context-types as they were defined in 1974).[3]

The second major use of the context tree has been to *organize the important components of some object.* For example, in the SACON system the substructures of the main structure correspond to components or regions of the object that have some uniform property, typically a specific geometry or material. Each substructure instance is considered *independently,* and conclusions about individual responses to stress loadings are summarized on the structure level to provide a "global" sense of the overall response of the structure. A recent, additional example of this use of a part-whole hierarchy is found in a system called LITHO (Bonnet, 1979), which interprets data from oil wells. In this system, each well is decomposed into a number of zones that the petrologist can distinguish by depth (Figure 27-4).

A context need not correspond to some physical object but may be an abstract entity. However, the relationships among contexts are explicitly

---

[2]Contexts may also be instantiated by explicit command, but the mechanism is less convenient.

[3]It is instructive to compare this structure with the original context tree described in Chapter 5; the MYCIN system has undergone at least three intermediate reorganizations of its static tree. Significantly, however, the *kinds* of objects in the tree have not changed substantially.

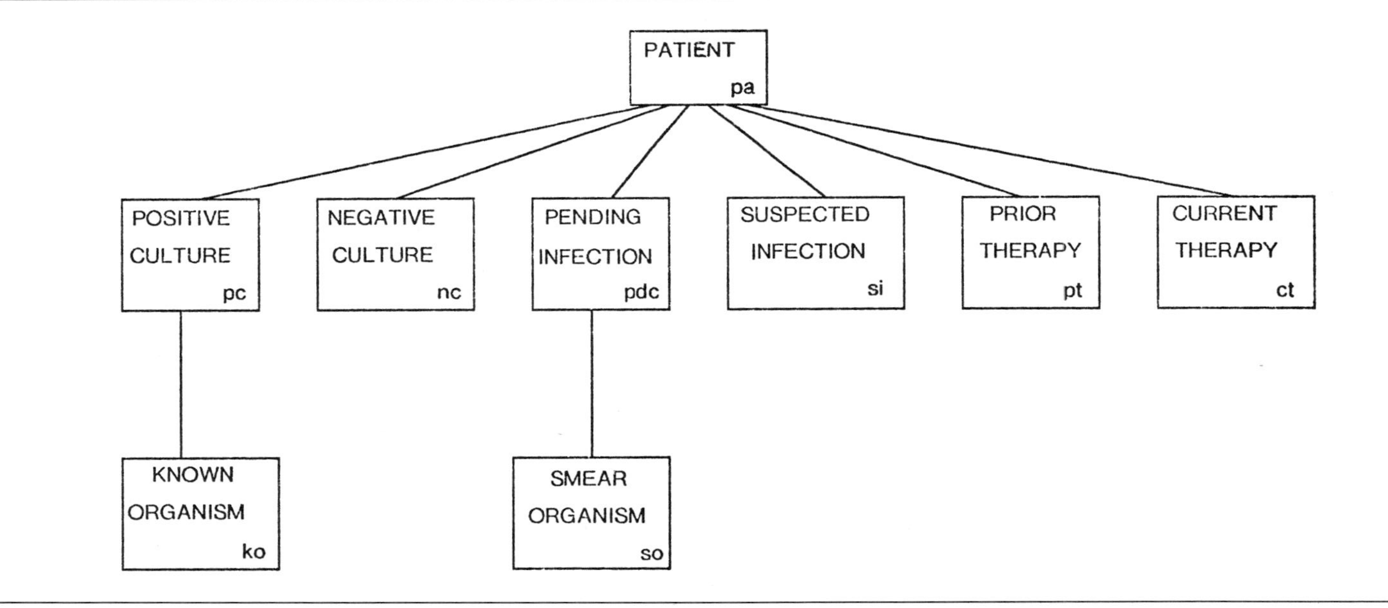

FIGURE 27-3 MYCIN's static tree.

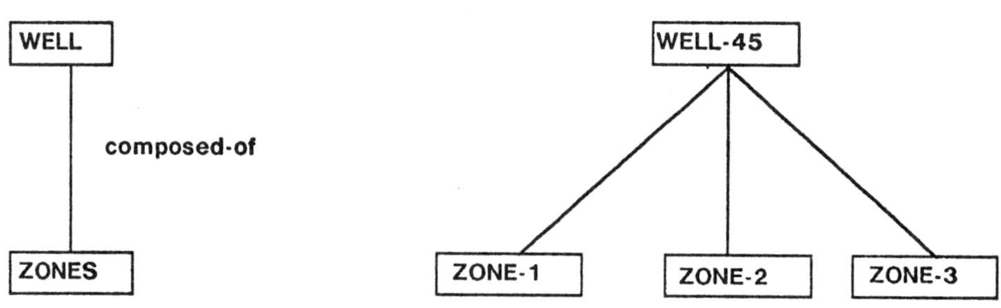

FIGURE 27-4 LITHO's static tree and an instance tree.

fixed by the tree of context-types. For this reason, physical objects, represented in this *part-whole fashion,* lend themselves more readily to the current context tree mechanism.

The last major use of the context tree, which is closely related to the part-whole use described above, has been to *represent important events or situations* that happen to an object. Thus, in the SACON system, a LOADING describes an anticipated scenario or maneuver (such as pounding or braking) to which the particular SUBSTRUCTURE is subjected. Each LOADING, in turn, is composed of a number of independent LOAD-COMPONENTS, distinguished by the direction and intensity of the applied force. Other uses of this organizational idea have been to represent individual past PREGNANCIES and current VISITS of a pregnant woman in the GRAVIDA system of Catanzarite (unpublished; see Figure 27-5) and the anticipated use of BLEEDING-EPISODES of a PATIENT in the CLOT system (Figure 27-6; see also Chapter 16).[4]

The primary reason for defining additional context-types in a consultant is to represent multiple instances of an entity during a case. Some users may like to define context-types that always have one instance and no more, primarily for purposes of organization, but this is often unnecessary (and even cumbersome).[5] For example, one might want to write rules that use various attributes of a patient's liver, but since there is always exactly one liver for a patient there is no need to have a liver context; any attribute of the liver can simply be viewed as an attribute of the patient.

Reference to parameters of contexts in *different* parts of an instance tree is currently very awkward. For example, in MYCIN, a particular drug may be associated somehow with a particular organism (Figure 27-7). However, this relationship between context-instances is *not* one that always holds

[4]It should be noted that use of the context mechanism to handle sequential visits in the GRAVIDA system is experimental and required the definition of numerous additional functions for this purpose. They are not currently in EMYCIN.

[5]Note, however, that separating unique concepts out into single contexts may provide more understandable rule translations due to the conventions of context-name substitutions in text generation. See Chapter 18 for further discussion of this point.

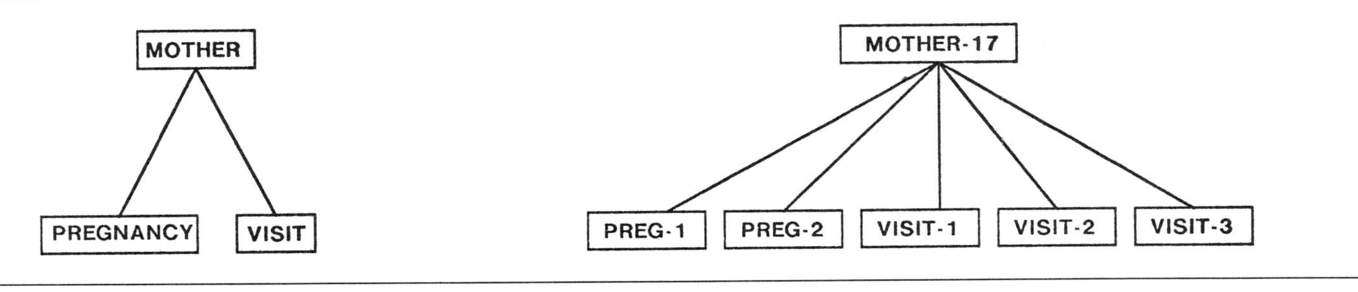

FIGURE 27-5 GRAVIDA's static tree and an instance tree.

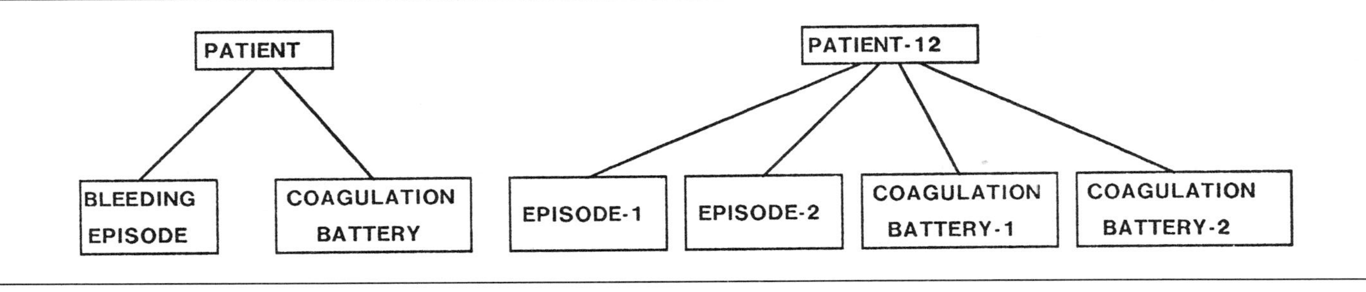

FIGURE 27-6 CLOT's static tree and an instance tree.

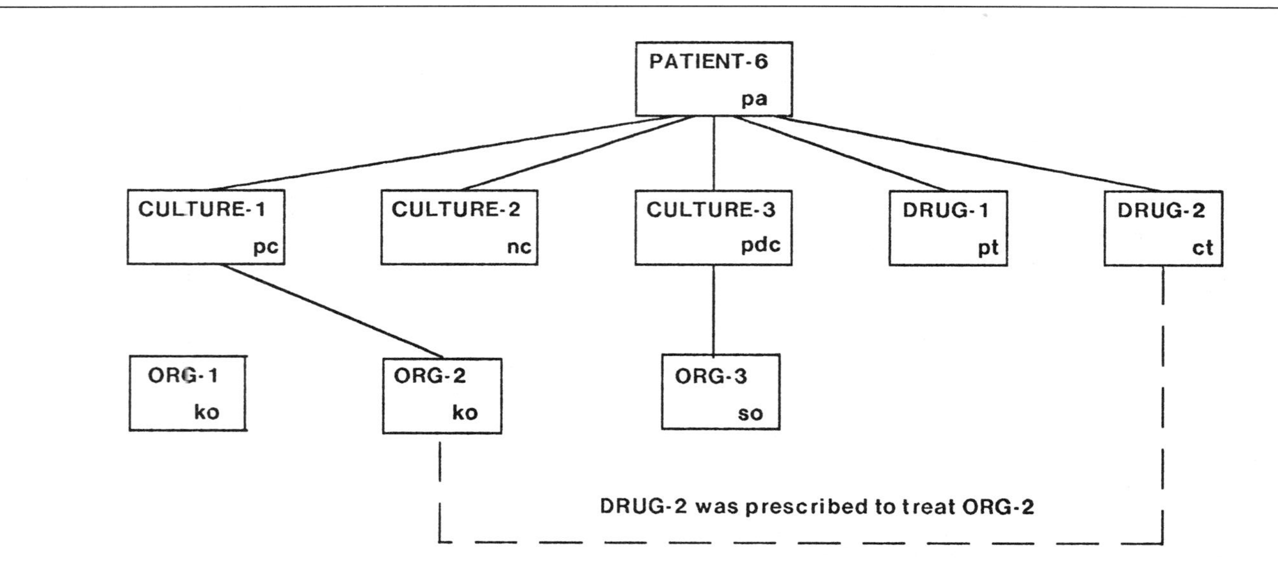

FIGURE 27-7 An example of a dynamic relationship between context-instances.

between all organisms and all drugs: not all drugs are prescribed to treat all identified organisms. This "prescribed for" relationship cannot be stated statically, independently of the case. Special predicate and action functions must be written to establish and manipulate these kinds of relationships between instances. It is best to avoid these interactions between disjoint parts of the tree during the initial design of the knowledge base.

Summing up our experience with this mechanism and considering its relative inflexibility, we offer this final caveat: for an initial system design, those using EMYCIN should start small and should use only one or two context-types. They should plan the structure of the consultant's context tree carefully before running the EMYCIN system, since restructuring a context tree is perhaps the most difficult and time-consuming knowledge-base construction task. Indeed, restructuring the context tree implies a complete restructuring of the rest of the knowledge base.

27.2 Grain Size of Rules

We had noticed that MYCIN's knowledge is "shallow" in the sense that its rules encode empirical associations but not theoretical laws. MYCIN lacks explicit representations of the "deep" understanding, such as an expert has, of causal mechanisms and reasoning strategies in medicine. MYCIN's rules do include some causal relations and definitions as well as structural relations, but all these are not cleanly separated from the heuristics and "compiled knowledge" that make up most of the rule set.

When we were building the initial system, we recognized that many rules were "broad-brush" treatments of complex processes, skipping from A to E in one leap and omitting any mention of B, C, and D in a chain such as A → B → C → D → E. We were focusing on rules whose "grain size" was of *clinical* significance. Even though finer-grained rules were often discussed, we consciously omitted them if the finer distinctions would not improve the program's ability to suggest appropriate treatments for infections or if they would not improve the understandability of the program for clinicians.[6] That is, the clinical significance of the conclusions determined the vocabulary of the rules. Thus, from the standpoint of performance, many causal mechanisms were not needed for reasoning from evidence to appropriate conclusions.

Examples of this collapsing of inference steps abound in all domains. For instance, physicians generally use a diuretic, such as furosemide, to treat edema or congestive heart failure without thinking twice about it. It is typically only when a patient fails to respond that the physician considers the mechanism of the drug's action in order to find, perhaps, another drug

[6]Note that physicians will be able to understand rules that medical students sometimes find confusing. See Chapter 20 for a further discussion of the grain size of rules.

to give with the first in order to produce the desired effect. Or, in a nonmedical domain, a mechanic often makes adjustments in response to manifestations of an automobile problem (e.g., adjusting the carburetor in response to stalling) and considers more detail only if the first few adjustments fail. An example from MYCIN is cited by Clancey in Chapter 29, in his discussion of the tetracycline rule: "If the patient is less than 8 years old, don't prescribe tetracycline." This rule lacks ties to the deeper understanding of drug action of which it is a consequence. Thus it is not only difficult for a student to remember, but also difficult for one to know how to modify or to know exactly how far the premise clause can be stretched safely.

We also recognized that many of the attributes mentioned in rules are not primitive observational terms in the same sense that values of laboratory tests are. For example, MYCIN asks whether a patient is getting better or worse in response to therapy, just as it asks for serum glucose levels. Obviously, there are a number of rules that could be written to infer whether the patient is better, mentioning such things as change in temperature, eating habits, and general coloring. That is, we chose a rule of the form A → B, with A as a primitive, rather than several rules in the following form:

$$\begin{array}{l} A_1 \rightarrow A \\ A_2 \rightarrow A \\ \vdots \\ A_n \rightarrow A \\ A \ \rightarrow B \end{array}$$

Neither of these shortcuts is a fatal flaw in the methodology of rule-based systems. Expanding the rule set to cover the richer knowledge physicians are known to hold would be possible, but time-consuming and unnecessary for improving MYCIN's advice in consultations. The consultation program, after all, was designed for use by physicians, and it seemed reasonable to leave some of the more basic observations up to them. However, as a result, there is considerable knowledge absent from MYCIN. As mentioned in Part Eight, successful tutoring depends on deep knowledge even more than successful consulting does.

27.3 Strategic, Structural, and Support Knowledge

The missing knowledge is of three classes: strategic, structural, and support. Strategic knowledge is an important part of expertise. MYCIN's built-in strategy is cautious: gather as much evidence as possible (without demanding new tests) for and against likely causes and then weigh the evidence. Operationally, this translates into exhaustive rule invocation whereby (a) all (relevant) rules are tried and (b) all rules whose left-hand sides match the case (and whose right-hand sides are relevant to problem-solving goals) have their right-hand sides acted upon. But under different circumstances, other strategies would be more appropriate. In emergencies, for example, physicians cannot take the time to gather much history data. Or, with recurring illness, physicians will order new tests and wait for the results. Deciding on the most appropriate strategy depends on medical knowledge about the context of the case. MYCIN's control structure is not concerned with resource allocation; it assumes that there is time to gather all available information that is relevant and time to process it. Thus MYCIN asks 20–70 questions and processes 1–25 rules between questions. We estimate that MYCIN executes about 50 rules per second (exclusive of I/O wait time). With larger amounts of data or larger numbers of rules, the control structure would need additional meta-rules that estimate the costs of gathering data and executing rules, in order to weigh costs against benefits. Also, in crisis situations or real-time data interpretation, the control structure would need to be concerned with the allocation of resources.[7]

One way to make strategic knowledge explicit is by putting it in *meta-rules,* as discussed in Chapter 28. They are rules of the same IF/THEN form as the medical rules, but they are "meta" in the sense that they talk *about* and reason *with* the medical rules. One of the interesting aspects of the meta-rule formalism, as Davis designed it, is that the same rule interpreter and explanation system work for meta-rules as for object-level rules. (Chapter 23 discussed the use of prototypes, or frames, for representing much of the same kind of knowledge about problem solving.) Making strategy knowledge explicit has come to be recognized as an important design consideration for expert systems (Barnett and Erman, 1982; de Kleer et al., 1977; Genesereth, 1981; Patil et al., 1981) because it can make a system's reasoning more efficient and more understandable.

Structural knowledge in medicine includes anatomical and physiological information about the structure and function of the body and its systems.[8] It is part of what we believe is needed for "deeper" reasoning about diagnosis. A structural model showing, *inter alia,* the normal connections of subparts can be used for reasoning about abnormalities. In contrast, representing this information in rules would force explicit mention of the

---

[7]In the AM and EURISKO programs (Lenat, 1976; 1983), Lenat has added information about maximum amounts of time to spend on various tasks, which keeps those programs from "overspending" computer time on difficult tasks of low importance. (EURISKO can also decide to change those time allocations.) In PROSPECTOR (Duda et al., 1978a), attention is focused on the rules that will add the most information, i.e., that will most increase or decrease the probability of the hypothesis being pushed. In Fox's system (Fox, 1981), the *estimated cost* of evaluating premises of rules helps determine which rules to invoke.

[8]More generally, we want to talk about the structure of any system or device we want an expert system to analyze, such as electronic circuits or automobiles.

abnormal situations and their manifestations. Thus there is a saving in the number of items represented explicitly in a rich structural model as opposed to an equally rich rule set. In medicine this point has been made by the Rutgers group (Kulikowski and Weiss, 1971) in the context of the CASNET program for diagnosing glaucomas. More recently, it is being advanced by Patil et al. (1981), Kunz (1983), Pople (1982), and others. In the domain of electronics almost everyone has noticed that a circuit diagram and causal knowledge are powerful pieces of knowledge to have [see, for example, Brown et al. (1974), Davis et al. (1982), Genesereth (1981), Grinberg, (1980)]. Structural knowledge also includes knowledge about the structure of the domain, e.g., the taxonomy of important concepts. This structure is an important reference point for guiding the problem solver in writing strategy rules.

Support knowledge includes items of information that are relevant for understanding a rule (or other knowledge structure). In early versions of MYCIN, we attached extra information to rules as justification for them or as historical traces of their evolution. For example, the *literature citations* provide credibility as well as pointers to more detailed information. The *names* of the persons who authored or edited a rule and the *dates* when it was created or edited are important pointers to persons responsible for the interpretation of the literature. The slot called "Justification" was created as a repository for the author's *comments* about why the rule was thought to be necessary in the first place. Additional support for a program's knowledge comes from deeper theoretical knowledge. Quantum chemistry, for example, could have been (but was not) referenced as support for DENDRAL's rules of mass spectrometry; pharmacology could have been (but was not) referenced to support MYCIN's rules of drug therapy. In general, support knowledge further explains the facts and relations of the domain knowledge. The contexts of tutoring and explanation demonstrate the need for support knowledge better than does the context of consultation because the additional support for rules is more relevant to *understanding* them than to *using* them (see Part Eight).

Recently, we have shifted our focus for this line of work from MYCIN to NEOMYCIN (Clancey and Letsinger, 1981), an updated version of the MYCIN knowledge base, representation, and control structure. In brief, it separates the diagnostic strategies clearly from the medical rules and facts used for diagnosing individual cases. By doing this, it can better serve as a basis for tutoring, as discussed in Chapter 26. NEOMYCIN was undertaken because of the issues noted in the following two chapters, but it is still too early to draw conclusions from the work.

28

Meta-Level Knowledge

Randall Davis and Bruce G. Buchanan

This chapter explores a number of issues involving representation and use of what we term *meta-level knowledge*, or knowledge about knowledge.[1] It begins by defining the term, then exploring a few of its varieties and considering the range of capabilities it makes possible. Four specific examples of meta-level knowledge are described, and a demonstration given of their application to a number of problems, including interactive transfer of expertise and the "intelligent" use of knowledge. Finally, we consider the long-term implications of the concept and its likely impact on the design of large programs. The context of this work is the TEIRESIAS program discussed in Chapter 9. In the earlier chapter we focused on the *use of* TEIRESIAS for knowledge acquisition. Here we focus on the classification and types of knowledge *used by* TEIRESIAS.

In the most general terms, meta-level knowledge is knowledge about knowledge. Its primary use here is to enable a program to "know what it knows," and to make multiple uses of its knowledge. As mentioned in Chapter 9, the program is not only able to use its knowledge directly, but may also be able to examine it, abstract it, reason about it, or direct its application.

This chapter discusses examples of meta-level knowledge classified along two dimensions: (i) specificity character (*representation-specific* vs. *domain-specific*), and (ii) source (*user-supplied* vs. *derived*). Representation-specific meta-level knowledge involves supplying a program with a store of knowledge dealing with the *form* of its representations, in particular, their design and organization. Traditionally, this design and organization infor-

This chapter is an expanded and edited version of a paper originally appearing in *Proceedings of the Fifth IJCAI,* 1977, pp. 920–928. Used by permission of International Joint Conferences on Artificial Intelligence, Inc.; copies of the *Proceedings* are available from William Kaufmann, Inc., 95 First Street, Los Altos, CA 94022.

[1]Following standard usage, knowledge about objects and relations in a particular domain will be referred to as *object-level knowledge.*

I. Knowledge about contents of rules in the knowledge base—Rule Models
II. Knowledge about syntax
  Of the representation of objects—Schemata
  Of predicate functions—Function Templates
III. Knowledge about strategies—Meta-Rules

FIGURE 28-1 Classification of meta-level knowledge in TEIRESIAS.

mation is present in a system only implicitly, for example, in the way a particular segment of code accesses data or the way a chunk of knowledge is encoded. Type declarations are a small step toward more explicit specification of this information, especially as they are used in extended data types and record structures. As we discuss below, this sort of information, along with a range of other facts about representation design, can be employed quite usefully if it is made explicit and made available to the system.

Domain-specific meta-level knowledge contains information dealing with the *content* of object-level knowledge, independent of its particular encoding. It might involve any kind of useful information about a chunk of knowledge, including its likely utility, range of applicability, speed or space requirements, capabilities, and side effects. The two examples given here deal with forms of meta-level knowledge that (i) offer information about global patterns and trends in the content of object-level knowledge, and (ii) provide strategic information, i.e., knowledge about how best to use other knowledge.

The examples described below also illustrate the difference between user-supplied and derived meta-level knowledge. The former is of course obtained from the user; the latter is derived by the system on the basis of information it already has. The user-supplied variety is used as a source for knowledge that the system could not have deduced on its own; the derived form allows the system to uncover useful characteristics of the knowledge base and to make maximal use of knowledge it already has.

As will become clear below, meta-level knowledge makes possible a number of interesting capabilities. The representation-specific variety supports knowledge acquisition, provides assistance on knowledge base maintenance, and makes possible multiple distinct uses of a single chunk of knowledge. The domain-specific type provides a site for embedding information about the most effective use of knowledge and can have a significant impact on both the efficiency displayed by a system and its level of performance. The examples also demonstrate that the source of the meta-level knowledge has an impact on system performance. In particular, the derived variety is shown to make possible a very simple but potentially useful form of closed-loop behavior.

We examine below the four instances of meta-level knowledge used by TEIRESIAS (shown in Figure 28-1) and review for each (i) the basic idea, explaining why it is a form of meta-level knowledge; (ii) a specific instance, detailing the information it contains; (iii) an example of how that information is used to support knowledge base construction, maintenance, or use; and (iv) the other capabilities it makes possible, including a limited form of self-knowledge.

28.1 Rule Models

28.1.1 Rule Models as Empirical Abstractions of the Knowledge Base

As described in Chapter 9, a rule model is an abstract description of a subset of rules, built from empirical generalizations about those rules. It is used to characterize a "typical" member of the subset and is composed of four parts. First, a list of examples indicates the subset of rules from which this model was constructed.

Next, a description characterizes a typical member of the subset. Since we are dealing in this case with rules composed of premise-action pairs, the description currently implemented contains individual characterizations of a typical premise and a typical action. Then, since the current representation scheme used in those rules is based on associative triples, we have chosen to implement those characterizations by indicating (a) which attributes "typically" appear in the premise (and in the action) of a rule in this subset and (b) correlations of attributes appearing in the premise (and in the action).[2] Note that the central idea is the concept of *characterizing a typical member of the subset.* Naturally, that characterization looks different for subsets of rules than it does for procedures, theorems, frames, etc. But the main idea of characterization is widely applicable and not restricted to any particular representational formalism.

The two remaining parts of the rule model are pointers to models describing more general and more specific rule models covering larger or smaller subsets of rules. The set of models is organized into a number of tree structures, each of the general form shown in Figure 28-2. This structure determines the subsets for which models will be constructed. At the root of each tree is the model made from all the rules that conclude about <attribute>; below this are two models dealing with all affirmative and all negative rules; and below this are models dealing with rules that affirm or deny specific values of the attribute. There are several points to note here. First, these models are not hardwired into the system, but are instead formed by TEIRESIAS on the basis of the current contents of the knowledge base. Second, whereas the knowledge base contains object-level rules about a specific domain, the rule models contain information about those

[2]Both of these are constructed via simple statistical thresholding operations.

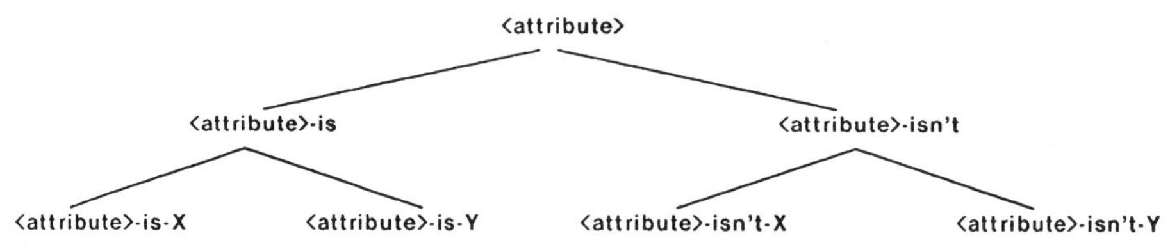

FIGURE 28-2 Organization of the rule models.

rules, in the form of empirical generalizations. As such, they offer a global overview of the regularities in the rules. The rule models are thus an example of derived, domain-specific meta-level knowledge.

28.1.2 Rule Model Example

Figure 28-3 shows an example of a rule model, one that describes the subset of rules concluding affirmatively about the area for an investment.[3] (Since not all details of implementation are relevant here, this discussion will omit some.) As indicated above, there is a list of rules from which this model was constructed, descriptions characterizing the premises and actions, and pointers to more specific and more general models. Each characterization in the description is shown split into its two parts, one concerning the presence of individual attributes and the other describing correlations. The first item in the premise description, for instance, indicates that "most" rules about the area of investment mention the attribute RETURNRATE in their premises; when they do mention it, they "typically" use the predicate functions SAME and NOTSAME; and the "strength," or reliability, of this piece of advice is 3.83.

The fourth item in the premise description indicates that when the attribute RETURNRATE (rate of return) appears in the premise of a rule in this subset, the attribute TIMESCALE "typically" appears as well. As before, the predicate functions are those usually associated with the attributes, and the number is an indication of reliability.

28.1.3 Use of Rule Models in Knowledge Acquisition

Use of the rule models to support knowledge acquisition occurs in several steps. First, as noted in Chapter 9, our model of knowledge acquisition is one of interactive transfer of expertise in the context of a shortcoming in

[3]These examples were generated by substituting investment terms for medical terms in examples from TEIRESIAS using MYCIN's medical knowledge.

```
MODEL FOR RULES CONCLUDING AFFIRMATIVELY ABOUT INVESTMENT AREA

EXAMPLES        ((RULE116 .33)
                 (RULE050 .70)
                 (RULE037 .80)
                 (RULE095 .90)
                 (RULE152 1.0)
                 (RULE140 1.0))

DESCRIPTION
 PREMISE        ((RETURNRATE SAME NOTSAME 3.83)
                 (TIMESCALE SAME NOTSAME 3.83)
                 (TREND SAME 2.83)

                 ((RETURNRATE SAME) (TIMESCALE SAME) 3.83)
                 ((TIMESCALE SAME) (RETURNRATE SAME) 3.83)
                 ((BRACKET SAME) (FOLLOWS NOTSAME SAME) (EXPERIENCE SAME) 1.50))

 ACTION         ((INVESTMENT-AREA CONCLUDE 4.73)
                 (RISK CONCLUDE 4.05)

                 ((INVESTMENT-AREA CONCLUDE) (RISK CONCLUDE) 4.73))

MORE-GENL       (INVESTMENT-AREA)

MORE-SPEC       (INVESTMENT-AREA-IS-UTILITIES)
```

FIGURE 28-3 Example of a rule model.

the knowledge base. The process starts with the expert challenging the system with a specific problem and observing its performance. If the expert believes its results are incorrect, there are available a number of tools that will allow him or her to track down the source of the error by selecting the appropriate rule model. For instance, if the problem is a missing rule in the knowledge base to conclude about the appropriate area for an investment, then TEIRESIAS will select the model shown in Figure 28-3 as the appropriate one to describe the rule it is about to acquire. Note that the selection of a specific model is in effect an expression by TEIRESIAS of its *expectations* concerning the new rule, and the generalizations in the model become predictions about the likely content of the rule.

At this point the expert types in the new rule (Figure 28-4), using the vocabulary specific to the domain. (In all traces, computer output is in mixed upper and lower case, while user responses are in boldface capitals.)

As mentioned in Chapter 9 and further described in Chapter 18, English text is understood by allowing keywords to suggest partial interpretations and intersecting those results with the expectations provided by the selection of a particular rule model. We thus have a data-directed process (interpreting the text) combined with a goal-directed process (the predictions made by the rule model). Each contributes to the end result, but it is their combination that is effective. TEIRESIAS displays the results of

```
The new rule will be called RULE383
        If:     1 - THE CLIENT'S INCOME TAX BRACKET IS 50%
            and 2 - THE CLIENT IS FOLLOWING UP ON MARKET TRENDS CAREFULLY
            and 3 -
        Then:   1 - THERE IS EVIDENCE (.8) THAT THE INVESTMENT AREA SHOULD BE HIGH
                    TECHNOLOGY
            and 2 -

This may take a few moments . . .
```

FIGURE 28-4 New rule as stated by the expert.

this initial interpretation of the rule (Figure 28-5). If there are mistakes (as there are in this case), a rule editor is available to allow the expert to indicate necessary changes. This is easily accomplished, since TEIRESIAS can often make an effective second choice by determining the likely source of error in its initial guess.

Once the expert is satisfied that TEIRESIAS has correctly understood what was said, it is the system's turn to see if *it* is satisfied with the content of the rule. The main idea is to use the rule model to see how well this new rule "fits into" the system's model of its knowledge—i.e., does it "look like" a typical rule of the sort expected?

If the expert agrees to the inclusion of a new clause, TEIRESIAS attempts to create it (Figure 28-6). The system relies on the context of the current dialogue (which indicates that the clause should deal with the amount of the client's investment experience) and the fact that the rule must work for this case or it won't fix the bug (it is not shown here, but earlier in the interaction the expert indicated that the client had a *moderate* amount of experience). TEIRESIAS' guess is not necessarily correct, of course, since the desired clause may be more general, but it is at least a plausible attempt.

It should be noted that there is nothing in this concept of "second-guessing" that is specific to the rule models as they are currently designed, or indeed to associative triples of rules as a knowledge representation. The most general and fundamental point was mentioned above—testing to see how something "fits into" the system's model of its knowledge. At this point

```
This is my understanding of your rule:

RULE383
      IF:     1) The client's income-tax bracket is 50%, and
              2) The market has followed a upward trend recently, and
              3) The client manages his assets carefully
      THEN:   There is evidence (.8) that the area of the investment should be high-technology
```

FIGURE 28-5 TEIRESIAS' first interpretation of the rule shown in Figure 28-4.

```
I hate to criticize, Randy, but did you know that most rules about what the area of investment might be, that mention-
        the income-tax bracket of the client, and
        how closely the client follows the market
ALSO mention -
        [A] - the amount of investment experience of the client
Shall I try to write a clause to account for [A]?
++** Y

How about -
        [A] The amount of investment experience of the client is moderate
Ok?
++** Y
```

FIGURE 28-6 TEIRESIAS' suggestion of an additional clause to the new rule based on the rule model shown in Figure 28-3.

the system might perform any kind of check for violations of any established prejudices about what the new chunk of knowledge should look like. Additional kinds of checks for rules might concern the strength of the inference, the number of clauses in the premise, etc. In general, this "second-guessing" process can involve any characteristic that the system may have "noticed" about the particular knowledge representation in use.

Automatic generation of rule models has several interesting implications, since it makes possible a synthesis of the ideas of model-based understanding and learning by experience. While both of these have been developed independently in previous AI research, their combination produces a novel sort of feedback loop: rule acquisition relies on the set of rule models to effect the model-based understanding process; this results in the addition of a new rule to the knowledge base; and this in turn triggers recomputation of the relevant rule model(s).

Note, first, that performance on the acquisition of a subsequent rule may be better, because the system's "picture" of its knowledge base has improved—the rule models are now computed from a larger set of instances, and their generalizations are more likely to be valid. Second, since the relevant rule models are recomputed each time a change is made to the knowledge base, the picture they supply is kept constantly up to date, and they will at all times be an accurate reflection of the shifting patterns in the knowledge base.

Finally, and perhaps most interesting, the models are not hand-tooled by the system architect or specified by the expert. They are instead formed by the system itself, and formed as a result of its experience in acquiring rules from the expert. Thus, despite its reliance on a set of models as a basis for understanding, TEIRESIAS' abilities are not restricted by a preexisting set of models. As its store of knowledge grows, old models can become more accurate, new models will be formed, and the system's stock of knowledge about its knowledge will continue to expand.

28.2 Schemata

28.2.1 The Need for Knowledge About Representations

As data structures go beyond the simple types available in most programming languages to extended data types defined by the user, they typically become rather complex. Large programs may have numerous structures that are complex in both their internal organization and their interrelationships with other data types in the system. Yet information about these details may be scattered in comments in system code, in documents and manuals maintained separately, and in the mind of the system architect. This presents problems to anyone changing the system. Consider, for example, the difficulties encountered in such a seemingly simple problem as adding a new instance of an existing data type to a large program. Just finding all of the necessary information can be a major task, especially for someone unfamiliar with the system.

One particularly relevant set of examples comes from the numerous approaches to knowledge representation that have been tried over the years. While the emphasis in discussions of predicate calculus, semantic nets, production rules, frames, etc., has naturally concerned their respective conceptual power, at the level of implementation each of these carries problems of data structure management.

Our second example of meta-level knowledge, then, is of the representation-specific variety and involves describing to a system a range of information about the representations it employs. The main idea here is, first, to view every knowledge representation in the system as an extended data type and to write explicit descriptions of them. These descriptions should include all of the information about structure and interrelations that is often widely scattered. Next, we devise a language in which all of this can be put in machine-comprehensible terms and write the descriptions in those terms, making this store of information available to the system. Finally, we design an interpreter for the language, so that the system can use its new knowledge to keep track of the details of data structure construction and maintenance.

The approach is based on the concept of a *data structure schema*, a device that provides a framework in which representations can be specified. The framework, like most, carries its own perspectives on its domain. One point it emphasizes strongly is the detailed specification of many kinds of information about representations. It attempts to make this specification task easier by providing ways of organizing the information and a relatively high-level vocabulary for expressing it.

Schema hierarchy: indicates categories of representations and their organization

Individual schema: describes structure of a single representation

Slot names: (the schema building blocks) describe implementation conventions

FIGURE 28-7 Levels of knowledge about representations.

28.2.2 Schema Example

There are three levels of organization of the information about representations (Figure 28-7). At the highest level, a schema hierarchy links the schemata together, indicating what categories of data structure exist in the system and the relationships among them. At the next level of organization are individual schemata, the basic units around which the information about representations is organized. Each schema indicates the structure and interrelationships of a single type of data structure. At the lowest level are the slot names (and associated structures) from which the schemata are built; these offer knowledge about specific conventions at the programming language level. Each of these three levels supplies a different sort of information; together they comprise an extensive body of knowledge about the structure, organization, and implementation of the representations.

The hierarchy is a generalization hierarchy (Figure 28-8) that indicates the global organization of the representations. It makes extensive use of the concept of inheritance of properties, so that a particular schema need represent only the information not yet specified by schemata above it in the hierarchy. This distribution of information also aids in making the network extensible.

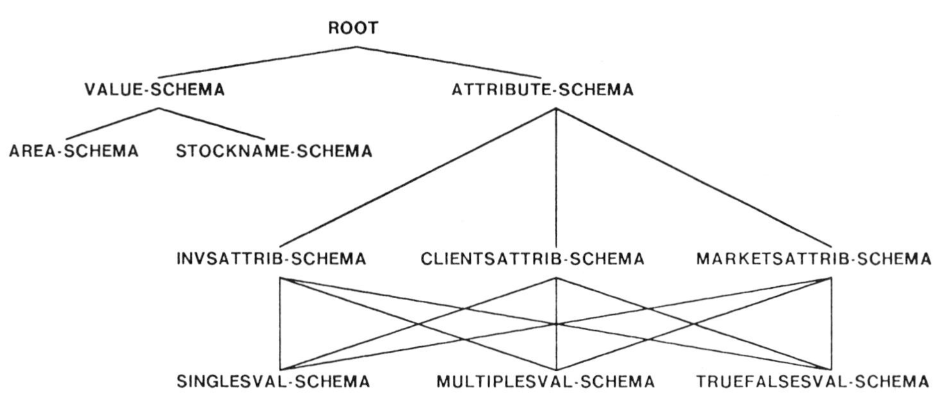

FIGURE 28-8 Part of the schema hierarchy.

Each schema contains several different types of information:

1. the structure of its instances,
2. interrelationships with other data structures,
3. a pointer to all current instances,
4. inter-schema organizational information, and
5. bookkeeping information.

Figure 28-9 shows the schema for a stock name; information corresponding to each of the categories listed above is grouped together. The first five lines in Figure 28-9 contain structure information and indicate some of the entries on the property list (PLIST) of the data structure that represents a stock name. The information is a triple of the form

<slot name> <blank> <advice>

The slot name labels the "kind" of thing that fills the blank and serves as a point around which much of the "lower-level" information in the system is organized. The blank specifies the format of the information required, while the advice suggests how to find it. Some of the information needed may be domain-specific, and hence must be requested from the expert. But some of it may concern completely internal conventions of representation, and hence should be supplied by the system itself, to insulate the domain expert from such details. The advice provides a way of indicating which of these situations holds in a given case.

```
STOCKNAME-SCHEMA
  PLIST          [( INSTOF STOCKNAME-SCHEMA                                    GIVENIT
                     SYNONYM (KLEENE (1 0) < ATOM >)                           ASKIT
                     TRADEDON (KLEENE (1 1 2) <(MARKET-INST FIRSTYEAR-INST)>)  ASKIT
                     RISKCLASS CLASS-INST                                      ASKIT
                    CREATEIT]

  RELATIONS      ( (AND* STOCKNAMELIST HILOTABLE)
                   (OR* CUMVOTINGRIGHTS)
                   (XOR* COMMON PFD CUMPFD PARTICPFD)
                   ((OR* PFD CUMPFD PARTICPFD) PFORATETABLE)
                   ((AND* CUMPFD) OMITTEDDIVS) )

  INSTANCES      (AMERICAN-MOTORS AT&T . . . XEROX ZOECON)

  FATHER         (VALUE-SCHEMA)

  OFF-SPRING     NIL

  DESCR          "the STOCKNAME-SCHEMA describes the format for a stock name"
  AUTHOR         DAVIS
  DATE           1115
  INSTOF         (SCHEMA-SCHEMA)
```

FIGURE 28-9 Schema for a stock name.

The next five lines in the schema (under RELATIONS) indicate its interrelations with other data structures in the system. The main point here is to provide the system architect with a way of making explicit all of the data structure interrelationships on which the design depends. Expressing them in a machine-accessible form makes it possible for TEIRESIAS to take over the task of maintaining them, as explained below.

The schemata also keep a list of all current instantiations of themselves (under INSTANCES), primarily for use in maintaining the knowledge base. If the design of a data structure requires modification, it is convenient to have a pointer to all current instances to ensure that they are similarly modified.

The next two lines (FATHER and OFF-SPRING) contain organizational information indicating how the stock name schema is connected to the schema hierarchy.

Finally, there are four slots for bookkeeping information to help keep track of a large number of data structures: each structure is tagged with the date of creation and author, along with a free-text description supplied by the author. In addition, each structure has a pointer to the schema of which it is an instance (note in this case that it is the schema itself that is the data structure being described by this information).

28.2.3 Use of Schemata in Knowledge Acquisition

Use of the schemata in knowledge acquisition relies on several ideas:

- Information in the schema is viewed as a guide to creating a new instance of the representation it describes.
- That guidance is supplied by (a) the structure description information, which is in the form of a prototype to be instantiated, and (b) the relations information, which is interpreted as pointers to a number of structures that may require updating to ensure that necessary data structure interrelations are maintained.
- It is this instantiation and interpretation process that drives the knowledge transfer dialogue.
- The advice present in the schema adds a level of sophistication to the dialogue.

For instance, suppose in the process of adding a new rule to the system the expert mentions a stock the system hasn't heard about yet. Learning about the new stock (i.e., creating a new instance of the concept of stock name) becomes a subproblem in the task of acquiring the new rule. The schema for the concept of stock name is retrieved and used as the basis for a dialogue that requests the necessary information from the expert. An abbreviated version of the dialogue is shown in Figure 28-10.

The new rule will be called RULE384
If 1 - **THE DESIRED RATE OF RETURN ON THE INVESTMENT IS GREATER THAN 10%**
2 - **THE AMOUNT OF INVESTMENT EXPERIENCE OF THE CLIENT IS MODERATE**
3 - **THE AREA OF THE INVESTMENT IS NATURAL RESOURCE DEVELOPMENT**
Then
1 - **THERE IS EVIDENCE (.5) THAT THE NAME OF THE STOCK TO INVEST IN IS GEORGIA PACIFIC**

Sorry, but I don't understand
THERE IS EVIDENCE (.5) THAT THE NAME OF THE STOCK TO INVEST IN IS GEORGIA PACIFIC
because these words are unknown: GEORGIA PACIFIC

{*TEIRESIAS finds it cannot generate any interpretations of the text, so it reprints the original line and specifies where the trouble is. This makes it possible for the expert to figure out what it is that is new to the system.*}

Would you care to try rephrasing that?
++** **Y**
(Please use *'s to mark what you think might be a new attribute or a new value of an existing attribute.)

1 - **THERE IS EVIDENCE (.5) THAT THE NAME OF THE STOCK TO INVEST IN IS * GEORGIA PACIFIC ***

{*While the language in this example is very simple, there are more complex cases where it would be quite hard to decide from the context what sort of new item the expert had in mind. To avoid the necessity for more sophisticated natural language handling, the expert is asked to mark off the new word or phrase with asterisks.*}

It looks as though
GEORGIA PACIFIC
refers to a new value of an attribute, correct?
++** **Y**
. . . is it the name of a stock?
++** **Y**

{*. . . and with the new item clearly marked, the system can then do some very simple pattern matching to decide what's going on.*}

Now please tell me a few things about it . . .

{*TEIRESIAS retrieves the schema for a stock, and "reads" it to find out what it needs to know about any stock.*}

On what markets is GEORGIA-PACIFIC traded?
The answer should be in the form of 1 or more of the following-
<market name> <year first traded>
[Type 1 set to a line, then an empty line when done.]
++** **NYSE 1945**
++** **PCE 1968**
++**

{*Each of the questions from the system is prompted by the attempt to fill in some component of the data structure being built, according to the representation conventions indicated by the schema.*}

What is the current risk classification of GEORGIA-PACIFIC?
The answer should be in the form of a
<risk classification>
++** **AMEX**

FIGURE 28-10 Excerpt of dialogue in which the system learns a new rule.

```
  Sorry, but the following are invalid -
      AMEX is not a recognized <risk classification>
  Please answer again [use the same answer if you really meant it].
++** BLUE-CHIP
++**
```

{TEIRESIAS now begins working on updating other data structures in response to the addition of the new stock name.}

```
Should this new item be added to-
      1 - the list of common stocks, or
      2 - the list of preferred stocks, or
      3 - the list of cumulative preferred stocks, or
      4 - the list of participating preferred stocks
Select one of the above
++** 3
[Adding GEORGIA-PACIFIC to CUMULATIVEPFD]
```

{One of these tasks involves adding the new stock to one of four mutually exclusive lists. (Several other necessary updates are also performed; these have been edited out here for brevity.)}

```
Ok, done with GEORGIA-PACIFIC now. . . Back to the rule.
```

{Having finished acquiring information about the new stock, the system returns to parsing the new rule, and with some help from the expert gets the correct result [the parsing process is omitted here, see Davis (1977) for a detailed example].}

```
This may take a few moments.

This is my understanding of your rule:
  If  1 - the desired rate of return for the investment is greater than 10%
      2 - the amount of investment experience of the client is moderate
      3 - the area of investment is natural-resource-development
  Then
      1 - there is evidence (.5) that the name of the stock to choose is georgia-pacific
```

FIGURE 28-10 continued

28.2.4 Other Uses of Schemata

The preceding subsection showed one instance of using schemata for maintenance of the knowledge base. They help ensure that one change to the knowledge base (adding a new instance of a known representation) will not violate necessary relationships between data structures. The schemata also support other capabilities. Besides being useful in maintaining the knowledge base, they offer a convenient mechanism for organizing and implementing data structure access and storage functions.

One of the ideas behind the design of the schemata is to use them as points around which to organize knowledge. The information about structure and interrelationships described above, for instance, is stored this way. In addition, access and storage information is also organized in this fashion. By generalizing the advice concept slightly, it is possible to effect all data structure access and storage requests in the appropriate schema. That is, code that needs to access a particular structure "sends" an access request, and the structure "answers" by providing the requested item.[4] This offers the well-known advantage of insulating the implementation of a data structure from its logical design. Code that refers only to the latter is far easier to maintain in the face of modifications to data structure implementation.

28.3 Function Templates

Associated with each predicate function in the system is a *template,* a list structure that resembles a simplified procedure declaration (Figure 28-11). It is representation-specific, indicating the order and generic type of the arguments in a typical call of that function. Templates make possible two interesting parallel capabilities: code generation and code dissection. Templates are used as a basis for the simple form of code generation alluded to in Chapter 9. Although details are beyond the scope of this chapter [see Davis (1976)], code generation is essentially a process of "filling in the blanks": processing a line of text in a new rule involves checking for keywords that implicate a particular predicate function, and then filling in its template on the basis of connotations suggested by other words in the text.

Function	*Template*
SAME	(object attribute value)

FIGURE 28-11 Template for the predicate function SAME.

Code dissection is accomplished by using the templates as a guide to extracting any desired part of a function call. For instance, as noted earlier, TEIRESIAS forms the rule models on the basis of the current contents of the knowledge base. To do this, it must be able to pick apart each rule to determine the attributes to which it refers. This could have been made possible by requiring that every predicate function use the same function call format (i.e., the same number, type, and order of arguments), but this would be too inflexible. Instead, we allow every function to describe its own calling format via its template. To dissect a function call, then, we need only retrieve the template for the relevant function and then use the template as a guide to dissecting the remainder of the form. The template in Figure 28-11, for instance, indicates that the *attribute* would be the second item after the function name. This same technique is also used by TEIRESIAS' explanation facility, where it permits the system to be quite precise in the explanations it provides.

[4]This was suggested by the perspective taken in work on SMALLTALK (Goldberg and Kay, 1976) and ACTORS (Hewitt et al., 1973). This style of writing programs has come to be known as object-oriented programming.

This approach also offers a useful degree of flexibility. The introduction of a new predicate function, for instance, can be totally transparent to the rest of the system, as long as its template can be written in terms of the available set of primitives such as attribute, value, etc. The power of this approach is limited primarily by this factor and will succeed to the extent that code can be described by a relatively small set of such primitive descriptors. While more complex syntax is easily accommodated (e.g., the template can indicate nested function calls), more complex semantics are more difficult (e.g., the appearance of multiple attributes in a function template can cause problems).

Finally, note that the templates also offer a small contribution to system maintenance. If it becomes necessary to modify the calling sequence of a function, for instance, we can edit just the template and have the system take care of effecting analogous changes to all current invocations of the function.

28.4 Meta-Rules

28.4.1 Meta-Rules—Strategies to Guide the Use of Knowledge

A second form of domain-specific meta-level knowledge is *strategy knowledge* that indicates how to use other knowledge. This discussion considers strategies from the perspective of *deciding which knowledge to invoke next* in a situation where more than one chunk of knowledge may be applicable. For example, given a problem solvable by either heuristic search or problem decomposition, a strategy might indicate which technique to use, based on characteristics of the problem domain and nature of the desired solution. If the problem decomposition technique were chosen, other strategies might be employed to select the appropriate decomposition from among several plausible alternatives.

This view of strategies is useful because many of the paradigms developed in AI admit (or even encourage) the possibility of having several alternative chunks of knowledge be plausibly useful in a single situation (e.g., production rules, logic-based languages, etc.). When a set of alternatives is large enough (or varied enough) that exhaustive invocation is infeasible, some decision must be made about which should be chosen. Since the performance of a program will be strongly influenced by the intelligence with which that decision was made, strategies offer an important site for the embedding of knowledge in a system.

A MYCIN-like system invokes rules in a simple backward-chaining fashion that produces an exhaustive depth-first search of an AND/OR goal tree. If the program is attempting, for example, to determine which stock would make a good investment, it retrieves all the rules that make a conclusion about that topic (i.e., they mention STOCKNAME in their action clauses). It then invokes each one in turn, evaluating each premise to see if the conditions specified have been met. The search is exhaustive because the rules are inexact: even if one succeeds, it was deemed to be a wisely conservative strategy to continue to collect all evidence about a subgoal.

The ability to use an exhaustive search is of course a luxury, and in time the base of rules may grow large enough to make this infeasible. At this point some choice would have to be made about which of the plausibly useful rules should be invoked. *Meta-rules* were created to address this problem. They are rules *about* object-level rules and provide a strategy for pruning or reordering object-level rules before they are invoked.

28.4.2 Examples of Meta-Rules

Figure 28-12 shows four meta-rules for MYCIN (reverting to medicine again for the moment). The first of them says, in effect, that in trying to determine the likely identities of organisms from a sterile site, rules that base their identification on other organisms from the same site are not likely to be successful. The second indicates that when dealing with pelvic abscess, organisms of the class *Enterobacteriacae* should be considered before gram-positive rods. The third and fourth are like the second in that they reorder relevant rules before invoking them.

It is important to note the character of the information conveyed by meta-rules. First, note that in all cases we have a rule that is making a conclusion about other rules. That is, where object-level rules conclude about the medical (or other) domain, meta-rules conclude about object-level rules. These conclusions can (in the current implementation) be of two forms. As in the first meta-rule, they can make deductions about the likely utility of certain object-level rules, or as in the second, they can indicate a partial ordering between two subsets of object-level rules.

Note also that (as in the first example) meta-rules make conclusions about the *utility* of object-level rules, not about their *validity*. That is, METARULE001 does not indicate circumstances under which some of the object-level rules are invalid [or even "very likely (.9)" to be invalid]. It merely says that they are likely not to be *useful;* i.e., they will probably fail, perhaps only after requiring extensive computation to evaluate their preconditions. This is important because it has an impact on the question of distribution of knowledge. If meta-rules did comment on validity, it might make more sense to distribute the knowledge in them, i.e., to delete the meta-rule and just add another premise clause to each of the relevant object-level rules. But since their conclusions concern utility, it does not make sense to distribute the knowledge.

Adding meta-rules to the system requires only a minor addition to MYCIN's control structure. As before, the system retrieves the entire list

```
METARULE001

IF   1) the culture was not obtained from a sterile source, and
     2) there are rules which mention in their premise a previous
        organism which may be the same as the current organism
THEN it is definite (1.0) that each of them is not going to be useful.

PREMISE:  ($AND (NOTSAME CNTXT STERILESOURCE)
                (THEREARE OBJRULES (MENTIONS CNTXT PREMISE
                'SAMEBUG) SET1))
ACTION:  (CONCLIST SET1 UTILITY NO TALLY 1.0)


METARULE002

IF   1) the infection is a pelvic-abscess, and
     2) there are rules which mention in their premise
        enterobacteriaceae, and
     3) there are rules which mention in their premise gram-positive rods,
There is suggestive evidence (.4) that the former should be done before
     the latter.

PREMISE:  ($AND (SAME CNTXT PELVIC-ABSCESS)
                (THEREARE OBJRULES(MENTIONS CNTXT PREMISE
                              ENTEROBACTERIACEAE) SET1)
                (THEREARE OBJRULES(MENTIONS CNTXT PREMISE GRAMPOS-RODS)
                              SET2))
ACTION:  CONCLIST SET1 DOBEFORE SET2 TALLY .4)


METARULE003

IF   1) there are rules which do not mention the current goal in
        their premise
     2) there are rules which mention the current goal in their
        premise
THEN it is definite that the former should be done before the latter.

PREMISE:  ($AND(THEREARE OBJRULES ($AND (DOESNTMENTION FREEVAR
                         ACTION CURGOAL))SET1)
                (THEREARE OBJRULES ($AND (MENTIONS FREEVAR PREMISE
                         CURGOAL)SET2))
ACTION:  (CONCLIST SET1 DOBEFORE SET2 1000)


METARULE004

IF   1) there are rules which are relevant to positive cultures, and
     2) there are rules which are relevant to negative cultures
THEN it is definite that the former should be done before the latter.

PREMISE:  ($AND(THEREARE OBJRULES ($AND (APPLIESTO FREEVAR POSCUL))
                          SET1)
                (THEREARE OBJRULES ($AND (APPLIESTO FREEVAR NEGCUL))
                          SET2))
ACTION:  (CONCLIST SET1 DOBEFORE SET2 1000)
```

FIGURE 28-12 Four meta-rules for MYCIN.

of rules relevant to the current goal (call the list L). But before attempting to invoke them, it first determines if there are any meta-rules relevant to the goal.[5] If so, these are invoked first. As a result of their actions, we may obtain a number of conclusions about the likely utility and relative ordering of the rules in L. These conclusions are used to reorder or shorten L, and the revised list of rules is then used. Viewed in tree-search terms, the current implementation of meta-rules can either prune the search space or reorder the branches of the tree.

28.4.3 Guiding the Use of the Knowledge Base

There are several points to note about encoding knowledge in meta-rules. First, the framework it presents for knowledge organization and use appears to offer a great deal of leverage, since much can be gained by adding to a system a store of (meta-level) knowledge about which chunk of object-level knowledge to invoke next. Considered once again in tree terms, we are talking about the difference between a "blind" search of the tree and one guided by heuristics. The advantage of even a few good heuristics in cutting down the combinatorial explosion of tree search is well known. Thus, where earlier sections were concerned about adding more object-level knowledge to improve performance, here we are concerned with giving the system more information about how to use what it already knows. Consider, too, that the definition of intelligence includes appropriate use of information. Even if a store of (object-level) information is not large, it is important to be able to use it properly. Meta-rules provide a mechanism for encoding strategies that can make this possible.

Second, the description given in the preceding subsection has been simplified in several respects for the sake of clarity. It discusses the augmented control structure, for example, in terms of two levels. In fact, there can be an arbitrary number of levels, each serving to direct the use of knowledge at the next lower level. That is, the system retrieves the list (L) of object-level rules relevant to the current goal. Before invoking this, it checks for a list (L′) of first-order meta-rules that can be used to reorder or prune L, etc. Recursion stops when there is no rule set of the next higher order, and the process unwinds, each level of strategies advising on the use of the next lower level. We can gain leverage at this higher level by encoding heuristics that guide the use of heuristics. That is, rather than adding more heuristics to improve performance, we might add more information at the next higher level about effective use of existing heuristics.

[5]That is, are there meta-rules directly associated with that goal? Meta-rules can also be associated with other objects in the system, but that is beyond the scope of this chapter. The issues of organizing and indexing meta-rules are covered in more detail elsewhere (Davis, 1976; 1978).

The judgmental character of the rules offers several interesting capabilities. It makes it possible, for instance, to write rules that make different conclusions about the best strategy to use and then rely on the underlying model of confirmation (Shortliffe and Buchanan, 1975) to weigh the evidence. That is, the strategies can "argue" about the best rule to use next, and the strategy that "presents the best case" (as judged by the confirmation model) will win out.

Next, recall that the basic control structure of the performance program is a depth-first search of the AND/OR goal tree sprouted by the unwinding of rules. The presence of meta-rules of the sort shown in Figure 28-12 means that this tree has an interesting characteristic at each node: when the system has to choose a path, there may be information stored that advises about the best path to take. There may therefore be available an extensive body of knowledge to guide the search, but that knowledge is not embedded in the code of a clever search algorithm. It is instead organized around the specific objects that form the nodes in the tree; i.e., instead of a smart algorithm, we have a "smart tree."

Finally, there are several advantages associated with the use of strategies that are goal-specific, explicit, and imbedded in a representation that is the same as that of the object-level knowledge. The fact that strategies are *goal-specific,* for instance, makes it possible to specify precise heuristics for a given goal, without imposing any overhead on the search for any other goals. That is, there may be a number of complex heuristics describing the best kinds of rules to use for a particular goal, but these will cause no computational overhead except in the search for that goal.

The fact that they are *explicit* means a conceptually cleaner organization of knowledge and an ease of modification of established strategies. Consider, for instance, alternative means of achieving the sort of partial ordering specified by the second meta-rule. There are several alternative schemes by which this could be accomplished, involving appropriate modifications to the relevant object-level rules and slight changes to the control structure. Such schemes, however, share several faults that can be illustrated by considering one such approach: an agenda with multiple priority levels like the one proposed in Bobrow and Winograd (1977).

In an agenda-driven system, rules are put on an agenda rather than dealt with in the form of a linear list of relevant rules in a partial ordering. Partial ordering could be accomplished simply by setting the priority of some rules higher than that of others; rules in subset A, for instance, might get priority 6, while those in subset B are given priority 5. But this technique presents two problems: it is both opaque and likely to cause bugs. It will not be apparent from looking at the code, for instance, *why* the rules in A were given a higher priority than that of the rules in B. Were they more likely to be useful, or is it desirable that those in A precede those in B no matter how useful they may be? Consider also what happens if, before we get a chance to invoke any of the rules in A, an event occurs that makes it clear that their priority ought to be reduced (for reasons unrelated to the desired partial ordering). If the priority of only the rules in A is adjusted, a bug arises, since the desired relative ordering may be lost.

The problem is that this approach tries to reduce a number of different, incommensurate factors to a single number, *with no record of how that number was reached.* Meta-rules offer one mechanism for making these sorts of considerations explicit, and for leaving a record of why a set of processes has been queued in a particular order. They also make subsequent modifications easier, since all of the information is in one place—changing a strategy can be accomplished by editing the relevant meta-rule, rather than by searching through a program for all the places where priorities have been set to effect that strategy.

Lastly, the use of a *uniform encoding of knowledge* makes the treatment of all levels the same. For example, second-order meta-rules require no machinery in excess of that needed for first-order meta-rules. It also means that all the explanation and knowledge acquisition capabilities developed for object-level rules can be extended to meta-rules as well. The first of these (explanation) has been done and works for all levels of meta-rules. Adding this to TEIRESIAS' explanation facility makes possible an interesting capability: in addition to being able to explain what it did, the system can also explain *how it decided to do what it did.* Knowledge in the strategies has become accessible to the rest of the system and can be explained in just the same fashion. We noted above that adding meta-level knowledge to the system was quite distinct from adding more object-level knowledge, since strategies contain information of a qualitatively different sort. Explanations based on this information are thus correspondingly different as well.

28.4.4 Broader Implications of Meta-Rules

The concept of strategies as a mechanism for deciding which chunk of knowledge to invoke next can be applied to a number of different control structures. We have seen how it works in goal-directed scheme, and it functions in much the same way with a data-directed process. In the latter case meta-rules offer a way of controlling the depth and breadth of the implications drawn from any new fact or conclusion. Pursuing this further, we can imagine making the decision to use a data- or goal-directed process itself as an issue to be decided by a collection of appropriate meta-rules. At each point in its processing, the system might invoke one set of meta-rules to choose a control structure, then use another set to guide that control structure. This can be applied to many control structures, demonstrating the range of applicability of the basic concept of strategies as a device for choosing what to do next.

28.4.5 Content-Directed Invocation

If meta-rules are to be used to select from among plausibly useful object-level rules, they must have some way of referring to the object-level rules. The mechanism used to effect this reference has implications for the flexibility and extensibility of the resulting system. To see this, note that the meta-rules in Figure 28-12 refer to the object-level rules by *describing* them and effect this description by direct examination of content. For instance, METARULE001 refers to *rules that mention in their premises previous organisms that may be the same as the current organism,* which is a description rather than an equivalent list of rule names. The set of object-level rules that meet this description is determined at execution time by examining the source code of the rules. That is, the meta-rule "goes in and looks" for the relevant characteristic, using the function templates as a guide to dissecting the rules. We have termed this *content-directed invocation.*

Part of the utility of this approach is illustrated by its advantages over using explicit lists of object-level rules. If such lists were used, then tasks would require extensive amounts of bookkeeping. After an object-level rule had been edited, for instance, we would have to check all the strategies that name it, to be sure that each such reference was still applicable to the revised rule. With content-directed invocation, however, these tasks require no additional effort, since the meta-rules effect their own examination of the object-level rules and will make their own determination of relevance.

28.5 Conclusions

We have reviewed four examples of meta-level knowledge and demonstrated their application to the task of building and using large stores of domain-specific knowledge. This has showed that supplying the system with a store of information about its representations makes possible a number of useful capabilities. For example, by describing the structure of its representations (schemata, templates), we make possible a form of transfer of expertise, as well as a number of facilities for knowledge base maintenance. By supplying strategic information (meta-rules), we make possible a finer degree of control over use of knowledge in the system. And by giving the system the ability to derive empirical generalizations about its knowledge (rule models), we make possible a number of useful abilities that aid in knowledge transfer.

The examples reviewed above illustrate a number of general ideas about knowledge representation and use that may prove useful in building large programs. We have, first, the notion that knowledge in programs should be made explicit and accessible. Use of production rules to encode the object-level knowledge is one example of this, since knowledge in them may be more accessible than that embedded in the code of a procedure. The schemata, templates, and meta-rules illustrate the point also, since each of them encodes a form of information that is, typically, either omitted entirely or at best is left implicit. By making knowledge explicit and accessible, we make possible a number of useful abilities. The schemata and templates, for example, support the forms of system maintenance and knowledge acquisition described above. Meta-rules offer a means for explicit representation of the decision criteria used by the system to select its course of action. Subsequent "playback" of those criteria can then provide a form of explanation of the motivation for system behavior [see Davis (1976) for examples]. That behavior is also more easily modified, since the information on which it is based is both clear (since it is explicit) and retrievable (since it is accessible). Finally, more of the system's knowledge and behavior becomes open to examination, especially by the system itself.

Second, there is the idea that programs should have access to their own representations. To put this another way, consider that over the years numerous representation schemes have been proposed and have generated a number of discussions of their respective strengths and weaknesses. Yet, in all these discussions, one entity intimately concerned with the outcome has been left uninformed: the program itself. What this suggests is that we ought to describe to the program a range of information about the representations it employs, including such things as their structure, organization, and use.

As noted, this is easily suggested but more difficult to do. It requires a means of describing both representations and control structures, and the utility of those descriptions will be strongly dependent on the power of the language in which they are expressed. The schemata and templates are the two main examples of the partial solutions we have developed for describing representations, and both rely heavily on the idea of a task-specific high-level language—a language whose conceptual primitives are task-specific. The main reason for using this approach is to make possible what we might call "top-down code understanding." Traditionally, efforts at code understanding [e.g., Waldinger and Levitt (1974), Manna (1969)] have attempted to assign meaning to the code of some standard programming language. Rather than take on this sizable task, we have used task-specific languages to make the problem far easier. Instead of attempting to assign semantics to ordinary code, we assigned a "meaning" to each of the primitives in the high-level language and represented it in one or more informal ways. Thus, for example, ATTRIBUTE is one of the primitives in the "language" in which templates are written; its meaning is embodied in procedures associated with it that are used during code generation and dissection [see Davis (1976) for details].

This convenient shortcut also implies a number of limitations. Most importantly, the approach depends on the existence of a finite number of "mostly independent" primitives. This means a set of primitives with only a few, well-specified interactions between them. The number of interactions should be far less than the total possible, and interactions that do occur should be uncomplicated (as, for example, the interaction between the concepts of attribute and value).

But suppose we could describe to a system its representations? What benefits would follow? The primary thing this can provide is a way of effecting multiple uses of the same knowledge. Consider, for instance, the multitude of ways in which the object-level rules have been used. They are executed as code in order to drive the consultation (see Part Two); they are viewed as data structures, and dissected and abstracted to form the rule models (Parts Three and Nine); they are dissected and examined in order to produce explanations (Part Six); they are constructed during knowledge acquisition (Part Three); and, finally, they are reasoned about by the meta-rules (Part Nine).

It is important to note here that the feasibility of such multiplicity of uses is based less on the notion of production rules *per se* than on the availability of a representation with a *small grain size* and a *simple syntax and semantics.* "Small" modular chunks of code written in a simple, heavily stylized form (though not necessarily a situation-action form) would have done as well, as would have any representation with simple enough internal structure and of manageable size. The introduction of greater complexity in the representation, or the use of a representation that encoded significantly larger "chunks" of knowledge, would require more sophisticated techniques for dissecting and manipulating representations than we have developed thus far. But the key limitations are size and complexity of structure, rather than a specific style of knowledge encoding.

Two other benefits may arise from the ability to describe representations. We noted earlier that much of the information necessary to maintain a system is often recorded in informal ways, if at all. If it were in fact convenient to record this information by describing it to the program itself, then we would have an effective and useful repository of information. We might see information that was previously folklore or informal documentation becoming more formalized and migrating into the system itself. We have illustrated above a few of the advantages this offers in terms of maintaining a large system.

This may in turn produce a new perspective on programs. Early scarcity of hardware resources led to an emphasis on minimizing machine resources consumed, for example, by reducing all numeric expressions to their simplest form by hand. More recently, this has meant a certain style of programming in which a programmer spends a great deal of time thinking about a problem first, trying to solve as much as possible by hand, and then abstracting out only the very end product of all of that effort to be embodied in the program. That is, the program becomes simply a way of manipulating symbols to provide "the answer," with little indication left of what the original problem was or, more importantly, what knowledge was required to solve it.

But what if we reversed this trend, and instead viewed a program as a place to store many forms of knowledge about both the problem and the proposed solution (i.e., the program itself)? This would apply equally well to code and data structures and could help make possible a wider range of useful capabilities of the sort illustrated above.

One final observation. As we noted at the outset, interest in knowledge-based systems was motivated by the belief that no single domain-independent paradigm could produce the desired level of performance. It was suggested instead that a large store of domain-specific (object-level) knowledge was required. We might similarly suggest that this too will eventually reach its limits and that simply adding more object-level knowledge will no longer, by itself, guarantee increased performance. Instead, it may be necessary to focus on building stores of meta-level knowledge, especially in the form of strategies for effective use of knowledge. Such "meta-level knowledge–based" systems may represent a profitable future direction for research.

29

Extensions to Rules for Explanation and Tutoring

William J. Clancey

As described in Part Eight, the success of MYCIN as a problem solver suggested that the program's knowledge base might be a suitable source of subject material for teaching students. This use of MYCIN was consistent with the design goals that the program's explanations be educational to naive users and that the representation be flexible enough to allow for use of the rules outside of the consultative setting. In theory, the rules acquired from human experts would be understandable and useful to students. The GUIDON program discussed in Chapter 26 was developed to push these assumptions by using the rules in a tutorial interaction with medical students.

In attempting to "transfer back" the experts' knowledge to students through GUIDON, we found that the experts' diagnostic approach and understanding of rules were not explicitly represented. GUIDON cannot justify the rules because MYCIN does not have an encoding of how the concepts in a rule fit together. GUIDON cannot fully articulate MYCIN's problem-solving approach because the structure of the search space and the strategy for traversing it are implicit in the ordering of rule concepts. Thus the seemingly straightforward task of converting a knowledge-based system into a computer-aided instruction program has led to a detailed reexamination of the rule base and the foundations on which rules are constructed, an epistemological study.

In building MYCIN, rule authors did not recognize a need to record the structured way in which they were fitting rule parts together. The rules are more than simple associations between data and hypotheses. Sometimes clause order counts for everything, and different orders can mean differ-

This chapter is an edited version of an article appearing in *Artificial Intelligence* 20: 215–251 (1983).

ent things. Also, some rules are present mostly to control the invocation of others. The uniformity of the representation obscures these various functions of clauses and rules. In looking beyond the surface of the rule representation to make explicit the intent of the rule authors, this paper has a purpose similar to Woods' "What's in a Link?" (1975) and Brachman's "What's in a Concept?" (1976). We ask, "What's in a Rule?"

In building GUIDON, we thought that we were simply being "applications engineers" by making use of MYCIN's explanation facility for a tutorial setting. As noted in Chapter 26, it was surprising to find out how little the explanation facility could accomplish for a student. Without a crisp characterization of what we expected an explanation to convey, the program was of questionable tutorial value. On the positive side, the study of these shortcomings led to a radical change in our conception of MYCIN's rules and supplied a new epistemological framework for building expert systems.

In this chapter we provide a review of MYCIN's explanatory capability and an overview of an epistemological framework for enhancing that capability. The following two sections examine in detail the problems of *justifying a rule* and *explaining an approach,* thereby elucidating the *support* and *strategic* aspects of the epistemological framework. Implications for performance of a consultation system and modifiability are considered briefly. Finally, in the last section, the framework is used to analyze other expert systems.

29.1 MYCIN's Explanation Capability

As already mentioned, MYCIN was designed so that it could explain its reasoning to the user. This means that it can describe its reasoning steps: how a request for data is related to a goal, how one goal leads to another, and how a goal is achieved. Figure 29-1 shows a consultation excerpt in which the program demonstrates a line of reasoning (chained goals) that lead backwards from the current question:

Is the patient a compromised host (Rule 343)	→	Is the patient immunosuppressed?[1]
(Rule 395)	→	Is the patient receiving steroids?
(Rule 543)	→	Is *E. coli* causing the meningitis?

[1]Read as "... compromised host (by Rule 343) answers the question 'Is the patient immunosuppressed?' ... "

```
   23) Is J.Smith a compromised host?
   ** WHY

[i.e. WHY is it important to determine whether J.Smith is a compromised host?]

[3.0] This will aid in determining whether J.Smith is immunosuppressed.
      If
          [3.1] J.Smith is not a compromised host
      then
          it is definite (1.0) that J.Smith is not immunosuppressed
      [RULE343]

   [back to question 23 . . .]
   ** WHY

[i.e. WHY is it important to determine whether J.Smith is immunosuppressed?]

[4.0]. . . in order to determine whether J.Smith has received corticosteroids.
      If
          [4.1] J.Smith is not immunosuppressed
      then
          it is definite (1.0) that J.Smith has not received corticosteroids.
      [RULE395]

   [back to question 23 . . .]
   ** WHY

[i.e. WHY is it important to determine whether J.Smith has received corticosteroids?]

[5.0]. . . in order to determine the organisms causing the infection.

      It has already been established that
          [5.1] the infection which requires therapy is meningitis, and
          [5.2] only circumstantial evidence is available for this case, and
          [5.3] the type of meningitis is bacterial.

      Therefore, if
          [5.4] J.Smith is receiving corticosteroids

      then
          there is evidence that the organisms causing the infection are:
              e.coli (.4), klebsiella-pneumoniae (.2), or pseudomonas-aeruginosa (.1)
      [RULE543]

   [back to question 23 . . .]
   ** NO
```

FIGURE 29-1 Consultation excerpt showing explanation capability. (User input in boldface capitals; all other text is printed by MYCIN.)

Figure 29-2 illustrates how, in the questioning session after the consultation, one can inquire further about the program's intermediate reasoning steps, including why it didn't ask about something. These are the explanation capabilities that we sought to exploit in a teaching program.

MYCIN's explanations are entirely in terms of its rules and goals. The question WHY means "Why do you want this information?" or "How is this information useful?" and is translated internally as "In what rule does this goal appear, and what goal does the rule conclude about?" Davis, who developed the explanation facility, pointed out that MYCIN did not have the knowledge to respond to other interpretations of a WHY question (Davis, 1976). He mentioned specifically the lack of rule justifications and planning knowledge addressed in this chapter.

In order to illustrate other meanings for the question WHY in MYCIN, we illustrate the rule set as a network of goals, rules, and hypotheses in Figure 29-3. At the top level are all of the system's *goals* that it might want to pursue to solve a problem (diagnostic and therapeutic decisions). Examples of goals, stated as questions to answer, are "What is the shape of the organism?" and "What organism is causing the meningitis?" At the second level are *hypotheses* or possible choices for each of the goals. Examples of hypotheses are "The organism is a rod." and "*E. coli* is causing the meningitis." At the third level are the *rules* that support each hypothesis. At the fourth level appear the *premises* of these rules, specific hypotheses that must be believed for the rule to apply. For example, for Rule 543 to apply (shown in Figure 29-1) it must be the case that the infection is meningitis, that the meningitis was caused by bacteria, that the patient is receiving steroids, and so on.

A key aspect of MYCIN's interpreter is that, when confronted with a hypothesis in a rule premise that it needs to confirm, it considers all related hypotheses by pursuing the more general goal. For example, attempting to apply Rule 543, the program will consider all rules that conclude about the infection, rather than just those that conclude that the infection is meningitis. Similarly, it will consider all rules that conclude about the kind of meningitis (viral, fungal, TB, or bacterial), rather than just those that hypothesize that the meningitis is bacterial.[2] These new goals deriving from rules can now be seen conceptually as level 1 goals, and the process recurs.

The links in Figure 29-3 and their ordering are points of flexibility in the rule representation. For example, the author of a rule defines each goal and its specific hypotheses (levels 1 and 2 and 4 and 5). Less trivially, it is the author's choice to define rules that link hypotheses to one another. For example, rules on level 3 link levels 2 and 4. We call the rationale behind this link the *justification of the rule*. GUIDON cannot teach rule justifications because they are not represented in MYCIN. Section 29.3 examines the nature of rule justifications and how a tutoring system can provide them.

---

[2]This is not inefficient, given the program's exhaustive search strategy and the fact that the other hypotheses will be referenced by other rules. Note also that some hypotheses, such as "the patient is receiving steroids," are not generalized but are represented as goals directly. Whether or not a hypothesis is represented as a yes/no parameter or as a "value" of a multi-valued parameter (such as "kind of meningitis") is a decision of the author of the rule, deriving from a pattern of hypotheses that he or she wishes to collapse for clarity into a more general goal. By this process of abstraction, a single multi-valued parameter dealing with kinds of surgery would replace individual yes/no parameters that specified "cardiac surgery," "neurosurgery," etc. These organizational decisions have no bearing on system performance, so the knowledge base is somewhat inconsistent in how these choices are made.

**** DID YOU CONSIDER WHETHER THE PATIENT WAS RECEIVING STEROIDS?**

RULE543 could have used:
    whether J.Smith has received corticosteroids.

Clause 4 of RULE543 "the patient has received corticosteroids" was already known to be false.

**** HOW DID YOU KNOW THAT THE PATIENT HAD NOT RECEIVED STEROIDS?**

RULE395 was used to conclude that J.Smith has not received corticosteroids.
    The last question asked before the conclusion was made was 23.

**** WHAT WAS QUESTION 23?**

Question 23 was asked in order to find out whether J.Smith is a compromised host
    in an effort to execute RULE343.

FIGURE 29-2 Excerpt from a question/answer session. (User input appears in boldface capitals.)

Next, the author's ordering of hypotheses in a rule's premise will affect the order in which goals are pursued (level 5). The rationale for this choice again lies outside of the rule network. Thus the program cannot explain why it pursues meningitis (goal 5.1 in Figure 29-1) *before* determining that the infection is bacterial (goal 5.3). Section 29.4 examines how this ordering constitutes a strategy and how it can be made explicit.

The order in which rules for a goal are tried (level 3) also affects the order in which hypotheses (and hence subgoals) are pursued (level 5). For example, Rule 535 considers whether the patient is an alcoholic; so if this rule is tried before Rule 543, alcoholism will be considered before steroids. As these goals cause questions to be asked of the user, it is evident that the ordering of questions is also determined by the ordering of rules as well as by the ordering of clauses in the premise of a rule.

Here there is no implicit author rationale, for rule order lies outside of the author's choice; it is fixed, and determined only by the order in which rules were entered into the system. As pointed out above, MYCIN does not *decide* to pursue the hypothesis "bacterial meningitis" before "viral meningitis"—it simply picks up the bag of rules that make some conclusion about "kind of meningitis" and tries them in numeric order. Hence rule order is the answer to the question "Why is one hypothesis considered before another?" And rule order is often the answer to "Why is one question asked before another?" Focusing on a hypothesis and choosing a question to confirm a hypothesis are not necessarily arbitrary in human reasoning. This raises serious questions about using MYCIN for interpreting a student's behavior and teaching him or her how to reason, as discussed in Section 29.4.[3]

---

[3]Meta-rules could have been used for ordering rules, as described in Chapter 28. The present chapter is a rethinking of the whole question.

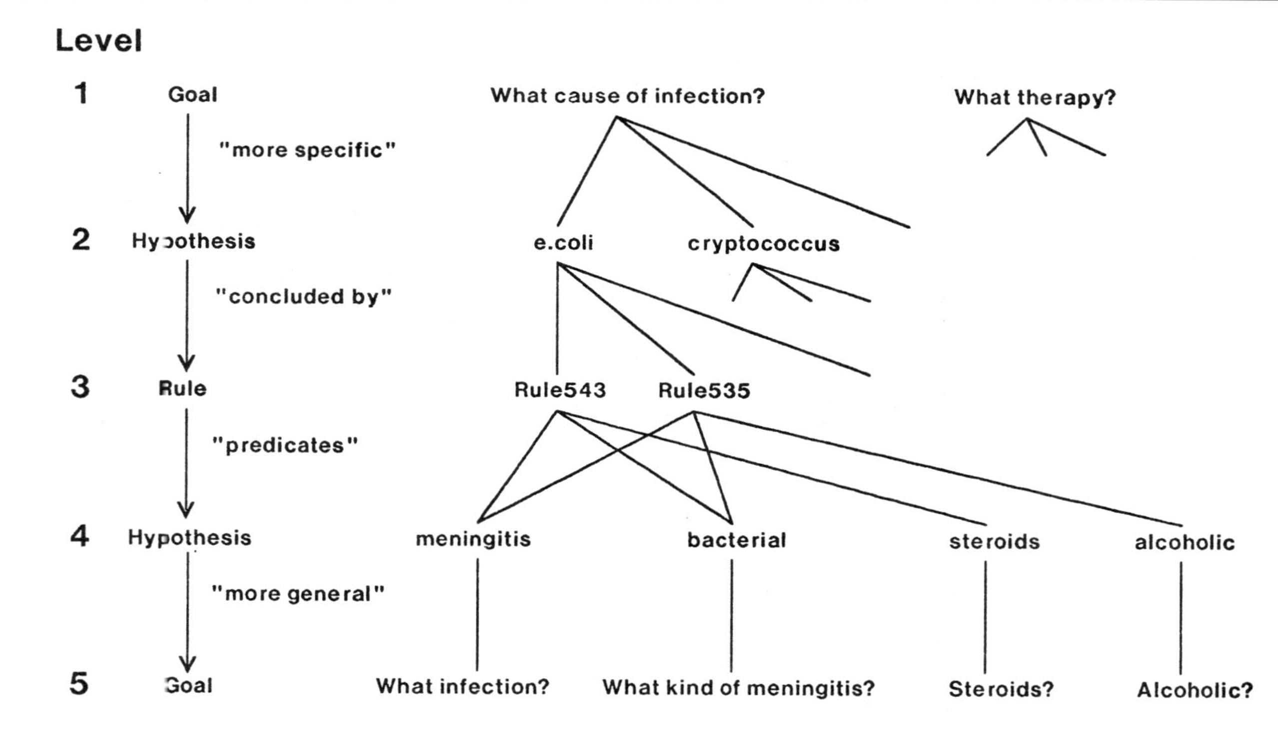

FIGURE 29-3 Rule set shown as a network linking hypotheses and goals.

To summarize, we have used a rule network as a device for illustrating aspects of MYCIN's behavior that it cannot explain. We are especially interested in making explicit the knowledge that lies behind the behavior that is not arbitrary but that cannot be explained because it is implicit in rule design. To do this, we will need some sort of framework for characterizing the knowledge involved, since the rule link itself is not sufficient. An epistemological framework for understanding MYCIN's rules is presented in the next section.

29.2 An Epistemological Framework for Rule-Based Systems

The framework presented in this section stems from an extensive study of MYCIN's rules. It is the basic framework that we have used for understanding physicians' explanations of their reasoning, as well as being a foundation for re-representing the knowledge in MYCIN's rules. As an illustration, we will consider in detail the steroids rule shown again in Figure 29-4.[4]

RULE543

IF: 1) The infection which requires therapy is meningitis,
2) Only circumstantial evidence is available for this case,
3) The type of the infection is bacterial,
4) The patient is receiving corticosteroids,
THEN: There is evidence that the organisms which might be causing the infection are e.coli (.4), klebsiella-pneumoniae (.2), or pseudomonas-aeruginosa (.1)

FIGURE 29-4 The steroids rule.

Figure 29-5 shows how this diagnostic heuristic is justified and incorporated in a problem-solving approach by relating it to strategic, structural, and support knowledge. Recalling Section 29.1, we use the term *strategy* to refer to a plan by which goals and hypotheses are ordered in problem solving. A decision to determine "cause of the infection" before "therapy to administer" is a strategic decision. Similarly, it is a strategic decision to pursue the hypothesis "*E. coli* is causing meningitis" before "*Cryptococcus* is causing meningitis." And recalling an earlier example, deliberately deciding to ask the user about steroids before alcoholism would be a strategic decision. These decisions all lie above the plane of goals and hypotheses,

[4]The English form of rules stated in this paper has been simplified for readability. Sometimes clauses are omitted. Medical examples are for purposes of illustration only.

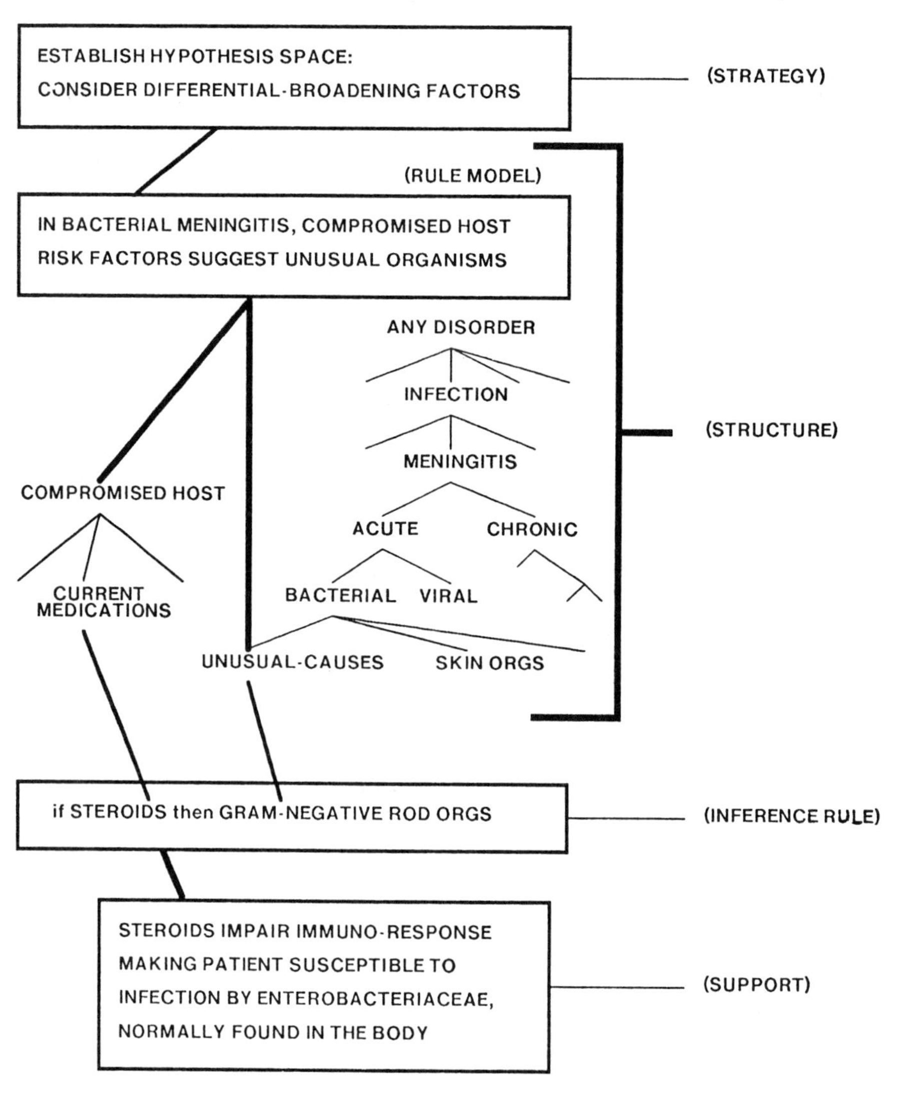

FIGURE 29-5 Augmenting a knowledge source with three kinds of meta-level knowledge: knowledge for indexing, justifying, and invoking a MYCIN rule.

and as discussed later, they can often be stated in domain-independent terms, e.g., "consider differential-broadening factors."

In order to make contact with the knowledge of the domain, a level of *structural knowledge* is necessary. Structural knowledge consists of abstractions that are used to index the domain knowledge. For example, one can classify causes of disease into common and unusual causes, for example, of bacterial meningitis. These concepts provide a *handle* by which a strategy can be applied, a means of referencing the domain-specific knowledge. For example, a strategy might specify considering common causes of a disease; the structural knowledge about bacterial meningitis allows this strategy to be instantiated in that context. This conception of structural knowledge follows directly from Davis' technique of *content-directed invocation* of knowledge sources (see Chapter 28). A handle is a means of indirect reference and is the key to abstracting reasoning in domain-independent terms. The discussion here elaborates on the nature of handles and their role in the explanation of reasoning.

The structural knowledge we will be considering is used to index two kinds of hypotheses: *problem features,* which describe the problem at hand (for example, whether or not the patient is receiving steroids is a problem feature); and *diagnoses,* which characterize the cause of the observed problem features. For example, acute meningitis is a diagnosis. In general, problem features appear in the premises of diagnostic rules, and diagnoses appear in the conclusions. Thus organizations of problem features and diagnoses provide two ways of indexing rule associations: one can use a strategy that brings certain diagnoses to mind and consider rules that support those hypotheses; or one can use a strategy that brings certain problem features to mind, gather that information, and draw conclusions (apply rules) in a data-directed way.

Figure 29-5 shows how a rule model, or *generalized rule,*[5] as a form of structural knowledge, enables either data-directed consideration of the steroids rule or hypothesis-directed consideration. Illustrated are partial hierarchies of problem features (compromised host factors) and diagnoses (kinds of infections, meningitis, etc.)—typical forms of structural knowledge. The specific organisms of the steroids rule are replaced by the set "gram-negative rods," a key hierarchical concept we use for understanding this rule.

Finally, the justification of the steroids rule, a link between the problem feature hypothesis "patient is receiving steroids" and the diagnostic hypothesis "gram-negative rod organisms are causing acute bacterial infectious meningitis," is based on a causal argument about steroids impairing the body's ability to control organisms that normally reside in the body. While this *support knowledge* is characteristically low-level or narrow in contrast with the strategical justification for considering compromised host risk factors, it still makes interesting contact with structural terms, such as the mention of *Enterobacteriaceae,* which are kinds of gram-negative rod organisms. In the next section, we will consider the nature of rule justifications in more detail, illustrating how structural knowledge enables us to make sense of a rule by tying it to the underlying causal process.

[5]Davis' rule models (Chapter 28), generated automatically, capture patterns, but they do not restate rules more abstractly as we intend here.

29.3 Explaining a Rule

Here we consider the logical bases for rules: what kinds of arguments justify the rules, and what is their relation to a mechanistic model of the domain? We use the terms "explain" and "justify" synonymously, although the sense of "making clear what is not understood" (explain) is intended more than "vindicating, showing to be right or lawful" (justify).

29.3.1 Different Kinds of Justifications

There are four kinds of justifications for MYCIN's rules: identification, cause, world fact, and domain fact. In order to explain a rule, it is first necessary to know what kind of justification it is based on.

1. Rules that use identifying properties of an object to classify it are called *identification rules.* Most of MYCIN's rules that use laboratory observations of an unknown are like this: "If the organism is a gram-negative, anaerobic rod, its genus may be bacteroides (.6)." Thus an identification rule is based on the properties of a class.
2. Rules whose premise and action are related by a causal argument are called *causal rules.* The causality can go in either direction in MYCIN rules: "symptom caused by disease" or, more commonly, "prior problem causes disease." Szolovits and Pauker (1978) suggest that it is possible to subdivide causal rules according to the scientific understanding of the causal link:
   a. *empirical association* (a correlation for which the process is not understood),
   b. *complication* (direction of causality is known, but the conditions of the process are not understood), and
   c. *mechanism* (process is well modeled).

   Most of MYCIN's causal rules represent medical complications that are not easily expressed as anatomical relations and physiological processes. The certainty factors in MYCIN's causal rules generally represent a mixture of probabilistic and cost/benefit judgment. Rather than simply encoding the strength of association between symptom and cause, a certainty factor also captures how important it is that a diagnosis be considered in therapy selection.
3. Rules that are based on empirical, commonsense knowledge about the world are called *world fact rules.* An example is "If the patient is male, then the patient is not pregnant." Other examples are based on social patterns of behavior, such as the fact that a young male might be a military recruit and thus be living in a crowded environment where disease spreads readily.

4. *Domain fact rules* link hypotheses on the basis of domain definitions. An example is "If a drug was administered orally and it is poorly absorbed in the GI tract, then the drug was not administered adequately." By definition, to be administered adequately a drug must be present in the body at high enough dosage levels. By using domain fact rules, the program can relate problem features to one another, reducing the amount of information it has to request from the user.

In summary, a rule link captures class properties, social and domain facts, and probabilistic and cost/benefit judgments. When a definition, property, or world fact is involved, simply saying this provides a reasonable explanation. But causal rules, with their connection to an underlying process of disease, require much more, so we will concentrate on them.

29.3.2 Levels of Explanation—What's Not in a Rule?

In this section we consider the problem of justifying a causal rule, the tetracycline rule:

> "If the patient is less than 8 years old, don't prescribe tetracycline."

This rule simply states one of the things that MYCIN needs to know to properly prescribe drugs for youngsters. The rule does not mention the underlying causal process (chelation, or drug deposition in developing bones) and the social ramifications (blackened permanent teeth) on which it is based. From this example, it should be clear that the justifications of MYCIN's rules lie outside of the rule base. In other words, the record of inference steps that ties premise to action has been left out. A few questions need to be raised here: Did the expert really leave out steps of reasoning? What is a justification for? And what is a good justification?

Frequently, we refer to rules like MYCIN's as "compiled knowledge." However, when we ask physicians to justify rules that they believe and follow, they very often can't explain why the rules are correct. Or their rationalizations are so slow in coming and so tentative that it is clear they are not articulating reasoning steps that are consciously followed. Leaps from data to conclusion are justified because the intermediate steps (like the process of chelation and the social ramifications) generally remain the same from problem to problem. There is no need to step through this knowledge—to express it conditionally in rules. Thus, for the most part, MYCIN's rules are not compiled in the sense that they represent a deliberate composition of reasoning steps by the rule authors. They are compiled in the sense that they are optimizations that leave out unnecessary steps—evolved patterns of reasoning that cope with the demands of ordinary problems.

If an expert does not think about the reasoning steps that justify a rule, why does a student need to be told about them? One simple reason

tetracycline in youngster
→ chelation of the drug in growing bones
→ teeth discoloration
→ undesirable body change
→ don't administer tetracycline

FIGURE 29-6 Causal knowledge underlying the tetracycline rule.

is so the student can remember the rule. A justification can even serve as memory aid (mnemonic) without being an accurate description of the underlying phenomena. For example, medical students have long been told to think in terms of "bacteria eating glucose" from which they can remember that low CSF (cerebrospinal fluid) glucose is a sign of a bacterial meningitis (as opposed to fungal or viral meningitis). The interpretative rule is learned by analogy to a familiar association (glucose is a food, and bacteria are analogous to larger organisms that eat food). This explanation has been discredited by biological research, but it is still a useful mnemonic.

Given that an accurate causal argument is usually expected, how is a satisfying explanation constructed? To see the difficulty here, observe that, in expanding a rule, there is seemingly no limit to the details that might be included. Imagine expanding the tetracycline rule by introducing three intermediate concepts as shown in Figure 29-6. The choice of intermediate concepts (the grain size of rules) is arbitrary, of course. For example, there is no mention of how the chelation occurs. What are the conditions? What molecules or ions are involved? There are arbitrarily many levels of detail in a causal explanation. To explain a rule, we not only need to know the intermediate steps, we also need to decide which steps in the reasoning need to be explained. Purpose (how deep an understanding is desirable) and prior knowledge are obviously important.

Conceptually, the support knowledge for a causal rule is a tree of rules, where each node is a reasoning step that can theoretically be justified in terms of finer-grained steps. The important thing to remember is that MYCIN is a flat system of rules. It can only state its immediate reasoning steps and cannot explain them on *any* level of detail.

29.3.3 Problem Features, the Hypothesis Taxonomy, and Rule Generalizations

A tree of rules seems unwieldy. Surely most teachers cannot expand on every reasoning step down to the level of the most detailed physical knowledge known. The explanation tree for the tetracycline rule, for example, quickly gets into chemical bonding theory. Explaining a rule (or under-

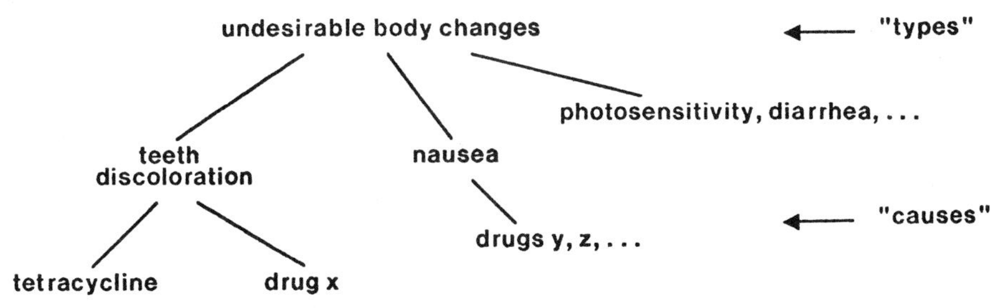

FIGURE 29-7 Problem feature hierarchy for contraindication rules.

standing one) does not require that every detail of causality be considered. Instead, a relatively high level of explanation is generally satisfying—most readers probably feel satisfied by the explanation that tetracycline causes teeth discoloration. This level of satisfaction has something to do with the student's prior knowledge.

For an explanation to be satisfying, it must make contact with already known concepts. We can characterize explanations by studying the kinds of intermediate concepts they use. For example, it is significant that most contraindication rules, reasons for not giving antibiotics, refer to "undesirable body changes." This pattern is illustrated hierarchically in Figure 29-7. The first level gives types of undesirable changes; the second level gives causes of these types of changes. Notice that this figure contains the last step of the expanded tetracycline rule and a leap from tetracycline to this step. The pattern connecting drugs to the idea of undesirable body changes forms the basis of an expectation for explanations: we will be satisfied if a particular explanation connects to this pattern. In other words, given an effect that we can interpret as an undesirable body change, we will understand why a drug causing that effect should not be given. We might want to know how the effect occurs, but here again, we will rest easy on islands of familiarity, just as we don't feel compelled to ask why people don't want black teeth.

To summarize, key concepts in rule explanations are abstractions that connect to a pattern of reasoning we have encountered before. This suggests that one way to explain a rule, to make contact with a familiar reasoning pattern, is to generalize the rule. We can see this more clearly from the viewpoint of diagnosis, which makes rich use of hierarchical abstractions.

Consider the following fragment from a rule we call the leukopenia rule:

> "If a complete blood count is available and the white blood count is less than 2.5 units, then the following bacteria might be

causing infection: e.coli (.75), pseudomonas-aeruginosa (.5), klebsiella-pneumoniae (.5)."

How can we explain this rule? First, we generalize the rule, as shown in Figure 29-8. The premise concepts in the rules on the left-hand side of levels 1 through 3 are problem features (cf. Section 29.2), organized hierarchically by different kinds of relations. Generally, a physician speaks loosely about the connections—referring to leukopenia both as a cause of immunosuppression as well as a kind of immunosuppression—probably because the various causes are thought of hierarchically.

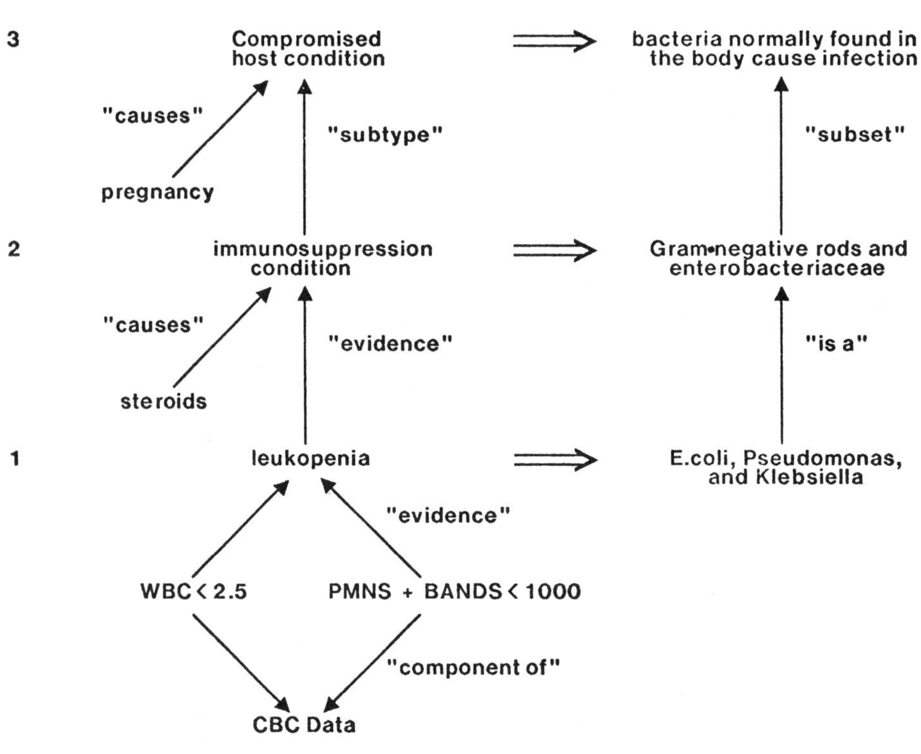

FIGURE 29-8 Generalizations of the leukopenia rule.

The relationships among CBC, WBC, and leukopenia reveal some interesting facts about how MYCIN's rules are constructed. WBC is one component of a complete blood count (CBC). If the CBC is not available, it makes no sense to ask for any of the components. Thus the CBC clause in the leukopenia rule is an example of a *screening clause*. Another example of a screening clause is the age clause in

> "If . . . age is greater than 17 and the patient is an alcoholic, then . . ."

Here the relation is a social fact; if the patient is not an adult, we assume that he is not an alcoholic. The third relation we observe is a subtype, as in

> "If . . . the patient has undergone surgery and the patient has undergone neurosurgery, then . . . "

All screening relations can be expressed as rules, and some are, such as

> "If the patient has not undergone surgery, then the patient has not undergone cardiac surgery."

(stated negatively, as is procedurally useful). The philosophy behind MYCIN's rule set is inconsistent in this respect; to be economical and to make the relationship between clauses explicit, all screening clauses should be expressed as world fact rules or hierarchies of parameters. Indeed, the age/alcoholic relation suggests that some of the relations are not definitional and should be modified by certainty factors.

Viewed as a semantic network representation, MYCIN's rules are links without labels. Even when rules explicitly link problem features, the *kind of relation* is not represented because MYCIN's rule language does not allow the link to be labeled. For example, a rule could state "If no CBC was taken, then WBC is not available," but MYCIN allows no way of saying that WBC is a *component of* CBC. Finally, when one problem feature serves as a redefinition of another, such as the relation between leukopenia and WBC, the more abstract problem feature tends to be left out altogether. "Leukopenia" is not a MYCIN parameter; the rule mentions WBC directly, another manifestation of knowledge compilation. *For purposes of explanation, we argue that problem features, their relations, and the nature of the link should be explicit.*

Returning to Figure 29-8, the action concepts, or *diagnostic hypotheses* shown on the right-hand side, are part of a large hierarchy of causes that the problem solver will cite in the final diagnosis. The links in this diagnosis space generally specify refinement of cause, although in our example they strictly designate subclasses. Generally, problem features are abstractions of patient states indicated by the observable symptoms, while the diagnosis space is made up of abstractions of causal processes that produce the symptoms. Paralleling our observations about rule problem features, we note that the relations among diagnostic hypotheses are not represented in MYCIN—nowhere in the knowledge base does it explicitly state that *E. coli* is a bacterium.

Now suppose that the knowledge in Figure 29-8 were available, how would this help us to explain the leukopenia rule? The idea is that we first restate the rule on a higher level. We point out that a low WBC indicates leukopenia, which is a form of immunosuppression, thus tying the rule to the familiar pattern that implicates gram-negative rods and *Enterobacteriaceae.* This is directly analogous to pointing out that tetracycline causes teeth discoloration, which is a form of undesirable body change, suggesting that the drug should not be given.

By re-representing Figure 29-8 linearly, we see that it is an expansion of the original rule:

WBC < 2.5 → leukopenia
→ immunosuppression
→ compromised host
→ infection by organisms found in body
→ gram-negative rods and *Enterobacteriaceae*
→ *E. coli, Pseudomonas,* and *Klebsiella*

The expansion marches up the problem feature hierarchy and then back down the hierarchy of diagnoses. The links of this expansion involve causality composed with identification, subtype, and subset relations. By the hierarchical relationships, a rule on one level "explains" the rule below it. For example, the rule on level 3 provides the detail that links immunosuppression to the gram-negative rods. By generalizing, we have made a connection to familiar concepts.

Tabular rules provide an interesting special case. The CSF protein rule shown in Figure 29-9 appears to be quite formidable. Graphing this rule as shown in Figure 29-10, we find a relatively simple relation that an expert states as "If the protein value is less than 40, I think of viral infections; if it is more than 100, I think of bacterial, fungal, or TB." This is the first level of generalization, the principle that is implicit in the rule. The second level elicited from the expert is "If the protein value is low, I think of an

---

RULE500 (The CSF Protein Rule)

IF: 1) The infection which requires therapy is meningitis,
2) A lumbar puncture has been performed on the patient, and
3) The CSF protein is known
THEN: The type of the infection is as follows:
If the CSF protein is:
a) less than 41 then: not bacterial (.5), viral (.7), not fungal (.6), not tb (.5);
b) between 41 and 100 then: bacterial (.1), viral (.4), fungal (.1);
c) between 100 and 200 then: bacterial (.3), fungal (.3), tb (.3);
d) between 200 and 300 then: bacterial (.4), not viral (.5), fungal (.4), tb (.4);
e) greater or equal to 300 then: bacterial (.4), not viral (.6), fungal (.4), tb (.4);

FIGURE 29-9 The CSF protein rule.

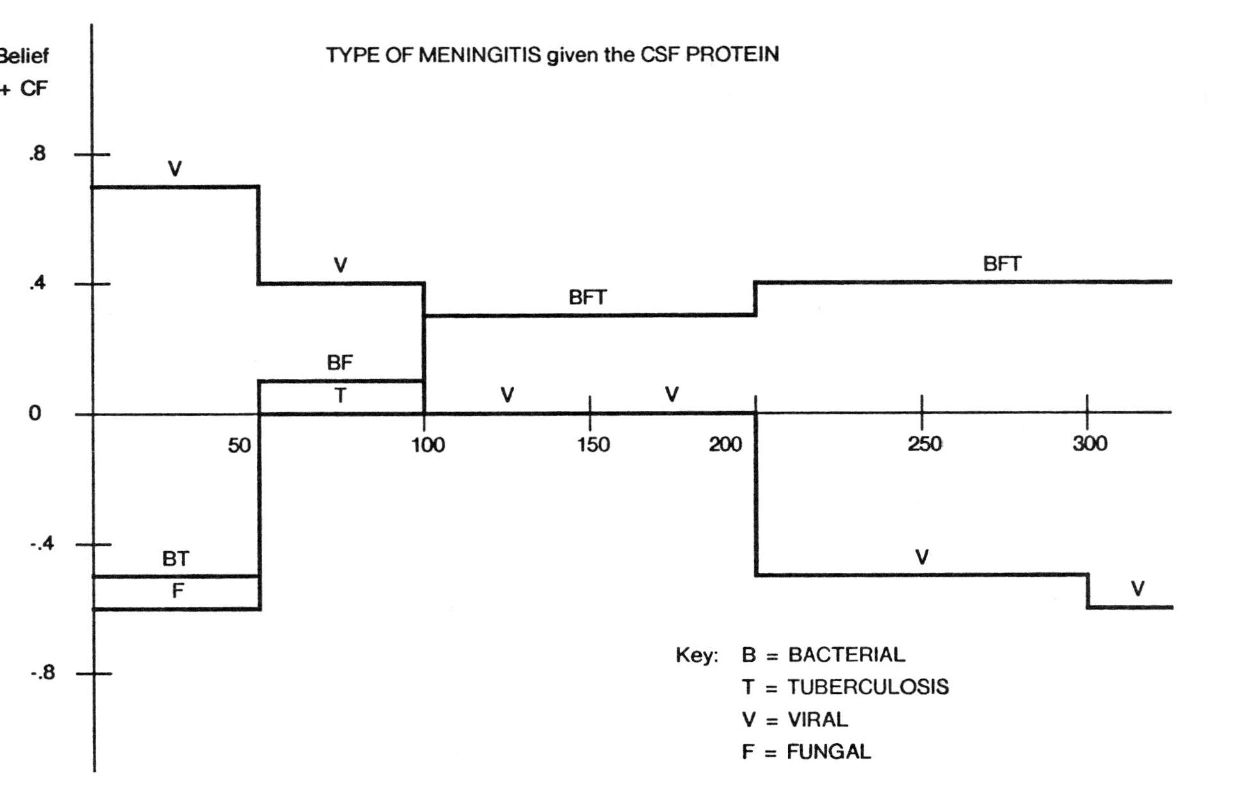

FIGURE 29-10 Graph of the conclusions made by the CSF protein rule (Figure 29-9).

acute process; if it is high, I think of a severe or long-term process."[6] Then, at the highest level, the expert states, "An infection in the meninges stimulates protein production." So in moving up abstraction hierarchies on both the premise and action sides of the rule (acute and chronic are subtypes of infection), we arrive at a mnemonic, just like "bacteria eat glucose." Abstractions of both the observations and the conclusions are important for understanding the rule.

We might be surprised that explanations of rules provide levels of *detail* by referring to more *general* concepts. We are accustomed to the fact that principled theoretical explanations of, say, chemical phenomena, refer to atomic properties, finer-grained levels of causality. Why should a rule explanation refer to concepts like "compromised host" or "organisms normally found in the body"? The reason is that in trying to understand a rule like the steroids rule, we are first trying to relate it to our understanding of what an infection is at a high, almost metaphorical level. In fact, there are lower-level "molecular" details of the mechanism that could be explained, for example, how steroids actually change the immunological system. But our initial focus as understanders is at the top level—to link the problem feature (steroids) to the global process of meningitis infection. We ask, "What makes it happen? What role do steroids play in the infectious meningitis process?"

The concept of "compromised host" is a label for a poorly understood causal pattern that has value because we can relate it to our understanding of the infection process. It enables us to relate the steroids or WBC evidence to the familiar metaphor in which infection is a war that is fought by the body against invading organisms.

> "If a patient is compromised, his or her defenses are down; he or she is vulnerable to attack."

In general, causal rules argue that some kind of process has occurred. We expect a top-level explanation of a causal rule to relate the premise of the rule to our most general idea of the process being explained. This provides a constraint for how the rule should be generalized, the subject of the next section.

29.3.4 Tying an Explanation to a Causal Model

MYCIN's diagnostic rules are arguments that a process has occurred in a particular way. There are many kinds of infections, which have different characteristics, but bacterial infections tend to follow the same script: entry of an organism into the body, passage of the organism to the site of infec-

[6]Bacterial meningitis is a severe, acute (short-term) problem, while fungal and TB meningitis are problems of long (chronic) duration.

tion, reproduction of the organism, and causation of observable symptoms. An explanation of a rule that concludes that an organism is causing an infection must demonstrate that this *generic process* has occurred. In short, this is the level of abstraction that the explanation must connect to.

A program was written to demonstrate this idea. The data parameters in MYCIN's 40 diagnostic rules for bacterial meningitis are restated as one or more of the steps of the infectious process script. This restatement is then printed as the explanation of the rule. For example, the program's explanation of the rule linking alcoholism to *Diplococcus* meningitis is:

> The fact that the patient is an alcoholic *allows access of organisms from* the throat and mouth *to* lungs (by reaspiration of secretions).
>
> The fact that the patient is an alcoholic *means that the patient is a compromised host, and so susceptible to infection.*

Words in italics in the first sentence constitute the pattern of "portal and passage." We find that the premise of a rule generally supplies evidence for only a single step of the causal process; the other steps must be inferred by default. For example, the alcoholic rule argues for passage of the *Diplococcus* to the lungs. The person reading this explanation must know that *Diplococcus* is normally found in the mouth and throat of any person and that it proceeds from the lungs to the meninges by the blood. The organism finds conditions favorable for growth because the patient is compromised, as stated in the explanation. In contrast, the leukopenia rule only argues for the patient being a compromised host, so the organisms are the default organisms, those already in the body, which can proceed to the site of infection.[7]

These explanations say which steps are enabled by the data. They place the patient on the path of an infection, so to speak, and leave it to the understander to fill in the other steps with knowledge of how the body normally works. This is why physicians generally refer to the premise data as "predisposing factors." To be understood, a rule must be related to the prior steps in a causal process, the general concepts that explain many rules.

The process of explanation is a bit more complicated in that causal relations may exist between clauses in the rule. We have already seen that one clause may screen another on the basis of world facts, multicomponent test relations, and the subtype relation. The program described here knows these relations and "subtracts off" screening clauses from the rule. Moreover, as discussed in Section 29.4, some clauses describe the context in which the rule applies. These, too, are made explicit for the explanation program and subtracted off. In the vast majority of MYCIN rules, only one premise clause remains, and this is related to the process of infection in the way described above.

---

[7]As physicians would expect, alcoholism also causes infection by gram-negative rods and *Enterobacteriaceae*. We have omitted these for simplicity. However, this example illustrates that a MYCIN rule can have multiple conclusions reached by different causal paths.

When more than one clause remains after the screening and contextual clauses have been removed, our study shows that a causal connection exists between the remaining clauses. We can always isolate one piece of evidence that the rule is about (for example, WBC in the leukopenia rule); we call this the *key factor* of the rule. We call the remaining clauses *restriction clauses.*[8] There are three kinds of relations between a restriction clause and a key factor:

- *A confirmed diagnosis explains a symptom.* For example, a petechial rash would normally be evidence for *Neisseria,* but if the patient has leukemia, it may be the disease causing the rash. Therefore, the rule states, "If the patient has a petechial rash (the key factor) and does not have leukemia (the restriction clause), then *Neisseria* may be causing the meningitis."
- *Two symptoms in combination suggest a different diagnosis than one taken alone.* For example, when both purpuric and petechial rashes occur, then a virus is a more likely cause than *Neisseria.* Therefore, the petechial rule also includes the restriction clause "the patient does not have a purpuric rash."
- *Weak circumstantial evidence is made irrelevant by strong circumstantial evidence.* For example, a head injury so strongly predisposes a patient to infection by skin organisms that the age of the patient, a weak circumstantial factor, is made irrelevant.

In summary, to explain a causal rule, a teacher must know the purposes of the clauses and connect the rule to abstractions in the relevant process script.

29.3.5 The Relation of Medical Heuristics to Principles

It might be argued that we must go to so much trouble to explain MYCIN's rules because they are written on the wrong level. Now that we have a "theory" for which intermediate parameters to include ("portal," "pathway," etc.), why don't we simply rewrite the rules?

The medical knowledge we are trying to codify is really on two levels of detail: (1) principles or generalizations, and (2) empirical details or specializations. MYCIN's rules are empirical. Cleaning them up by representing problem feature relationships explicitly would give us the same set of rules at a higher level. But what would happen if process concepts were incorporated in completely new reasoning steps, for example, if the rule set related problem features to hypotheses about the pathway the organism took through the body? It turns out that reasoning backwards in terms of

[8]Restriction clauses are easy to detect when examining the rule set because they are usually stated negatively.

a causal model is not always appropriate. As we discovered when explaining the rules, not all of the causal steps of the process can be directly confirmed; we can only assume that they have occurred. For example, rather than providing diagnostic clues, the concept of "portal of entry and passage" is very often deduced from the diagnosis itself.

According to this view, principles are good for summarizing arguments, and good to fall back on when you've lost grasp on the problem, but they don't *drive the process* of medical reasoning. Specifically, (1) *if a symptom needs to be explained (is highly unusual), we ask what could cause it* ("Strep-viridans? It is normally found in the mouth. How did it get to the heart? Has the patient had dental work recently?"); (2) *to "prove" that the diagnosis is correct (after it has been constructed), we use a causal argument* ("He has pneumonia; the bacteria obviously got into the blood from the lungs."). Thus causal knowledge can be used to provide feedback that everything fits.

It may be difficult or impossible to expect a set of diagnostic rules both to serve as concise, "clincher" methods for efficiently getting to the right data and still to represent a model of disease. Put another way, a student may need the model if he or she is to understand new associations between disease and manifestations, but will be an inefficient problem solver if he or she always attempts to convert that model directly to a subgoal structure for solving ordinary problems. Szolovits and Pauker (1978) point out that these "first principles" used by a student are "compiled out" of an expert's reasoning.

In meningitis diagnosis, the problem is to manage a broad, if not incoherent, hypothesis set, rather than to pursue a single causal path. The underlying theory recedes to the background, and the expert tends to approach the problem simply in terms of weak associations between observed data and bottom-line conclusions. This may have promoted a rule-writing style that discouraged introducing intermediate concepts such as leukopenia, even where they might have been appropriate.

29.4 Teaching Problem-Solving Strategy

A *strategy* is an approach for solving a problem, a plan for ordering methods so that a goal is reached. It is well accepted that strategic knowledge must be conveyed in teaching diagnostic problem solving. As Brown and Goldstein (1977) say:

> Without explicit awareness of the largely tacit planning and strategic knowledge inherent in each domain, it is difficult for a person to "make sense of" many sequences of behavior as described by a story, a set of instructions, a problem solution, a complex system, etc. . . . The teacher should articulate

for that domain the higher-order planning knowledge and strategic knowledge for formulating and revising hypotheses about what something means.

Strategic knowledge is general, much like the principles of mechanism we discussed earlier; both relate to processes that have structure. Thus it is not sufficient to show a student only MYCIN's solution, the *surface structure* of the program; we must explain why the rules are invoked in a particular order.

Here it is clear how *teaching* how to do something differs from merely *explaining* how something was done: we want the student to be able to replicate what he or she observes, to solve similar problems independently. This is why mnemonics are useful when justifying a rule. Regarding strategy, we must again address human foibles and preference: we must teach a strategy that a human can follow.

The main points of this section are:

- MYCIN's strategy is different from a physician's strategy;
- MYCIN's strategic knowledge is embedded in the rules, indistinguishable from screening and problem feature clauses;
- A domain-independent representation of strategy is useful for teaching and for purposes of economy.

29.4.1 Surface and Deep Structure of MYCIN

A person trying to understand a MYCIN consultation observes that pieces of data are requested by the program as shown in Figure 29-11. Conceptually, these questions are terminals hanging below an AND node in a subgoal tree, as shown in Figure 29-12. Following the terminology of Brown and Goldstein (1977), a rule node is a *method* for achieving a goal (e.g., "organisms that might be causing the infection") by asking questions or pursuing a set of subgoals to achieve. Therefore, the tree of rules and subgoals is part of a deep-structured trace that they postulate is constructed when the understander makes sense of the surface problem solution.

It is not sufficient for a student to know all of the possible methods he or she can bring to bear on a problem. He or she generally needs a *plan* for solving the problem, that is, needs schemata for kinds of problems that can be tackled using different *approaches* or lines of reasoning. A plan sets up a rational sequence of methods that might get you closer to the solution, but without guarantees.

The hypothetico-deductive strategy used in medical problem solving constitutes a plan for focusing on hypotheses and selecting confirmatory questions (Elstein et al., 1978). However, the methods selected in Figure 29-12 (Rules 511 through 578) have been applied in a fixed, arbitrary order—not planned by the rule author. MYCIN has no "deep structure"

31) Has Pt538 ever undergone any type of surgery?
** **YES**
32) Does Pt538 have a history of NEUROSURGERY?
** **NO**
33) Does Pt538 live in a crowded environment?
** **NO**
34) Do you suspect recent alcoholic history in Pt538?
** **NO**
35) Is meningitis a hospital-acquired infection?
** **YES**
36) Is Pt538's clinical history consistent with EPIGLOTTITIS?
** **NO**
37) Is Pt538's clinical history consistent with OTITIS-MEDIA?
** **NO**
38) Has Pt538 ever undergone splenectomy?
** **NO**
39) Is Pt538 a burn patient?
** **YES**

FIGURE 29-11 Excerpt from a MYCIN consultation showing requests for relevant data.

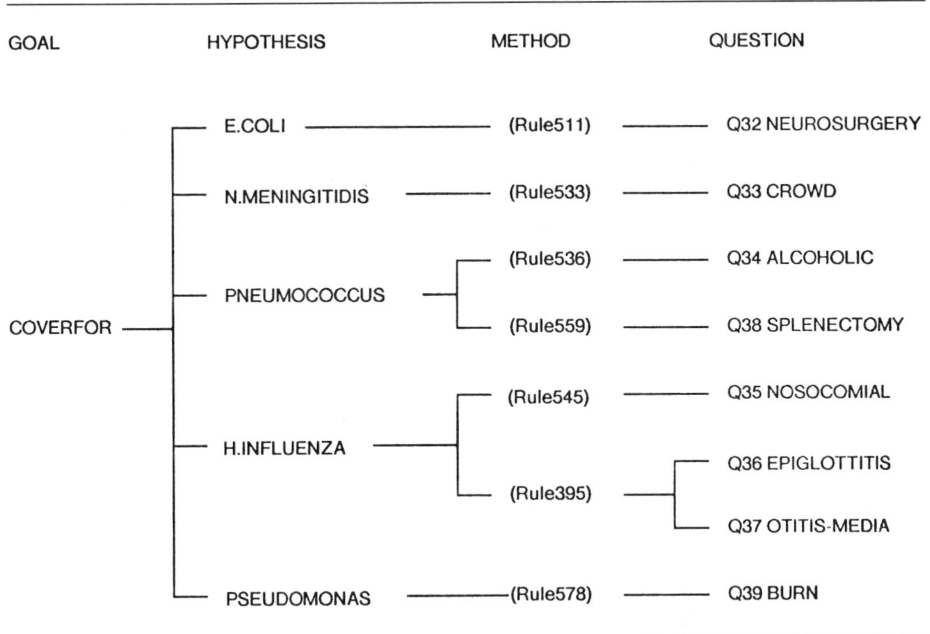

FIGURE 29-12 Portion of the AND/OR tree corresponding to the questions shown in Figure 29-11 (reorganized according to the hypothesis each rule supports).

RULE092 (The Goal Rule)

IF: 1) Gather information about cultures taken from the patient and therapy he is receiving,
2) Determine if the organisms growing on cultures require therapy
3) Consider circumstantial evidence for additional organisms that therapy should cover
THEN: Determine the best therapy recommendation

RULE535 (The Alcoholic Rule)

IF: 1) The infection which requires therapy is meningitis,
2) Only circumstantial evidence is available for this case,
3) The type of meningitis is bacterial,
4) The age of the patient is greater than 17 years, and
5) The patient is an alcoholic,
THEN: There is evidence that the organisms which might be causing the infection are diplococcus-pneumoniae (.3) or e.coli (.2)

FIGURE 29-13 The goal rule and the alcoholic rule.

plan at this level; the program is simply applying rules (methods) exhaustively. This lack of similarity to human reasoning severely limits the usefulness of the system for teaching problem solving.

However, MYCIN does have a problem-solving strategy above the level of rule application, namely the control knowledge that causes it to pursue a goal at a certain point in the diagnosis. We can see this by examining how rules interact in backward chaining. Figure 29-13 shows the goal rule and a rule that it indirectly invokes. In order to evaluate the third clause of the goal rule, MYCIN tries each of the COVERFOR rules; the alcoholic rule is one of these (see also Figure 29-12). We call the goal rule a *task rule* to distinguish it from inference rules. Clause order counts here; this is more a procedure than a logical conjunction. The first three clauses of the alcoholic rule, the *context clauses,* also control the order in which goals are pursued, just as is true for a task rule. We can represent this hidden structure of goals by a tree which we call the *inference structure* of the rule base (produced by "hanging" the rule set from the goal rule). Figure 29-14 illustrates part of MYCIN's inference structure.[9,10]

The program's strategy comes to light when we list these goals in the order in which the depth-first interpreter makes a final decision about them. For example, since at least one rule that concludes "significant" (goal 4 in Figure 29-14) mentions "contaminant" (goal 3), MYCIN applies *all* of the "contaminant" rules before making a final decision about "significant." Analyzing the entire rule set in a similar way gives us the ordering (shown in Figure 29-14):

[9]Some definitions of terms used in the following discussion: TREATFOR = organisms to be treated, based on direct laboratory observation; COVERFOR = organisms to be treated, based on circumstantial evidence; SIGNIFICANT = this organism merits therapeutic attention, based on the patient's degree of sickness and validity of culture results; CONTAMINANT = the finding of this organism is spurious; it was probably introduced during sampling from the cultured site of the body, as a blood culture might include skin organisms.

[10]We leave out the goals REGIMEN and TREATFOR because they are just placeholders for task rules, like subroutine names.

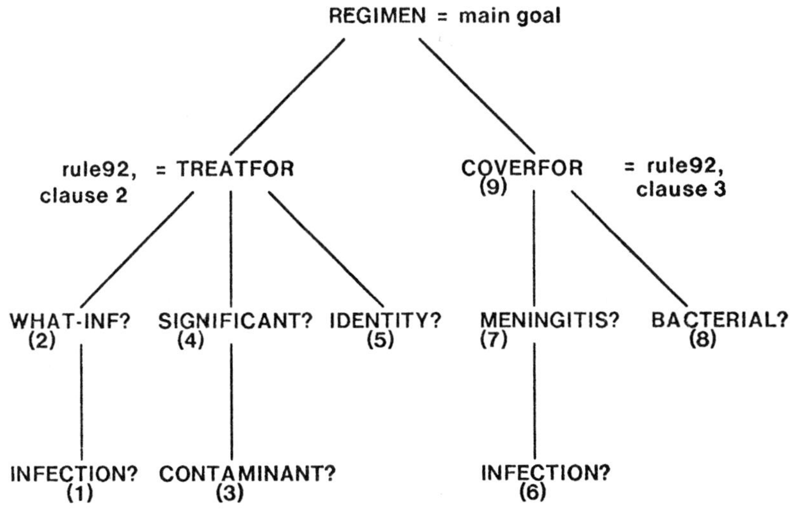

FIGURE 29-14 Portion of MYCIN's inference structure. (Numbers give the order in which nonplaceholder goals are achieved by the depth-first interpreter.)

1. Is there an infection?
2. Is it bacteremia, cystitis, or meningitis?
3. Are there any contaminated cultures?
4. Are there any good cultures with significant growth?
5. Is the organism identity known?
6. Is there an infection? (already done in Step 1)
7. Does the patient have meningitis? (already done in Step 2)
8. Is it bacterial?
9. Are there specific bacteria to cover for?

MYCIN's diagnostic plan is in two parts, and both proceed by top-down refinement. This demonstrates that a combination of structural knowledge (the taxonomy of the diagnosis space—infection, meningitis, bacterial, *Diplococcus* . . .) and strategic knowledge (traversing the taxonomy from the top down) is procedurally embedded in the rules. In other words, we could write a program that interpreted an explicit, declarative representation of the diagnosis taxonomy and domain-independent form of the strategy to bring about the same effect.

At this level, MYCIN's diagnostic strategy is not a complete model of how physicians think, but it could be useful to a student. As the quote from Brown and Goldstein would indicate, and as has been confirmed in GUIDON research, teachers do articulate both the structure of the problem

META-RULE002

IF: 1) The infection is pelvic-abscess, and
2) There are rules which mention in their premise enterobacteriaceae, and
3) There are rules which mention in their premise gram-positive rods,
THEN: There is suggestive evidence (.4) that the former should be done before the latter

FIGURE 29-15 A MYCIN meta-rule.

space and the nature of the search strategy to students. This means that we need to represent explicitly the fact that the diagnosis space is hierarchical and to represent strategies in a domain-independent form. If a strategy is not in domain-independent form, it can be taught by examples, but not explained.

29.4.2 Representing Strategic Knowledge in Meta-Rules

How might we represent domain-independent strategic knowledge in a rule-based system? In the context of the MYCIN system, Davis pursued the representation of strategic knowledge by using *meta-rules* to order and prune methods (Chapter 28). These meta-rules are invoked just before the object-level rules are applied to achieve a goal. An example of an infectious disease meta-rule is shown in Figure 29-15 (see Figure 28-12 for other examples). Observe that this is a *strategy* for pursuing a goal. In particular, this meta-rule might be associated with the goal "identity of the organism." It will be invoked to order the rules for every subgoal in the search tree below this goal; in this simple way, the rule sets up a line of reasoning. This mechanism causes some goals to be pursued before others, orders the questions asked by the system, and hence changes the surface structure of the consultation.

Although meta-rules like this can capture and implement strategic knowledge about a domain, they have their deficiencies. Like the performance rules we have examined, Davis's domain-dependent examples of meta-rules leave out knowledge important for explanation. Not only do they leave out the domain-specific support knowledge that justifies the rules, they leave out the domain-independent strategic principles that GUIDON should teach. In short, meta-rules provide the *mechanism* for controlling the use of rules, but not the domain-independent *language* for making the strategy explicit.

The implicit strategic principle that lies behind Meta-Rule 002 is that common causes of a disorder should be considered first. The structural knowledge that ties this strategy to the object-level diagnostic rules is an explicit partitioning of the diagnosis space taxonomy, indicating that the group of organisms called *Enterobacteriaceae* are more likely than gram-positive rod organisms to cause pelvic infections. This is what we want to teach the student. One can imagine different common causes for different infection types, requiring different meta-rules. But if all meta-rules are as specific as Meta-Rule 002, principles will be compiled into many rules redundantly and the teaching points will be lost.

What does a domain-independent meta-rule look like, and how is it interfaced with the object-level rules? To explore this question, we have reconfigured the MYCIN rule base into a new system, called NEOMYCIN (Clancey and Letsinger, 1981). Briefly, meta-rules are organized hierarchically (again!) into tasks, such as "group and refine the hypothesis space." These rules manage a changing hypothesis list by applying different kinds of knowledge sources, as appropriate. Knowledge sources are essentially the object-level rules, indexed in the taxonomy of the diagnosis space by a domain-independent structural language.

For example, one meta-rule for achieving the task of pursuing a hypothesis is "If there are unusual causes, then pursue them."[11] Suppose that the current hypothesis is "bacterial meningitis." The program will use the structural label "unusual causes" to retrieve the nodes "gram-negative rods," "enterobacteriaceae," and "listeria," add them to the hypothesis list, and pursue them in turn. When there are no "unusual causes" indicated, the meta-rule simply does not apply. Pursuing gram-negative rods, the program will find that leukopenia is a relevant factor, but will first ask if the patient is a compromised host (Figure 29-8), modeling a physician's efficient casting of wider questions.

Other terms in the structural language used by NEOMYCIN's domain-independent meta-rules are

1. process features, such as *extent* and *location* of disease;
2. the *enabling step* of a causal process;
3. *subtype*;
4. *cause*;
5. *trigger association*;
6. *problem feature screen*; and structural properties of the taxonomy, such as *sibling*.

In effect, the layer of structural knowledge allows us to separate out *what* the heuristic is from *how* it will be used. How domain-specific heuristics like MYCIN's rules should be properly integrated with procedural, strategic knowledge is an issue at the heart of the old "declarative/procedural

[11]This rule appears after the rule for considering common causes, and the ordering is marked as strategically significant. Domain-independent meta-rules have justifications, organization, and strategies for using them. Their justification refers to properties of the search space and the processor's capabilities.

controversy" (Winograd, 1975). We conclude here that, for purposes of teaching, the hierarchies of problem features and of the diagnosis space should be represented explicitly, providing a useful means for indexing the heuristics by both premise and action. A structural language of cause, class, and process can connect this domain-specific knowledge to domain-independent meta-rules, the strategy for problem solving.

29.4.3 Self-Referencing Rules

Self-referencing rules provide an interesting special example of how problem-solving strategies can be embedded in MYCIN's rules. A rule is self-referencing if the goal concluded by the action is also mentioned in the premise. An example is the aerobicity rule shown in Figure 29-16.[12]

RULE086

IF: 1) The aerobicity of the organism is not known, and
2) The culture was obtained more than 2 days ago,
THEN: There is evidence that the aerobicity of the organism is obligate-aerob (.5) or facultative (.5)

FIGURE 29-16 The aerobicity rule.

This rule is tried only after all of the non–self-referencing rules have been applied. The cumulative conclusion of the non–self-referencing rules is held aside, then the self-referencing rules are tried, using in each rule the tentative conclusion. Thus the first clause of Rule 86 will be true only if none of the standard rules made a conclusion. The effect is to reconsider a tentative conclusion. When the original conclusion is changed by the self-referencing rules, this is a form of nonmonotonic reasoning (Winograd, 1980). We can restate MYCIN's self-referencing rules in domain-independent terms:

- *If nothing has been observed, consider situations that have no visible manifestations.* For example, the aerobicity rule: "If no organism is growing in the culture, it may be an organism that takes a long time to grow (obligate-aerob and facultative organisms)."
- The self-referencing mechanism makes it possible to state this rule without requiring a long premise that is logically exclusive from the remainder of the rule set.

[12]Aerobicity refers to whether an organism can grow in the presence of oxygen. A facultative organism can grow with or without oxygen; an anaerobic organism cannot grow with oxygen present; and an obligate-aerob is aerobic only in a certain stage of growth. Note that the rule is self-referencing in that aerobicity is mentioned in both the premise and the conclusion.

- *If unable to make a deduction, assume the most probable situation.* For example: "If the gram stain is unknown and the organism is a coccus, then assume that it is gram-positive."
- *If there is evidence for two hypotheses, A and B, that tend to be confused, then rule out B.* For example: "If there is evidence for TB and fungal, and you have hard data for fungal, rule out TB."

Like Meta-Rule 002, self-referencing rules provide a useful mechanism for controlling the use of knowledge, but they leave out both the domain-dependent justification and the general, domain-independent reasoning strategy of which they are examples. These rules illustrate that strategy involves more than a search plan; it also takes in principles for reasoning about evidence. It is not clear that a teacher needs to state these principles explicitly to a student. They tend to be either common sense or almost impossible to think about independently of an example. Nevertheless, they are yet another example of strategic knowledge that is implicit in MYCIN's rules.

29.5 Implications for Modifiability and Performance

MYCIN achieved good problem-solving performance even without having to reason about the structural, strategic, and support knowledge we have been considering. However, there are situations in which knowledge of justification and strategy allows one to be a more flexible problem solver, to cope with novel situations, in ways that MYCIN cannot. Knowing the basis of a rule allows you to know when not to apply it, or how to modify it for special circumstances. For example, knowing that tetracycline won't kill the young patient but the infection might, you may have to dismiss social ramifications and prescribe the drug. You can deliberately break the rule because you understand the assumptions underlying it.

There will also be problems that cannot be diagnosed using MYCIN's rules. For example, several years ago *Coccidioides* meningitis strangely appeared in the San Francisco Bay Area. We would say that this "violates all the rules." To explain what was happening, one has to reason about the underlying mechanisms. The organisms were traveling from the San Joaquin Valley to the Bay Area by "freak southeastern winds," as the newspapers reported. The basic mechanism of disease was not violated, but this time the patients didn't have to travel to the Valley to come in contact with the disease. A human expert can understand this because he or she can fit the new situation to the model. Examples like these make us realize that

AI systems like MYCIN can only perform some of the functions of an expert.

Regarding modifiability, the process of reconfiguring MYCIN's rules in NEOMYCIN's terms required many hours of consultation with the original rule authors in order to unravel the rules. As shown in this paper, the lack of recorded principles for using the representation makes it difficult to interpret the purposes of clauses and rules. The strategy and overall design of the program have to be deduced by drawing diagrams like Figure 29-14. Imagine the difficulty any physician new to MYCIN would have modifying the CSF protein table (Figure 29-9); clearly, he or she would first need an explanation from the program of why it is correct.

We also need a principled representation to avoid a problem we call *concept broadening*. When intermediate problem abstractions are omitted, use of goals becomes generalized and weakened. This happened in MYCIN as the meaning of "significance" grew to include both "evidence of infection" and "noncontaminated cultures." As long as the rule author makes an association between the data and some parameter he or she wants to influence, it doesn't matter for correct performance that the rule is vague. But vague rules are difficult to understand and modify.

A rule base is built and extended like any other program. Extensive documentation and a well-structured design are essential, as in any engineering endeavor. The framework of knowledge types and purposes that we have described would constitute a "typed" rule language that could make it easier for an expert to organize his or her thoughts. On the other hand, we must realize that this meta-level analysis may impose an extra burden by turning the expert into a taxonomist of his or her own knowledge—a task that may require considerable assistance, patience, and tools.

29.6 Application of the Framework to Other Systems

To illustrate further the idea of the strategy, structure, and support framework and to demonstrate its usefulness for explaining how a program reasons, several knowledge-based programs are described below in terms of the framework. For generality, we will call inference associations such as MYCIN's rules *knowledge sources* (KS's). We will not be concerned here with the representational notation used in a program, whether it be frames, production rules, or something else. Instead, we are trying to establish an understanding of the knowledge contained in the system: what kinds of inferences are made at the KS level, how these KS's are structured explicitly in the system, and how this structure is used by strategies for invoking KS's. This is described in Table 29-1.

TABLE 29-1 Examples of Various Types of Knowledge Structures in Several AI Systems

System	*Domain*	*KS example*	*Strategy*	*Structure*	*Support*
DENDRAL (Buchanan and Feigenbaum, 1978)	Chemistry, mass spectrometry analysis	Identification rules relating functional groups to spectral peaks	Aggregation heuristics build superatoms and generate all plausible interstitial structures	Family trees of functional groups (ketones, ethers, etc.)	Molecular chemistry
HEARSAY II (Erman et al., 1980)	Speech understanding	Hypothesizing words from syllable level	Policy KS's control hypothesizing words to generate thresholds (data-directed)	Hierarchy of interpretation levels with links to KS's	Grammar identification properties of phonemes, syllables, and words
AM (Lenat, 1976)	Concept formation, mathematical discovery	Rules to create concepts and fill in facets	Activity heuristics propose tasks (priority agenda focuses heuristics)	Hierarchy of heuristics associated with most general concept/context to which they apply	Theory of interestingness, chiefly based on generalizing and specializing
MOLGEN (Stefik, 1979)	Molecular genetics, experiment planning	Specific lab techniques: input objects → molecular changes and byproducts	Determine differences, sketch plan, refine steps (message passing)	Hierarchy of laboratory operation types (used by refinement design operator)	Processes of molecular biology
CENTAUR (Aikins, 1983)	Medical diagnosis, pulmonary function	Disease component → evidence for prototype	Hypothesis-directed, top-down refinement (agenda)	Hierarchy of disease prototypes	Disease patterns, biological processes
NEOMYCIN (Clancey and Letsinger, 1981)	Medical diagnosis, diseases causing neurological symptoms	Data → evidence for disease process or *causal* state/category	Grouping and refining list of hypotheses (meta-rules focus pursuit)	Multiple hierarchies of etiological processes	Disease patterns, biological processes

29.6.1 The Character of Structural Knowledge

One product of this study is a characterization of different ways of structuring KS's for different strategical purposes. In all cases, the effect of the structural knowledge is to provide a handle for separating out what the KS is from when it is to be applied.[13]

The different ways of structuring KS's are summarized here according to the processing rationale:

- *Organize KS's hierarchically by hypothesis for consistency in data-directed interpretation.* In DENDRAL, if a functional group is ruled out, more specific members of the family are not considered during forward-directed, preliminary interpretation of spectral peaks. Without this organization of KS's, earlier versions of DENDRAL could generate a subgroup as a plausible interpretation while ruling out a more general form of the subgroup, as if to say "This is an ethyl ketone but not a ketone." (Buchanan et al., 1970).
- *Organize KS's hierarchically by hypothesis to eliminate redundant effort in hypothesis-directed refinement.* In DENDRAL, the family trees prevent the exhaustive structure generator from generating subgroups whose more general forms have been ruled out. The same principle is basic to most medical diagnosis systems that organize diagnoses in a taxonomy and use a top-down refinement strategy, such as CENTAUR and NEOMYCIN.
- *Organize KS's by multiple hypothesis hierarchies for efficient grouping (hypothesis-space splitting).* Besides using the hierarchy of generic disease processes (infectious, cancerous, toxic, traumatic, psychosomatic, etc.), NEOMYCIN groups the same diseases by multiple hierarchies according to disease process features (organ system involved, spread in the system, progression over time, etc.). When hypotheses are under consideration that do not fall into one confirmed subtree of the primary etiological hierarchy, the group and differentiate strategy is invoked to find a process feature dimension along which two or more current hypotheses differ. A question will then be asked, or a hypothesis pursued, to differentiate among the hypotheses on this dimension.
- *Organize KS's for each hypothesis on the basis of how KS data relates to the hypothesis, for focusing on problem features.* In NEOMYCIN, additional relations make explicit special kinds of connections between data and hypotheses, such as "this problem feature is the enabling causal step for this diagnostic process," and meta-rules order the selection of questions (invocation of KS's) by indexing them indirectly through these relations. For example, "If an enabling causal step is known for the hypothesis to be confirmed, try to confirm that problem feature." The meta-rules that

[13]In this section, the term *hypothesis* generally refers to a diagnostic or explanatory interpretation made by a KS (in terms of some model), although it can also be a hypothesis that a particular problem feature is present.

reference these different relations ("enabling step," "trigger," "most likely manifestation") are ordered arbitrarily. Meta-meta-rules don't order the meta-rules because we currently have no theoretical basis for relating the first-order relations to one another.

- *Organize KS's into data/hypothesis levels for opportunistic triggering at multiple levels of interpretation.* HEARSAY's blackboard levels (sentence, word sequence, word, etc.) organize KS's by the level of analysis they use for data, each level supplying data for the hypothesis level above it. When new results are posted on a given level, KS's that "care about" that level of analysis are polled to see if they should be given processing time. *Policy KS's* give coherence to this opportunistic invocation by affecting which levels will be given preference. CRYSALIS (Engelmore and Terry, 1979) (a program that constructs a three-dimensional crystal structure interpretation of x-ray crystallographic data) takes the idea a step further by having multiple planes of blackboards; one abstracts problem features, and the other abstracts interpretations.
- *Organize KS's into a task hierarchy for planning.* In MOLGEN, laboratory operators are referenced indirectly through tasks that are steps in an abstract plan. For example, the planning level *design decision* to refine the abstract plan step MERGE is accomplished by indexing laboratory operators by the MERGE task (e.g., MERGE could be refined to using a ligase to connect DNA structures, mixing solutions, or causing a vector to be absorbed by an organism). Thus tasks in planning are analogous to hypotheses in interpretation problems.
- *Organize KS's into a context specialization hierarchy for determining task relevance.* In AM, relevant heuristics for a task are inherited from all concepts that appear above it in the specialization hierarchy. Thus AM goes a step beyond most other systems by showing that policy KS's must be selected on the basis of the kind of problem being solved. Lenat's work suggests that this might be simply a hierarchical relationship among kinds of problems.

The above characterizations of different organizations for knowledge are a first step toward a vocabulary or language for talking about indirect reference of KS's. It is clear that strategy and structure are intimately related; to make this clearer, we return to the earlier topic of explanation.

Teaching a strategy might boil down to saying "think in terms of such-and-such a structural vocabulary in order to get this strategical task done"—where the vocabulary is the indexing scheme for calling KS's to mind. So we might say, "Think in terms of families of functional subgroups in order to rule out interpretations of the spectral peaks." Or, "Consider process features when diseases of different etiologies are possible." That is, teaching a strategy involves in part the *teaching of a perspective for relating KS's hierarchically* (e.g., "families of functional subgroups" or "disease process features") and then *showing how these relations provide leverage for managing a large amount of data or a large number of hypotheses.* The explanation of the sought-after leverage must be in terms of some task for carrying the problem forward, thus tying the structuring scheme to the overall process of what the problem solver is trying to do. Thus we say "to rule out interpretations" or "to narrow down the problem to one etiological process" or (recalling Figure 29-4) "to broaden the spectrum of possibilities." In this way, we give the student a meta-rule that specifies what kind of vocabulary to consider for a given strategical task.

Davis' study of meta-rules (Chapter 28) suggested a need for a vocabulary of meta-rule knowledge. His examples suggested just a few conceptual primitives for describing refinement (ordering and utility of KS's) and a few primitives for describing object-level knowledge (KS input and output). All of the strategies in our examples deal with ordering and utility criteria for KS's; so we have nothing to add there. All of the examples given here reference KS's by the data they act upon, the hypotheses they support or the tasks they accomplish, except for AM, which references KS's by their scope or domain of applicability. What is novel about the analysis here is the focus on *relations* among hypotheses and among data.

From our domain-independent perspective, strategical knowledge selects KS's on the basis of the causal, subtype, process, or scoping relation they bear to hypotheses or data currently thought to be relevant to the problem at hand. Thus our meta-rules make statements like these:

1. "Consider KS's that would demonstrate a prior cause for the best hypothesis."
2. "Don't consider KS's that are subtypes of ruled-out hypotheses."
3. "Consider KS's that abstract known data."
4. "Consider KS's that distinguish between two competing kinds of processes."
5. "Consider KS's relevant to the current problem domain."

To summarize, the structural knowledge we have been studying consists of relations that hierarchically abstract data and hypotheses. These relations constitute the vocabulary by which domain-independent meta-rules invoke KS's. The key to our analysis is our insistence on domain-independent statement of meta-rules—a motivation deriving from our interest in explanation and teaching.

29.6.2 Explicitness of Strategical Knowledge

Another consideration for explanation is whether or not the strategy for invoking KS's is explicit. To some extent, system designers are not generally interested in representing high-level strategies that are always in effect and never reasoned about by the program. Instead, they are satisfied if their system can be programmed in the primitives of their representation language to bring about the high-level effect they are seeking. For example, top-down refinement is "compiled into" CENTAUR's hierarchy itself by the control steps that specify on each level what to do next (e.g., "After confirming obstructive airways disease, determine the subtype of obstructive airways disease."). By separating control steps from disease inferences, Aikins improved the explanation facility, one of the goals of CENTAUR. However, the rationale for these control steps is not represented—it is just as implicit as it was in PUFF's contextual clauses. In contrast, NEOMYCIN's "explore and refine" task clearly implements top-down refinement through domain-independent meta-rules. However, these meta-rules are ordered to give preference to siblings before descendents—an example of an implicit strategy.

One common way of selecting KS's is on the basis of numerical measures of priority, utility, interestingness, etc. For example, CENTAUR, like many medical programs, will first request the data that give the most weight for the disease under consideration. Thus the weight given to a KS is another form of indexing by which a strategy can be applied. If we wish to explain these weights, we should ideally replace them by descriptors that "generate" them, and then have the strategy give preference to KS's having certain descriptors. NEOMYCIN's meta-rules for requesting data (described above) are a step in this direction.

MOLGEN's "least-commitment" meta-strategy is a good example of implicit encoding by priority assignment. The ordering of tasks specified by least commitment is "Look first for differences, then use them to sketch out an abstract plan, and finally refine that plan. . . . " This ordering of tasks is implicit in the numerical priorities that Stefik has assigned to the design operators in MOLGEN. Therefore, an explanation system for MOLGEN could not explain the least-commitment strategy but could only say that the program performed one task before another because the priority was higher for the former.

29.6.3 Absence of Support Knowledge

We have little to say about support knowledge in these systems because none of them represents it. That is, the causal or mathematical models, statistical studies, or world knowledge that justifies the KS's is not used during reasoning. As discussed in Section 29.5, this limitation calls into question the problem-solving flexibility or "creativeness" of these programs. In any case, the knowledge is not available for explanation.

29.6.4 Summary

The strategy/structure/support framework can be applied to any knowledge-based system by asking certain questions: What are the KS's in the system, i.e., what kinds of recognition or construction operations are performed? How are the KS's labeled or organized, by data/constraint or by hypothesis/operation? Is this indexing used by the interpreter or by explicit strategical KS's, or is it just an aid for the knowledge engineer? What theoretical considerations justify the KS's? Is this knowledge represented? With this kind of analysis, it should be clear how the knowledge represented needs to be augmented or decomposed if an explanation facility is to be built for the system. Quite possibly, as in MYCIN, the representational notation will need to be modified as well.

29.7 Conclusions

The production rule formalism is often chosen by expert system designers because it is thought to provide a perspicuous, modular representation. But we have discovered that there are points of flexibility in the representation that can be easily exploited to embed structural and strategic knowledge in task rules, context clauses, and screening clauses. Arguing from a teacher's perspective, we showed that hierarchies of problem features and diagnoses, in addition to a domain-independent statement of strategy, are useful to justify rules and teach approaches for using them. Also, when a rule is causal, satisfactory explanations generalize the rule in terms of an underlying process model. This same knowledge should be made explicit for purposes of explanation, ease of modification, and potential improvement of problem-solving ability.

Characterizing knowledge in three categories, we concluded that MYCIN's rules were used as a programming language to embed strategic and structural principles. However, while context and screening clauses are devices that don't precisely capture the paths of expert reasoning, the basic connection between data and hypothesis is a psychologically valid association. As such, the "core rules" represent the experts' knowledge of causal processes in proceduralized form. Their knowledge is not necessarily compiled into this form, but may be compiled with respect to causal models that may be incomplete or never even learned. For this reason, support knowledge needs to be represented in a form that is somewhat redundant to the diagnostic associations, while structure and strategy can be directly factored out and represented declaratively.

The lessons of this study apply to other knowledge-based programs, including programs that do not use the production rule representation. The first moral is that one cannot simply slap an interactive front end onto a good AI program and expect to have an adequate teaching system. Similarly, an explanation system may have to do more than just read back reasoning steps and recognize questions: it may be useful to abstract the reasoning steps, relating them to domain models and problem-solving strategies.

Other knowledge bases could be studied as artifacts to evaluate the expressiveness of their representation. Is the design of the inference structure explicit? Can it be reasoned about and used for explanation? Where are the choice points in the representation and what principles for their use have not been represented explicitly? For rule-based systems one should ask: What is the purpose of each clause in the rule and why are clauses ordered this way? Why is this link between premise and conclusion justified? Under what circumstances does this association come to mind?

Finally, future knowledge engineering efforts in which the knowledge of experts is codified could benefit from an epistemology that distinguishes KS's from meta-level knowledge of three kinds—strategy, structure, and support knowledge. Relative to that framework, then, it makes sense to ask about the appropriateness of representing knowledge using rules, units, or other notations. When the system fails to behave properly, changes to *either* the epistemology or the rules should be entertained. In fact, this is a cyclic process in which changes are made to the rules that subtly tear at the framework, and after incorporating a series of changes, a new, better epistemology and revised notation can be arrived at. (For example, a single MYCIN rule might seem awkward, but a pattern such as 40 rules having the same first 3 clauses suggests some underlying structure to the knowledge.) Thus a methodology for converging on an adequate epistemology comes in part from constant cycling and reexamining of the entire *system* of rules.

The epistemology that evolved from attempts to reconfigure MYCIN's rules is NEOMYCIN's etiological taxonomy, multiple disease process hierarchies, data that trigger hypotheses, etc., plus the domain-independent task hierarchy of meta-rules. In our use of terms like "problem feature," we have moved very far from MYCIN's too abstract concept of "clinical parameter," which did not distinguish between data and hypotheses. Our epistemology provides an improved basis for interpreting expert reasoning, a valuable foundation for knowledge engineering, as echoed by Swanson et al. (1977):

> Three aspects of the expert's adaptation are especially important to the design of decision support systems: the generative role of basic principles of pathophysiology, the hierarchical structure of disease knowledge, and the heuristics used in coping with information processing demands.

These categories of knowledge provide a framework for understanding an expert. We ask, "What *kind* of knowledge is the expert describing?" This framework enables us to focus our questions so that we can separate out detailed descriptions of the expert's causal model from both the associations that link symptom to disorder and the strategies for using this knowledge.

29.8 Postscript: How the Rule Formalism Helped

Despite some apparent shortcomings of MYCIN's rule formalism noted in this chapter and throughout the book, we must remember that the program has been influential because it works well. The uniformity of representation has been an important asset. With knowledge being so easy to encode, it was perhaps the simple parameterization of the problem that made MYCIN successful. The program could be built and tested quickly at a time when little was known about building expert systems. Finally, the explicit codification of medical knowledge, now taken for granted in expert systems, allows examination of, and improvement upon, the knowledge structures.

PART TEN

Evaluating Performance

30

The Problem of Evaluation

Early in the development of MYCIN we felt the need to assess formally the program's performance. By 1973 we had already run perhaps a hundred cases of bacteremia through the system, revising the knowledge base as needed whenever problems were discovered. At the weekly project meetings Cohen and Axline were increasingly impressed by the validity of the program's recommendations, and they encouraged the design of an experiment to assess its performance on randomly selected cases of bacteremic patients. There was a uniform concern that it would be inadequate to assess (or report) the work on the basis of anecdotal accolades alone—an informal approach to evaluation for which many efforts in both AI and medical computer science had been criticized.

30.1 Three Evaluations of MYCIN

Shortliffe accordingly designed and executed an experiment that was reported as a chapter in his dissertation (Shortliffe, 1974). Five faculty and fellows in the Stanford Division of Infectious Diseases were asked to review and critique 15 cases for which MYCIN had offered therapy advice. Each evaluator ran the first of the 15 cases through MYCIN himself (in order to get a feeling for how the program operated) and was then given printouts showing the questions asked and the advice generated for each of the other 14 cases. Questions were inserted at several places in the typescripts so that we could assess a variety of features of the program:

- its ability to decide whether a patient required treatment;
- its ability to determine the significance of isolated organisms;
- its ability to determine the identity of organisms judged significant;
- its ability to select therapy to cover for the list of most likely organisms;
- its overall consultative performance.

The design inherently assumed that the opinions of recognized experts provided the "gold standard" against which the program's performance should be assessed. For reasons outlined below, other criteria (such as the actual organisms isolated or the patient's response to therapy) did not seem appropriate. Despite the encouraging results of this experiment (hereafter referred to as Study 1), several problems were discovered during its execution:

- The evaluators complained that they could not get an adequate "feel" for the patients by merely reading a typescript of the questions MYCIN asked (and they therefore wondered how the program could do so).
- Because the evaluators knew they were assessing a computer program, there was evidence that they were using different (and perhaps more stringent) criteria for assessing its performance than they would use in assessing the recommendations of a human consultant.
- MYCIN's "approval rating" of just under 75% was encouraging but intuitively seemed to be too low for a truly expert program; yet we had no idea how high a rating was realistically achievable using the gold standard of approval by experts;
- The time required from evaluators was seen to be a major concern; the faculty and fellows agreed to help with the study largely out of curiosity, but they were all busy with other activities and some of them balked at the time required to thoroughly consider the typescripts and treatment plans for all 15 cases.
- Questions were raised regarding the validity of a study in which the evaluators were drawn from the same environment in which the program was developed; because of regional differences in prescribing habits and antimicrobial sensitivity patterns, some critics urged a study design in which MYCIN's performance in settings other than Stanford could be assessed.

Many of these problems were addressed in the design of our second study, also dealing with bacteremia, which was undertaken in the mid-1970s and for which a published report appeared in 1979 (Yu et al., 1979a). This time the evaluators were selected from centers around the country (five from Stanford, five from other centers) and were paid a small honorarium in an effort to encourage them to take the time required to fill out the evaluation forms. Because the evaluators did not have an opportunity to run the MYCIN program themselves, we deemphasized the actual appearance of a MYCIN typescript in this study (hereafter referred to as Study 2). Instead, evaluators were provided with copies of each of the 15 patients' charts up to the time of the therapy decisions (with suitable precautions taken to preserve patient anonymity). They once again knew they were evaluating a computer program, however. In addition, although the forms were designed to allow evaluators to fill them out largely by using checklists, the time required to complete them was still lengthy if the physician was careful in the work, and there were once again long delays in getting the evaluation forms back for analysis. In fact, despite the "motivating honorarium," some of the evaluators took more than 12 months to return the booklets.

Although the MYCIN knowledge base for bacteremia had been considerably refined since Study 1, we were discouraged to find that the results of Study 2 once again showed about 75% overall approval of the program's advice. It was clear that we needed to devise a study design that would "blind" the evaluators to knowledge of which advice was generated by MYCIN and that would simultaneously allow us to determine the overall approval ratings that could be achieved by experts in the field. We began to wonder if the 75% figure might not be an upper limit in light of the controversy and stylistic differences among experts.

As a result, our meningitis study (hereafter referred to as Study 3) used a greatly streamlined design to encourage rapid turnaround in evaluation forms while keeping evaluators unaware of what advice was proposed by MYCIN (as opposed to other prescribers from Stanford). Study 3 is the subject of Chapter 31, and the reader will note that it reflects many of the lessons from the first two studies cited above. With the improved design we were able to demonstrate formally that MYCIN's advice was comparable to that of infectious disease experts and that 75% is in fact *better* than the degree of agreement that could generally be achieved by Stanford faculty being assessed under the same criteria.

In the next section we summarize some guidelines derived from our experience. We believe they are appropriate when designing experiments for the evaluation of expert systems. Then, in the final section of this chapter, we look at some previously unpublished analyses of the Study 3 data. These demonstrate additional lessons that can be drawn and on which future evaluative experiments may build.

30.2 A Summary of Evaluation Considerations

The three MYCIN studies, plus the designs for ONCOCIN evaluations that are nearing completion, have taught us many lessons about the validation of these kinds of programs. We summarize some of those points here in an effort to provide guidelines of use to others doing this kind of work.[1]

[1]Much of this discussion is based on Shortliffe's contribution to Chapter 8 of *Building Expert Systems*, edited by R. Hayes-Roth, D. Lenat, and D. Waterman (Hayes-Roth, Waterman and Lenat, 1983).

30.2.1 Dependence on Task, System, Goals, and Stage of Development

Most computing systems are developed in response to some human need, and it might therefore be logical to emphasize the system's response to that need in assessing whether it is successful. Thus there are those who would argue that the primary focus of a system evaluation should be on the task for which it was designed and the quality of its corresponding performance. Other aspects warranting formal evaluation are often ignored. It must accordingly be emphasized that there are diverse components to the evaluation process. We believe that validation is most appropriately seen as occurring in stages as an expert system develops over time.

The MYCIN work, however, has forced us to focus our thinking on the evaluation of systems that are ultimately designed to perform a real-world task, typically to be used by persons who are not computer scientists. Certainly one of our major goals has been the development of a useful system that can have an impact on society by becoming a regularly used tool in the community for which it is designed. Although we have shown in earlier chapters that many basic science problems typically arise during the development of such systems, in this section we will emphasize the staged assessment of the developing tool (rather than techniques for measuring its scientific impact as a stimulus to further research). We have organized our discussion by looking at the "what?", "when?", and "how?" of evaluating expert systems.

30.2.2 What to Evaluate?

As mentioned above, at any stage in the development of a computing system several aspects of its performance could be evaluated. Some are more appropriate than others at a particular stage. However, by the time a system has reached completion it is likely that every aspect will have warranted formal assessment.

Decisions/Advice/Performance

Since accurate, reliable advice is an essential component of an expert consultation system, it is usually the area of greatest research interest and is logically an area to emphasize in evaluation. However, the mechanisms for deciding whether a system's advice is appropriate or adequate may be difficult to define or defend, especially since expert systems tend to be built precisely for those domains in which decisions are highly judgmental. It is clear that no expert system will be accepted by its intended users if they fail to be convinced that the decisions made and the advice given are pertinent and reliable.

Correct Reasoning

Not all designers of expert systems are concerned about whether their program reaches decisions in a "correct" way, so long as the advice that it offers is appropriate. As we have indicated, for example, MYCIN was not intended to simulate human problem solving in any formal way. However, there is an increasing realization that expert-level performance may require heightened attention to the mechanisms by which human experts actually solve the problems for which the expert systems are being built. It is with regard to this issue that the interface between knowledge engineering and psychology is the greatest, and, depending on the motivation of the system designers and the eventual users of the expert program, some attention to the mechanisms of reasoning that the program uses may be appropriate during the evaluation process. The issue of deciding whether or not the reasoning used by the program is "correct" will be discussed further below.

Discourse (I/O Content)

Knowledge engineers now routinely accept that parameters other than correctness will play major roles in determining whether or not their systems are accepted by the intended users (see Chapter 32). The nature of the discourse between the expert system and the user is particularly important. Here we mean such diverse issues as:

- the choice of words used in the questions and responses generated by the program;
- the ability of the expert system to explain the basis for its decisions and to customize those explanations appropriately for the level of expertise of the user;
- the ability of the system to assist the user when he or she is confused or wants help; and
- the ability of the expert system to give advice and to educate the user in a congenial fashion so that the frequently cited psychological barriers to computer use are avoided.

It is likely that issues such as these are as important to the ultimate success of an expert system as is the quality of its advice. For this reason such issues also warrant formal evaluation.

Hardware Environment (I/O Medium)

Although some users, particularly when pressed to do so, can become comfortable with a conventional typewriter keyboard to interact with computers, this is a new skill for other potential users and frequently not one they are motivated to learn. For that reason we have seen the development of light pen interfaces, touch screens, and specialized keypads, any of which may be adequate to facilitate simple interactions between users and systems. Details of the hardware interface often influence the design of the system software as well. The intricacies of this interaction cannot be ignored in system evaluation, nor can the mundane details of the user's reaction to the terminal interface. Once again, it can be difficult to design evaluations in which dissatisfaction with the terminal interface is isolated as a variable, independent of discourse adequacy or decision-making performance. As we point out below, one purpose of staged evaluations is to eliminate some variables from consideration during the evolution of the system.

Efficiency

Technical analyses of system behavior are generally warranted. Underutilized CPU power or poorly designed methods for accessing disk space, for example, may introduce resource inefficiencies that severely limit the system's response time or cost effectiveness. Inefficiencies in small systems are often tolerable to users, but will severely limit the potential for those systems to grow and still remain acceptable.

Cost Effectiveness

Finally, and particularly if it is intended that an expert system become a widely used product, some detailed evaluation of its cost effectiveness is necessary. A system that requires an excessive time commitment by the user, for example, may fail to be accepted even if it excels at all the other tasks we have mentioned. Few AI systems have reached this stage in system evolution, but there is a wealth of relevant experience in other computer science areas. Expert systems must be prepared to embark on similar studies once they reach an appropriate stage of development.

30.2.3 When to Evaluate?

The evaluation process is a continual one that should begin at the time of system design, extend in an informal fashion through the early stages of development, and become increasingly formal as a developing system moves toward real-world implementation. It is useful to cite nine stages of system development, which summarize the evolution of an expert system.[2] They are itemized in Table 30-1 and discussed in some detail below.

---

[2]These implementation steps are based on a discussion of expert systems in Shortliffe and Davis (1975).

TABLE 30-1 Steps in the Implementation of an Expert System

1. Top-level design with definition of long-range goals
2. First version prototype, showing feasibility
3. System refinement in which informal test cases are run to generate feedback from the expert and from users
4. Structured evaluation of performance
5. Structured evaluation of acceptability to users
6. Service functioning for extended period in prototype environment
7. Follow-up studies to demonstrate the system's large-scale usefulness
8. Program changes to allow wide distribution of the system
9. General release and distribution with firm plans for maintenance and updating

As mentioned above, it is important for system designers to be explicit about their long-range goals and motives for building an expert system. Thus the first stage of a system's development (Step 1), the initial design, should be accompanied by explicit statements of what the measures of the program's success will be and how failure or success will be evaluated. It is not uncommon for system designers to ignore this issue at the outset. If the evaluation stages and long-range goals are explicitly stated, however, they will necessarily influence the early design of the expert system. For example, if explanation capabilities are deemed to be crucial for the user community in question, this will have important implications for the system's underlying knowledge representation.

The next stage (Step 2) is a demonstration that the design is feasible. At this stage there is no attempt to demonstrate expert-level performance. The goal is, rather, to show that there is a representation scheme appropriate for the task domain and that knowledge-engineering techniques can lead to a prototype system that shows some reasonable (if not expert) performance on some subtask of that domain. An evaluation of this stage can be very informal and may simply consist of showing that a few special cases can be handled by the prototype system. Successful handling of the test cases suggests that with increased knowledge and refinement of the reasoning structures a high-performance expert system is possible.

The third stage (Step 3) is as far as many systems ever get. This is the period in which informal test cases are run through the developing system, the system's performance is observed, and feedback is sought from expert collaborators and potential end users. This feedback serves to define the major problem areas in the system's development and guides the next iteration in system development. This iterative process may go on for months or years, depending on the complexity of the knowledge domain, the flexibility of the knowledge representation, and the availability of techniques adequate to cope with the domain's specific control or strategic processes. One question is constantly being asked: how did this system do on this case? Detailed analyses of strengths and weaknesses lead back to further research; in this sense evaluation is an intrinsic part of the system development process.

Once the system is performing well on most cases with which it is presented, it is appropriate to turn to a more structured evaluation of its decision-making performance. This evaluation can be performed without assessing the program's actual utility in a potential user's environment. Thus Step 4 is undertaken if the test cases being used in Step 3 are found to be handled with skill and competence, and there accordingly develops a belief that a formal randomized study will show that the system is capable of handling almost any problem from its domain of expertise. Only a few expert systems have reached this stage of evaluation. The principal examples are studies of the PROSPECTOR program developed at SRI International (Gaschnig, 1979) and the MYCIN studies described earlier in this chapter. It should be emphasized that a formal evaluation with randomized case selection may show that the expert system is in fact not performing at an expert level. In this case, new research problems or knowledge requirements are defined, and the system development returns to Step 3 for additional refinement. A successful evaluation at Step 4 is desirable before a program is introduced into a user environment.

The fifth stage (Step 5), then, is system evaluation in the setting where the intended users have access to it. The principal question at this stage is whether or not the program is acceptable to the users for whom it was intended. Essentially no expert systems have been formally assessed at this stage. The emphasis in Step 5 is on the discourse abilities of the program, plus the hardware environment that is provided. If expert-level performance has been demonstrated at Step 4, failure of the program to be accepted at Step 5 can be assumed to be due to one of these other human factors.

If a system is formally shown to make good decisions and to be acceptable to users, it is appropriate to introduce it for extended periods in some prototype environment (Step 6). This stage, called *field testing,* is intended largely to gain experience with a large number of test cases and with all the intricacies of on-site performance. Careful attention during this stage must be directed toward problems of scale; i.e., what new difficulties will arise when the system is made available to large numbers of users outside of the direct control of the system developers? Careful observation of the program's performance and the changing attitudes of those who interact with it are important at this stage.

After field testing, it is appropriate to begin follow-up studies to demonstrate a system's large-scale usefulness (Step 7). These formal evaluations often require measuring pertinent parameters before and after introducing the system into a large user community (different from the original prototype environment). Pertinent issues are the system's efficiency, its cost effectiveness, its acceptability to users who were not involved in its early experimental development, and its impact on the execution of the task with which it was designed to assist. During Step 7 new problems may be discovered that require attention before the system can be distributed (Step

8). These may involve programming changes or modifications required to allow the system to run on a smaller or exportable machine.

Finally, the last stage in system development is general release as a marketable product or in-house tool (Step 9). Inherent at this stage are firm plans for maintaining the knowledge base and keeping it current. One might argue that the ultimate evaluation takes place at this stage when it is determined whether or not the system can succeed in broad use. However, a system's credibility is likely to be greater if good studies have been done in the first eight stages so that there are solid data supporting any claims about the quality of the program's performance.

30.2.4 How to Evaluate?

It would be folly to claim that we can begin to suggest detailed study designs for all expert systems in a single limited discussion. There is a wealth of information in the statistical literature, for example, regarding the design of randomized controlled trials, and much of that experience is relevant to the design of expert system evaluations. Our intention here, therefore, is to concentrate on those issues that complicate the evaluation of expert systems in particular and to suggest pitfalls that must be considered during study design.

We also wish to distinguish between two senses of the term *evaluation*. In computer science, system evaluation often is meant to imply optimization in the technical sense—timing studies, for example. Our emphasis, on the other hand, is on a system's performance at the specific consultation task for which it has been designed. Unlike many conventional programs, expert systems do not deal with deterministic problems for which there is clearly a right or wrong answer. As a result, it is often not possible to demonstrate in a straightforward fashion that a system is "correct" and then to concentrate one's effort on demonstrating that it reaches the solution to a problem in some optimal way.

Need for an Objective Standard

Evaluations require some kind of "gold standard"—a generally accepted correct answer with which the results of a new methodology can be compared. In the assessment of new diagnostic techniques in medicine, for example, the gold standard is often the result of an invasive procedure that physicians hope to be able to avoid, even though it may be 100% accurate (e.g., operative or autopsy results, or the findings on an angiogram). The sensitivity and specificity of a new diagnostic liver test based on a blood sample, for example, can best be assessed by comparing test results with the results of liver biopsies from several patients who also had the blood test; if the blood test is thereby shown to be a good predictor of the results of the liver biopsy, it may be possible to avoid the more invasive procedure in future patients. The parallel in expert system evaluation is obvious; if we can demonstrate that the expert system's advice is comparable to the gold standard for the domain in question, it may no longer be necessary to turn to the gold standard itself if it is less convenient, less available, or more expensive.

Can the Task Domain Provide a Standard?

In general there are two views of how to define a gold standard for an expert system's domain: (1) what eventually turns out to be the "correct" answer for a problem, and (2) what a human expert says is the correct answer when presented with the same information as is available to the program. It is unfortunate that for many kinds of problems with which expert systems are designed to assist, the first of these questions cannot be answered or is irrelevant. Consider, for example, the performance of MYCIN. One might suggest that the gold standard in its domain should be the identity of the bacteria that are ultimately isolated from the patient, or the patient's outcome if he or she is treated in accordance with (or in opposition to) the program's recommendation. Suppose, then, that MYCIN suggests therapy that covers for four possibly pathogenic bacteria but that the organism that is eventually isolated is instead a fifth rare bacterium that was totally unexpected, even by the experts involved in the case. In what sense should MYCIN be considered "wrong" in such an instance? Similarly, the outcome for patients treated for serious infections is not 100% correlated with the correctness of therapy; patients treated in accordance with the best available medical practice may still die from fulminant infection, and occasionally patients will improve despite inappropriate antibiotic treatment. Accordingly, we said that MYCIN performed at an expert level and was "correct" if it agreed with the experts, even if both MYCIN and the experts turned out to be wrong. The CADUCEUS program has been evaluated by comparing the diagnoses against those published on selected hard cases from the medical literature (Miller et al., 1982).

Are Human Experts Evaluated?

When domain experts are used as the objective standard for performance evaluation, it is useful to ask whether the decisions of the experts themselves are subjected to rigorous evaluations. If so, such assessments of human expertise may provide useful benchmarks against which to measure the expertise of a developing consultation system. An advantage of this approach is that the technique for evaluating experts is usually a well-accepted basis for assessing expertise and thus lends credibility to an evaluation of the computer-based approach.

Informal Standards

Typically, however, human expertise is accepted and acknowledged using less formal criteria, such as level of training, recommendations of previous clients, years of experience in a field, number of publications, and the like. [Recently, Johnson et al. (1981) and Lesgold (1983) have studied measures of human expertise that are more objective.] Testimonials regarding the performance of a computer program have also frequently been used as a catalyst to the system's dissemination, but it is precisely this kind of anecdotal selling of a system against which we are arguing here. Many fields (e.g., medicine) will not accept technological innovation without rigorous demonstration of the breadth and depth of the new product's capabilities. Both we and the PROSPECTOR researchers encountered this cautious attitude in potential users and designed their evaluations largely in response to a perceived need for rigorous demonstrations of performance.

Biasing and Blinding

In designing any evaluative study, considerations of sources of bias are of course important. We learned this lesson when evaluating MYCIN, and, as mentioned earlier, this explains many of the differences between the bacteremia evaluation (Study 2) and the meningitis study (Study 3). Many comments and criticisms from Study 2 evaluators reflected biases regarding the proper role for computers in medical settings (e.g., "I don't think the computer has an adequate sense of how sick this patient is. You'd have to see a patient like this in order to judge."). As a result, Study 3 mixed MYCIN's recommendations with a set of recommendations from nine other individuals asked to assess the case (ranging from infectious disease faculty members to a medical student). When national experts later gave opinions on the appropriateness of therapeutic recommendations, they did not know which proposed therapy (if any) was MYCIN's and which came from the faculty members. This "blinded" study design removed an important source of potential bias, and also provided a sense of where MYCIN's performance lay along a range of expertise from faculty to student.

Controlling Variables

As we pointed out in the discussion of *when* to evaluate an expert system, one advantage of a sequential set of studies is that each can assume the results of the experiments that preceded it. Thus, for example, if a system has been shown to reach optimal decisions in its domain of expertise, one can assume that the system's failure to be accepted by its intended users in an experimental setting is a reflection of inadequacies in an aspect of the system *other* than its decision-making performance. One key variable that could account for system failure can be "removed" in this way.

Realistic Standards of Performance

Before assessing the capabilities of an expert system, it is necessary to define the minimal standards that are acceptable for the system to be called a success. It is ironic that in many domains it is difficult to decide what level of performance qualifies as expert. Thus it is important to measure the performance of human experts in a field if they are assessed by the same standards to be used in the evaluation of the expert system. As we noted earlier, this point was demonstrated in the MYCIN evaluations. In Studies 1 and 2, MYCIN's performance was approved by a majority of experts in approximately 75% of cases, a figure that seemed disappointingly low to us. We felt that the system should be approved by a majority in at least 90% of cases before it was made available for actual clinical use. The blinded study design for the subsequent meningitis evaluation (Study 3), however, showed that even infectious disease faculty members received at best a 70–80% rating from other experts in the field. Thus the 90% figure originally sought may have been unrealistic in that it inadequately reflected the extent of disagreement that can exist even among experts in a field such as clinical medicine.

Sensitivity Analysis

A special kind of evaluative procedure that is pertinent for work with expert systems is the analysis of a program's sensitivity to slight changes in knowledge representation, inference weighting, etc. Similarly, it may be pertinent to ask which interactive capabilities were necessary for the acceptance of an expert consultant. One approach to assessing these issues is to compare two versions of the system that vary the feature under consideration. An example of studies of this kind are the experiments that we did to assess the certainty factor model. As is described in Chapter 10 (Section 10.3), Clancey and Cooper showed that the decisions of MYCIN changed minimally from those reported in the meningitis evaluation (Chapter 31) over a wide range of possible CF intervals for the inferences in the system. This sensitivity analysis helped us decide that the details of the CF's associated with rules mattered less than the semantic and structural content of the rules themselves.

Interaction of Knowledge: Preserving Good Performance When Correcting the Bad

An important problem, discussed in Chapter 7, can be encountered when an evaluation has revealed system deficiencies and new knowledge has been added to the system in an effort to correct these. In complex expert systems, the interactions of new knowledge with old can be unanticipated and lead to detrimental effects on problems that were once handled very well by the system. An awareness of this potential problem is crucial as system builders iterate from Step 3 to Step 4 and back to Step 3 (see Table 30-1). One method for protecting against the problem is to keep a library of old cases available on-line for batch testing of the system's decisions. Then, as changes are made to the system in response to the Step 4 evaluations of the program's performance, the old cases can be run through the revised version to verify that no unanticipated knowledge interactions have been introduced (i.e., to show that the program's performance on the old cases does not deteriorate).

Realistic Time Demands on Evaluators

A mundane issue that must be considered anyway, since it can lead to failure of a study design or, at the very least, to unacceptable delays in completing the program's assessment, is the time required for the evaluators to judge the system's performance. If expert judgments are used as the gold standard for adequate program performance, the opinions of the experts must be gathered for the cases used in the evaluation study. A design that picks the most pertinent two or three issues to be assessed and concentrates on obtaining the expert opinions in as easy a manner as possible will therefore have a much better chance of success. We have previously mentioned the one-year delay in obtaining the evaluation booklets back from the experts who had agreed to participate in the Study 2 bacteremia evaluation. By focusing on fewer variables and designing a checklist that allowed the experts to assess program performance much more rapidly, the meningitis evaluation was completed in less than half that time (Chapter 31).

30.3 Further Comments on the Study 3 Data

When the Study 3 data had been analyzed and published (Chapter 31), we realized there were still several lingering questions. The journal editors had required us to shorten the data analysis and discussion in the final report. We also had asked ourselves several questions regarding the methodology and felt that these warranted further study.

Accordingly, in 1979 Reed Letsinger (then a graduate student in our group) undertook an additional analysis of the Study 3 data. What follows is largely drawn from an internal memo that he prepared to report his findings. The reader should be familiar with Chapter 31 before studying the sections below.

30.3.1 Consistency of the Evaluators

The eight national evaluators in Study 3 could have demonstrated internal inconsistency in two ways. Since each one was asked first to indicate his own decision, he could be expected to judge as acceptable any of the prescribers' decisions that were identical to his own. The first type of inconsistency would occur if this expectation were violated. Among the 800 judgments in the Study 3 data (8 evaluators × 10 prescribers × 10 patients), 15 instances of this type of inconsistency occurred. Second, since several prescribers would sometimes make the same decision regarding a patient, another form of inconsistency would occur if an evaluator were to mark identical treatments for the same patient differently for different prescribers. Since the evaluators had no basis for distinguishing among the subjects (prescribers), such discrepancies were inherently inconsistent. Twenty-two such instances occurred in the Study 3 data set.

These numbers indicate that 37 out of the 800 data points (4.6%) could be shown to be in need of correction on the basis of these two tests. Such a figure tells us something about the reliability of the data—clearly pertinent in assessing the study results. We have wondered about plausible explanations for these kinds of inconsistencies. One is that the evaluators were shown both the *drugs* recommended by the prescribers *and* the recommended *doses*. They were asked to base their judgment of treatment acceptability on drug selection alone, but we did ask separately for their opinion on dosage to help us assess the adequacy of MYCIN's dosing algorithms (see Chapter 19). It appeared in retrospect, however, that the evaluators sometimes ignored the instructions and discriminated between two therapy prescriptions that differed only in the doses of the recommended drugs. These judgments are thus only inconsistent in the sense that they reflect judgments that the evaluators were not supposed to be making. The problem reflects the inherent tension between our wanting to get as much possible information from evaluators and the risks in introducing new variables or data that may distract evaluators from the primary focus of the study. Another methodologic point here is that such design weaknesses may be uncovered by making some routine tests for consistency.

30.3.2 Agreement Among Evaluators

The tendency of the experts to agree with one another has a direct impact on the power of the study to discriminate good performance from bad. Consider two extreme cases. At one end is the case where on the average the evaluators agree with each other just as much as they disagree. This means that on each case the prescribers would tend to get scores around the midpoint—in the case of the MYCIN study, around 4 out of 8. The cumulative scores would then cluster tightly around the midpoint of the possible range, e.g., around 40 out of 80. The differences between the quality of performance of the various subjects would be "washed out," the scores would all be close to one another, and consequently, it would be very unlikely that any of the differences between scores would be significant. At the other extreme, if the evaluators always agreed with each other, the only "noise" in the data would be contributed by the choice of the sample cases. Intermediate amounts of disagreement would correspondingly have intermediate effects on the variability of the scores, and hence on the power of the test to distinguish the performance capabilities of the subjects.

A rough preliminary indication of the extent of this agreement can be derived from the MYCIN data. A judgment situation consists of a particular prescriber paired with a particular case. Thus there are 100 judgment situations in the present study, and each receives a score between 0 and 8, depending on how many of the evaluators found the performance of the subject acceptable on the case. The range between 0 and 8 is divided into three equal subranges, 0 to 2, 3 to 5, and 6 to 8. A judgment situation receiving a score in the first of these ranges may be said to be generally unacceptable, while those receiving scores in the third range are generally acceptable. The situations scoring in the middle range, however, cannot be decided by a two-thirds majority rule, and so may be considered to be undecided due to the evaluators' inability to agree. It turns out that 53 out of the 100 judgment situations were undecided in this sense in the MYCIN study.

For a more accurate indication of the level of this disagreement, the evaluators can be paired in all possible combinations, and the percentage of judgment situations in which they agree can be calculated. The mean of this percentage across all pairs of evaluators reflects how often we should expect two experts to agree on the question of whether or not the performance of a prescriber is acceptable (when the experts, the prescriber, and the case are chosen from populations for which the set of evaluators, the set of subjects, and the set of cases used in the study are representative samples). In the MYCIN study, this mean was 0.591. Thus, if the evaluators, prescribers, and cases used in this study are representative, we would in general expect that if we choose two infectious disease experts and a judgment situation at random on additional cases, the two experts will disagree on the question of whether or not the recommended therapy is acceptable 4 out of every 10 times!

Before such a number can be interpreted, more must be known about the pattern of agreement. One question is how the disagreement was distributed across the subjects and across the cases. It turns out that the variation across subjects was remarkably low for the MYCIN data, with a standard deviation of less than 6 percentage points. The standard deviation across cases was slightly higher—just under 10 percentage points. Very little of the high level of disagreement among the graders can be attributed to the idiosyncracies of a few subjects or of a few cases. If it had turned out that a large amount of the disagreement focused on a few cases or a few subjects, they could have been disregarded, and the power of the study design increased.

A second question that can be raised is to what extent the disagreements result from differing tolerance levels among the different evaluators for divergent recommendations. A quick and crude measure of this tolerance level is simply the percentage of favorable responses the evaluators gave. The similarity between the tolerance levels of two graders can be measured by the difference between those percentages. It is then possible to rank all the pairs of evaluators in terms of the degree of similarity of their tolerance levels, just as it is possible to rank pairs of evaluators by their agreements. The extent to which the tendency of the evaluators to agree or disagree with one another can be explained by the variation in their tolerance levels can be measured by the correlation between these two rankings. With the MYCIN study, the Spearman rank correlation coefficient turns out to be 0.0353 with no correction for ties. This is not significantly greater than 0. If there had been a significant correlation, the scores given by the evaluators could have been weighted in order to normalize the effects due to different tolerance levels. The actual disagreement among the evaluators would then have been reduced.

A third possibility is that different groups of experts represent different schools of thought on solving the type of problems represented in our sample. If so, there should be clusters of evaluators, all of whose members agree with each other more than usual, while members of different clusters tend to disagree more than usual. There was some slight clustering of this sort in the MYCIN data. Evaluators 1, 3, and 4 all agreed with each other more often than the mean of 0.591, as did 2 and 6, and matching any member of the first group with any member of the second gives an agreement of less than the mean. However, evaluator 8 agreed with all five of these evaluators more than 0.591. These clusterings are probably real, but they cannot account for very much of the tendency of the evaluators to disagree. If significant clustering had been uncovered, the data could have been reinterpreted to treat the different "schools" of experts as additional variables in the analysis. Within each of these "schools," the agreement would then have been considerably increased.

In retrospect we now realize that the design of the MYCIN study would have permitted several different kinds of patterns to be uncovered, any one of which could have been used as a basis for increasing the agreement among the evaluators, and hence the power of the test. Unfortunately, none of these patterns actually appeared in the MYCIN data.

30.3.3 Collapsing the Data

The previous discussion of the tendency of the experts to agree with one another is subject to at least one objection. Suppose that, for a particular case, four of the ten prescribers made the same recommendation, and expert e1 agreed with the recommendation while expert e2 did not. Then e1 and e2 would be counted as disagreeing four times, when in fact they are only disagreeing over one question. If a large number of the cases lead to only a few different responses, then it might be worth lumping together the prescribers that made the same therapy recommendation. Then the experts will be interpreted as judging the responses the subjects made, rather than the subjects themselves. As is noted in the next section, this kind of collapsing of the data is useful for other purposes as well.

Deciding whether two treatments are identical may be nontrivial. Sometimes the responses are literally identical, but in other cases the responses will differ slightly, although not in ways that would lead a physician with a good understanding of the problem to accept one without also accepting the other. One plausible criterion is to lump together two therapy recommendations for a case if no evaluator accepts one without accepting the other. A second test is available when one of the evaluators gives a recommendation that is identical to one of the prescriber's recommendations. Recommendations that that evaluator judged to be equivalent to his own can then be grouped with the evaluator's recommendation, so long as doing so does not conflict with the first criterion. In using either of these tests, the data should first be made consistent in the manner discussed in Section 30.3.1.

Using these tests, the ten subjects in the ten cases of the MYCIN study reduced to an average of 4.2 different therapy recommendations for each case, with a standard deviation of 1.55 and a range from 2 to 6. This seems to be a large enough reduction to warrant looking at the data in this collapsed form.

30.3.4 Judges as Subjects

With the collapsing of prescribers into therapies, it may be possible to identify an evaluator's recommendation with one or more of the prescribers' recommendations. By then eliminating that evaluator from the rank of judges, his recommendation can be considered judged by the other evaluators. In this way the evaluators may be used as judges of each other, thereby allowing comparisons with the rankings of the original prescribers. This does not always work, since sometimes an evaluator's recommendation cannot be identified with any of the prescribers'. In Study 3, 9 out of 80 evaluator-generated therapies could not be judged as identical to any of the prescribers' recommendations.

Measuring the evaluators' performance against each other in this manner provides another indication of the extent of disagreement among them. It also produces more scores that can be (roughly) compared to the percentage scores of the prescribers. In Study 3, 8 more scores can be added to the 10 assigned to the prescribers, giving a field of 18 scores. The analysis of variance or chi-square was run on this extended population.

The new analysis showed that the mean score for the evaluators was

0.699, which is both higher than the mean agreement (0.591) and higher than the mean of the prescribers' scores (0.585). This latter fact is to be expected, since the subjects included people who were chosen for the study because their level of expertise was assumed to be lower than that of the evaluators. Nevertheless, half of the evaluators scored above the highest-scoring prescriber (while the other half spread out evenly over the range between the top-ranking subject and the eighth-ranking subject). The fact that agreement between the evaluators looks higher on this measure than it does on other measures indicates that much of the disagreement was over therapies that none of the evaluators themselves recommended.

It is interesting to ask why the evaluators ranked higher in this analysis than the Stanford faculty members among the prescribers, many of whom would have qualified as experts by the criteria we used to select the national panel. A plausible explanation is the method by which the evaluators were asked to indicate their own preferred treatment for each of the ten cases. As is described in Chapter 31, for each case the expert was asked to indicate a choice of treatment on the first page of the evaluation form and *then* to turn the page and rank the ten treatments that were recommended by the prescribers. There was no way to force the evaluators to make a commitment about therapy before turning the page, however. It is therefore quite possible that the list of prescribers' recommendations served as "memory joggers" or "filters" and accordingly influenced the evaluators' decisions regarding optimal therapy for some of the cases. Since none of the prescribers was aware of the decisions made by the other nine subjects, the Stanford faculty members did not benefit from this possible advantage. We suspect this may partly explain the apparent differences in ratings among the Stanford and non-Stanford experts.

30.3.5 Summary

The discussion in this section demonstrates many of the detailed subanalyses that may be performed on a rich data set such as that provided by Study 3. Information can be gathered on interscorer reliability of the evaluation instrument, and statistical techniques are available for detecting correlations and thereby increasing the reliability (and hence the power) of the test.

31

An Evaluation of MYCIN's Advice

Victor L. Yu, Lawrence M. Fagan, Sharon Wraith Bennett, William J. Clancey, A. Carlisle Scott, John F. Hannigan, Bruce G. Buchanan, and Stanley N. Cohen

A number of computer programs have been developed to assist physicians with diagnostic or treatment decisions, and many of them are potentially very useful tools. However, few systems have undergone evaluation by independent experts. We present here a comparison of the performance of MYCIN with the performance of clinicians. The task evaluated was the selection of antimicrobials for cases of acute infectious meningitis before the causative agent was identified.

MYCIN was originally developed in the domain of bacteremias and then expanded to include meningitis. Its task is a complicated one; it must decide whether and how to treat a patient, often in the absence of microbiological evidence. It must allow for the possibility that any important piece of information might be unknown or uncertain. In deciding which organisms should be covered by therapy, it must take into account specific clinical situations (e.g., trauma, neurosurgery), host factors (e.g., immunosuppression, age), and the possible presence of unusual pathogens (e.g., *F. tularensis* or *Candida nonalbicans*). In selecting optimal antimicrobial therapy to cover all of the most likely organisms, the system must consider antimicrobial factors (e.g., efficacy, organism susceptibility) and relative contraindications (e.g., patient allergies, poor response to prior therapy).

When knowledge about a new area of infectious disease is incorporated into MYCIN's knowledge base, the system's performance is evaluated

---

This chapter is an edited version of an article originally appearing in *Journal of the American Medical Association* 242: 1279–1282 (1979).

to show that its therapeutic regimens are as reliable as those that an infectious disease specialist would recommend. An evaluation of the system's ability to diagnose and treat patients with bacteremia yielded encouraging results (Yu et al., 1979a). The results of that study, however, were difficult to interpret because of the potential bias in an unblinded study and the disagreement among the infectious disease specialists as to the optimal therapeutic regimen for each of the test cases.

The current study design enabled us to compare MYCIN's performance with that of clinicians in a blinded fashion. This study involved a two-phase evaluation. In the first phase, several *prescribers,* including MYCIN, prescribed therapy for the test cases. In the second phase of the evaluation, prominent infectious disease specialists, the *evaluators,* assessed these prescriptions without knowing the identity of the prescribers or knowing that one of them was a computer program.[1]

31.1 Materials and Methods

Ten patients with infectious meningitis were selected by a physician who was not acquainted with MYCIN's methods or with its knowledge base pertaining to meningitis. All of the patients had been hospitalized at a county hospital affiliated with Stanford, were identified by retrospective chart review, and were diagnostically challenging. Two criteria for case selection ensured that the ten cases would be of diverse origin: there were to be no more than three cases of viral meningitis, and there was to be at least one case from each of four categories, tuberculous, fungal, viral, and bacterial (including at least one with positive gram stain of the cerebrospinal fluid and at least one with negative gram stain). A detailed clinical summary of each case was compiled. The summary included the history, physical examination, laboratory data, and the hospital course prior to therapeutic intervention. These summaries were used to run the MYCIN consultations. Only the information contained in the summaries was used as input to MYCIN, and no modifications were made to the program.

These same summaries were presented to five faculty members in the Division of Infectious Diseases in the Departments of Medicine and Pediatrics at Stanford University, to one senior postdoctoral fellow in infectious diseases, to one senior resident in medicine, and to one senior medical student. The resident and student had just completed a six-week rotation

[1]We wish to thank the following infectious diseases specialists who participated in this study: Donald Armstrong, M.D.; John E. Bennet, M.D.; Ralph D. Feigin, M.D.; Allan Lavetter, M.D.; Phillip J. Lerner, M.D.; George H. McCracken, Jr., M.D.; Thomas C. Merigan, M.D.; James J. Rahal, M.D.; Jack S. Remington, M.D.; William S. Robinson, M.D.; Penelope J. Shackelford, M.D.; Paul F. Wehrle, M.D.; and Anne S. Yeager, M.D.

in infectious diseases. None of these individuals was associated with the MYCIN project. The seven Stanford physicians and the medical student were asked to prescribe an antimicrobial therapy regimen for each case based on the information in the summary. If they chose not to prescribe antimicrobials, they were requested to specify which laboratory tests (if any) they would recommend for determining the infectious etiology. There were no restrictions concerning the use of textbooks or any other reference materials, nor were any time limits set for completion of the prescriptions.

Ten prescriptions were compiled for each case: that actually given to the patient by the treating physicians at the county hospital, the recommendation made by MYCIN, and the recommendations of the medical student and of the seven Stanford physicians. In the remainder of this chapter, MYCIN, the medical student, and the eight physicians will be referred to as *prescribers.*

The second phase of the evaluation involved eight infectious disease specialists at institutions other than Stanford, hereafter referred to as *evaluators,* who had published clinical reports dealing with the management of infectious meningitis. They were given the clinical summary and the set of ten prescriptions for each of the ten cases. The prescriptions were placed in random order and in a standardized format to disguise the identities of the individual prescribers. The evaluators were asked to make their own recommendations for each case and then to assess the ten prescriptions. The 100 prescriptions (10 each by 10 prescribers) were classified by each evaluator into the following categories:

Equivalent: the recommendation was identical to or equivalent to the evaluator's own recommendation (e.g., treatment of one patient with nafcillin was judged equivalent to the use of oxacillin);

Acceptable alternative: the recommendation was different from the evaluator's, but he considered it to be an acceptable alternative (e.g., the selection of ampicillin in one case was considered to be an acceptable alternative to penicillin);

Not acceptable: the evaluator found the recommendation unacceptable or inappropriate (e.g., the recommendation of chloramphenicol and ampicillin in one case was considered to be unacceptable by all evaluators who thought the patient had tuberculosis and who prescribed antituberculous therapy).

The 800 assessments (100 each by 8 evaluators) were analyzed as follows. A one-way analysis of variance (ANOVA) was used to analyze the overall difference effects between MYCIN and the other prescribers. The Tukey studentized range test was used to demonstrate individual differences between prescribers following attainment of significance. A similar analysis of variance was used to measure evaluator variability.

TABLE 31-1 Ratings of Antimicrobial Selection Based on Evaluator Rating and Etiologic Diagnosis

Prescribers	*No. (%) of items in which therapy was rated acceptable* by an evaluator (n=80)*	*No. (%) of items in which therapy was rated acceptable* by majority of evaluators (n=10)*	*No. of cases in which therapy failed to cover a treatable pathogen (n=10)*
MYCIN	52 (65)	7 (70)	0
Faculty-1	50 (62.5)	5 (50)	1
Faculty-2	48 (60)	5 (50)	1
Infectious disease fellow	48 (60)	5 (50)	1
Faculty-3	46 (57.5)	4 (40)	0
Actual therapy	46 (57.5)	7 (70)	0
Faculty-4	44 (55)	5 (50)	0
Resident	36 (45)	3 (30)	1
Faculty-5	34 (42.5)	3 (30)	0
Student	24 (30)	1 (10)	3

*Therapy was classified as acceptable if an evaluator rated it as equivalent or as an acceptable alternative.

31.2 Results

The evaluators' ratings of each prescriber are shown in the second column of Table 31-1. Since there were 8 evaluators and 10 cases, each prescriber received 80 ratings from the evaluators. Sixty-five percent of MYCIN's prescriptions were rated as acceptable by the evaluators. The corresponding mean rating for the five faculty specialists was 55.5% (range, 42.5% to 62.5%). A significant difference was found among the prescribers; the hypothesis that each of the prescribers was rated equally by the evaluators is rejected (standard F test, $F = 3.29$ with 9 and 70 *df;* $p < 0.01$).

Consensus among evaluators was measured by determining the number of cases ($n = 10$) in which the prescriber received a rating of acceptable from the majority (five or more) of experts (third column of Table 31-1). Seventy percent of MYCIN's therapies were rated as acceptable by a majority of the evaluators. The corresponding mean ratings for the five faculty prescribers was 44% (range, 30% to 50%). MYCIN failed to win a rating of acceptable from the majority of evaluators in three cases. MYCIN prescribed penicillin for a case of meningococcal meningitis, as did four evaluators. However, four other evaluators prescribed penicillin with chloramphenicol as initial therapy before identification of the organism, and they rated MYCIN's therapy as not acceptable. MYCIN prescribed penicillin as treatment for group B *Streptococcus;* however, most evaluators selected ampicillin and gentamicin as initial therapy. MYCIN prescribed penicillin as treatment for *Listeria;* however, most evaluators used combinations of two drugs.

There were seven instances in which prescribers selected antimicrobial therapy that failed to cover a treatable pathogen (fourth column of Table 31-1). Five instances involved a case of tuberculous meningitis in which ineffective antibacterials (ampicillin, penicillin, and chloramphenicol) or no antimicrobials were prescribed. The other two instances included a case of meningococcal meningitis where one prescriber failed to prescribe any antimicrobial therapy and a case of cryptococcal meningitis where flucytosine was prescribed in inadequate dosage as the sole therapy.

31.3 Comment

In clinical medicine it may be difficult to define precisely what constitutes appropriate therapy. Our study used two criteria for judging the appropriateness of therapy. One was simply whether or not the prescribed therapy would be effective against the offending pathogen, which was ultimately identified (fourth column of Table 31-1). Using this criterion, five prescribers (MYCIN, three faculty prescribers, and the actual therapy given the patient) gave effective therapy for all ten cases. However, this was not the sole criterion, since failure to cover other likely pathogens and the hazards of overprescribing are not considered. The second criterion used was the judgment of eight independent authorities with expertise in the management of meningitis (second and third columns of Table 31-1). Using this criterion, MYCIN received a higher rating than any of the nine human prescribers.

This shows that MYCIN's capability in the selection of antimicrobials for meningitis compares favorably with the Stanford infectious disease specialists, who themselves represent a high standard of excellence. Three of the Stanford faculty physicians would have qualified as experts in the management of meningitis by the criteria used for the selection of the national evaluators.

Of the five prescribers who never failed to cover a treatable pathogen (fourth column of Table 31-1), MYCIN and the faculty prescribers were relatively efficient and selective as to choice and number of antibiotics prescribed. In contrast, while the actual therapy prescribed by the physicians caring for the patient never failed to cover a treatable pathogen, their therapeutic strategy was to prescribe several broad-spectrum antimicrobials. In eight cases, the physicians actually caring for the patient prescribed two or three antimicrobials; in six of these eight cases, one or no antimicrobial would have sufficed. Overprescribing of antimicrobials is not necessarily undesirable, since redundant or ineffective antimicrobial therapy can be discontinued after a pathogen has been identified. However, an optimal clinical strategy attempts to limit the number and spectrum of antimicrobials prescribed to minimize toxic effects of drugs and superinfection while selecting antimicrobials that will still cover the likely pathogens.

The primary limitation of our investigation is the small number of cases studied. This was a practical necessity, since we had to consider the time required for the evaluators to analyze 10 complex cases and rate 100 therapy recommendations. Although only 10 patient histories were used, the selection criteria provided for diagnostically diverse and challenging cases to evaluate MYCIN's accuracy. The selection of consecutive or random cases of meningitis admitted to the hospital might have yielded a limited spectrum of meningitis cases that would not have tested fully the capabilities of either MYCIN or the Stanford physicians. In addition to our evaluation, the program has undergone extensive testing involving several hundred cases of retrospective patient histories, prospective patient cases, and literature cases of meningitis. These have confirmed its competence in determining the likely identity of the pathogen, selecting an effective drug at an appropriate dosage, and recommending further diagnostic studies (a capability not evaluated in the current study).

Because of the diagnostic complexities of the test cases, unanimity in all eight ratings in an individual case was difficult to achieve. For example, in one case, although the majority of evaluators agreed with MYCIN's selection of antituberculous drugs for initial therapy, two evaluators did not and rated MYCIN's therapy as not acceptable. Six of the ten test cases had negative CSF smears for any organisms, so in these cases antimicrobial selection was made on a clinical basis. It is likely that if more routine cases had been selected, there would have been greater consensus among evaluators.

The techniques used by MYCIN are derived from a subfield of computer science known as artificial intelligence. It may be useful to analyze some of the factors that contributed to the program's strong performance. First, the knowledge base is extremely detailed and, for the domain of meningitis, is more comprehensive than that of most physicians. The knowledge base is derived from clinical experience of infectious disease specialists, supplemented by information gathered from several series of cases reported in the literature and from hundreds of actual cases in the medical records of three hospitals.

Second, the program is systematic in its approach to diagnosis. A popular maxim among physicians is "One has to think of the disease to recognize it." This is not a problem for the program; rare diseases are never "forgotten" once information about them has been added to the knowledge base, and risk factors for specific meningitides are systematically analyzed. For example, the duration of headache and other neurological symptoms for one week before hospital admission was a subtle clue in the diagnosis of tuberculous meningitis. The program does not overlook relevant data but also does not require complete and exact information about the patient. For example, in a case involving a patient with several complex medical problems, the presence of purpura on physical examination was an important finding leading to the diagnosis of meningococcal meningitis. However, even if the purpura were absent or had been overlooked, MYCIN would have treated empirically for meningococcal meningitis on the basis of the patient's age and CSF analysis.

Third, since the program is based on the judgments of experienced clinicians, it reflects their understanding of the diagnostic importance of various findings. The program does not jump to conclusions on the basis of an isolated finding, nor does it neglect to ask for key pieces of information. Abnormal findings or test results are interpreted with respect to the clinical setting.

Finally, the system is up to date; frequent additions and modifications ensure its currentness. The meningitis knowledge base incorporates information from the most recent journal articles and the current experience of an infectious diseases division. Therapy selection and dosage calculations are derived from prescribing recommendations more recent than those in any textbook. (This was a factor in a case for which, at the time of this study, the recommendation of low-dose amphotericin B therapy combined with flucytosine was available only in recent issues of specialty journals.)

Because MYCIN compared favorably with infectious disease experts in this study, we believe that it could be a valuable resource for the practicing physician whose clinical experience for specific infectious diseases may be limited. The data demonstrate the program's reliability. However, further investigations in a clinical environment are warranted. Questions concerning the program's acceptability to practicing physicians and its impact on patient care, as well as issues of cost and legal implications, remain to be answered. Other capabilities of MYCIN that may assist the practicing physician include the following:

1. Identifying each of the potential pathogens with an estimate of its likelihood in causing the disease (Chapter 5).
2. Recommending antimicrobial dosages, considering weight, height, surface area, and renal function. Separate dosage regimens are given for the neonate, infant, child, and adult. Intrathecal dosage regimens are also given (Chapter 19).
3. Checking for contraindications of specific drugs, including pregnancy, liver disease, and age (Chapter 6).
4. Graphing predicted serum concentrations for aminoglycosides with relation to the expected minimal inhibitory concentration of the organism (Chapter 19).
5. Justifying its recommendation in response to queries by the physician (Chapter 18).

The methodology of the evaluation is of interest because it was developed in an attempt to analyze clinical decisions for which there is no clear right or wrong choice. Since most areas of medicine are characterized by a variety of acceptable approaches, even among experts, the technique used here may be generally useful in assessing the quality of decision making by other computer programs.

PART ELEVEN

Designing for Human Use

32

Human Engineering of Medical Expert Systems

Although we have frequently referred to human engineering issues throughout this book and have considered them from the outset in our design of MYCIN and its descendents, we have also noted that MYCIN was never used routinely in patient-care settings. Yes, the program was able to explain its reasoning, and this seemed likely to heighten its acceptability. And yes, we spent much time attending to detail so that (a) user aids were available at any time through the use of HELP and question mark commands, (b) the system automatically corrected spelling errors when it was "obvious" what the user meant, and (c) a physician could enter only the first few characters of a response if what was entered uniquely defined the intended answer. However, there were still significant barriers that prevented us from undertaking the move to formal implementation.

Some of these barriers were unrelated to human engineering issues, viz., the need for an enhanced knowledge base in other areas of infectious disease at a time when both Axline and Yu were departing from Stanford, the difficulty of obtaining funding for knowledge base enhancement when the program itself had become both large and competent, and our own lack of enthusiasm for implementation studies once we had come to identify some of the computer science inadequacies in MYCIN's design and preferred to work on those in a new environment. All of these might have been ignored, however, since MYCIN was fully operational and could have been tested clinically with relatively little incremental effort. What dissuaded us from doing so was the simple fact that we *knew* the program was likely to be unacceptable, for mundane reasons quite separate from its excellent decision-making performance. Most of these issues were related to logistical and human-engineering problems in the program's introduction. We have described these pragmatic considerations elsewhere (Shortliffe, 1982a) and have indicated how they influenced our decision to turn our attention to the development of a new system for clinical oncology (see Chapter 35). We will briefly summarize these points here.

First, although there was a demonstrated need for a system like MYCIN (see the data on antibiotic use outlined in Chapter 1), we did not feel there was a *recognized* need on the part of individual practitioners. Most physicians seem to be quite satisfied with their criteria for antibiotic selection, and we were unconvinced that they would be highly motivated to seek advice from MYCIN, particularly in light of the other problems noted below.

Our second concern was our inability to integrate MYCIN naturally into the daily activities of practitioners. The program required a special incremental effort on their part: once they had decided to consider giving a patient an antibiotic, it would have been necessary to find an available terminal, log on, and then respond to a series of questions (many of which were simply transcriptions of lab results already known to be available on other computers at Stanford). Linkage of SUMEX (MYCIN's "home" computer) to Stanford lab machines was considered but rejected because of lack of resources to do so and the realization that a research machine like SUMEX would still have been unable to offer high-quality reliable service to physician users. When the machine was heavily loaded, annoying pauses between MYCIN's questions were inevitable, and a total consultation could have required as long as 30 minutes or an hour. This was clearly unacceptable and would have led to rejection of the system despite its other strong features. Slight annoyances, such as the requirement that the physicians type their answers, would have further alienated users. Adapting MYCIN to run on its own machine was an unrealistic answer because of the computational resources needed to run a program of that size (at that time) and our lack of interest in trying to adapt the code for a non-Interlisp environment.[1]

Thus, as of late 1978, MYCIN became a static system, maintained on SUMEX for demonstration purposes and for student projects but no longer the subject of active research. In addition, in the subsequent five years its knowledge base has become rapidly outdated, particularly with regard to antimicrobial agents. The "third-generation" cephalosporins have been introduced in the intervening years and have had a profound effect on antibiotic selection for a number of common problems in infectious disease (because of their broad spectrum and low toxicity relative to older agents). This point emphasizes the need for knowledge base maintenance mechanisms once expert systems are introduced for routine use in dynamic environments, where knowledge may change rapidly over time.

Even though MYCIN is no longer a subject of active work, the experiments described in this book have been a productive source of new insights. In this final section to the book, we describe related pieces of work that show some of the ways in which MYCIN has influenced our research

[1]The CONGEN program within DENDRAL had just been recoded from Interlisp to BCPL, and we were acutely aware of the manpower investment it took by someone intimately familiar with the design and code. This effort could only have been undertaken under the conviction that the result would be widely used.

activities in the areas of human engineering and user attitudes. Our new work on ONCOCIN, for example, has been based on underlying knowledge structures developed for MYCIN but has been augmented and revised extensively because of our desire to overcome the barriers that prevented the clinical implementation of MYCIN. Our attitude on the importance of human factors in designing and building expert systems is reflected in the title of a recent editorial we prepared on the subject: "Good Advice is Not Enough" (Shortliffe, 1982b).

32.1 The Interface Language for Physicians

It was never our intention to become enmeshed in the difficult problems of understanding unconstrained English. Work in computational linguistics achieved important results during the 1960s and 1970s, but we saw the problems as being extremely difficult and were afraid that our progress in other areas would be slowed if we became overly involved in building language capabilities for MYCIN. We *did* spend time ensuring that the program could express itself in English, but this was not difficult because of the stereotypic form of the rules and the power of LISP. We totally avoided any need for the program to understand natural language during the consultation (depending instead on HOW, WHY, and EXPLAIN commands as described in Chapter 18), but we did build a simple question-answering (QA) system that was available electively at the end of the advice session. Although it was possible to get answers to most questions using the QA module, the system was not very robust, and it took new users some time to learn how to express themselves so that they would be understood. Once again, the capability that was developed for question answering (which was borrowed for the TEIRESIAS work; see Chapter 9) was greatly facilitated by the highly structured and uniform techniques for knowledge representation that we had used.

It is important to note that our desire to avoid natural language processing accounts in large part for the decision to use goal-directed (backward-chained) reasoning in MYCIN. If we had simply allowed the user to start a consultation by describing a patient, it would have been necessary that MYCIN understand such text descriptions before beginning forward-chained invocation of rules. By using a backward-chained approach, MYCIN controlled the dialogue and therefore could ask specific questions that generally required one- or two-word answers.

From a human-engineering viewpoint, this decision was suboptimal, even though, ironically, it was made to avoid language-understanding problems that we knew would have annoyed physician users. The problem that resulted from having MYCIN control the dialogue was the inability of the user to volunteer information, meaning that he or she had to wait for MYCIN to ask about what was known to be a crucial point. Alain Bonnet, a postdoctoral fellow from France, was fascinated by this problem when he visited our group in the mid-1970s. He decided to look for ways in which MYCIN's knowledge structures could be augmented to permit volunteered information about a patient at the beginning of a consultation session. His work on this subsystem, known as BAOBAB, is described in Chapter 33. The complexity of the issues that needed to be addressed in building such a capability are clear in that article. Fascinating though the work was, BAOBAB never functioned at a performance level sufficiently high to justify its incorporation into MYCIN.

Despite the limitations of its language capabilities, we are generally pleased with the ability of MYCIN and the EMYCIN systems to appear to converse in English through the use of rather simple techniques of text generation and understanding. This conversational appearance of the program is due to the combined efforts of several project members and to the flexibility of the underlying knowledge structures used. Issues in computational linguistics in the EMYCIN environment continue to be fruitful areas of investigation for student projects. As recently as 1980, a medical student and research assistant, Lou Sanner, added code to MYCIN that was able to generate prose summaries of patients from our library of old cases. His generalized approach to the problem was added to EMYCIN and generates prose descriptions of stored cases from any EMYCIN domain. An example of one of his MYCIN case translations is shown in Figure 32-1.

32.2 Assessing Physicians' Attitudes

As many of the early papers in this volume indicate, we proceeded through the 1970s with the firm conviction that AI techniques offered potential solutions to problems that had limited physicians' acceptance of advice-giving systems. We were especially convinced that explanation capabilities were crucial for user acceptance and that this single failing in particular largely accounted for the rejection of systems based solely on statistical approaches. As is discussed in Chapter 30, we could not *prove* that explanations would make a difference unless we implemented a consultation system in a clinical environment where controlled studies could be undertaken. Thus we had depended on our intuitions and appealed to others to believe in what we felt was an obvious requirement for optimal systems.

In 1980, however, a combination of events encouraged us to undertake a formal analysis of physicians' attitudes. We had toyed with the idea for several years but had been discouraged by the time and resources necessary

A summary is now being generated:
[consultation of 7-May-77 6:00PM]

Pt600 is a 33 year old Caucasian female with clinical evidence of otitis media who has neurological signs of 5 hours and symptoms of 1 day duration. She is febrile and weighs 70 kgm. She has impaired renal function. She is 4 + sick (on a scale of 4). The patient is thought to have a csf infection symptomatic for 1 day.

TEST RESULTS:

CBC:	WBC	25K		PMNS	85%	Bands	12%
CSF:	WBC	12500		PMNS	98%		
	glucose		25		(blood glucose 140)		
	protein	450					

recent serum creatinine 1

CULTURES:	When obtained:	Organisms
csf	6 hours ago	Gramneg rod Grampos coccus in pairs

DRUGS:

Erythromycin was started (oral) 30 hours ago.

FIGURE 32-1 Example of a MYCIN case summary.

to do such a study well. In August of 1980 Stanford hosted the annual Workshop on Artificial Intelligence in Medicine, and we organized a two-day tutorial program so that local physicians who were interested could learn about this emerging discipline. In addition, funding from the Henry J. Kaiser Family Foundation allowed us to support a questionnaire-based project to assess physicians' attitudes. Finally, a doctoral student in educational psychology, Randy Teach, joined the project that summer and brought with him much-needed skills in the areas of statistics, study design, and the use of computer-based statistical packages.

The resulting study used the physicians who were attending the AIM tutorial as subjects, with a control group of M.D.'s drawn from the surrounding community. Chapter 34 summarizes the results and concludes with design recommendations derived from the data analysis. The reader is referred to that chapter for details; however, it is pertinent to reiterate here that a program's ability to give explanations for its reasoning was judged to be the single most important requirement for an advice-giving system in medicine. This observation accounts for our continued commitment to research on explanation, both in the ONCOCIN program (Langlotz and Shortliffe, 1983) and in current doctoral dissertations from the Heuristic Programming Project (Cooper, 1984; Kunz, 1984). Other results of the attitude survey reemphasize the importance of human-engineering issues (such as ease of use and access) in the design of acceptable consulting systems.

32.3 Clinical Implementation of an Expert System

It seems appropriate that we close a book about the MYCIN "experiments" with a description of ONCOCIN, MYCIN's most recent descendent. The problem domain for this program was selected precisely because it seemed to offer an excellent match between the problem-solving task involved and the set of pragmatic considerations that we outlined at the beginning of this chapter. Chapter 35 describes ONCOCIN's task domain in some detail and discusses the knowledge structures and architecture used to heighten its clinical effectiveness. However, Chapter 35 does not discuss the logistics of implementation that are among the newest lessons learned by our group. Thus what follows here is a description of our experience with ONCOCIN's implementation. Much of the discussion is drawn from a recent paper written by members of the ONCOCIN project (Bischoff et al., 1983). The reader may find it useful to study the technical description in Chapter 35 before reading this discussion of what has happened since the system was introduced for clinical use.

ONCOCIN assists physicians with the management of patients enrolled in experimental plans (called protocols) for treating cancer with chemotherapy. The system has been in limited use in the Stanford Oncology Clinic since May of 1981. The potential utility of such a system has been recognized at several major cancer treatment centers, and other groups have been developing systems to assist with similar tasks (Horwitz et al., 1980; Blum et al., 1980; Wirtschafter et al., 1980). Since the core of knowledge about oncology protocols is defined in protocol documents, the domain of cancer chemotherapy has the advantage of having a readily available source of structured knowledge of the field. The ongoing involvement of oncologists with ONCOCIN, both as research colleagues and as potential users, has provided additional expertise and highly motivated collaboration in knowledge base development. We currently have encoded the protocols for Hodgkin's disease, non-Hodgkin's lymphoma, breast cancer, and oat cell carcinoma of the lung[2] and will be adding all of the other treatment protocols employed at Stanford. It should be emphasized that the resulting computer-based protocols include both the specific rules gleaned from the protocol documents *and* some additional judgmental expertise from our experts, who have defined the ways in which the system ought to respond to unusual or aberrant situations.[3]

[2]The oat cell protocol is the most complex protocol at Stanford. It was implemented to verify that our representation scheme would apply to essentially any of the protocols currently in use. However, it has not yet been released for routine use, pending its thorough testing.

[3]In order to design a program that could be operational in the short term, our initial design plan was consciously to avoid major theoretical barriers such as management of inexact reasoning and generalized methods for temporal reasoning.

32.3.1 System Design

ONCOCIN's system design is a result of the combined efforts of an interdisciplinary group of computer scientists, clinicians, statisticians and support staff, totaling 29 individuals. System design began in July of 1979. From the outset, the logistics of how a consultation system could fit into the busy oncology clinic were a crucial design consideration; one of our first tasks was to study the flow of information within the clinic. We asked the oncology fellows about their attitudes regarding computers and asked them to assess the potential role of such technology in the oncology clinic. A Stanford industrial engineer with experience in the area of human factors was consulted during the iterative phase of interface design. Programmers would offer mock demonstrations to those with little or no computer expertise. After getting comments and suggestions on the demonstration, modifications were made, and a new mock-up was presented. This process was repeated until all felt satisfied with the interaction. Design decisions of this type were discussed at regular research meetings involving both physicians and computer scientists.

The design of the reasoning program, which is written in Interlisp and uses AI representation techniques (see Chapter 35), was affected by our desire to create a system that provides rapid response. The original ONCOCIN prototype used keyboard-oriented interactive programs borrowed from EMYCIN. As was mentioned earlier in this chapter, we knew from our previous work, however, that this type of interaction would be too tedious and time-consuming for a busy clinic physician. A physician using MYCIN often had to wait while questions were generated and rules were tried. The use of the EMYCIN interface, however, enabled us to create the program's knowledge base and to evaluate its therapy recommendations while we were concurrently deciding on the interface design. The ultimate interface incorporates a fast display program that is separate from the AI reasoning program (Gerring et al., 1982). Thus ONCOCIN is actually a set of independent programs that run in parallel and communicate with each other.

A major design goal was to have ONCOCIN used directly by physicians at the time of a patient's visit to the clinic for chemotherapy. One way to encourage physicians' involvement was to make the system easily accessible while providing a variety of hard-copy reports that had previously either not existed or required manual preparation. A computer-generated summary sheet is produced in the morning for each scheduled patient enrolled in one of the protocols handled by the computer. The summary sheet is attached to the patient's chart and serves as a reminder of the patient's diagnosis and stage, expected chemotherapy, and any recent abnormal laboratory values or toxicities. A centrally located video display terminal is used by the oncologist after the patient has been examined. The physician interacts with ONCOCIN's high-speed data acquisition program (the *Interviewer*). While the clinician is entering data through the Interviewer, that program is passing pertinent answers to the reasoning program (the *Reasoner*), which uses the current patient data, the past history, and the protocol assignment to formulate a treatment plan. By the time data entry is complete, the Reasoner has generally completed its plan formulation and has passed the results back to the Interviewer, which in turn displays the recommendation to the user. The physician can then agree with or modify the system's treatment recommendation, make adjustments to the laboratory and x-ray tests suggested for the patient by ONCOCIN, and end the session. Progress notes are produced on a printer near the ONCOCIN terminal so they can be easily removed, verified and signed by the physician, and then placed in the hospital chart. After the session the computer also generates an *encounter sheet,* which lists the tests to be ordered, when they should be scheduled, and when the patient should return to the clinic for his or her next visit. This information is generated on a second printer located at the front desk, where these activities are scheduled.

The system design attempts to prevent the computer system from being perceived as an unwanted intrusion into the clinic. The physician/computer interaction takes the place of a task that the physician would otherwise perform by hand (the manual completion of a patient flow sheet) and requires only 5 to 7 minutes at the terminal. A training session of 30 minutes has been adequate for physicians to achieve independent use of the system, and the hard-copy reports assist the physicians with their responsibilities. Because we were eager to make the system as flexible as possible and to simulate the freedom of choice available to the physicians when they fill out the flow sheets by hand, the program leaves the users largely in control of the interaction. Except for the patient's white cell count, platelet count, and information about recent radiation therapy (key issues in determining appropriate therapy), the physicians may enter whatever information they feel is pertinent, leaving some fields blank if they wish. An important evaluative issue that we are accordingly investigating is whether ONCOCIN encourages more complete and accurate recording of the flow sheet data despite the user's ability to skip entries if he or she wishes to do so. Users may enter data into the flow sheet format in whatever order they prefer, skipping forward or backward and changing current or old answers. This approach is radically different from that used in MYCIN in that the physician decides what information to enter and the reasoning can proceed in a data-directed fashion. Data entry in a flow sheet format avoids the problems of natural language understanding that prevented this approach in MYCIN.

32.3.2 Terminal Interface

The system incorporates a special terminal interface to ensure that a busy clinician can find ONCOCIN fast and easy to use, as well as simple to learn. The physician interacts with a high-speed (9600 baud) video display ter-

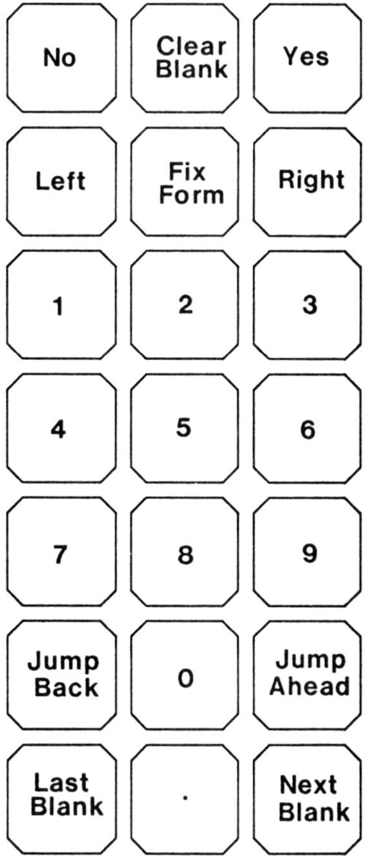

FIGURE 32-2 ONCOCIN's 21-key pad.

minal with multiple windows, simulating the appearance of the conventional paper flow sheet. Simulation of the form makes the interaction more comfortable and familiar.

A customized keyboard was designed for data entry. It allows the physician to enter the flow sheet information using a 21-key pad (Figure 32-2), which is located to the right of a conventional terminal keyboard. We considered light pens and touch screens but felt that they were either too expensive or too unreliable at the present time. Furthermore, a simple key pad was adequate for our needs. The layout of the key pad is simple and self-explanatory. Ten of the keys make up a number pad, which is laid out the same way as the numbers on push-button telephones. Our human factors consultant recommended this arrangement because we could safely assume user experience with push-button telephones, while user experience with a calculator-style number pad would be likely to be more limited. The other keys on the pad are "Yes" and "No" keys, and cursor control keys. The labels on the cursor control keys suggest that the user is filling in the blanks on a paper form, for example, "Next Blank," "Clear Blank," "Jump Ahead," etc. Our human factors consultant suggested using this terminology instead of terms including the word "Field" (e.g., "Next Field"), which are information-processing terminology and not as intuitive for naive computer users. This decision reflects our general effort to avoid computer jargon in talking with physicians, printing text on the terminal screen, or communicating with them in memos.

32.3.3 Display Design

The design of the display is derived from the paper flow sheet used for many years for protocol data gathering and analysis. The display screen is divided into four sections as indicated in Figure 32-3:

a. the *explanation field,* which presents the justification for the recommendation indicated by the user-controlled cursor location (the black block in the figure)

b. the *message field,* which identifies the patient and provides a region for sending pertinent messages from ONCOCIN to the physician

c. the *flow sheet,* which displays a region of the conventional hard copy flow sheet; the display includes columns for past visits, and the physician enters data and receives recommendations in the right-hand column

d. the *soft key identifiers,* labels that indicate the special functions associated with numbered keys across the top of the terminal keyboard

Note that when the physician is entering patient data, the explanation field specifies the range of expected entries for the item with which the cursor is aligned. When the system has recommended therapy (as in Figure 32-3), the explanation field provides a brief justification of the drug dosage indicated by the cursor location.

32.3.4 Integration into the Clinic

To make ONCOCIN's integration into the clinic as smooth as possible, we scheduled clinic meetings led by the oncology members of our research team. At one early meeting to announce that the system would soon be available, we gave a system demonstration and held a discussion of our project goals. Individual training sessions were then scheduled to teach each physician how to use the system. These orientation sessions were brief and informative. They stressed that the physician is the ultimate decision

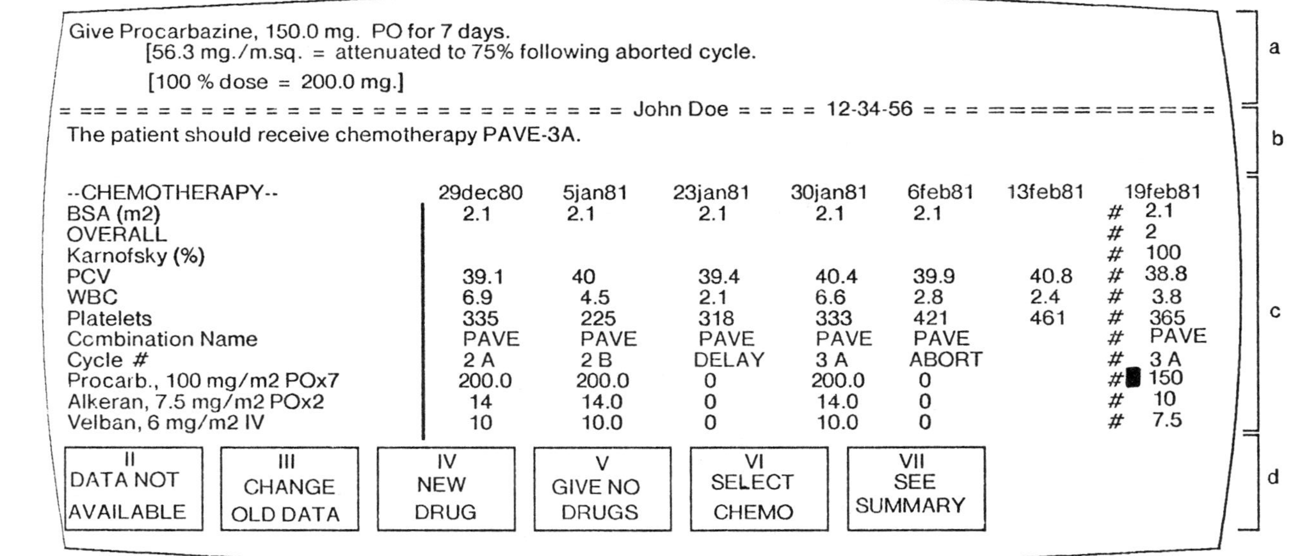

FIGURE 32-3 Sample ONCOCIN screen.

maker about the patient's care, and that the computer-based consultant is intended to remind the physician about the complex details of the protocols and to collect patient data. Members of our group meet with oncology faculty and physicians occasionally to give them progress reports on our research.

We also enlisted the help of a data manager who is responsible for training sessions, ensures that on-line patient records are current, and sees that the system runs smoothly. The data manager is available whenever the system is running in the clinic and offers assistance when necessary. This role has proved to be particularly crucial. The data manager is the most visible representative of our group in the clinic (other than the collaborating oncologists themselves). The person selected for this role therefore must be responsible, personable, tactful, intelligent, aware of the system's goals and capabilities, and able to communicate effectively with the physicians. If the person in this role is unable to satisfy these qualifications, he or she can make system use seem difficult, undesirable, and imposing to the physician users.

Integration of the system into the clinic was planned as a gradual process. When the system was first released, the program handled a small number of patients and protocols. As the program became more familiar to the physicians, we added more patients to the system. We are in the process of adding new protocols, which in turn will mean additional patients being handled on the computer. ONCOCIN was initially available only three mornings per week. It is now available whenever patients who are being followed on the computer are scheduled. This plan for slow integration of the system into the clinic has made ONCOCIN's initial release less disruptive to the clinic routine than it would have been if we had attempted to incorporate a comprehensive system that handled all patients and protocols from the onset. This method of integration has also allowed us to fine-tune our system early in its development, based on responses and suggestions from our physician users.

32.3.5 Responses and Modifications to the System

After the system's initial release, the data manager and the collaborating oncologists collected comments and suggestions from the physicians who used the system. We have made numerous program changes in response to suggestions for modifications and desirable new features. We have also conducted a number of formal studies to evaluate the impact of the system on physicians' attitudes, the completeness and accuracy of data collection, and the quality of the therapeutic decisions.

We soon learned that some of our initial design decisions had failed to anticipate important physician concerns. For example, if the Reasoner needed an answer to a special question not on the regular flow sheet form, our initial approach was to have the Interviewer interrupt data entry to request this additional information. The physicians were annoyed by these interruptions, so we modified the scheme to insert the question less obtrusively on a later section of the flow sheet, and to stop forcing the physician to answer such questions.

Another concern was that ONCOCIN was too stringent about its drug dosage recommendations, requesting justifications from the physician even for minor changes. We needed to take into account, for example, that a different pill size might decrease or increase a dose slightly and yet would be preferable for a patient's convenience. We subsequently obtained from the oncologists on our team ranges for each chemotherapeutic agent, within which any dosage modifications could be considered insignificant. Such minor modifications no longer generate requests for justification.[4] We also modified the program to recommend the same dose that the physician prescribed during a prior visit if that recommendation is within the acceptable range calculated by the program.

Some system users also asked whether the program could generate a progress note for the patient's visit. When we developed this feature and installed a small printer to prepare these notes in duplicate, use of the system was immediately made more desirable because this capability saved the physician the time required to dictate a note. This feature also helps to encourage the physician to enter relevant data completely and accurately because the quality of the resulting progress note is dependent on the data entry process.

When the system was first released, it was available only on the three mornings per week when the majority of lymphoma patients were seen (the computer, a DEC System 2020, is used at other times by other members of our research community). This allowed us to provide rapid response time through an arrangement for high-priority use of the computer. Since some lymphoma protocol patients were seen at other times, however, there were continuing problems in keeping the computer-based files up to date and thus in establishing ONCOCIN's role as a reliable aid for the management of that subset of patients. In response to this problem, we have made the system available whenever a patient known to the system is seen in the clinic. When the physician initiates a consultation, the program checks to see if the computer response is likely to be slow and, if so, prints out a warning to that effect. The physician may then either abort the session or proceed with the anticipation that the interaction will take longer than usual. We have found that the physicians understand and appreciate this feature and will often continue despite the delays.

---

[4]Current research is also investigating an adaptation of ONCOCIN's recommendation scheme whereby it will critique the physician's own therapy plan and give advice only when specifically requested to do so (Langlotz and Shortliffe, 1983).

32.3.6 Lessons Learned

It is clear that in order for a computer-based consultant to be effective in a clinical setting, the overall system design must take into account both the needs of the intended users and the constraints under which they function. This is the central theme of the lessons that we have learned from the MYCIN and ONCOCIN experiences. The program must be designed to satisfy a need for consultation and to provide this assistance in a fast, easy-to-use, and tactful manner. It should ideally avoid an incremental time commitment or an increase in the responsibilities of its users, or they will tend to resist its use. We have found that providing extra information-processing services, such as printing progress notes for the physicians, significantly heightens the system's appeal.

For ONCOCIN to have an effective role as a physician's assistant, providing both data management functions and consultations on patient treatment, it needs to be part of the daily routine in the clinic. Because of the limited number of patients and protocols currently on the system, ONCOCIN is still an exception to the daily routine; this will change as more protocols are encoded and the system is transferred to dedicated hardware. We are planning to move ONCOCIN to a personal workstation (a LISP machine capable of handling large AI programs) so that it will be self-contained. As it becomes the principal record-keeping system in the oncology clinic and enables the oncologists to receive useful advice for essentially all of their patient encounters, ONCOCIN will become successfully integrated into the clinic setting. The next stage will be to disseminate the system, mounted on single-user workstations, into other settings outside Stanford.

Physician involvement in the design of ONCOCIN has been crucial in all aspects of the system development. The collaborating oncologists provide answers to questions that are unclear from the protocol descriptions, evaluate the program's recommendations to ensure they are reasonable, offer useful feedback during the development of the user interface, and provide advice about how the computer-based consultation system can best fit into the clinic setting. Their collaboration and that of the computer scientists, medical personnel, and others in our interdisciplinary group (all of whom are committed to the creation of a clinically useful consultation tool) have combined to create a system for which limited integration into a clinical setting has been accomplished. We expect that total integration will be feasible within the next few years.

33

Strategies for Understanding Structured English

Alain Bonnet

Psychological work on memory, in particular by Bartlett (1932), has led to the conclusion that people faced with a new situation use large amounts of highly structured knowledge acquired from previous experience. Bartlett used the word *schema* to refer to this phenomenon. Minsky (1975), in his famous paper, proposed the notion of a *frame* as a fundamental structure used in natural language understanding, as well as in scene analysis. I will use the former term in the rest of this chapter, in spite of its general connotation.

The main thesis defended by Bartlett was that the phenomena of memorization and remembering are both constructive and selective. The hypothesis has more recently been revived by psychologists working on discourse structure (Collins, 1978; Bransford and Franks, 1971; Kintsch, 1976). Various experiments performed on subjects who were told stories and then asked to describe what they remembered showed that people not only forget facts but add some. Moreover, they are unable to distinguish between what they have actually heard and what they have inferred. People hearing a story make assumptions, which they might revise or refine as more information comes in, either confirmatory or contradictory. Making such assumptions entails building (or retrieving) models of the expected text contents. A corollary of this process is that if the story adequately fits the model people have in mind, the story will be understood more easily.

Although it is difficult to give a formal definition of what constitutes a coherent text, it is an accepted notion that sentences that comprise it are

---

This chapter is based on a technical memo (HPP-79-25) from the Heuristic Programming Project, Department of Computer Science, Stanford University. Used with permission.

linked by cause-effect relationships, chronological orderings, and the like. Flashbacks are not contradictory with coherence, but they can make the text more difficult to comprehend. Texts dealing with specific domains seem to be structured in terms of topic. Consequently, an important problem to face is recognizing the different topics and deciding when a *shift in topic* occurs.

Several frame-based languages, such as KRL (Bobrow and Winograd, 1977), the "units package" (Stefik, 1979), and FRL (Roberts and Goldstein, 1977), implement the basic concepts underlying frames, or schemata. A schema contains slots. They can be viewed as variables that will be bound to data. Each slot contains "facets" (FRL), "aspects" (units package), or "descriptors" (KRL), which specify how to fill the slots, for example, specifying the type of values acceptable (numeric, strings of characters), the range of possible values, values to assign by default, or attached procedures describing what to do if the slot is filled in (this is a way to make inferences). Slots may be organized into hierarchical schemata, in which case values may be inherited from one schema to a more specialized one. This hierarchy and concomitant inheritance avoids any duplication of common properties.

BAOBAB is an experimental natural language interface to the MYCIN system and is based on the idea that clusters of topics can be represented in framelike structures. Its design has been inspired by observations regarding text coherence, shifts in topic, temporal orderings, etc. Figure 33-1 shows a short dialogue between a physician and the program. The English that is generated is somewhat stilted, but its main purpose is to be nonambiguous. In this chapter are presented the principles and methods that permitted the implementation of a program with these capabilities.

33.1 Related Work and Goals

AI researchers have explored a variety of strategies to recognize shifts in topic occurring during dialogues or written texts. One issue faced is the necessity to narrow the space of possible referents of a linguistic object by focusing at different levels of detail. Thus Grosz (1977) studied the role of focus in the interpretation of utterances and its relation to domain structure. She used the task structure to resolve definite noun phrases in task-oriented dialogues. Sidner (1979) extended this work to determine the use of focusing in the resolution of pronoun references and other kinds of anaphora occurring in dialogues. Rosenberg (1977) has studied how themes are linked via references in newspaper articles.

Another major reason for focusing is to avoid combinatorial explosion. The fear of such an explosion is mainly motivated by the large number of inferences that may be made if all possible frames are activated. In fact,

```
I am ready

** THIS IS A 26 YEAR OLD MALE PATIENT

My understanding is:
The age of the patient is 26
The sex of the patient is male

** FIVE DAYS AGO, HE HAD RESPIRATORY-TRACT SYMPTOMS

What is his name?

** JO

My understanding is:
The name of the patient is Jo
Respiratory-tract is one of the symptoms that the patient had

** A COUPLE OF DAYS BEFORE THE ADMISSION, HE HAD A MALAISE

Please give me the date of admission

** MARCH 12, 1979

My understanding is:
The patient was admitted at the hospital 3 days ago
Malaise is one of the symptoms that the patient had 5 days ago
```

FIGURE 33-1 Short sample dialogue. The physician's inputs appear in capital letters after the double asterisks.

some of the frames might rule out others, thus enabling the space of possible inferences to be pruned. This issue has also been raised by Charniak (1978). Embodying world knowledge in frames (Minsky, 1975) or scripts (Abelson, 1973; Schank and Abelson, 1975) led to the development of programs that achieved a reasonably deep level of understanding, for example, GUS (Bobrow et al., 1977), NUDGE (Goldstein and Roberts, 1977), FRUMP (DeJong, 1977) and SAM (Cullingford, 1977).

BAOBAB and the other programs mentioned so far have a common feature: they do not interpret sentences in isolation. Rather, they interpret in the context of an ongoing discourse and, hence, use discourse structure. BAOBAB also explores issues of (a) what constitutes a model for structured texts and (b) how and when topic shifts occur. However, BAOBAB is interested neither in inferring implicit facts that might have occurred temporally between facts explicitly described in a text nor in explaining intentions of characters in stories (main emphases of works using scripts or plans). Our program focuses instead on coherence of texts, which is mainly a task of detecting anomalies, asking the user to clarify vague pieces of information or disappointed expectations, and suggesting omissions. The domain of application is patient medical summaries, a kind of text for which language-processing research has mainly consisted of filling in formatted grids without demanding any interactive behavior (Sager, 1978). BAOBAB's objectives are to understand a summary typed in "natural medical jargon" by a physician and to interact by asking questions or displaying what it has understood.

The program uses a model of the typical structure of medical summaries, which consists of a set of related schemata, described below. BAOBAB uses both its medical knowledge and its model of the usual description of a medical case to interpret the dialogue or the text and to produce an internal structure usable by MYCIN. The program then uses this information to guide a standard consultation session.

BAOBAB behaves like a clerk or a medical assistant who knows what a physician has to describe and how a malady is ordinarily presented. It reacts to violations of the model, such as a description that ignores symptoms or that fails to mention results of cultures that have been drawn. It does not attempt to use its knowledge to infer any diagnosis but, in certain cases, can draw inferences that will facilitate MYCIN's task. BAOBAB uses these capabilities to establish relationships between the concepts stated. This facilitates interpretations of what is said. For example, BAOBAB knows that "semi-coma" refers to the state of consciousness of the patient and "hyperthyroidism" to a diagnosis. One use of the program would be to allow the physician to volunteer information before or during the consultation. This feature would respond to the common frustration expressed by some users who object to having to wait for MYCIN to ask a key question before they can tell it about a crucial symptom.

BAOBAB consists of (a) a parser that maps the surface input into an internal representation, (b) a set of schemata that provide a model of the kind of information that the program is ready to accept and of the range of inferences that it will be able to draw, (c) episode-recognition strategies that allow appropriate focusing on particular pieces of the texts, and (d) an English-text generator used to display in a nonambiguous fashion what has been understood. As described in Chapter 5, this generator was already available in MYCIN. The main emphasis here will therefore be on the description of schemata and schema-activation strategies. These techniques have been successfully implemented, using Interlisp (Teitelman, 1978), in a program connected with MYCIN's data base and running on the SUMEX computer at Stanford.

33.2 Schemata and Their Relations

Medical summaries can be viewed as sequences of episodes that correspond to phrases, sentences, or groups of sentences dealing with a single topic. Each such topic may be represented by a schema. Processing and understanding a text consist of mapping episodes in the text onto the schemata that constitute the model. Matching a schema can be discontinuous; that is, two episodes referring to the same schema need not necessarily be juxtaposed (they might be separated by an episode referring to another schema). We will refer to this phenomenon as a *temporary schema-shift*.

A typical scenario is as follows. The medical case is introduced with general information, such as the date and the reason for admission to the hospital. Then the patient is presented (name, age, . . .). Symptoms (noted by the patient) and signs (observed by the physician) are described. A physical exam is usually performed, and cultures are taken for which results are pending or available. The structure of such a text can be captured in a sequence of schemata, one of which is shown in Figure 33-2. These texts are usually well structured. Redundancies can appear, but discrepancies are rather rare (although they must be detected when they occur). Expectations are usually satisfied.

A typical BAOBAB schema contains domain-specific knowledge and resembles a frame (Minsky, 1975) or script (Schank and Abelson, 1975) or unit (Stefik, 1979). Relevant slots define expected values, default values, and attached procedures. Attributes relating to the same topic are gathered into these schemata. There is some overlap between them (such as WEIGHT, which can occur in the identification of the patient as well as in the results of a physical exam). Each schema contains two types of slots: global slots (comments, creation date, author's name, how to recognize the schema, what is the preferred position of the schema within summaries) and individual slots (which correspond to MYCIN's clinical parameters). Each individual slot contains *facets* specifying how to fill it in or what actions to take when it has been filled in (by procedural attachment).

Global slots are mainly used to decide whether a part of the text being analyzed suggests or confirms a schema or how the confirmation of one schema causes another one to be abandoned. The slots CONFIRMED-BY and SUGGESTED-BY point to lists of slots belonging to the schema. The first defines the schema (characteristic slots), whereas the other is nonessential for confirming the schema. The slots TERMINATED-BY and PREF-FOLLOWED-BY specify relationships of mutual exclusion and partial ordering between schemata. All these slots are described in more detail in the section devoted to strategies for activating schemata. Nonglobal slots are always attributes grouped within a schema. Each is, in turn, a schema whose slots are the facets mentioned above (Roberts and Goldstein, 1977).

33.2.1 An Example of a Schema

In the $DESCRIPT schema (Figure 33-2), the first three global slots (AUTHOR, CREATION-DATE, and COMMENT) are used for documentation, whereas the next four are used to define strategies for schema-shifts (see below). Then six individual slots (corresponding to parameter names) define the schema. Each of them is described by subslots, or facets, some of which (e.g., EXPECT, TRANS, LEGALVALS, CHECK, PROMPT) already exist in the structure of MYCIN's knowledge base. Others have been

```
$DESCRIPT
---------

  AUTHOR: BONNET
  CREATION-DATE: OCT-10-78
  COMMENT: Patient identification
  CONFIRMED-BY: (NAME AGE SEX RACE)
  TERMINATED-BY: ($SYMPTOM)
  SUGGESTED-BY: (WEIGHT HEIGHT)
  PREF-FOLLOWED-BY: ($SYMPTOM)

NAME
          EXPECT: ANY
          TRANS: ("the name of" *)
          TOBEFILLED: T
          WHENFILLED: DEMONNAME
AGE
          EXPECT: POSNUMB
          TRANS: ("the age of" *)
          CHECK: (CHECK VALU 0 100.0 (LIST "Is the patient really"
                   VALU "years old?") T)
          TOBEFILLED: T
          WHENFILLED: SETSTATURE
SEX
          EXPECT: (MALE FEMALE)
          TRANS: ("the sex of" *)
          TOBEFILLED: T
          WHENFILLED: SEXDEMON
RACE
          EXPECT: (CAUCASIAN BLACK ASIAN INDIAN LATINO OTHER)
          TRANS: ("the race of" *)
WEIGHT
          EXPECT: POSNUMB
          TRANS: ("the weight of" *)
          CHECK: (CHECK VALU LIGHT HEAVY (LIST "Does the patient
                   really weigh" VALU "kilograms?") T)
HEIGHT
          EXPECT: POSNUMB
          CHECK: (CHECK VALU SMALL TALL (LIST "Is the patient
                   really" VALU "centimeters tall?") T)
                        .
                        .
                        .
```

FIGURE 33-2 Schema of a patient description.

created to allow the program to intervene during the course of the dialogue. For example, when the slot TOBEFILLED holds the value T (true), it means that the value of the variable must be asked if the physician does not provide it. The WHENFILLED feature specifies a procedure to run as soon as the slot is filled in. This is the classic way of making inferences. For example, SETSTATURE specifies narrower ranges of weight and height for a patient according to his or her age.

33.2.2 Facets

Expected and legal values. EXPECT is used for single-valued parameters, whereas LEGALVALS is used for multi-valued parameters (see Chapter 5). They both give a list of possible values for an attribute.

Linguistic information. TRANS always contains a phrase in English describing the parameter; it is used for generating translations of rules and other semantic entities. PROMPT contains a question, in English, that asks the user about the corresponding parameter. It is used, in addition to the usual way MYCIN asks for information, to clarify a concept recognized as "fuzzy." For example, entry of the clause "THE PATIENT DRINKS 6 CANS OF BEER EVERY MORNING" leads BAOBAB to ask "Is the patient alcoholic?" since MYCIN has no explicit knowledge about alcoholic beverages, but can recognize such keywords as drink or alcohol. CHECK contains a question that can be used to request verification whenever a value outside the normal range has been given.

TOBEFILLED. If the TOBEFILLED facet of an attribute is set to T (true), it means that the slot has to be filled. Concretely, this means that if the slot has not yet been filled when the schema is abandoned, the attached request will be carried out. This does not necessarily mean that the parameter is essential from a clinical point of view; it may be essential for communication purposes.

33.2.3 Procedural Attachment

In BAOBAB, there are two kinds of procedural attachment. The first, called WHENFILLED, allows associated actions to be carried out depending on conditions local to the slot. It is analogous to the "demons" of Selfridge (1959) or Charniak (1972). The second kind of attachment, called PREDICATE, is used to specify how to fill a slot and is mentioned last. These facets allow BAOBAB to:

a. *Produce inferences.* If the attribute of a clause that has just been built has an attached procedure, it can trigger the building of another clause; for example, INFERFEVER is run as soon as the temperature is known and can lead to a clause such as "The patient is not febrile."

b. *Narrow a range of expected values.* Consider, for example, the weight of a patient. This has *a priori* limits, by default, of 0 and 120 kilograms. This range is narrowed according to the age of the patient as soon as the latter is known.

c. *Make predictions.* An event like "a lumbar puncture" can cause predictions about "CSF data" (not about their values, but about the fact that they will be mentioned). These predictions will be checked, and appropriate questions will be asked if they remain unfulfilled as the dialogue proceeds.

d. *Dynamically modify the grammar.* A semantic category like <PATIENT> can be updated by the name of the patient as soon as it is known. This update is done by the procedure DEMONNAME as indicated in Figure 33-2.

e. *Specify how to fill a slot.* Sometimes a procedure expresses the most convenient way to match a category. This kind of procedure has been called a "servant." For example, the best way to match a <VALUE> is to know that it points to its corresponding <ATTRIBUTE>. This is much simpler than examining the list of 500 values in the dictionary.

33.2.4 Default Values

BAOBAB distinguishes among three kinds of default values:

a. Some parameters have default values that are negations of symptoms; for example, TEMPERATURE has "98.6 F" as a default value (negation of fever), and STATE-OF-CONSCIOUSNESS has "alert" as a default value (negation of altered consciousness).

b. Other parameters depend on the result of a medical exam or procedure, and in such cases the default value is simply "unknown." Pointing out an unknown value to the physician might remind him or her that the procedure has in fact been carried out and that a result should have been mentioned. An example of such a default value is that for the parameter STATE-OF-CHEST, which depends on an x-ray.

c. Finally, some parameters inherit a value from another variable; for example, the date of a culture might reasonably be the date of admission to the hospital (if the infection is not hospital-acquired).

Note that any default value assumed by the program is explicitly stated. This feature allows the user to override the default value when in disagreement with it (a mandatory feature because a default value might be used later by the consultation program and therefore be taken into account in the formation of the diagnosis).

33.3 The Grammar

In a technical domain, where specialists write for specialists, terseness of style is widespread (e.g., "T 101.4 rectal"). Thus a syntactic parsing does not provide enough additional information to justify its use for text comprehension. Instead, a computer program can use a semantically oriented grammar. This grammar makes the parsing process unambiguous and therefore efficient. Discussions of this point can be found in Burton (1976) and Hendrix (1976).

BAOBAB's parser uses a context-free augmented grammar [cf. the augmented transition network of Woods (1970)]. A grammar rule specifies (1) the syntax, (2) a semantic verification of the parsed tree resulting from the syntactic component, and (3) a response expression used to build one or several clauses. The grammar is divided into specific and nonspecific rules.

Specific grammar rules are associated with the slots of schemata and describe the way these can be mentioned at the surface level. Categories used in the rules are things such as <PATIENT>, <SIGN>, and <DIAGNOSIS>. This link between the grammar and the schemata provides a means to try, by priority, those grammar rules that are appropriate to the schema under consideration. Furthermore, it provides a means to postpone the risk of combinatorial explosion due to the large number of grammar rules (due to the specificity of the categories used in the productions).

Nonspecific grammar rules use general concepts such as <ATTRIBUTE>, <OBJECT>, and <VALUE>, which are commonly used to represent knowledge in systems. This kind of rule is general enough to be used in other domains; but once the syntax has been recognized, these rules must undergo a semantic check in order to verify that, say, values and attributes fit together, hence the importance of the augmentation of the grammar mentioned above.

Specific grammar rules enable the system to recognize peculiar constructs. For example, "120/98" and "98 F" do not belong to well-known syntactic classes but have to be recognized as values for blood pressure and temperature. Grammar rules such as

<VITAL> → <BP> <HIGH/LOW>

<VITAL> → <TEMP><TEMPNUM>|<TEMP><NUM>(DEGREES)

are used to parse "BP 130/94" or "T 98 F." The category <TEMPNUM> has an attached procedure, a specific piece of code that recognizes "F" as Fahrenheit, detaches it from "98," verifies that 98 is a reasonable value for a temperature, and finally returns "98 degrees" as the value of the temperature.

The following are examples of the "syntax" of purely semantic rules:

<sentence> → <patient> <experience> <symptom> <time>

<symptom> → <modifier> <symptom>

<patient> → patient | <name>

<name> → (the name of the patient, usually encountered at the beginning of the text)

<experience> → complain of | experience | <have>

<symptom> → headache | malaise | chill | . . .

<modifier> → severe | painful | . . .

<have> → has | had | . . .

<time> → <num> <time-unit> ago | on <date>

<time-unit> → day | week | . . .

<num> → 1|2|3| . . .

<date> → a date recognized by an associated LISP function

This subset of the grammar enables the program to recognize inputs such as the following:

1. NAPOLEON COMPLAINED OF SEVERE HEADACHE 3 DAYS AGO
2. BILL EXPERIENCED MALAISE ON SEPT-22-1978
3. JANE HAD CHILLS ON 10/10/78

Examples of purely syntactic rules are as follows:

<SENTENCE> → <NP> <VP>

<NP> → <NOUN> | <ADJ> <NOUN> | <DET> <ADJ> <NOUN> | <DET> <NOUN> |. . .

<VP> → <VERB> | <VERB> <NP> | <VERB> <PREPP>

<PREPP> → <PREP> <NP>

where <NP> stands for noun phrase, <VP> for verb phrase, <DET> for determiner, <PREPP> for prepositional phrase and <PREP> for preposition. The set of rules enables the system to recognize input sentence 1 above (except for the notion of time), as shown in the syntactic tree of Figure 33-3.

When the semantic component interprets such a syntactic tree, it checks that <NOUN> is matched by a person (whereas the direct use of <PATIENT> would make useless such a verification). Input sentences such as the following would thus be rejected:

4. THE BOAT COMPLAINED OF HEADACHE
5. BILL COMPLAINED OF A SEVERE LEG

Numerous systems use a representation based on the notion of object-

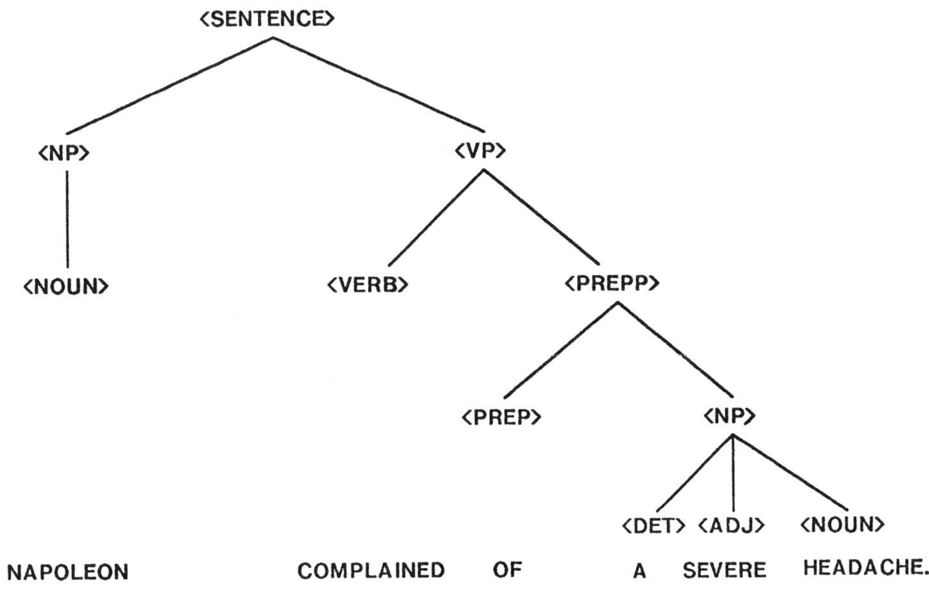

FIGURE 33-3 A conventional syntactic tree.

attribute-value triples with an optional associated predicate-function. In such domains, one can define grammar rules such as:

<SENTENCE> → <OBJECT/ATTRIBUTE> <PREDICATE-FUNCTION> <VALUE>

<OBJECT/ATTRIBUTE> → <ATTRIBUTE> OF <OBJECT> | <OBJECT> <ATTRIBUTE>

<OBJECT> → PATIENT | CULTURE | ORGANISM | . . .

<ATTRIBUTE> → ISATTRIBUTE (attached procedure specifying how to recognize an attribute)

<PREDICATE-FUNCTION> → <SAME> | <NOTSAME> | . . .

<SAME> → IS | HAS | . . .

<VALUE> → ISVALUE (attached procedure specifying how to recognize the value of an attribute)

Such "syntactico"-semantic rules enable the recognition of input sentences such as:

6. THE TEMPERATURE OF THE PATIENT IS 99

7. THE MORPHOLOGY OF THE ORGANISM IS ROD

The complete form of the <SENTENCE> rule is displayed below. The first line is the syntax, the second is the augmentation, and the third is the response. CHECKAV (check attribute value) is a function of two arguments, <ATTRIBUTE> and <VALUE>, that returns "true" if the value matches the attribute, in which case the response expression is produced; otherwise, the semantic interpretation has failed.

```
((<OBJECT/ATTRIBUTE> <PREDICATE-FUNCTION> <VALUE>)
 ((CHECKAV <ATTRIBUTE> <VALUE>)
  (LIST <PREDICATE-FUNCTION> <ATTRIBUTE> <VALUE>)))
```

It is interesting to note that the predicate function is usually a verb phrase, and the <ATTRIBUTE> OF <OBJECT> sequence a noun phrase, as is <VALUE>. This means that a syntactic structure is being implicitly used.

The interpreter progresses in a left-to-right and top-down fashion, with backtracking. Whenever a grammar rule is satisfied but a part of the input remains to be analyzed, the remaining part is given back to the control structure, which then can invoke special processes; for example, a conjunction at the head of the remaining input can trigger an attempt to resolve it as an elliptical input. Thus in "ENGLISH PEOPLE LOVE BLONDS AND DRINK TEA," the second part can be analyzed as "English people drink tea." The algorithm implemented for handling elliptical inputs has been inspired by LIFER (Hendrix, 1976). When an input fails to be recognized, the interpreter assumes that a part of the input is missing or implicit, and it looks at the preceding utterance. If parts of the input match categories used in the grammar rule satisfied by the earlier input, it then assumes that the parts that have no correspondence in the new input can be repeated.

33.4 Schema-Shift Strategies

A language describing choices between schemata, and therefore schema-shift strategies, should include an attempt to answer the following questions: How is a schema focused, confirmed, or abandoned? What are the links between schemata (such as exclusive or sequencing relations)?

33.4.1 Suggest vs. Confirm

Bullwinkle makes the distinction [Bullwinkle (1977); see also Sidner (1979)] between potential and actual shifts of focus, pointing out that the cues suggesting a new frame must be confirmed by a subsequent statement in order to avoid making unnecessary shifts. This phenomenon is handled in a different fashion in BAOBAB. Instead of waiting for the suggestion to be confirmed, a qualitative distinction is made between the slots of a frame. The ones marked as suggesting but not confirming are regarded as weak clues and will not lead to a shift of focus, whereas the ones marked as confirming (hence suggesting) are sufficiently strong clues to command the shift. This distinction can be illustrated by the following two examples:

1. "The patient was found comatose. She was admitted to the hospital. A lumbar puncture was performed. She denied syncope or diplopia . . ."
2. "The patient was found comatose. He was admitted to the hospital. The protein from CSF was 58 mg% . . ." (CSF = cerebrospinal fluid)

In Example 1, the lumbar puncture suggests CSF results that are not given (weak clue). In Example 2, a detail of CSF results (strong clue) is given directly ("the protein"). In other words, the physician jumps into detail, and the frame is directly confirmed.

33.4.2 Top-down vs. Bottom-up

Sometimes the schema is explicitly announced, as in "results of the culture." This is a name-driven invocation of the schema. More often, the instantiation of the schema is content-driven. The clues used are the attributes associated with the schema, their expected values (if any), and other concepts that might suggest the frame. For example, "skin" is related to "rash," which belongs to the physical exam frame. These are indeed very simple indices. Research on more sophisticated methods for recognizing the relevant schema, such as discrimination nets, have been suggested (Charniak, 1978).

33.4.3 Termination Conditions

A simple case in which a schema can be terminated is when all of its slots have been filled. This is an ideal situation, but it does not occur very often. Another case is when the intervention of a schema implies that another schema is out of focus, which could be, but is not necessarily, the result of chronological succession. In general, this phenomenon occurs when the speaker actually starts the plot after setting the characters of the story. There is no standard way to decide when the setting is finished. However, as soon as the story actually starts, the setting could be closed and possibly completed with default values or with the answers to questions about whatever was not clear or omitted. A TERMINATED-BY slot has been created to define which schemata can explicitly terminate others; for example, the $SYMPTOM schema usually closes the $DESCRIPT schema (name, age, sex, race), as it is very unlikely that the speaker will give the sex of the patient in the middle of the description of the symptoms. This fact is due to the highly constrained nature of the domain.

33.4.4 Termination Actions

When a schema is terminated, the program infers all the default values of the unfilled slots. It also checks whether the expectations set during the story have been fulfilled. These actions can be performed only when a shift has been detected or at the end of the dialogue; otherwise, the program might ask too early about information that the user will give later. In the case where a schema has been exhausted (all its slots filled), an *a priori* choice with regard to the predicted next schema is made. This choice is possible by using a PREFERABLY-FOLLOWED-BY pointer that, in the absence of a bottom-up (data-driven) trigger for the next schema, decides in a top-down fashion which schema is the most probable to follow at a given point.

33.4.5 Schema-Grammar Links

Specific grammar rules described earlier are always associated with clinical parameters and therefore with schemata. This link is interesting from two points of view:

a. The interpreter takes advantage of this relationship to try specific rules in order of decreasing probability of relevance to the schema currently in focus. There is no quantitative notion of probability, but the preferred sequencing causes the trial according to priority not only of grammar rules associated with the activated schema, but also of the ones of the preferred successor, in case an unforeseen shift occurs. Rules are reordered whenever a schema-shift occurs, which explains why the more disorganized presentations of a text take longer to be parsed.

b. The parser can examine the content of a schema during the semantic interpretation of an input. For example, it can check the correspondence of an attribute and a value. It can also trigger a question whose answer is needed to interpret the current input. Therefore, there is a two-way connection between schemata and the grammar. This link is one of the key ideas underlying the interactive behavior of the program.

33.4.6 Comparison with Story-Grammars

Other methods have been proposed to take advantage of the coherent structure of texts. Psychologists and linguists have attempted to draw a parallel between the structure linking sentences within a text and the structure linking words within sentences. The notion of story-grammars, or text-grammars, grew out of this analogy, leading to the representation as context-free rules of the regularities appearing in such simple texts as fables.

Rumelhart (1975) describes a story as an introduction followed by episodes. An episode is an event followed by a reaction. A reaction is an internal response followed by an overt response, etc. A simple observation supporting the parallel is that two sentences in sequence usually bear some kind of relation to each other (often implicit); otherwise, the juxtaposition would be somewhat bizarre. Recognizing a paragraph as a sequence of sentences "at a syntactic level" leads to building a tree structure that may be further used by a semantic component.

The limits of the analogy between phrase structure and text structure can be easily ascertained. Winograd (1977) underlines the limits of a generative approach by pointing out that "there are interwoven themes and changes of scene which create a much more complex structure than can be handled with a simple notion of constituency." Furthermore, even if one can give an exhaustive list of words satisfying <NOUN>, it is difficult to determine how to match a <CONSEQUENCE> or an <OVERT-RESPONSE>. It follows that whether or not the process of a grammar rule has been satisfied is not easy to define. Even if we can predict that a determiner will precede an adjective or a noun, it is much more difficult to foresee that an *emotion* will be followed by a *reaction,* or at least not with the same regularity. It also seems that the "syntactic" category of a phrase is strongly domain-dependent. A given sentence may be a *consequence* or a *reason* according to the context. This phenomenon occurs less frequently with traditionally syntactic categories.

In addition, flashbacks are commonly used when people tell stories. In particular, a consequence might very well precede an explanation of an event. Chronological order is not often respected, as in "Van Gogh had difficulties to wake up. He had drunk a lot the night before." Along the same lines, elliptical phenomena (incomplete inputs) seem difficult to resolve; if one can determine the missing part of a sentence by reference to the syntactic structure of the preceding sentence, it is not easy to guess the nonstated event that has caused a reaction. The "syntactic" categories of text-grammars correspond more or less to schemas. The model defined in BAOBAB merely defines a partial ordering, or links of a preferred ordering between schemata. It follows that the *introduction* may be absent or that *signs* may precede *symptoms* without the text being regarded as incoherent. Violations of the idealistic model only cause requests for clarification or additional information. They make the comprehension process more difficult but do not halt it.

33.5 Direction for Future Work

The BAOBAB grammar is currently not very large (about 200 rules), and only seven schemata have been implemented. In order to be able to parse more complicated texts efficiently, ones involving symptoms that might imply different infections (with interactions between them), a computer program will need more sophisticated clues to determine which schema is the most appropriate to apply and in what priority. Furthermore, certain concepts are currently ignored because their relevance to medical knowledge is not always straightforward. For example, an infection acquired by a member of the patient's family or even the patient's occupation could give hints to the physician during the early stages of the diagnostic formulation, but these are not currently used.

33.6 Sample Sessions

The following examples demonstrate BAOBAB's capabilities as a natural language interface for describing cases to MYCIN. The physician types the input in upper case after the double asterisks; BAOBAB's responses are in lower case. An actual summary written by a physician has been chosen. It is slightly simplified, broken down into inputs, and given as a dialogue to facilitate the interactions. A few italicized comments have been inserted in parentheses to clarify points. Names of schemata start with the symbol $.

In the first example, the exposition of the summary does not satisfy the model (mainly because expectations are not fulfilled), which therefore causes interventions from the program. Questions are asked, analogous to the way in which MYCIN asks them. In the other two examples, the model is satisfied; the dialogue follows a normal course.

33.6.1 First Example

** A 19 YEAR OLD BOY WITH PETECHIAL RASH, LETHARGY AND POSITIVE BRUDZINSKI'S SIGN.

Patient's name?

(The $DESCRIPT schema has been activated by the beginning of the input. Then there is a schema-shift which generates the request for the missing name.)

** BILL

My understanding is:

The name of the patient is Bill
The age of the patient is 19 years
The sex of the patient is male
Petechial is one of the types of rash which the patient has
Lethargy is one of the symptoms that the patient had
Brudzinski is one of the signs that the patient showed

** HE HAD AN LP

My understanding is:
A lumbar puncture has been performed on the patient

** BYE

(Unfulfilled expectations trigger requests for CSF results.)

What is the total WBC count of the CSF?

** 9500

What percent of the WBCs in the CSF were polys?

** 70

What is the protein value (mg/100cc) in the CSF?

** 32

What is the glucose value (milligrams percent) in the CSF?

** 12

.
.
.

33.6.2 Second Example

** REASONS FOR ADMISSION: CHILLS HEADACHE MALAISE *(sets up expectations)*

So I will expect chill headache malaise as values for symptoms

** DATE OF ADMISSION: DECEMBER 25 1978

My understanding is that:
the patient was admitted at the hospital 4 days ago

** HISTORY OF THE PRESENT ILLNESS *(announces the $IDENTIFICATION schema)*

Ok.

** PAT IS A 26 YEAR OLD CAUCASIAN FEMALE

My understanding is that:
the age of the patient is 26 years
the race of the patient is Caucasian
the sex of the patient is female
the name of the patient is Pat

** ONE DAY PRIOR TO ADMISSION SHE EXPERIENCED CHILLS AND HEADACHE *(shift to $SYMPTOMS)*

My understanding is that:
chill is one of the symptoms that the patient had 5 days ago
headache is one of the symptoms that the patient had 5 days ago

(time inferences)

** ONE DAY AFTER SHE HAD A MALAISE

My understanding is that:

malaise is one of the symptoms that the patient had 4 days ago

** A LUMBAR PUNCTURE WAS PERFORMED *(weak clue to $LABDATA)*

My understanding is that:
a lumbar puncture has been performed on the patient

** SHE DENIED SYNCOPE OR PHOTOPHOBIA *($SYMPTOMS and $SIGNS)*

My understanding is that:
syncope is not one of the symptoms that the patient had
photophobia is not one of the symptoms that the patient had

** SOCIAL HISTORY: OCCASIONAL ALCOHOL USE

Do you suspect recent alcoholic history in Pat? *(clarification)*

** NO

My understanding is that:
the patient is not an alcoholic

** PHYSICAL EXAM *(announces $EXAM)*

Ok.

** WEIGHT 110 POUNDS

My understanding is that:
the weight of the patient is 49.9 kgms

** TEMP 101 DEGREES P 90 BP 110/75 RR 28

My understanding is that:
the temperature of the patient is 101
the pulse of the patient is 90
the blood pressure of the patient is 110/75
the respiratory rate of the patient is 28 breaths/minute

** SKIN NORMAL *(leads to a clause via inference)*

My understanding is that:
the patient does not have a rash or cutaneous lesions

** NECK: MARKED NUCHAL RIGIDITY *(another inference)*

My understanding is that:
meningismus is one of the signs that the patient showed

** BRUDZINSKI'S SIGN WAS POSITIVE

My understanding is that:
Brudzinski is one of the signs that the patient showed

** LAB DATA *(announces $LABDATA)*

Ok.

** CSF RESULTS *(sets a context)*

Ok.

** WBC 9500 *(understood in context)*

My understanding is that:
the WBC from the CSF is 9500

** PROTEIN 56

My understanding is that:
the CSF protein is 56

** GLUCOSE 45 MG%

My understanding is that:
the CSF glucose value is 45

** PERIPHERAL CBC (sets another context)

Ok.

** WBC 23.5 (understood in context)

My understanding is that:
the white count from the patient's peripheral
CBC (in thousands) is 23.5

** THE VALUE OF WBC IS 22.5 (corrects a mistyping)

Instead of 23.5 ? (making sure that it was meant)

** YES

My new understanding is that: The white count from
the patient's peripheral CBC (in thousands) is 22.5

** BYE

I have assumed the following by default: (inferences by default)
the state of consciousness of the patient is alert
the patient's X-ray is not abnormal
the patient is not immunosuppressed
Do you agree?

** THE PATIENT IS IMMUNOSUPPRESSED (overrides a default value)

My new understanding is that: The patient is immunosuppressed
Do you agree?

** YES

bye.

33.6.3 Third Example

** REASONS FOR ADMISSION: HEADACHE, LETHARGY AND FEVER

So I will expect HEADACHE LETHARGY FEBRILE as symptoms

** DATE OF ADMISSION ON MARCH 14

That was 6 days ago.
My understanding is
the patient was admitted at the hospital 6 days ago

** BARBARA IS A 3 YAER OLD WHITE FEMALE

=YEAR (automatic spelling correction)
My understanding is
the age of the patient is 3 years
the race of the patient is Caucasian
the sex of the patient is female
the name of the patient is Barbara

** ONE DAY PRIOR TO ADMISSION, SHE BECAME LETHARGIC

My understanding is
lethargy is one of the symptoms that the patient had 7 days ago

** SHE COMPLAINED OF HEADACHE AND HAD A TEMPERATURE OF 101 DEGREES

My understanding is
headache is one of the symptoms that the patient had
the temperature of the patient is 101
the patient is febrile

** A PHYSICIAN OBTAINED A COMPLETE BLOOD COUNT

My understanding is
the results of a recent CBC of the patient are available

** A LUMBAR PUNCTURE WAS PERFORMED

My understanding is
a lumbar puncture has been performed on the patient

** WEIGHT 39 LBS

My understanding is
the weight of the patient is 17.7 kgms

** HEIGHT 1.03 METER

Is the patient really 103.0 centimeters tall? *(asking for confirmation because that seems tall for 3 years)*
(Y or N) ** YES

My understanding is
the height of the patient is 103 cms

** BP 120/70 P 140

My understanding is
the blood pressure of the patient is 120/70
the pulse of the patient is 140

** RR 28 T 101 *(redundancy, the temperature was already known)*

My understanding is
the respiratory rate of the patient is 28

** SKIN: PETECHIAE ON FACE AND SHOULDERS

My understanding is
petechial is one of the types of rash which the patient has

** NECK: DEFINITE MENINGISMUS

My understanding is
meningismus is one of the signs that the patient showed

** LAB DATA: CSF RESULTS *(announces lab results; no clause is built)*

Ok.

** WBC 110 WITH 96% POLYS *(interpretation in the context of CSF)*

My understanding is
the WBC from the CSF is 110
the percent of PMN's in the CSF is 96

** PROTEIN 25 MG% AND GLUCOSE 95

My understanding is
the CSF protein is 25
the CSF glucose value is 95

** PERIPHERAL CBC

Ok.

** WBC 12300

Is the white count from the patient's peripheral CBC (in thousands) really 12300?
(the physician forgot that a number of thousands was expected)

** NO

Please enter the right value now

** 12.3

My understanding is

```
the white count from the patient's peripheral CBC (in thousands) is 12.3

** WITH 76% POLYS AND 1% BANDS

My understanding is
the percent of PMN's in the CBC is 76
the percent of peripheral WBC's which are immature in the CBC is 1

** SIMULTANEOUS BLOOD GLUCOSE: 170

My understanding is
the simultaneous blood glucose value is 170

** BYE

I have assumed the following by default:

the state of consciousness of the patient is alert
the patient has not shown symptoms of mumps
it is unknown whether the patient's X-ray is abnormal
the patient does not have a rash or cutaneous lesions
the patient does not have evidence of ocular nerve dysfunction
the patient is not an alcoholic
the patient is not immunosuppressed
it is unknown whether the patient does have a TB risk factor
the patient is not a compromised host
the patient does not live in a crowded environment
the patient has not been recently exposed to a contagious disease
the patient has not undergone surgery
the infection was not acquired while the patient was hospitalized
the patient has not been seriously burned
there is not evidence of congenital malformation involving the central nervous system
the patient is not a diabetic
the patient is not a premature infant
it is unknown whether the patient has had an injury or insult to, or defect in the central nervous system

You can change any of them if you disagree

** SHE HAS UNDERGONE SURGERY

I suppose it should replace the patient has not undergone surgery
Right?

** YES
Ok.

** GOOD-BYE
```

33.7 Conclusion

The strategies outlined in this chapter could be applied to a broad range of structured texts. The approach rests on the assumption that the texts' scenarios can be seen as sequences of episodes, identifiable by the program, in order to be integrated into appropriate schemata. Therefore, clustering attributes into framelike structures must make sense in the domain of application. The episodes could simultaneously refer to several schemata; that is, the associated schemata could have slots in common. Furthermore, it should be possible to define partial-ordering links between schemata.

The relationships could be rather loose, but the more constrained they are, the better this feature would work.

Expert systems usually need some kind of understanding to communicate in natural jargon with their users (expert, consultant, and/or student). The technique described here—breaking the knowledge down into schemata that correspond to different pieces of texts, associating semantic grammar rules with the schemata, and using strategies for recognizing episode shifts—should be generally applicable in such domains.

34

An Analysis of Physicians' Attitudes

Randy L. Teach and Edward H. Shortliffe

Despite the promise of medical computing innovations, many health care professionals have expressed skepticism about the computer's role as an aid to clinicians. A number of barriers have been noted. For example, Friedman and Gustafson (1977) have suggested that system designers tend to develop systems that are neither convenient for physicians nor responsive to their needs. Glantz (1978) has questioned the trade-off in costs and benefits for most medical computing applications, including computer-assisted consultations. Schwartz (1970) has noted that physicians are wary of formal decision aids because they perceive such tools to be a threat to their jobs and to their professional stature. He has also suggested that physicians are concerned about their ability to learn how to use computer systems (Schwartz, 1979), but that they simultaneously fear the prospect of being "left behind" if they fail to keep current. Other observers (Eisenberg, 1974; Weizenbaum, 1976) have questioned the role of computers as clinical consultation systems, suggesting that computer-based consultants may be an inappropriate use of computing technology that will inevitably degrade and debase the human function.

Observations such as these are generally based on personal experience without benefit of formal studies of physicians' attitudes. The few available studies have sought physicians' opinions regarding computing technology in general, but have tended not to specifically examine attitudes regarding the clinical introduction of computers. One early study (Mayne et al., 1968) found little physician interest or faith in the role of computing technology. However, Startsman and Robinson (1972) and others (Day, 1970; Resnikoff

This chapter is based on an article originally appearing in *Computers in Biomedical Research* 14: 542–558 (December 1981).

et al., 1967) have reported supportive physician attitudes. A follow-up to the Startsman and Robinson study by Melhorn and coworkers (1979) produced almost identical results, but also noted that physicians might be reluctant to accept the clinical use of computing technology.

Motivation for the Current Study

Our study was motivated by the belief that the future of research in medical computing, particularly the development of computer-based consultation systems, depends on improving our understanding of the needs, expectations and performance demands of clinicians. The previous studies had not specifically addressed these issues. Our study used a questionnaire, similar in format to the instrument developed by Startsman and Robinson (1972) but different in content. One modification was to limit the scope of our survey by focusing only on physicians' attitudes regarding clinical consultation systems. Previous studies had been more general in their focus and had surveyed a broader range of opinion. We chose this more limited focus because several research groups currently developing medical consultation systems are concentrating on physician users and have recognized the need for better information about the concerns and performance demands of clinicians. Another change was the inclusion of statements designed to ascertain the performance capabilities that physicians consider necessary for a consultation program to be clinically acceptable. Previous studies had not addressed this important aspect. We hoped that with these modifications the study would yield results from which guidelines could be formulated to help medical computing experts design more acceptable clinical consultation systems.

Relationship Between Physicians' Characteristics and Attitudes

A second objective of the study was to test the common assumption that prior experience with computers affects attitudes about the clinical use of computing technology. We therefore included measures of both computing experience and *knowledge* of computing concepts in the questionnaire. A number of other demographic variables were also included.

Impact of a Medical Computing Course on Attitudes

A third objective was to assess the impact of an intensive medical computing course on physicians' attitudes. The authors of both of the previous major studies (Startsman and Robinson, 1972; Melhorn et al., 1979), as well as others (Levy, 1977), had speculated that intensive educational efforts might result in increased acceptance of medical computing by physicians. Partly to test this assumption, we designed a medical computing tutorial and measured its impact on the attitudes of the physician attendees.[1] The tutorial faculty consisted of 15 physicians and computer scientists who are active researchers in the development of computer-based clinical consultation systems. Presentations encompassed the researcher's work, goals, and perspective on the role of computer-assisted decision making in clinical medicine. An introductory session was included to introduce physicians to general computing concepts and terminology.

34.1 Methods

34.1.1 Instrument

A survey instrument (questionnaire) was developed to measure physicians' attitudes regarding computer-based consultation systems. Attitudes were measured by the instrument along three dimensions: (1) the *acceptability* of different medical computing applications; (2) *expectations* about the effect of computer-based consultation systems on medicine; and (3) *demands* regarding the performance capabilities of consultation systems. Every effort was made to include items representative of the design issues that are currently being considered by medical computing experts. We performed extensive pilot testing of the questionnaire prior to its use in the study.

Acceptance was measured by asking physicians about eight real or imagined medical computing applications. The applications ranged from computer-based medical records to the use of computers as substitutes for physicians in underserved areas (Table 34-1). The Expectation- and Demand-scales included statements about medical computing, emphasizing the potential role of computer-based consultation systems. Each statement used a Likert-type scale in which respondents were instructed to mark one of five categories: (1) strongly disagree, (2) somewhat disagree, (3) not sure, (4) somewhat agree, (5) strongly agree.

The Expectation-scale (E-scale) included 17 statements and was designed to measure physicians' opinions about how computer-based consultations are likely to affect the practice of medicine (i.e., how computers *will* affect medical practice).[2] The Demand-scale (D-scale) of 15 statements

[1]The tutorial was offered by the Departments of Medicine and Computer Science at Stanford University in August of 1980. It was organized in conjunction with the Sixth Annual Workshop on Artificial Intelligence in Medicine, which was sponsored by the Division of Research Resources of the NIH.

[2]The statements are shown in Table 34-3. For identification purposes in this paper, each is identified by an E followed by a number. The letter E denotes that the statement belongs to the Expectation-scale.

sought physicians' opinions regarding the most desirable performance capabilities for computer-based consultation systems (i.e., what computers *should* be able to do).[3] The possible range of ratings for statements on both the E- and D-scales is -2 to $+2$. On the E-scale a positive rating means that respondents felt that the stated effect is not likely to occur, and a negative rating means that they felt that the effect is likely. On the D-scale a positive rating means that the item was judged to be an important capability for computer-based clinical systems, and a negative rating means that it is judged to be unimportant.

A set of background questions was also included on the questionnaire. These included items about medical specialty, type of practice (academic medicine or private practice), number of years since receiving the M.D. degree, percentage of time devoted to research, and extent of prior experience with computers. All questions in this group contained fixed response categories. A second set of 22 questions asked respondents to indicate their (self-reported) level of *knowledge* about computers and computer science concepts.

34.1.2 Participants

Two samples of physicians were included in the study. One included registrants for the tutorial mentioned above. The 85 physicians who filled out the questionnaire represented 90% of the physicians registered for the tutorial. Twenty-nine nonphysician attendees who were engaged in either basic medical research or medical computing also returned survey forms.

By announcing that the course was appropriate for physicians with little or no knowledge of medical computing, we hoped to attract a cross section of physicians. Although continuing medical education (CME) credit was also available, we were aware that the backgrounds and attitudes of these physicians might contrast with those who chose not to attend the tutorial. Therefore, a second sample of physicians was selected from Stanford Medical School clinical faculty and from Stanford-affiliated physicians practicing in the surrounding community.

34.1.3 Procedure

The questionnaire was included in the preregistration packet that was mailed to all tutorial registrants approximately one month before the course. A cover letter asked respondents to complete and return the questionnaire as soon as possible so that the results could be used to guide the

[3]The Demand-scale statements are shown in Table 34-5. Each statement is identified by a D followed by a number.

speakers' presentations. At the end of the tutorial, participants were asked to complete the same questionnaire for a second time. A respondent-selected code number facilitated matching of pretutorial and posttutorial results. To encourage open and unbiased responses, the respondents were assured of anonymity.

The second sample, stratified by medical specialty, was randomly selected from the roster of Stanford Medical School faculty and affiliated community physicians. These individuals, 57 faculty members and 92 affiliated physicians, received a questionnaire with a cover letter requesting their help with the research study and assuring them of anonymity. The letter also invited them to participate in the tutorial and instructed them to return the registration form instead of the questionnaire if they wished to do so. None chose to register.[4] A follow-up letter was sent to the entire 149-member sample three weeks after the original mailing to maximize questionnaire return. Sixty-one questionnaires of the original 149 were eventually returned (41%).

Nonparametric Chi-square analysis was used to compare the tutorial and nontutorial samples. Reliability of the attitude scales was determined on a subsample of ten subjects (Cronbach, 1970). Internal consistency of the scales was calculated by correlating odd and even items and correcting the resulting correlations using the Spearman-Brown formula (Cronbach, 1970). Means and standard deviations were computed for each of the individual statements included on the three attitude scales. The Expectation- and Demand-scales were subjected to factor analysis to identify meaningful subgroupings of statements. Principal factoring with iteration was employed (Nie et al., 1975). Simplification of the factor structure was obtained by oblique rotation with delta set equal to zero. Analysis of variance was used to compare the attitudes of physicians with different backgrounds and knowledge of medical computing. Analysis of variance was also used to compare pretutorial and posttutorial ratings.

34.2 Results

34.2.1 Characteristics of Physicians Studied

The final sample of 146 physicians included subsamples of 85 tutorial participants and 61 physicians who were associated with Stanford University Medical Center but who chose not to participate in the tutorial (control group). Of the combined sample, 43% were in medical fields (internal

[4]All recipients had also received an initial announcement for the course several weeks earlier, and none had registered in response to the initial mailing.

medicine, family practice, pediatrics, general practice), 27% were from surgical fields (general surgery, surgical subspecialties, obstetrics/gynecology, anesthesiology), and 30% were from other specialties (primarily radiology and pathology). There was no significant difference between the two subsamples (Chi-square = 5.16, $p > .05$).

Of the combined sample, 44% were academicians, 45% were in private practice, and 11% were Stanford house staff.[5] Differences between the subsamples (Chi-square = 6.28, $p < .01$) were due to the separation of the house staff group from the academic subgroup. A separate analysis of house staff responses to the questionnaire items revealed that they had response patterns almost identical to those of the academicians. Incorporation of the house staff into the academic category resulted in comparable frequencies for the attendees and controls (Chi-square = 4.93, $p > .05$).

Of the combined sample, 31% had fewer than 10 years of experience since graduating from medical school, 22% 10 to 20 years, and 47% more than 20 years. Differences between the attendees and controls were not significant (Chi-square = 3.24, $p > .20$). While 43% of subjects reported that they devoted no time to research, 27% devoted less than a third of their time, and only 30% devoted more than a third of their time to research. The difference between attendee and control groups was not significant (Chi-square = 5.73, $p > .05$). Finally, 46% reported no computing experience, 32% had had some experience (i.e., at least running "canned" computer programs), and 22% reported extensive experience including the design of computing systems. There was no significant difference between the tutorial attendees and the controls (Chi-square = 3.17, $p > .20$).

34.2.2 Acceptance Ratings

The options for the Acceptance question are shown in Table 34-1. Physicians had an average Acceptance rating of 5.5 applications out of the 8 included on the scale. The table shows that support for the 5 major applications exceeded 80% of respondents.

Medical speciality was the only characteristic that was significantly predictive of a respondent's Acceptance of computing applications. Table 34-2 shows that surgeons were less accepting of medical computing applications than either of the other two subgroups. There was no significant difference in the Acceptance rating between tutorial and nontutorial participants, private practice and academic physicians, those with several years in practice and those who had recently graduated, physicians engaged in research and those who were not, or physicians with and without computing experience.

---

[5]All house-staff subjects were tutorial attendees rather than members of the control group.

TABLE 34-1 Physicians' Acceptance of Medical Computing Applications

% Acceptance	Medical Records	HIS*	Patient Monitoring	Diagnostic Consults	Therapy Consults	Physical Exams	M.D. Substitute†	M.D. Licensure‡
		97%						
	83%	XXXX			83%			
	XXXX	XXXX	80%	81%	XXXX			
	XXXX	XXXX	XXXX	XXXX	XXXX			
	XXXX	XXXX	XXXX	XXXX	XXXX			
	XXXX	XXXX	XXXX	XXXX	XXXX			52%
	XXXX	XXXX	XXXX	XXXX	XXXX	36%		XXXX
	XXXX	XXXX	XXXX	XXXX	XXXX	XXXX	32%	XXXX
	XXXX	XXXX	XXXX	XXXX	XXXX	XXXX	XXXX	XXXX
	XXXX	XXXX	XXXX	XXXX	XXXX	XXXX	XXXX	XXXX
	XXXX	XXXX	XXXX	XXXX	XXXX	XXXX	XXXX	XXXX

*Hospital Information Systems
†Substituting for physicians in medically underserved areas
‡Testing physicians for relicensure

TABLE 34-2 Scheffe Comparison of Acceptance Ratings for Subgroups of Medical Specialists

Specialty	*Mean*	*Standard deviation*	*Significance*
1. Medical	6.03	1.55	1 vs. 2 → $p < .01$
2. Surgical	4.35	1.82	2 vs. 3 → $p < .01$
3. Other	5.67	1.84	
Total	5.45	1.84	

34.2.3 Expectation Ratings

Table 34-3 displays the ratings and standard deviations for each statement on the Expectation-scale. The statements are listed in order of their average ratings, from those outcomes that physicians thought were the most likely to occur to those that were expected to occur less frequently. The average Expectation rating for physicians was slightly positive ($X = .42$). This was comparable to that of the nonphysician sample, shown in the right-hand column. Only 3 of the 17 statements received negative ratings (i.e., were judged likely to occur), including fears about the possibility that consultation systems will increase government control of medicine, concerns that systems will increase the cost of care, and expectations that patients will blame the computer program for ineffective treatment decisions. On the other hand, physicians felt strongly that consultation systems would neither interfere with their efficiency nor force them to adapt their thinking to the reasoning process used by the computer program. They also felt that the use of consultation systems would *not* reduce the need for either specialists or paramedical personnel.

Subgroups of physicians displayed significant differences in their Expectations about how computer-assisted consultations will affect medical practice. The means and standard deviations for all the significant findings are summarized in Table 34-4. A significance level of .01 was used for each analysis in order to maintain an overall significance level of less than .06. The Expectations of tutorial registrants were on the average more positive than those of the nontutorial group, although neither group thought that consultation programs would adversely affect medical practice. Physicians in academic settings and those in training indicated overall positive Expectations, whereas private practice physicians tended to hold slightly negative Expectations. Young doctors expressed more positive Expectations than did physicians with 10 to 20 years of experience, although the recent graduates were no more positive than physicians with at least 20 years experience. Experience with computers was positively related to Expectations, as was Knowledge about computing concepts.

TABLE 34-3 Means and Standard Deviations (in Parentheses) for Ratings of Expectation Statements

	Physicians *n = 146*	*Nonphysicians* *n = 29*
E1. *Will* increase government control of physicians' practices	−.26 (1.23)	.15 (.95)
E2. *Will* be blamed by patients for errors in management	−.23 (1.15)	−.30 (1.10)
E3. *Will* increase the cost of care	−.14 (1.07)	.44 (1.09)
E4. *Will* threaten personal and professional privacy	.02 (1.41)	.50 (1.45)
E5. *Will* result in serious legal and ethical problems (e.g., malpractice)	.32 (1.06)	−.04 (.98)
E6. *Will* threaten the physician's self-image	.32 (1.23)	.15 (1.01)
E7. *Will* be hard for physicians to learn	.34 (1.17)	.85 (.95)
E8. *Will* result in reliance on cookbook medicine and diminish judgment	.43 (1.34)	.92 (1.14)
E9. *Will* diminish the patient's image of the physician	.45 (1.16)	.74 (1.10)
E10. *Will* be unreliable because of computer "malfunctions"	.51 (1.09)	1.07 (.83)
E11. *Will* dehumanize medical practice	.53 (1.34)	1.04 (1.09)
E12. *Will* depend on knowledge that cannot easily be kept up to date	.53 (1.20)	1.00 (1.00)
E13. *Will* alienate physicians because of electronic gadgetry	.62 (1.03)	.41 (1.08)
E14. *Will* force physician to think like computer	.73 (1.15)	1.19 (1.00)
E15. *Will* reduce the need for paraprofessionals	.83 (.91)	.82 (1.08)
E16. *Will* reduce the need for specialists	.99 (1.07)	1.11 (1.09)
E17. *Will* result in less efficient use of physician's time	1.05 (.84)	1.56 (.58)
Total scale =	.42	.68

TABLE 34-4 Scheffe Comparisons of Expectations for Physicians with Different Characteristics

Characteristic	*Groups*	*Mean*	*Standard deviation*	*Significance*
Totals		.41	.59	
Professional orientation	1. Academic	.55	.58	1 vs. 2 → $p < .01$
	2. Private	.22	.59	3 vs. 2 → $p < .01$
	3. Training	.64	.48	
Clinical experience	1. < 10 yrs.	.59	.52	
	2. 10 to 20 yrs.	.18	.54	1 vs. 2 → $p < .01$
	3. > 20 yrs.	.39	.63	
Computing experience	1. Little or none	.24	.62	1 vs. 3 → $p < .01$
	2. Moderate	.50	.58	
	3. Extensive	.63	.47	

34.2.4 Demand Ratings

Table 34-5 depicts statements on the Demand-scale, ordered from most to least important according to the average rating each received. Physicians' Demands were significantly less than those of the nonphysicians, although the ranked ordering of each Demand statement was almost the same for the two groups. A system's ability to explain its advice was thought to be its most important attribute. Second in importance was a system's ability to understand and update its own knowledge base. Improving the cost effectiveness of tests and therapies was also important. Physicians did not think that a system has to display either perfect diagnostic accuracy or perfect treatment planning to be acceptable. On the other hand, they would not accept the use of a consultation system as a standard for acceptable medical practice, nor would they recommend reducing the amount of technical knowledge that physicians have to know just because a consultation system is available. The differences found among physician subgroups on the Expectation-scale were not evident on the Demand-scale.

A test-retest reliability coefficient of $r = .94$ was obtained across two administrations of the three scales: Acceptance, Expectations, and Demands. The split-half reliability for the D-scale was only $r = .70$, and that of the E-scale was $r = .83$. These rather modest split-half reliabilities suggested to us that the scales were measuring more than one aspect of physicians' attitudes. In order to better understand the structure of physicians' attitudes measured, these scales were subjected to factor analysis. Five major groups of statements (factors) were extracted from the combined scales and are described below. Correlations among them were low, ranging from .01 to .19, except for Factors 1 and 5, which correlated at .31. The factors accounted for 45% of the total variance of the combined scales.

TABLE 34-5 Means Ratings and Standard Deviations (in Parentheses) for Demand Statements

	Physicians *n = 146*	*Nonphysicians* *n = 129*
D1. *Should* be able to explain their diagnostic and treatment decisions to physician users	1.42 (.80)	1.78 (.42)
D2. *Should* be portable and flexible so that physician can access them at any time and place	1.14 (.81)	1.52 (.51)
D3. *Should* display an understanding of their own medical knowledge	.99 (.94)	1.48 (.80)
D4. *Should* improve the cost efficiency of tests and therapies	.85 (.99)	1.11 (1.58)
D5. *Should* automatically learn new information when interacting with medical experts	.84 (1.02)	1.41 (.75)
D6. *Should* display common sense	.75 (1.20)	1.11 (.97)
D7. *Should* simulate physicians' thought processes	.64 (1.16)	.93 (1.07)
D8. *Should* not reduce the need for specialists	.46 (1.18)	.70 (1.07)
D9. *Should* demand little effort from physician to learn or use	.35 (1.20)	1.19 (.92)
D10. *Should* respond to voice command and not require typing	.26 (1.23)	.56 (1.05)
D11. *Should* not reduce the need for paraprofessionals	.26 (1.06)	.85 (1.03)
D12. *Should* significantly reduce amount of technical knowledge physician must learn and remember	−.08 (1.34)	.00 (1.49)
D13. *Should* never make an error in treatment planning	−.25 (1.33)	−.22 (1.34)
D14. *Should* never make an incorrect diagnosis	−.45 (1.31)	−.26 (1.46)
D15. *Should* become the standard for acceptable medical practice	−.80 (1.13)	.00 (1.07)
Total scale =	.44	.81

TABLE 34-6 Intercorrelation of Physicians' Computing Knowledge, Acceptance, Expectations, and Demands

	Demands	Expectations	Knowledge
Acceptance	.27*	.26*	.27*
Knowledge	.08	.26*	
Expectations	.05		

*$p < .001$

Factor 1 includes statements E7, E8, E11, E13, and E17 (Table 34-3). It relates to Expectations about how physicians might be personally affected by a consultation system. All of these statements received positive ratings (i.e., the outcomes were judged to be unlikely) ranging from .34 to 1.05. Factor loadings for the statements ranged from .43 to .59.[6]

Factor 2 includes statements D1, D2, D3, D5, and D6 from the D-scale (Table 34-5). The factor is composed of the performance Demands thought by physicians to be the most important. Ratings of the statements ranged from .75 to 1.42. Factor loadings for the statements ranged from .41 to .65.

Factor 3 relates to Demands about system accuracy. It includes statements D13 and D14, which were rated relatively unimportant by the respondents. Factor loadings were .84 and .89, respectively.

Factor 4 includes statements from both scales and relates to physicians' attitudes regarding the effect of computing systems on the need for health care personnel. It includes statements E15, E16, D8, and D11. The factor reflects the opinion that consultation systems will not and should not affect the need for either specialists or paraprofessionals.

Factor 5 includes statements E1, E4, E5, E6, E8, E9, and E11 from the E-scale. It is similar to Factor 1 because statements E8 and E11 relate to both factors; however, its focus appears to be slightly different. Whereas Factor 1 related to the individual practitioner, Factor 5 is concerned with the effect of consultation programs on medical practice in general. Factor loadings ranged from −.70 to −.41.

Nearly the same pattern of differences among physicians was found for the factors as was found for the full-scale ratings. Individual differences in Expectations on Factors 1 and 5 were related to differences in knowledge about computer concepts, experience with computers, time in medical practice, professional orientation, and tutorial participation. Individual differences were not found on ratings of the other three factors.

Table 34-6 shows the relationship between the scale ratings and Knowledge about computers and medical computing concepts. Acceptance was

[6]Factor loadings can range from −1.0 to +1.0 and indicate the degree of relationship between each statement and the factor.

moderately related to Knowledge, Expectations, and Demands. Knowledge was also related to Expectations but not to Demands, and Expectations were unrelated to Demands. These results are consistent with the differences reported above for the analyses of variance.

34.2.5 Tutorial Findings

Of the tutorial participants, 50% completed the posttutorial questionnaire. The posttutorial sample did not differ from the pretutorial group on any of the sample characteristics including medical specialty, professional orientation, years of medical experience, time devoted to research, or computing experience.

The tutorial affected physicians in two ways. First, it significantly increased their self-reported knowledge about computing concepts from a mean of 15.0 concepts to a mean of 25.5 concepts ($p < .001$). Second, it raised the level of their performance Demands from a mean of .44 to a mean of .72 ($p < .01$), although the relative importance of the individual statements did not change. Physicians' Expectations did not change overall; although Factor 1 did show a slight change in the positive direction (i.e., the outcomes were judged less likely than they had been before the course), the difference was not enough to be statistically significant. The mean posttutorial Acceptance rating of 6.0 was not significantly different from the tutorial registrants' pretutorial rating of 5.8. Also, participation in the tutorial did not alter the relatively low pretutorial Acceptance ratings of the surgical specialists.

34.3 Discussion

The study we have described had three principal goals: (1) to measure physicians' attitudes regarding consultation systems, (2) to compare the attitudes of subgroups of physicians, including those who chose to attend a medical computing tutorial and those who did not, and (3) to assess the impact of the continuing education course on the attitudes and knowledge of the physicians who enrolled. In this section, we discuss some of the results relevant to each of these goals.

34.3.1 Attitudes of Physicians

There was no significant difference in demographics or computing knowledge between the tutorial attendees and the control group. The overall analysis of physicians' attitudes was therefore based on responses from all physicians surveyed. The respondents were selective in their Acceptance of computing applications. Applications that were presented as aids to clinical practice were more readily accepted than those that involved the automation of clinical activities traditionally performed by physicians themselves. The distinction between a clinical *aid* and a *replacement* seems to be important to physicians and suggests design criteria and preferred modes for the introduction of computing innovations. This perspective is consistent with historical attitudes regarding the adoption of other kinds of technological innovation. For example, computerized axial tomography has been widely accepted largely because it functions as a remarkably useful clinical *tool*, providing physicians with faster and more reliable information, but it in no way infringes on the physician's patient-management role. In contrast, automated history-taking systems have not received widespread acceptance, despite their accuracy and reliability. We suspect that one reason physicians have resisted their use is because they are perceived as a threat to a traditional clinical function.

Some observers have speculated that many physicians oppose computer-based decision aids because they fear a loss of job security and prestige. The study results do not support this viewpoint. The physicians surveyed believe that consultation systems will not reduce the need for either specialists or paraprofessionals. Furthermore, they do not feel that either a physician's self-image or the respect he or she receives from patients will be reduced by the use of this kind of system. They are worried that consultation systems may increase the cost of care, although they believe that the programs should be designed to decrease costs. This Expectation may reflect past experience with new technologies that have generally increased cost, at least initially, but have eventually been accepted because of perceived improvement in patient care. In light of the generally positive Expectations of physicians, as demonstrated in this study, it is unlikely that the acceptance of a medical consultation system will depend solely on its ability to reduce the cost of care; the crucial factor, rather, is likely to be the system's ability to improve the quality of patient care or to simplify its delivery.

The results from the Demand-scale indicate, however, that for a system to improve patient care in an acceptable fashion, it must be perceived as a tool that will *assist* physicians with management decisions. It is clear that physicians will reject a system that dogmatically offers advice, even if it has impressive diagnostic accuracy and an ability to provide reliable treatment plans. Physicians seem to prefer the concept of a system that functions as much like a human consultant as possible.

34.3.2 Comparisons Among Subgroups

Physicians' Expectations about the effect of computer-assisted consultation systems on medical practice were generally positive, although considerable differences among physicians were noted. The finding that physicians with prior computing experience have more positive Expectations regarding the effects of consultation systems supports the belief of other investigators, although even the groups with little or no experience generally had positive attitudes. The slightly more positive Expectations of academic physicians may be a source of encouragement to medical computing researchers because this kind of system development typically depends on support from the academic community. However, the more negative Expectations of private practice physicians and of those who chose not to attend the tutorial are worrisome. These groups represent the majority of practitioners in the country and are, in particular, the physicians for whom many of the research systems are designed.[7] Furthermore, although many of their concerns, such as worries about increased government control of medical practice, defy direct attention by the medical computing researcher, an increased awareness of them may lead to more sensitive design decisions and more tactful introduction of new systems.

34.3.3 Effect of the Tutorial

The tutorial experience had a small but significant effect on physicians' Demands and also produced a substantial increase in their knowledge about computing concepts. The results from the Demand-scale were of particular interest. Physicians apparently gained new insights from the tutorial into the potential use and capabilities of medical computing and increased their performance Demands accordingly. These opinions regarding the attributes of acceptable computing systems were surprisingly uniform across physician subgroups both before and after the tutorial. Our interpretation of this result is that physicians are serious about these Demands and that consultation systems are not likely to be clinically effective, regardless of the accuracy of their advice, until these capabilities have been incorporated.

On the other hand, the tutorial had no significant effect on physicians' Acceptance of computer applications or on their Expectations regarding the effect of consultation systems on medical practice. The failure of the tutorial to change the Acceptance rating is not surprising because the pretutorial ratings were already very high. It is possible that an expanded set of applications on the Acceptance scale, particularly applications that involve the automation of traditional physician functions, would have produced a different result. Similarly, the Expectations of the tutorial registrants were markedly positive prior to the tutorial and were not significantly changed as a result of the course. Before the survey we were concerned that the Expectations of the course participants might decline

[7]Although our study included physicians with different backgrounds and interests (e.g., medical specialty, time devoted to research), we cannot generalize with certainty from our results to the national community of physicians. Our self-selected tutorial participants were almost all academic or academically affiliated, and our nontutorial (control) sample was selected from a similar population.

on the posttutorial questionnaire; it was possible that the physicians in the audience would begin to worry about the effects of certain applications after being exposed to the problems and uncertainties experienced by the medical computing researchers. Instead, the attendees apparently understood both the potential and the problems associated with designing consultation programs and took a more positive approach by increasing their Demands for more humanlike performance from the systems.

Although physicians with positive Expectations could be distinguished from those with negative ones on the basis of their knowledge about computing concepts prior to the tutorial, increasing their knowledge about these concepts did not change their Expectations. Since physicians with negative Expectations were also the least likely to participate voluntarily in our CME program, the effectiveness of CME in increasing the acceptance of clinical computing among the most resistant physicians is questionable. However, the study results indicate that computing applications have already obtained a strong core of support among some physicians. This support may even be deeper than we had expected because, for the physicians we surveyed, it extended to the belief that medical computing should be considered an area of basic medical research, comparable to biochemistry and immunology. In response to a question on this subject included at the end of the questionnaire, 75% of the pretutorial and control group physicians agreed that medical computing should be considered an area of basic medical research, and another 14% were undecided. We believe that this uniformly positive response may have been influenced by the administration of the questionnaire, and physicians asked the same question without the context provided by the survey instrument might respond less favorably. On the other hand, even physicians with minimal computing experience seem likely to accept the fundamental research component of medical computer science if it is pointed out to them. This suggests a strong educational message that must be conveyed to the medical community regarding the research role of the discipline.

34.4 Recommendations

The results of this survey counter the common impression that physicians tend to be resistant to the introduction of clinical consultation systems. Although we have polled physicians only from the immediate vicinity of our medical center, there is no reason to assume that a nationwide survey would achieve markedly different results. We have found that a significant segment of the medical community believes that assistance from computer-based consultation systems will ultimately benefit medical practice. However, a major concern at present is whether system developers can respond adequately to physician demands for performance capabilities that extend beyond currently available computer science techniques. In light of these results, the following recommendations may be helpful.

1. Strive to *minimize changes to current clinical practices.* The system should ideally replace some current clinical function, thereby avoiding the need for an *additive* time commitment by the physician. The system should ideally be available when and where physicians customarily make decisions.
2. Concentrate some of the research effort on *enhancing the interactive capabilities* of the expert system. The more natural these capabilities, the more likely it is that the system will be used. At least four features appear to be highly desirable:
   a. *Explanation.* The system should be able to justify its advice in terms that are understandable and persuasive. In addition, it is preferable that a system adapt its explanation to the needs and characteristics of the user (e.g., demonstrated or assumed level of background knowledge in the domain). A system that gives dogmatic advice is likely to be rejected.
   b. *Common sense.* The system should "seem reasonable" as it progresses through a problem-solving session. Some researchers argue that the program's operation should therefore parallel the physician's reasoning processes as much as possible. There is a growing body of knowledge about the psychological underpinnings of medical problem solving (Elstein et al., 1978), and systems that draw on these insights are likely to find an improved level of acceptance by the medical community.
   c. *Knowledge representation.* The knowledge in the system should be easy to bring up to date, and this often seriously constrains the format for storing information in the computer. A challenging side issue is the automatic "learning" of new knowledge of the domain, either through interaction with expert physicians or through "experience" once the system is in regular use.
   d. *Usability.* The system should be easy to learn and largely self-documenting. The mode of interaction may be the key to acceptability, and effective methods for understanding text or spoken language should dramatically increase the utility of clinical systems. For routine activities, it is preferable that use of the system be as easy as pressing a button.
3. Recognize that *100% accuracy is neither achievable nor expected.* Physicians will accept a system that functions at the same level as a human expert, as long as the interactive capabilities noted above are a component of the consultative process.
4. Consider carefully the *most appropriate criteria for assessing a clinical consultation system.* Not all medical computer programs should be judged

on the same basis, and cost-effectiveness may appropriately be a secondary concern when a system can be shown to significantly improve the quality of patient care or the efficiency of its delivery.

5. When designing systems, *consider the concerns and demands that physicians express* about consultation systems. These should be used to guide both the development and the implementation of the systems of the future. It is increasingly recognized that it takes only one shortcoming to render an otherwise well-designed system unacceptable.

The considerations outlined here place severe demands on current computing capabilities. Many of the issues that we have cited, and that were included on the Demand-scale in the survey, are capabilities that are beyond the current state of the art in computer science. They thus help delineate some of the important basic research issues for future work in medical computing.

35

An Expert System for Oncology Protocol Management

Edward H. Shortliffe, A. Carlisle Scott, Miriam B. Bischoff, A. Bruce Campbell, William van Melle, and Charlotte D. Jacobs

This chapter describes an oncology protocol management system, named ONCOCIN after its domain of expertise (cancer therapy) and its historical debt to MYCIN. The program is actually a set of interrelated subsystems, the primary ones being:[1]

1. the *Reasoner*, a rule-based expert consultant that is the core of the system; and
2. the *Interviewer*, an interface program that controls a high-speed terminal and the interaction with the physicians using the system.

The Interviewer is described in some detail in Chapter 32. This chapter describes the problem domain and the representation and control techniques used by the Reasoner. We also contrast ONCOCIN with EMYCIN

This chapter is based on an article originally appearing in *Proceedings of the Seventh IJCAI*, 1981, pp. 876–881. Used by permission of International Joint Conferences on Artificial Intelligence, Inc.; copies of the *Proceedings* are available from William Kaufmann, Inc., 95 First Street, Los Altos, CA 94022.

[1]Each program runs in a separate fork under the TENEX or TOPS-20 operating systems, thereby approximating a parallel processing system architecture. Another program, the *Interactor*, handles interprocess communication. There is also a process that provides background utility operations such as file backup. This chapter does not describe these aspects of the system design or their implementation. Details are available elsewhere (Gerring et al., 1982).

(Chapter 15), explaining why the EMYCIN formalism was inadequate for our purposes, even though it did strongly influence the system's rule-based design.

35.1 Overview of the Problem Domain

ONCOCIN is designed to assist clinical oncologists in the treatment of cancer patients. Because the optimal therapy for most cancers is not yet known, clinical oncology research is commonly based on complex formal experiments that compare the therapeutic benefits and side effects (toxicity) of proposed alternative disease treatments. "Cancer" is a general term for many diseases having different prognoses and natural histories. A treatment that is effective against one tumor may be ineffective against another. Thus a typical cancer research center may conduct many simultaneous experiments, each concerned with a different kind of cancer and its optimal therapy (i.e., the treatment plan with the best chance of cure, remission, or reduction in tumor size and the least chance of serious side effects).

Each of these experiments is termed a *protocol.* Patients with a given tumor must meet certain eligibility criteria before they are accepted for treatment on the protocol; ineligible patients are treated in accordance with the best state-of-the-art therapy and are therefore not part of a formal clinical experiment.[2] Patients accepted for protocol treatment, on the other hand, are randomly assigned to receive one of two or more possible treatments. The experiment requires close monitoring of each patient's clinical response and treatment toxicity. These data are tallied for all patients treated under the alternate regimens, and in this way the state of the art is updated over time.

Each protocol is described in a detailed document, often 40 to 60 pages in length, which specifies the alternate therapies being compared and the data that need to be collected. Therapies may require as many as eight to ten drugs, given simultaneously or in sequence, continuously or intermittently. In addition, pharmacologic therapy may be combined with appropriate surgery or radiation therapy. No single physician is likely to remember the details in even one of these protocol documents, not to mention the 30 to 60 protocols that may be used in a major cancer center (any one of which may be used to guide treatment of the patients under the care of a single physician). Although an effort is made to have the documents available in the oncology clinics when patients are being treated for their

[2]Unfortunately, for many tumors the best state-of-the-art therapy may cause intolerable toxicity or be only partially effective. That is why there is a constant search for improved therapeutic plans.

tumors, it is often the case that a busy clinic schedule, coupled with a complex protocol description, leads a physician to rely on memory when deciding on drug doses and laboratory tests. Furthermore, solutions for all possible treatment problems cannot be spelled out in protocols. Physicians use their own judgment in treating these patients, resulting in some variability in treatment from patient to patient. Thus patients being treated on a protocol do not always receive therapy in exactly the manner that the experimental design suggests, and the data needed for formal analysis of treatment results are not always completely and accurately collected. In some cases, patients suffer undue toxicity or are undertreated simply because protocol details cannot be remembered, located, or are not explicitly defined.

The problems we have described reach far beyond the oncology clinic at Stanford Medical Center. There are now several institutions designing protocol management systems to make the details of treatment protocols readily available to oncologists and to insure that complete and accurate data are collected.[3] ONCOCIN is superficially similar to some of the developing systems, but both its short- and long-term goals are unique in ways we describe below. One overriding point requires emphasis: in order to achieve its goals, ONCOCIN must be used directly by busy clinicians; the implications of this constraint have pervaded all aspects of the system design.

35.2 Research Objectives

The overall goals of the ONCOCIN project are

1. to demonstrate that a rule-based consultation system with explanation capabilities can be usefully applied and can gain acceptance in a busy clinical environment;
2. to improve the tools currently available, and to develop new tools, for building knowledge-based expert systems for medical consultation; and
3. to establish both an effective relationship with a specific group of physicians and a scientific foundation, which will together facilitate future research and implementation of computer-based tools for clinical decision making.

[3] A memo from the M.I.T. Laboratory for Computer Science (Szolovits, 1979) describes a collaboration between M.I.T. and oncologists who have been building a protocol management system at Boston University (Horwitz et al., 1980). They are planning to develop a program for designing *new* chemotherapy protocols. To our knowledge, this is the only other project that proposes to use AI techniques in a clinical oncology system. However, the stated goals of that effort differ from those of ONCOCIN.

Hence ONCOCIN's research aims have two parallel thrusts: to perform research into the basic scientific issues of applied artificial intelligence, and to develop a clinically useful oncology consultation tool. The AI component of the work emphasizes the following:

1. the implementation and evaluation of recently developed techniques designed to make computer technology more natural and acceptable to physicians;
2. extension of the methods of rule-based consultation systems so that they can interact with a large data base of time-oriented clinical information;
3. the design of a generalized control structure, separate from the domain knowledge, with the hope that the general system can be usefully applied in other problem areas with similar tasks;
4. continuation of basic research into mechanisms for making decisions based on data trends over time;
5. the design of a rapid, congenial interface that can bring a high-performance AI system to a group of users who are not experienced with AI or with computers in general; and
6. the development of techniques for assessing knowledge base completeness and consistency (see Chapter 8).

35.3 System Overview

The ONCOCIN system will eventually contain knowledge about most of the protocols in use at the Oncology Clinic at Stanford Medical Center. Although protocol knowledge is largely specified in a written document, many questions arise in translating the information into a computer-based format. Knowledge base development has therefore been dependent on the active collaboration of Stanford oncologists. We have started by encoding the knowledge contained in the protocols for treatment of Hodgkin's disease and the non-Hodgkin's lymphomas.[4] In generating its recommendation, the system uses initial data about the patient's diagnosis, results of current laboratory tests, plus the protocol-specific information in its knowledge base. As information is acquired, it is stored on-line in files associated with the patient.

After examining a patient, the physician uses a video display terminal to interact with ONCOCIN's data-acquisition program (the Interviewer;

[4]We also implemented the complex protocol for treating oat cell carcinoma of the lung. Because the oat cell protocol is the most complex at Stanford, and it took only a month to encode the relevant rules, we are hopeful that the representation scheme we have devised will be able to manage, with only minor modifications, the other protocols we plan to encode in the future.

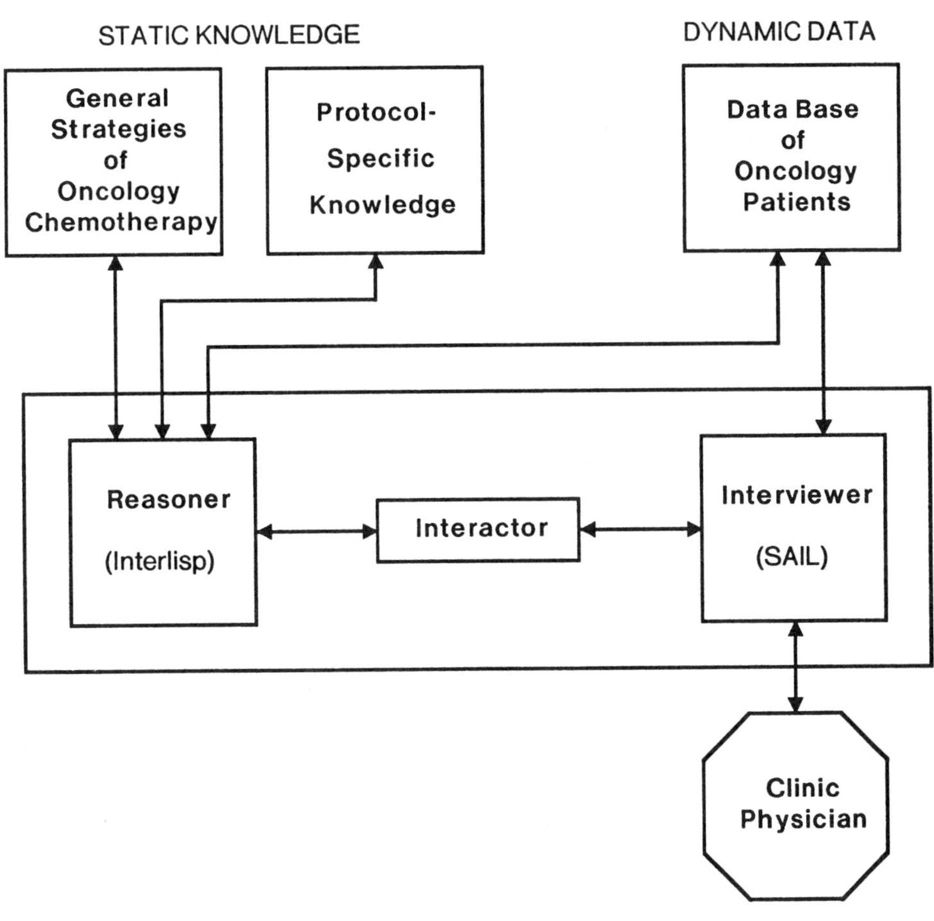

FIGURE 35-1 Overview of ONCOCIN.

see Chapter 32), reviewing time-oriented data from the patient's previous visits to the clinic, entering information regarding the current visit, and receiving recommendations, generated by the Reasoner, of appropriate therapy and tests. The Reasoner and Interviewer are linked with one another as shown in Figure 35-1. Each is able to use a data base of prior patient data. In addition, the Reasoner has access to information regarding the execution of chemotherapy protocols (control blocks) and specific information (rules) about the chemotherapy being used to treat the patient. Before terminating an interaction, the physician can examine the explanation provided with each recommendation.[5] The physician may approve

[5]We have chosen a representation that had also facilitated early work to allow ONCOCIN to offer a justification for any intermediary conclusions that the system made in deriving the advice (Langlotz and Shortliffe, 1983).

or modify ONCOCIN's recommendation; any changes are noted by the system and kept available for future review. ONCOCIN also provides hard-copy backup to complement the on-line interaction and facilitate communication among clinic personnel.

35.4 The Reasoner

35.4.1 Why Not EMYCIN?

ONCOCIN's Reasoner communicates with the Interviewer during a consultation. Although EMYCIN's interactive routines provided a means for us to develop a prototype system quickly, the need to interact eventually with a specialized interface program is one of several reasons that we chose to build most of ONCOCIN from scratch rather than to implement it as a new EMYCIN system (Chapter 15). Other important differences between ONCOCIN's application and the domains for which EMYCIN systems have been built include the following:

1. ONCOCIN requires serial consideration of patients at intervals typically spread over many months. Each clinic visit is a new data point, and conventional EMYCIN context trees and case data tables do not easily accommodate multiple measurements of the same attribute over time.
2. Expert-level advice from ONCOCIN also requires inference rules based on assessment of temporal trends for a given parameter.[6] Because EMYCIN assumes that a consultation is to be given at a single point in time, it does not provide a mechanism for assessing trends or interacting with a data bank of past information on a case.
3. ONCOCIN does not require many of the capabilities provided by EMYCIN. For example, the simplified interaction mediated through the Interviewer allows questions to be answered directly without dealing with the complexities of natural language understanding.
4. Because of the nature of the interaction with the Interviewer, ONCOCIN needs to operate in a data-driven mode. Although EMYCIN has a limited allowance for forward chaining of rules, it would be inconvenient to force a largely data-driven reasoning process into the EMYCIN format.

[6]This same point led to the development of Fagan's VM system (Chapter 22), a rule-based program that was influenced by EMYCIN but differed in its detailed implementation because of the need to follow trends in patients under treatment in an intensive care unit. The development of similar capabilities for ONCOCIN is an active area of research at present.

35.4.2 Representation

Knowledge about the oncology domain is represented using five main data structures: contexts, parameters, data blocks, rules, and control blocks.[7] In addition, we use a high-level description of each of these structures to serve as a template for guiding knowledge acquisition during the definition of individual instances.[8]

Contexts represent concepts or entities of the domain about which the system needs static knowledge. Individual contexts are classified by type (e.g., disease, protocol, or chemotherapy) and can be arranged hierarchically. During a consultation, a list of "current" contexts is created as information is gathered. These current contexts together provide a high-level description of the patient in terms of known chemotherapeutic plans. This description serves to focus the system's recommendation process.

Parameters represent the attributes of patients, drugs, tests, etc., that are relevant for the protocol management task (e.g., white blood count, recommended dose, or whether a patient has had prior radiotherapy). Each piece of information accumulated during a consultation is represented as the value of a parameter. There are three steps in determining the value of a parameter. First, the system checks to see if the value can be determined by *definition* in the current context. If not, the *"normal" method* of finding the value is used: if the parameter corresponds to a piece of laboratory data that the user is likely to know, it is requested from the user; otherwise, rules for concluding the parameter are tried. Finally, the system may have a (possibly context-dependent) *default value* that is used in the event that the normal mechanism fails to produce a value, or the user may be asked to provide the answer as a last resort.[9]

Data blocks define logical groupings of related parameters (e.g., initial patient data or laboratory test results). A data block directs the system to treat related parameters as a unit when requesting their values from the Interviewer, storing the values on a patient's file, or retrieving previously stored values.

Rules are the familiar productions used in MYCIN and other rule-based systems; they may be invoked in either data-driven or goal-directed mode. A rule concludes a value for some parameter on the basis of values of other parameters. A rule may be designated as providing a definitional

[7]There are a few additional data structures designed to coordinate the interaction between the Reasoner and the Interviewer.

[8]The knowledge base editor is based on the similar programs designed and implemented for EMYCIN. A graphics editor has also been developed for use on the LISP machine workstations to which we intend to transfer ONCOCIN (Tsuji and Shortliffe, 1983).

[9]This "pure" description of ONCOCIN's technique for assigning values to parameters is actually further complicated by the free-form data entry allowed in the Interviewer. The details of how this is handled, and the corresponding relationship to control blocks, will not be described here.

value or a default value as defined above. The rules are categorized by the context in which they apply.

As in EMYCIN systems, rules are represented in a stylized format so that they may be translated from Interlisp into English for explanation purposes.[10] This representation scheme more generally allows the system to "read" and manipulate the rules. It has also facilitated the development of programs to check for consistency and completeness of the rules in the knowledge base (Chapter 8).

Below are the English translations of two ONCOCIN rules. Note that Rule 78 provides a default value for the parameter "attenuated dose."[11]

RULE075

To determine the current attenuated dose for all drugs in MOPP or for all drugs in PAVe:

IF: 1) This is the start of the first cycle after cycle was aborted, and
2) The blood counts do not warrant dose attenuation
THEN: Conclude that the current attenuated dose is 75 percent of the previous dose.

RULE078

After trying all other methods to determine the current attenuated dose for all drugs:

IF: The blood counts do warrant dose attenuation
THEN: Conclude that the current attenuated dose is the previous dose attenuated by the minimum of the dose attenuation due to low WBC and the dose attenuation due to low platelets.

Control blocks serve as high-level descriptions of the system's methods for performing tasks. Each contains an ordered set of steps to be used for accomplishing a specific task (e.g., formulating a therapeutic regimen or calculating the correct dose of a drug). Note that this data structure allows us to separate control descriptions explicitly from decision rules, a distinction that was often unclear in EMYCIN systems. Because we wish to be able to explain any action that ONCOCIN takes, control blocks can be translated into English using the same translation mechanism that is used to translate rules, for example:

ADVISE

To make a recommendation about treating the patient:
1) Formulate a therapeutic regimen.
2) Determine the tests to recommend.
3) Determine suggestions about the patient.
4) Determine the time till the patient's next visit.

DOSE

To calculate the correct dosage of the drug:
1) Determine the current attenuated dose.
2) Determine the units in which the drug should be measured.
3) Determine the maximum allowable dose of the drug.
4) Determine the route of administration.
5) Determine the number of days for which the drug should be given.
6) Compute the dose based upon body surface area.

---

[10]In keeping with the philosophy reflected in other systems we have designed, ONCOCIN is able to produce natural language explanations for its recommendations. See also the critiquing work of Langlotz and Shortliffe (1983).

[11]PAVe and MOPP are acronyms for two of the drug combinations used to treat Hodgkins' disease.

To summarize the differences between ONCOCIN's rules and those used in MYCIN and other EMYCIN systems:

1. Control is separated from domain knowledge, although process information is still codified in a modular format using control blocks.
2. The contextual information, which defines the setting in which a rule can be applied, is separated from the main body of the rule and used for screening rules when they are invoked (see next section).
3. Rules are subclassified to distinguish the major mechanisms by which the values of parameters can be determined (definitional, normal, and default rules).

35.4.3 Control

When a user specifies the task that ONCOCIN is to perform, the corresponding control block is invoked. This simply causes the steps in the control block to be taken in sequence. These steps may entail the following:

1. *Fetching a data block,* either by loading previously stored data or by requesting them from the user. This causes parameter values to be set, resulting in data-directed invocation of rules that use those parameters (and that apply in the current context).
2. *Determining the value of a parameter.* This causes goal-directed invocation of the rules that conclude the value of the parameter (and apply in the current context). Definitional rules are applied first, then the normal rules, and if no value has been found by these means, the default rules are tried. If a rule that is invoked in a goal-directed fashion uses some parameter whose value is not yet known, that parameter's value is determined so that the rule can be evaluated. In addition, concluding the value of any parameter, either by the action of rules or when information is entered by the user, may cause data-directed invocation of other rules.
3. *Invoking another control block.*
4. *Calling a special-purpose function* (which may be domain-dependent).

The effects of this control mechanism contrast with the largely backward-chained control used in MYCIN and other EMYCIN systems. Figure 35-2 shows the goal-oriented procedure used in EMYCIN. All invocation of rules results because the value of a specific parameter is being sought. Rules used to determine the value of that parameter can be referenced in any order, although ordering is maintained for the assessment of the parameters occurring in the conditional statements in each rule's premise. Antecedent (data-driven) rules are used when the user's response to a question, or (less commonly) the conclusion from another rule, triggers

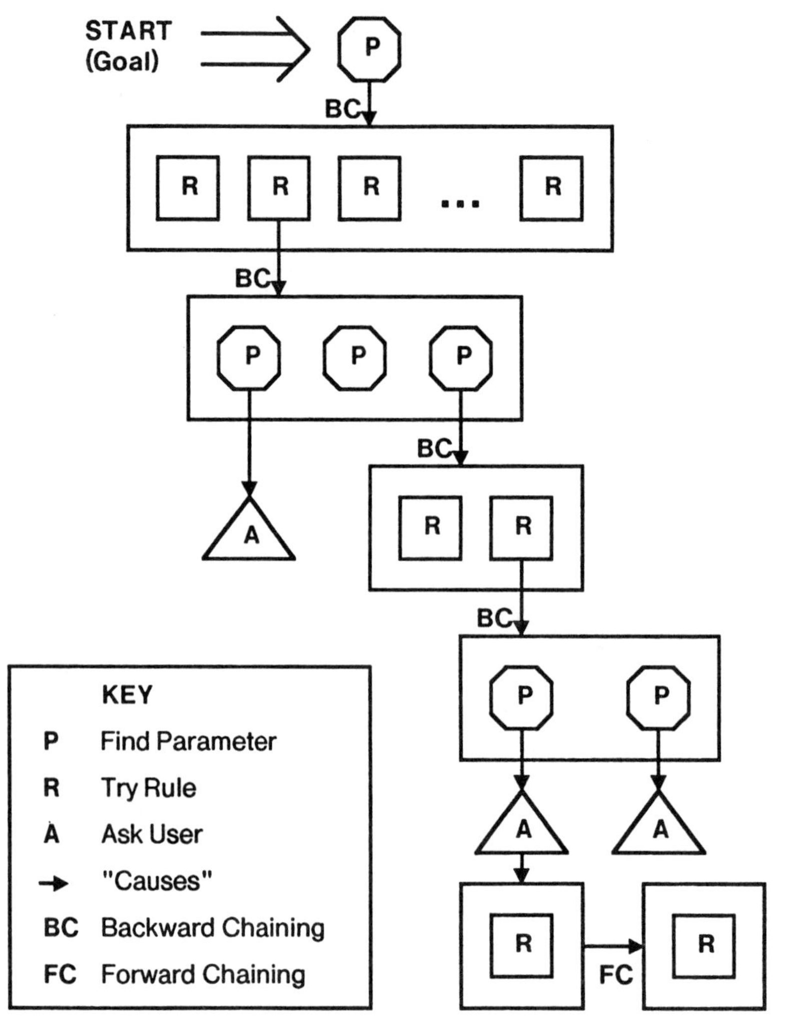

FIGURE 35-2 Control in EMYCIN.

one of the system's forward-chained rules. These rules can only be used as antecedent rules, they typically have single conditions in their premises, and repeated forward chaining is permitted only if one rule concludes with certainty that the premise of another is true.

In ONCOCIN (Figure 35-3), on the other hand, initial control is derived from the control block invoked in response to the task selected by the user. Forward chaining and backward chaining of rules are intermingled,[12] and any rule can be used in either direction.

[12]The broken line in Figure 35-3 outlines the portion of the ONCOCIN control structure that is identical to that found in EMYCIN (Figure 35-2).

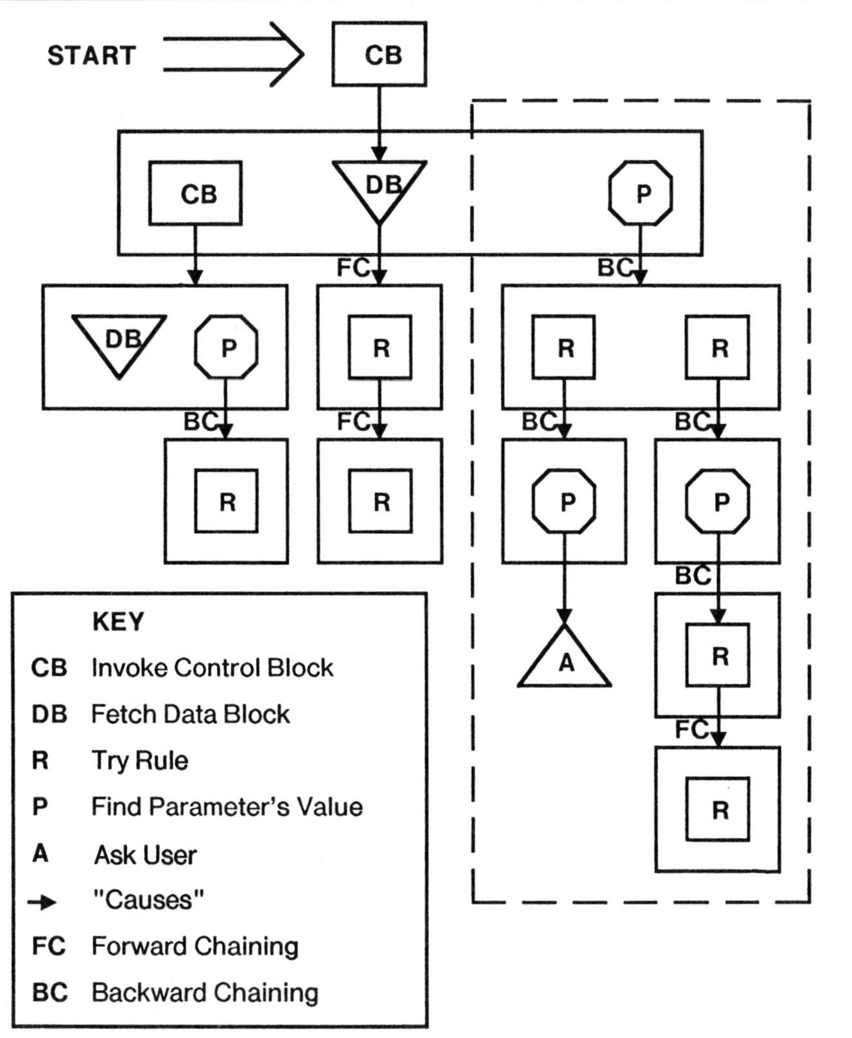

FIGURE 35-3 Control in ONCOCIN.

35.5 Why Artificial Intelligence Techniques?

We have learned from the MYCIN experience, and in building other EMYCIN systems as well, that a major part of each development effort has been the encoding of poorly understood knowledge. Enlisting the time and enthusiasm of domain experts has often been difficult, yet progress is usually impossible without active collaboration. Thus there is great appeal to a domain in which much of the needed knowledge is already recorded in thorough, albeit lengthy and complicated, documents (viz., the protocol descriptions that are written for every cancer therapy clinical experiment). Much of the appeal of the ONCOCIN problem domain is the availability of detailed documents that we can study and use for knowledge base development.

As we noted earlier, several other centers have begun to develop protocol management systems, but none has chosen to use techniques drawn from artificial intelligence. Complicated though the chemotherapy protocols may be, they are largely algorithmic, and other groups have been able to encode much of the knowledge using less complex representation techniques. Our reasons for choosing an AI approach for encoding the knowledge of oncology chemotherapy are varied.[13] It should be stressed that all protocols have important loopholes and exceptions; when an aberrant situation arises for a patient being treated, the proper management is typically left unspecified. For example, the lymphoma protocols with which we have been most involved to date include several rules of the following form:

IF: there is evidence of disease extension
THEN: refer the patient to lymphoma clinic

IF: there is significant toxicity to vincristine
THEN: consider substituting velban

As shown here, the protocols often defer to the opinions of the attending physicians without providing guidelines on which they might base their decisions. Hence there is no standardization of responses to unusual problems, and the validity of the protocol analysis in these cases is accordingly subject to question. One goal is to develop approaches to these more complex problems that characterize the management of patients being treated for cancer. It is when these issues are addressed that the need for AI techniques is most evident and the task domain begins to look similar in complexity to the decision problems in a system like MYCIN. Rules will eventually have uncertainty associated with them (we have thus far avoided the need for certainty weights in the rules in ONCOCIN), and close collaboration with experts has been required in writing new rules that are *not* currently recorded in chemotherapy protocols or elsewhere. In addition, however, AI representation and control techniques have already allowed us to keep the knowledge base flexible and easily modified. They have also allowed us to develop explanation capabilities and to separate kinds of knowledge explicitly in terms of their semantic categories (Langlotz and Shortliffe, 1983; Tsuji and Shortliffe, 1983).

[13]Because we need a high-speed interface to ensure the system's acceptance by physicians, we have been forced to design a complex system architecture with asynchronous processes. We have also wanted to allow each process to run in whatever computer language seems most appropriate for its task. ONCOCIN subprocesses are currently written in Interlisp, SAIL, and assembler (Gerring et al., 1982). We have not described the total system or our reasons for making these design decisions, but we believe the structure is necessary to achieve acceptance of the system in a clinical setting.

35.6 Conclusion

In summary, the project seeks to identify new techniques for bringing large AI programs to a clinical audience that would be intolerant of systems that are slow or difficult to use. The design of a novel interface that uses both custom hardware and efficient software has heightened the acceptability of ONCOCIN. Formal evaluations are underway to allow us to determine both the effectiveness and the acceptability of the system's clinical advice.

For the present we are trying to build a useful system to which increasingly complex decision rules can be added. We are finding, as expected, that the encoding of complex knowledge that is not already stated explicitly in protocols is arduous and requires an enthusiastic community of collaborating physicians. Hence we recognize the importance of one of our research goals noted earlier in this report: to establish an effective relationship with a specific group of physicians so as to facilitate ongoing research and implementation of advanced computer-based clinical tools.

PART TWELVE

Conclusions

36

Major Lessons from This Work

In this book we have presented experimental evidence at many levels of detail for a diverse set of hypotheses. As indicated by the chapter and section headings, the major themes of the MYCIN work have many variations. In this final chapter we will try to summarize the most important results of the work presented. This recapitulation of the lessons learned should not be taken as a substitute for details in the sections themselves. We provide here an abstraction of the details, but hope it also constitutes a useful set of lessons on which others can build. The three main sections of this chapter will

- reiterate the main goals that provide the context for the experimental work;
- discuss the experimental results from each of the major parts of the book; and
- summarize the key questions we have been asked, or have asked ourselves, about the lessons we have learned.

If we were to try to summarize in one word why MYCIN works as well as it does, that word would be *flexibility*. By that we mean that the designers' choices about programming constructs and knowledge structures can be revised with relative ease and that the users' interactions with the system are not limited to a narrow range in a rigid form. While MYCIN was under construction, we tried to keep in mind that the ultimate system would be *used* by many doctors, that the knowledge base would be *modified* by several experts, and that the code itself would be *programmed* by several programmers.[1] In hindsight, we now see many areas of inflexibility in MYCIN and EMYCIN. For example, the knowledge acquisition system in EMYCIN requires that the designer of a new system express taxonomic knowledge in a combination of rules and contexts; no facile language is provided for talking about such structures. We lose some expressive power because MYCIN's[2] representation of all knowledge in rules and tables does not separate causal links from heuristics. And MYCIN's control structure forecloses the possibility of tight control over the sequence of rules and procedures that should be invoked together. Thus we are recommending that the principle of flexibility be pushed even farther than we were able to do during the last decade.

Two important ingredients of a flexible system are *simplicity* and *modularity*. We have discussed the simplicity of both the representation and control structure in MYCIN, and the modularity of the knowledge base. While simple structures are sometimes frustrating to work with, they do allow access from many other programs. For example, explanation and knowledge acquisition are greatly facilitated because the rules and backward chaining are syntactically simple (without much additional complication in their actual implementation). The semantics of the rules also appear simple, to users at least, because they have been defined that way by persons in the users' own profession.

The modularity of MYCIN's knowledge representation also contributed to its success. The rules were meant to be individual chunks of knowledge that could be used, understood, or modified independently of other rules. McCarthy, in his paper on the Advice Taker (McCarthy, 1958), set as one requirement of machine intelligence that a program be modifiable by giving it declarative statements about new facts and relations. It should not be necessary to reprogram it. That has been one of the goals of all work on knowledge programming, including our own. MYCIN's rules can be stated to the rule editor as new relations and are immediately incorporated into the definition of the system's behavior.

Modularity includes separation of individual "chunks" of knowledge from one another and from the program that interprets them. But it also implies a structuring of the knowledge that allows indexing from many perspectives. This facilitates editing, explanation, tutoring, and interpreting the individual chunks in ways that simple separation does not. In the

---

[1]As mentioned, LISP provided a good starting place for the development of a system like MYCIN because its programming constructs need not be fixed in type and size and it allows the building of data structures that are executable as code. At the time of system construction, a designer often needs to postpone making commitments about data structures, data types, sizes of lists, and so forth until experimenting with a running prototype. At the time the knowledge base for an expert system is under construction, similar degrees of flexibility are required to allow the program to improve incrementally. At the time a system is run, it needs flexibility in its I/O handling, for example, to correct mistakes and provide different assistance to different users.

[2]In much of this chapter, what we say about the design of MYCIN carries over to EMYCIN as well.

case of MYCIN's rule-based structure, both the elements of data in a rule's premises and the elements of the rule's conclusion are separated and indexed. However, it is now clear that more structuring of a knowledge base than MYCIN supports will allow indexing chunks of knowledge still further, for example to explain the strategies under which rules are interpreted or to explain the relationships among premise clauses.

36.1 Two Sets of Goals

It must be emphasized that the MYCIN experiments were inherently interdisciplinary, and we were thus guided by two distinct sets of issues: medical goals and artificial intelligence goals. They can be seen as two sides of the same coin. We were trying to build an AI system capable of high-performance problem solving in medicine. Yet each side made its own demands, and we were often forced to allocate resources to satisfy one or the other set of concerns.

On the medical side we wanted to demonstrate the sufficiency of symbolic inference rules in medical problems for which statistical and numerical methods had mostly been used previously. We were also trying to find methods that would allow programs to focus on therapy, as well as on diagnosis. We were explicitly trying to address recognized problems in medical practice and found considerable evidence that physicians frequently err in selecting antimicrobial agents. We were trying to develop a consultation model with which physicians would be comfortable because it mirrored their routine interactions with consultants in practice. And we were trying to develop a system that *could* and *would* be used in hospitals and private practice.

On the AI side, as we have said, the primary motivation was to explore the extent to which rules could be used to achieve expert-level problem solving. In DENDRAL, situation-action rules had been used to encode much of the program's knowledge about mass spectrometry, but considerably more knowledge resided in LISP procedures. In MYCIN, we wanted to use rules exclusively, to see if this could be done in a problem area as complex as medicine. The overriding principle guiding us was the belief that the flexibility of a program was increased by separating medical knowledge from procedures that manipulate and reason with that knowledge. We believed that by making the representation more flexible, it would be easier to build more powerful programs in domains where programs grow by accretion.

The previous chapters reflect this duality of goals. It is important to recognize the tensions this duality introduced in order to understand adequately both the descriptions of the experimental work in this book and the underlying motivations for the individual research efforts.

36.2 Experimental Results

Although we were not always explicitly aware of the hypotheses our work was testing, in retrospect a number of results can be stated as consequences of the experiments performed. The nature of experiments in AI is not well established. Yet, as we said in the preface, an experimental science grows by experimentation and analysis of results. The experiments reported here are not nearly as carefully planned as are, for example, clinical trials in medicine. However, once some uncharted territory has been explored, it is possible to review the path taken and the results achieved.

We have used the phrase "MYCIN-like system" in many places to characterize rule-based expert systems, and we have tried throughout the book to say what these are. In summary, then, let us say what we mean by rule-based systems. They are expert systems whose primary mode of representation is simple conditional sentences; they are extensions of production systems in which the concepts are closer in grain size to concepts used by experts than to psychological concepts. Rule-based systems are deductively not as powerful as logical theorem-proving programs because their only rule of inference is *modus ponens* and their syntax allows only a subset of logically well-formed expressions to be clauses in conditional sentences. Their primary distinction from logic-based systems is that rules define facts in the context of how they will be used, while expressions in logic-based systems are intended to define facts independently of their use.[3] For example, the rule A → B in a rule-based system asserts only that fact A is evidence for fact B.

Rule-based systems are primarily distinguished from frame-based systems by their restricted syntax. The emphasis in a rule is on the inferential relationship between facts (for example, "A is evidence for B" or "A causes B"). In a frame the emphasis is on characterizing concepts by using links of many types (including evidential relations).

Rule-based systems are sometimes characterized as "shallow" reasoning systems in which the rules encode no causal knowledge. While this is largely (but not entirely) true of MYCIN, it is not a necessary feature of rule-based systems. An expert may elucidate the causal mechanisms underlying a set of rules by "decompiling" the rules (see Section 29.3.2 for a discussion of decompiling the knowledge on which the tetracycline rule is based). The difficulties that one encounters with an expanded rule set are knowledge engineering difficulties (construction and maintenance of the knowledge base) and not primarily difficulties of representation or interpretation. However, the causal knowledge thus encoded in an expanded rule set would be usable only in the context of the inference chains in which it fits

[3]This way of making the distinction was pointed out by John McCarthy in a private communication.

and would not be as generally available to all parts of the reasoning system as one might like. A circuit diagram and the theoretical knowledge underneath it, in contrast, can be used in many different ways.

Winston (1977) summarized the main features of MYCIN as follows:

1. MYCIN can help physicians diagnose infections.
2. MYCIN is a backward-chaining deduction system.
3. MYCIN computes certainty factors.
4. MYCIN talks with the consulting physician in English.
5. MYCIN can answer a variety of questions about its knowledge and behavior.
6. MYCIN can assimilate new knowledge interactively.

While this is a reasonable summary of what the program can do, it stops short of analyzing how the main features of MYCIN work or why they do not work better. The analysis presented here is an attempt to answer those questions. Not all of the experiments have positive results. Some of the most interesting results are negative, occasionally counter to our initial beliefs. Some experiments were conceived but never carried out. For example, although it was explicitly our initial intention to implement and test MYCIN on the hospital wards, this experiment was never undertaken. Instead the infectious disease knowledge base was laid to rest in 1978[4] despite studies demonstrating its excellent decision-making performance. This decision reflects the unanticipated lessons regarding clinical implementation (described in Part Eleven) that would not have been realized without the earlier work.

Finally, a word about the organization of this section on results. We have described the lessons mostly from the point of view of what we have learned about building an intelligent program. We were looking for ways to build a high-performance medical reasoning program, and we made many choices in the design of MYCIN to achieve that goal. For the program itself, we had to choose (1) a model of diagnostic reasoning, (2) a representation of knowledge, (3) a control structure for using that knowledge, and (4) a model of how to tolerate and propagate uncertainty. We also had to formulate (5) a methodology for building a knowledge base capable of making good judgments. Our working hypothesis, then, was that the choices we made were sufficient to build a program whose performance was demonstrably good.[5] If we had failed to demonstrate expert-level performance, we would have had reason to believe that one or more of our choices had been wrong. In addition, other aspects of the program were

---

[4]Much of the MYCIN-inspired work reported in this volume was done after this date, however.

[5]Note that sufficiency is a weak claim. We do not claim that any choice we made is *necessary*, nor do we claim that our choices cannot be improved.

also tested: (6) explanation and tutoring, (7) the user interface, (8) validation, (9) generality, and (10) project organization. The following ten subsections review these ten aspects of the program and the environment in which it was constructed.

36.2.1 The Problem-Solving Model

From the point of view of MYCIN's reasoning, the program is best viewed as an example of the *evidence-gathering paradigm*. This can be seen as a form of search, in which the generator is not constructing complex hypotheses from primitive elements but is looking at items from a predefined list. For diagnosis, MYCIN has the names of 120 organisms. (Twenty-five of the possible causes are explicitly linked to evidence through rules, the rest can be reasoned about through links in tables or links to prior cultures. Properties of all of them must be known, including their sensitivities to each of the drugs.) Logically speaking, MYCIN could run down the list one at a time and test each hypothesis by asking what evidence there is for or against it. This would not produce a pleasing consultation, but it would provide the same diagnoses.

This sort of evidence gathering can be contrasted with heuristic search in which a *generator* of hypotheses defines the search space, as in DENDRAL. It also differs from generate-and-test programs in that hypotheses are not considered (or tested) unless there is evidence pointing to them.

Solutions to problems posed to EMYCIN systems are interpretations of the data. EMYCIN implicitly assumes that there is no unique solution to a problem, but that the evidence will support several plausible conclusions from a fixed list. (This is partly because of the uncertainty in both the data and the rules.) The size of the solution space is thus 2^N where N is the number of single conclusions on the fixed list. In MYCIN there are 120 organism names on the list of possible identities. However, it is unlikely that more than a half-dozen organism identities will have sufficient evidence to warrant covering for them. If we assume that MYCIN will cover for the top six candidate organisms in each case, the number of possible combinations[6] in a solution is more like

$$\binom{120}{6}$$

or about 10^9. Obviously, the method of evidence gathering does not generate all of them.

[6]The number of medically meaningful conclusions is actually much fewer because certain combinations are implausible or nearly impossible.

We have used EMYCIN to build systems in a variety of domains of medicine and engineering. An appropriate application of the evidence-gathering model seems to meet most of the following criteria:

- a classification problem in which data are explained or "covered" by hypotheses from a predefined list;
- a problem that is partly defined by explaining, once, a snapshot of data (as opposed to continuous monitoring problems in which hypotheses are revised frequently as more data are collected);
- a problem of sufficient difficulty that practitioners often turn to textbooks or experts for advice;
- a problem of sufficient difficulty that experts require time for reasoning—their solutions are not instantaneous (but neither do they take dozens of hours);
- a problem of narrow enough scope that a knowledge base can be built and refined in a "reasonable" time (where the resources available and the importance of the problem partly define reasonableness);
- a problem that can be defined in a "closed world," i.e., with a vocabulary that covers the problem description space but is still bounded and "reasonably" small.

Additional characteristics of problems suitable for this kind of solution are listed in Section 36.2.9 on the generality of the EMYCIN framework.

36.2.2 Representation

One of MYCIN's most encouraging lessons for designers of expert systems is the extent to which good performance can be attained with the simple syntax of fact triples and conditional rules. MYCIN's rules are augmented with a context tree around which the dialogue is organized, but other EMYCIN systems (e.g., PUFF) use a degenerate tree of only one kind of object. Also, many rules were encoded in a "shorthand" form (as entries in tables). CF's were added to the simple rule form in MYCIN, but again, other EMYCIN systems (e.g., SACON) perform well with categorical rules (all CF's = 1). For many problems, the simple syntax of fact triples and conditional associations among facts is quite appropriate. In Chapter 3 (Section 3.2) we summarized many additional production system enhancements that were developed for MYCIN.

On the other hand, our experience using EMYCIN to build several expert systems has suggested some negative aspects to using such a simple representation for all the knowledge. The associations that are encoded in rules are elemental and cannot be further examined (except through the symbolic text stored in slots such as JUSTIFICATION or AUTHOR). A reasoning program using only homogeneous rules with no internal distinctions among them thus fails to distinguish among:

Chance associations (e.g., proportionally more left-handed than right-handed persons have been infected by *E. coli* at our institution)

Statistical correlations (e.g., meningococcal meningitis outbreaks are correlated with crowded living conditions)

Heuristics based on experience rather than precise statistical studies (e.g., oral administration of drugs is less reliable in children than are injections)

Causal associations (e.g., streptomycin can cause deafness)

Definitions (e.g., all *E. coli* are gram-negative rods)

Knowledge about structure (e.g., the mouth is connected to the pharynx)

Taxonomic knowledge (e.g., viral meningitis is a kind of infection)

The success of MYCIN, which generally does not distinguish among these types of associations, demonstrates that it is possible to build a high-performance program within a sparse representation of homogeneous rules (augmented with a few other knowledge structures). Nevertheless, limited experience with CENTAUR, WHEEZE, NEOMYCIN, and ONCOCIN leads us to believe that the tasks of building, maintaining, and understanding the knowledge base will be easier if the types of knowledge are separated. This becomes especially pertinent during knowledge acquisition (as described in Part Three) and when teaching the knowledge base to students (Part Eight).

Every formalism limits the kinds of things that can be expressed. From the start we were trying to balance expressive power against simplicity and modularity. As in DENDRAL, in MYCIN we departed from a "pure" production rule representation by allowing complex predicates in the left-hand sides of rules and complex actions in the right-hand sides. All of the inferential knowledge was still kept in rules, however. Every rule was augmented with additional information, using property lists. We used the premise and action properties of rule names for inferential knowledge and used the other properties for bookkeeping, literature references, and the like.[7] Meta-rules can reference the values of any of these slots, to focus attention within the backward-chaining flow of control, thereby making it more sensitive to global context.

Many problems require richer distinctions or finer control than MYCIN-like rules provide. A more general representation, such as frames, allows a system designer to make the description of the world more complex. In frames, for instance, it is easier to express the following:

---

[7]This is the major distinction between our rules and frames. Inference about inheritance of values is not handled implicitly in MYCIN, as it would be in a frame-based system, but is explicitly dealt with in the action parts of the rules (using the context tree). However, there is considerable similarity in the augmented form of MYCIN's rules and frames, and in their expressive power. Although frames are typically used to represent single concepts, whereas rules represent inferential relationships, the structural similarities between these encoding techniques suggest that frame-based and rule-based representations are not a strict dichotomy.

- Procedural knowledge—sequencing tasks
- Control knowledge—when to invoke knowledge sources
- Knowledge of context—the general context in which elements of the knowledge base are relevant
- Inheritance of properties—automatic transfer of values of some slots from parent concepts to offspring
- Distinctions among types of links—parent and offspring concepts may be linked as
    - class and instance
    - whole and part
    - sct and subset

The loss of simplicity in the frame representation, however, may complicate the inference, explanation, and knowledge acquisition routines. For example, inheritance of properties will be handled (and explained) differently depending on the type of link between parent and offspring concepts.

There is a trade-off between simplicity and expressive power. A simpler representation is easier to use but constrains the kinds of things a system builder might want to say. There is also a trade-off between generality and the power of knowledge acquisition tools. An unconstrained representation may have the expressive power of a programming language such as LISP or assembly language, but it can be more difficult to debug. There is considerable overlap among the alternative representation methods, and current work in AI is still experimenting with different ways of making this trade-off.

36.2.3 Control of Inferences

A strong result from the MYCIN experiment is that simple backward chaining (goal-driven reasoning) is adequate for reasoning at the level of an expert. As with DENDRAL, it was somewhat surprising that high performance could be achieved with a simple well-known method. The quality of performance is the same as (and the line of reasoning logically equivalent to) that of data-driven or other control strategies. The main virtues of a goal-driven control strategy are simplicity and ability to focus requests for data. It is simple enough to be explained quickly to an expert writing rules, so that he or she has a sense of how the rules will be used. And it allows explanations of a line of reasoning that are generally easily understood by persons requesting advice.

Internally, backward chaining is also simple. Rules are checked for applicability (i.e., the LHS's are matched against the case data to see if the RHS's should be executed) if and only if the RHS's are relevant to the subgoal under consideration. Relevance is determined by an index created automatically at the time a rule is created, so rule invocation is highly focused. For example, a new rule A → B will be added to the UPDATEDBY list associated with parameter B; then when subgoal B is under consideration only the rules on this list are tried.

We also needed to focus the dialogue, and we did it by introducing the context tree to guide the subgoal selection.[8] In addition, we needed to overcome some of the sensitivity to the *order* of clauses in a rule dictating the order in which subgoals were pursued and questions were asked. Thus the preview mechanism (Chapter 3) was developed to check all clauses of a rule to see if any are known to be false before chaining backward on the first clause. Once the preview mechanism was implemented, we found we could avoid the appearance of stupidity by introducing antecedent rules in order to make definitional inferences immediately upon receiving some data, for example:

SEX OF PT IS MALE → PREGNANCY OF PT IS NO

Then, regardless of where a clause about pregnancy occurred in a rule's premise, the above antecedent relation would keep the backward-chaining control structure from pursuing earlier clauses needlessly for male patients. Without the antecedent rule, however, nonpregnancy would not be known for males until the pregnancy clause caused backward chaining and the above relation (as a consequent rule) caused the system to check the sex of the patient. Without the preview mechanism, earlier clauses would have been pursued (and unnecessary lines of reasoning possibly generated) before the relevance of the patient's sex was discovered.

The main disadvantage of this control strategy is that users cannot interrupt to steer the line of reasoning by volunteering new information. A user can become frustrated, knowing that the system's present line of reasoning will turn out to be fruitless as a result of data that are going to be requested later. This human-engineering issue is discussed again in Section 36.2.7.

We carried the idea of separating knowledge from inference procedures a step further when we separated control strategies from the rule invocation mechanism. One of the elegant points about this experiment is the use of the same rule formalism to encode strategy rules as we use for the medical rules, with attendant use of the same explanation procedures. In Part Nine we discuss writing meta-rules for controlling inference using the same rule formalism, interpreter, and explanation capabilities. There is sufficient generality in this formalism to support meta-level reasoning, as well as meta-meta-level reasoning and beyond. We needed to add some new predicates to talk *about* rules and rule sets. And we needed one change in the interpreter to check for higher-level rules before executing rules

[8]Recall that the context tree was introduced for two other reasons as well: to allow MYCIN to keep track of multiple instances of the same kind of object, and to allow the program to understand hierarchical relationships among entities.

applicable to a subgoal. We did not experiment enough with meta-rules to determine how much expressive power they offer. However, both CENTAUR and NEOMYCIN give some indication of the control and strategy knowledge we need in medical domains, some of which appears difficult to represent in meta-rules because we lack a rich vocabulary for talking about sequences of tasks. Although meta-rules were designed to prune or reorder the set of rules gathered up by the backward-chaining control routine, their implementation is clean because they reference rules at the next lower level by content and not by name; i.e., they do *not* require specification of an explicit sequence of rules to be invoked in order (e.g., Rule 50 then Rule 71 then Rule 39).

Meta-rules allow separation of types of knowledge in ways that are difficult to capture in medical rules alone. Some diagnostic strategies were initially built into the inference procedure, such as exhaustive invocation of rules—an inherently cautious strategy that is appropriate for this medical context but not for all. Sometimes, though, we wanted MYCIN to be more sensitive to context; the age of the patient, for example, may indicate that some rules can be ignored.[9] Meta-rules work because they can examine the contents of rules at the next lower level and reason about them. This is part of the benefit of the flexibility provided by LISP and the simplicity of the rule syntax.

We have little actual experience with meta-rules in MYCIN, however. Because of the cautious strategy of invoking all relevant rules, we found few opportunities for using them. The one or two meta-rules that made good medical sense could be "compiled out" by moving their contents into the rules themselves. For example, "do rules of type A before those of type B" can be accomplished by manually ordering rules on the UPDATEDBY list or manually ordering clauses in rules. The system overhead of *determining* whether there are any meta-rules to guide rule invocation is a high price to pay if all of the rules will be invoked anyway. So, although their potential power for control was demonstrated, their actual utility is being assessed in subsequent ongoing work such as NEOMYCIN (Clancey, 1983).

36.2.4 Inexact Inference

MYCIN is known partly for its model of inexact inference (the CF model), a one-number calculus for propagating uncertainty through several levels of inference from data to hypotheses. MYCIN's performance shows that, for some problems at least, degrees of evidential support can be captured adequately in a single number,[10] and a one-number calculus can be devised

[9]This was not done with meta-rules, however, because it could easily be handled by the preview mechanism and judicious use of screening clauses.

[10]Although the CF model was originally based on separate concepts of belief and disbelief (as defined for MB and MD in Chapter 11), recall that even then the net belief is reflected in a single number and only one number is associated with each inferential rule.

to propagate uncertainty. The one number we actually use is a combination of disparate factors, most importantly strength of inference and utility considerations. Theoretically, it would have made good sense to keep those separate. Heuristically and pragmatically, we were unable to acquire as many separate numbers as we would have needed for Bayesian probability calculations followed by calculations of expected values (utilities) associated with actions and outcomes.

The CF in a rule measures the *increased* strength of the conclusion. In effect, we asked the medical experts "How much more strongly do you believe the conclusion *h after* you know the premises *e* are true than you did before?" If we were dealing strictly with probabilities, which we are not, then the CF for positive evidential support would be a one-number approximation to

$$\frac{P(h|e) - P(h)}{1 - P(h)}$$

The one-number calculus achieves the goals we sought, although without the precision that many persons desire. The combining of uncertainty depends on relatively small numbers of rules being applicable at any point. Otherwise, many small pieces of evidence ultimately boost the support of every hypothesis to 0.99 and we lose distinctions among strengths of support for hypotheses. The effect of the propagation is a modestly accurate clustering of hypotheses by gross measures of evidential strength (HIGH, MEDIUM, LOW, NONE). But within a cluster the ranking of hypotheses is too dependent on the subjectiveness of the CF's, as well as on the certainty propagation scheme, to be taken precisely.

The focus of a decision-making aid, however, needs to be on recommendations for action. Thus it needs costs and benefits, as well as probabilities, associated with various outcomes. When MYCIN recommends treating for *Streptococcus,* for example, it has combined the likelihood of strep with the risk of failing to treat for it. For this reason we now realize it is perhaps more appropriate to think of CF's as measures of *importance* rather than of probability or strength of belief. That is, they measure the increased importance of acting on the conclusion of a rule in light of new evidence mentioned in the premise. For example, self-referencing rules mention the same parameter in both premise and action parts:

$$A \;\&\; B \;\&\; C \rightarrow A$$

Such a rule is saying, in effect, that if you already have reason to believe A, and if B and C are likely in this case, then increase the importance of A. In principle, we could have separated probabilities from utilities. In practice, that would have required more precision than infectious disease experts were willing or able to supply.

The discontinuity around the 0.2 threshold is not a necessary part of the CF model. It was added to the implementation to keep the backward-chaining control structure from expending effort for very small gain. In a data-driven system the data would all be gathered initially, and the inferences, however weak, could be propagated exhaustively. In a goal-driven system, however, the 0.2 threshold is a heuristic that precludes unnecessary questions. In the rule

$$A \,\&\, B \,\&\, C \rightarrow D$$

if any clause is not "true enough," the subsequent clauses will not be pursued. If clause A, after tracing, has not accumulated evidence over the 0.2 threshold then the system will not bother to ask about clauses B and C. In brief, the threshold was invented for purposes of human engineering since it shortens a consultation and reduces the number of questions asked of the user.

This value of the threshold is arbitrary, of course. It should simply be high enough to prevent the system from wasting its time in an effort to use very small pieces of evidence. With a sick patient, there is a little evidence for almost every disease, so the threshold also helps to avoid covering for almost every possible problem. The threshold has to be low enough, on the other hand, to be sure that important conclusions are considered. Once the 0.2 threshold was chosen, CF's on rules were sometimes set with it in mind. For example, two rules concluding *Streptococcus*, each at the CF = 0.1 level, would not be sufficient alone to include *Streptococcus* in the list of possible causes to consider further.[11]

Because we are not dealing with probabilities, or even with "pure" strength of inference alone, our attempt to give a theoretical justification for CF's was flawed. We based it on probability theory and tried to show that CF's could be related to probabilities in a formal sense. Our desiderata for the CF combining function were based on intuitions involving confirmation, not just probabilities, so it is not surprising, in retrospect, that the justification in terms of formal probability theory is not convincing (see Chapter 12). So the CF model must be viewed as a set of heuristics for combining uncertainty and utility, and not as a calculus for confirmation theory. As we noted in Chapter 13, the Dempster-Shafer theory of evidence offers several potential advantages over CF's. However, simplifying assumptions and approximations will be necessary to make it a computationally tractable approach.

In a deductive system the addition of new facts, as axioms, does not change the validity of theorems already proved. In many interesting problem areas, such as medical diagnosis, however, new knowledge can invalidate old conclusions. This is called nonmonotonic reasoning (McDermott

[11] See the exchange of messages at the end of Chapter 10 for a discussion of how this situation arose in the development of the meningitis knowledge base.

and Doyle, 1980) because new inferences are not always adding new conclusions monotonically to the accumulating knowledge about a problem. In MYCIN, early conclusions are revised as new data are acquired—for example, what looked like an infection of one type on partial evidence looks like another infection after more evidence is accumulated. The problems of nonmonotonicity are mostly avoided, though, because MYCIN gathers evidence for and against many conclusions, using CF's to adjust the strength of evidence of each, and only decides at the end which conclusions to retain. As pointed out in Section 29.4.3, self-referencing rules can change conclusions after all the evidence has been gathered and thus may be considered a form of nonmonotonic reasoning.

Quantification of "Soft" Knowledge

We know that the medical knowledge in MYCIN is not precise, complete, or well codified. Although some of it certainly is mathematical in nature, it is mostly "soft" in the sense that it is judgmental and empirical, and there are strong disagreements among experts about the formulation of what is known. Nevertheless, we needed a way of representing the strength of associations in rules and of calculating the strength with which numerous pieces of evidence support a conclusion. We first looked for a calculus of imprecise concepts that did not involve combining numbers. For example, a few pieces of weakly suggestive evidence would combine into moderately suggestive evidence, and many pieces would be strongly suggestive. But how many? And how do the different qualitative degrees combine? We did not like the idea of discrete categories of strength since it introduces discontinuities in the combinations. So we looked for a continuous function that was not overly sensitive to small changes in degrees.

In working with CF's, we found that quantifying soft knowledge does not require fine levels of precision (Chapter 10). That is why this calculus can be used in a practical domain. With several rules providing evidence for a conclusion, the CF's could be written rather roughly and still give the desired effect. We later showed that, for the MYCIN domain, experts did not have to use more than four or five degrees of evidential strength, even though we provided a continuous scale from 0 to 1.

We discovered two styles of rule composition. The first follows our initial belief that rules can be written independently of one another. The CF's are set by experts based on their accumulated experience of how much more likely or important the conclusion is after the premises are known than it is before they are known. This assumes that CF's do not need to be precisely set because (a) the knowledge itself is not precise and (b) about as many rules will have CF's that are "too high" as will have ones that are "too low" (in some undefinable, absolute sense). The second style of setting CF's is more tightly controlled. Each new empirical association of evidence

Data:
- Erroneous
- Incomplete

Rules:
- Erroneous (or only partly correct)
- Incomplete

Conceptual framework (domain-dependent and domain-independent parts):
- Incorrect vocabulary of attributes, predicates, and relations
- Incorrect inference structure
- Incomplete set of concepts
- Incomplete logical structure

FIGURE 36-1 Sources of uncertainty in rule-based systems.

with a conclusion, in this view, requires examining rules with similar evidence or similar conclusions to see how strong the association should be, relative to the others. For example, to set the CF on a new rule, A → Z, one would look at other rules such as:

$$X \rightarrow Z \text{ (CF} = 0.2)$$

$$Y \rightarrow Z \text{ (CF} = 0.8)$$

Then, if evidence A is about as strong as Y (0.8) and much stronger than X (0.2), the new CF should be set around the 0.8 level. The exchange of messages at the end of Chapter 10 reflects the controversy that arose in our group over these two styles of CF assignment.

In both cases, the sensitivity analysis mentioned in Chapter 10 convinced us that the rules we were putting into MYCIN were not dependent on precise values of CF's. That realization helped persons writing rules to see that they could be indifferent to the distinction between 0.7 and 0.8, for example, and the system would not break down.

Corrections for Uncertainty

There are many "soft" or ill-structured domains, including medical diagnosis,[12] in which formal algorithmic methods do not exist (Pople, 1982). In diagnostic tasks there are several sources of uncertainty besides the heuristic rules themselves. These are summarized in Figure 36-1.

[12]There are so-called *clinical algorithms* in medicine, but they do not carry the guarantees of correctness that characterize mathematical or computational algorithms. They are decision flow charts in which heuristics have been built into a branching logic so that paramedical personnel can use them to provide good care in many commonly occurring situations.

In an empirical domain, the measurements, observations, and terms used to describe data may be erroneous. Instruments sometimes need recalibrating, or electronic noise in the line can produce spurious readings. Some tests are notoriously unreliable. Similarly, observers sometimes make mistakes in noticing or recording data. Among these mistakes is the failure to describe correctly what one sees. This ranges from checking the wrong box to choosing words poorly. The data are often incomplete as well. Tests with the most diagnostic value and least cost or inconvenience are done first, as a matter of general strategy. At any time, there are always more tests to be done (if only to redo an old one) and always new observations to be made (if only to observe the same variables for a few more hours). But some action must eventually be taken on the best available data, even in the absence of complete information.

With the rules, too, it is impossible to guarantee correctness and completeness (Chapter 8). This is not the fault of the expert supplying the rules; it is inevitable in problem areas in which the knowledge is soft.

Finally, the whole conceptual framework may be missing some critical concepts and may contain constructs that are at the wrong level of detail. Domain-independent parts of the framework that may introduce errors into the problem-solving process include the inference structure and the calculus for combining inexact inferences. The domain-dependent aspects of the problem-solving framework include the vocabulary and the conceptual hierarchies used to relate terms. Some questions of chemistry, for example, require descriptions of molecules in terms of electron densities and cannot be answered with a "ball and stick" vocabulary of molecular structure. Similarly, expert performance in medical domains will sometimes require knowledge of causality or pathophysiologic mechanism, which is not well represented in MYCIN-like rules (see Chapter 29).

The best answer we have found for dealing with uncertainty is redundancy. By that we mean using multiple, overlapping sources of knowledge to reach conclusions, and using the overlaps as checks and balances on the correctness of the contributions made by different knowledge sources. In MYCIN we try to exploit the overlaps in the information contributed by laboratory and clinical data, just as physicians must. For example, a high fever and a high white cell count both provide information about the severity of an infection. On the assumption that the correct data will point more coherently to the correct conclusions than incorrect data will, we expect the erroneous data to have very little effect after all the evidence has been gathered. The *absence* of a few data points will also have little overall effect if other, overlapping evidence has been found. Overlapping inference paths, or redundancy in the rules, also helps correct problems of a few incorrect or missing inferences. With several lines of reasoning leading from data to conclusions, a few can be wrong (and a few can be missing), and the system still ends up with correct conclusions.

We recognize that introducing redundant data and inference rules is at odds with the independence assumptions of the CF model. We did not want the system to fail for want of one or two items of information. When we encounter cases with missing evidence, a redundant reasoning path ensures the robustness of the system. In cases where the overlapping pieces of evidence are all present, however, nothing inside the system prevents it from using the dependent information multiple times. We thus have to correct for this in the rule set itself. The dependencies may be syntactic—for example, use of the same concept in several rules—in which case an intelligent editor can help detect them. Or they may be semantic—for example, use of causally related concepts—in which case physicians writing or reviewing the rules have to catch them.

In the absence of prior knowledge about which data will be available for all cases, we felt we could not insist on a vocabulary of independent concepts for use in MYCIN's rules. Therefore, we had to deal with the pragmatic difficulty of sometimes having too little information and sometimes having overlapping information. Our solution is also pragmatic, and not entirely satisfactory: (a) check for subsumed and overlapping rules during knowledge entry so that they can be separated explicitly; (b) cluster dependent pieces of evidence in single rules as much as possible; (c) organize rules hierarchically so that general information will provide small evidence and more specific information will provide additional confirmation, taking notice of the dependencies involved in using both general and specific evidence; (d) set the CF's on dependent rules (including rules in the hierarchy) to take account of the possibilities of reasoning with redundant paths if all data are *included* and reasoning with a unique path if most data are *missing*.

The problems of an incomplete or inappropriate conceptual scheme are harder to fix. In some cases where we have tried, the EMYCIN framework has appeared to be inappropriate, e.g., a constraint satisfaction problem (MYCIN's therapy algorithm) and problems involving tight procedural control (VM and ONCOCIN). In these instances, we have abandoned this approach to the problem because substantial changes to the conceptual scheme would have required rethinking the definitions of all parts of EMYCIN. The domain-dependent parts are under the control of the experts, though, and can be varied more easily. Not surprisingly, experts with whom we have collaborated seem to prefer working largely within one framework. In MYCIN, for example, there was not a lot of mixing of, say, clinical concepts (such as temperature) and theoretical concepts (such as the effect of fever on cellular metabolism). If the conceptual scheme is inappropriate for the problem, then there is no hope at present for incorporating a smooth correction mechanism. We are always tempted to add more parameters and rules before making radical changes in the whole conceptual framework and approach to the problem, so we will be slow to discover corrections for fundamental limitations.

36.2.5 Knowledge Base Construction and Maintenance

One of the major lessons of this and other work on expert systems is that large knowledge bases must be built incrementally. In many domains, such as medicine, the knowledge is not well codified, so it is to be expected that the first attempts to build a knowledge base will result in approximations. As noted earlier, incremental improvements require flexible knowledge structures that allow easy extensions. This means not only that the syntax should be relatively simple but that the system should allow room for growth. Rapid feedback on the consequences of changes also facilitates improvements. A knowledge base that requires extra compilation steps before it can be tried (especially long ones) cannot grow easily or rapidly.

Knowledge acquisition is now seen as the critical bottleneck in building expert systems. We came to understand through this work that the knowledge-engineering process can be seen as a composite of three stages:

1. knowledge base conceptualization (problem definition and choice of conceptual framework);
2. knowledge base construction (within the conceptual framework); and
3. knowledge base refinement (in response to early performance).

In each stage, the limiting factors are (a) the expressive power of the representation, (b) the extent to which knowledge of the domain is already well structured, (c) the ability of the expert to formulate new knowledge based on past experience, (d) the power of the editing and debugging tools available, and (e) the ability of the knowledge engineer to understand the basic structure and vocabulary of the domain and to use the available tools to encode knowledge and modify the framework.

Our experiments focus largely on the refinement stage.[13] Within this stage, the model that we have found most useful is that of debugging in context; an expert can more easily critique a knowledge base and suggest changes to it in the context of specific cases than in the abstract. Initial formulations of rules are often too general since the conceptualization stage appropriately demands generality. Such overgeneralizations can often best be found and fixed empirically, i.e., by running cases and examining the program's conclusions.

One important limitation of our model is its failure to address the problem of integrating knowledge from different experts. For some extensions to the knowledge base there is little difference between refinement by one expert or many. For extensions in which different experts use different concepts (not just synonyms for the same concept), we have no tools

[13]Some work in progress on the ROGET program (Bennett, 1983) attempts to build an intelligent, interactive tool to aid in conceptualization and construction of EMYCIN systems in new domains.

for reaching a consensus.[14] As suggested in Part Three, the best solution we found for this problem was designating a knowledge base "czar" who was responsible for maintaining coherence and consistency of the knowledge base. The process is facilitated, however, by techniques for comparing new rules with previously acquired knowledge and for performing high-level analyses of large portions of the knowledge base (Chapter 8). We found that this static analysis was insufficient, at least in domains in which nonformal, heuristic reasoning is essential. The best test of strength of a knowledge base appears to be empirical. Nevertheless, a logical analysis can provide important cues to persons debugging or extending a knowledge base, for example, in indicating gaps in logical chains of rules.

There are other models for transferring expertise to a program besides knowledge engineering. The war horse of AI is programming each new performance program using LISP (or another favorite language). This is euphemistically called "custom crafting" or, more recently, "procedural embedding of knowledge." In general, it is slower and the result is usually less flexible than with knowledge engineering, as we learned from DENDRAL.

Another model is based on a direct dialogue between expert and program. This would, if successful, eliminate the need for a knowledge engineer to translate and transform an expert's knowledge. Our attempts to reduce our dependence on knowledge engineers, however, have been largely unsuccessful. Some of the tools built to aid the maintenance of a knowledge base (e.g., the ARL editor; see Chapter 15) have been used by both experts and knowledge engineers. TEIRESIAS (Chapter 9) provides a model by which experts can refine a knowledge base without assistance from a knowledge engineer. For very simple domains such tools can probably suffice for use by experts with little training. As the complexity of a domain grows, however, the amount of time experts can spend seems to shrink. So far, the only way we have found around this dilemma is for knowledge engineers to act as "transducers" to help transform experts' knowledge into usable form.

Other models of knowledge acquisition that we considered leave the expert as well as the knowledge engineer out of the transfer process. Two such models are reading and induction. In the reading model, a program scans the literature looking for facts and rules that ought to be included in the knowledge base. We had considered using the parser described in Chapter 33 to read simplified transcriptions of journal articles. But the difficulties described in that chapter led us to believe that there was as much intellectual effort in transcribing articles for such purposes as in formulating rules directly.[15]

---

[14]We do record the author of each rule with date, justification, and literature citations, but these are not used by the program except as text strings to be printed.

[15]More recent work by others at Stanford explores the use of knowledge-based techniques for inferring new medical knowledge from a large data base of patient information (Blum, 1982).

We did not have the resources to experiment with induction in the MYCIN domain. We kept statistics on rule invocations and found them to be somewhat useful in revealing patterns to the knowledge engineers. For example, rules that are never invoked over a set of test cases may be either covering rare circumstances—in which case they are left unchanged—or failing to match because of errors in the left-hand sides—in which case they are modified. Learning new rules by induction is a difficult task when the performance program chains several rules together to link data to conclusions. In these cases, the so-called credit assignment problem—specifically, the problem of deciding which rules are at fault in case of poor performance—demands considerable expertise. In TEIRESIAS, credit assignment was largely turned over to the expert for this reason.

Since knowledge engineering was our primary mode of knowledge acquisition, we found that some interactive tools for building, editing, and checking the knowledge base gave needed assistance to the system builders. This is sometimes referred to as *knowledge programming*—the construction of complex programs by adding declarative statements of knowledge to an inference framework. The emphasis is on transferring the domain-specific knowledge into a framework and not on building up the framework in the first place from LISP programming constructs. At worst, this is accomplished by an expert using an on-line text editor. This is primitive, but if the expert is comfortable with the syntax and the problem-solving framework, a complex system can still be built more quickly than it could if the expert were forced to write new code, keeping track of array indices and go-to loops. There are many higher levels of assistance possible. Considerable error checking can be done on the syntax, and even more help can be provided by an intelligent assistant that understands some of the semantics of the domain. Knowledge programming, with any level of assistance, is one of the powerful ideas to come out of AI work in the 1970s.

36.2.6 Explanation and Tutoring

When we began this work, there had been little attempt in AI to provide justifications of a program's conclusions because programs were mostly used only by their designers. PARRY (Colby, 1981) had a selective trace that allowed designers to debug the system and casual users to understand its behavior. DENDRAL's Predictor also had a selective trace that could explain the origins of predicted data points, but it was used only for debugging. As part of our goal of making MYCIN acceptable to physicians, we tried from the start to provide windows into the contents of the knowledge base and into the line of reasoning. Our working assumption was that physicians would not ask a computer program for advice if they had to treat the program as an unexaminable source of expertise. They normally ask questions of, or consult, other physicians partly for education to help with future cases and partly for clarification and understanding of the present case. We believe that initial acceptance of an advice-giving system depends on users being able to understand why it provides the advice that it does (Chapter 34). Moreover, physicians are sensitive to well-established legal guidelines that argue against prescribing drugs without understanding why (or whether) they are appropriate.

The Model

The model of explanation in MYCIN is to "unwind the goal stack" in response to a WHY question. That is, when a user wants to know why an item of information is needed, MYCIN's answer is to show the rule(s) that caused this item to be requested. Answers to successive WHY questions show successively higher rules in the stack. For example, in the reasoning chain

$$A \rightarrow B \rightarrow C \rightarrow D \rightarrow E$$

MYCIN chains backward from goal E to the primary element A. A user who wants to know why A is requested will see the rule A → B. A second WHY question (i.e., "WHY do you want to know B?") will cause MYCIN to show the rule B → C, and so on. Keeping a simple history list of rule invocations is adequate for producing reasonable explanations of the program's line of reasoning, in part because reasoning is explicitly goal-directed. The goals and subgoals provide an overall rationale for the invocation of rules. The history list captures the context in which information is sought as well as the purpose for which it is sought.

But questions asking why MYCIN requests a particular piece of information provide only a small window on the reasoning process. The complementary HOW questions extend the view somewhat by allowing a user to ask how a fact has already been established or will later be pursued. The same history list provides the means for answering HOW questions during a consultation. For example, a user may be told that item A_2 is needed because B is the current goal and there is a rule of the form

$$A_1 \ \& \ A_2 \ \& \ A_3 \rightarrow B$$

where A_1 is already known (or believed) to be true. Then the user may ask how A_1 is known and will then see the rules that concluded it (or be told that it is primary information entered at the terminal if no rules were used). Similarly, the user may ask how A_3 will be pursued if the condition regarding A_2 is satisfied.

Explanations can be much richer. For example, they can provide insights into the structure of the domain or the strategy behind the line of reasoning. All of these extensions require more sophistication than is embodied in looking up and down a history list. This is a minimal explanation system. It provides reasons that are only as understandable as the rules are, and some can be rather opaque. Looking up or down the goal stack is not always appropriate, but this is all MYCIN can do. Sometimes, for instance, a user would like a justification for a rule in terms of the underlying theory but cannot get it. Moreover, MYCIN has no model of the user and thus cannot distinguish, say, a student's question from a physician's. These issues were discussed at length in Chapters 20 and 29.

At the end of a consultation, a user may ask questions about MYCIN's conclusions (final or intermediate) and will receive answers much like those given during the consultation. General questions about the knowledge base may also be asked. In order to get MYCIN to answer WHY NOT questions about hypotheses that were rejected or never considered, more reasoning apparatus was needed. Since there is no history of rules that were *not* tried, MYCIN needs to read the rules to see which ones might have been relevant and then to determine why they were not invoked.

Tutoring

We had initially assumed that physicians and students would learn about infectious disease diagnosis and therapy by running MYCIN, especially if they asked why and how. This mode of teaching was too passive, however, to be efficient as a tutorial system, so we began to investigate a more active tutor, GUIDON. The program has two parts: (a) the knowledge base used by MYCIN, and (b) a set of domain-independent tutorial rules and procedures.

We originally assumed that a knowledge base that is sufficient for high-performance problem solving would also be sufficient for tutoring. This assumption turned out to be false, and this negative result spawned revisions in our thinking about the underlying representation of MYCIN's knowledge. We concluded that, for purposes of teaching, and for explanation to novices, the facts and relations known to MYCIN are not well enough grounded in a coherent model of medicine (Chapter 29). MYCIN's knowledge is, in a sense, compiled knowledge. It performs well but is not very comprehensible to students without the concepts that have been left out. For example, a MYCIN rule such as

$$A \rightarrow B$$

may be a compilation of several associations and definitions:

$$A \rightarrow A_1$$

$$A_1 \rightarrow A_2$$

$$A_2 \rightarrow B$$

If A_1 and A_2 are not observable phenomena or quantities routinely measured, the only association that matters for clinical practice is $A \rightarrow B$. A student *would* gain some benefit from remembering MYCIN's compiled knowledge, but the absence of an underlying model makes it difficult to remember a scattered collection of rules. Additional knowledge of the structure of the domain, and of problem-solving strategies, provides the "glue" by which the rules are made coherent. Recent work at M.I.T. by Swartout (1983) and Patil et al. (1981) has further emphasized this point.

We also believe that an intelligent tutoring program can be devised such that medical knowledge and pedagogical knowledge are explicitly separated. The art of pedagogy, however, is also poorly codified and evokes at least as much controversy as the art of medicine. GUIDON has directed meaningful dialogues with both the MYCIN and SACON knowledge bases, so its pedagogical knowledge (tutoring rules; see Chapter 26) is not specific to medical education. Some of the knowledge about teaching is procedural because the sequence of actions is often important. Thus the pedagogical knowledge is a mixture of rules and stylized procedures.

36.2.7 The User Interface

Consultation Model

We chose to build MYCIN on the model of a physician-consultant who gives advice to other physicians having questions about patient care. Was it a good choice?

Here the answer is ambiguous. From an AI point of view, the consultation model is a good paradigm for an interactive decision-making tool because it is so clear and simple. The program controls the dialogue, much as a human consultant does, by asking for specific items of data about the problem at hand. Thus the program can understand short English responses to its questions because it knows what answers are reasonable at each point in the dialogue. Moreover, it can ask for as much—and only as much—information as is relevant. Also, the knowledge base can be highly specialized because the context of the consultation can be carefully controlled.

A disadvantage of the consultation model as implemented in MYCIN, however, is that it prevents a user from volunteering pertinent data.[16] Although the approach avoids the need for MYCIN to understand free-text data entry, physicians can find it irritating if they are unable to offer key pieces of information and must wait for the program to ask the right question.[17] In addition, MYCIN asks a lot of questions (around 50 or 60,

[16]Our one attempt to permit volunteered information (Chapter 33) was of limited success, largely because of the complexity of getting a computer to understand free text.

[17]The ability to accept volunteered information is a major feature of the PROSPECTOR model of interaction embodied in KAS (Reboh, 1981).

usually), and the number increases as the knowledge base grows. Few physicians want to type answers to that many questions—in fact, few of them want to type anything. With current technology, then, the consultation model increases the cost of getting advice beyond acceptable limits. Clinicians would rather phone a specialist and discuss a case verbally. Moreover, the consultation model sets up the program as an "expert" and leaves the users in the undesirable position of asking a machine for help. In some professions this may be acceptable, but in medicine it is difficult to sell.

One way to avoid the need for typing so many answers is to tap into on-line patient data bases. Many of MYCIN's questions, for example, could be answered by looking in automated laboratory records or (as PUFF now does) could be gathered directly from medical instruments (Aikins et al., 1983). Another way is to wait for advanced speech understanding and graphical input.

The consultation model assumes a cooperative and knowledgeable user. We attempted to make the system so robust that a user cannot cause an unrecoverable error by mistake. But the designers of any knowledge base still have to anticipate synonyms and strange paths through the rules because we know of no safeguards against malice or ignorance. Some medically impossible values are still not caught by MYCIN.[18] If users are cooperative enough to be careful about the medical correctness of what they type, MYCIN's implementation of the consultation model is robust enough to be helpful.

Other Models of Interaction

DENDRAL does not engage a user in a problem-solving dialogue as MYCIN does. Instead, it accepts a set of constraints (interactively defined) that specify the problem, then it produces a set of solutions. This might be called the *"hired gun" model* of interaction: specify the target, accept the results, and don't ask questions.

Recently we have experimented with a *critiquing model* for the ONCOCIN program, an attempt to respond to some of the limitations of the traditional consultation approach. In the critiquing model, a user states his or her own management plan, or diagnosis, and the program interrupts only if the plan is judged to be significantly inferior to what the program would have recommended (Langlotz and Shortliffe, 1983).

The *monitoring model* of the VM program (Chapter 22) follows much the same interactive strategy as that of ONCOCIN—offering advice only when there is a need. In addition, it periodically updates and prints a summary and interpretation of the patient's condition.

---

[18]For example, John McCarthy (maliciously) told MYCIN that the site of a culture was amniotic fluid—for a male patient—and MYCIN incorrectly accepted it (McCarthy, 1983). Nonmedical users (including one of the authors) have found similar "far-out bugs" as a consequence of sheer ignorance of medicine.

English Understanding

We attempted to design a satisfactory I/O package without programming extensive capabilities for understanding English. One of the pleasant surprises was the extent to which relatively simple sentence parsing and generating techniques can be used. In ELIZA, Weizenbaum (1967) showed that a disarmingly natural conversation can be produced by a program with no knowledge of the subject matter. We wanted to avoid the extensive effort of designing a program for understanding even a subset of unrestricted English. Thus we used roughly the same techniques used in ELIZA and in PARRY (Colby, 1981). Our main concern at the beginning was that the subset of English used by physicians was too broad and varied to be handled by simple techniques. This concern was unfounded. Subsequently, we have come to believe that the more technical the domain, the more stylized the communication. Then keyword and phrase matching are sufficient for understanding responses to questions and for parsing questions asked by users. As long as the program is in control of the dialogue, there is little problem with ambiguity because the types of responses a user can give are determined by the program's questions. Even in a mode in which a user asks questions about any relevant topic (Chapter 18), simple parsing techniques are usually adequate because (a) the range of relevance is rather restricted and (b) terms with ambiguity within this range are few in number and are disambiguated by other terms with unique meanings that serve to fix the context.

We did find, however, that our simple parser was not sufficient for understanding many facts presented at once in a textual description of a patient (Chapter 33). The facts picked out of the text were largely correct, but we missed many. We could successfully restrict the syntax of questions a person can ask without overly restricting the nature of the questions. But we found no general forms for facts that gave us assurance that the program could understand the wide variety of verbs used in case descriptions.

There are several shortcomings in MYCIN'S interface that could antagonize physicians.[19] First, it requires that a user *type*. There is a tantalizing possibility of speech-understanding interfaces that accept sentences in large vocabularies from multiple speakers. But these are not here yet, and certainly were only glimmers on the horizon in 1975. Second, MYCIN requires users to provide information that they know is stored on other computers in the same building. We were prepared to string cables among the computers, but the effort and expense were not justified as long as MYCIN was only a research program. Third, as we have noted, MYCIN does not accept volunteered information. Although we experimented with

[19]The lessons learned regarding the limitations of MYCIN's interface have greatly influenced the design of our recent ONCOCIN system (Chapters 32 and 35). That system's domain was selected largely because it provides a natural mechanism for allowing the physician to volunteer patient information (i.e., the flow sheet), and because data can be entered using a special keypad rather than the full terminal keyboard.

programs to permit this kind of interaction (Chapter 33), the theoretical issues involved prevented robust performance and discouraged us from incorporating the facility on a routine basis. Besides, eventually MYCIN asks all questions that it considers relevant, so, in a logical sense, volunteered information is unnecessary. From the users' point of view, however, MYCIN is often too fully in control of the dialogue. Users would like to be able to steer the line of reasoning and get the program to focus on a few salient facts at the beginning. Fourth, as mentioned above, we believe it is important to provide a window into the line of reasoning and the knowledge base. The window that we provide is narrow, however, and lacks the flexibility and clarity that would let a physician see quickly why MYCIN reasons as it does. Part of the difficulty is that the rules provided as explanations often mix strategy and tactics and thus are difficult to understand in isolation. Our more recent work on explanation has begun to look at issues such as these (Chapter 20).

36.2.8 Validation

There are many dimensions to the question "How good is MYCIN?" We have looked in detail at two: (a) How good is MYCIN's performance? and (b) What features would make such systems acceptable to physicians?

Decision-Making Performance

We experimented with three evaluations of MYCIN, each refined in light of our experience with the previous one, and believe that something much like Turing's test can demonstrate the level of performance of an expert system. In the third evaluation, we asked outside experts to rate the conclusions reached by MYCIN, several Stanford faculty, house staff, and students—on the same set of randomly selected, hard cases. Then, as in Turing's test (Turing, 1950), we looked at the statistics of how the outside experts rated MYCIN's performance relative to that of the Stanford faculty and the others. The conclusion from these studies is that MYCIN recommends therapeutic actions that are as appropriate as those of experts on Stanford's infectious disease faculty—as judged by experts not at Stanford. (More precisely, the outside experts disagreed with MYCIN's recommendation no more often than they disagreed with the recommendations of the Stanford experts.)

Although they are reasonably conclusive, studies such as this are expensive. Considerable research time was consumed in the design and execution of the MYCIN studies, and we required substantial contributed time from Stanford faculty, house staff, and students and from outside experts. Moreover, we learned from the earlier studies that we needed to separate the quality of advice from other factors affecting the utility and acceptance of the program. Thus the final study provides no information about whether the system would be used in practice, what the cost-benefit trade-offs would be, etc. However, we believe that high performance is a *sine qua non* for an expert system and thus deserves separate evaluation early in a program's evolution (see Chapter 8 of Hayes-Roth et al., 1983).

Acceptability

Unfortunately, we still have not fully defined the circumstances under which physicians will use a computer for help with clinical decision making. Only in the recent ONCOCIN work (Chapters 32 and 35) have we shown that physicians can be motivated to use decision aids in carefully selected and refined environments. In the original MYCIN program we had hoped to provide intelligent assistance to clinicians and to be able to demonstrate that the use of a computer reduced the number (and severity of consequences) of inappropriate prescriptions for antibiotics. Physicians in a teaching hospital, however, may not *need* assistance with this problem to the same extent as others—or, even if they do, they do not *want* it. So we found ourselves designing a program largely for physicians not affiliated with universities, with whom we did not interact daily.

In a survey of physicians' opinions (Chapter 34), we confirmed our impression that explanations are necessary for acceptance. If an assistant is unable to explain its line of reasoning, it will not gain the initial confidence of the clinicians who have to take responsibility for acting on its therapy recommendations. There is an element of legal liability here and an element of professional pride. A physician must understand the alternative possible causes of a problem and the alternative treatments, or else he or she may be legally negligent. Also, professionals will generally believe they are right until given reason to think otherwise. We also found that high performance alone was not sufficient reason for a practicing physician (or engineer or technician) to use a consultation program (Shortliffe, 1982a). We thought that finding a medical problem that is not solved well (and finding documentation of the difficulties) was the right starting place. What we failed to see was that adoption of a new tool is not based solely on demonstrated need coupled with demonstrated high performance of the tool. In retrospect, that was naive. Acceptability is different from high performance (Shortliffe, 1982b).

36.2.9 Generality

One of the most far-reaching sets of experiments in this work involved the generalizability of the MYCIN representation scheme and inference engine. We believed the skeletal program could be used for similar problem-solving tasks in other domains, but no amount of analysis and discussion could have been as convincing as the working demonstrations of EMYCIN in several different areas of medicine, electronics, tax advising, and software consulting. Making the inference engine domain-independent meant we had to write the rule interpreter so that it manipulates only the symbols named in the rules and makes no semantic transformations except as specified in the knowledge base.

However, there are a number of assumptions about the *type* of problem being solved that are built into EMYCIN. We assume, for instance, that the problem to be solved is one of analyzing a static collection of data (a "snapshot"), weighing all relevant evidence for and against competing hypotheses, and recommending some action. The whole formalism loses strength when it is stretched outside the limits of its design. We see parallels with earlier efforts to build a general problem solver; however, the generality of EMYCIN is intended to be strongly bounded.

There is no mystery to how a system (such as MYCIN) can be generalized (to EMYCIN) so that it is applicable to many problems in other domains: *keep the reasoning processes and the knowledge base separate.* However, some of the limiting characteristics of the data, the reasoning processes, the knowledge base, and the solutions are worth repeating.

The Data

EMYCIN was designed to analyze a static collection of data. The data may be incomplete, interdependent, incorrect ("noisy"), and even inconsistent. A system built in EMYCIN can, if the knowledge base is adequate, resolve ambiguities and cope with uncertainty and imprecision in the data. EMYCIN does assume, however, that there is only one set of data to analyze and that new data will not arrive later from experiments or monitoring. The number of elements of data in the set has been small—roughly 20–100—in the cases analyzed by MYCIN and other EMYCIN systems. But there seems to be no reason why more data cannot be accepted.

Reasoning Processes

EMYCIN is set up to reason backward from a goal to the data required to establish it. It can also do some limited forward reasoning within this context. It thus requests the data it needs when they are not otherwise available.

It is an evidence-gathering system, collecting evidence for and against potentially relevant conclusions. It is not set up to reason in other ways, for example, by generating hypotheses from primitive elements and testing them, by instantiating a template, or by refining a high-level description through successive abstraction levels. It can propagate uncertainty from the data, through uncertain inference rules, to the conclusions. Backtracking is not supported because the system follows all relevant paths.

Overall, the reasoning is assumed to be analytic and not synthetic. Diagnostic and classification tasks fit well; construction and planning tasks do not. The piece of MYCIN that constructs a therapy plan within constraints, for example, was coded as a few rules that call for evaluating specialized procedures (Chapter 6). It is a complex constraint satisfaction problem, with symbolic expressions of constraints. It was not readily coded in MYCIN-like rules because of the numerous comparison operations (for example, "minimizing").

An interpretation of the data, for instance "the diagnosis of the problem," is the usual goal in EMYCIN systems. In at least one case (SACON; see Chapter 16), however, a solution can have a somewhat more prescriptive flavor. Given a description of a problem, SACON does not solve it directly but rather describes what the user should do to solve it. The prescription of what to do "covers" the data in much the same way as a diagnosis covers the data. Because the evidence-gathering model fit this problem, it was not necessary to treat it as a constraint satisfaction problem.

Knowledge Base

The form of knowledge is assumed primarily to be situation-action rules and fact triples (with CF's). Other knowledge structures, such as tables of facts and specialized procedures, are included as well. Since the knowledge base is indexed and is small relative to the rest of the program, the size of the knowledge base should not be a limiting factor for most problems. MYCIN's knowledge base of 450 rules and about 1000 additional facts (in tables) is the largest with which we have had experience, although ONCOCIN is almost that large and is growing rapidly.

Solutions

As mentioned in the discussion of evidence gathering, the solutions are assumed to be subsets of elements from a predefined list. There are 120 organisms in MYCIN's list of possible causes. In this problem area, the evidence is generally considered insufficient for a precise determination of a unique solution or a strictly ordered list of solutions. Because the evidence is almost certainly incomplete in the first 24–48 hours of a severe infection, both MYCIN and physicians are expected to "cover for" a set of most likely and most risky causes. It is not expected that someone can uniquely identify "the cause" of the problem when the data are suggestive but still leave the problem underdetermined.

36.2.10 Project Organization

Funding

Funding for the research presented here was not easy to find because of the duality of goals mentioned above. Clinically oriented agencies of the government were looking for fully developed programs that could be sent to hospitals, private practices, military bases, or space installations. They saw the initial demonstration with bacteremia as a sign that ward-ready programs could be distributed as soon as knowledge of other infections was added to MYCIN. And they seemed to believe that transcribing sentences from textbooks into rules would produce knowledge bases with clinical expertise. Other funding agencies recognized that research was still required, but we failed to convince them that both medical *and* AI research were essential. We felt that the kinds of techniques we were using could help codify knowledge about infectious diseases and could help define a consensus position on issues about which there are differences of medical opinion. But we also felt that the AI techniques themselves needed analysis and extension before they could be used for wholesale extensions to medical knowledge. More generally, we saw medicine as a difficult real-world domain that is typical of many other domains. Failing to find an agency that would support both lines of activity, we submitted separate proposals for the dual lines. After the initial three years of NIH support for MYCIN, only the AI line was funded by the NSF, ONR, and DARPA (in the efforts that produced EMYCIN, GUIDON, and NEOMYCIN). By 1977 our medical collaborators were in transition for other reasons anyway, so we largely stopped developing the infectious disease knowledge base.[20]

Technology Transfer

When we began, we believed in the "better mousetrap" theory of technology transfer: build a high-performance program that solves an important problem, and the world will transfer the technology. We have learned that several elements of this naive theory are wrong. First, there is a bigger difference between acceptability and performance than we appreciated, as mentioned above. Second, there has to be a convenient mechanism of transfer. MYCIN ran only in Interlisp under the TENEX and TOPS-20

[20]That is not to say, however, that all medical efforts stopped. Shortliffe rejoined the project in 1979 and began defining and implementing ONCOCIN. Clancey needed to reformulate MYCIN's knowledge base in a form more suitable for tutoring (NEOMYCIN) and enlisted the help of Dr. Tim Beckett. Several medical problem areas were investigated and prototype systems were built using EMYCIN. These include pulmonary function testing (PUFF), blood clotting disorders (CLOT), and complications of pregnancy (GRAVIDA). And several masters and doctoral students have continued to use medicine as a test-bed for ideas in AI and decision making, causal reasoning, representation and learning. Several projects undertaken after 1977 are included in the present volume.

operating systems. Since hospital wards and physicians' offices do not have access to the same equipment that computer science laboratories do, we would have had to rewrite this large and complex system in another language to run on smaller machines. We were not motivated to undertake this task. Now, however, smaller, cheaper machines are available that do run Interlisp and other dialects of LISP, so technology transfer is much more feasible than when MYCIN was written.

Stability

We were fortunate with MYCIN in finding stability in (a) the goals of the project, (b) the code, and (c) the system environment.

The group of researchers defining the MYCIN project changed as students graduated, as interests changed, and as career goals took people out of our sphere. Shortliffe, Buchanan, Davis, Scott, Clancey, Fagan, Aikins, and van Melle formed a core group, however, that maintained a certain continuity. Even with a fluid group, we found stability in the overall goal of trying to build an AI system with acknowledged medical expertise. Those who felt this was too narrow a goal moved on quickly, while others found this sharp focus to be an anchor for defining their own research. Another anchor was the code itself. Much of any individual's code is opaque to others, and MYCIN contains its share of "patches" and "hacks." Yet because the persons writing code felt a responsibility to leave pieces of program that could be maintained and modified by others, the programming practices of most of the group were ecologically sound.[21] Finally, the stability of Interlisp, TENEX, and the SUMEX-AIM facility contributed greatly to our ability to build a system incrementally. Without this outside support, MYCIN could not have expanded in an orderly fashion and we would have been forced to undertake massive rewrites just to keep old code running.

36.3 Key Questions and Answers

We realize that a book of this size, describing several experiments that are interrelated in complex and sometimes subtle ways, may leave the reader asking exactly what has been learned by the research and what lessons can be borrowed by others already working in the field or about to enter it. This final chapter has attempted to summarize those lessons, but we feel the need to close with a brief list of frequently asked questions and our

[21]Bill van Melle, Carli Scott, and Randy Davis especially enforced this ethic. In particular, van Melle's system-building tools helped maintain the integrity of a rapidly changing, complex system.

answers to them. The responses are drawn from the work described in earlier chapters but are also colored by our familiarity with other work in AI (particularly research on expert systems). Despite the brevity and simplicity of the questions and answers, we feel that they do summarize the key lessons learned in the MYCIN experiments. For those readers who like to start at the end when deciding whether or not to read a book, we hope that the list will pique their curiosity and motivate them to start reading from the beginning.

- *Is a production rule formalism sufficient for creating programs that can reason at the level of an expert?*

  Yes, although we discovered many limitations and modified the "pure" production rule formalism in several ways in order to produce a program that met our design criteria.

- *Is backward chaining a good model of control for guiding the reasoning and the dialogue in consultation tasks?*

  Yes, particularly when the input data must be entered by the user, although for efficiency and human-engineering reasons it is desirable to augment it with forward chaining and meta-level control as well.

- *Is the evidence-gathering model useful in other domains?*

  Yes, there are many problems in which evidence must be gathered and weighed for a set of possible hypotheses. Infectious disease diagnosis is typical of many problems in having a prestored list of hypotheses that defines the search space. It is not the only useful model for hypothesis formation, however. In other problem areas, hypotheses can be synthesized from smaller elements and then evidence gathered for them in a manner closer to the generate-and-test approach. Or evidence can be gathered during the generation of hypotheses, as in the heuristic search model used in DENDRAL.

- *Is the CF model of inexact reasoning sufficiently precise for expert-level performance?*

  Yes, at least in domains where the evidence weights are used to cluster sets of most likely hypotheses rather than to select the "best" from among them. Some domains demand, and supply, finer precision than the CF model supports, but we felt we lost little information in reasoning with the infectious disease rules using the CF model. We would need to perform additional experiments to determine the breadth of the model's applicability, but we recognize that a calculus of more than one number allows finer distinctions.

- *What is the best way to build a large knowledge base?*

  Knowledge engineering is, for now. Because the problem areas we consider most appropriate for plausible reasoning are those that are not already completely structured (e.g., in sets of equations), constructing a knowledge base requires defining some new structures. Filling out a knowledge base, then, requires considerable testing and refinement in order to forge a robust and coherent set of plausible rules. Knowledge engineering requires a substantial investment in time for both the knowledge engineer and domain expert, but there are currently no better methods for transferring expertise to expert systems.

- *Were we successful in generalizing the problem-solving framework beyond the domain of infectious diseases?*

  Yes, EMYCIN has been demonstrated in many different problem areas. It has limitations, but its value in system building is more dependent on the structural match of the problem to the task of diagnosis than it is on the specific knowledge structures of the subject area.

- *Can the contents of an EMYCIN knowledge base be effectively used alone for tutoring students and trainees?*

  No, the knowledge base does not contain a rich enough model of the causal mechanisms, support knowledge, or taxonomies of a domain to allow a student to build a coherent picture of how the rules fit together or what the best problem-solving strategies are.

- *Is the consultation model of interaction a good one for a decision-making aid for physicians?*

  For physicians the tradeoff between time and benefit is the key consideration. A lengthy consultation will only be acceptable if there are major advantages for the patient or physician to be gained by using the system. For most applications, therefore, a decision-making aid should be integrated with routine activities rather than called separately for formal consultations. For practitioners in other fields, however, the consultation model may be quite acceptable.

- *Is a simple key word and phrase parser powerful enough for natural language interaction between users and a system in a technical domain?*

  Yes, as long as the user can tolerate a stylized interaction and tries to phrase responses and requests in understandable ways. The approach is probably not sufficient, however, for casual users who seldom use a system and accordingly have no opportunity to learn its linguistic idiosyncrasies.

- *Can we prove the correctness of conclusions from MYCIN?*

  No, because the heuristics carry no guarantees. However, we can demonstrate empirically how well experts judge the correctness of a program's conclusions by using a variant of Turing's test.

- *Why is MYCIN not used routinely and why are the rules not published?*

  Although MYCIN gives good advice and has been a marvelous source of new knowledge about expert systems and their design, computers that run Interlisp are still too expensive, and there are enough deficiencies in MYCIN's breadth of knowledge and user interface that it would not be a cost-effective tool for physicians to use on such narrow problem areas as meningitis and bacteremia. We have been asked why we have not published MYCIN's rules about infectious diseases as a service to physicians and medical students, even though the system itself is not available. The long answer is in Chapter 29, but the short answer is that it would not be a service. The rules, as written, do not separate the "key" factors from the context-setting factors, they omit many causal mechanisms that relate key factors with conclusions, and they (together with the rule interpreter) embody a strategy of medical diagnosis that is never explicit. They are not readable as text, nor were they intended to be. They make more sense in the context of *use* than they do in isolation.

- *Why does MYCIN work so well?*

  There are many reasons. First, the task was carefully chosen to increase the likelihood of success: infectious disease therapy selection is a combinatorial problem within a restricted (and relatively small) vocabulary, with time available for several seconds of reasoning, and with available local expertise. Also, there is not just one unique solution to a problem, but a set of acceptable conclusions. Second, the simple, modular knowledge structures we used were designed to be easily understood and changed. Thus the knowledge base could be built incrementally with rapid feedback, i.e., without losing much time to radical changes in underlying data structures and access functions. (In addition, the knowledge structures could be used for multiple interrelated purposes, thereby exploiting and further demonstrating the power and utility of a modular representation scheme.) Third, the research team was dedicated and highly motivated to make MYCIN work. Six doctoral dissertations on MYCIN and related programs resulted from these efforts, with at least as much effort expended by others not working for degrees.

Epilog

Although the "MYCIN gang" has disbanded, the excitement of creating the constellation of programs described in this book is still evident. The legacy of this group is a set of results that others can build on. We are proud to have been active in the definition and development of MYCIN and are enriched by having worked with such an outstanding group of individuals.

Appendix: Annotated Typescript of a Sample MYCIN Consultation

A.1 Instructions for Users at the Start of an Infectious Disease Consultation (Optional)

[Here, as elsewhere, the responses typed by the user follow a double-asterisk prompt.]

MYCIN 3-Jun-78 . . .

Special options (type ? for help):
**

Instructions? (Y or N)
** YES

This is a computer program named MYCIN that has been designed to advise you regarding an appropriate choice of infectious disease therapy. It is understood that you have a patient who may have an infection. Please answer the following questions, terminating each response with RETURN. To correct typing errors, use the DELETE key to delete single characters, <ctrl>W to delete a word, and <ctrl>Q to delete the whole line.

If you are not certain of your answer, you may modify the response by inserting a certainty factor (a number from 1 to 10) in parentheses after your response. Absolute certainty (10) is assumed for every unmodified answer. It is likely that some of the following questions cannot be answered with certainty.

You may change an answer to a previous question in two ways. If the program is waiting for a response from you (that is, has typed **), enter CHANGE followed by the number(s) of the question(s) whose answers will be altered. You may also change a previous answer at any time (even when the program is not waiting for a response from you) by typing <ctrl>F (Fix), which will cause the program to interrupt its computation and ask what you want to change. (If the response to <ctrl>F is not immediate, try typing the RETURN key in addition.) Try to avoid going back because the process requires reconsidering the patient from the beginning and therefore may be slow.

Note that you may also enter UNK (for UNKnown) if you do not know the answer to a question, ? if you wish to see a more precise definition of the question or some examples of recognized responses, ?? if you want to see all recognized responses, the word RULE if you would like to see the decision rule which has generated the question being asked, the word WHY if you would like to see a more detailed explanation of the question, or the letters QA if you would like to interrupt the consultation in order to ask questions regarding the decisions made so far in the consultation. If you are ever puzzled about what options are available to you during a consultation, enter the word HELP and a list of options will be listed for you.

Sample Response [user input follows the **]
Does the patient have a risk factor for tuberculosis?
**?

One or more of the following are considered risk factors for TB: a) positive PPD (5TU), b) history of close contact with a person having active TB, c) household member with a past history of active TB, d) chest X-ray showing apical scarring, e) granulomas seen on biopsy of any organ tissue.

expected responses are: YES NO
Enter HELP for user options.
** YES

SUMMARY:
(type ctrl-O to abort printout)

UNK -	Answer not known.
? -	Rephrases the question and gives examples of recognized responses.
?? -	Prints a list of all recognized responses.
RULE -	Prints the current decision rule.
QA -	Program enters question-answering mode.
CHANGE # -	Go back and re-request answer to question number #.
COMMENT -	Enter comments about any aspect of the system's performance. Your comments will be forwarded to those in charge of the MYCIN program.
WHY -	Gives high-level explanation of the current reasoning chain that provoked this question.
HOW # -	Explains HOW the system will achieve a goal referred to by number # in a previous explanation.
EXPLAIN -	Provides a more detailed explanation of a previous answer given by a WHY command.
FORGET -	Resets the explanation of the reasoning chain back to lowest level, as if you never used the WHY/EXPLAIN commands.
STOP -	Halts the program without completing the consultation.
SAVE -	Halts the program, saving the current patient on a disk file, retrievable at a later date.
HELP -	Prints this list.

A.2 Infectious Disease Consultation Session

[This is a typescript of a MYCIN consultation on an actual patient treated at Stanford. MYCIN was not used to suggest treatment. Spaces have been added for readability, and comments (in italics) have been inserted. Otherwise it is a verbatim transcript. User's responses follow double asterisks.]

--------PATIENT-538--------
1) Patient's name:
** PT538 *[Name, age, sex, and race are always asked because they are INITIALDATA.]*
2) Age:
** 34 YEARS
3) Sex:
** MAEL
=MALE *[MYCIN corrects misspellings.]*
4) Race:
** WHY *[The user asks for an explanation. In this instance it is trivial.]*

[i.e. WHY is it important to determine the race of PATIENT-538?]

[1.0] The race of a patient is one of the 5 standard parameters that identify
a patient.
This may be useful later in the consultation. For example, it is
relevant in determining the organisms (other than those seen on cultures
or smears) which might be causing the infection.

[back to question 4...]
** CAUCASIAN *[This is the answer to the question about race.]*

Please supply one answer under each heading. If your response is not

understood, you will be prompted by the standard questioning method.
(enter ? for normal prompting, * for questions that are not applicable.)

Please enter the results of positive cultures using the following table.

site	culture number	date collected	date| positive	method| of collection [urine,sputum only]

5)**DONE

[The next question asks for several items in tabular form since they are found together in the hospital record.]

Please enter the results of pending cultures in the following table.

site	culture number	date collected	stain| examined	method of| collection [urine,sputum only]

6)** CSF 1234 30-Jan-77 YES *

stain of smear	morph|

[MYCIN follows up on the stain of the smear and the morphology.]

[type DONE if no organism was seen on the smear]

7)**DONE

[No information about stain or morphology is available. MYCIN now follows up question 6, asking about other positive cultures.]

site	cul #	date coll.	smear examined?|	coll. method|

8)**DONE *[There are no more positive cultures.]*

Please enter negative cultures in the following table.

site	culture number	date| collected	method of| collection [urine,sputum only]

9)**DONE *[There are no negative cultures.]*

10) Do you suspect Pt538 may have an infection at a site from which you have not obtained culture specimens?
** NO

Please enter information on current antimicrobials.

drug name	route of administration	date| started
11)** CEPHALOTHIN	IV	23-Jan-77

12)**DONE

Please enter information on prior antimicrobials.

drug name	route of administration	date| started	date| stopped

13)**DONE

[Considering organisms (other than those isolated from cultures) which might be present. . .]

14) Has Pt538 recently had symptoms of persistent headache or other abnormal neurologic symptoms (dizziness, lethargy, etc.)?
** YES
15) Has Pt538 recently had objective evidence of abnormal neurologic signs (nuchal rigidity, coma, seizures, etc.) documented by physician observation or examination?
** YES

The CSF cultures will be considered to be associated with MENINGITIS.

16) Please give the date on which clinical evidence (symptoms, signs, or laboratory tests) of the meningitis first appeared.
** 29-Jan-77 22:15
17) Does Pt538 have an abnormal chest X-ray?
** NO
18) Does Pt538 have one or more of the following risk factors for TB: a) positive intermediate strength PPD, b) history of close contact with a person with active TB, c) a household member with a past history of active TB, d) apical scarring on chest X-ray, e) history of granulomas on biopsy of liver, lymph node, or other organs?
** NO
19) Does Pt538 have any cutaneous lesions or rash on physical examination?
** NO
20) Does Pt538 have evidence of ocular nerve dysfunction?
** NO
21) Is Pt538 a compromised host (e.g. alcoholic, sickle-cell-disease, immunosuppressed)?
** YES
22) Is Pt538 immunosuppressed (e.g. corticosteroid therapy, cytotoxic drug therapy, radiation therapy, leukemia, lymphoma)?
** NO
23) For how many days has Pt538 had abnormal neurologic signs?
** 7.2 HOURS

[Note that the answer was given in hours. MYCIN has to be flexible enough to convert units.]

24) For how many days has Pt538 had neurologic symptoms?
** 1 DAYS
25) Has Pt538 had recent evidence of tender or enlarged salivary glands?
** NO
26) Has Pt538 been exposed to any contagious disease recently (e.g. meningococcal disease, mumps) ?
** NO

Please enter CSF findings in the following table

	CSF WBC	Percent PMN	Protein	CSF Glucose	Peripheral Glucose
27)**	100	99	280	5	UNKNOWN

[Note that some information is missing.]

28) Do you know the results of a recent CBC of Pt538?
** YES

Please enter CBC results in the following table

	WBC in 1000's	Percent PMN	Percent BANDS
29)**	1.9	UNKNOWN	UNKNOWN

30) Has Pt538 had any injury or insult to, or defect in the central-nervous-system (excluding neurosurgery)?
** NO
31) Has Pt538 ever undergone any type of surgery?
** YES
32) Does Pt538 have a history of NEUROSURGERY?
** NO
33) Does Pt538 live in a crowded environment?
** NO
34) Do you suspect recent alcoholic history in Pt538?
** NO
35) Is meningitis a hospital-acquired infection?
** WHY

[This is a more interesting question, requiring presentation of the rule that caused question 35 to be asked. Note that the first five clauses of the rule have been investigated and question 35 is motivated by the last clause. MYCIN first rephrases the question to give the user its interpretation of the WHY.]

[i.e. WHY is it important to determine whether the infection was acquired while the patient was hospitalized?]

[2.0] This will aid in determining the organisms (other than those seen on
cultures or smears) which might be causing the infection.
It has already been established that
[2.1] the infection which requires therapy is meningitis, and
[2.2] organisms were not seen on the stain of this pending CSF culture,
and
[2.3] the type of the infection is bacterial, and
[2.4] neurosurgery is not one of the relevant items from the history
of Pt538, and
[2.5] the age of Pt538 is greater than 10 days
Therefore, if
[2.6] the infection was acquired while the patient was hospitalized
then
there is evidence that the organisms (other than those seen on
cultures or smears) which might be causing the infection is e.coli
(.75) staphylococcus-coag-pos (.3) pseudomonas-aeruginosa (.3)
klebsiella-pneumoniae (.5)
Author: Yu
[RULE545]

[back to question 35. . .]

[MYCIN now requests the answer to question 35 again. Instead of answering, the user asks how clause 2.3 was confirmed.]

** HOW 2.3

[i.e. HOW was it established that the type of the infection is bacterial?]

[Rather than printing the contents of the rules, MYCIN shows the rule numbers and the strength of positive and negative evidence from each rule.]

The following rules concluded about:
the likelihood that the type of the infection is bacterial

	Rule	Yes	No
[2.7]	RULE148	(.19)	
[2.8]	RULE500	(.51)	
[2.9]	RULE501	(.95)	
[3.0]	RULE502	(.97)	
[3.1]	RULE526	(.98)	
[3.2]	RULE504	(.97)	
[3.3]	RULE524	(.98)	

Thus, it has been established that the type of the infection is bacterial.

[back to question 35...]
** HOW 2.5

[i.e. HOW was it established that the age of pt538 is greater than 10 days?]

In answer to question 2 you said that the age of pt538 is 34 years

Thus, it has been established that the age of pt538 is greater than 10 days.

[back to question 35. . .]
** Y
36) Is Pt538's clinical history consistent with EPIGLOTTITIS?
** NO
37) Is Pt538's clinical history consistent with OTITIS-MEDIA?
** NO
38) Has Pt538 ever undergone splenectomy?
** NO
39) Is Pt538 a burn patient?
** WHY *[Another explanation is requested.]*

[i.e. WHY is it important to determine whether PATIENT-538 has been seriously
burned?]

[4.0] This will aid in determining the organisms (other than those seen on
cultures or smears) which might be causing the infection.
It has already been established that
[4.1] the infection which requires therapy is meningitis, and
[4.2] organisms were not seen on the stain of this pending CSF culture,
and
[4.3] the type of the infection is bacterial
Therefore, if
[4.4] pt538 has been seriously burned
then
there is suggestive evidence (.5) that pseudomonas-aeruginosa is one
of the organisms (other than those seen on cultures or smears)
which might be causing the infection
Author: Yu
[RULE578]

[back to question 39. . .]
** WHY *[In this case, the user asks another WHY question, backing up the subgoal tree.]*

[i.e. WHY is it important to determine the organisms (other than those seen
on cultures or smears) which might be causing the infection?]

[5.0] ... in order to determine the therapeutic regimen of PATIENT-538.
If
[5.1] information has been gathered about organisms isolated from the
patient, organisms noted on smears of the patient, negative
cultures of the patient, suspected infections without
microbiological evidence, current drugs of the patient and prior drugs of the patient, and
[5.2] an attempt has been made to deduce the organisms which require
therapy, and
[5.3] You have given consideration to organisms (other than those
seen in cultures or smears) which might be present, and found
at least one organism which requires therapy.
then
determine the best therapy recommendation from among the drugs likely
to be effective against the significant organisms
[RULE092]

[back to question 39. . .]
** Y

[MYCIN now prints its intermediate conclusions about the likely causes of the infection.]

I have found evidence (RULE545 RULE557) that treatment should cover for E.coli
causing meningitis.
I have found evidence (RULE545 RULE557 RULE578) that treatment should cover
for Pseudomonas-aeruginosa causing meningitis.
I have found evidence (RULE545 RULE557) that treatment should cover for
Klebsiella-pneumoniae causing meningitis.
I have found evidence (RULE507) that treatment should cover for Diplococcus-
pneumoniae causing meningitis.

[Now MYCIN begins to ask questions related to appropriate therapy.]

40) Does Pt538 have focal neurological signs?
** UNKNOWN

[Some questions are motivated by the organism under consideration. Thus the following lines sometimes provide useful contextual information to a user.]

[Determining which drugs are desirable for use against the E.coli. . .]
[Determining which drugs are desirable for use against the Pseudomonas-
aeruginosa. . .]

[Determining which drugs are desirable for use against the Klebsiella-pneumoniae. . .]
[Determining which drugs are desirable for use against the Diplococcus-pneumoniae. . .]

My therapy recommendations will be designed to treat for organisms that either are very likely or, although less likely, would have a significant effect on therapy selection if they were present. It is important to cover for the following probable infection(s) and associated organism(s):

INFECTION-1 is MENINGITIS

+ <ITEM-1> E.COLI [from clinical evidence only]
+ <ITEM-2> PSEUDOMONAS-AERUGINOSA [from clinical evidence only]
+ <ITEM-3> KLEBSIELLA-PNEUMONIAE [from clinical evidence only]
+ <ITEM-4> DIPLOCOCCUS-PNEUMONIAE [from clinical evidence only]

41) Does Pt538 have a clinically significant allergic reaction to any antimicrobial agent?
** NO
[Considering AMPICILLIN-AND-GENTAMICIN for use against INFECTION-1...]
42) Do you have reason to suspect that Pt538 may have impaired renal function?
** NO

43) Pt538's weight in kilograms (or <number> POUNDS):
** 70

[Finally, MYCIN prints the best therapy it has found to maximize the chances of effective coverage of the cause(s) of the infection while minimizing the number of drugs, their toxicity, and side effects.]

[REC-1] My preferred therapy recommendation is as follows:
In order to cover for Items <1 2 3 4>:
Give the following in combination:
1) AMPICILLIN
Dose: 3.5g (28.0 ml) q4h IV [calculated on basis of 50 mg/kg]

2) GENTAMICIN
Dose: 119 mg (3.0 ml, 80mg/2ml ampule) q8h IV [calculated on basis of 1.7 mg/kg plus consider giving 5 mg q24h Intrathecal
Comments: Monitor serum concentrations

Since high concentrations of penicillins can inactivate aminoglycosides, do not mix these two antibiotics in the same IV bottle.

Do you wish to see the next choice therapy?

** YES *[Other therapies can be examined.]*

Which, if any, of the above drugs do you wish eliminated from consideration?
** AMPICILLIN

[Considering GENTAMICIN for use against INFECTION-1...]
[Considering PENICILLIN for use against INFECTION-1...]

[REC-2] Next best therapy recommendation:
In order to cover for Items <1 2 3>:
Give: GENTAMICIN
Dose: 119 mg (3.0 ml, 80mg/2ml ampule) q8h IV [calculated on basis of 1.7 mg/kg] plus consider giving 5 mg q24h Intrathecal
Comments: Monitor serum concentrations

In order to cover for Item <4>:
Give: PENICILLIN
Dose: 3.5 million units (7.0 ml) q4h IV [calculated on basis of 50000 units/kg]

RECOMMENDATION-2 is equivalent to RECOMMENDATION-1.

Would you like to see details of this comparison?
** YES

Looking at the coverage of the 'most likely' items, we see that:

RECOMMENDATION-1 consists of 1 first choice drug (AMPICILLIN for ITEM-1 and ITEM-4) and 1 third choice drug (GENTAMICIN for ITEM-1, ITEM-2 and ITEM-3)

RECOMMENDATION-2 consists of 1 first choice drug (PENICILLIN for ITEM-4) and 1 third choice drug (GENTAMICIN for ITEM-2, ITEM-1 and ITEM-3)

ORGANISMS	RECOMMENDATION-1	RECOMMENDATION-2
'most likely'	Drug -- Choice Ranking	Drug -- Choice Ranking
ITEM-1	AMPICILLIN-AND-GENTAMICIN--1st	GENTAMICIN--3rd
ITEM-2	GENTAMICIN--2nd	GENTAMICIN--2nd
ITEM-3	GENTAMICIN--3rd	GENTAMICIN--3rd
ITEM-4	AMPICILLIN--1st	PENICILLIN--1st

(The desirability of a drug is defined to be its lowest ranking for the items it covers.)

Do you wish to see the next choice therapy?
** NO

A.3 Answers to User's Questions About This Consultation and About the Knowledge Base

Please ask any simple-English questions regarding the above consultation session or the overall knowledge of the consultation system. When discussing the consultation above, please refer to organisms, cultures, etc. by their numeric names (e.g., ORGANISM-1). Questions which were asked during the consultation may be specified by the numbers that preceded them above, (e.g., WHY DID YOU ASK QUESTION 1?). Control-O will abort type-out, or cancel the current question. Type HELP for a list of the options available. Enter the word STOP when you have no further questions.

Type HELP for the list of question options.

** HELP

QA-OPTIONS:
(Type ctrl-O to abort printout)

ADVICE --	Prints suggestions for using the QA system effectively.
QT --	Prints examples of question types recognized by the system.
EQ <numbers> --	Prints an explanation of the specified question(s) from the consultation, e.g., EQ 8 13.
LP <object type> --	Prints list of attributes associated with object type, e.g., LP CULTURE. (Object types are patient, infection, culture, organism, and drug.)
PR <numbers> --	Prints specified rule(s), e.g., PR 373 49 87 2.
EXPLTHER --	Prints a short description of the therapy program
REC --	Prompts user for alternative therapy RECommendation and compares it to MYCIN's recommendation.
RX <infection> <organism identities> --	Prints treatment lists for specified organisms causing the indicated infection, e.g., RX MENINGITIS ENTEROCOCCUS.
JUSTIFICATION --	When rules are printed out, include their justifications.
LITERATURE --	When rules are printed out, include their literature references.
NOJUST --	Stop giving justification and/or literature with rules.
TERSE --	Print rules in terse format.
VERBOSE --	Turns off terse printing of rules.
STOP --	Escape from QA-module.
HELP --	Prints this list.

** JUSTIFICATION

** LITERATURE

** WHY DID YOU TREAT E.COLI?

ITEM-1 is E.coli associated with meningitis. I decided to treat ITEM-1 on
the basis of clinical evidence only.

The following rules concluded about:
the likelihood that e.coli is one of the organisms (other than those
seen on cultures or smears) which might be causing the infection

RULE545 was used to conclude that e.coli is one of the organisms (other than
those seen on cultures or smears) which might be causing the infection
(.74). The last question asked before the conclusion was made was 35.
RULE557 was used to conclude that e.coli is one of the organisms (other than
those seen on cultures or smears) which might be causing the infection
(.93). The last question asked before the conclusion was made was 37.

[A summary of why E. coli was treated shows the parameters associated with E. coli as a likely cause of the infection.]

The parameters most frequently used in these rules were:
the infection which requires therapy
whether a smear of the culture was examined
whether organisms were seen on the stain of the culture
the type of the infection

Would you like a summary of ALL the parameters used by these rules?
** YES

Parameter (rules with this parameter)

the white count from the patient's peripheral CBC (in thousands) (557)
whether the results of a recent CBC of the patient are available (557)
whether the infection was acquired while the patient was hospitalized (545)
the age of the patient (545)
the relevant items from the history of the patient (545)
the type of the infection (545, 557)
whether organisms were seen on the stain of the culture (545, 557)
whether a smear of the culture was examined (545, 557)
the infection which requires therapy (545, 557)

[The next question is about MYCIN's knowledge in general, not about the conclusions drawn for the case just discussed.]

** HOW DO YOU USE THE TYPE OF THE INFECTION?
The following rules use:
the type of the infection

154, 578, 574, 572, 570, 565, 564, 559, 557, 553, 551, 549, 547, 545, 543, 541,
539, 537, 535, 533, 531, 529, 523, 520, 519, 517, 515, 513, 511, 507, 300,
289, 288, 287, 280, 174, 167

The parameter most frequently concluded by these rules is:
the organisms (other than those seen on cultures or smears) which might
be causing the infection

Would you like a summary of ALL the parameters concluded by these rules?
** NO

Which of the rules do you wish to see?
** 280

RULE280

[This rule applies to all cultures, and is tried in order to find out about
the organisms (other than those seen on cultures or smears) which might
be causing the infection]

If: 1) The infection which requires therapy is meningitis, and
2) The type of the infection is fungal, and
3) Organisms were not seen on the stain of the culture, and
4) The patient is not a compromised host, and
5) The patient has been to an area that is endemic for coccidiomycoses, and
6) The race of the patient is one of: black asian indian, and
7) The cryptococcal antigen in the CSF was not positive
Then: There is suggestive evidence (.5) that cryptococcus is not one of the
organisms (other than those seen on cultures or smears) which
might be causing the infection
Author: YU
Justification: Dark-skinned races, especially Filipino, Asian, and Black (in
that order) have an increased susceptibility to coccidiomycoses
meningitis.
Literature: Stevens, D.A. et al. Miconazole in Coccidiomycosis. Am J Med,
60:191-202, Feb 1976.

A.4 Therapy Recommendation Consultation Session

[If the infection and organism identities are known, MYCIN can still be helpful in recommending appropriate therapy.]

MYCIN 3-Jun-78 . . .

Special options (type ? for help):
** REC

Instructions? (Y or N)
** YES

This program recommends therapy for a patient with infectious diseases. You will be asked a few facts about the patient which will be used to determine the dosages and appropriateness of giving certain antibiotics. Then you will be prompted for the infection(s) that you want treated and the organism(s) which you feel may be responsible for each infecton.

MYCIN cannot make a recommendation without knowing the infection(s) and organism(s) to be treated. Other information is requested for the purpose of refining therapy selection, but is not essential; you may answer UNKNOWN to any of these questions.

Case 2, AA, 47-24-3l, VMC, A 3 year old female with one day history of headache, lethargy, fever to 104. L.P.: Protein 25, glucose 95 110 cells with 96% polys. Pe: Meningismus, petechiae on arms and shoulders.

28-NOV-77 11:05:51
[consultation of 23-JUN-76 12:00]

--------PATIENT-683--------
1) Patient's name: (first-last)
** PT683
2) Age:
** 3.5
3) Sex:
** FEMALE
4) Is Pt683 currently receiving therapy with any antimicrobial agent?
** NO

```
  5) During the present illness, has Pt683 been treated with an
     antimicrobial agent which is no longer being administered?
  ** NO
Infection: MENINGITIS
Organism: VIRUS
    [Determining which drugs are desirable for use against the Virus. . .]
  Are there any other organisms which might be causing this meningitis?
** YES
Organism: HEMOPHILUS-INFLUENZAE
  6) Has the lab reported the in-vitro antibiotic sensitivities of the
     hemophilus-influenzae causing the meningitis (ITEM-2)?
  ** N
    [Determining which drugs are desirable for use against the Hemophilus-
        influenzae. . .]
  7) Does Pt683 have a clinically significant allergic reaction to any
     antimicrobial agent?
  ** NO
  Are there any other organisms which might be causing this meningitis?
** YES
Organism: NEISSERIA-MENINGITIDIS
8) Has the lab reported the in-vitro antibiotic sensitivities of the
   neisseria-meningitidis causing the meningitis (ITEM-3)?
** N
  [Determining which drugs are desirable for use against the Neisseria-
      meningitidis. . .]
Are there any other organisms which might be causing this meningitis?
** NO
Are there additional infections for which you want therapy recommendations?
** NO

INFECTION-1 is MENINGITIS

  + ...           VIRUS Supportive therapy.
  + <ITEM-2>      HEMOPHILUS-INFLUENZAE
  + <ITEM-3>      NEISSERIA-MENINGITIDIS

[Considering AMPICILLIN-AND-CHLORAMPHENICOL for use against INFECTION-1. . .]
  9) What is the most recent creatinine clearance in ml/min which you feel
     is a true representation of Pt683's renal function?
  ** UNKNOWN
  10) What is the most recent serum creatinine of Pt683 (in mg/100ml)?
  ** UNKNOWN

  11) Pt683's weight in kilograms (or <number> POUNDS):
  ** 17.7
[REC-1] My preferred therapy recommendation is as follows:
  In order to cover for Items <2 3>:
    Give the following in combination:
    1) AMPICILLIN
    Dose: 886 mg (7.0 ml) q4h IV [calculated on basis of 50 mg/kg]
    [The dose should be modified in SEVERE renal failure. I can adjust
        the dose only if a creatinine clearance or a serum creatinine
        is obtained, and the patient's weight is known.]

    2) CHLORAMPHENICOL
    Dose: 443 mg (4.4 ml) q6h IV [calculated on basis of 25 mg/kg]
```

Please ask any simple-English questions regarding the above consultation session or the overall knowledge of the consultation system. When discussing the consultation above, please refer to organisms, cultures, etc. by their numeric names (e.g. ORGANISM-1). Questions which were asked during the consultation may be specified by the numbers that preceded them above, (e.g., WHY DID YOU ASK QUESTION 1?). Control-O will abort type-out, or cancel the current question. Type HELP for a list of the options available. Enter the word STOP when you have no further questions.

Type HELP for the list of question options.

** JUSTIFICATION

** LITERATURE

[MYCIN can compare its recommendation against one that the user would like to consider.]

** REC
For each item in turn, enter the drug you would have prescribed in RECOMMENDATION-1.
In order to minimize the number of drugs in your recommendation, you may not want to prescribe therapy for every item. Items which represent the most likely organisms are indicated with a plus sign (+).

+ ITEM-1—the virus **
+ ITEM-2—the hemophilus-influenzae ** CARBENICILLIN
+ ITEM-3—the neisseria-meningitidis ** CARBENICILLIN

[Checking for contraindications. . .]
[Considering CARBENICILLIN for use against INFECTION-1. . .]
[No contraindications found. . .]

[Now comparing your prescription to MYCIN's. . .]

ORGANISMS	MYCIN's regimen	Your regimen
"most likely"	Drug -- Choice Ranking	Drug -- Choice Ranking
ITEM-2	AMPICILLIN-AND-CHLORAMPHENICOL--1st	CARBENICILLIN--3rd
ITEM-3	AMPICILLIN--1st	CARBENICILLIN--2nd

(The desirability of a drug is defined to be its lowest ranking for the items it covers.)

[Giving one drug is often preferable to giving two. In this case, however, the one would not be as effective.]

Your recommendation for the most likely organism(s) is not optimal, since your prescription of 1 third choice drug (CARBENICILLIN for ITEM-3 and ITEM-2) should be avoided.

[You may refer to your regimen as RECOMMENDATION-2 in later questions.]

** STOP

References

Abelson, R. 1973. The structure of belief systems. In *Computer Models of Thought and Language,* eds. R. C. Schank and K. M. Colby, pp. 287–339. San Francisco: Freeman.

Adams, J. B. 1976. A probability model of medical reasoning and the MYCIN model. *Mathematical Biosciences* 32: 177–186. (Appears as Chapter 12 in this volume.)

Aiello, N. 1983. A comparative study of control strategies for expert systems: AGE implementation of three variations of PUFF. In *Proceedings of the Third National Conference on Artificial Intelligence,* pp. 1–4.

Aiello, N., and Nii, H. P. 1981. AGE-PUFF: A simple event-driven program. Report no. HPP-81-25, Computer Science Department, Stanford University

Aikins, J. S. 1979. Prototypes and production rules: An approach to knowledge representation for hypothesis formation. In *Proceedings of the 6th International Joint Conference on Artificial Intelligence* (Tokyo), pp. 1–3. (Appears with revisions as Chapter 23 of this volume.)

———. 1980. Prototypes and production rules: a knowledge representation for computer consultations. Ph.D. dissertation, Stanford University. (Also Stanford Report no. STAN-CS-80-814.)

———. 1983. Prototypical knowledge for expert systems. *Artificial Intelligence* 20(2): 163–210.

Aikins, J. S., Kunz, J. C., Shortliffe, E. H., and Fallat, R. J. 1983. PUFF: An expert system for interpretation of pulmonary function data. *Computers and Biomedical Research* 16: 199–208.

Allen, J. 1978. *Anatomy of LISP.* New York: McGraw-Hill.

Anderson, J. 1976. *Language, Memory and Thought.* Hillsdale, NJ: Erlbaum.

Anthony, J. R. 1970. Effect on deciduous and permanent teeth of tetracycline deposition in utero. *Postgraduate Medicine* 48(4): 165–168.

Barker, S. F. 1957. *Induction and Hypothesis: A Study of the Logic of Confirmation.* Ithaca, NY: Cornell University Press.

Barnett, J. A. 1981. Computational methods for a mathematical theory of evidence. In *Proceedings of the 7th International Joint Conference on Artificial Intelligence* (Vancouver, B.C.), pp. 868–875.

Barnett, J. A., and Erman, L. 1982. Making control decisions in an expert system is a problem-solving task. Technical report, Information Sciences Institute, University of Southern California.

Barr, A., and Feigenbaum, E. A. (eds.). 1981, 1982. *The Handbook of Artificial Intelligence* (vols. 1, 2). Los Altos, CA: Kaufmann.

Barr, A., Beard, M., and Atkinson, R. C. 1976. The computer as a tutorial laboratory: The Stanford BIP project. *International Journal of Man-Machine Studies* 8: 567–596.

Bartlett, F. C. 1932. *Remembering: A Study in Experimental and Social Psychology.* Cambridge, U.K.: Cambridge University Press.

Bennett, J. S. 1983. ROGET: A knowledge-based consultant for acquiring the conceptual structure of an expert system. Report no. HPP-83-24, Computer Science Department, Stanford University.

Bennett, J. S., and Goldman, D. 1980. CLOT: A knowledge-based consultant for bleeding disorders. Report no. HPP-80-7, Computer Science Department, Stanford University.

Bennett, J. S., and Hollander, C. R. 1981. DART: An expert system for computer fault diagnosis. In *Proceedings of the 7th International Joint Conference on Artificial Intelligence* (Vancouver, B.C.), pp. 843–845.

Bennett, J. S., Creary, L., Engelmore, R., and Melosh, R. 1978. SACON: A knowledge-based consultant for structural analysis. Report no. HPP-78-23, Computer Science Department, Stanford University.

Bischoff, M., Shortliffe, E. H., Scott, A. C., Carlson, R. W., and Jacobs, D. 1983. Integration of a computer-based consultant into the clinical setting. In *Proceedings of the 7th Symposium on Computer Applications in Medical Care* (Baltimore, MD), pp. 149–152.

Blum, B. I., Lenhard, R., and McColligan, E. 1980. Protocol directed patient care using a computer. In *Proceedings of 4th Symposium on Computer Applications in Medical Care* (Washington, D.C.), pp. 753–761.

Blum, R. L. 1982. Discovery and representation of causal relationships from a large time-oriented clinical database: The RX project. Ph.D. dissertation, Stanford University. (Also in *Computers and Biomedical Research* 15: 164–187.)

Bobrow, D. G. 1968. Natural language input for a computer problem-solving system. In *Semantic Information Processing,* ed. M. Minsky, pp. 146–226. Cambridge, MA: MIT Press.

Bobrow, D. G., and Winograd, T. 1977. An overview of KRL, a knowledge representation language. *Cognitive Science* 1: 3–46.

Bobrow, D. G., Kaplan, R. M., Kay, M., Norman, D., Thompson, H., and Winograd, T. 1977. GUS: A frame-driven dialog system. *Artificial Intelligence* 8: 155–173.

Bobrow, R. J., and Brown, J. S. 1975. Systematic understanding: Synthesis, analysis and contingent knowledge in specialized understanding systems. In *Representation and Understanding: Studies in Cognitive Science,* eds. D. G. Bobrow and A. Collins, pp. 103–129. New York: Academic Press.

Bonnet, A. 1981. LITHO: An expert system for lithographic analysis. Internal working paper, Schlumberger Corp., Paris, France.

Boyd, E. 1935. *The Growth of the Surface Area of the Human Body.* Minneapolis: University of Minnesota Press.

Brachman, R. J. 1976. What's in a concept: Structural foundations for semantic networks. Report no. 3433, Bolt Beranek and Newman.

Bransford, J., and Franks, J. 1971. The abstraction of linguistic ideas. *Cognitive Psychology* 2: 331–350.

Brown, J. S., and Burton, R. R. 1978. Diagnostic models for procedural bugs in mathematical skills. *Cognitive Science* 2: 155–192.

Brown, J. S., and Goldstein, I. P. 1977. Computers in a learning society. Testimony for the House Science and Technology Subcommittee on Domestic and International Planning, Analysis and Cooperation, October, 1977.

Brown, J. S., and VanLehn, K. 1980. Repair theory: A generative theory of bugs in procedural skills. *Cognitive Science* 4(4): 379–426.

Brown, J. S., Burton, R. R., and Zydbel, F. 1973. A model-driven question-answering system for mixed-initiative computer-assisted instruction. *IEEE Transactions on Systems, Man, and Cybernetics* SMC-3(3): 248–257.

Brown, J. S., Burton, R. R., and Bell, A. G. 1974. SOPHIE: A sophisticated instructional environment for teaching electronic troubleshooting (an example of AI in CAI). Report no. 2790, Bolt Beranek and Newman.

Brown, J. S., Burton, R., Miller, M., de Kleer, J., Purcell, S., Hausmann, C., and Bobrow, R. 1975. Steps toward a theoretic foundation for complex knowledge-based CAI. Report no. 3135, Bolt Beranek and Newman.

Brown, J. S., Rubenstein, R., and Burton, R. 1976. Reactive learning environment for computer-aided electronics instruction. Report no. 3314, Bolt Beranek and Newman.

Brown, J. S., Burton, R. R., and de Kleer, J. 1982. Pedagogical, natural language, and knowledge engineering techniques in SOPHIE I, II, and III. In *Intelligent Tutoring Systems,* eds. D. Sleeman and J. S. Brown, pp. 227–282. London: Academic Press.

Bruce, B. C. 1975. Generation as a social action. In *Proceedings of the Conference on Theoretical Issues in Natural Language Processing,* pp. 74–77.

Buchanan, B. G., and Duda, R. O. 1983. Principles of rule-based expert systems. In *Advances in Computers* (vol. 22), ed. M. C. Yovits, pp. 164–216. New York: Academic Press.

Buchanan, B. G., and Feigenbaum, E. A. 1978. DENDRAL and Meta-DENDRAL: Their applications dimension. *Artificial Intelligence* 11: 5–24.

Buchanan, B. G., and Mitchell, T. 1978. Model-directed learning of production rules. In *Pattern-Directed Inference Systems,* eds. D. Waterman and F. Hayes-Roth, pp. 297–312. New York: Academic Press.

Buchanan, B. G., Sutherland, G., and Feigenbaum, E. A. 1970. Rediscovering some problems of artificial intelligence in the context of organic chemistry. In *Machine Intelligence 5,* eds. B. Meltzer and D. Michie, pp. 209–254. Edinburgh, U.K.: Edinburgh University Press.

Buchanan, B. G., Mitchell, T. M., Smith, R. G., and Johnson, C. R., Jr. 1978. Models of learning systems. In *Encyclopedia of Computer Science and Technology* 11, ed. J. Belzer, pp. 24–51. New York: Marcel Dekker.

Bullwinkle, C. 1977. Levels of complexity in discourse for anaphora disambiguation and speech act interpretation. In *Proceedings of the 5th International Joint Conference on Artificial Intelligence* (Cambridge, MA), pp. 43–49.

Burton, R. R. 1976. Semantic grammar: An engineering technique for constructing natural language understanding systems. Report no. 3453, Bolt Beranek and Newman.

———. 1979. An investigation of computer coaching for informal learning activities. *International Journal of Man-Machine Studies* 11: 5–24.

Burton, R. R., and Brown, J. S. 1982. An investigation of computer coaching for informal learning activities. In *Intelligent Tutoring Systems,* eds. D. Sleeman and J. S. Brown, pp. 79–98. New York: Academic Press.

Carbonell, J. R. 1970a. AI in CAI: An artificial-intelligence approach to computer-assisted instruction. *IEEE Transactions on Man-Machine Systems,* MMS-11: 190–202.

———. 1970b. Mixed-initiative man-computer instructional dialogues. Report no. 1971, Bolt Beranek and Newman.

Carbonell, J. R., and Collins, A. M. 1973. Natural semantics in artificial intelligence. In *Advance Papers of the 3rd International Joint Conference on Artificial Intelligence* (Stanford, CA), pp. 344–351.

Carden, T. S. 1974. The antibiotic problem (editorial). *New Physician* 23: 19.

Carnap, R. 1950. The two concepts of probability. In *Logical Foundations of Probability,* pp. 19–51. Chicago: University of Chicago Press.

———. 1962. The aim of inductive logic. In *Logic, Methodology, and Philosophy of Science,* eds. E. Nagel, P. Suppes, and A. Tarski, pp. 303–318. Stanford, CA: Stanford University Press.

Carr, B., and Goldstein, I. 1977. Overlays: A theory of modeling for CAI. Report no. 406, Artificial Intelligence Laboratory, Massachusetts Institute of Technology.

Chandrasekaran, B., Gomez, F., Mittal, S., and Smith, J. 1979. An approach to medical diagnosis based on conceptual schemes. In *Proceedings of the 6th International Joint Conference on Artificial Intelligence* (Tokyo), pp. 134–142.

Charniak, E. 1972. Toward a model of children's story comprehension. Report no. AI TR-266, Artificial Intelligence Laboratory, Massachusetts Institute of Technology.

———. 1977. A framed painting: The representation of a common sense knowledge fragment. *Journal of Cognitive Science* 1(4): 355–394.

———. 1978. With a spoon in hand this must be the eating frame. In *Proceedings of the 2nd Conference on Theoretical Issues in Natural Language Processing,* pp. 187–193.

Charniak, E., Riesbeck, C., and McDermott, D. 1980. *Artificial Intelligence Programming.* Hillsdale, NJ: Erlbaum.

Chi, M. T. H., Feltovich, P. J., and Glaser, R. 1980. Representation of physics knowledge by experts and novices. Report no. 2, Learning Research and Development Center, University of Pittsburgh.

Ciesielski, V. 1980. A methodology for the construction of natural language front ends for medical consultation systems. Ph.D. dissertation, Rutgers University. (Also Technical Report no. CBM-TR-112.)

Clancey, W. J. 1979a. Dialogue management for rule-based tutorials. In *Proceedings of the 6th International Joint Conference on Artificial Intelligence* (Tokyo), pp. 155–161.

———. 1979b. Transfer of rule-based expertise through a tutorial dialogue. Ph.D. dissertation, Computer Science Department, Stanford University. (Also Stanford Report no. STAN-CS-769.)

———. 1979c. Tutoring rules for guiding a case method dialogue. *International Journal of Man-Machine Studies* 11: 25–49. (Edited version appears as Chapter 26 of this volume.)

———. 1981. Tutoring rules for guiding a case method dialogue. In *Intelligent Tutoring Systems,* eds. D. H. Sleeman and J. S. Brown, pp. 201–225. New York: Academic Press. (Same as Clancey, 1979c.)

———. 1983a. The advantages of abstract control knowledge in expert system design. In *Proceedings of the 3rd National Conference on Artificial Intelligence* (Washington, D.C.), pp. 74–78.

———. 1983b. The epistemology of a rule-based expert system: A framework for explanation. *Artificial Intelligence* 20: 215–251. (Appears as Chapter 29 in this volume.)

———. 1984. Methodology for building an intelligent tutoring system. In *Methods and Tactics in Cognitive Science,* eds. W. Kintsch, J. R. Miller, and P. G. Polson. Hillsdale, NJ: Erlbaum. Forthcoming.

Clancey, W. J., and Letsinger, R. 1981. NEOMYCIN: Reconfiguring a rule-based expert system for application to teaching. In *Proceedings of the 7th International Joint Conference on Artificial Intelligence* (Vancouver, B.C.), pp. 829–836.

Clark, K. L., and McCabe, F.G. 1982. PROLOG: a language for implementing expert systems. In *Machine Intelligence,* eds. J. Hayes, D. Michie, and Y. Pao, pp. 455–470. New York: John Wiley.

Cohen, P. R., and Feigenbaum, E. A. (eds.). 1982. *The Handbook of Artificial Intelligence* (vol. 3). Los Altos, CA: Kaufmann.

Cohen, S. N., Armstrong, M. F., Briggs, R. L., Chavez-Pardo, R., Feinberg, L. S., Hannigan, J. F., Hansten, P. D., Hunn, G. S., Illa, R. V., Moore, T. N., Nishimura, T. G., Podlone, M. D., Shortliffe, E. H., Smith, L. A., and Yosten, L. 1974. Computer-based monitoring and reporting of drug interactions. In *Proceedings of MEDINFO IFIP Conference* (Stockholm, Sweden), pp. 889–894.

Colby, K. M. 1981. Modeling a paranoid mind. *Behavioral and Brain Sciences* 4(4): 515–560.

Colby, K. M., Parkinson, R. C., and Faught, B. 1974. Pattern-matching rules for the recognition of natural language dialogue expressions. Report no. AIM-234, Stanford Artificial Intelligence Laboratory, Stanford University.

Collins, A. 1976. Processes in acquiring knowledge. In *Schooling and Acquisition of Knowledge,* eds. R. C. Anderson, R. J. Spiro, and W. E. Montague, pp. 339–363. Hillsdale, NJ: Erlbaum.

———. 1978. Fragments of a theory of human plausible reasoning. In *Proceedings of the 2nd Conference on Theoretical Issues in Natural Language Processing,* pp. 194–201.

Conchie, J. M., Munroe, J. D., and Anderson, D. O. 1970. The incidence of staining of permanent teeth by the tetracyclines. *Canadian Medical Association Journal* 103: 351–356.

Cooper, G. F. 1984. NESTOR: A medical decision support system that integrates causal, temporal, and probabilistic knowledge. Ph.D. dissertation, Computer Science Department, Stanford University. Forthcoming.

Cronbach, L. J. 1970. *Essentials of Psychological Testing.* New York: Harper and Row.

Cullingford, R. 1977. Script application: Computer understanding of newspaper stories. Ph.D. dissertation, Yale University.

Cumberbatch, J., and Heaps, H. S. 1973. Application of a non-Bayesian approach to computer aided diagnosis of upper abdominal pain. *International Journal of Biomedical Computing* 4: 105–115.

Cumberbatch, J., Leung, V. K., and Heaps, H. S. 1974. A non-probabilistic method for automated medical diagnosis. *International Journal of Biomedical Computing* 5: 133–146.

Davis, R. 1976. Applications of meta-level knowledge to the construction, maintenance, and use of large knowledge bases. Ph.D. dissertation, Computer Science Department, Stanford University. (Reprinted with revisions in Davis and Lenat, 1982.)

———. 1977a. Generalized procedure calling and content-directed invocation. *SIGPLAN Notices* 12(8): 45–54.

———. 1977b. Interactive transfer of expertise: Acquisition of new inference rules. In *Proceedings of the 5th International Joint Conference on Artificial Intelligence* (Cambridge, MA), pp. 321–328.

———. 1978. Knowledge acquisition in rule-based systems: Knowledge about representations as a basis for system construction and maintenance. In *Pattern-Directed Inference Systems,* eds. D. A. Waterman and F. Hayes-Roth, pp. 99–134. New York: Academic Press.

———. 1979. Interactive transfer of expertise: Acquisition of new inference rules. *Artificial Intelligence* 12: 121–158. (Edited version appears as Chapter 9 of this volume.)

———. 1980. Meta-rules: Reasoning about control. *Artificial Intelligence* 15: 179–222.

———. 1984. Diagnosis based on structure and function: Paths of interaction and the locality principle. *Artificial Intelligence:* forthcoming.

Davis, R., and Buchanan, B. G. 1977. Meta-level knowledge: Overview and applications. In *Proceedings of the 5th International Joint Conference on Artificial Intelligence* (Cambridge, MA), pp. 920–927. (Edited version appears as Chapter 28 of this volume.)

Davis, R., and Lenat, D. B. 1982. *Knowledge-Based Systems in Artificial Intelligence.* New York: McGraw-Hill.

Davis, R., Buchanan, B., and Shortliffe, E. 1977. Production rules as a representation for a knowledge-based consultation system. *Artificial Intelligence* 8(1): 15–45.

Davis, R., Shrobe, H., Hamscher, W., Wieckert, K., Shirley, M., and Polit, S. 1982. Diagnosis based on description of structure and function. In *Proceedings of the National Conference on Artificial Intelligence* (Pittsburgh, PA), pp. 137–142.

Day, E. 1970. Automated health services: Reprogramming the doctor. *Methods of Information in Medicine* 9: 116–121.

de Dombal, F. T. 1973. Surgical diagnosis assisted by computer. *Proceedings of the Royal Society of London* V-184: 433–440.

de Dombal, F. T., Leaper, D. J., Horrocks, J. C., Staniland, J. R., and McCann, A. P. 1974. Human and computer aided diagnosis of abdominal pain: Further report with emphasis on the performance of clinicians. *British Medical Journal* 1: 376–380.

de Dombal, F. T., Horrocks, J. C., and Staniland, J. R. 1975. The computer as an aid to gastroenterological decision making. *Scandinavian Journal of Gastroenterology* 10: 225–227.

de Finetti, B. 1972. *Probability, Induction, and Statistics: The Art of Guessing.* New York: Wiley.

deJong, G. 1977. Skimming newspaper stories by computer. Report no. 104, Computer Science Department, Yale University.

de Kleer, J., Doyle, J., Steele, G., and Sussman, G. 1977. AMORD: Explicit control of reasoning. In *Proceedings of the Symposium on Artificial Intelligence and Programming Languages,* pp. 116–125. Reprinted in *SIGPLAN Notices,* vol. 12, and *SIGART Newsletter,* no. 64.

Delfino, A. B., Buchs, A., Duffield, A. M., Djerassi, C., Buchanan, B. G., Feigenbaum, E. A., and Lederberg, J. 1970. Applications of artificial intelligence for chemical inference VI. Approach to a general method of interpreting low resolution mass spectra with a computer. *Helvetica Chimica Acta* 53: 1394–1417.

Deutsch, B. G. 1974. The structure of task-oriented dialogs. In *IEEE Symposium for Speech Recognition,* pp. 250–253.

Ditlove, J., Weidmann, P., Bernstein, M., and Massry, S. G. 1977. Methicillin nephritis. *Medicine* 56: 483–491.

Duda, R. O., and Shortliffe, E. H. 1983. Expert systems research. *Science* 220: 261–268.

Duda, R. O., Hart, P. E., and Nilsson, N. J. 1976. Subjective Bayesian methods for rule-based inference systems. In *AFIPS Conference Proceedings of the 1976 National Computer Conference,* vol. 45 (New York), pp. 1075–1082.

Duda, R. O., Hart, P. E., Barrett, P., Gaschnig, J., Konolige, K., Reboh, R., and Slocum, J. 1978a. Development of the PROSPECTOR consultant system for mineral exploration. Final report for SRI projects 5821 and 6415, Artificial Intelligence Center, SRI International.

Duda, R. O., Hart, P. E., Nilsson, N. J., and Sutherland, G. L. 1978b. Semantic network representations in rule-based inference systems. In *Pattern-Directed Inference Systems,* eds. D. A. Waterman and F. Hayes-Roth, pp. 203–221. New York: Academic Press.

Edelmann, C. M., Jr., and Barnett, H. L. 1971. Pediatric nephrology. In *Diseases of the Kidney,* eds. M. B. Strauss and L. G. Welt, p. 1359. Boston: Little, Brown.

Edwards, L. D., Levin, S., and Lepper, M. H. 1972. A comprehensive surveillance system of infections and antimicrobials used at Presbyterian-St. Luke's Hospital—Chicago. *American Journal of Public Health* 62: 1053–1055.

Edwards, W. 1972. N = 1: Diagnosis in unique cases. In *Computer Diagnosis and Diagnostic Methods,* ed. J. A. Jacquez, pp. 139–151. Springfield, IL: Thomas.

Eisenberg, L. 1974. Don't lean on the computer. *Physician's World* (April).

Elstein, A. S., Shulman, L. S., and Sprafka, S. A. 1978. *Medical Problem Solving: An Analysis of Clinical Reasoning.* Cambridge, MA: Harvard University Press.

Engelmore, R. S., and Terry, A. 1979. Structure and function of the CRYSALIS system. In *Proceedings of the 6th International Joint Conference on Artificial Intelligence* (Tokyo), pp. 250–256.

Erman, L. D., Hayes-Roth, F., Lesser, V. R., and Reddy, D. R. 1980. The Hearsay-II speech-understanding system: Integrating knowledge to resolve uncertainty. *Computing Surveys* 12: 213–253.

Evans, A., Jr. 1964. An ALGOL 60 compiler. In *Annual Review of Automatic Programming* (vol. 4), ed. R. Goodman, pp. 87–124. New York: Macmillan.

Fagan, L. 1980. VM: Representing time-dependent relations in a clinical setting. Ph.D. dissertation, Computer Science Department, Stanford University.

Fagan, L. M., Kunz, J. C., Feigenbaum, E. A., and Osborn, J. J. 1979. Representation of dynamic clinical knowledge: Measurement interpretation in the intensive care unit. In *Proceedings of the 6th International Joint Conference on Artificial Intelligence* (Tokyo), pp. 260–262. (Edited version appears as Chapter 22 of this volume.)

Falk, G. 1970. Computer interpretation of imperfect line data. Report no. AIM-132, Artificial Intelligence Laboratory, Stanford University.

Faught, W. F. 1977. Motivation and intensionality in a computer simulation model. Report no. AIM-305, Artificial Intelligence Laboratory, Stanford University.

Feigenbaum, E. A. 1963. Simulation of verbal learning behavior. In *Computers and Thought,* eds. E. A. Feigenbaum and J. Feldman, pp. 297–309. New York: McGraw-Hill.

———. 1978. The art of artificial intelligence: Themes and case studies of knowledge engineering. In *AFIPS Conference Proceedings of the 1978 National Computer Conference,* vol. 47 (Anaheim, CA), pp. 227–240.

Feigenbaum, E. A., Buchanan, B. G., and Lederberg, J. 1971. On generality and problem solving: A case study involving the DENDRAL program. In *Machine Intelligence 6,* eds. B. Meltzer and D. Michie, pp. 165–190. New York: American Elsevier.

Feldman, J. A., Low, J. R., Swinehart, D. C., and Taylor, R. H. 1972. Recent developments in SAIL: An ALGOL-based language for artificial intelligence. In *AFIPS Conference Proceedings of the 1972 Fall Joint Computer Conference,* vol. 41 (Anaheim, CA), pp. 1193–1202.

Feltovich, P. J., Johnson, P. E., Moller, J. H., and Swanson, D. B. 1980. The role and development of medical knowledge in diagnostic expertise. Paper presented at the annual meeting of the American Educational Research Association, 1980.

Feurzeig, W., Munter, P., Swets, J., and Breen, M. 1964. Computer-aided teaching in medical diagnosis. *Journal of Medical Education* 39: 746–755.

Fisher, L. S., Chow, A. W., Yoshikawa, T. T., and Guze, L. B. 1975. Cephalothin and cephaloridine therapy for bacterial meningitis. *Annals of Internal Medicine* 82: 689–693.

Floyd, R. 1961. A descriptive language for symbol manipulation. *Journal of the Association for Computing Machinery* 8: 579–584.

Fox, M. 1981. Reasoning with incomplete knowledge in a resource-limited environment: Integrating reasoning and knowledge acquisition. In *Proceedings of the 7th International Joint Conference on Artificial Intelligence* (Vancouver, B.C.), pp. 313–318.

Franke, E. K., and Ritschel, W. A. 1976. A new method for quick estimation of the absorption rate constant for clinical purposes using a nomograph. *Drug Intelligence and Clinical Pharmacy* 10: 77–82.

Friedman, L. 1981. Extended plausible inference. In *Proceedings of the 7th International Joint Conference on Artificial Intelligence* (Vancouver, B.C.), pp. 487–495.

Friedman, R. B., and Gustafson, D. H. 1977. Computers in clinical medicine: A critical review (guest editorial). *Computers and Biomedical Research* 10: 199–204.

Garvey, T. D., Lowrence, J. D., and Fischler, M. A. 1981. An inference technique for integrating knowledge from disparate sources. In *Proceedings of the 7th International Joint Conference on Artificial Intelligence* (Vancouver, B.C.), pp. 319–325.

Gaschnig, J. 1979. Preliminary performance analysis of the PROSPECTOR consultant system for mineral exploration. In *Proceedings of the 6th International Joint Conference on Artificial Intelligence* (Tokyo), pp. 308–310.

Genesereth, M. R. 1981. The use of hierarchical models in the automated diagnosis of computer systems. Report no. HPP-81-20, Computer Science Department, Stanford University.

Gerring, P. E., Shortliffe, E. H., and van Melle, W. 1982. The Interviewer/Reasoner model: An approach to improving system responsiveness in interactive AI systems. *AI Magazine* 3(4): 24–27.

Gibaldi, M., and Perrier, D. 1975. *Pharmacokinetics.* New York: Marcel Dekker.

Ginsberg, A. S. 1971. Decision analysis in clinical patient management with an application to the pleural effusion syndrome. Report no. R-751-RC-NLM, Rand Corporation.

Glantz, S. A. 1978. Computers in clinical medicine: A critique. *Computer* 11: 68–77.

Glesser, M. A., and Collen, M. F. 1972. Toward automated medical decisions. *Computers and Biomedical Research* 5: 180–189.

Goguen, J. A. 1968. The logic of inexact concepts. *Synthese* 19: 325–373.

Goldberg, A., and Kay, A. 1976. Smalltalk-72 user's manual. Report no. SSL 76-6, Learning Research Group, Xerox PARC, Palo Alto, CA.

Goldstein, I. P. 1977. The computer as coach: An athletic paradigm for intellectual education. Report no. 389, Artificial Intelligence Laboratory, Massachusetts Institute of Technology.

———. 1978. Developing a computational representation of problem solving skills. Report no. 495, Artificial Intelligence Center, Massachusetts Institute of Technology.

Goldstein, I. P., and Roberts, B. R. 1977. NUDGE: A knowledge-based scheduling program. In *Proceedings of the 5th International Joint Conference on Artificial Intelligence* (Cambridge, MA), pp. 257–263.

Gorry, G. A. 1973. Computer-assisted clinical decision making. *Methods of Information in Medicine* 12: 45–51.

Gorry, G. A., and Barnett, G. O. 1968. Experience with a model of sequential diagnosis. *Computers and Biomedical Research* 1: 490–507.

Gorry, G. A., Kassirer, J. P., Essig, A., and Schwartz, W. B. 1973. Decision analysis as the basis for computer-aided management of acute renal failure. *American Journal of Medicine* 55: 473–484.

Grayson, C. J. 1960. *Decision Under Uncertainty: Drilling Decisions by Oil and Gas Operators.* Cambridge, MA: Harvard University Press.

Greiner, R., and Lenat, D. B. 1980. A representation language language. In *Proceedings of the 1st Annual National Conference on Artificial Intelligence* (Stanford, CA), pp. 165–169.

Grinberg, M. R. 1980. A knowledge based design system for digital electronics. In *Proceedings of the 1st Annual National Conference on Artificial Intelligence* (Stanford, CA), pp. 283–285..

Grosz, B. 1977. The representation and use of focus in a system for understanding dialogs. In *Proceedings of the 5th International Joint Conference on Artificial Intelligence* (Cambridge, MA), pp. 67–76.

Gustafson, D. H., Kestly, J. J., Greist, J. H., and Jensen, N. M. 1971. Initial evaluation of a subjective Bayesian diagnostic system. *Health Services Research* 6: 204–213.

Harré, R. 1970. Probability and confirmation. In *The Principles of Scientific Thinking,* pp. 157–177. Chicago: University of Chicago Press.

Hartley, J., Sleeman, D., and Woods, P. 1972. Controlling the learning of diagnostic tasks. *International Journal of Man-Machine Studies* 4: 319–340.

Hasling, D. W., Clancey, W. J., Rennels, G. D. 1984. Strategic explanations for a diagnostic consultation system. *International Journal of Man-Machine Studies:* forthcoming.

Hayes-Roth, F., and McDermott, J. 1977. Knowledge acquisition from structural descriptions. In *Proceedings of the 5th International Joint Conference on Artificial Intelligence* (Cambridge, MA), pp. 356–362.

Hayes-Roth, F., Waterman, D., and Lenat, D. (eds.). 1983. *Building Expert Systems.* Reading, MA: Addison-Wesley.

Hearn, A. C. 1971. Applications of symbol manipulation in theoretical physics. *Communications of the Association for Computing Machinery* 14(8): 511–516.

Heiser, J. F., Brooks, R. E., and Ballard, J. P. 1978. Progress report: A computerized psychopharmacology advisor (abstract). In *Proceedings of the 11th Collegium Internationale Neuro-Psychopharmacologicum* (Vienna), p. 233.

Helmer, O., and Rescher, N. 1960. On the epistemology of the inexact sciences. Report no. R-353, Rand Corporation.

Hempel, C. G. 1965. Studies in the logic of confirmation. In *Aspects of Scientific Explanation and Other Essays in the Philosophy of Science,* pp. 3–51. New York: Free Press.

Hendrix, G. G. 1976. The Lifer manual: A guide to building practical natural language interfaces. Report no. 138, Artificial Intelligence Center, Stanford Research Institute.

———. 1977. A natural language interface facility. *SIGART Newsletter* 61: 25–26.

Hewitt, C. 1972. Description and theoretical analysis (using schemata) of PLANNER: A language for proving theorems and manipulating models in a robot. Ph.D. dissertation, Massachusetts Institute of Technology.

Hewitt, C., Bishop, P., and Steiger, R. 1973. A universal modular ACTOR formalism for artificial intelligence. In *Advance Papers of the 3rd International Joint Conference on Artificial Intelligence* (Stanford, CA), pp. 235–245.

Hilberman, M., Kamm, B., Tarter, M., and Osborn, J. J. 1975. An evaluation of computer-based patient monitoring at Pacific Medical Center. *Computers and Biomedical Research* 8: 447–460.

Horwitz, J., Thompson, H., Concannon, T., Friedman, R. H., Krikorian, J., and Gertman, P. M. 1980. Computer-assisted patient care management in medical oncology. In *Proceedings of the 4th Symposium on Computer Applications in Medical Care* (Washington, D.C.), pp. 771–780.

Jaynes, J. 1976. *The Origin of Consciousness in the Breakdown of the Bicameral Mind.* Boston: Houghton Mifflin.

Jelliffe, R. W., and Jelliffe, S. M. 1972. A computer program for estimation of creatinine clearance from unstable serum creatinine levels, age, sex, and weight. *Mathematical Biosciences* 14: 17–24.

Johnson, P. E., Duran, A., Hassebrock, F., Moller, J., Prietula, M., Feltovich, P. J., and Swanson, D. B. 1981. Expertise and error in diagnostic reasoning. *Cognitive Science* 5(3): 235–283.

Kahneman, D., Slovic, P., and Tversky, A. 1982. *Judgment under Uncertainty: Heuristics and Biases.* Cambridge, U.K.: Cambridge University Press.

Keynes, J. M. 1962. *A Treatise on Probability.* New York: Harper and Row.

Kintsch, W. 1976. Memory for prose. In *The Structure of Human Memory,* ed. C. Cofer, pp. 90–113. San Francisco: Freeman.

Koffman, E. B., and Blount, S. E. 1973. Artificial intelligence and automatic programming in CAI. In *Advance Papers of the 3rd International Joint Conference on Artificial Intelligence* (Stanford, CA), pp. 86–94.

Kulikowski, C., and Weiss, S. 1971. Computer-based models of glaucoma. Report no. 3, Computers in Biomedicine, Department of Computer Science, Rutgers University.

———. 1982. Representation of expert knowledge for consultation: The CASNET and EXPERT projects. In *Artificial Intelligence in Medicine,* ed. P. Szolovits, pp. 21–55. Boulder, CO: Westview Press.

Kunin, C. M. 1973. Use of antibiotics: A brief exposition of the problem and some tentative solutions. *Annals of Internal Medicine* 79: 555–560.

Kunz, J. C. 1984. Use of AI, simple mathematics, and a physiological model for making medical diagnoses and treatment plans. Ph.D. dissertation, Stanford Heuristic Programming Project, Stanford University. Forthcoming.

Kunz, J. C., Fallat, R. J., McClung, D. H., Osborn, J. J., Votteri, B. A., Nii, H. P., Aikins, J. S., Fagan, L. M., and Feigenbaum, E. A. 1979. A physiological rule-based system for interpreting pulmonary function test results. In *Proceedings of Computers in Critical Care and Pulmonary Medicine,* pp. 375–379.

Kunz, J. C., Shortliffe, E. H., Buchanan, B. G., and Feigenbaum, E. A. 1984. Computer-assisted decision making in medicine. *The Journal of Medicine and Philosophy* 9: 135–160.

Langlotz, C. P., and Shortliffe, E. H. 1983. Adapting a consultation system to critique user plans. *International Journal of Man-Machine Studies* 19: 479–496.

Leaper, D. J., Horrocks, J. C., Staniland, J. R., and de Dombal, F. T. 1972. Computer-assisted diagnosis of abdominal pain using estimates provided by clinicians. *British Medical Journal* 4: 350–354.

Ledley, R. S. 1973. Syntax-directed concept analysis in the reasoning foundations of medical diagnosis. *Computers in Biology and Medicine* 3: 89–99.

Lenat, D. B. 1975. Beings: Knowledge as interacting experts. In *Advance Papers of the 4th International Joint Conference on Artificial Intelligence* (Tbilisi, USSR), pp. 126–133.

———. 1976. AM: An artificial intelligence approach to discovery in mathematics as heuristic search. Ph.D. dissertation, Computer Science Department, Stanford University. (Stanford Reports nos. CS-STAN-76-570 and AIM-286. Reprinted with revisions in Davis and Lenat, 1982.)

———. 1983. Theory formation by heuristic search. The nature of heuristics II: Background and examples. *Artificial Intelligence* 21: 31–59.

Lesgold, A. M. 1983. Acquiring expertise. Report no. PDS-5, Learning Research and Development Center, University of Pittsburgh. (Also forthcoming in *Tutorials in Learning and Memory,* eds. J. R. Anderson and S. M. Kosslyn. San Francisco: Freeman.)

Lesser, R. L., Fennell, R. D., Erman, L. D., and Reddy, D. R. 1974. Organization of the HEARSAY II speech understanding system. In *Contributed Papers of the IEEE Symposium on Speech Recognition* (Pittsburgh, PA), pp. 11–21.

———. 1975. Organization of the HEARSAY II speech understanding system. *IEEE Transactions on Acoustics, Speech, and Signal Processing* ASSP-23: 11–23.

Levy, A. H. 1977. Is informatics a basic medical science? In *MEDINFO 77,* pp. 979–981. Amsterdam: North-Holland.

Linde, C. 1978. The organization of discourse. In *Style and Variables in English,* eds. T. Shopen and J. M. Williams. Cambridge, MA: Winthrop Press.

Linde, C., and Goguen, J. A. 1978. Structure of planning discourse. *Journal of Social Biological Structure* 1: 219–251.

Lindsay, R. K., Buchanan, B. G., Feigenbaum, E. A., and Lederberg, J. 1980. *Applications of Artificial Intelligence for Organic Chemistry: The DENDRAL Project.* New York: McGraw-Hill.

Luce, R. D., and Suppes, P. 1965. Preference, utility, and subjective probability. In *Handbook of Mathematical Psychology,* eds. R. D. Luce, R. R. Bush, and E. Galanter, pp. 249–410. New York: Wiley.

Manna, Z. 1969. The correctness of programs. *Journal of Computer and System Sciences* 3: 119–127.

MARC Corporation. 1976. *MARC User Information Manual.* Palo Alto, CA: MARC Analysis Research Corporation.

Mayne, J. G., Weksel, W., and Scholtz, P. N. 1968. Toward automating the medical history. *Mayo Clinic Proceedings* 43(1): 1–25

McCarthy, J. 1958. Programs with common sense. In *Proceedings of the Symposium on the Mechanisation of Thought Processes,* pp. 77–84. (Reprinted in *Semantic Information Processing,* ed. M. L. Minsky, pp. 403–409. Cambridge, MA: MIT Press, 1968.)

———. 1983. Some expert systems need common sense. Invited presentation for the New York Academy of Sciences Science Week Symposium on Computer Culture, April 5–8, 1983. *Annals of the New York Academy of Science:* forthcoming.

McCarthy, J., Abrahams, P. J., Edwards, D. J., Hart, T. P., and Levin, M. I. 1962. *LISP 1.5 Programmer's Manual.* Cambridge, MA: MIT Press.

McDermott, D. V. and Doyle, J. 1980. Non-monotonic logic I. *Artificial Intelligence* 13: 41–72.

Melhorn, J. M., Warren, K. L., and Clark, G. M. 1979. Current attitudes of medical personnel towards computers. *Computers and Biomedical Research* 12: 327–334.

Michie, D. 1974. *On Machine Intelligence.* New York: John Wiley and Sons.

Miller, R. A., Pople, H. E., and Myers, J. D. 1982. INTERNIST-1: An experimental computer-based diagnostic consultant for general internal medicine. *New England Journal of Medicine* 307(8): 468–476.

Minsky, M. L. 1975. A framework for representing knowledge. In *The Psychology of Computer Vision,* ed. P. H. Winston, pp. 211–277. New York: McGraw-Hill.

Model, M. L. 1979. Monitoring system behavior in a complex computational environment. Ph.D. dissertation, Stanford University. (Also Technical Report no. CS-79-701.)

Moran, T. P. 1973a. The symbolic imagery hypothesis: A production system model. Ph.D. dissertation, Computer Science Department, Carnegie-Mellon University.

———. 1973b. The symbolic nature of visual imagery. In *Advance Papers of the 3rd International Joint Conference on Artificial Intelligence* (Stanford, CA), pp. 472–477.

Moses, J. 1971. Symbolic integration: The stormy decade. *Communications ACM* 8: 548–560.

Muller, C. 1972. The overmedicated society: Forces in the marketplace for medical care. *Science* 176: 488–492.

Mulsant, B., and Servan-Schreiber, D. 1984. Knowledge engineering: A daily activity on a hospital ward. *Computers and Biomedical Research* 17: 71–91.

Neu, H. C., and Howrey, S. P. 1975. Testing the physician's knowledge of antibiotic use. *New England Journal of Medicine* 293: 1291–1295.

Newell, A. 1973. Production systems: Models of control structures. In *Visual Information Processing,* ed. W. G. Chase, pp. 463–526. New York: Academic Press.

———. 1983. The heuristic of George Polya and its relation to artificial intelligence. In *Methods of Heuristics,* eds. R. Groner, M. Groner, and W. F. Bischof. Hillsdale, NJ: Erlbaum.

Newell, A., and Simon, H. A. 1972. *Human Problem Solving.* Englewood Cliffs, NJ: Prentice-Hall.

Nie, N. H., Hull, C. H., Jenkins, J. C., Steinbrenner, K., and Bent, D. H. 1975. *SPSS: Statistical Package for the Social Sciences.* New York: McGraw-Hill.

Nii, H. P., and Feigenbaum, E. A. 1978. Rule-based understanding of signals. In *Pattern-Directed Inference Systems,* eds. D. A. Waterman and F. Hayes-Roth, pp. 483–501. New York: Academic Press.

Nii, H. P., Feigenbaum, E. A., Anton, J. J., and Rockmore, A. J. 1982. Signal-to-symbol transformation: HASP/SIAP case study. *AI Magazine* 3(2): 23–35.

Nilsson, N. J. 1971. *Problem Solving Methods in Artificial Intelligence.* New York: McGraw-Hill.

Norusis, M. J., and Jacquez, J. A. 1975a. Diagnosis I. Symptom nonindependence in mathematical models for diagnosis. *Computers and Biomedical Research* 8: 156–172.

———. 1975b. Diagnosis II. Diagnostic models based on attribute clusters: A proposal and comparisons. *Computers and Biomedical Research* 8: 173–188.

O'Brien, T. E. 1974. Excretion of drugs in human milk. *American Journal of Hospital Pharmacology* 31: 844–854.

Osborn, J. J., Beaumont, J. C., Raison, A., and Abbott, R. P. 1969. Computation for quantitative on-line measurement in an intensive care ward. In *Computers in Biomedical Research,* eds. R. W. Stacey and B. D. Waxman, pp. 207–237. New York: Academic Press.

Papert, S. 1970. Teaching children programming. In *IFIP Conference on Computer Education.* Amsterdam: North-Holland.

Parry, M. F., and Neu, H. C. 1976. Pharmacokinetics of ticarcillin in patients with abnormal renal function. *Journal of Infectious Disease* 133: 46–49.

Parzen, E. 1960. *Modern Probability Theory and Its Applications.* New York: Wiley.

Patil, R. S., Szolovits, P., and Schwartz, W. B. 1981. Causal understanding of patient illness in medical diagnosis. In *Proceedings of 7th International Joint Conference on Artificial Intelligence* (Vancouver, B. C.), pp. 893–899.

———. 1982. Information acquisition in diagnosis. In *Proceedings of the National Conference on Artificial Intelligence* (Pittsburgh, PA), pp. 345–348.

Pauker, S. P., and Pauker, S. G. 1977. Prenatal diagnosis: a directive approach to genetic counseling using decision analysis. *Yale Journal of Biological Medicine* 50: 275–289.

Pauker, S. G., and Szolovits, P. 1977. Analyzing and simulating taking the history of the present illness: Context formation. In *IFIP Working Conference on Computational Linguistics in Medicine,* eds. W. Schneider and A. L. Sagvall-Hein, pp. 109–118. Amsterdam: North-Holland.

Pauker, S. G., Gorry, G. A., Kassirer, J. P., and Schwartz, W. B. 1976. Toward the simulation of clinical cognition: Taking a present illness by computer. *American Journal of Medicine* 60: 981–995.

Peterson, O. L., Andrews, L. P., Spain, R. S., and Greenberg, B. G. 1956. An analytic study of North Carolina general practice. *Journal of Medical Education* 31: 1–165.

Pipberger, H. V., McCaughan, D., Littman, D., Pipberger, H. A., Cornfield, J., Dunn, R. A., Batchelor, C. D., and Berson, A. S. 1975. Clinical application of a second generation electrocardiographic computer program. *American Journal of Cardiology* 35: 597–608.

Politakis, P. G. 1982. Using empirical analysis to refine expert system knowledge bases. Ph.D. dissertation, Computer Science Research Laboratory, Rutgers University. (Also Technical Report no. CBM-TR-130.)

Polya, G. 1957. *How To Solve It: A New Aspect of Mathematical Method.* Princeton, NJ: Princeton University Press.

Pople, H. E., Jr. 1977. The formation of composite hypotheses in diagnostic problem solving: An exercise in synthetic reasoning. In *Proceedings of the 5th International Joint Conference on Artificial Intelligence* (Cambridge, MA), pp. 1030–1037.

———. 1982. Heuristic methods for imposing structure on ill-structured problems: The structuring of medical diagnostics. In *Artificial Intelligence in Medicine,* ed. P. Szolovits, pp. 119–190. Boulder, CO: Westview Press.

Popper, K. R. 1959. Corroboration, the weight of evidence. In *The Logic of Scientific Discovery,* pp. 387–419. New York: Scientific Editions.

Post, E. 1943. Formal reductions of the general combinatorial problem. *American Journal of Mathematics* 65: 197–268.

Ramsey, F. P. 1931. *The Foundations of Mathematics and Other Logical Essays.* London: Kegan Paul.

Reboh, R. 1981. Knowledge engineering techniques and tools in the PROSPECTOR environment. Report no. 243, Artificial Intelligence Center, SRI International, Menlo Park, CA.

Reddy, D. R., Erman, L. D., Fennell, R. D., and Neely, R. B. 1973. The HEARSAY speech-understanding system: An example of the recognition process. In *Advance Papers of the 3rd International Joint Conference on Artificial Intelligence* (Stanford, CA), pp. 185–193.

Reimann, H. H., and D'Ambola, J. 1966. The use and cost of antimicrobials in hospitals. *Archives of Environmental Health* 13: 631–636.

Reiser, J. F. 1975. BAIL: A debugger for SAIL. Report no. AIM-270, Artificial Intelligence Laboratory, Stanford University.

Resnikoff, M., Holland, C. H., and Stroebel, C. F. 1967. Attitudes toward computers among employees of a psychiatric hospital. *Mental Hygiene* 51: 419.

Resztak, K. E., and Williams, R. B. 1972. A review of antibiotic therapy in patients with systemic infections. *American Journal of Hospital Pharmacy* 29: 935–941.

Rieger, C. 1976. An organization of knowledge for problem solving and language comprehension. *Artificial Intelligence* 7: 89–127.

Roberts, A. W., and Visconti, J. A. 1972. The rational and irrational use of systemic microbial drugs. *American Journal of Hospital Pharmacy* 29: 828–834.

Roberts, B., and Goldstein, I. P. 1977. The FRL manual. Report no. 409, Artificial Intelligence Laboratory, Massachusetts Institute of Technology.

Rosenberg, S. 1977. Frame-based text processing. Report no. 431, Artificial Intelligence Laboratory, Massachusetts Institute of Technology.

Ross, P. 1972. Computers in medical diagnosis. *CRC Critical Review of Radiological Science* 3: 197–243.

Rubin, M. I., Bruck, E., and Rapoport, M. 1949. Maturation of renal function in childhood: Clearance studies. *Journal of Clinical Investigation* 28: 1144.

Rumelhart, D. 1975. Notes on a schema for stories. In *Representation and Understanding: Studies in Cognitive Science,* eds. D. G. Bobrow and A. Collins, pp. 211–236. New York: Academic Press.

Rychener, M. D. 1975. The student production system: A study of encoding knowledge in production systems. Technical report, Computer Science Department, Carnegie-Mellon University.

Sager, N. 1978. Natural language information formatting: The automatic conversion of texts in a structured data base. In *Advances in Computers* (vol. 17), ed. M. C. Yovits, pp. 89–162. New York: Academic Press.

Salmon, W. C. 1966. *The Foundations of Scientific Inference.* Pittsburgh, PA: University of Pittsburgh Press.

———. 1973. Confirmation. *Scientific American* 228: 75–83.

Savage, L. J. 1974. *Foundations of Statistics.* New York: Wiley.

Schank, R., and Abelson, R. 1975. Scripts, plans and knowledge. In *Advance Papers of the 4th International Joint Conference on Artificial Intelligence* (Tbilisi, USSR), pp. 151–158.

Scheckler, W. E., and Bennett, J. V. 1970. Antibiotic usage in seven community hospitals. *Journal of the American Medical Association* 213: 264–267.

Schefe, P. 1980. On foundations of reasoning with uncertain facts and vague concepts. *International Journal of Man-Machine Studies* 12: 35–62.

Scheinok, P. A., and Rinaldo, J. A. 1971. System diagnosis: The use of two different mathematical models. *International Journal of Biomedical Computing* 2: 239–248.

Schwartz, G. J., Haycock, G. B., Edelmann, C. M., Jr., and Spitzer, A. 1976. A simple estimate of glomerular filtration rate in children derived from body length and plasma creatinine. *Pediatrics* 58: 259–263.

Schwartz, W. B. 1970. Medicine and the computer: The promise and problems of change. *New England Journal of Medicine* 283: 1257–1264.

———. 1979. Decision analysis: A look at the chief complaint. *New England Journal of Medicine* 300: 556.

Schwartz, W. B., Gorry, G. A., Kassirer, J. P., and Essig, A. 1973. Decision analysis and clinical judgements. *American Journal of Medicine* 55: 459–472.

Scott, A. C., Clancey, W. J., Davis, R., and Shortliffe, E. H. 1977. Explanation capabilities of knowledge-based production systems. *American Journal of Computational Linguistics* Microfiche 62. (Appears as Chapter 18 of this volume.)

Scragg, G. W. 1975a. Answering process questions. In *Advance Papers of the 4th International Joint Conference on Artificial Intelligence* (Tbilisi, USSR), pp. 435–442.

———. 1975b. Answering questions about processes. In *Explorations in Cognition,* eds. D. A. Norman and D. E. Rumelhart. San Francisco: Freeman.

Selfridge, O. 1959. Pandemonium: A paradigm for learning. In *Proceedings of Symposium on Mechanisation of Thought and Processes,* pp. 511–529. Teddington, U.K.: National Physics Laboratory.

Shackle, G. L. S. 1952. *Expectation in Economics.* Cambridge, U.K.: Cambridge University Press.

———. 1955. *Uncertainty in Economics and Other Reflections.* Cambridge, U.K.: Cambridge University Press.

Shafer, G. 1976. *A Mathematical Theory of Evidence.* Princeton, NJ: Princeton University Press.

Shortliffe, E. H. 1974. MYCIN: A rule-based computer program for advising physicians regarding antimicrobial therapy selection. Ph.D. dissertation, Stanford University. (Reprinted with revisions as Shortliffe, 1976.)

———. 1976. *Computer-Based Medical Consultations: MYCIN.* New York: American Elsevier.

———. 1980. Consultation systems for physicians: The role of artificial intelligence techniques. In *Proceedings of the 3rd National Conference of the Canadian Society for Computational Studies of Intelligence* (Victoria, B.C.), pp. 1–11. (Also in *Readings in Artificial Intelligence,* eds. B. Webber and N. Nilsson, pp. 323–333. Menlo Park, CA: Tioga Press, 1981.)

———. 1982a. Computer-based clinical decision aids: Some practical considerations. In *Proceedings of the AMIA Congress 82* (San Francisco, CA), pp. 295–298.

———. 1982b. The computer and medical decision making: Good advice is not enough (guest editorial). *IEEE Engineering in Medicine and Biology Magazine* 1(2): 16–18.

Shortliffe, E. H., and Buchanan, B. G. 1975. A model of inexact reasoning in medicine. *Mathematical Biosciences* 23: 351–379.

Shortliffe, E. H., and Davis, R. 1975. Some considerations for the implementation of knowledge-based expert systems. *SIGART Newsletter* 55: 9–12.

Shortliffe, E. H., Axline, S. G., Buchanan, B. G., Merigan, T. C., and Cohen, S. N. 1973. An artificial intelligence program to advise physicians regarding antimicrobial therapy. *Computers and Biomedical Research* 6: 544–560.

Shortliffe, E. H., Axline, S. G., Buchanan, B. G., and Cohen, S. N. 1974. Design considerations for a program to provide consultations in clinical therapeutics. In *Proceedings of the 13th San Diego Biomedical Symposium* (San Diego, CA), pp. 311–319.

Shortliffe, E. H., Davis, R., Axline, S. G., Buchanan, B. G., Green, C. C., and Cohen, S. N. 1975. Computer-based consultations in clinical therapeutics: Explanation and rule acquisition capabilities of the MYCIN system. *Computers and Biomedical Research* 8: 303–320.

Shortliffe, E. H., Buchanan, B. G., and Feigenbaum, E. A. 1979. Knowledge engineering for medical decision making: A review of computer-based clinical decision aids. *Proceedings of the IEEE* 67: 1207–1224.

Siber, G. R., Echeverria, P., Smith, A. L., Paisley, J. W., and Smith, D. H. 1975. Pharmacokinetics of gentamicin in children and adults. *Journal of Infectious Diseases* 132: 637–651.

Sidner, C. 1979. A computational model of co-reference comprehension in English. Ph.D. dissertation, Massachusetts Institute of Technology.

Simmons, H. E., and Stolley, P. D. 1974. This is medical progress? Trends and consequences of antibiotic use in the United States. *Journal of the American Medical Association* 227: 1023–1026.

Sleeman, D. H. 1977. A system which allows students to explore algorithms. In *Proceedings of the 5th International Joint Conference on Artificial Intelligence* (Cambridge, MA), pp. 780–786.

Slovic, P., Rorer, L. G., and Hoffman, P. J. 1971. Analyzing use of diagnostic signs. *Investigative Radiology* 6: 18–26.

Smith, D. H., Buchanan, B. G., Engelmore, R. S., Duffield, A. M., Yeo, A., Feigenbaum, E. A., Lederberg, J., and Djerassi, C. 1972. Applications of artificial intelligence for chemical inference VIII: An approach to the computer interpretation of the high resolution mass spectra of complex molecules: Structure elucidation of estrogenic steroids. *Journal of the American Chemical Society* 94: 5962–5971.

Sprosty, P. J. 1963. The use of questions in the diagnostic problem solving process. In *The Diagnostic Process,* ed. J. A. Jacquez, pp. 281–308. Ann Arbor, MI: University of Michigan School of Medicine.

Startsman, T. S., and Robinson, R. E. 1972. The attitudes of medical and paramedical personnel towards computers. *Computers and Biomedical Research* 5: 218–227.

Stefik, M. 1979. An examination of a frame-structured representation system. In *Proceedings of the 6th International Joint Conference on Artificial Intelligence* (Tokyo), pp. 845–852.

Stevens, A. L., Collins, A., and Goldin, S. 1978. Diagnosing students' misconceptions in causal models. Report no. 3786, Bolt Beranek and Newman.

Swanson, D. B., Feltovich, P. J., and Johnson, P. E. 1977. Psychological analysis of physician expertise: Implications for design of decision support systems. In *MEDINFO 77,* pp. 161–164. Amsterdam: North-Holland.

Swartout, W. R. 1981. Explaining and justifying expert consulting programs. In *Proceedings of the 7th International Joint Conference on Artificial Intelligence* (Vancouver, B.C.), pp. 815–822.

———. 1983. A system for creating and explaining expert consulting programs. *Artificial Intelligence* 21: 285–325.

Swinburne, R. G. 1970. Choosing between confirmation theories. *Philosophy of Science* 37: 602–613.

———. 1973. *An Introduction to Confirmation Theory.* London: Methuen.

Szolovits, P. 1979. Artificial intelligence and clinical problem solving. Report no. MIT/LCS/TM-140, Laboratory for Computer Science, Massachusetts Institute of Technology.

Szolovits, P., and Pauker, S. G. 1978. Categorical and probabilistic reasoning in medical diagnosis. *Artificial Intelligence* 11: 115–144.

Teach, R. L. 1984. Patterns of explanation and reasoning in clinical medicine: Implications for improving the performance of expert computer systems. Ph.D. dissertation, Stanford University. Forthcoming.

Teitelman, W. 1978. *Interlisp Reference Manual.* Palo Alto, CA: Xerox Palo Alto Research Center.

Tesler, L. G., Enea, H. J., and Smith, D. C. 1973. The LISP70 pattern matching system. In *Advance Papers of the 3rd International Joint Conference on Artificial Intelligence* (Stanford, CA), pp. 671–676.

Trigoboff, M. 1978. IRIS: A framework for the construction of clinical consultation systems. Ph.D. dissertation, Department of Computer Science, Rutgers University.

Tsuji, S., and Shortliffe, E. H. 1983. Graphical access to the knowledge base of a medical consultation system. In *Proceedings of AAMSI Congress 83* (San Francisco), pp. 551–555.

Turing, A. M. 1950. Computing machinery and intelligence. *Mind* 59: 433–460. (Reprinted in *Computers and Thought,* eds. E. A. Feigenbaum and J. Feldman. New York: McGraw-Hill, 1963.)

Tversky, A. 1972. Elimination by aspects: A theory of choice. *Psychology Review* 79: 281–299.

van Melle, W. 1974. Would you like advice on another horn? MYCIN project internal working paper, Stanford University.

———. 1980. A domain-independent system that aids in constructing knowledge-based consultation programs. Ph.D. dissertation, Computer Science Department, Stanford University. (Stanford Reports nos. STAN-CS-80-820 and HPP-80-22. Reprinted as van Melle, 1981.)

———. 1981. *System Aids in Constructing Consultation Programs.* Ann Arbor, MI: UMI Research Press.

van Melle, W., Scott, A. C., Bennett, J. S., and Peairs, M. 1981. The EMYCIN manual. Report no. HPP-81-16, Computer Science Department, Stanford University.

Waldinger, R., and Levitt, K. N. 1974. Reasoning about programs. *Artificial Intelligence* 5: 235–316.

Warner, H. R., Toronto, A. F., Veasey, L. G., and Stephenson, R. 1961. A mathematical approach to medical diagnosis: Application to congenital heart disease. *Journal of the American Medical Association* 177(3): 177–183.

Warner, H. R., Toronto, A. F., and Veasy, L. G. 1964. Experience with Bayes' theorem for computer diagnosis of congenital heart disease. *Annals of the New York Academy of Science* 115: 2.

Waterman, D. A. 1970. Generalization learning techniques for automating the learning of heuristics. *Artificial Intelligence* 1: 121–170.

———. 1974. Adaptive production systems. Complex Information Processing Working Paper, Report no. 285, Psychology Department, Carnegie-Mellon University.

———. 1978. Exemplary programming. In *Pattern-Directed Inference Systems,* eds. D. A. Waterman and F. Hayes-Roth, pp. 261–280. New York: Academic Press.

Weiner, J. L. 1979. The structure of natural explanation: Theory and application. Report no. SP-4305, System Development Corporation.

———. 1980. BLAH: A system which explains its reasoning. *Artificial Intelligence* 15: 19–48.

Weiss, C. F., Glazko, A. J., and Weston, J. K. 1960. Chloramphenicol in the newborn infant. *New England Journal of Medicine* 262: 787–794.

Weiss, S. M., Kulikowski, C. A., Amarel, S., and Safir, A. 1978. A model-based method for computer-aided medical decision-making. *Artificial Intelligence* 11: 145–172.

Weizenbaum, J. 1967. Contextual understanding by computers. *Communications of the Association for Computing Machinery* 10(8): 474–480.

———. 1976. *Computer Power and Human Reason: From Judgment to Calculation.* San Francisco: Freeman.

Wilson, J. V. K. 1956. Two medical texts from Nimrud. *IRAQ* 18: 130–146.

———. 1962. The Nimrud catalogue of medical and physiognomical omina. *IRAQ* 24: 52–62.

Winograd, T. 1972. Understanding natural language. *Cognitive Psychology* 3: 1–191.

———. 1975. Frame representations and the procedural/declarative controversy. In *Representation and Understanding, Studies in Cognitive Science,* eds. D. G. Bobrow and A. Collins, pp. 185–210. New York: Academic Press.

———. 1977. A framework for understanding discourse. Report no. AIM-297, Artificial Intelligence Laboratory, Stanford University.

———. 1980. Extended inference modes in reasoning by computer systems. *Artificial Intelligence* 13: 5–26.

Winston, P. H. 1970. Learning structural descriptions from examples. Report no. TR-76, Project MAC, Massachusetts Institute of Technology.

———. 1977. *Artificial Intelligence.* Reading, MA: Addison-Wesley.

———. 1979. Learning and reasoning by analogy. *Communications of the Association for Computing Machinery* 23(12): 689–703.

Winston, P. H., and Horn, B. 1981. *LISP*. Reading, MA: Addison-Wesley.

Wirtschafter, D. D., Gams, R., Ferguson, C., Blackwell, W., and Boackle, P. 1980. Clinical protocol information system. In *Proceedings of the 4th Symposium on Computer Applications in Medical Care* (Washington, D.C.), pp. 745–752.

Woods, W. A. 1970. Transition network grammars for natural language analysis. *Communications of the Association for Computing Machinery* 13(10): 591–606.

———. 1975. What's in a link: Foundations for semantic networks. In *Representation and Understanding: Studies in Cognitive Science,* eds. D. G. Bobrow and A. Collins, pp. 35–82. New York: Academic Press.

Yu, V. L., Buchanan, B. G., Shortliffe, E. H., Wraith, S. M., Davis, R., Scott, A. C., and Cohen, S. N. 1979a. An evaluation of the performance of a computer-based consultant. *Computer Programs in Biomedicine* 9: 95–102.

Yu, V. L., Fagan, L. M., Wraith, S. M., Clancey, W. J., Scott, A. C., Hannigan, J. F., Blum, R. L., Buchanan, B. G., and Cohen, S. N. 1979b. Antimicrobial selection by a computer: A blinded evaluation by infectious disease experts. *Journal of the American Medical Association* 242(12): 1279–1282. (Appears as Chapter 31 of this volume.)

Zadeh, L. A. 1965. Fuzzy sets. *Information and Control* 8: 338–353.

———. 1975. Fuzzy logic and approximate reasoning. *Synthese* 30: 407–428.

———. 1978. Fuzzy sets as a basis for a theory of possibility. *Fuzzy Sets and Systems* 1: 3–28.

Name Index

Subject Index